EDITION

4

The Effective Reader

D. J. Henry

Daytona State College

Boston   Columbus   Indianapolis   New York   San Francisco   Upper Saddle River
Amsterdam   Cape Town   Dubai   London   Madrid   Milan   Munich   Paris   Montréal   Toronto
Delhi   Mexico City   São Paulo   Sydney   Hong Kong   Seoul   Singapore   Taipei   Tokyo

Editor-in-Chief: Eric Stano
Editorial Assistant: Jamie Fortner
Senior Development Editor: Melissa Parkin
Head of Marketing: Roxanne McCarley
Senior Supplements Editor: Donna Campion
Executive Digital Producer: Stefanie A. Snajder
Digital Editor: Sara Gordus
Digital Content Specialist: Julia Pomann
Production Manager: Ellen MacElree
Project Coordination, Text Design, and Electronic Page Makeup: Cenveo® Publisher Services
Cover Designer/Manager: Wendy Ann Fredericks
Cover Photo: © LattaPictures/Getty Images
Senior Manufacturing Buyer: Dennis J. Para
Printer/Binder: LSC Communications/Crawfordsville
Cover Printer: Lehigh-Phoenix Color/Hagerstown

Credits and acknowledgments borrowed from other sources, and reproduced, with permission, in this textbook appear on pages C-1 to C-3.

3   17

www.pearsonhighered.com

Student ISBN-13: 978-0-321-84565-8
Student ISBN-10: 0-321-84565-X
A la Carte ISBN-13: 978-0-321-96568-4
A la Carte ISBN-10: 0-321-96568-X

Brief Contents

Detailed Contents

4   Implied Main Ideas and Implied Central Ideas   155

9 Fact and Opinion   403

10 Tone and Purpose   451

11 Inferences   499

12 The Basics of Argument   549

PART

2 Additional Readings   657

PART

3

Combined-Skills Tests   749

PART

4

Reading Enrichment (Available Only in *The Effective Reader* eTEXT)

Appendix: Reading Graphics in Textbooks

Preface

Dear Colleagues:

The story of Annie Sullivan and Helen Keller is one of my favorite success stories. Annie patiently, lovingly tapped thousands of words into Helen's palm, knowing that Helen's stubborn rebellion would melt once the flame of knowledge was ignited. These two remarkable women and their teaching and learning relationship serve as reminders of two ideals: reading empowers an individual life, and our work as instructors is of great and urgent importance. Many of our students come to us needing to reinforce the basic skills that make effective reading and clear thinking possible. Too often they struggle with text structure and feel uncertain about their comprehension. However with solid instruction and guided practice, these students can discover the power and pleasure of reading. *The Effective Reader,* Fourth Edition, has been designed to address these challenges.

New to This Edition

A number of changes have been made to *The Effective Reader*, Fourth Edition, all of which are designed to help students become effective readers and critical thinkers.

■ **Integration with—and enhanced feedback through—MyReadingLab.** A hallmark change in this edition is the book's integration with MyReadingLab. Students now have the option of taking both the Review and Mastery Tests that appear at the conclusion of each chapter in Part 1—as well as the Combined-Skills Tests in Part 3—in MyReadingLab. By taking the Review Tests and Combined-Skills Tests in MyReadingLab, students will receive automatic feedback as to why certain answers are right and others wrong. The Mastery Tests do not include feedback online and therefore serve as a true test of students' mastery. This integration also offers the additional benefit of helping instructors more easily track and monitor their students' work through the tests and their mastery of the skills.

- **Additional Opportunities for Practice and Instruction of *The Effective Reader*, Fourth Edition, available in MyReadingLab.** While the printed text contains five Combined Skills Tests in Part 3, an additional five Tests—with feedback—can also be found in MyReadingLab. In addition, a special appendix on Reading Graphics in Textbooks can be found in the Pearson eText, which is located on the left hand navigation bar within MyReadingLab.

- **New Information Literacy Applications.** Designed to help develop students' research capabilities—and focused by the skill being taught in that chapter—these new activities break information literacy down into manageable chunks. Located after the Practices and before the Review Tests, this feature helps students learn how to identify a need for new knowledge, how to locate and analyze new information, and how to apply that information to a specific situation.

- **New Summary Responses.** Introduced in Chapter 5 ("Supporting Details") and appearing after Review Tests 3 and 4, the Summary Responses connect reading to writing, deepen students' comprehension, and lay the groundwork for responding to the "What Do You Think?" feature.

- **Chapter Review Cards.** These cards—which make studying more accessible and efficient by distilling chapter content down to the fundamentals—have now been integrated into each of the relevant chapters for greater ease of use.

- **New Passages and Readings Throughout.** As with every edition, we have replaced short passages as well as longer readings throughout the text to ensure that the reading is engaging to each new wave of students. The following are just *some* examples of the many new readings that now appear in the text:

"Special Effects" by Louis Giannetti

"Beware of Groupthink" by Joseph A. DeVito

"Making Ethical Choices" by Lydia E. Anderson and Sandra B. Bolt

"Dreams Vary" by Philip G. Zimbardo, Robert L. Johnson, and Vivian McCann Hamilton

"Culture" by John D. Carl

"Helicopter Parents" by Mary Ann A. Schwartz

"Social Networking Sites: Online Friendships Can Mean Offline Peril" by The Federal Bureau of Investigation

"Toys R Us" by Bucky McMahon

"To the Power of a Persevering Teacher" by D.J. Henry

"I am Adam Lanza's Mother" by Liza Long

"Psychological Disorders" by Richard J. Gerrig and Philip G. Zimbardo

Guiding Principles

Every edition of *The Effective Reader* has been written to develop in students the essential abilities that will enable them to become stronger readers and critical thinkers.

Practice and Feedback

The best way to learn is to do. Thus, one of the primary aims of this text is to give students plentiful opportunities to practice, practice, practice! Every concept introduced in the book is accompanied by an explanation of the concept, an example with explanation of the example, and one or more practice exercises. Each chapter also contains brief skill applications, four review tests, four mastery tests, and a chapter review.

High-Interest Reading Selections

For many, enthusiasm for reading is stimulated by material that offers high-interest topics written in a fast-paced style. Every effort has been made to provide reading passages in examples, reviews, and tests that students will find lively and engaging. Topics are taken from issues arising out of popular culture and textbooks—some examples are movies, weight loss, sports figures, depression, interpersonal relationships, nutrition, inspirational and success stories, role models, stress management, and exercise—all written in active language using short, lively sentences. A special effort was made to include a variety of passages from textbooks across the curriculum. The main goal is to give students the opportunity to interact with authentic voices of writers in everyday life, working life, and academic life.

Integration of the Reading Process and Reading Skills

Effective readers blend individual reading skills into a reading process such as SQ3R. Before reading, effective readers skim for new or key vocabulary or main ideas. They create study questions and make connections to their prior knowledge. During reading, effective readers check their comprehension. For example, they annotate the text. They notice thought patterns and the relationship between ideas. They read for the answers to the questions they created before reading. After reading, effective readers use outlines, concept maps, and summaries to review what they have read and deepen their understanding. Students are taught to integrate each skill into a reading process in Part 1. In Chapter 1, "A Reading System for Effective Readers," students are introduced to SQ3R. In every other Part 1 chapter, students actively apply SQ3R strategies in "Before Reading About" and "After Reading About" activities. "Before Reading About" activities are pre-reading exercises that appear at the beginning of each chapter. These activities guide the student to review important concepts studied in earlier chapters, build on prior knowledge, and preview upcoming material. "After Reading About" activities are review activities that appear after the review tests in each chapter. These activities guide the student to reflect upon his or her achievements and assume responsibility for learning. Since many students are visual learners, the "Before Reading About" and "After Reading About" activities are signaled with reading process icons.

Comprehensive Approach

The Effective Reader, Fourth Edition, offers several levels of learning. First, students are given an abundance of practice. They are able to focus on individual reading skills through a chapter-by-chapter workbook approach. In each chapter of Part 1, Review Test 4 offers a multi-paragraph passage with items on all the skills taught up to that point. In addition, Chapter 1, "A Reading System for Effective Readers," teaches students how to apply their reading skills to the reading process before, during, and after reading by using SQ3R. Students also learn to apply all skills in combination in Part 2, "Additional Readings," and Part 3, "Combined-Skills Tests." The aim is to provide our students with varied and rich opportunities to learn and practice reading skills and to apply reading processes.

Chapter Features

Each chapter in Part 1 has several important features that help students become effective readers.

- **Learning Outcomes.** Each chapter opens with learning outcomes to help students preview and assess their progress as they master chapter content.
- **"Before Reading About . . .":** "Before Reading About . . ." activities appear at the beginning of Chapters 2–13 in Part 1. These activities are prereading

exercises based on SQ3R: they review important concepts studied in earlier chapters, build on prior knowledge, and preview the chapter. The purpose of "Before Reading About . . ." is to actively teach students to develop a reading process that applies individual reading skills as they study.

- **"After Reading About . . .":** "After Reading About . . ." activities appear after Review Test 4 in Chapters 2–13 of Part 1. Based on SQ3R, "After Reading About . . ." activities teach students to reflect on their achievements and assume responsibility for their own learning. These activities ask students reflective questions to check their comprehension of the skill taught in the chapter. Students learn to integrate individual reading skills into a reading process; they learn the value of reviewing material; and finally, students create a learning journal that enables them to see patterns in their behaviors and record their growth as readers.

- **Instruction, example, explanation, and practice.** Each chapter skill is broken down into components, and each component is introduced and explained. Instruction is followed by an example, an explanation of the example, and a practice. Each section has its own instruction, example, explanation, and practice exercises.

**Textbook
Skills**

- **Textbook Skills.** In the last section in each chapter, students are shown the ways in which the skills they are learning apply to reading textbooks. These activities, signaled by the icon to the left, present material from a textbook reading and direct students to apply the chapter's skill to the passage or visual. In a concerted effort to prepare students to be effective readers in their content courses, activities that foster textbook skills across the curriculum are also carefully woven throughout the entire textbook. The Textbook Skills icon signals these activities.

- **Visual Vocabulary.** The influence of technology and the media on reading is evident in the widespread use of graphics in newspapers, magazines, and textbooks. Throughout this textbook, visual vocabulary is presented as part of the reading process, and students interact with these visuals by completing captions or answering skill-based questions. The aim is to teach students to value photos, graphs, illustrations, and maps as important sources of information.

- **Review Tests.** Each chapter has four Review Tests—which can also be found in MyReadingLab—where they are accompanied by feedback. Review Tests 1 through 3 are designed to give ample opportunity for practice with the specific skill taught in the chapter; Review Test 4 offers a multi-paragraph passage with combined-skills questions based on all the skills taught up to and including that particular chapter. Review

Tests 3 and 4 also give "What Do You Think?" writing prompts so that teachers have the opportunity to guide students as they develop critical thinking skills.

- **Mastery Tests.** Each chapter includes four Mastery Tests, which are also found in MyReadingLab. Most of the Mastery Tests are based on excerpts from science, history, psychology, social science, and literature textbooks.

- **Chapter Review.** A chapter review is included for each chapter, distilling the most important concepts down for students and helping them take responsibility for their own learning. In this edition, these chapter reviews appear with their relevant chapters.

The Pearson Teaching and Learning Package

The Effective Reader, Fourth Edition, is supported by a series of innovative teaching and learning supplements. Ask your Pearson sales representative for a copy, or download the content for certain ancillaries at www.pearsonhighered.com/irc. Your sales representative will provide you with the username and password to access these materials.

- **MyReadingLab** is an online, mastery-based system created specifically for students learning to become effective readers. It not only offers students the opportunity to take the Review, Mastery, and Combined-Skills Tests from *The Effective Reader* in an online setting (with feedback accompanying the Review and Combined-Skills Tests), it also offers a wealth of *additional* instruction (in different modalities), remediation, and practice. The site's flexible nature allows instructors to easily assign exercises and establish due dates according to their syllabus, or it can immerse students in a completely personalized, adaptive experience that targets the competencies on which they need to work to succeed. Regardless of the way MyReadingLab is integrated into the course, it offers instructors powerful and easy-to-use tracking and reporting features, facilitating the demonstration of improved and measurable learning outcomes among their students.

- **The Annotated Instructor's Edition (AIE)** is a replica of the student text, with all answers included. ISBN 0-321-96559-0

- **The Instructor's Manual and Test Bank**, prepared by Mary Dubbe and Loretta Rodgers, features teaching strategies for each textbook chapter, plus additional readings that engage students with a variety of learning styles and encourage active learning through class, group, and independent practices. Each chapter includes an introduction designed to hook the students, reproducible handouts, and study-strategy cards. Also included are a ten-item quiz for each chapter. A supplemental section provides a sample syllabus, readability calculations for each reading in *The Effective Reader*, Fourth Edition, five book quizzes to encourage independent reading, and a scaffolded book review form. ISBN 0-321-96569-8

- **The PowerPoint Slides**, developed by Mary Dubbe, offers a deck of book-specific slides to augment and complement an instructor's lecture, whether delivered live in classroom or online. ISBN 0-321-96571-X

- **The Lab Manual**, prepared by Mary Dubbe, is designed as a student workbook and provides a collection of 65 activities that provide additional practice, enrichment, and assessment for the skills presented in *The Effective Reader*, Fourth Edition. The activities for each chapter include practice exercises, one review test, and two mastery tests that mirror the design of *The Effective Reader*, Fourth Edition, and emphasize the reading skills and applications students need in order to succeed in college. The lab activities give students realistic practice, encourage them to use the strategies they have learned, and offer an opportunity for students to continue to build a base of general, background knowledge. This lab manual can be used to strengthen students' reading skills, to allow them to assess their own progress, and to measure their success and readiness for college level reading. ISBN 0-321-98854-X

Alternative Formats

The Effective Reader, Fourth Edition, is offered in several different formats to give instructors and students the flexibility of using the very same material in different settings and at different price points:

- **A la Carte.** This unbound, binder-ready version of the text gives students the option of integrating their own notes with textbook material, and it enables them to only carry only the relevant chapter of the text to class. It is available at 2/3 the net price of the bound text.

- **CourseSmart eText.** Available through www.coursesmart.com, this online version of the text—which offers complete pages fidelity with the print edition—is available at different, discounted price points depending on the duration of access.

Acknowledgments

As I worked on the fourth edition of this reading series, I felt an overwhelming sense of gratitude and humility for the opportunity to serve the learning community as a textbook author. I would like to thank the entire Pearson team for their dedication to providing the best possible materials to foster literacy. To every person, from the editorial team to the representatives in the field, all demonstrate a passion for students, teachers, and learning. It is a joy to be part of such a team. Special thanks are due to the following: Eric Stano, Editor-in-Chief, Developmental Reading and Writing; Kathy Smith with Cenveo® Publisher Services for her tireless devotion to excellence; and Ellen MacElree and the entire production team for their work ethic and gracious attitudes. I would also like to thank Mary Dubbe and Loretta Rodgers for authoring the Lab Manual and the Instructor's Manual that supplement this reading series.

For nearly twenty-five years, I worked with the most amazing group of faculty from across the State of Florida as an item-writer, reviewer, or scorer of state-wide assessment exams for student learning and professional certification. The work that we accomplished together continues to inform me as a teacher, writer, and consultant. I owe a debt of gratitude to this group who sacrificed much for the good of our students.

Finally, I would like to gratefully recognize the invaluable insights provided by the following colleagues and reviewers. I deeply appreciate their investment of time and energy: Julia Erben, Gulf Coast Community College; Suzanne Franklin, Johnson County Community College; Richard Gair, Valencia College; Sondra Grove, Portland Community College; Valerie Hennen, Gateway Technical School; Valerie Hicks, The Community College of Baltimore County; Martha Hofstetter, Delaware Technical & Community College; Janice Johnson, Missouri State University—West Plains; Kelly Johnson, Front Range Community College; Kimberly Jones, College of Southern Idaho; Morita Lance, Leeward Community College; Debbie McCarty, MCC–Maple Woods; Vicki Raine, MCC–Penn Valley; Frederia Whitlow Sampson, Albany Technical College; and Jacquelyn Warmsley, Tarrant County College.

D .J. Henry
Daytona Beach, Florida

PART

1

Becoming an Effective Reader

A Reading System for Effective Readers

(LO) LEARNING OUTCOMES

After studying this chapter, you should be able to:

- (LO1) Define Prior Knowledge
- (LO2) Use the Three Phases of the Reading Process with SQ3R
- (LO3) Before Reading: Survey and Question
- (LO4) During Reading: Read and Annotate
- (LO5) After Reading: Recite and Review
- (LO6) Develop Textbook Skills: Ask and Answer Questions Before, During, and After Reading.
- (LO7) Apply Information Literacy Skills: Academic, Personal, and Career Applications of the Reading Process

Many people think that reading involves simply passing our eyes over words in the order they appear on the page. But reading is much more than that. Once we understand the **reading process**, we can follow specific steps and apply strategies that will make us effective readers. The most important aspect of being an effective reader is being an active reader.

Reading is an active process during which you draw information from the text to create meaning. When you understand what you've read, you've achieved **comprehension** of the material.

Comprehension is an understanding of what has been read.

Active reading means that you ask questions, find answers, and react to an author's ideas. Before we examine the reading process in detail, it is important to talk about the role of prior knowledge.

Define Prior Knowledge

LO1 We all have learned a large body of information throughout a lifetime of experience. This body of information is called **prior knowledge**.

Knowledge is gained from experience and stored in memory. Every day, our prior knowledge is expanded by what we experience. For example, a small child hears the word *hot* as her father blows on a spoonful of steaming soup. The hungry child grabs for the bowl and cries as some of the hot liquid spills on her hand. The child has learned and will remember the meaning of *hot*.

> **Prior knowledge** is the large body of information that is learned throughout a lifetime of experience.

The following graphic illustrates specific ways to connect to prior knowledge in each phase of the reading process. Connecting to prior knowledge increases comprehension.

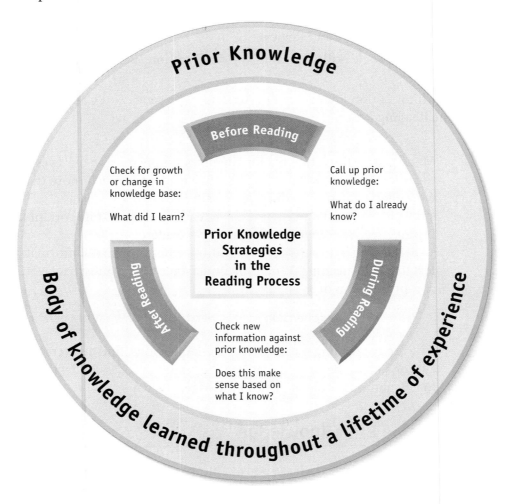

Prior Knowledge

Body of knowledge learned throughout a lifetime of experience

Before Reading

Check for growth or change in knowledge base:

What did I learn?

Call up prior knowledge:

What do I already know?

Prior Knowledge Strategies in the Reading Process

After Reading

During Reading

Check new information against prior knowledge:

Does this make sense based on what I know?

> **EXAMPLE** Read the following paragraph. In the space provided, list any topics from the paragraph about which you already have prior knowledge.

Physical and Mental Fitness

Just as physical exercise builds up the body, mental exercise builds the mind. None of us expects to be able to suddenly run a marathon or lift heavy weights without training. And our bodies rarely take on that lean, toned look without physical effort. However, as we exercise our bodies, they become stronger and leaner. Likewise, as we exercise our minds through reading and writing, our mental abilities become stronger and more efficient.

_____

_____

EXPLANATION If you know about psychology and the issues linked to mental well-being, then this paragraph makes more sense to you than it would to someone who does not understand the complexity suggested by the expression "mental fitness." However, even if you do not know much about psychology, you may have helpful prior knowledge about some of the other ideas in the passage. For example, most of us have seen the effects of working out on the human body. Our prior knowledge about physical fitness helps us understand the kind of commitment we must make to building our own mental fitness.

The more prior knowledge we have about a topic, the more likely we are to understand that topic. This is why effective readers build their knowledge base by reading often! ◀

Practice 1

Read the following paragraph from a college health textbook. Then answer the questions that follow it.

Textbook
Skills

Toxic Fumes: Cigarette Smoke

¹Most of the compounds in cigarette smoke are gaseous, and many of them are toxic. ²By far the most hazardous of these gases is carbon monoxide, the same gas that is emitted from the exhaust pipe of a car. ³The difference is that there are community or statewide standards to keep carbon monoxide auto emissions within a safe level, whereas no standards exist for cigarette smoke. ⁴The amount of carbon monoxide that stays in a

smoker's blood is related to activity levels. [5]During the day, carbon monoxide remains in the blood for two to four hours; during sleep, however, it remains for up to eight hours.

— Adapted from Pruitt, B. E., and Jane J. Stein. *Healthstyles: Decisions for Living Well*, 2nd ed., p. 185 © 1999. Printed and electronically reproduced by permission of Pearson Education, Inc., Upper Saddle River, New Jersey.

1. What did you already know about carbon monoxide? That is, what was your prior knowledge? _____

    _____

2. What did you already know about cigarette smoke? _____

    _____

3. When you think of carbon monoxide, what do you think of? Describe ideas and experiences that come to mind. _____

    _____

4. When you think of cigarette smoke, what do you think of? Describe ideas and experiences that come to mind. _____

    _____

5. Was this an easy passage to understand? How does your prior knowledge affect your understanding of this passage? _____

    _____

6. List any parts of the passage you had no prior knowledge of: _____

    _____

LO2 Use the Three Phases of the Reading Process with SQ3R

Triggering prior knowledge is a reading skill that you as an active reader can turn into a reading strategy by using it as you read. **Reading** is best described as a process defined by three distinct phases. Each phase has its own thinking steps. SQ3R is a reading system that connects to prior knowledge and offers strategies for each phase of the reading process. The following graphic illustrates the phases of the reading process through SQ3R. Effective readers repeat or move among phases as needed to repair comprehension.

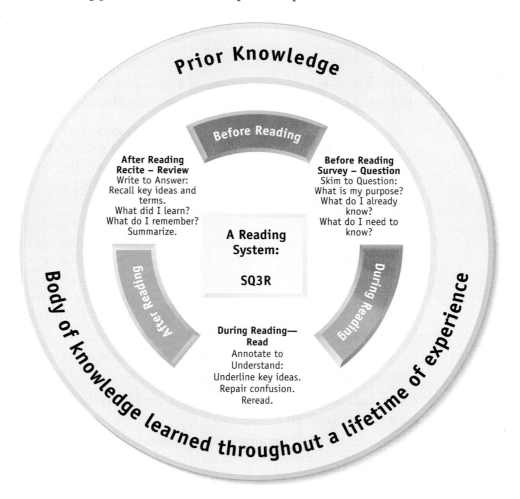

Prior Knowledge

Before Reading

After Reading
Recite – Review
Write to Answer:
Recall key ideas and
terms.
What did I learn?
What do I remember?
Summarize.

Before Reading
Survey – Question
Skim to Question:
What is my purpose?
What do I already
know?
What do I need to
know?

**A Reading
System:**

SQ3R

After Reading

During Reading

**During Reading—
Read**
Annotate to
Understand:
Underline key ideas.
Repair confusion.
Reread.

Body of knowledge learned throughout a lifetime of experience

SQ3R stands for Survey, Question, Read, Recite, and Review.

LO3 Before Reading: Survey and Question

Survey

Quickly look over, or **skim,** the reading passage for clues about how it is organized and what it is going to talk about or teach you.

To skim effectively, look at *italic* and **bold** type and take note of titles, the introduction, and headings. Also look at pictures and graphs. Finally, read the first paragraph, summaries, and questions. Each of these clues provides important information.

Question

To aid in comprehension, ask questions before you read. The following list of prereading questions can be used in most reading situations:

- What is the passage about? The answer to this question will lead you to the main point the author is making. Sometimes the author will state the main idea in a topic sentence; other times the main idea will be implied. Chapter 3 gives in-depth instruction and practice on identifying and locating stated main ideas, and Chapter 4 teaches how to grasp main ideas that are not stated but only implied.

- How is the material organized? The answer to this question will help you identify and follow the thought pattern the author has used so that the ideas flow smoothly and logically. Chapters 7 and 8 offer detailed explanations about and practice with the following thought patterns: time, space, listing, classification, comparison and contrast, cause and effect, generalization and example, and definition and example.

- What do I already know about this idea? (What is my prior knowledge?)

- What is my purpose for reading?

- What is my reading plan? Do I need to read everything, or can I just skim for the information I need?

- What are the most important parts to remember?

▶ **EXAMPLE** Before you read the following passage word for word, look over the passage and fill in the following information.

1. What is the passage about? _____

   _____

2. What do I already know about this topic? _____

   _____

3. What is my purpose for reading? That is, why am I reading this? What do I need to remember? _____

_____

_____

4. What ideas in the passage are in *italics* or in **bold** type? _____

_____

_____

Textbook
Skills

The Problems of Designer Drugs

Designer drugs are produced in chemical laboratories or made in homes and sold illegally. These drugs are easy to produce from available raw material. The drugs themselves were once technically legal because the law had to specify the exact chemical structure of an illegal drug. However, there is now a law in place that bans all chemical cousins of illegal drugs.

Collectively known as **club drugs**, these dangerous substances include *Ecstasy*, *Special K*, and *Rohypnol*. Although users may think of them as harmless, research has shown that club drugs can produce a range of unwanted effects. Some of these effects include hallucinations, paranoia, amnesia, and in some cases, death. Some club drugs work on the same brain mechanisms as alcohol and therefore can dangerously boost the effects of both substances. Because the drugs are odorless and tasteless, people can easily slip them into drinks. Some of them have been associated with sexual assaults and for that reason are referred to as *date rape drugs*.

—Adapted from Donatelle, Rebecca J.,
Health: The Basics 5th ed., pp. 181–182.

EXPLANATION

1. What is the passage about? The title of the passage gives us a clue: "The Problems of Designer Drugs." So does the first paragraph. By quickly looking at the terms in *italic* and **bold** print, you can see that this passage is about the dangers of designer drugs, also known as club drugs.

2. What do I already know about this topic? This answer will vary for each of you. Some of you may know someone who has used or been a victim of designer drugs; thus you already know a great deal that will help you understand this passage. Others may not have any experience with illegal drugs. Yet most of you probably know someone who has struggled with alcoholism or misuse of legal drugs. So you can connect your experience to the information in the passage.

3. What is my purpose for reading? I need to know what is so dangerous about designer drugs.

4. What are the words in *italic* and **bold** type? *Designer drugs, club drugs, Ecstasy, Special K, Rohypnol,* and *date rape drugs*. Simply by writing the highlighted words in a list, you have begun to summarize the author's main point (for more on summarizing, see pages 660–661). ◁

LO4 During Reading: Read and Annotate

After you have surveyed and asked questions about the text, it's time to read the entire passage.

Read

As you read, think about the importance of the information by continuing to ask questions:

- Does this new information agree with what I already knew?
- Do I need to change what I thought I knew?
- What is the significance of this information? Do I need to remember this?

In addition to asking questions while you read, acknowledge and resolve any confusion as it occurs.

- Create questions based on the headings, subheadings, and words in **bold** type and *italics*.
- Reread the parts you don't understand.
- Reread when your mind drifts during reading.
- Read ahead to see if the idea becomes clearer.
- Determine the meaning of words from the context.
- Look up new or difficult words.
- Think about ideas even when they differ from your own.

Annotate

Make the material your own. Make sure you understand it by repeating the information.

- Create a picture in your mind or on paper.
- Mark your text by underlining, circling, or otherwise highlighting topics, key terms, and main ideas. (See pages 658–659 for more information about how to annotate a text.)
- Restate the ideas in your own words.
- Write out answers to the questions you created based on the headings and subheadings.
- Write a summary of the section or passage.

⊘ EXAMPLE

A. Before you read the following passage from a college science textbook, survey the passage and answer the following questions.

1. What is the passage about? _____

_____

2. What do I already know about this passage? What is my prior knowledge?

_____

_____

3. What is important about this passage? What do I need to remember?

_____

_____

4. What words in **bold** type will help me remember what I need to know?

_____

Textbook
Skills

B. Once you have surveyed the information, read the passage. During reading, monitor your understanding: (1) highlight key words and ideas; (2) answer questions based on the ideas in **bold** print.

---

5. What new or difficult words do I need to look up?

6. What is color resemblance?

7. What are some examples of color resemblance?

8. What is countershading?

9. What is an example of countershading?

Hiding to Live: Animal Camouflage

[1]Animals in danger of being hunted and killed have evolved ways to camouflage themselves. [2]Perhaps the simplest type of camouflage is **color resemblance**, in which an animal's color matches the color of its background. [3]Color resemblance is illustrated by green aphids that live on vegetation, gray-brown lizards inhabiting sandy areas, and black beetles that cling to the bark of trees.

[4]Another type of camouflage is **countershading**. [5]Without markings, an object will reflect more light—and appear lighter—on its top surface than on its bottom surface. [6]This difference makes an animal stand out against its background. [7]Countershading, or the placement of darker markings on the top of the animal, reduces the reflection and allows the animal to blend into its background. [8]For example, most fish are darkest on their top sides and consequently less visible when alive than when dead and floating belly up.

—Adapted from Maier, Richard, *Comparative Animal Behavior: An Evolutionary and Ecological Approach*, pp. 148–149.

EXPLANATION

A. **Before Reading: Survey and Question**

1. What is the passage about? Types of camouflage used by animals

2. What do I already know about this passage? What is my prior knowledge? Answers will vary.

3. What is important about this passage? What do I need to remember? Wording will vary: the ways in which camouflaging helps an animal survive

4. What words are in **bold** type? Color resemblance and countershading

B. **During Reading: Read and Annotate**

5. What are the new or difficult words I need to look up? Answers will vary.

6. What is color resemblance? A type of camouflage in which an animal's color matches the color of its background

7. What are some examples of color resemblance? <u>Green aphids, gray-brown lizards, and black beetles</u>

8. What is countershading? <u>Markings on the top of the animal that are darker than those on the bottom</u>

9. What is an example of countershading? <u>Most fish</u>

10. Identify any ideas you needed to reread to understand. <u>Answers will vary</u>.

LO5 After Reading: Recite and Review

Once you have read the entire selection, go back over the material to review and respond to it.

Recite

As part of your review, take time to think and write about what you have read.

- Connect new information to your prior knowledge about the topic.
- Form opinions about the material and the author.
- Record changes in your opinions based on the new information.
- Write about what you have read. What do you think about what you have read?

Review

- Summarize the most important parts (for more information about how to summarize, see pages 660–661).
- Revisit and answer the questions raised by headings and subheadings.
- Review new words and their meanings based on the way they were used in the passage.

Practice 2

Now that you have learned about each of the three phases of the reading process, practice putting all three together. Think before, during, and after reading. Apply SQ3R to the following passage. Remember the steps:

- **Survey:** Look over the whole passage.
- **Question:** Ask questions about the content. Predict how the new information fits in with what you already know about the topic.

- **Read:** Continue to question, look up new words, reread, and create pictures in your mind.
- **Recite:** Restate the ideas in your own words. Take notes: Write out questions and answers, definitions of words, and new information.
- **Review:** Think about what you have read and written. Use writing to capture your opinions and feelings about what you have read.

Before Reading: Survey and Question

Skim the passage from a college law textbook, and answer the following questions:

1. What is this passage about? _____

   _____

2. What do I already know about this information? _____

   _____

3. What do I need to remember? _____

   _____

4. What ideas are in **bold** type? _____

   _____

Before you go on: Use the words you listed in item 4 to create questions. Write the questions in the boxes beside the textbook passage. You will write your answers in these same boxes during reading.

During Reading: Read and Annotate

As you read, highlight key ideas and answer the questions you created from the ideas in **bold** type.

Sources of U.S. Law

5. _____

   _____

   _____

   _____

[1]Because the United States was once a British colony, our legal system is based primarily on the common-law philosophy. [2]The concept of *stare decisis* plays a major role in the development of our laws. [3]*Stare decisis* means that prior court decisions control subsequent cases with the same or similar facts.

6. _____

_____

_____

_____

7. _____

_____

_____

8. _____

_____

⁴However, not all U.S. law results from cases decided by judges. ⁵The U.S. system of law is regulated by a written **constitution** as well as by laws enacted by duly elected representatives. ⁶These laws are known as **codes** or statutory laws. ⁷U.S. laws are categorized according to their source as constitutional law, case law, **statutory law**, or administrative regulations. ⁸These sources of law are found in both the federal and state legal systems.

—Hames, Joanne and Ekern, Yvonne,
Introduction to Law, 4th ed. p. 24.

After Reading: Recite and Review

9. How does *stare decisis* relate to the word *decide*? _____

_____

10. What is the most important point to remember from this passage?

_____

_____

LO6 Develop Textbook Skills: Ask and Answer Questions Before, During, and After Reading

Textbook
Skills

A vast number of textbooks use titles, headings, **bold** print, and *italics* to organize ideas. An effective reader applies the questioning and reciting steps to these pieces of information. For example, before reading, notice titles and headings. Use titles and headings to create questions. Write these questions out. During or after reading, write out the answers to these questions. After reading, use the questions and answers as a review quiz.

> **EXAMPLE** Before you read the following passage from a college communications textbook, skim the information and write out five questions based on the title and words in *italic* print. After you read, answer the questions you created before you read.

Communication Context

[1]Communication exists in a context that determines, to a large extent, the meaning of any verbal or nonverbal message. [2]The same words or behaviors may have totally different meanings when they occur in different contexts. [3]For example, the greeting "How are you?" means "Hello" to someone you pass regularly on the street but "Is your health improving?" to a friend in the hospital. [4]A wink to an attractive person on a bus means something completely different from a wink that signifies a put-on or a lie. [5]Divorced from the context, it's impossible to tell what meaning was intended from just examining the signals.

[6]The context will also influence what you say and how you say it. [7]You communicate differently depending on the specific context you're in. [8]Contexts have at least four aspects: physical, cultural, social-psychological, and temporal or time.

- [9]The *physical context* is the tangible or concrete environment, the room, park, or auditorium; you don't talk the same way at a noisy football game as you do at a quiet funeral.
- [10]The *cultural context* involves the lifestyles, beliefs, values, behavior, and communication of a group; it is the rules of a group of people for considering something right or wrong.
- [11]The *social-psychological context* has to do with the status relationships among speakers, the formality of the situation, the norms of a group or organization; you don't talk the same way in the cafeteria as you would at a formal dinner at your boss's house.
- [12]The *temporal context* is a message's position within a sequence of events; you don't talk the same way after someone tells you about the death of a close relative as you do after someone reveals they've won the lottery.
- [13]These four contexts interact—each influences and is influenced by the others. [14]For example, arriving late for a date (temporal context) may lead to changes in the degree of friendliness (social-psychological context), which would depend upon the culture of you and your date (cultural context) and may lead to changes in where you go on the date (physical context).

—DeVito, Joseph A., *Essentials of Human
Communication*, 7th ed., pp. 7–8.

1. Question: _____

_____

Answer: _____

_____

2. Question: _____

_____

Answer: _____

_____

3. Question: _____

_____

Answer: _____

_____

4. Question: _____

_____

Answer: _____

_____

5. Question: _____

_____

Answer: _____

_____

EXPLANATION Compare your questions and answers to the ones given here.

1. *Question:* How does context influence communication?

Answer: The meanings of words and actions often vary because they are based on or influenced by the situation in which they occur.

2. *Question:* What is physical context?

Answer: Physical context is the place where the communication takes place, such as at home, in a park, or in a classroom.

3. *Question:* What is cultural context?

    Answer: Cultural context is a way of life of a group, including beliefs, values, rules, and communication.

4. *Question:* What is social-psychological context?

    Answer: Social-psychological context is the status relationships among speakers, the formality of the situation, and the standards of the group.

5. *Question:* What is temporal context?

    Answer: Temporal context is the timing of the message in a sequence of events.

    The phrase "four aspects" suggests a list. And the list includes special terms, definitions of the terms, and examples of the terms. ⊙

Practice 3

Before you read the following passage from a college nutrition textbook, skim the information and write three questions based on the words in **bold** print. During reading, annotate the text. After you read, answer the questions you created before you read.

Grains, Glorious Whole Grains

¹There are three edible parts in a kernel of grain: the bran, the endosperm, and the germ. ²The **bran** or outer shell of the wheat kernel is rich in fiber, B vitamins, phytochemicals, and trace minerals such as chromium and zinc. ³The **germ** or seed of the kernel is a nutritional powerhouse providing vitamin E, heart-healthy fats, and plenty of B vitamins. ⁴The **endosperm**, or starchy component of the grain, contains protein, B vitamins, and some fiber, although not as much as bran.

⁵Depending upon which parts of the kernel are used, grain products can be divided into two main categories: **refined grains** and **whole grains**. ⁶In refined grains, such as wheat or white bread and white rice, the grain kernel goes through a milling process that strips out the bran and germ, leaving only the endosperm of the kernel in the end product. ⁷As a result, some, though not all, of the B vitamins, iron, phytochemicals, and dietary fiber are removed.

⁸To restore some of the nutrition lost from refined grains, **enriched grains** have folic acid, thiamin, niacin, riboflavin, and iron added to them. ⁹This improves their nutritional quality somewhat, but the fiber and the

phytochemicals are lost. [10]Though refined grains can still be a good source of complex carbohydrates, you can think of *refined* as having left some of nutrition *behind*. [11]From a health standpoint, what was left behind may end up being the most important part of the kernel.

[12]Whole-grain foods, such as whole-wheat bread, white whole-wheat bread, brown rice, and oatmeal, contain all three parts of the kernel.

—Blake, Joan, *Nutrition and You*, 2nd ed., p. 98.

VISUAL *VOCABULARY*

The outer shell of a wheat kernel is called a _____.

a. bran
b. germ

1. Question: _____

   Answer: _____

   _____

2. Question: _____

   Answer: _____

   _____

3. Question: _____

   Answer: _____

   _____

   _____

Apply Information Literacy Skills

 ## Academic, Personal, and Career Applications of the Reading Process

Information literacy is the ability to recognize a need for information, and to then identify, locate, evaluate, and effectively use that information to resolve an issue or problem. Information literacy is the set of skills needed to find, retrieve, analyze, and use information. Effective use of the reading process is an information literacy skill that can be applied to academic, personal, and career issues or situations.

Academic Application

Assume you are taking a college history course. Your professor has given you a list of terms to study for the midterm exam. You have located the following paragraph in your history textbook that defines several of these key terms.

- **Before Reading:** Skim the passage and record at least three questions you will read to answer based on the key terms in **bold** print.
- **During Reading:** Highlight the details that answer each of your pre-reading questions.
- **After Reading:** In the space following the passage, record the answers to your pre-reading questions based on the key terms in **bold** print.

Pre-Reading Questions: _____

_____

Theoretical Foundations of American Government

[1]To understand the type of government we have today, we will look at the theories of government that influenced the Framers. [2]The Framers drafted the Constitution and created the United States of America.

Social Contract Theory

[3]Even before the Pilgrims arrived in the New World, they saw the necessity for a **social contract**, an agreement among the people signifying their consent to be governed. [4]While at sea, they wrote a document

called the **Mayflower Compact**. [5]This compact listed the scope of their government and its expectations of citizens. [6]This document was based on a social contract theory of government. [7]Two English theorists of the seventeenth century, Thomas Hobbes (1588–1679) and John Locke (1632–1704), built on conventional notions about the role of government and the relationship of the government to the people in proposing a **social contract theory** of government. [8]They argued that all individuals were free and equal by natural right. [9]This freedom, in turn, required that all people give their consent to be governed.

Key Terms: _____

_____

_____

_____

_____

Personal Application

Assume you are a parent or friend of a 10-year-old video game enthusiast. You want to give this young person a video game as a present for a special occasion. You have selected three possible games, but you are not sure if any is appropriate. The games are *Chronicles of Vampires: Origins*, rated E10+; *Rayman Brain Games*, rated EC; and *Twisted Metal*, rated M. To help you make your decision, you have found the following information on the Internet.

- **Before Reading:** Skim the passage and record the questions you have as a consumer.
- **During Reading:** Highlight the details that answer each of your pre-reading questions.
- **After Reading:** In the space following the passage, record your decision and the reasons for your choice of game for the 10-year-old.

Pre-Reading Questions: _____

_____

_____

Game Ratings Symbols

[1]The Entertainment Software Rating Board (ESRB) ratings are designed to provide concise and impartial information about the content in computer and video games. [2]Thus, consumers, especially parents, can make an informed purchase decision. [3]ESRB ratings have two equal parts. [4]Rating symbols suggest age appropriateness for the game. [5]Content descriptors indicate elements in a game that may have triggered a particular rating and/or may be of interest or concern. [6]To take full advantage of the ESRB rating system, it's important to check both the rating symbol (on the front of the box) and the content descriptors (on the back). [7]Following are the ESRB Rating Symbols:

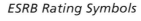

ESRB Rating Symbols

[8]Titles rated **EC (Early Childhood)** have content that may be suitable for ages 3 and older. [9]Contains no material that parents would find inappropriate.

[10]Titles rated **E (Everyone)** have content that may be suitable for ages 6 and older. [11]Titles in this category may contain minimal cartoon, fantasy or mild violence and/or infrequent use of mild language.

[12]Titles rated **E10+ (Everyone 10 and older)** have content that may be suitable for ages 10 and older. [13]Titles in this category may contain more cartoon, fantasy or mild violence, mild language and/or minimal suggestive themes.

[14]Titles rated **T (Teen)** have content that may be suitable for ages 13 and older. [15]Titles in this category may contain violence, suggestive themes, crude humor, minimal blood, simulated gambling, and/or infrequent use of strong language.

[16]Titles rated **M (Mature)** have content that may be suitable for persons ages 17 and older. [17]Titles in this category may contain intense violence, blood and gore, sexual content and/or strong language.

[18]Titles rated **AO (Adults Only)** have content that should only be played by persons 18 years and older. [19]Titles in this category may include prolonged scenes of intense violence and/or graphic sexual content and nudity.

[20]Titles listed as **RP (Rating Pending)** have been submitted to the ESRB and are awaiting final rating. [21](This symbol appears only in advertising prior to a game's release.)

—From "Game Rating Symbols," *Game Ratings and Descriptor Guide*. Reprinted by permission of the Entertainment Software Rating Board (ESRB). The ESRB rating icons are registered trademarks of the Entertainment Software Association.

Decision and Reasons: _____

_____

_____

_____

_____

_____

Career Application

Assume you work in the human resources department of a local company. Your supervisor has appointed you to a committee whose purpose is to update the employee manual. You have been asked to learn about the U.S. government's policy on age discrimination. You have found on the Internet the following memo published by the U.S. Equal Employment Opportunity Commission.

- **Before Reading:** Skim the memo and record at least three questions you will read to answer.
- **During Reading:** Highlight the details that answer each of your pre-reading questions.
- **After Reading:** In the space following the passage, record the key ideas you have learned that you want to share with the committee.

Pre-Reading Questions: _____

_____

_____

_____

Age Discrimination

[1]Age discrimination involves treating someone (an applicant or employee) less favorably because of his age. [2]The Age Discrimination in Employment Act (ADEA) only forbids age discrimination against people who are age 40 or older. [3]It does not protect workers under the age of 40. [4]However, some states do have laws that protect younger workers from age discrimination.

[5]It is not illegal for an employer or other covered entity to favor an older worker over a younger one, even if both workers are age 40 or older. [6]Discrimination can occur when the victim and the person who inflicted the discrimination are both over 40.

Age Discrimination & Work Situations

[7]The law forbids discrimination when it comes to any aspect of employment. [8]This includes hiring, firing, pay, job assignments, promotions, layoff, training, fringe benefits, and any other term or condition of employment.

Age Discrimination & Harassment

[9]It is unlawful to harass a person because of his or her age. [10]Harassment can include, for example, offensive remarks about a person's age. [11]The law doesn't prohibit simple teasing, offhand comments, or isolated incidents that aren't very serious. [12]However, harassment is illegal when it is so frequent or severe that it creates a hostile or offensive work environment. [13]In addition, harassment is illegal when it results in an adverse employment decision (such as the victim being fired or demoted). [14]The harasser can be the victim's supervisor, a supervisor in another area, a coworker. [15]In addition, a harasser can be someone who is not an employee of the employer, such as a client or customer.

Age Discrimination & Employment Policies/Practices

[16]An employment policy or practice that applies to everyone, regardless of age, can be illegal if it has a negative impact on applicants or employees age 40 or older and is not based on a reasonable factor other than age.

—U.S. Equal Employment Opportunity Commission <http://www1.eeoc.gov//laws/types/age.cfm?renderforprint=1>

Key Ideas: _____

_____

_____

_____

_____

REVIEW TEST 1

Score (number correct) _____ × 20 = _____%

Visit MyReadingLab to take this test online and receive feedback and guidance on your answers.

Before Reading

Survey the following paragraph from a college geology textbook. Then, using the words in **bold** print, create five questions to guide your reading.

What Is an Earthquake?

[1]Earthquakes are natural geologic phenomena caused by the sudden and rapid movement of a large volume of rock. [2]The violent shaking and destruction caused by earthquakes are the result of rupture and slippage along fractures in Earth's crust called **faults**. [3]Larger quakes result from the rupture of larger fault segments. [4]The origin of an earthquake occurs at depths between 5 and 700 kilometers, at the **focus**. [5]The point at the surface directly above the focus is called the **epicenter**.

[6]During large earthquakes, a massive amount of energy is released as **seismic waves**—a form of elastic energy that causes vibrations in the material that transmits them. [7]Seismic waves are analogous to waves produced when a stone is dropped into a calm pond. [8]Just as the impact of

the stone creates a pattern of waves in motion, an earthquake generates waves that radiate outward in all directions from the focus. [9]Even though seismic energy dissipates rapidly with increasing distance, sensitive instruments located around the world detect and record these events.

—Tarbuck, Frederick K., Edward J. Lutgens, and Dennis G. Tasa. *Essentials of Geology*, 11th ed., pp. 336–337.

1. _____

2. _____

3. _____

4. _____

5. _____

REVIEW TEST 2

Score (number correct) _____ × 25 = _____%

Visit MyReadingLab to take this test online and receive feedback and guidance on your answers.

Using SQ3R, read the following passage from the college textbook *Introduction to Hospitality Management*. Then complete the study chart.

Decision-Making Styles

Textbook
Skills

[1]Decision makers differ in their way of thinking; some are rational and logical, whereas others are intuitive and creative. [2]Rational decision makers look at the information in order. [3]They organize the information and make sure it is logical and consistent. [4]Only after carefully studying all of the given options do they finally make the decision. [5]Intuitive thinkers, on the other hand, can look at information that is not necessarily in order. [6]They can make quick decisions based on their spontaneous creativity and intuition. [7]Although a careful analysis is still required, these types of people are comfortable looking at all solutions as a whole as opposed to studying each option separately.

[8]The second dimension in which people differ is each individual's **tolerance for ambiguity**. [9]Managers who have a high tolerance for ambiguity are lucky in that they save a lot of time while making a decision. [10]These individuals can process many thoughts at the same time.

[11]Unfortunately, some managers have a low tolerance for ambiguity. [12]These individuals must have order and consistency in the way they organize and process the information so as to minimize ambiguity.

[13]Upon review of the two dimensions of decision making, ways of thinking and tolerance for ambiguity, and their subdivisions, four major decision-making styles become evident:

1. [14]The **directive style** entails having a low tolerance for ambiguity as well as being a rational thinker. [15]Individuals who fall into the category of having a directive decision-making style are usually logical and very efficient. [16]They also have a primary focus on the short run and are relatively quick decision makers. [17]Directive decision makers value speed and efficiency, which can cause them to be remiss in assessing all alternatives, such that decisions are often made with minimal information.

2. [18]Decision makers who have an **analytic style** of decision making have a large tolerance for ambiguity. [19]Compared to directive decision makers, these people require more information before making their decisions and, consequently, they consider more alternatives. [20]Individuals with an analytic style are careful decision makers, which gives them leeway to adapt or cope with unique situations.

3. [21]Decision makers who have a **conceptual style** of decision making look at numerous alternatives and are typically very broad in their outlook. [22]Their focus is on the long run of the decision made. [23]These individuals are typically creative and often find creative solutions to the problem with which they are dealing.

4. [24]Decision makers who work well with others are said to have a **behavioral style** of decision making. [25]This entails being receptive to suggestions and ideas from others as well as being concerned about the achievements of their employees. [26]They commonly communicate with their coworkers through meetings. [27]These individuals try to avoid conflict as often as possible, because acceptance by others is very important to them.

[28]At least one of these decision-making styles is always used by managers. [29]However, decision makers often combine two or more styles to make a decision. [30]Most often a manager will have one dominant decision-making style and use one or more other styles as alternates. [31]Flexible individuals vary their decision-making styles according to each unique situation. [32]If the style is to consider riskier options (analytic style) or if the decision is made based on suggestions from subordinates (behavioral

style), each style will eventually bring the decision maker to the optimal solution for the unique problem he or she is facing.

—Walker, John R., *Introduction to Hospitality Management*, 3rd ed., pp. 565–567.

The decision makers who have a(n) _____ style search out information in order to make a thoughtful decision.

a. directive
b. analytic
c. conceptual
d. behavioral

Study Chart for "Decision-Making Styles"

Style	Traits
1. _____	_____
	_____
	_____
	_____
	_____
2. _____	_____
	_____
	_____
	_____
3. _____	_____
_____	_____
	_____
4. _____	_____
_____	_____
	_____
	_____

REVIEW TEST 3

Score (number correct) _____ × 10 = _____%

Visit MyReadingLab to take this test online and receive feedback and guidance on your answers.

Before, During, and After Reading

A. Before you read, survey the following passage from a college health textbook, and then answer the questions given here.

Textbook Skills

1. What is the passage about? _____

_____

2. What are the ideas in *italics* or in **bold** print? _____

_____

3. What do I already know about this idea? _____

_____

4. What do I need to remember? _____

_____

_____

B. Read the passage. As you read, answer the questions in the left margin.

Aging: Physical Changes

¹Although the **physiological** consequences of aging can differ in severity and timing, certain typical changes occur as a result of the aging process. ²The changes that occur to skin and bones illustrate what can be expected.

Skin

5. What does **physiological** mean? _____

_____

_____

³As a normal consequence of aging, the skin becomes thinner and loses elasticity. ⁴This loss occurs most in the outer surfaces. ⁵Fat deposits, which add to the soft lines and shape of the skin, diminish. ⁶Starting at age 30, lines develop on the forehead as a result of smiling, squinting, and other facial

6. What are some of the effects of aging on the *skin*?

_____

_____

_____

_____

_____

7. What are some of the effects of aging on *bones*?

_____

_____

_____

8. What is *osteoporosis*?

_____

_____

_____

_____

_____

expressions. [7]These lines become more obvious, with added "crow's feet" around the eyes, during the 40s. [8]During a person's 50s and 60s, the skin begins to sag and lose color, leading to **pallor** in the 70s. [9]Body fat in underlying layers of skin tends to shift away from limbs and into the trunk region of the body. [10]Age spots become more numerous because of patches of excessive pigments under the skin.

Bones

[11]Throughout the life span, bones are continually changing because of the accumulation and loss of minerals. [12]By the third or fourth decade of life, mineral loss from bones becomes more prevalent than mineral accumulation. [13]The result is weakness and porosity (diminishing density) of bony tissue. [14]This loss of minerals, such as calcium, occurs in both sexes. [15]However, it is much more common in females. [16]Loss of calcium can lead to **osteoporosis**, a disease marked by low bone density and structural deterioration of bone tissue. [17]These fragile, porous bones are prone to fracture. [18]This condition, however, can occur at any age.

—Adapted from Donatelle, Rebecca J. *Health: The Basics*, 5th ed., p. 387.

C. After reading, answer the following questions.

9. In sentence 8, what does the term *pallor* refer to?

_____

_____

10. What could a person do to minimize the impact of osteoporosis?

_____

_____

SUMMARY RESPONSE

Respond to the passage by answering the following question: What is the author's most important idea? Restate the author's ideas in your own words. Begin your summary response with the following: *The most important idea of "Aging: Physical Changes" by Donatelle is . . .*

WHAT DO YOU THINK?

What do you think about the aging process? In what ways do our choices affect the aging process? Assume you are a camp counselor to a group of pre-teens. Write a paragraph or two that you may use to introduce this issue to your group. In your paragraph include the following information:

- Explain the aging process on skin and bones.
- Explain how healthy habits promote healthy skin and bones throughout life.

VISUAL *VOCABULARY*

The best meaning of the word **melanin** as used in the caption below is _____.

a. a vitamin
b. a natural sunscreen
c. dark skin color

▲ Melanin is a pigment that offers protection against UV rays for dark-skinned people. In contrast, fair-skinned people are much less protected and more susceptible to aging and diseases of the skin.

REVIEW TEST 4

Score (number correct) _____ × 20 = _____%

Visit MyReadingLab to take this test online and receive feedback and guidance on your answers.

Before reading: Survey the following passage from a college psychology text-book. Study the words in the Vocabulary Preview; then skim the passage, noting the words in **bold** print. Answer the Before Reading questions that follow the passage. Then read the passage and answer the After Reading question that follows.

Vocabulary Preview

debilitating (1): devastating
neurons (11): nerve cells
neurotransmitter (12): a substance that transmits or carries nerve impulses

Textbook
Skills

Parkinson's Disease

[1]The connection between the brain and behavior is seen in the **debilitating** effects of Parkinson's disease, a brain disorder. [2]Parkinson's afflicts about half a million Americans from every slice of life—from celebrity Michael J. Fox to the lady next door.

[3]The physical effects are obvious. [4]The hands of people with Parkinson's disease shake; they may move slowly, *lethargically*, with a stooped posture and shuffling walk; their limbs often seem frozen in position and resist attempts to bend them. [5]Along with the physical effects, Parkinson's disease also takes an emotional and social toll.

[6]A piano tuner named John had to stop working because he developed Parkinson's disease. [7]He had difficulty controlling his movements, and his behavior changed as well. [8]He became so listless that he rarely left his house. [9]He missed meals. [10]And he started to contract various minor illnesses, which worsened his other symptoms.

[11]All these changes, physical and behavioral, were caused directly or indirectly by the death of certain **neurons** in John's brain. [12]In the brains of people with Parkinson's disease, cells that produce the **neurotransmitter** dopamine have died. [13]Dopamine plays a key role in the areas of the brain that are involved in planning movements. [14]When patients take a drug that helps produce dopamine, symptoms decrease, often for a long period of time.

[15]When John's neurons no longer produced enough dopamine, the working of his brain was affected, and his muscle control was impaired. [16]His shaky hands made it almost impossible for him to tune pianos, so John had to retire. [17]After he gave up the work he loved, he became depressed. [18]He began to think of himself as diseased. [19]As a consequence, he lost interest in going out. [20]He stopped seeing many people, who in turn stopped seeing, and helping, him. [21]The events in his brain influenced his feelings about himself and his relationships with other people.

—Adapted from Kosslyn, Stephen M. and Robin S. Rosenberg, *Psychology: The Brain, The Person, The World*, p. 52.

Before Reading Questions

Complete the following sentence by filling in the blanks with the title of the passage and the words in the Vocabulary Preview:

The (**1**) _____ symptoms of (**2**) _____ are caused by the death of (**3**) _____ in the brain that produce the (**4**) _____ dopamine.

After Reading Question

5. What are the physical, emotional, and social effects of Parkinson's disease?

_____

_____

_____

SUMMARY RESPONSE

Respond to the passage by answering the following question: What is the author's most important idea? Restate the author's ideas in your own words. Begin your summary response with the following: *The most important idea of "Parkinson's Disease" by Kosslyn is . . .*

Assume you are volunteering with the local Rotary Club. This group is sponsoring a 5-mile run/walk to raise money for Mario Gomez, an electrician and father of four who is suffering from a debilitating illness (such as Parkinson's disease, cancer, etc.). As a volunteer, you have been asked to write a letter that will go out to local businesses. Include the following information in your letter:

- Explain some of the emotional and physical effects of the disease.
- Describe the financial expenses of treating this illness.
- Ask for donations.
- Explain how the funds raised will benefit him.

After Reading About a Reading System for Effective Readers

Now that you have read and studied a reading system for effective readers, take time to reflect on what you have learned before you begin the Mastery Tests. Think about your learning and performance by answering the following questions. Write your answers in your notebook.

- How has my knowledge base or prior knowledge about the reading process changed?
- Based on my studies, how do I think I will perform on the Mastery Test(s)? Why do I think my scores will be above average, average, or below average?
- Would I recommend this chapter to other students who want to learn more about the reading process? Why or why not?

Test your understanding of what you have learned about a reading system for effective readers by completing the Chapter 1 Review.

Name _____ Section _____

Date _____ **Score** (number correct) _____ × 25 = _____%

Visit MyReadingLab to take this test online and receive feedback and guidance on your answers.

Textbook Skills

Before you read, skim the following passage from a college humanities textbook. Also, look over the blank chart labeled "Q and A Study Chart for 'The Beginnings of Culture.'" Write four questions in the "Question" column of the chart. **As you read**, annotate the text for details that answer your questions. **After you read**, record your answers in the "Answer" column of the chart. Use your own words.

The Beginnings of Culture

[1]*Culture* can be defined as a way of living practiced by a group of people and passed on from one generation to the next. [2]It took thousands of years for cultures to develop into full-blown civilizations. [3]A civilization is distinct from a culture. [4]A *civilization* has the ability to organize itself thoroughly as a social, economic, and political entity by means, especially, of written language. [5]Written language did not come into being until about 3000 BCE, after human culture shifted from its hunter-gatherer origins to agriculture-based communities. [6]As cultures became more stable and permanent, they became capable of producing not only pottery but metal work, monumental architecture, and literature.

Mesopotamia

[7]In the Tigris and Euphrates valleys of the Fertile Crescent, a series of competing cultures arose. [8]First, in the late fourth century BCE, the Sumerians built monumental ziggurats dedicated to the gods and developed a system of writing. [9]They were succeeded by the Akkadians and Babylonians, the last of whom developed a code of law preserved in a carved stone monument. [10]The first epic poem to survive, the *Epic of Gilgamesh*, originated in these cultures. [11]Most cultures that arose in the Fertile Crescent were polytheistic (believing in many gods). [12]However, the Hebrew religion was monotheistic (believing in one god). [13]The written word was central to their culture and lives in their book of law, the *Torah*.

Egypt

[14]The predictable cycle of flood and sun, and with it the annual deluge of the Nile River valley, helped to create, in Egypt, a strong cultural belief in the stability and balance of all things. [15]Each night the sun god Re, with whom the Egyptian kings were strongly identified, descends into darkness only to rise again, as does the Nile, on a yearly basis. [16]Each person's soul or life force (the ka) was believed to follow this same cycle. [17]And as a result, most surviving Egyptian art and architecture is devoted to burial and the afterlife, the cycle of life, death, and rebirth.

China and India

[18]In the river valleys of China and India other civilizations arose. [19]In China, the Qin dynasty unified the country and built a Great Wall to protect it. [20]During the Shang

dynasty, a philosophical and religious tradition arose that emphasized the balance of opposites embodied in the yin-yang symbol. [21]This tradition led to the development of the *Dao de jing* and Confucianism. [22]The *Dao de jing (The Way and Its Power)* is a book of 81 poems that aid the individual to let go of self through contemplation and to enter the flow of life. [23]Confucianism is a way of life based on self-discipline and proper relations among people. [24]In India, the Hindu religion developed, which also emphasizes the sacred rhythms of creation and destruction, birth, death, and rebirth.

—Adapted from Sayre, Henry M., *Discovering the Humanities*, p. 32.

Q and A Study Chart for "The Beginnings of Culture"

Questions (Before Reading)	Answers (After Reading)
1. _____	_____
_____	_____
_____	_____
_____	_____
2. _____	_____
_____	_____
_____	_____
_____	_____
	_____
3. _____	_____
_____	_____
_____	_____
_____	_____
	_____
4. _____	_____
_____	_____
_____	_____
_____	_____
	_____

Name _____ Section _____

Date _____ **Score** (number correct) _____ × 20 = _____%

Visit MyReadingLab to take this test online and receive feedback and guidance on your answers.

Read the following passage from a college sociology textbook. **Before you read,** skim the questions at the end of the passage. **As you read,** annotate the text. **After you read,** answer the questions.

Gender and the Workplace

[1]Today, women make up almost half of the United States' paid labor force and more than half of all married couples depend on two incomes. [2]While it's now accepted and necessary for women to work, the types of jobs as well as the compensation for these jobs remain different for men and women. [3]Three theoretical models—the human capital model, the choice model, and the patriarchy model—attempt to explain these discrepancies.

[4]The **human capital model** assumes that men and women bring different natural skills to the workplace. [5]For example, society perceives men to have more mechanical skills, thus they make better engineers. [6]Because society considers women to be more nurturing, they are assumed to be better teachers. [7]Such an argument suggests it is not discrimination to hire men to do jobs for which they are more suited. [8]This explains why men seem to have advantages in higher-income professions, such as medicine, engineering, and law.

[9]The **choice model** explains the income gap by analyzing the kinds of jobs women choose. [10]Women choose to major in social work or elementary education, therefore knowingly entering fields that pay less. [11]This argument suggests that if you choose a career that pays very little, you have only yourself to blame.

[12]The **patriarchy model** assumes that we have a male-dominated society that doesn't allow women to hold upper-tier jobs or steers them away from such careers early in life. [13]For example, when discussing majors with an enrollment counselor, students may experience stereotypical gender role expectations. [14]Male students are asked to consider business or engineering. [15]Female students are asked about education or communication fields as possible professions.

[16]The patriarchy mode supports the idea of a **glass ceiling**, or the invisible barrier that prevents women from reaching the executive suite. [17]For example, few women become the CEOs of large companies. [18]On the 2009 Fortune 500 list, women headed only 15 companies. [19]Cornell

Sociology professor Shelley J. Correll studied labor distribution by sex and found that cultural beliefs about gender shape both male and female attitudes about their abilities. [20]If this is the case, our ideas about gender may need to undergo a radical change before the income gap between men and women disappears.

—Carl, John D., *Think Sociology,* 11th ed., p. 198.

1. What are the three theoretical models that explain the difference between men's and women's pay?

   _____

   _____

2. How does the human capital model explain the difference?

   _____

   _____

3. How does the choice model explain the difference?

   _____

   _____

4. How does the patriarchy model explain the difference?

   _____

   _____

5. What is the glass ceiling?

   _____

   _____

Name _____ Section _____

Date _____ **Score** (number correct) _____ × 20 = _____ %

Visit MyReadingLab to take this test online and receive feedback and guidance on your answers.

Using SQ3R, read the following passage from a personal finance textbook.

Advantages and Disadvantages of Credit

Textbook
Skills

Background on Credit

[1]Credit represents funds a creditor provides to a borrower that the borrower will repay in the future with interest. [2]The funds borrowed are sometimes referred to as the principal, so we segment repayment of credit into interest and principal payments. [3]Credit is frequently extended to borrowers as a loan with set terms such as the amount of credit provided and the maturity date when the credit will be repaid. [4]For most types of loans, interest payments are made periodically (such as every quarter or year), and the principal payment is made at the maturity date, when the loan is to be terminated.

Advantages of Using Credit

[5]Individuals borrow funds when the dollar amount of their purchases exceeds the amount of their available cash. [6]Many individuals use borrowed funds to purchase a home or car or to pay their tuition fees. [7]In contrast, others use credit (such as a credit card) for convenience when making day-to-day purchases.

Disadvantages of Using Credit

[8]There can be a high cost to using credit. [9]If you borrow too much money, you may have difficulty making your credit card payments. [10]It is easier to obtain credit than to pay it back. [11]And having a credit line can tempt you to make impulse purchases that you cannot afford. [12]College students are carrying credit cards in record numbers. [13]Eighty-three percent of all students have at least one credit card, and the average credit card balance is $2,327. [14]Many students make minimum payments on their credit cards while in school with the expectation that they will be able to pay off their balance once they graduate and are working full-time. [15]Yet the accumulating interest fees catch many by surprise, and the debt can quickly become difficult to manage. [16]Today's graduating students have an average of $20,402 in combined education loan and credit card balances. [17]If you are unable to repay the credit you receive, you may not

be able to obtain credit again or will have to pay a very high interest rate to obtain it. [18]Your ability to save money will also be reduced if you have large credit payments. [19]If spending and credit card payments exceed your net cash flows, you will need to withdraw savings to cover the deficiency.

[20]Warren Buffett, a successful billionaire investor, recently offered financial advice to some students. [21]He told them that they will not make financial progress if they are borrowing money at 18 percent (a typical interest rate on credit cards). [22]In recent years, more than 1 million people in the United States have filed for bankruptcy each year. [23]A primary reason for these bankruptcies is that the individuals obtained more credit than they could repay. [24]Even if obtaining credit at a high interest rate does not cause personal bankruptcy, it limits the potential increase in personal wealth.

1. What is this passage about? _____

_____

Complete the following concept map with information from the passage.

Impact of Credit Payments on Saving

USE OF CREDIT

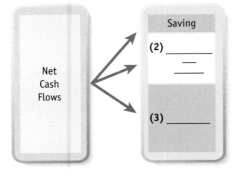

NO USE OF CREDIT

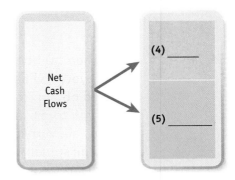

—Text and Figure Adapted from Madura, Jeff, *Personal Finance Update*, 2nd ed., pp. 186–188.

Name _____ Section _____

Date _____ **Score** (number correct) _____ × 10 = _____%

Visit MyReadingLab to take this test online and receive feedback and guidance on your answers.

A. Using SQ3R, read the following passage from a college psychology textbook. Answer the questions in the left margin.

Textbook
Skills

1. What are mnemonic devices?

_____

_____

_____

2. What are interactive images?

_____

_____

_____

3. What are acronyms?

_____

_____

_____

_____

4. What are initialisms?

_____

_____

_____

Mnemonic Devices

[1]**Mnemonic devices** are strategies that improve memory. [2]Mnemonics can easily double your recall and are well worth the effort of learning. [3]Mnemonic devices not only help you learn something in the first place, but should you forget it, you will be able to relearn it more effectively.

[4]Probably the single most effective mnemonic device is the use of **interactive images.** [5]Forming images of objects interacting will improve memory even without any effort to learn the material. [6]For example, if you want to learn someone's first name, visualize someone else you already know who has the same first name. [7]Then imagine that person interacting with your new acquaintance in some way. [8]You might envision them fighting or hugging.

[9]Another effective mnemonic device is the use of acronyms. [10]**Acronyms** are words made from the first letters of the important words in a phrase. [11]Acronyms can be pronounced. [12]One example is NOW, for the National Organization for Women. [13]**Initialisms** are simply the initial letters of words in a phrase that probably do not combine to make a word, such as DNA for deoxyribonucleic acid. [14]Initialisms may be easier to make up. [15]The idea of using both acronyms and initialisms is to create a single unit that can be "unpacked" as a set of cues for something more complicated.

—Adapted from Kosslyn, Stephen M. and Robin S. Rosenberg, *Psychology: The Brain, The Person, The World*, pp. 228–229.

B. Using SQ3R, read the following paragraph taken from a college literature text-book.

Textbook
Skills

Hyperbole and Understatement

[1]Most of us, from time to time, emphasize a point with a statement containing an exaggeration: "Faster than greased lightning," "I've told him a thousand times." [2]We speak, then, not literal truth but use a figure of speech called **overstatement** or **hyperbole**. [3]Poets, too, being fond of emphasis, often exaggerate for effect. [4]Instances are Marvell's claim of a love that should grow "vaster than empires and more slow." [5]Another is John Burgon's description of Petra: "A rose-red city, half as old as time." [6]Overstatement can also be used for humor. [7]Take, for instance, the fat woman's boast (from a blues song): "Every time I shake, some skinny gal loses her home." [8]The opposite is **understatement**, which is a figure of speech that implies more than is said. [9]For example, Robert Frost's line "One could do worse than be a swinger of birches" uses understatement. [10]All through the poem, he has suggested that to swing on a birch tree is one of the most deeply satisfying activities in the world.

—Adapted from Kennedy, X. J. and Dana Gioia, *Literature:
An Introduction to Fiction, Poetry, and Drama*, 8th ed.,
Interactive Edition p. 867.

5. What is this passage about? _____

_____

Complete the concept map with information from the paragraph.

Figure of Speech	Definition	Example
Overstatement or hyperbole	6. _____	7. _____
8. _____	9. _____	10. _____

1 Summary of Key Concepts of a Reading System for Effective Readers

LO1 LO2
LO3 LO4
LO5 LO6

Assess your comprehension of prior knowledge and the reading process.

- Comprehension is _____.

- Prior knowledge is _____

    _____.

- Use prior knowledge to _____:

    - _____ by asking, "What do I already know about this topic?"

    - Check _____ against your prior knowledge by asking, "Does this make sense based on what I know?"

    - Check for _____ in your knowledge base by asking, "What did I learn?"

- The reading process has three phases: _____

    _____.

- SQ3R, an acronym for a reading process, stands for _____

    _____. SQ3R activates prior knowledge and offers strategies for each phase of the reading process:

    - Before Reading, _____: Skim _____

        _____. Ask questions such as

        _____

        _____

    - During Reading, _____ key words and ideas. Repair confusion. Reread.

    - After Reading, Recite and Review: Recall _____. Summarize. Answer questions such as _____

        _____

Test Your Comprehension of a Reading System for Effective Readers

Respond to the following questions and prompts.

(LO1) (LO5) (LO6) (LO7)   In your own words, what is prior knowledge? _____

_____

(LO2) (LO3) (LO4) (LO5)   Create a graph or draw a picture to illustrate SQ3R.

(LO1) (LO2) (LO3) (LO4) (LO5) (LO6) (LO7)   Describe your reading process. How did you read before you studied this chapter? Will you change your reading process? If so, how? If not, why not?

_____

_____

_____

_____

_____

Vocabulary and Dictionary Skills

CHAPTER 2

LO LEARNING OUTCOMES

After studying this chapter you should be able to:

- **LO1** Define Vocabulary
- **LO2** Analyze Context Clues: A SAGE Approach
- **LO3** Develop Textbook Skills: Using a Glossary
- **LO4** Analyze Word Parts: Roots, Prefixes, Suffixes
- **LO5** Use an Online Dictionary
- **LO6** Develop Textbook Skills: Learning Content Words and Textbook Definitions
- **LO7** Apply Information Literacy Skills: Academic, Personal, and Career Applications of Vocabulary and Dictionary Skills

Before Reading About Vocabulary Skills

Chapter 1 taught you the importance of surveying material before you begin reading by skimming the information for **bold** or *italic* type. Throughout this textbook, key ideas are emphasized in bold or italic print where they appear in the passage; often they are also set apart visually in a box that gives the definition or examples of the term. Skim the chapter for key ideas in boxes that will help you understand vocabulary skills. Refer to these boxes and create at least six questions that you can answer as you read the chapter. Write your questions in the following spaces (record the page number for the key term in each question):

_____ (page _____)

_____ (page _____)

_____ (page _____)

_____ (page _____)

_____ (page _____)

Compare the questions you created with the following questions. Then write the ones that seem most helpful in your notebook, leaving enough space between each question to record the answers as you read and study the chapter.

What is vocabulary? (page 46) What is a context clue? (page 47) What are word parts? (page 58) What kind of information does a dictionary provide? (page 66) What is a glossary? (page 53) How will each of these skills help me develop my vocabulary? (pages 46 and 58)

LO1 Define Vocabulary

Words are the building blocks of meaning. Have you ever watched a child with a set of building blocks such as Legos? Hundreds of separate pieces can be joined together to create buildings, planes, cars, or even spaceships. Words are like that, too. A word is the smallest unit of thought. Words properly joined create meaning.

> **Vocabulary** is all the words used or understood by a person.

How many words do you have in your **vocabulary**? If you are like most people, by the time you are 18 years old, you know about 60,000 words. During your college studies, you will most likely learn an additional 20,000 words. Each subject you study will have its own set of words. There are several ways to study vocabulary.

LO2 Analyze Context Clues: A SAGE Approach

Effective readers interact with new words in a number of ways. One way is to use **context clues**. The meaning of a word is shaped by its context. The word *context* means "surroundings." The meaning of a word is shaped by the words surrounding it—its context. Effective readers use context clues to learn new words.

> A **context clue** is the information that surrounds a new word, and is used to understand its meaning.

There are four types of context clues:

- Synonyms
- Antonyms
- General context
- Examples

Notice that when the first letters of each context clue are put together, they spell the word **SAGE**. The word *sage* means "wise." Using context clues is a wise—a SAGE—reading strategy.

Synonyms

A **synonym** is a word that has the same or nearly the same meaning as another word. Many times, an author will place a synonym near a new or difficult word as a context clue to the word's meaning. Usually, a synonym is set off with a pair of commas, a pair of dashes, or a pair of parentheses before and after it.

Synonym Signal Words	
or	*that is*

⊙ **EXAMPLES** Each of the following sentences has a key word in **bold** type. In each sentence, underline the signal word or words and then circle the synonym for the word in **bold**.

1. At times, we pursue an activity as an end in itself, simply because it is enjoyable, not because of an attached award. We are pulled by **intrinsic motivation**, that is, internal incentives.

2. Other times, we act to gain a reward outside ourselves or to avoid some undesirable consequence. We are pulled by **extrinsic motivation** or external incentives.

EXPLANATIONS

1. The signal words *that is* clue the reader that the synonym for *intrinsic motivation* is *internal incentives*.

2. The signal word *or* clues the reader that the synonym for *extrinsic motivation* is *external incentives*.

VISUAL *VOCABULARY*

Exercise balls provide a better work-out because their _____ instability causes more of the body's muscles to respond.

   a. extrinsic
   b. intrinsic

Practice 1

Textbook Skills

Each of the following sentences from a college textbook contains a word that is a synonym for the word in **bold** type. Underline the signal words and circle the synonym in each sentence.

1. Directional terms allow medical workers to explain exactly where one body structure is in relation to another. For example, the forehead is **superior** to, that is, above the nose.

2. The navel is **inferior** to—or below—the breastbone.

3. The heart is **posterior** to (behind) the breastbone.

4. The breastbone is **anterior** to, or in front of, the spine.

—Marieb, Elaine N., *Essentials of Human Anatomy and Physiology*, 9th ed., p. 18.

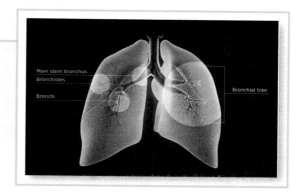

VISUAL VOCABULARY

This image of the lungs is from the _____ view.

    a. superior
    b. anterior

Antonyms

An **antonym** is a word that has the opposite meaning of another word. Antonyms help you see the shade of a word's meaning by showing you what the original word is *not*. The following contrast words often act as signals that an antonym is being used.

Antonym Signal Words		
but	*instead*	*unlike*
however	*not*	*yet*
in contrast	*on the other hand*	

Sometimes antonyms can be found next to the new word. In those cases, commas, dashes, or parentheses set them off. At other times, antonyms are placed in other parts of the sentence to emphasize the contrast between the ideas.

> EXAMPLES In each sentence, underline the signal word and circle the antonym for the word in **bold** type. In the blank, write the letter of the word that best defines the word in **bold**.

_____a_____ **1.** During dinner, Anne Marie let out a long, loud burp that **mortified** her mother but (amused) her friends.
    a. embarrassed   c. silenced
    b. killed   d. delighted

_____ **2.** Suzanne's tone was surprisingly **flippant**, in contrast to her usual respectful manner.

    a. polite   c. funny

    b. sassy   d. loud

EXPLANATIONS

1. The signal word *but* clues the reader that the antonym is *amused*. The best definition of the word *mortified* is (a) *embarrassed*.

2. The signal words *in contrast* clue the reader that the antonym is *respectful*. The best definition of the word *flippant* is (b) *sassy*.

Practice 2

In each sentence, underline the signal word and circle the antonym for the word in **bold** type. In the blank, write the letter of the word that best defines the word in **bold**.

_____ **1.** Please leave the kitchen **immaculate**, not filthy, when you finish your meal preparations.

    a. messy   c. spotless

    b. well-stocked   d. cool

_____ **2.** Maxine acted **smug** when instead she should have been humble.

    a. joyful   c. calm

    b. depressed   d. conceited

_____ **3.** At the beginning of Dickens's novel *A Christmas Carol*, the character Scrooge has a **mercenary** nature, but by the story's end, he has become a generous spirit.

    a. carefree   c. greedy

    b. angry   d. curious

General Context

Often you will find that the author has not provided either a synonym clue or an antonym clue. In that case, you will have to rely on the general context of the passage to figure out the meaning of the unfamiliar word. This requires you to read the entire sentence or to read ahead for a few sentences for information that will help you understand the new word.

Information about the word can be included in the passage in several ways. Sometimes a definition of the word may be provided. Vivid word pictures or descriptions of a situation can provide a sense of the word's meaning. Sometimes you may need to figure out the meaning of an unknown word by using logic and reasoning skills.

> **EXAMPLES** In the blank, write the letter of the word that best defines the word in **bold** type.

_____ **1.** To ensure safety, written and road tests should be **mandatory** for everyone who seeks a driver's license for the first time; no exceptions should be allowed.

    a. optional   c. required
    b. difficult   d. debated

_____ **2.** Instead of being placed in adult prisons, where they often become more antisocial by mixing with hardened criminals, youth who have been convicted of crimes should be placed in programs that **rehabilitate** them.

    a. restore to useful life
    b. punish for good reason
    c. exhaust in order to break the spirit
    d. entertain

EXPLANATIONS

1. The best meaning of the word *mandatory* is (c) *required*. Clues from the sentence are the words *ensure* and *no exceptions should be allowed*.

2. The best meaning of the word *rehabilitate* is (a) *restore to useful life*. The passage suggests that placing young people in adult prisons just makes them tougher; the contrast word *instead* indicates that the word *rehabilitate* must mean something different. ◁

Practice 3

Each of the following sentences has a word in **bold** type. In the blank, write the letter of the word that best defines the word in **bold**.

_____ **1.** Jamie **speculated** about how much weight he wanted to gain during the three-month bodybuilding program he was beginning.

    a. knew   c. worried
    b. wondered   d. celebrated

_____ **2.** Losing weight too quickly—more than a pound or two a week—can be **detrimental** to long-term weight control and good health.
   a. helpful   c. harmful
   b. odd   d. pleasing

_____ **3.** Many employers use yearly bonuses and raises as **incentives** to encourage work habits that go beyond expectations.
   a. dreams   c. barriers
   b. tricks   d. motivators

Examples

Many times an author will show the meaning of a new or difficult word by providing an example. Signal words indicate that an example is coming.

Example Signal Words
consists of   for example   for instance   including   such as

Colons and dashes can also indicate examples.

> **EXAMPLES**   Using example clues, choose the correct meaning of the word in **bold** type.

_____ **1.** The American presidency has suffered **infamous** events such as the Watergate scandal of Richard Nixon and the impeachment of Bill Clinton by the House of Representatives.
   a. exciting, little-known
   b. boring, well-known
   c. tarnishing, well-known
   d. frightening, little-known

_____ **2.** Some authors use **pseudonyms**; for example, famous American author Mark Twain's real name was Samuel Clemens.
   a. typists   c. ghost writers
   b. mental tricks   d. pen names

EXPLANATIONS

   1. The best meaning of the word *infamous* is (c) *tarnishing, well-known*.

   2. The best meaning of the word *pseudonyms* is (d) *pen names*.

Practice 4

Using example clues, choose the correct meaning of the word in **bold** type.

_____ **1.** Baseball figure Yogi Berra's humor was based on using **malapropisms**; for instance, one of his most famous lines is "If you see a fork in the road, take it."

    a. misuses of words   c. social situations
    b. personal attacks   d. nature jokes

_____ **2. Rigorous** programs, such as boot camps and outward-bound programs, help develop character in the individuals who take part in them.

    a. required   c. difficult
    b. lengthy   d. abusive

LO3 Develop Textbook Skills: Using a Glossary

Textbook
Skills

Each subject or content area, such as science, mathematics, or English, has its own specialized vocabulary. Therefore, some textbooks provide an extra section in the back of the book called a *glossary* that alphabetically lists all the specialized terms with their definitions as they were used throughout the textbook. Other textbooks may provide short glossaries within each chapter; in these cases, the glossaries may appear in the margins or in highlighted boxes, listing the words in the order that they appear on the page. The meanings given in a glossary are limited to the way in which the word or term is used in that content area.

> A **glossary** is a list of selected terms with their definitions as used in a specific area of study.

Glossaries provide excellent opportunities to use strategies before and after reading. Before reading, skim the section for specialized terms (usually these words are in **bold** or *italic* print). Checking the words and their meanings triggers prior knowledge or establishes meaning that will deepen your comprehension. In addition, you can create vocabulary review lists using glossary terms by paraphrasing or restating the definition in your own words. These vocabulary lists can be used after reading to review and test your recall of the material.

Textbook
Skills

◉ EXAMPLE The following selection is from a college psychology textbook. Before reading, use the glossary to complete the vocabulary review list. Then read the passage. After reading, answer the questions.

GLOSSARY

algorithm a set of steps that, if followed methodically, will guarantee the solution to a problem.

heuristic a rule of thumb that does not guarantee the correct answer to a problem but offers a likely shortcut to it.

representation a way of looking at a problem.

strategy an approach to solving a problem, determined by the type of representation used and the processing steps to be tried.

Algorithms and Heuristics: Getting From Here to There

[1]To solve a problem you need a **strategy**, an approach to solving a problem determined by the type of **representation** used and the processing steps to be tried. [2]There are two types of strategies: algorithms and heuristics. [3]Let's say you heard about a fantastic price being offered on a hit alternative music CD by an independent record store, but you don't know the name of the store. [4]You could try to find it by calling every relevant listing in the yellow pages. [5]This process involves using an **algorithm**, a set of steps that if followed methodically will guarantee the right answer. [6]But you may not have time to call every store. [7]Instead, you might guess that the record store is in a part of town where many students live. [8]In this case, having reduced the list of candidates to those located near the campus, you might find the store after calling only a few. [9]This process reflects use of a **heuristic**, a rule of thumb that does not guarantee the correct answer but offers a likely shortcut to it. [10]One common heuristic is to divide a big problem into parts and solve them one at a time.

—Adapted from Kosslyn, Stephen M. and Robin S. Rosenberg, *Psychology: The Brain, The Person, The World*, p. 206.

Before Reading

1. _____ an approach to solving a problem based on a way of looking at a problem and the steps taken to solve the problem

2. _____ a series of systematic steps that assures the right answer

3. heuristic _____

_____

After Reading

_____ 4. Which sentence uses most of the words listed in the glossary?

_____ 5. Which problem-solving strategy is described in the following example? Kimberly couldn't find the rice, but started in aisle 3 first, because she thought it might be with the pasta. Then she tried aisle 10, because she thought it might be with the international foods.

—Kosslyn & Rosenberg, *Psychology: The Brain, The Person, The World*, p. 236.

    a. algorithm   b. heuristic

EXPLANATION

1. A *strategy* is an approach to solving a problem based on a way of looking at a problem and the steps taken to solve the problem. Note that the paraphrase (restatement) of the definition for strategy draws on information given in the definition for *representation*.

2. *Algorithm* is a series of systematic steps that assures the right answer.

3. Compare your paraphrase of the definition for *heuristic* with the following: *use of prior knowledge or experience that is likely to lead to the solution more quickly.*

4. Sentence 1 uses most of the words listed in the glossary. Sentence 1 also states the main idea of the paragraph, the point the author is making.

5. Kimberly used (b), the heuristic approach. This approach is an experimental, trial-and-error approach in contrast to the algorithm, which approaches problem solving using proven formulas. The importance of glossaries is evident when you consider that this question about Kimberly came directly from the psychology textbook's chapter review. Textbook reviews and course tests often include questions about the key terms listed in glossaries. ◄

Practice 5

Textbook
Skills

The following selection is from a college anatomy and physiology textbook. Before reading, use the glossary to complete your vocabulary review list. Then read the passage. After reading, answer the questions.

Energy

[1]In contrast to matter, energy is massless and does not take up space. [2]It can be measured only by its effects on matter. [3]Energy is commonly defined as the ability to do work or to put matter into motion. [4]When energy is actually doing work (moving objects), it is referred to as **kinetic** (kĭ-neh′tik) **energy**. [5]Kinetic energy is displayed in the constant movement of the tiniest particles of matter (atoms) as well as in larger objects, such as a bouncing ball.

GLOSSARY

chemical energy energy form stored in chemical bonds that hold atoms together

electrical energy energy form resulting from the movement of charged particles

energy the ability to do work

kinetic energy energy of motion

mechanical energy energy form directly involved with putting matter into motion

potential energy stored energy

radiant energy energy of the electromagnetic spectrum, which includes heat, light, ultraviolet waves, infrared waves, and other forms

[6]When energy is inactive or stored (as in the batteries of an unused toy), it is called **potential energy**. [7]All forms of energy exhibit both kinetic and potential work capacities.

[8]Actually, energy is a physics topic, but it is difficult to separate matter and energy. [9]All living things are built of matter, and to grow and function they require a continuous supply of energy. [10]Thus, matter is the substance, and energy is the mover of the substance. [11]Because this is so, it is worth taking a brief detour to introduce the forms of energy the body uses as it does its work.

Forms of Energy

- [12]**Chemical energy** is stored in the bonds of chemical substances. [13]When the bonds are broken, the (potential) stored energy is unleashed and becomes kinetic energy (energy in action). [14]For example, when gasoline molecules are broken apart in your automobile engine, the energy released powers your car. [15]In like manner, all body activities are "run" by the chemical energy harvested from the foods we eat.

- [16]**Electrical energy** results from the movement of charged particles. [17]In your house, electrical energy is the flow of electrons along the wiring. [18]In your body, an electrical current is generated when charged particles (called ions) move across cell membranes. [19]The nervous system uses electrical currents called nerve impulses to transmit messages from one part of the body to another.

- [20]**Mechanical energy** is energy directly involved in moving matter. [21]When you ride a bicycle, your legs provide the mechanical energy that moves the pedals. [22]We can take this example one step further back: As the muscles in your legs shorten, they pull on your bones, causing your limbs to move (so that you can pedal the bike).

- [23]**Radiant energy** travels in waves; that is, it is the energy of the electromagnetic spectrum, which includes X rays, infrared radiation (heat energy), visible light, radio, and ultraviolet waves. [24]Light energy, which stimulates the retinas of your eyes, is important in vision. [25]Ultraviolet waves cause sunburn, but they also stimulate our bodies to make vitamin D.

—Marieb, Elaine N., *Essentials of Human Anatomy and Physiology*, 9th ed., pp. 27–28.

Before Reading

Establish or activate prior knowledge. Use the glossary to fill in each blank with the appropriate word.

The ability to do work—**(1)** _____—takes on many forms. While there is the energy of motion, or **(2)** _____ energy, there is also **(3)** _____ or stored energy. In addition, there are four basic forms of energy. The movement of charged particles creates **(4)** _____ energy. Chemical bonds store **(5)** _____ energy. **(6)** _____ energy is directly involved with causing matter to move. And **(7)** _____ energy travels in many forms of waves.

After Reading

Recall and review information and test your comprehension by filling in the blanks with information from the passage.

_____ **8.** The muscles in the human body causing the limbs to move and legs pedaling a bicycle illustrate
a. potential energy.
b. electrical energy.
c. mechanical energy.
d. radiant energy.

_____ **9.** The human nervous system uses
a. mechanical energy.
b. electrical energy.
c. radiant energy.
d. chemical energy.

_____ **10.** What are the two work abilities exhibited by all forms of energy?
a. kinetic and potential
b. kinetic and mechanical
c. radiant and chemical
d. potential and electrical

VISUAL *VOCABULARY*

Fire is a form of _____ energy.

a. chemical
b. electrical
c. mechanical
d. radiant

LO4 Analyze Word Parts: Roots, Prefixes, Suffixes

Just as ideas are made up of words, words are also made up of smaller parts. *Word parts* can help you learn vocabulary more easily and quickly. In addition, knowing the meaning of the parts of words helps you understand a new word when you see it in context.

Many words are divided into the following three parts: *roots, prefixes*, and *suffixes*.

Root	The basic or main part of a word. Prefixes and suffixes are added to roots to make a new word. Example: *press* means "press."
Prefix	A group of letters with a specific meaning added to the beginning of a word (root) to make a new word. Example: ***com**press* means "press together."
Suffix	A group of letters with a specific meaning added to the end of a word (root) to make a new word. Example: *press**ure*** means "act of pressing."

Effective readers understand how the three word parts join together to make additional words. The following chart lists a few of the most common prefixes, roots, and suffixes in the English language. To improve your vocabulary, memorize these word parts.

Commonly Used Word Parts		
Word Part:	**Meaning**	**Sample Word**
Prefix		
anti-	against	antisocial
de-	opposite	defrost
in-, im-	in, not	inside, impossible
pre-	before	predawn
sub-	under	subgroup
un-	not	unheard

Commonly Used Word Parts

Word Part:	Meaning	Sample Word
Root		
cred	to believe	credible
dic-, dit-, dict-	to say	dictation
ducere-, duct-, duc-	to draw or lead	conduct
graph-, graf-	to write, draw	graph
mittere-, mit-, mis-, mise-	to put or send	remit
scribe-, script-	to write	scripture
stare-, stat-	to stand	stature
Suffix		
-able, -ible	can be done	capable
-ate	cause to be	graduate
-al	having traits of	practical
-er	comparative, one who	higher, controller
-ic	having the traits of	simplistic
-less	without	effortless
-ous, -eous, -ious	possessing qualities of	joyous
-y	characterized by	honestly

⊙ **EXAMPLES** Look at the following root, prefix, and suffix. Make two new words by combining the word parts. The meaning of each part is in parentheses. You don't have to use all the parts to make a word.

Prefix:	*in-*	(not)
Root:	*vis*	(see)
Suffix:	*-ible*	(capable of)

1. _____   **2.** _____

EXPLANATIONS

1. The root and suffix combine to form the word *visible*, which means "capable of being seen," as in the following sentence: *Carmen's joy was visible in her smile.*

...g ...itted between neurons by one or more of a large group of chemical substances known as **neurotransmitters**.

—Wood, Wood, & Boyd, *Mastering the World of Psychology,* 3rd ed., p. 42.

2. All three word parts combine to form the word *invisible,* which means "not capable of being seen," as in the following sentence: *Josie was so embarrassed that she wished she were invisible.* ◄

Practice 6

Identify the word parts for each of the following words. Circle prefixes and suf

3. According to one study, **recidivism** rates show that nearly 70% of young adults paroled from prison in 22 states during 1978 were rearrested for serious crimes one or more times within six years of their release.

—Schmalleger, Frank J., *Criminal Justice Today:
An Introductory Text for the 21st Century,*
10th ed., pp. 472–473.

4. Worse, still, observed the authors of the study, was the fact that 40% of **recidivists** would have been in prison at the time of readmission to prison if they had served the maximum term of their original sentence.

—Schmalleger, *Criminal Justice Today,* 10th ed.,
pp. 472–473.

Prefixes

A **prefix** is a group of letters with a specific meaning added to the beginning of a word or root to make a new word. Though the basic meaning of a root is not changed, a prefix changes the meaning of the word as a whole. For example, the prefix *ex-* means "out of" or "from." When placed in front of the root *tract* (which means "pull" or "drag"), the word *extract* is formed. *Extract* means "pull or drag out." The same root *tract* joined with the prefix *con-* (which means "with" or "together") creates the word *contract*. A *contract* legally pulls people together to accomplish something.

The importance of prefixes can be seen in the family of words that comes from the root *ject*, which means "throw." Look over the following examples of prefixes and their meanings. Note the change in the meaning of the whole word based on the meaning of the prefix.

Prefix	Meaning	Root	Meaning	Example
e-	out of, from	*ject*	throw	*eject*
in-	in, into			*inject*
re-	back, again			*reject*

◎ **EXAMPLES** Using the meanings of the prefixes, root, and context clues, put each word into the sentence that best fits its meaning. Use each word once.

Prefix	Meaning		Root	Meaning
ex-	out of, from		*pel*	push, drive
pro-	forward, in favor of			

> *pel* = **push, drive**
>
> expel   propel

1. The sorority threatened to _____ Danielle because she would not join in hazing new members.

2. Len Watson used his family's name and fortune to _____ him into a seat in the Senate.

EXPLANATIONS

1. The sorority wanted to "drive out" Danielle because she refused to conform.

2. Len used his family's success to push him forward into becoming a senator. ◁

Practice 8

Textbook Skills

Study the word parts in the chart. Next, read the four sentences taken from a college textbook. Then define the vocabulary words in **bold** print based on information from the word chart and the general sense of the sentences. Write your definitions in the given spaces.

Prefix	Meaning	Root	Meaning	Suffix	Meaning
intra-	within, inside			*-ive*	of, belonging to,
peri-	around, surrounding	*operis*	labor		quality of
pre-	before	*opus*	work		
post-	after				

1. Surgery encompasses three phases referred to as the **perioperative** period.

_____

2. The first phase, the **preoperative** phase, begins when the decision to have surgery is made and ends when the client is transferred to the operating table.

_____

3. The second phase, the **intraoperative** phase, begins when the client is transferred to the operating table and ends when the client is admitted to the post-anesthesia care unit or recovery room.

_____

4. The third phase, the **postoperative** phase, begins with the admission of the client to the recovery room and ends when healing is complete.

_____

—Adapted from Potter, Patricia, et al.,
Fundamentals of Nursing, 8th ed., p. 940.

Suffixes

A **suffix** is a group of letters with a specific meaning added to the end of a word or root to make a new word. Though the basic meaning of a root does not change, a suffix can change the type of word and the way a word is used. Look at the following set of examples:

Root	Meaning	Suffix	Meaning	Word
psych	mind	*-ology*	study	*psychology*
		-ist	person	*psychologist*
		-ical	possessing or expressing a quality	*psychological*

> **EXAMPLES** Using the meanings of the root, suffixes, and context clues, put each of the words in the box into the sentence that best fits its meaning. Use each word once.

Root	Meaning	Suffix	Meaning
tact	touch	*-ful*	full of
		-ile	of, like, related to, being
		-less	without
		-ly	in such a manner

tact = touch	
tactfully	tactile

1. Many blind people rely on their _____ sense to read braille.

2. I don't know how to tell you this _____, but your zipper is down.

EXPLANATIONS

1. Many blind people use the tips of their fingers to feel words written in braille; they are using their *tactile* sense, their sense of touch.

2. The speaker would like to have a gentle touch and deliver the embarrassing news about the zipper *tactfully*. ◄

Practice 9

Study the word parts in the chart. Next, read the four sentences taken from a college textbook. Then define the vocabulary words in **bold** print based on information from the word chart and the general sense of the sentences. Write your definitions in the given spaces. Wording may vary.

Root	Meaning	Suffix	Meaning
socius	companion, ally, associate	-al	quality of
		-ist	one who
		-ology	study of
		-ity, -ty	quality, condition, state of

Textbook
Skills

1. Auguste Comte, the founder of sociology, stressed that the scientific method should be applied to the study of **society**.

   _____

2. **Sociology** only recently appeared on the human scene.

   _____

3. Sociology grew out of **social** upheaval.

   _____

4. Comte believed that **sociologists** would reform the entire society, making it a better place to live.

—Adapted from Henslin, James M., *Sociology: Down-to-Earth Approach*, 9th ed., pp. 8–9.

LO5 Use an Online Dictionary

Experts believe that most English-speaking adults know and use between 25,000 and 50,000 words. That seems like a large number, yet the English language has over a million words. Effective readers use a dictionary to understand new or difficult words. Overall, there are two basic types of dictionaries: the print dictionary and the online dictionary.

Most dictionaries provide the following information:

- Spelling (how the word and its different forms are spelled)
- Pronunciation (how to say the word)
- Part of speech (the function of the word)
- Definition (the meaning of the word)
- Synonyms (words that have similar meanings)
- Etymology (the history of the word)

All print dictionaries have guide words at the top of each page. However, dictionaries differ from each other in the way they give other information about words. Each dictionary will explain how to use its resources in the first few pages of the book.

Online dictionaries are easy to access and easy to use, and all offer a wide range of similar learning resources. For example, note the resources offered in the homepage tabs of Merriam-Webster.com.

Click on a specific tab to see information for the word in that resource. Then, click on the search button.

| Dictionary | Thesaurus | Medical | Encyclo. | New! Spanish Central ▶ |

Type your term into the search box.

Source: Search bar reprinted by permission from *Merriam-Webster's Collegiate® Dictionary*, 11th Edition. © 2013 by Merriam-Webster, Inc. (www.Merriam-Webster.com)

How to Access and Read an Online Dictionary Entry

Each online dictionary varies in ways to access its resources. Preview several online dictionaries. Browse their sites to see which resources seem most helpful to you. Two highly popular free online dictionaries are Merriam-Webster.com and Dictionary.com. The examples in this discussion about how to use online dictionaries are taken from Merriam-Webster.com.

Search Box

An online dictionary offers a search box on its homepage.

Source: Search bar and definition of "cognition" reprinted by permission from *Merriam-Webster's Collegiate® Dictionary*, 11th Edition. © 2013 by Merriam-Webster, Inc. (www.Merriam-Webster.com)

The following screenshot is the main entry resulting from the search for the word *cognition*. The annotated screenshot identifies the various types of information given about the word. Note that you can click on terms that are in **bold** in the dictionary entries to receive more information. Each following section of instruction explores each type of information.

Main Entry: Types of Information

Source: Definition of "cognition" reprinted by permission from *Merriam-Webster's Collegiate® Dictionary*, 11th Edition. © 2013 by Merriam-Webster, Inc. (www.Merriam-Webster.com)

Spelling and Syllables

The spelling of the main word is given first in **bold** type. The word is also divided into syllables. The word *cognition* has three syllables: cog·ni·tion.

⊘ **EXAMPLES** Use an online dictionary to break the following words into sylla-bles. Place a dot (·) between the syllables.

1. intermit _____

2. pedagogy _____

EXPLANATIONS

1. *Intermit* has three syllables: *in-ter-mit.*

2. *Pedagogy* has four syllables: *ped-a-go-gy.* ⊘

Practice 1 0

Use an online dictionary to break the following words into syllables. Place a dot (·) between the syllables.

1. scavenger _____

2. tundra _____

Pronunciation

Pronunciation symbols indicate the sounds of consonants and vowels. Dictionar-ies provide pronunciation keys so that you will understand the symbols used in the pronunciation guide to a word. Following is a sample pronunciation key found on Merriam-Webster.com.

Pronunciation Symbols
Click on any linked word below to hear the pronunciation.

\ ə \ as **a** in abut	\ g \ as **g** in go	\ r \ as **r** in red
\ ˈə ˌə \ as **u** in abut	\ h \ as **h** in hat	\ s \ as **s** in less
\ ᵊ \ as **e** in kitten	\ i \ as **i** in hit	\ sh \ as **sh** in shy
\ ər \ as **ur/er** in further	\ ī \ as **i** in ice	\ t \ as **t** in tie
\ a \ as **a** in ash	\ j \ as **j** in job	\ th \ as **th** in thin
\ ā \ as **a** in ace	\ k \ as **k** in kin	\ t̲h̲ \ as **th** in the
\ ä \ as **o** in mop	\ k̲ \ as **ch** in ich dien	\ ü \ as **oo** in loot
\ au̇ \ as **ou** in out	\ l \ as **l** in lily	\ u̇ \ as **oo** in foot
\ b \ as in baby	\ m \ as **m** in murmur	\ v \ as **v** in vivid
\ ch \ as **ch** in chin	\ n \ as **n** in own	\ w \ as **w** in away
\ d \ as **d** in did	\ ŋ \ as **ng** in sing	\ y \ as **y** in yet
\ e \ as **e** in bet	\ ō \ as **o** in go	\ yü \ as **you** in youth
\ ˈē ˌē \ as **ea** in easy	\ ȯ \ as **aw** in law	\ yu̇ \ as **u** in curable
\ ē \ as **y** in easy	\ ȯi \ as **oy** in boy	\ z \ as **z** in zone
\ f \ as **f** in fifty	\ p \ as **p** in pepper	\ zh \ as **si** in vision

Source: Pronunciation symbols reprinted by permission from *Merriam-Webster's Collegiate® Dictionary*, 11th Edition. © 2013 by Merriam-Webster, Inc. (www.Merriam-Webster.com).

Note that each letter and symbol is followed by a sample word. The sample word tells you how that letter and symbol sounds. For example, the long *a* sounds like *a* in *ace*. And the short *a* has the sound of the *a* in *ash*.

Different dictionaries use different symbols in their pronunciation keys, so be sure to check the key of the dictionary you are using.

▷ **EXAMPLES**　Go to Merriam-Webster.com to answer questions about the following words.

_____　**1.** con·sign (\kən-'sīn\)

The *i* in *consign* sounds like the *i* in
a. sit.
b. ice.

_____　**2.** de·vi·ate (\'dē-vē-ˌāt)

The *a* in *deviate* sounds like the *a* in
a. mat.
b. day. ◁

Practice 11

Go to Merriam-Webster.com. Find and write in the spelled pronunciation.

1. performance _____

2. bacteria _____

Parts of Speech

Parts of speech indicate how a word functions in a sentence. Dictionary entries tell you what part of speech a word is—noun, verb, adjective, and so on. The part of speech is abbreviated and printed in italics. Your dictionary provides a full list of abbreviations. The following are the most common abbreviations for the parts of speech.

Parts of Speech			
adj	adjective	*n*	noun
adv	adverb	*prep*	preposition
conj	conjunction	*pron*	pronoun
interj	interjection	*v, vi, vt*	verb

Read again the sample dictionary entry for *cognition*.

Online dictionaries state the part of speech or function of a word in various ways. First, the part of speech always appears in the main entry, as in the following screenshot of *cognition*.

Part of speech

Source: Part of speech "cognition," reprinted by permission from *Merriam-Webster's Collegiate® Dictionary*, 11th Edition. © 2013 by Merriam-Webster, Inc. (www.Merriam-Webster.com).

Second, the part of speech is also stated for each of the various forms of a given word. In Merriam-Webster.com, scroll down the page from the main entry until you see the related forms of the word. Notice that as the word changes in its function or part of speech, it also varies in the number of syllables.

Third, some online dictionaries list definitions based on the parts of speech. For example, Merriam-Webster.com lists 35 entries for the word *talk*. The list is organized by part of speech, starting with 4 definitions of its verb form and 8 definitions of its noun form.

EXAMPLES Use an online dictionary to identify the parts of speech for each of the following words. A word may be used as more than one part of speech.

1. complement _____

2. before _____

3. fly _____

EXPLANATION Merriam-Webster.com offers a main entry for each part of speech of the word.

Practice 12

Use an online dictionary to identify the parts of speech for each of the following words. A word may be used as more than one part of speech.

1. graph _____

2. angle _____

3. degree _____

Definitions

Most words have more than one meaning. When there is more than one definition, each meaning is numbered. Many times the dictionary will also provide examples of sentences in which the word is used.

> **EXAMPLES** Three definitions are given for the word *degree*. In the spaces provided, write the number of the definition that best fits its meaning in each sentence.

1. A step or stage in a process

2. A unit of measurement for angles and curves

3. A title conferred on students by a college, university, or professional school upon completion of a program of study

_____ **A.** Joanne changed her physical fitness activities by degrees; she began with short 5-minute walks and built up to 30-minute walks every day of the week.

_____ **B.** John received his associate of arts degree from a community college and his bachelor of arts degree from a four-year university.

_____ **C.** If two triangles are similar, their corresponding angles have the same number of degrees.

EXPLANATION The definition that best fits its meaning in each sentence: A (1); B (3); C (2).

Practice 13

Here are two words, their definitions, and sentences using the words based on their various definitions. In the spaces provided, write the number of the definition that best fits each sentence. Note that one definition is not used.

A. **factor: 1** something that brings about a result, ingredient; **2** one who acts or transacts the business of another; **3** a number that will divide into another number exactly

_____ **1.** The *factors* of 10 are 1, 2, and 5.

_____ **2.** The doctor discovered that pollen was a *factor* in Justine's sinus condition.

B. **plot: 1** *n* a small area of planted ground; **2** *n* the plan or main story of a literary work; **3** *v* to mark or note on as if on a map or chart

_____ **3.** I love to read a novel with a fast-paced *plot.*

_____ **4.** The graph of an equation is a drawing that *plots* all its solutions.

_____ **5.** Grandmother worked in the vegetable *plot* all morning.

LO6 Develop Textbook Skills: Learning Content Words and Textbook Definitions

Content Words

Textbook Skills

Many students think they should be able to pick up a textbook and simply read it. However, a textbook is written for a content or subject area, such as math, history, or English. Each content area has its own vocabulary. For example, a history textbook takes a different approach from that of a literature textbook. Different courses may use the same words, but the words often take on a new or different meaning in the context of the content area.

> **EXAMPLES** The following sentences all use the word *parallel.* Write the letter of the course that would use the word in the context in which it appears.

_____ **1.** The brain appears to be a parallel processor, in which many different groups of neuron circuits work on different tasks at the same time.
a. mathematics   c. history
b. English   d. psychology

_____ **2.** Some writers use parallel structure of words and phrases for a balanced and smooth flow of ideas.
a. mathematics   c. history
b. English   d. psychology

_____ **3.** Parallel lines never intersect.
a. mathematics   c. history
b. English   d. psychology

EXPLANATIONS Use context clues to determine your answers.

1. The word *parallel* in this sentence is used in the study of the mind. So this term is used in a psychology class (d).

2. The word *parallel* in this sentence is used in an English class (b). Parallel structure refers to the repetition of words and phrases that are equal in their forms.

3. The word *parallel* in this sentence is used in a mathematics class (a). Parallel lines can run side by side without meeting. ◀

Textbook Definitions

You do not always need to use the dictionary to find the meaning of a word. In fact, many textbooks contain words or word groups that you cannot find in a dictionary. The content word is usually typed in bold or italic print. The definition follows, and many times an example is given. Context clues are helpful.

▷ **EXAMPLES** Read the following passage from a psychology textbook. Then answer the questions that follow it.

Textbook Skills

Disconfirmation is a communication pattern in which you ignore a person's presence as well as that person's communications. You say, in effect, that the person and what she or he has to say aren't worth serious attention. Disconfirming responses often lead to loss of self-esteem. Note that disconfirmation is not the same as rejection. In **rejection**, you disagree with the person; you indicate your unwillingness to accept something the other person says or does. In disconfirming someone, however, you deny that person's significance; you claim that what this person says or does simply does not count.

—DeVito, Joseph A., *The Interpersonal Communication Book*, 10th ed., p. 171.

1. A communication pattern in which you ignore a person's presence as well as that person's communications is _____.

2. An unwillingness to accept something the other person says or does is _____.

EXPLANATIONS The author knows that these words, or the specific uses of these words, may be new for many students, so the words are set in **bold** print and definitions are given.

1. disconfirmation   2. rejection

Practice 14

Read each of the following textbook passages. Then write the definition for each of the words in **bold** print.

Textbook
Skills

1. To say that $x + 4 <$ (is less than) 10 and $x <$ (is less than) 6 are **equivalent** is to say that they have the same solution set. For example, the number 3 is a solution to $x + 4 < 10$. It is also a solution for $x < 6$. The number -2 is a solution of $x < 6$. It is also a solution of $x + 4 < 10$. Any solution of one is a solution of the other; they are equivalent.

—Bittinger, Marvin L. and Beecher, Judith A.,
*Introductory and Intermediate Algebra:
A Combined Approach, 2nd ed.*, p. 143.

_____

2. To borrow the useful terms of the English novelist E. M. Forster, characters may seem **flat** or round. A **flat** character has only one outstanding trait or feature: for example, the stock character of the mad scientist, with his lust for absolute power and his crazily gleaming eyes.

—Adapted from Kennedy X. J. and Gioia, Dana,
Literature, 8th ed., p. 78.

_____

3. **Codependence** refers to a self-defeating relationship pattern in which a person is "addicted to the addict."

—Donatelle, Rebecca J. and Davis, Lorraine G.,
Access to Health, 7th ed., p. 321.

_____

_____

Visual Vocabulary

Textbook
Skills

Textbooks often make information clearer by providing a visual image such as a graph, chart, or photograph. Take time to study these visual images and their captions to figure out how each one ties in to the information given in words.

⊘ **EXAMPLES** Study the following flow chart from a college psychology textbook. Then use information from the flow chart to fill in the blanks in the paragraph that explains the flow chart in greater detail.

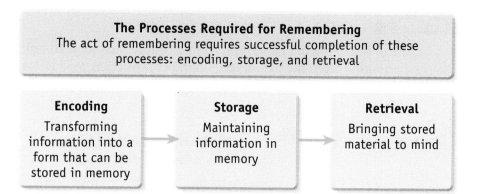

The Processes Required for Remembering
The act of remembering requires successful completion of these processes: encoding, storage, and retrieval

Encoding
Transforming information into a form that can be stored in memory

Storage
Maintaining information in memory

Retrieval
Bringing stored material to mind

Psychologists think of memory as involving three cognitive processes: **(1)** _____, **(2)** _____, and **(3)** _____. The first process, **(4)** _____, is the transformation of information into a form that can be stored. For example, if you witness a car crash, you might try to form a mental picture of it to enable yourself to remember it. The second process, **(5)** _____, involves keeping or maintaining information. For **(6)** _____ information to be stored, some physiological change must take place in the brain—a process called consolidation. The final process, **(7)** _____, occurs when information is brought to mind. To remember something, you must perform all three processes— **(8)** _____ the information, **(9)** _____ it, and then **(10)** _____ it.

—Wood et al., *Mastering the World of Psychology*, 3rd ed., p. 178.

EXPLANATIONS The flow chart contains all the information you needed to fill in the blanks in the paragraph. As you compare your answers to the following, note the change in suffixes based on how certain words are used in context:
(1) encoding; (2) storage; (3) retrieval; (4) encoding; (5) storage; (6) encoded; (7) retrieval; (8) encode; (9) store; and (10) retrieve. ◂

Practice 15

Read the following paragraph from a college biology textbook. Then, using information from the paragraph, fill in the flow chart to illustrate the ideas in the paragraph.

The Scientific Method Is the Basis for Scientific Inquiry

[1]The scientific method proceeds step-by-step. [2]It begins when someone makes an **observation** of an interesting pattern or phenomenon. [3]The observation, in turn, prompts the observer to ask a **question** about what was observed. [4]Then, after a period of contemplation (that

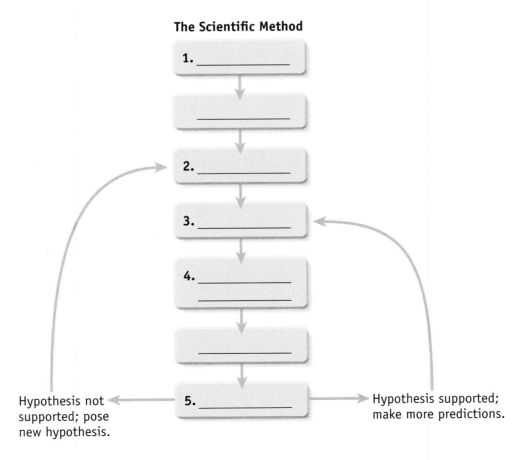

The Scientific Method

1. _____

_____

2. _____

3. _____

4. _____
_____

_____

Hypothesis not supported; pose new hypothesis. ← 5. _____ → Hypothesis supported; make more predictions.

perhaps also includes reflecting on the scientific work of others who have considered related questions), the person proposes an answer to the question, an explanation for the observation. [5]This proposed explanation is a **hypothesis**. [6]A good hypothesis leads to a **prediction**, typically expressed in "if … then" language. [7]The prediction is tested with further observations or with **experiments**. [8]These experiments produce results that either support or refute the hypothesis, and a **conclusion** is drawn about it. [9]A single experiment is never an adequate basis for a conclusion; the experiment must be repeated not only by the original experimenter but also by others.

—Audesirk, Teresa, Audesirk, Gerald, and Byers, Bruce E., *Life on Earth,* 5th ed., p. 3.

Apply Information Literacy Skills

 ## Academic, Personal, and Career Applications of Vocabulary and Dictionary Skills

Effective use of vocabulary and dictionary skills are basic information literacy skills. Vocabulary and dictionary skills are vital to success in academic, personal, and career situations. In your academic, personal, and career lives, you will come across many unfamiliar words. Thus, you will use the skills that you learned in this chapter in several ways:

- Recognize your own need to comprehend a new word or term.
- Find and interpret the meanings of new words or terms.
- Apply the new word or term to the specific situation.

Academic Application

Assume you are taking a college biology course. Your textbook provides three vocabulary resources: (1) Key terms are highlighted in bold print and defined in the text. (2) Each chapter summary lists key vocabulary and identifies the page number where the term appears in the text. (3) The last section of the textbook is a glossary of all key terms highlighted in bold in the text.

- **Before Reading:** (1) Skim the passage. Note the "Chapter Summary: Key Terms." (2) Identify three key terms to learn. (3) Create a word chart to use before, during, and after reading. Consider use of context clues (SAGE), word parts, an online dictionary, and/or textbook resources:

- **During Reading:** Highlight the definitions of the key terms identified before reading.

- **After Reading:** In the space following the passage, complete the word chart with details from the passage.

Before Reading: Need to Know Key Terms: ———————————————

——

Before Reading: My Word Chart

Context Clues, Word Parts, Dictionary, Textbook Resources: ——————————

——

Chapter Summary: Key Terms

aerobic (71)	cytoplasmic fluid (60)	metabolically (105)	molecule (2,3)
anaerobic (71)	enzymes (104)	metabolism (105)	
ATP (103)	eukaryotic (62)	mitochondrion (71)	

Mitochondria Use Energy Stored in Food Molecules to Produce ATP

[1]All eukaryotic cells contain **mitochondria** (singular, mitochondrion), which are sometimes called the "powerhouses of the cell." [2]These power-houses extract energy from food molecules and store it in the high-energy bonds of ATP. [3]Different amounts of energy can be released from a food molecule, depending on how it is broken down. [4]The breakdown of food molecules begins with enzymes in the cytoplasmic fluid. [5]This process does not use oxygen. [6]This **anaerobic** ("without oxygen") breakdown does not convert much food energy into ATP energy. [7]Mitochondria enable a eu-karyotic cell to use oxygen to break down high-energy molecules even further. [8]These **aerobic** ("with oxygen") reactions generate energy much more effectively. [9]About 16 times as much ATP is generated by aerobic metabolism in the mitochondria than by anaerobic metabolism in the

cytoplasmic fluid. **10**Not surprisingly, mitochondria are found in large numbers in metabolically active cells, such as muscle. **11**And they are less abundant in cells that are less active, such as those of cartilage.

—Adapted from Audesirk, Teresa, Audesirk, Gerald, and Byers, Bruce E., *Biology: Life on Earth with Physiology*, 9th ed., p. 71.

After Reading

Complete the following chart with three key terms identified before reading. List the resources you used to complete the chart.

		Biology Word Chart		
Term	**Part of Speech**	**Word Parts**	**Definition**	**Use in Sentence**

Vocabulary Resources:

Personal Application

Assume you are buying a car from an individual rather than a car lot. The owner has presented you with a bill of sale. The following is an excerpt from the document.

- **Before Reading:** Skim the passage and underline at last three key terms that you need to know. Use an online dictionary to look up the meanings of these words.

- **During Reading:** Highlight details related to the key terms you identified before reading.

- **After Reading:** In the space following the passage, use your own words to state the meaning of the key words you identified before reading.

Vehicle Bill of Sale

[1] I, J. Smith of 3 Home Lane, Lake View, Texas, hereby certify that I am the lawful owner of this vehicle and have the authority to sell it. [2] I hereby acknowledge the receipt of $3,000 in the form of cash, from Lola Reed, as full payment for the purchase of said vehicle, which is sold "AS IS." [3] I do hereby grant, sell and transfer full ownership of this vehicle to the buyer. [4] I certify that this vehicle, at the time of sale, is free from all encumbrances, taxes, fees and liens except as those specified on the Title or listed below; and that, I (Seller) will defend and be held fully responsible for such lawful claims and demands with respect to the vehicle, if any.

Key Terms and Definitions: _____

_____

_____

Career Application

Assume you have decided to start your own small business. You want to deduct business expenses from your income tax. Read the following section from an online document provided by the Internal Revenue Service.

- **Before Reading:** Skim the text and underline the key terms you need to know. Use an online dictionary to look up the meanings of these words.

- **During Reading:** Highlight details related to the key terms you identified before reading.

- **After Reading:** In the space following the passage, use your own words to state the meaning of the key words you identified before reading.

Cost Recovery

[1]You can elect to deduct or amortize certain business start-up costs. [2]Although you generally cannot take a current deduction for a capital expense, you may be able to recover the amount you spend through depreciation, amortization, or depletion. [3]These recovery methods allow you to deduct part of your cost each year. [4]In this way, you are able to recover your capital expense.

—Internal Revenue Service. "What Can I Deduct?" *Publication 535 (2010), Business Expenses.* Department of Treasury. <http://www.irs.gov/publications/p535/index.html>

Key Terms and Definitions: _____

_____

_____

REVIEW TEST 1

Score (number correct) _____ × 10 = _____%

Visit MyReadingLab to take this test online and receive feedback and guidance on your answers.

Context Clues

A. Use context clues. Select the letter of the best meaning for each word in **bold** type. Then identify the context clue you used.

_____ **1.** Manny's attendance **dwindled**, until he finally stopped coming altogether.
   a. lessened   c. enhanced
   b. improved   d. ended

_____ **2.** The context clue used for the word *dwindled* in sentence 1:
   a. synonym   c. general context
   b. antonym   d. example

_____ **3.** Researchers have learned to control or eliminate many **blights** such as smallpox and the bubonic plague.
   a. barriers   c. diseases
   b. tests   d. mysteries

_____ **4.** The context clue used for the word *blights* in sentence 3:
   a. synonym
   b. antonym
   c. general context
   d. example

B. Using context clues, write the definition for each word in **bold** type. Choose definitions from the box. Use each definition once.

complicated	environment	range
disagreement	illnesses	smooth-talking

5. Few singers can boast of a musical **repertoire** like that of Elvis Presley, who easily mastered gospel, ballads, and rock and roll.

_____

6. In a democratic society, individuals who disagree with government are allowed to voice their **dissent** by writing, speaking, and even marching in the streets.

_____

7. Washing hands with warm, sudsy water is an important step in the fight against **infirmities** caused by unseen germs.

_____

8. Con artists cheat countless numbers of us with their **glib** promises and high-pressure sales tactics.

_____

9. The handmade lacework on the tablecloth has a beautiful and **intricate** design of roses and scallops.

_____

10. Central Florida alligators enjoy a **habitat** of spring-fed waterways, sandy beaches with fallen logs, and shallow wetlands for hunting and nesting.

_____

Copyright © 2015 Pearson Education, Inc.

REVIEW TEST 2

Score (number correct) _____ × 10 = _____%

Visit MyReadingLab to take this test online and receive feedback and guidance on your answers.

Dictionary and Glossary Skills

A. Look over the following entry from Merriam-Webster.com. Then mark each numbered item **T** if it is true or **F** it is false based on the entry.

> **om·niv·o·rous** 🔊 *adjective* \äm-ˈniv-rəs, -ˈni-və-\
> : eating both plants and animals
> : eager to learn about many different things
>
> Full Definition of OMNIVOROUS   Cite! ℞+1
> **1** : feeding on both animal and vegetable substances
> **2** : avidly taking in everything as if devouring or consuming
> <an *omnivorous* reader>
> — **om·niv·o·rous·ly** *adverb*

Source: Definition of "omnivorous" reprinted by permission from *Merriam-Webster's Collegiate® Dictionary, 11th Edition.* © 2013 by Merriam-Webster, Inc. (www.Merriam-Webster.com).

_____ **1.** The entry gives one form of the word *omnivorous*.

_____ **2.** Someone's mind can be *omnivorous*.

_____ **3.** *Omnivorous* has three syllables.

_____ **4.** The *ou* in *omnivorous* sounds like the *ou* in *out*.

_____ **5.** *Omnivorous* is a noun.

REVIEW TEST 3

Score (number correct) _____ × 20 = _____%

Visit MyReadingLab to take this test online and receive feedback and guidance on your answers.

Read the following passage from a college film studies textbook. Answer the questions that follow.

Special Effects

[1]If William Shakespeare were alive today, he would be **enthralled** by the ability of computer-generated imagery (CGI) to create fantastic, brave

new worlds, where the magical is commonplace. [2]This digital technology, perfected in the 1990s, revolutionized special effects. [3]Although it's very expensive, costing hundreds of thousands of dollars for only a few minutes of screen time, eventually CGI will save film producers millions.

[4]In the past, whole scenes often had to be reshot because of technical glitches. [5]For example, if a modern building or auto appeared in a period film, the scene had to be recut or even rephotographed. [6]Today, such details can be removed digitally. [7]So can a microphone that accidentally dips into the frame. [8]Even sweat on an actor's face can be **effaced** by an F/X technician.

[9]Computer-generated images can be stored for future use, when they can be digitally altered with new costumes, new backgrounds or foregrounds, or with a totally different atmosphere, as in the magical landscapes in *The Lord of the Rings* trilogy. [10]In fact, physical sets don't even have to be constructed in some instances, since images containing the sets can be created on a computer.

[11]Even realistic movies can benefit from this technology. [12]In *Forrest Gump*, a handful of extras were digitally expanded into a cast of thousands. [13]In the ultrarealistic Holocaust drama, *The Pianist*, the events take place during the World War II era, yet director Roman Polanski used CGI for several scenes—the bombed-out ruins of a city street, a character falling from a tall building, aircraft streaking across the skies.

[14]Traditional animation, with its time-consuming, hand-drawn cel images, is being replaced by computers, which produce images that are created digitally, not *à mano*. [15]CGI has produced a new "look" in animation, less detailed, more sculptural, more *plastique*—like the streamlined images of *Shrek*, *The Polar Express*, and *The Incredibles*.

[16]Acting has also been affected by this technology, though not usually in a positive way. [17]In *Star Wars*, for example, actors often performed in front of F/X bluescreens rather than with other actors, who were later digitally added to the shot by computer technicians. [18]Some critics have complained that such acting is often cold and mechanical, with none of the human subtleties that can be found in scenes where performers are actually interacting.

[19]Digital editing is also much easier than traditional methods. [20]Instead of handling a physical filmstrip and making actual cuts, modern editors need only to press a button to cut from one shot to another.

[21]In addition, CGI technology will eventually make film distribution and exhibition cheaper. [22]Today, film prints can cost up to $2,000 apiece. [23]A mainstream American movie can be shown simultaneously on 2,000 screens, costing $4 million just for the cost of prints. [24]In the future, movies will be stored on digital disks, like a DVD, and will cost only a few dollars to manufacture. [25]Distributors will also save on shipping fees. [26]Instead of

the heavy reels of traditional movies, costing thousands of dollars to ship by bus, plane, or rail, in the future, a lightweight disk will be sent to movie theaters for only a few dollars. [27]Projection equipment will basically consist of a commercial DVD machine, not the **cumbersome**, expensive, mechanical projectors that have dominated film exhibition for over 100 years.

[28]The biggest danger of this technology, of course, is that it will fall into the hands of moneygrubbing hacks with the artistic sensibilities of gnats. [29]It's already happened. [30]The world's screens are dominated by soulless movies full of sound and fury, signifying nothing: pointless chases, explosions, **gratuitous** violence, explosions, lots of speed, explosions, and just for good measure, more explosions. [31]The story is usually predictable, the acting bereft of nuance, the sentiments banal. [32]But the special effects are **impeccable**. [33]In short, film artists interested in F/X materials need to be just as talented as artists in any other style or genre or technology. [34]It's what they do with the technology artistically that counts, not the technology per se.

—Gianetti, Louis, *Understanding Movies*,
12th ed., pp. 33–34.

_____ **1.** The best meaning of **enthralled** in sentence 1 is
  a. puzzled.   c. frustrated.
  b. upset.   d. fascinated.

_____ **2.** The best meaning of **effaced** in sentence 8 is
  a. erased.   c. monitored.
  b. produced.   d. increased.

_____ **3.** The best meaning of **cumbersome** in sentence 27 is
  a. easy to operate.   c. modern.
  b. hard to handle.   d. noisy.

_____ **4.** The best meaning of **gratuitous** in sentence 30 is
  a. frightening.   c. unnecessary.
  b. exciting.   d. extraordinary.

_____ **5.** The best meaning of **impeccable** in sentence 32 is
  a. ordinary.   c. perfect.
  b. visual.   d. interesting.

SUMMARY RESPONSE

Restate the author's most important idea in your own words using some of the words in **bold** print. Begin your summary response with the following: *The most important idea of "Special Effects" by Gianetti is …*

WHAT DO YOU THINK?

Do you agree with the author that too many movies rely just on special effects, and do not have interesting stories or acting? Assume you write a blog where you discuss and review movies. Write an article to post on your blog that discusses this topic. Consider the following points as you write:

- State your opinion about this topic.
- Support your opinion with specific examples of movies.

REVIEW TEST 4

Score (number correct) _____ × 10 = _____%

Visit MyReadingLab to take this test online and receive feedback and guidance on your answers.

Vocabulary Skills

Textbook Skills

Before reading: Survey the following passage from a college geography textbook. Answer the **Before Reading** questions that follow the passage. **After reading:** Check the answers you gave before reading to make sure they are accurate. Then respond to the "What Do You Think?" prompt to discuss and write about what you have read.

Vocabulary Preview

metallic (sentence 16): made of, containing metal

radius (sentence 16): a straight line extending from the center of a circle to its edge or from the center of a sphere to its surface

latitude (sentence 22): an imaginary line joining points on Earth's surface that are all of equal distance north or south of the equator

microorganisms (sentence 25): a tiny organism such as a virus or bacteria that can only be seen under a microscope

Earth's Physical Systems

[1]Geographers study natural processes in terms of four systems: the atmosphere, the hydrosphere, the lithosphere, and the biosphere, which encompasses all of Earth's living organisms.

[2]The **atmosphere** is a thin layer of gases surrounding Earth to an altitude of less than 480 kilometers (300 miles). [3]Pure, dry air in the lower atmosphere contains about 78 percent nitrogen and 21 percent oxygen

by volume. [4]It also includes about 0.9 percent argon (an inert gas) and 0.38 percent carbon dioxide. [5]Air is a mass of gas molecules held to Earth by gravity creating pressure. [6]Variations in air pressure from one place to another cause winds to blow, as well as create storms, and control **precipitation** or rainfall patterns.

[7]The **hydrosphere** is the water realm of Earth's surface. [8]Water can exist as a vapor, liquid, or ice, such as the oceans, surface waters on land (lakes, streams, and rivers), groundwater in soil and rock, water vapor in the atmosphere, and ice in glaciers. [9]Over 97 percent of the world's water is in the oceans in liquid form. [10]The oceans sustain a large quantity and variety of marine life in the form of both plants and animals. [11]Seawater supplies water vapor to the atmosphere, which returns to Earth's surface as rainfall and snowfall. [12]These are the most important sources of fresh water, which is essential for the survival of plants and animals. [13]Water changes temperature very slowly, so oceans also moderate seasonal extremes of temperature over much of Earth's surface. [14]Oceans also provide humans with food and a surface for transportation.

[15]The **lithosphere** is the solid Earth, composed of rocks and **sediments**—such as clay, silt, pebbles, or sand—overlying them. [16]Earth's core is a dense, metallic sphere about 3,500 kilometers (2,200 miles) in **radius**. [17]Surrounding the core is a **mantle** (or layer) about 2,900 kilometers (1,800 miles) thick. [18]A thin, brittle outer shell, the crust is 8 to 40 kilometers (5 to 25 miles) thick. [19]The lithosphere consists of Earth's crust and a portion of upper mantle directly below the crust, extending down to about 70 kilometers (45 miles). [20]Powerful forces deep within Earth bend and break the crust to form mountain chains and shape the crust to form continents and ocean basins. [21]The shape of Earth's crust influences climate. [22]If the surface of Earth were completely smooth, then temperature, winds, and precipitation would form orderly bands at each latitude.

[23]The **biosphere** consists of all living organisms on Earth. [24]The atmosphere, lithosphere, and hydrosphere function together to create the environment of the biosphere, which extends from the depths of the oceans through the lower layers of atmosphere. [25]On the land surface, the biosphere includes giant redwood trees, which can extend up to 110 meters (360 feet), as well as the **microorganisms** that live many meters down in the soil, in deep caves, or in rock fractures.

[26]These four spheres of the natural environment interact in many ways. [27]Plants and animals live on the surface of the lithosphere, where

they obtain food and shelter. [28]The hydrosphere provides water to drink and physical support for aquatic life. [29]Most life forms depend on breathing air, and birds and people also rely on air for transportation. [30]All life forms depend on inputs of solar energy.

[31]Humans also interact with each of these four spheres. [32]We waste away and die if we are without water. [33]We pant if oxygen levels are reduced in the atmosphere, and we cough if the atmosphere contains pollutants. [34]We need heat, but excessive heat or cold is dangerous. [35]We rely on a stable lithosphere for building materials and fuel for energy. [36]We derive our food from the rest of the biosphere.

—Bergman, Edward and Renwick, William H.,
*Introduction to Geography: People, Places,
and Environment*, 4th ed., p. 19.

Before Reading

A. Use context clues to answer the following questions.

_____ **1.** In sentence 6, the word **precipitation** means
   a. storm.   c. rainfall.
   b. air pressure.   d. gas.

_____ **2.** Identify the context clue used for the word **precipitation** in sentence 6.
   a. synonym   c. general context
   b. antonym   d. example

_____ **3.** In sentence 15, the word **sediments** means
   a. layers.   c. sands.
   b. rocks.   d. deposits.

_____ **4.** Identify the context clue used for the word **sediments** in sentence 15.
   a. synonym   c. general context
   b. antonym   d. example

_____ **5.** In sentence 17, the word **mantle** means
   a. garment.   c. core.
   b. layer.   d. metal.

_____ **6.** Identify the context clue used for the word **mantle** in sentence 17.
   a. synonym   c. general context
   b. antonym   d. example

B. Study the following word chart. Then match the word to its definition.

Root	Meaning
atmos	vapor, breath
bio	life
hydra	water
lith	stone
sphaera	globe, ball

_____ **7.** atmosphere   a. the part of Earth that is water

_____ **8.** biosphere   b. the solid outer layer of the Earth

_____ **9.** hydrosphere   c. the area of the Earth that is inhabited by living things

_____ **10.** lithosphere

                                 d. gases surrounding the Earth

VISUAL *VOCABULARY*

The Grand Canyon in Arizona represents Earth's _____.

a. atmosphere
b. hydrosphere
c. lithosphere

SUMMARY RESPONSE

Restate the author's most important idea in your own words using some of the words in bold print. Begin your summary response with the following: *The most important idea of "Earth's Physical Systems" by Bergman and Renwick is …*

WHAT DO YOU THINK?

Assume you are taking a college course in geography, and your class has been asked to write a report about the health of Earth's four systems in your local community. For example, what is the state of the hydrosphere where you live?

Are the lakes, rivers, or ocean near you clean and healthy, or polluted? Assume your report counts as 10% of your final grade, but also write your report as a letter to the editor of the local newspaper.

After Reading About Vocabulary and Dictionary Skills

The reading system you learned in Chapter 1 is an excellent study system that will help you comprehend and retain large sections of information, such as this textbook chapter about vocabulary skills. Now that you have studied the chapter, take time to reflect on what you have learned before you begin the Mastery Tests. Stop and think about your learning and performance by answering the following questions. Write your answers in your notebook.

- How has my knowledge base or prior knowledge about vocabulary and dictionary skills changed?
- Based on my studies, how do I think I will perform on the Mastery Test(s)? Why do I think my scores will be above average, average, or below average?
- Would I recommend this chapter to other students who want to learn more about vocabulary and dictionary skills? Why or why not?

Test your understanding of what you have learned about vocabulary and dictionary skills by completing the Chapter 2 Review.

Name _____ Section _____

Date _____ **Score** (number correct) _____ × 25 = _____%

Visit MyReadingLab to take this test online and receive feedback and guidance on your answers.

A. Look over the following entry from Merriam-Webster.com. Then mark each numbered item **T** if it is true or **F** it is false based on the entry.

as·cet·ic 🔊 *adjective* \a-'se-tik, a-\

  : relating to or having a strict and simple way of living that avoids physical pleasure

Full Definition of ASCETIC 🏷 Cite! ℞+1

1 : practicing strict self-denial as a measure of personal and especially spiritual discipline

2 : austere in appearance, manner, or attitude

  — **ascetic** *noun*
  — **as·cet·i·cal·ly** 🔊 *adverb*
  — **as·cet·i·cism** 🔊 *noun*

  📖 See ascetic defined for English-language learners »
  See ascetic defined for kids »

Variants of ASCETIC

as·cet·ic 🔊 also **as·cet·i·cal** 🔊

Examples of ASCETIC

- an *ascetic* diet of rice and beans
- Patterson's collection begins on the walls of the stairway to his basement. "That's where Cindy draws the line. That's probably a real good idea," he says. Mattsson, *ascetic* for a bachelor, imposes the same rule on himself. LeBeau, who has never been married, is much less restrained. —Tom Harpole, *Air & Space*, December 1999/January 2000

  [+] more

Origin of ASCETIC

  Greek *askētikos,* literally, laborious, from *askētēs* one that exercises, hermit, from *askein* to work, exercise

  First Known Use: 1646

Source: Definition, variants and origin of "ascetic" reprinted by permission from *Merriam-Webster's Collegiate® Dictionary*, 11th Edition. © 2013 by Merriam-Webster, Inc. (www.Merriam-Webster.com).

_____ 1. The word *ascetic* comes from a Greek word meaning "laborious."

_____ 2. The word *ascetic* can be used as a noun or as an adjective.

_____ 3. The word *ascetic* has four syllables.

_____ 4. The *e* in *ascetic* sounds like the *e* in *eat*.

Name _____ Section _____

Date _____ **Score** (number correct) _____ × 10 = _____%

Visit MyReadingLab to take this test online and receive feedback and guidance on your answers.

Read the following passage, adapted from a college mathematics textbook. Use context clues and the graphs to write the definitions for each word in **bold** type. Choose definitions from the box. One answer will be used twice.

Integers and the Real World

Textbook Skills

[1]A **set** is a collection of objects. [2]For our purposes, we will most often be considering sets of numbers. [3]The set of **natural numbers** are those numbers to the right of zero. [4]The **whole numbers** are the natural numbers with 0 included. [5]We can represent these two sets of numbers on a visual called a **number line**.

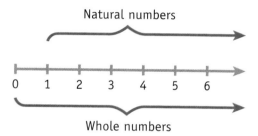

Natural numbers

0   1   2   3   4   5   6

Whole numbers

[6]We create a new set of numbers called *integers* by starting with the whole numbers, 0, 1, 2, 3, and so on. [7]For each natural number 1, 2, 3, and so on, we obtain a new number to the left of the zero on the number line: [8]For the number 1, there will be an opposite number −1 (negative 1); for the number 2, there will be an opposite number −2 (negative 2); and so on. [9]We call these new numbers to the left of zero **negative integers**. [10]The natural numbers are also called **positive integers**. [11]The set of **integers** equals { ... −5, −4, −3, −2, −1, 0, 1, 2, 3, 4, 5 ... }.

[12]Integers relate to many real-world problems and situations. [13]The following example will help you get ready to turn problem situations that use integers into mathematical language.

group
{ 0, 1, 2, 3, 4, 5 ...}
{ 1, 2, 3, 4, 5 ...}

{ ... –5, –4, –3, –2, –1}
graph
natural numbers, zero, and
    the opposites of natural numbers

{ 1, 2, 3, 4, 5 ...}
natural numbers

1. In sentence 1, **set** means _____.

2. In sentence 3, **natural numbers** means _____.

3. In sentence 4, **whole numbers** means _____.

4. In sentence 5, a **number line** is a _____ of sets of numbers.

5. In sentence 9, **negative integers** means _____.

6. In sentence 10, **positive integers** means _____.

7. In sentence 10, a synonym for **positive integers** is _____.

8. In sentence 11, **integers** means _____

_____.

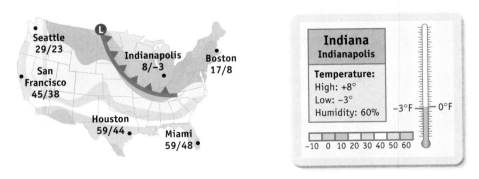

—Text and figure from Bittinger, Marvin L.; Beecher, Judith A., *Introductory and Intermediate Algebra: A Combined Approach,* 2nd ed., p. 13.

9–10. Use the temperature map to answer the following questions.

9. The low temperature in Indianapolis is 3 degrees below zero. Which integer corresponds to this situation? _____

10. The high temperature in Indianapolis is 8 degrees above zero. Which integer corresponds to this situation? _____

Name _____ Section _____

Date _____ **Score** (number correct) _____ × 10 = _____%

Visit MyReadingLab to take this test online and receive feedback and guidance on your answers.

A. Read the following passage, adapted from a college psychology textbook. Use context clues to write the definition for each word in **bold** type. Choose definitions from the box. You will not use all of the definitions.

Personality Types and Traits

Textbook Skills

¹It has long been clear that people differ in personality. ²The earliest known reason given for these individual differences is the humoral theory. ³This **premise** was first put forth by the Greek physician Galen in the second century. ⁴He based his beliefs on the then-current medical beliefs that had **originated** with the ancient Greeks. ⁵The body was thought to contain four humors, or fluids: yellow bile, black bile, phlegm, and blood. ⁶People were classified according to the disposition caused by the **predominance** or power of one of those humors in the body. ⁷Choleric people, who had an excess of yellow bile, were bad-tempered and **irritable**. ⁸Melancholic people, who had an excess of black bile, had gloomy and pessimistic natures. ⁹Phlegmatic people, whose bodies had large amounts of phlegm, were sluggish, calm, and unexcitable. ¹⁰Sanguine people had a **preponderance** of blood, which made them cheerful and passionate.

—Adapted from Carlson, Neil and William Buskist, *Psychology: Science of Behavior*, 5th ed., p. 449.

begun	great amount	offered
easily angered	idea	stopped
good-natured	influence	weakness

1. In sentence 3, **premise** means _____.

2. In sentence 4, **originated** means _____.

3. In sentence 6, **predominance** means _____.

4. In sentence 7, **irritable** means _____.

5. In sentence 10, **preponderance** means _____.

B. Read the following passage, adapted from a college health textbook. Use context clues and word parts to write the definition for each word in **bold** type. Choose definitions from the box. Use each definition once.

The Pathogens: Routes of Transmission

Textbook
Skills

¹**Pathogens** enter the body in several ways. ²They may be **transmitted** by direct contact between infected persons, such as by kissing, or by indirect contact such as by touching the object an infected person has had contact with. ³The hands are probably the greatest source of infectious disease transmission. ⁴You may also **autoinoculate** yourself, or transmit a pathogen from one part of your body to another. ⁵For example, you may touch a sore on your lip that is teeming with viral herpes and then transmit the virus to your eye when you scratch your itchy eyelid.

⁶Pathogens are also transmitted by airborne contact; you can breathe in air that carries a particular pathogen. ⁷Pathogens are also passed through foodborne infection if you eat something **contaminated** by **microorganisms**.

—Donatelle, Rebecca J., *Health: The Basics*, 5th ed., p. 348. © 2003.

Prefix	Meaning	Root	Meaning	Suffix	Meaning
auto-	self	*mit*	send	*-ate*	make, do, cause
con-	with	*ocul*	eye, bud	*-gen*	cause
in-	into	*organ*	work	*-ism*	being
micro-	small	*path*	disease		
trans-	across	*tamin*	spoil		

germs   poisoned   to infect another
life forms too small to be   spread   part of one's body
   seen by the naked eye

6. In sentence 1, **pathogens** means _____.

7. In sentence 2, **transmitted** means _____.

8. In sentence 4, **autoinoculate** means _____.

9. In sentence 7, **contaminated** means _____.

10. In sentence 7, **microorganisms** means _____.

_____.

Name _____ Section _____

Date _____ **Score** (number correct) _____ × 10 = _____%

Visit MyReadingLab to take this test online and receive feedback and guidance on your answers.

Vocabulary Skills

A. Using the information in the chart and the context of each sentence, select the word that best fits the meaning of the sentence. Use each word once.

Prefix	Meaning	Root	Meaning	Suffix	Meaning
carni-	flesh	ent	intestines	-al	possessing or expressing a quality
dys-	bad, impaired	function	perform	-ery	state, condition
omni-	all	nocturn	night	-ous	possessing the qualities of
		vor	devour, feed		

carnivorous   dysentery   dysfunctional   nocturnal   omnivores

1. Some birds such as eagles and ospreys are _____, with diets consisting of fish and small animals.

2. Julia is suffering with _____ because of water she drank in the jungle.

3. Just like a bat, my son Chip is a _____ creature who prefers to sleep during the day.

4. Most _____ have two types of teeth: sharp, tearing teeth for eating meat and flat, grinding teeth for eating plants.

5. If I don't get enough sleep, I become completely _____.

B. Using the information from the chart and the context of each sentence, select the word that best fits the meaning of the sentence. Use each word once.

Prefix	Meaning	Root	Meaning	Suffix	Meaning
e-	out of, from	ject	throw	-ile	capability
pro-	forward, in favor of	pellere	to drive	-ion	action, state

ejection   ejects   projectile   projects   propel

6. Because mother _____ her fears into action, she taught all of us the Heimlich maneuver as a safety precaution.

7. The Heimlich maneuver is an emergency procedure that _____ foreign objects from a choking victim's airway.

8. The maneuver causes the _____ of the foreign object by forcing quick bursts of air up from the abdomen.

9. Sometimes a strong burst of air turns the object that is blocking the air passage into a _____ as it shoots out of the victim's mouth.

10. Place a clenched fist and hands together just below the sternum; use inward and upward thrusts to _____ the object from the air passage.

2 Summary of Key Concepts of Vocabulary and Dictionary Skills

 Assess your comprehension of vocabulary and dictionary skills.

- **Vocabulary** is _____.

- Four of the most common types of context clues are as follows:

    - A **synonym** is _____
      _____.

    - An **antonym** is a _____.

    - The **general context** clue requires that you read _____
      _____.

    - **Example** clues are often introduced with _____
      _____.

- The three basic word parts are as follows:

    - The _____, the main part of the word.

    - The _____, the group of letters with a specific meaning
      added to the beginning of a word to make a new word.

    - The _____, the group of letters with a specific meaning
      added to the end of a word to make a new word.

- A dictionary entry contains the following information:

    - _____ of the word or term

    - _____ indicating the sounds of consonants and
      vowels of a word

    - _____ indicating the function of a word

    - _____ indicating the history of the word

- Each subject matter has its own _____.

Test Your Comprehension of Vocabulary and Dictionary Skills

Respond to the following questions and prompts.

LO1 LO2 LO3 LO4 LO5 LO6 LO7 In your own words, what is vocabulary? Identify the most helpful skill you have learned. _____

_____

LO2 LO6 LO7 Demonstrate your use of context clues. Use the headings below and create a chart based on the four types of context clues. Then complete the chart with new words you have come across recently as you read for this class, another class, or any reading situation.

Type of Clue	New Word	Meaning of Word	Source Sentence of Word

LO3 LO6 LO7 Go to the Vocabulary Preview in Review Test 4 on page 86. Choose a word or set of words to learn. Then demonstrate your ability to decode the meaning of words using word parts. Use the model of a word web below to create your own web of words linked by word parts. Use a family of words you have come across recently as you read for this class, another class, or any reading situation.

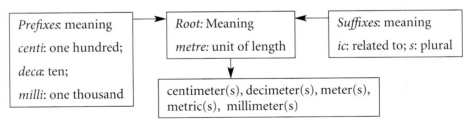

Prefixes: meaning
centi: one hundred;
deca: ten;
milli: one thousand

Root: Meaning
metre: unit of length

Suffixes: meaning
ic: related to; *s:* plural

centimeter(s), decimeter(s), meter(s), metric(s), millimeter(s)

LO3 LO5 LO6 LO7 Demonstrate your use of an online dictionary. Use the headings below and create a chart based on information found in an online dictionary. Then complete the chart with new words you have come across recently as you read for this class, another class, or any reading situation.

Word	Etymology	Part of Speech	Definition	Source Sentence of Word

Stated Main Ideas

3

(LO) LEARNING OUTCOMES

After studying this chapter, you should be able to:

LO1 Identify the Traits of a Main Idea

LO2 Identify the Topic of a Paragraph

LO3 Identify a Topic Sentence

LO4 Analyze the Flow of Ideas and Identify Placement of Topic Sentences

LO5 Recognize the Central Idea and the Thesis Statement

LO6 Develop Textbook Skills: Identify Topics, Main Ideas, and Central Ideas in Textbooks

LO7 Apply Information Literacy Skills: Academic, Personal, and Career Applications of Stated Main Ideas

Before Reading About Stated Main Ideas

Effective use of the reading process relies on developing questions about the material that will guide you as you read. Using the learning outcomes above, create at least five questions that you can answer as you study the chapter. Write your questions in the following spaces:

_____ (page _____)

_____ (page _____)

_____ (page _____)

_____ (page _____)

_____ (page _____)

Compare the questions you created based on the learning outcomes with the following questions. Then write the ones that seem the most helpful in your notebook, leaving enough space between each question to record the answers as you read and study the chapter.

What are the traits of a main idea? (below) What is the difference between a topic and a topic sentence? (p. 108) How is the flow of ideas related to the placement of topic sentences? (p. 114) What is the central idea? (p. 123) What is the difference between the central idea and a topic sentence? (p. 123)

LO1 Identify the Traits of a Main Idea

> A **main idea** is the author's controlling point about the topic. It usually includes the topic and the author's attitude or opinion about the topic, or the author's approach to the topic.

To identify the main idea, ask yourself two questions:

- Who or what is the paragraph about? The answer is the *topic*. The topic can be stated in just a few words.
- What is the author's controlling point about the topic? The answer is the *main idea*. The main idea is stated in one sentence.

Consider these questions as you read the following paragraph from a health textbook.

Textbook
Skills

The Cool-Down Period

The cool-down period is an important part of an exercise workout for several reasons. The cool-down involves reducing the intensity of exercise to allow the body to recover from the workout. During vigorous exercise such as jogging, a lot of blood is pumped to the legs, and there may not be enough to supply the heart and brain; failure to cool down properly may result in dizziness, fainting, and, in rare instances, a heart attack. By gradually reducing the level of physical activity, blood flow is directed back to the heart and brain.

—Adapted from Pruitt, B. E., & Stein, Jane J., *Health Styles*, 2nd ed., p. 169.

- Who or what is the paragraph about? The topic of the paragraph is "the cool-down period of an exercise workout."
- What is the author's controlling point about the topic? The controlling point is that it "is an important part." Putting topic and controlling point together, the main idea is "The cool-down period is an important part of an exercise workout for several reasons."

To better understand the traits of a main idea, compare a passage to a well-planned house of ideas. The *topic* or general subject matter is the roof. The roof covers all the rooms of the house. The *main idea* is the frame of the house, and the supporting details are the different rooms. The following diagram shows the relationship of the ideas:

Topic: Cool-down period

Main Idea (stated in a topic sentence):

The cool-down period is an important part of an exercise workout for several reasons.

Supporting Details:

Cool-down allows the body to recover from the workout.	No cool-down may result in dizziness, fainting, and, in rare instances, a heart attack.	Cool-down directs blood flow back to the heart and brain.

Each of the supporting details explains why the cool-down period is an important part of an exercise workout.

L02 Identify the Topic of a Paragraph

When you ask the question "Who or what is the paragraph about?" you must be sure that your answer is neither too general nor too specific. A general subject needs specific ideas to support or explain it. However, no single paragraph can discuss all the specific ideas linked to a general idea. So an author narrows the general subject to a topic that needs a specific set of ideas to support it. For example, the very general subject "music" can be narrowed to "hip-hop music." And the specific details related to hip-hop music might include the different rappers, ranging from Jay Z to Lil Wayne to Kanye West. In fact, a piece of writing dealing with the general topic "music" will include a very different set of specific ideas than the narrower topic of "hip-hop music." The more general category of music might include classical music and country music, for example. Or it might include symphonies, marching bands, and barber shop quartets.

Often an author shows the relationship between the topic and the specific details by repeating the topic throughout the paragraph as new pieces of information about the topic are introduced. To identify the topic, an effective reader often skims the material for this recurring idea. Skimming for the topic allows you to grasp the relationship among a general subject, the topic, and specific details.

> **EXAMPLE** Skim the following paragraph. Circle the topic as it recurs throughout the paragraph. Answer the question that follows.

A Sincere Apology

[1]A sincere apology is a powerful human experience. [2]A sincere apology is a peace offering that honors the importance of the wronged one's feelings. [3]It defuses anger and fosters healing. [4]A genuine apology offers closure to a painful past and openness to a future built on forgiveness and empathy. [5]A genuine "I'm sorry" accepts the blame for wrongdoing and the painful results. [6]Consider the following example: as a child, Debra suffered greatly because of her abusive, alcoholic father. [7]At the age of 17, she left her father's house, and they had no contact for many years. [8]On her thirty-fifth birthday, Debra received a letter from her father, offering her a long, emotional apology. [9]Their relationship began healing that day. [10]To be brave and wise enough to apologize sincerely is to accept a lesson from life and a unique peace based on self-respect.

_____ Which of the following best states the topic?
   a. apologizing
   b. a sincere apology
   c. the importance of the wronged one's feelings

EXPLANATION "Apologizing" is too general, for it could cover insincere apologies, how to apologize, or what to do if someone will not accept an apology. "The importance of the wronged one's feelings" is too narrow. This idea is a supporting detail, just one of the reasons an apology is so powerful. The topic of this paragraph is (b), "a sincere apology." You should have circled the following phrases: "sincere apology" (sentence 1), "sincere apology" (sentence 2), "genuine apology" (sentence 4), "genuine 'I'm sorry'" (sentence 5), and "apologize sincerely" (sentence 10). Note that the author used the synonym "genuine" to vary the wording of the topic. In addition, note that the title of the paragraph stated the topic. Authors often use titles to relay the topic of the material.

Practice 1

Skim each of the following paragraphs and circle the topic as it recurs throughout the paragraph. Then identify the idea that correctly states the topic. (_Hint:_ one idea is too general to be the topic; another idea is too specific.)

_____ 1.   ¹Many myths exist about the causes of acne. ²Chocolate and greasy foods are often blamed, but foods seem to have little effect on the development and course of acne in most people. ³Another common myth is that dirty skin causes acne; however, blackheads and other acne lesions are not caused by dirt. ⁴Finally, stress does not cause acne.

—Adapted from National Institute of Arthritis and Musculoskeletal and Skin Diseases, "Questions and Answers about Acne."

   a. dirty skin
   b. causes of acne
   c. myths about what causes acne

_____ 2.   ¹Playing rigorous sports in the heat can lead to several types of heat injuries. ²The first type of heat-related illness is dehydration, which is a lack of body fluids. ³The second type is heat exhaustion. ⁴Heat exhaustion has numerous effects, including nausea, dizziness, weakness, headache, pale and moist skin, heavy perspiration, normal or low body temperature, weak pulse, dilated pupils, disorientation, and fainting spells. ⁵A third type of heat injury is heat stroke. ⁶Heat stroke can lead to headaches, dizziness, confusion, and hot dry skin, possibly leading to vascular collapse, coma, and death. ⁷Each of these heat injuries can be prevented.

—Adapted from National Institute of Arthritis and Musculoskeletal and Skin Diseases, "Childhood Sports Injuries and Their Prevention."

   a. types of heat injuries
   b. injuries
   c. heatstroke

_____ 3.   ¹Older people benefit from volunteer work in several ways. ²First, being a volunteer improves the overall quality of an older person's life; it gives meaning and purpose to their lives. ³Second, older persons who volunteer have fewer medical problems than other people their age who are not as active. ⁴Older persons stay physically active when they volunteer; thus they do not suffer as often from heart disease and diabetes. ⁵Finally, volunteer work helps keep the brain active, and an active brain helps protect the memory as people age.

—Adapted from Administration on Aging, "Older Volunteers Leading the Way."

   a. volunteer work
   b. benefits of volunteer work for older people
   c. fewer medical problems

Textbook
Skills

_____ **4.**   [1]The barriers to women's advancement to top positions in the workforce are often very subtle, giving rise to the phrase _**glass ceiling**_. [2]In explaining "why women aren't getting to the top," one observer argues that "at senior management levels, competence is assumed. [3]What you are looking for is someone who fits, someone who gets along, someone you trust. [4]Now that's subtle stuff. [5]How does a group of men feel that a woman is going to fit in? [6]I think it's very hard." [7]Or as a woman bank executive says, "The men just don't feel comfortable." [8]There are many explanations for the glass ceiling, all controversial. [9]For example, some say that women choose staff assignments rather than fast-track, operating-head assignments. [10]Others claim that women are cautious and unaggressive in corporate politics. [11]Finally, some believe that women have lower expectations about peak earnings and positions, and these expectations become self-fulfilling.

—Dye, Thomas, _Politics in America, 5th ed._, Upper Saddle
River: Pearson Education, 2003, p. 589.

a. working women
b. women's low expectations about earnings
c. the glass ceiling for women

A "glass ceiling" is

_____ an invisible barrier preventing women from rising to the highest positions in the workforce.

_____ the sexual harassment a woman faces on the job.

_____ a popular architectural design for large office complexes.

Textbook
Skills

_____ **5.** [1]Intellectual blocks involve obstacles to knowledge. [2]You may find yourself unable to solve a problem for two reasons. [3]First, you may be blocked because you lack information. [4]Second, you may be blocked because you have incorrect or incomplete information. [5]When you buy a car, for example, you can be blocked by being unaware of various cars' performance ratings, repair records, or safety features. [6]Or you may be blocked because you have only one-sided information—the information given by the salesperson. [7]Or maybe you simply don't know enough about cars to buy one with confidence.

—Adapted from DiYanni, Robert, and Pat C. Hoy II, *The Scribner Handbook for Writers*, 3rd ed., p. 65.

    a. intellectual blocks

    b. incorrect information

    c. problem solving

LO3 Identify a Topic Sentence

Most paragraphs have three parts:

- A topic (the general idea or subject)
- A main idea (the controlling point the author is making about the topic, often stated in a topic sentence)
- Supporting details (the specific ideas to support the main idea)

Think again of the house of ideas that a writer builds. Remember, the main idea *frames* the specific ideas. Think of all the different rooms in a house: the kitchen, bedroom, bathroom, living room. Each room is a different part of the house. The frame determines the space for each room and the flow of traffic between rooms. Similarly, the main idea determines how much detail is given and how one detail flows into the next. The main idea of a paragraph is usually stated in a single sentence called the **topic sentence**. The topic sentence—the stated main idea—is unique in two ways.

First, the topic sentence contains two types of information: the topic and the author's controlling point, which restricts or qualifies the topic. At times, the controlling point may be expressed as the author's opinion using biased words. (For more information on biased words see Chapter 9, "Fact and Opinion.") For example, in the topic sentence "A sincere apology is a powerful human experience," the biased words "sincere" and "powerful" limit and control the topic "apology."

Other times, the controlling point may express the author's thought pattern, the way in which the thoughts are going to be organized. (For more information on words that indicate thought patterns, see Chapters 7 and 8.) For example, the topic sentence "Playing rigorous sports in the heat can lead to several types of heat injuries" uses the phrase "several types" to reveal that the author will control the topic by classifying or dividing the topic into types.

Often, an author will use both biased words and a thought pattern to qualify or limit the topic. For example, the topic sentence "Older people benefit from volunteer work in several ways" combines the biased word "benefit" and the phrase "several ways" to indicate that a list of positive examples and explanations will follow.

These qualifiers—words that convey the author's bias or thought pattern—helped you correctly identify the topic in the previous section. An important difference between the topic and the topic sentence is that the topic sentence states the author's main idea in a complete sentence.

> A **topic sentence** is a single sentence that states the topic and words that qualify the topic by revealing the author's opinion about the topic or the author's approach to the topic.

The second unique trait of the topic sentence is its scope: the topic sentence is a general statement that all the other sentences in the paragraph explain or support. A topic sentence states an author's opinion or thought process, which must be explained further with specific supporting details. For example, in the paragraph about the cool-down period after a workout, the topic and the author's controlling point about the topic are stated in the first sentence. Each of the other sentences in the paragraph gives a different reason to explain why the cool-down period is an important part of an exercise workout:

Topic	Author's attitude	Author's thought pattern
↓	↓	↓

The *cool-down period* is an *important part* of an exercise workout for *several reasons*.

First reason	Second reason	Third reason
Cool-down allows the body to recover from the workout.	No cool-down may result in dizziness, fainting, and, in rare instances, a heart attack.	Cool-down directs blood flow back to the heart and brain.

> **Supporting details** are specific ideas that *develop*, *explain*, or *support* the main idea.

The supporting details of a paragraph are framed by the main idea, and all work together to explain or support the author's view of the topic. As an effective reader, you will see that every paragraph has a topic, a main idea, and supporting details. It is much easier to tell the difference between these three parts of a passage once you understand how each part works. A topic, as the general subject of the paragraph, can be expressed in a word or phrase. The main idea contains both the topic and the author's controlling point about the topic and can be stated in one sentence called the topic sentence. The supporting details are all the sentences that state reasons and explanations for the main idea. To locate the topic sentence of a paragraph ask yourself two questions:

- Which sentence contains qualifiers that reveal the author's controlling point—that is, the author's attitude about the topic or approach to the topic?
- Do all the specific details in the passage support this statement?

> **EXAMPLE**

A. The following group of ideas presents a topic, a main idea, and two supporting details from an article posted on a popular website that offers health information. Circle the topic and underline the author's controlling point. Then answer the questions.

✗ a. (Chronic Fatigue Syndrome) (CFS) is marked by extreme fatigue that has lasted at least six months; is not the result of ongoing effort; is not substantially relieved by rest; and causes a substantial drop in daily activities.

(b.) Despite an intensive, nearly 20-year search, the cause of CFS remains unknown.

c. Much of the ongoing research into a cause has centered on the roles that the immune, endocrine, and nervous systems may play in CFS.

d. CFS is not caused by depression, although the two illnesses often coexist.

—United States Department of Health and Human Services. "Risk Factors for CFS." Centers for Disease Control and Prevention.

___b___ 1. Which of the following best states the topic?
    a. symptoms of CFS   c. definition of CFS
    ✗ causes of CFS

___b___ 2. Which sentence is the stated main idea?

B. Read the following paragraph. Circle the topic and underline the author's controlling point. Then answer the questions.

In Love with Sodas

[1]According to *Beverage Digest*, in 2009, the U.S. carbonated soft drink market totaled 9.4 billion cases. [2]Not surprisingly, the U.S. consumes the most sodas per person of any place in the world. [3]The American love for sodas alarms many health experts. [4]Research shows that drinking too many sodas can cause a wide range of health concerns. [5]For example, according to the Center for Science in the Public Interest, sodas are the single biggest source of calories in the American diet. [6]An average serving of 12 ounces of a soda contains 155 calories, 35 to 38 milligrams of caffeine, and around 40 grams of sugar. [7]Sodas provide about 7 percent of calories in most adult diets. [8]And teenagers get 15 percent of their total calories from sodas. [9]No wonder the number of obese people in America is growing. [10]Alarmingly, animal studies reveal that phosphorus, a common ingredient in soda, can deplete bones of calcium. [11]And two recent human studies suggest that girls who drink more soda are more prone to broken bones. [12]This finding supports the fear that drinking too many sodas may lead to osteoporosis later in life. [13]Finally, according to the Academy for General Dentistry, the acids in sodas are harmful to teeth. [14]Exposing teeth to sodas, even for a short period of time, causes dental erosion. [15]And long-term exposure can lead to significant enamel loss.

1. What is the topic of the paragraph? _____

2. Which sentence is the topic sentence that states the main idea? _____

VISUAL *VOCABULARY*

Osteoporosis causes a weakness and softness of _____, making them more prone to fracture.

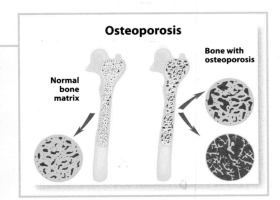

Osteoporosis

Normal bone matrix

Bone with osteoporosis

A. **1.** Item (b) "causes of CFS" is the best statement of the topic. Three of the four sentences refer to causes of CFS. Note that the topic is stated with just a few words—a phrase, not a complete sentence.

2. The main idea is best stated by item (b) "Despite an intensive, nearly 20-year search, the cause of CFS remains unknown." This sentence is the only statement that is broad enough to be relevant to all the other ideas. For example, item (a) introduces the general topic "CFS" by stating a definition of CFS based on its major symptom. Items (c) and (d) are supporting details that offer two views about the causes of CFS.

B. **1.** The word "soda" occurs 13 times within 15 sentences. When you ask *Who or what is this paragraph about?* the recurring word "soda" becomes the obvious answer. However, another idea is also repeated or referenced in almost every sentence: "health problem." So the best statement of the topic would include both ideas as in "The Health Risks of Drinking Too Many Sodas."

2. The topic sentence of the paragraph is sentence 4, "Research shows that drinking too many sodas can cause a wide range of health concerns." The first three sentences introduce the topic and its importance. Sentences 5 through 15 explain the possible health problems caused by drinking too many sodas. ◄

Practice 2

A. Each of the following groups of ideas contains a topic, a main idea, and two supporting details. In each group, first identify the topic. Then identify the stated main idea. (*Hint:* circle the topic and underline the author's controlling point in each group.)

Group 1

   a. A successful sales approach is sincere, optimistic, and confident.
   b. Use a sincere smile and an optimistic attitude to attract a potential customer.
   c. Look your customer directly in the eye and speak confidently and clearly at an easy-to-listen-to pace.

   _____a_____ **1.** Which of the following best states the topic?
        a. successful sales approach
        b. sales
        c. optimism

   _____a_____ **2.** Which sentence is the stated main idea?

Group 2

a. Malcolm X was a controversial African American activist during the civil rights era.
b. Malcolm X, born Malcolm Little, changed his name to protest bigotry.
c. Malcolm X, the son of a Baptist minister, became a member of the Black Muslim organization.

_____ *a*   **3.** Which of the following best states the topic?
   a. Malcolm X
   b. bigotry
   c. civil rights era

_____ *a*   **4.** Which sentence is the stated main idea?

Group 3

a. The collapse sinkhole is a common type of sinkhole in Florida.
b. It forms with little warning and leaves a deep, steep-sided hole.
c. Collapse sinkholes occur because of the weakening of the rock of the aquifer by erosion.

VISUAL *VOCABULARY*

The aquifer is _____.

a. a naturally occurring deep well of water
b. a body of porous sediment or rock, consisting of sand, shell, or limestone, that allows water to move underground

▲ Sinkholes form in a natural process of dissolving and eroding limestone that makes up the aquifer system.

Source: "Low Ground Waters Can Lead to Sinkholes." *Streamlines*, Fall 2000. Used by permission of the St. Johns River Water Management District, Palatka, Fla.

_____C_____ **5.** Which of the following best states the topic?
a. deep, steep hole
b. sinkholes
c. a collapse sinkhole

_____a_____ **6.** Which sentence is the stated main idea?

B. Read the following passage from a college textbook. Then answer the questions that follow.

Tattoos

Textbook
Skills

¹Tattoos are made by using a needle to deposit pigment in the dermis. ²Tattooing is an ancient practice believed to have originated around 10,000 years ago. ³These days, tattoos are symbols of club membership for some men (street gangs, the military, fraternities); other people view them as symbols of individuality. ⁴In recent years, more women have acquired tattoos as a means of expression and for cosmetic purposes; permanent eyeliner and tattooed liplines now account for over 125,000 tattoos a year.

⁵But what if a tattoo becomes unfashionable or the pigment migrates? ⁶Tattoo removal has been and still is a pain—both physically and financially. ⁷Until recently, once you had one, you were stuck with it, because attempts at removal—dermabrasion, cryosurgery (freezing), or applying caustic chemicals—left nasty scars. ⁸Using new laser-based technologies, dermatologists have no problem destroying the black or blue pigments in tattoos applied a generation ago, but newer, multicolored tattoos pose a larger problem. ⁹The multitude of pigments in tattoos today require several different lasers to be used over seven to nine treatments spaced about a month apart, each costing $75 to $150. ¹⁰The cost in pain is roughly equal to getting tattooed in the first place. ¹¹Nonetheless, tattoo removal across the United States is skyrocketing.

¹²Tattoos present some other risks. ¹³The FDA has some regulations concerning the composition of tattoo pigments, but their safety is not well established. ¹⁴Indeed, studies of dyes collected from tattooing studios have been found to contain cancer-causing agents that could be activated during tattoo removal. ¹⁵Statutory regulations vary widely (from none to complete prohibition) from state to state. ¹⁶Still, in each case, needles are used and bleeding occurs, and practitioners' competence varies significantly. ¹⁷If the practitioner does not adhere to strict sterile procedures, tattooing can spread infections. ¹⁸The risk of hepatitis C infection

(a chronic liver infection) is 15 times higher in people who have been tattooed than in those who have not. [19]So if you're thinking about getting a
tattoo, look into it carefully, and weigh your alternatives.

—Marieb, Elaine N., *Essentials of Human Anatomy &*
Physiology, 9th ed., p. 113.

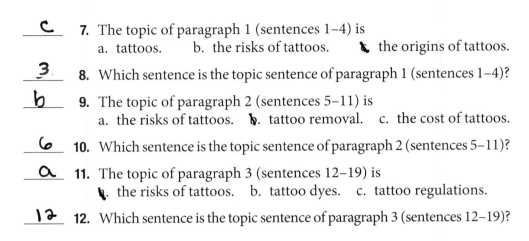

___C___ **7.** The topic of paragraph 1 (sentences 1–4) is
    a. tattoos.   b. the risks of tattoos.   ⟍ the origins of tattoos.

___3___ **8.** Which sentence is the topic sentence of paragraph 1 (sentences 1–4)?

___b___ **9.** The topic of paragraph 2 (sentences 5–11) is
    a. the risks of tattoos.   ⟍. tattoo removal.   c. the cost of tattoos.

___6___ **10.** Which sentence is the topic sentence of paragraph 2 (sentences 5–11)?

___a___ **11.** The topic of paragraph 3 (sentences 12–19) is
    ⟍. the risks of tattoos.   b. tattoo dyes.   c. tattoo regulations.

___12___ **12.** Which sentence is the topic sentence of paragraph 3 (sentences 12–19)?

LO4 # Analyze the Flow of Ideas and Identify Placement of Topic Sentences

So far, many of the paragraphs you have worked with in this textbook have
placed the topic sentence/main idea as the first sentence in the paragraph. The
three parts of a paragraph have flowed from general to specific ideas: the topic,
the main idea stated in a topic sentence, and the supporting details. However,
not all paragraphs put the main idea first. In fact, a topic sentence can be placed
at the **beginning** of a paragraph, **within** a paragraph, or at the **end** of a paragraph. The placement of the topic sentence controls the flow of ideas. In a sense,
when a writer builds a house of ideas, the floor plan—the flow of ideas—changes
based on the location of the topic sentence. One of the first things an effective
reader looks for is the location of the topic sentence.

Topic Sentence at the Beginning of a Paragraph

Remember that the topic sentence is the one sentence that is general enough to
include all the ideas in the paragraph. So a topic sentence that begins a paragraph signals a move from general ideas to specific ideas. This flow from general to specific, in which an author begins with a general statement and moves

to specific reasons and supports, is also known as deductive reasoning. Articles in encyclopedias and news stories in magazines and newspapers typically use the deductive flow of ideas. The chart below shows this flow from general to specific ideas.

Main idea: topic sentence
Supporting detail
Supporting detail
Supporting detail
Supporting detail

> **EXAMPLE** Read the following paragraph and identify its topic sentence. Remember to ask, "Does this sentence cover all the ideas in the paragraph?"

The Painful, Pesky Fire Ant

[1]Fire ants are painful and destructive pests. [2]The fire ant earned its name because of its venom. [3]The insect uses a wasplike stinger to inject the venom, which causes a painful burning sensation and leaves tiny, itching pustules. [4]The ants will swarm over anyone or anything that disturbs their nests. [5]In addition to causing pain, fire ants damage many crops by eating the plants and by protecting other insects that damage crops. [6]Fire ants are attracted to soybeans, eggplant, corn, okra, strawberries, and potatoes.

Topic sentence: _____1_____

VISUAL *VOCABULARY*

Swarm can be used as a verb and as a noun. Write a definition for each use. Use your dictionary if you want to.

Verb: _____

Noun: _____

_____

EXPLANATION   The topic sentence of this paragraph is sentence 1: "Fire ants are painful and destructive pests." All the other sentences explain the ways in which fire ants are painful and destructive. Notice how the passage first presents the general idea of fire ants as "painful and destructive." Next the details focus on the pain they cause, and then on the harm they do. ◁

Topic Sentence Within a Paragraph

Topic sentences within a paragraph can be near the beginning or in the middle of the paragraph.

Near the Beginning

A paragraph does not always start with the topic sentence. Instead, it may begin with a sentence or two that give a general overview of the topic. These introductory sentences are used to get the reader interested in the topic. They also lead the reader to the topic sentence. Sometimes introductory sentences tell how the ideas in one paragraph tie in to the ideas of earlier paragraphs. At other times, the introductory sentences give background information about the topic.

The flow of ideas remains deductive as it moves from general ideas (the introduction) and main idea (topic sentence) to specific ideas (supporting details). Human interest stories and editorials in magazines and newspapers, as well as academic papers, often rely on this flow of ideas. The following diagram shows this flow from general to specific ideas:

Introductory sentence
Main idea: topic sentence
Supporting detail
Supporting detail
Supporting detail

▷ **EXAMPLE**   Read the following paragraph and identify its topic sentence. Remember to ask, "Does this sentence cover all the ideas in the passage?"

Ice Cream Myths

[1]Ice cream reigns as a rich, delicious treat enjoyed by the majority of Americans. [2]Many myths exist about the origin of this well-loved

concoction of sugar and ice. [3]The three most common myths involve an explorer and two members of royalty. [4]One popular legend has the famous explorer Marco Polo bringing water ices from China to Italy. [5]Another myth claims that Catherine de Medici of Florence took her sorbetto recipes with her when she married Henry II and became queen of France in 1533. [6]The third popular myth credits Charles I of England with a formula for "frozen milk" he bought from a French chef in the 17th century.

Topic sentence: ____**3**____

EXPLANATION Sentence 3 is the topic sentence of this paragraph. Sentence 1 offers a simple but true background statement about the topic. The purpose of this sentence is to get the reader's attention. Sentence 2 introduces the topic "myths about the origin" (of ice cream). Sentences 4–6 are the supporting details that discuss the three myths. ◁

In the Middle

At times, an author begins a paragraph with a few attention-grabbing details. These details are placed first to stir the reader's interest in the topic. The flow of ideas no longer follows the deductive pattern of thinking because the material now moves from specific ideas (supporting details) to a general idea (the topic sentence) to specific ideas (additional supporting details). Creative essays and special interest stories that strive to excite reader interest often employ this approach. Television news stories frequently begin with shocking details to hook the viewer and prevent channel surfing. The following diagram shows this flow of ideas:

Supporting detail
Supporting detail
Main idea: topic sentence
Supporting detail
Supporting detail

EXAMPLE Read the following paragraph and identify its topic sentence. Remember to ask, "Does this sentence cover all the ideas in the passage?"

Prestige Pricing

[1]For many consumers, a high price indicates good quality. [2]Although this is not always the case, many consumers make this association when products are complex, have a strong brand identity, or are services with which they are unfamiliar. [3]The less they know about a product, the more consumers rely on price as an indicator of quality. [4]Businesses have to be careful not to lower their prices too much, otherwise a product may be perceived as low quality. [5]This is certainly not the case with prestige pricing. [6]Prestige pricing (also known as premium pricing), is the practice of charging a high price to invoke perceptions of high quality and privilege. [7]For those brands for which prestige pricing may apply, the high price itself is a motivator for consumers. [8]The higher perceived value because of the higher price actually increases demand and creates a higher price that becomes self-sustaining. [9]Some people have called this the snob effect. [10]Examples of this strategy include the pricing of cars made by Mercedes-Benz, Lexus, and Rolls-Royce.

—Solomon, Michael R., Poatsy, Mary Anne, and Martin, Kendall, *Better Business,* 2nd ed., p. 419.

Topic sentence: ___6___

EXPLANATION In sentences 1 through 4, the author offers background information that explains customers' usual perception of how cost is related to quality. Sentence 5 moves the focus to a special application of this perception and the topic of the paragraph: prestige pricing. In sentence 6, the author then states the main idea about prestige pricing: some businesses charge a high price to invoke the perception of high quality. Sentences 7 through 10 explain this idea further and give examples of products that use this strategy.

Topic Sentence at the End of a Paragraph

Sometimes an author waits until the end of the paragraph to state the topic sentence and main idea. This approach can be very effective, for it allows the details to build up to the main idea. The pattern is sometimes called climactic order.

The flow of ideas is known as inductive, as the author's thoughts move from specific (supporting details) to general (the topic sentence). Inductive reasoning is often used in math and science to generate hypotheses and theories, and to discover relationships between details. In addition, inductive reasoning is often used in argument (for more about argument, see Chapters 12 and 13). Politicians and advertisers use this approach to convince people to agree with their ideas or to buy their products. If a politician begins with a general statement such as "Taxes must be raised," the audience may strongly disagree. Then they may not listen to the specific reasons about why taxes must be raised. However, if the politician begins with the details and leads up to the main idea, people are more likely to listen. For example, people are more likely to agree that roads need to be repaired. Once they hear the specific details, they may then agree to raise taxes. Inductive reasoning is the process of arriving at a general understanding based on specific details. The following diagram shows the ideas moving from specific to general.

Supporting detail
Supporting detail
Supporting detail
Supporting detail
Main idea: topic sentence

▶ **EXAMPLE** Read the following paragraph and identify its topic sentence. Remember to ask, "Does this sentence cover all the ideas in the passage?"

A Personal Journey

[1]Every summer, my mother and I journeyed from our home in Florida to the farm in Mississippi on which she was raised. [2]However, the summer of my twenty-second year, we began our trip from Alabama instead of Florida. [3]The entire Mississippi clan had traveled over to witness my graduation from Judson College. [4]As a first-generation college graduate, I just knew I knew more than any of them, especially my mother. [5]Relief, joy, and a sense of freedom flooded me as Mother suggested I drive her car and she ride with Aunt Kaye. [6]Every so often, I purposefully lagged behind the caravan, lit up a cigarette, and smoked as I pleased—no matter that smoking was absolutely forbidden in Mother's car. [7]The cross-breeze from the rolled-down windows and my flicking the butts out the front window guaranteed

she would never know. ⁸Late that evening, as we unloaded the back seat, we both came upon a startling discovery at the same time: a deep burn hole the size of a knuckle. ⁹One of the butts had blown back in and lodged in the back seat. ¹⁰Silence loomed. ¹¹Then Mother said, "People are more important than things; I will not let this ruin this special time for us." ¹²In a blink, I traveled from pride to shame to redemption. ¹³Mother's one moment of mercy taught me more than four years of college.

Topic sentence: _13_

EXPLANATION   Sentences 1 through 11 tell the story of the author's journey to her mother's birthplace. The details of the story show the author's immaturity. In sentence 12, the author makes a statement that connects the physical trip and her journey of personal growth. Sentence 13 is the topic sentence. It clearly states the point the author is making, and it sums up the lesson of the story. Starting the passage with the details of the author's journey makes the idea much more interesting. Ending the passage with the main idea is very powerful.

Topic Sentence at the Beginning and the End of a Paragraph

A paragraph may start and end by stating one main idea in two different sentences. Even though these two sentences state the same idea, they usually word the idea in different ways. A topic sentence presents the main idea at the beginning of the paragraph. Then, at the end of the paragraph, the main idea is stated again, this time using different words. This flow of ideas is based on the age-old advice given to writers to "tell the reader what you are going to say; say it; then tell the reader what you said." Many essays written by college students rely on this presentation of ideas. The following diagram shows this flow of ideas:

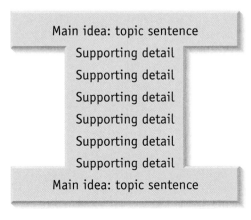

Main idea: topic sentence
Supporting detail
Supporting detail
Supporting detail
Supporting detail
Supporting detail
Supporting detail
Main idea: topic sentence

▸ **EXAMPLE** Read the following paragraph and identify its topic sentences. Remember to ask, "Do these sentences cover all the ideas in the passage?"

> [1]Using art as a form of therapy calls for a level of concentration that allows a person to relieve the pain of mental or emotional stress. [2]Art therapy is not limited to painting or drawing but can include dance, photography, music, writing, or any other art form. [3]The main goal of art therapy is healing through self-expression. [4]It allows a person to use visual means to explore feelings and emotions, to make the unseen seen, to discover how the mind works. [5]Art therapy does not require artistic ability, nor does it demand high artistic products. [6]Indeed, art therapy focuses on the process, not the product. [7]Art is therapy; art heals.

Topic sentences: ___1 and 7___

EXPLANATION Sentences 1 and 7 both state the main idea of the passage: Art therapy is healing. Notice how the wording changes at the end of the passage. Repeating the main idea makes the point much stronger and more likely to be remembered. ◂

Practice 3

Read the following paragraphs and identify the topic sentence(s). Remember to ask, "Do these sentences cover all the ideas in the paragraph?"

Believe in Tomorrow

> [1]If you had one wish, what would it be? [2]Would you wish for fame or for fortune? [3]The organization known as Believe in Tomorrow strives to grant the wishes and improve the quality of the lives of thousands of critically ill children and their families. [4]Just what are the wishes of these children? [5]One little girl in 1982 had just one wish as she faced a life-threatening illness: a pair of green roller skates. [6]Brian Morrison met that wish, and his simple act of compassion was the beginning of the Grant-a-Wish foundation. [7]That foundation is now named Believe in Tomorrow National Children's Foundation. [8]The foundation serves over 38,000 children each year and offers services that help ease pain, reduce loneliness, and bring joy over the course of their treatment. [9]Services include hospital housing for families, emotional support and networking, pain management, and once-in-a-lifetime adventures. [10]Each program is designed to inspire children and their families to focus on the promise of the future.

1. Topic sentence: ___3___

How to Prepare for a Natural Disaster

[1]Do you live in an area prone to tornados, flooding, hurricanes, fires, or earthquakes? [2]The best way to survive a natural disaster is to prepare for one. [3]The following steps offer an organized way to prepare for a natural disaster. [4]First, store a supply of disaster necessities. [5]Store water, non-perishable food items such as canned goods and packaged food that doesn't require cooking, and a survival-first aid kit of flashlights, radios, new batteries, extra clothing, and an emergency supply of your important medications. [6]Next, prepare your family and home. [7]Identify safe spots in your home. [8]Post a list of emergency contact numbers including the fire department, local hospital, your doctor, family members, and neighbors. [9]Protect your pets by creating disaster kits for them as well. [10]Third, prepare your car. [11]Keep your car well-maintained and ready to go. [12]Stock your car with emergency items such as a flashlight and first aid kit. [13]Fourth, make sure you have insurance and emergency funds. [14]Check your insurance policy to be sure you are covered for the types of disasters likely to occur in your area. [15]For example, in some areas, flood and wind insurance is extra. [16]Also make sure you have some spare money available in case of an emergency. [17]By following these few, simple steps, you will be better able to deal with a natural disaster.

2. Topic sentences: _____3 and 17_____

You've Got Spam: How to "Can" Unwanted E-Mail

[1]Do you receive lots of junk e-mail messages from people you don't know? [2]It's no surprise if you do. [3]As more people use e-mail, marketers are increasingly using e-mail messages to pitch their products and services. [4]Some consumers find unsolicited commercial e-mail, also known as spam, annoying and time consuming; others have lost money to bogus offers that arrived in their e-mail in-box. [5]An e-mail spammer buys a list of e-mail addresses from a list broker, who compiles it by "harvesting" addresses from the Internet. [6]Following are five simple suggestions to help reduce the amount of spam you receive. [7]First, try not to display your e-mail address in public. [8]This includes newsgroup postings, chat rooms, websites, or in an online service's membership directory. [9]Second, check the privacy policy when you submit your address to a website. [10]Third, read and understand the entire form before you send personal information through a website. [11]Fourth, use two e-mail addresses: one for personal messages and one for newsgroups and chat rooms.

[12]Finally, use an e-mail filter; your e-mail account may provide a tool to block potential spam.

—Adapted from Federal Trade Commission, "You've Got Spam: How to 'Can' Unwanted E-Mail."

3. Topic sentence: ___6___

Business Planning

[1]In 1958, college-aged brothers Dan and Frank Carney borrowed $600 from their mother to open a pizza parlor in Wichita, Kansas. [2]This venture marked the inception of the Pizza Hut empire. [3]The brothers had neither a formal business plan nor a clear vision of the path their business would take. [4]In fact, the Carneys simply gave away pizza on their opening night to garner the public's interest. [5]Although it was impulsive, their gimmick worked. [6]Less than a year later, the boys incorporated and opened their first franchise unit in Topeka, Kansas. [7]Within the next 10 years, more than 150 franchises opened nationwide, and one international franchise opened in Canada. [8]However, in 1970, the company's growth became explosive. [9]Pizza Hut went public, and the brothers quickly became overwhelmed. [10]"We about lost control of the operations," Frank Carney said in 1972. [11]"Then we figured out that we had to learn how to plan." Ultimately, Frank and Dan developed a plan that kept operations constant and under control. [12]They also created a corporate strategy that enticed PepsiCo to purchase Pizza Hut in 1977. [13]At that time, Pizza Hut sales had reached $436 million a year. [14]The Carneys' story is a success; however, if they had developed a clear business plan from the beginning, they may have been better prepared to handle their company's incredible growth.

—Solomon, Michael R., Poatsy, Mary Anne, and Martin, Kendall, *Better Business*, 2nd ed., pp. 198–199.

4. Topic sentence: ___14___

L05 Recognize the Central Idea and the Thesis Statement

Just as a single paragraph has a main idea, longer passages made up of two or more paragraphs also have a main idea. You encounter these longer passages in articles, essays, and textbooks. In longer passages, the main idea is called the **central idea.** Often the author will state the central idea in a single sentence called the **thesis statement.**

> The **central idea** is the main idea of a passage made up of two or more paragraphs.
>
> The **thesis statement** is a sentence that states the topic and the author's controlling point about the topic for a passage of two or more paragraphs.

You find the central idea of longer passages the same way you locate the main idea or topic sentence of a paragraph. The thesis statement is the one sentence that is general enough to include all the ideas in the passage.

> EXAMPLE Read the following passage from a college communications textbook and identify the thesis statement, which states the central idea.

Textbook
Skills

Supportive Responses

¹Listening stops when you feel threatened. ²No one likes to be proven wrong in front of others, criticized, or ignored. ³Defensive individuals are usually more concerned with protecting their self-concept and saving face than promoting communication. ⁴The more defensive a person becomes, the less able he is to perceive his partner's motives, values, and emotions.

⁵Your goal is to create situations that foster open communication in a supportive climate. ⁶Supportive responses are based on several behaviors that encourage problem solving and build healthy relationships. ⁷First, be aware of the use of "I" and "you." ⁸Instead of saying, "You're never around when I need you," a supportive response says, "I felt frustrated and needed your help." ⁹Second, focus on solving problems instead of placing blame. ¹⁰Third, show empathy instead of indifference. ¹¹And finally, be open-minded to the views of others instead of asserting your own view as the only or correct one.

—Adapted from Brownell, Judi. *Listening: Attitudes, Principles, and Skills*, 2nd ed., p. 284.

Thesis statement: ___6___

EXPLANATION The first four sentences introduce the need to know about the topic "supportive responses." These sentences are designed to hook the reader's interest in the topic. Sentence 5 is a link between the need to know and the author's central idea, which is stated in the next sentence. Sentence 6 is the central idea of the passage. It is the only sentence general enough to include most of the details in the passage. Note that sentence 6 includes the topic "supportive responses" and the author's controlling point about the topic; they are "behaviors that encourage problem solving and build healthy relationships." Sentences 7 through 11 are supporting details that list the supportive responses. ◉

Practice 4

Read the following passage from a college psychology textbook and identify the thesis statement, which states the central idea.

Taste and Smell Go Hand in Hand

[1]With only five or six taste categories, how can we taste so many flavors? [2]The secret lies in the fact that our taste perception is biased strongly by our sense of smell, which explains why we find food much less tasty when our noses are stuffed.

[3]Far more than we realize, we find certain foods "delicious" because of their smell. [4]Indeed, we perceive a combination of taste and smell.

[5]If you're not persuaded, try this exercise. [6]Buy some multiflavored jelly beans, open the bag, and close your eyes so you can't see which flavor you're picking. [7]Then pinch your nose with one hand and pop a jelly bean in your mouth. [8]At first you won't be able to identify the flavor. [9]You'll only be able to tell that it's sweet. [10]Then release your fingers from your nose and you'll soon be able to perceive the jelly bean's flavor.

—Lilienfield, Scott O., Lynn, Steven J., Namy, Laura L., and Woolf, Nancy J., *Psychology: A Framework for Everyday Thinking*, p. 133.

Thesis statement: _2_

LO6 ## Develop Textbook Skills: Identify Topics, Main Ideas, and Central Ideas in Textbooks

Textbook Skills

Textbooks identify topics in the title of each chapter. An excellent study strategy is to read a textbook's table of contents, a listing of all the chapters' titles, which are the general topics covered in the textbook. In addition to providing topics in chapter titles, textbooks also identify topics within each chapter. Other publications, such as newspapers and magazines, also use titles and headings to point out topics.

Textbook authors often state the topic of a passage or paragraph in a heading. For example, titles of graphs often help readers identify the main idea of the graph by stating the topic. Identifying the topic in a heading makes it easier to find the main idea and supporting details.

> **EXAMPLE** Assume you are enrolled in a college-level business course. Your professor has assigned Chapter 9 in your business textbook to read before your next class. Your professor has also stressed the importance of psychologist Abraham Maslow. Complete the following activities as if you were preparing for class.

A. Skim the table of contents for Chapter 9. Answer the question.

   _**b**_   **1.** "Maslow's Hierarchy of Needs" is a model that explains
      a. the importance of satisfaction and morale.
      b. motivation in the workplace.
      c. strategies for enhancing job satisfaction and motivation.
      d. managerial styles and leadership.

B. Read the textbook passage and study the graphic about "Maslow's Hierarchy of Needs." Answer the questions that follow.

Maslow's Hierarchy of Needs Model

[1]Psychologist Abraham Maslow's hierarchy of human needs model proposed that people have several different needs that they attempt to satisfy in their work. [2]He classified these needs into five basic types. [3]He also suggested that they be arranged in the hierarchy of importance. [4]According to Maslow, needs are hierarchical because lower-level needs must be met before a person will try to satisfy higher-level needs.

[5]Once a set of needs has been satisfied, it ceases to motivate behavior. [6]This is the sense in which the hierarchical nature of lower- and higher-level needs affects employee motivation and satisfaction. [7]For example, if you feel secure in your job, a new pension plan will probably be less important to you than the chance to make new friends and join an informal network among your coworkers.

[8]If, however, a lower-level need suddenly becomes unfulfilled, most people immediately refocus on that lower level. [9]Suppose, for example, you are seeking to meet your self-esteem needs by working as a divisional manager at a major company. [10]You learn that your division and, consequently, your job may be eliminated. [11]Then, you might very well find the promise of job security at a new firm as motivating as a promotion once would have been at your old company.

[12]Maslow's theory recognizes that because different people have different needs, they are motivated by different things. [13]Unfortunately, it provides few specific guidelines for action in the workplace. [14]Furthermore, research has found that the hierarchy varies widely, not only for different people but also across different cultures.

Maslow's Hierarchy of Needs

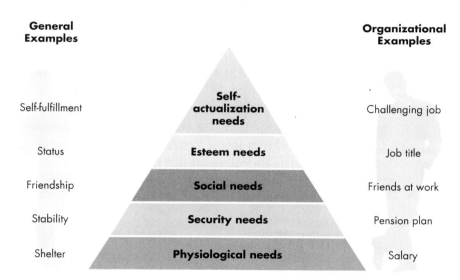

—Adapted from Griffin & Ebert, *Business*, 8th ed., pp. 244–245, and line art based on Maslow, Abraham H., Frager, Robert D., and Fadiman, James, *Motivation and Personality*, 3rd ed.

___d___ 2. The topic of this passage is
a. Maslow's Hierarchy of Needs.
b. Abraham Maslow.
c. work satisfaction.
d. Maslow's hierarchy of needs in the workplace.

___a___ 3. The central idea of the passage is stated in
a. sentence 1.   c. sentence 8.
b. sentence 5.   d. sentence 12.

_____C_____ 4. The best synonym for the word **Hierarchy** in the title of the graphic "Maslow's Hierarchy of Needs" is

a. list.   c. levels.

b. group.   d. demands.

EXPLANATIONS

A. **1.** "Maslow's Hierarchy of Needs" is a model that explains (b) "motivation in the workplace."

B. **2.** The topic of this passage is (d) "Maslow's Hierarchy of Needs in the Workplace."

3. The central idea of the passage is stated in (a) sentence 1.

4. The best synonym for the word **Hierarchy** in the title of the graphic "Maslow's Hierarchy of Needs" is (c) "levels." ◀

Practice 5

Assume you are enrolled in a college-level criminal justice course. Your professor has assigned Chapter 15 as a reading assignment on which you will be quizzed during your next class meeting. As you review your class notes, you notice that your professor has repeatedly stressed the following two topics: "Categories of children in the system" and "Court jurisdiction over young offenders." Complete the following activities as if you were preparing for the quiz.

A. Skim the table of contents for Chapter 15. Answer the question.

_____ **1.** "Categories of Children in the Juvenile Justice System" is a subtopic of
   a. Juvenile Justice throughout History.
   b. The Legal Environment.
   c. The Juvenile Justice Process Today.
   d. The Post-Juvenile Court Era.

B. Read the following passage and study the graphic from the textbook *Criminal Justice Today*. Answer the questions that follow.

Categories of Children in the Juvenile Justice System

[1]By the time of the Great Depression, most states had expanded juvenile statutes to include the following six categories of children. [2]These categories are still used today in most jurisdictions to describe the variety of children subject to juvenile court jurisdiction.

- [3]**Delinquent children** are those who violate the criminal law. [4]If they were adults, the word criminal would be applied to them.

- [5]**Undisciplined children** are said to be beyond parental control, as evidenced by their refusal to obey legitimate authorities, such as school officials and teachers. [6]They need state protection.

- [7]**Dependent children** typically have no parents or guardians to care for them. [8]Their parents are deceased, they were placed for adoption, or they were abandoned in violation of the law.

- [9]**Neglected children** are those who do not receive proper care from their parents or guardians. [10]They may suffer from malnutrition or may not be provided with adequate shelter.

- [11]**Abused children** are those who suffer physical abuse at the hands of their custodians. [12]This category was later expanded to include emotional and sexual abuse.

- [13]**Status offender** is a special category that embraces children who violate laws written only for them. [14]In some states, status offenders are referred to as persons in need of supervision (PINS).

[15]**Status offenses** include behavior such as truancy, vagrancy, running away from home, and incorrigibility. [16]The youthful "status" of juveniles is a necessary element in such offenses. [17]Adults, for example, may "run away from home" and not violate any law. [18]Runaway children, however, are subject to apprehension and juvenile court processing because state laws require that they be subject to parental control.

[19]Status offenses were a natural outgrowth of juvenile court philosophy. [20]As a consequence, however, juveniles in need of help often faced procedural dispositions that treated them as though they were delinquent. [21]Rather than lowering the rate of juvenile incarceration, the juvenile court movement led to its increase. [22]Critics of the juvenile court movement quickly focused on the abandonment of due process rights, especially in the case of status offenders, as a major source of problems. [23]Detention and incarceration, they argued, were inappropriate options here because children had not committed crimes.

Limit of Juvenile Court Jurisdiction Over Young Offenders, By State

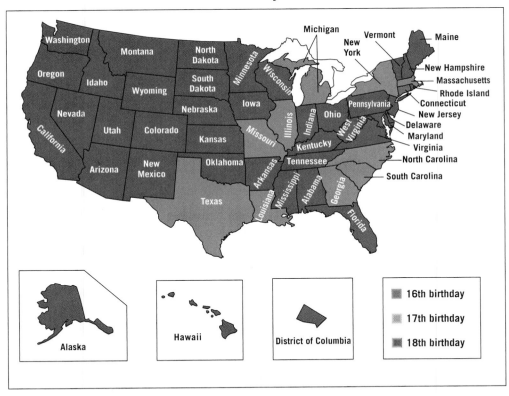

—Schmalleger, Frank J. *Criminal Justice Today: An Introductory Text for the 21st Century*, 10th ed., p. 562.

_____ **2.** The topic of this passage is
  a. juveniles.
  b. the legal system.
  c. legal classification of juveniles.
  d. juvenile offenses.

_____ **3.** The central idea of the passage is stated in
  a. sentence 1.   c. sentence 15.
  b. sentence 2.   d. sentence 22.

_____ **4.** The best synonym for the word **Jurisdiction** in the title of the graphic "Limit of Juvenile Court Jurisdiction Over Young Offenders, By State" is
  a. area.   c. ruling.
  b. authority.   d. official.

Apply Information Literacy Skills

 ## Academic, Personal, and Career Applications of Stated Main Ideas

The ability to identify a stated main idea is one component of information literacy. Along with having strong vocabulary skills, being able to locate and evaluate a stated main idea is an important part of accessing information. Information literacy is the ability to recognize the need to know the main idea, and then to locate, evaluate, and effectively apply that information to your situation. In your academic, personal, and career lives, you will come across various forms of documents such as essays, articles, reports, memos, or e-mails. You will be expected to understand and respond to the stated main idea of these documents. Thus, you will use the skills that you have learned in this chapter in several ways:

- Recognize your own need to know a stated main idea.
- Locate a stated main idea.
- Restate the author's stated main idea in your own words.
- Apply the stated main idea to your specific situation.

Academic Application

Assume you are taking a college course, Introduction to Health. Part of your study plan is to record key points in the chapter in your notebook as you read.

- **Before Reading:** Skim the passage. Circle the topic as it recurs. Create a question based on the topic. Keep in mind that the topic may recur with the use of synonyms.

- **During Reading:** Underline the topic sentence and details that answer the pre-reading question.
- **After Reading:** In the space following the passage, restate the author's main idea by answering your pre-reading question with information from the passage.

Pre-reading Question: _____

_____

Characteristics of Healthy Relationships

[1]Satisfying and stable relationships share certain identifiable traits, such as good communication, intimacy, friendship, and other factors. [2]A key ingredient is trust, the degree of confidence each person feels in a relationship. [3]Without trust, intimacy will not develop, and the relationship will likely fail. [4]Trust includes three fundamental elements.

1. [5]Predictability means that you can predict your partner's behavior, based on the knowledge that he or she acts in consistently positive ways.
2. [6]Dependability means that you can rely on your partner to give support in all situations, particularly those in which you feel threatened with hurt or rejection.
3. [7]Faith means that you feel absolutely certain about your partner's intentions and behavior.

[8]Trust can develop even when it is initially lacking. [9]This requires opening yourself to others, which carries the risk of hurt or rejection.

—Donatelle, Rebecca J. *Access to Health*, 12th ed., p. 121.

Author's Main Idea: _____

_____

Personal Application

Assume you are the parent of a young woman who will be living away from home for the first time. You are concerned that she could become a victim of identity theft. You have found a government website with the following information that you want to share with her.

- **Before Reading:** Skim the passage. Then rate this article from 1 to 5, with 5 being most helpful and 1 being least helpful.

- **During Reading:** Underline the topic sentence and the most important details of support.

- **After Reading:** In the space following the passage, write an e-mail to advise your daughter of what you have learned. In your own words, state the main idea and key points she should know.

Financial Fraud and Theft:
How to Protect Yourself

[1]Identity theft or "ID theft" occurs when an individual learns someone's Social Security number (SSN), bank account information or other details that can be used to go on a buying or borrowing binge. [2]Consumers can take four precautions. [3]First, protect personal information. [4]Protect your Social Security number, bank account and credit card numbers, PINs (personal identification numbers), passwords and other personal information. [5]Never provide this information in response to a phone call, a fax, a letter or an e-mail you've received. [6]Second, keep your financial trash "clean." [7]Don't throw away old ATM or credit card receipts, bank statements, tax returns or other documents containing personal information without shredding them first. [8]ID thieves pick through trash bins looking for trash they can turn into cash. [9]Third, use extra care with personal information on a computer or over the Internet. [10]Never provide bank, credit card or other sensitive information when visiting a Web site that doesn't explain how your personal information would be protected, including its use of "encryption" to safely transmit and store data. [11]Guard against e-mail requests to "update" or "confirm" personal information. [12]Reputable organizations that already have your online information won't contact you to verify account information online that they already have. [13]Finally, beware of offers that seem too good to be true. [14]Con artists often pose as charities or business people offering jobs, rewards or other "opportunities." [15]Be extremely suspicious of any offer that involves "easy money" or "quick fixes." [16]Avoid any pressure to make a quick decision, to send money, or provide bank account information before you receive anything in return.

—"Financial Fraud and Theft: How to Protect Yourself."
Federal Deposit Insurance Corporation. 16 Jan. 2012.
<http://www.fdic.gov/consumers/consumer/news
/cnspr05/fraud.html>

E-mail of Advice: _____

_____

_____

_____

Career Application

Assume you are a new, local employee for a hotel chain with worldwide locations. You desire to become part of the management team and advance in the company. The following excerpt is from the hotel's employee handbook.

- **Before Reading:** Skim the passage. Predict how this information will help you advance in the company.
- **During Reading:** Underline the thesis sentence.
- **After Reading:** In the space following the passage, reflect on how you will use performance reviews to help you advance in the company.

Pre-Reading Prediction: _____

_____

Employee Handbook: Employee Performance Reviews

[1]Supervisors will conduct performance reviews and planning sessions with all regular full-time and regular part-time employees. [2]The initial review occurs at the end of the first 90 days of employment. [3]Supervisors may call for informal reviews and planning sessions more often as needed.

[4]The purpose of performance reviews and planning sessions are for the supervisor and the employee to discuss current job tasks, encourage and recognize achievement, set work-related goals, and discuss methods for meeting set goals.

[5]Wage and salary increases are tied to performance. [6]An employee's performance reviews and planning sessions will have a direct impact on any changes in his/her compensation. [7]Therefore, employees are expected to carefully prepare for and fully participate in these reviews.

[8]After the first review, performance reviews occur semi-annually.

After Reading Reflection: _____

_____

_____

REVIEW TEST 1

Score (number correct) _____ × 20 = _____%

Visit MyReadingLab to take this test online and receive feedback and guidance on your answers.

Topics, Main Ideas, and Supporting Details

A. Each of the following groups of ideas includes one topic, one main idea, and two supporting details. In each group, first identify the topic. Then identify the stated main idea. (*Hint:* circle the topic and underline the author's controlling point in each group.)

Group 1

A. Procrastination has two possible causes.

B. Many people may procrastinate because they have a fear of failure, and if they don't begin a task or project, they can't fail at it.

C. Others may procrastinate out of laziness; these careless workers have not yet developed a strong work ethic.

_____ **1.** Which of the following best states the topic?
  a. laziness
  b. procrastination
  c. a strong work ethic

_____ **2.** Which sentence best states the main idea?

Group 2

A. A snake can control its body temperature in two ways.

B. First, a snake can darken its skin to absorb higher levels of solar heat; once its body reaches a suitable temperature, the snake can lighten its skin color.

C. A snake also spreads and flattens its body as it lies at a right angle to the sun's rays to expose more of its body and raise its temperature; to reduce its body temperature, a snake lies parallel to the sun's rays or moves into the shade.

—Adapted from Robert Smith and Thomas Smith, *Elements of Ecology*. Upper Saddle River: Pearson Education, 2000, p. 11a.

_____ **3.** Which of the following best states the topic?
   a. body temperature   c. a snake's body temperature
   b. snakes

_____ **4.** Which sentence best states the main idea?

B. Read the paragraph. Then answer the question.

[1]First Monday, Mississippi's largest flea market, and one of the nation's oldest, is a long-standing success that offers something for everybody. [2]Established in 1893, this open market was originally located on Ripley's downtown court square, but it is now stationed south of the city limits across from the county fairgrounds. [3]First Monday sits on over 50 acres and offers hundreds of booths that house vendors and assorted items for sale. [4]The variety of goods ranges from unique and hard-to-find items to new and used products, antiques, crafts, and much more, including pets. [5]First Monday is open the Saturday and Sunday preceding the first Monday of each month, and buyers travel hundreds of miles to trade there. [6]Admission is free, and the grounds provide dining facilities, electrical hookups, showers, a laundry room, table rental, cable TV hookup, and early-morning church services.

_____ **5.** Which sentence states the main idea of the paragraph?
   a. sentence 1   c. sentence 5
   b. sentence 2   d. sentence 6

REVIEW TEST 2

Score (number correct) _____ × 25 = _____ %

Visit MyReadingLab to take this test online and receive feedback and guidance on your answers.

Topics, Main Ideas, and Supporting Details

Read the following passage from a college humanities textbook. Answer the questions that follow.

The Frankenstein Monster

[1]Many attempts have been made by science to control Nature—in particular, to destroy or at least to weaken Atlantic hurricanes and Pacific cyclones. [2]On one occasion the experiment went so badly that one hurricane split into two. [3]A few centuries before this unfortunate incident, Mary Wollstonecraft Shelley (1797–1851), wife of the famous poet, wrote *Frankenstein*, or *The Modern Prometheus*, a fantasy novel that warned against meddling with Nature. [4]Her fable has since become a classic and added terminology to

our vocabularies. [5]We speak of anything that goes terribly awry as a "Frankenstein monster" and the creator of a product that backfires as a "regular Doctor Frankenstein." [6]The novel also spawned innumerable films.

[7]The youthful novelist based her story on the ancient myth of Prometheus, one of an early species of human being that was half human, half god. [8]His godly nature caused him to seek unlimited power, a power equal to that of the gods. [9]He attempted to steal fire from them but was caught in the act and sentenced to an eternity of anguish in which he was chained to a rock while a vulture ate his liver, a torture that could never end because the devoured liver always grew back.

[10]Mary Shelley's version of the myth has for its central character Victor Frankenstein, who is not the mad scientist of the well-known movie adaptations but a sensitive, gentle person intrigued from childhood by science (then called "natural philosophy") and eager to learn everything that could possibly be learned in order to create a better life for all people. [11]As he matures, he finds himself particularly concerned with the way the body functions.

> [12]*Wealth was an inferior object, but what glory would attend the discovery if I could but banish disease from the human frame, and render man invulnerable to any but a violent death.*

[13]Yet, he asked himself, how am I to find the secret of immortality unless I first learn where life comes from?

[14]Like her husband and other romantic writers, Mary Shelley saw Nature as a wondrous mystery full of almost divine secrets. [15]She and Percy Bysshe Shelley, whom she married at the age of sixteen, especially loved the grandeur of lakes and mountains. [16]Switzerland, the locale of the novel, was her favorite spot on earth. [17]For her, Nature was to be admired, adored, worshiped, but never analyzed, always to be left alone. [18]The tragic flaw of Victor Frankenstein is that he wants to be more than a *part* of Nature. [19]Not content with understanding how the spark of life enters lifeless matter—from electricity, he is convinced—he must take a further step. [20]He will assemble parts of cadavers into an eight-foot superman who will represent the perfection of the species and live forever.

[21]The outcome of his experiment is, as everyone knows, not what he expected.

> [22]*I had selected his features as beautiful.* [23]*Beautiful—Great God!* [24]*His yellow skin scarcely covered the work of muscles; and arteries beneath; his hair was of a lustrous black, and flowing; his teeth of a pearly whiteness; but these luxuriances only formed a horrid contrast with his watery eyes, and seemed almost of the same colour as the dun white sockets in which they were set.*

²⁵Nonetheless, the "daemon," as the author calls him, is at first kind and gentle. ²⁶He is a creature of Nature; and the author believes Nature, undisturbed, is good at heart—a fervent attitude shared today by those who believe that gas-house emissions, offshore drilling, and other humanly engineered projects are not harmful to the environment. ²⁷Yet society will not leave the daemon alone. ²⁸Because of his frightening appearance, he is rejected, scorned, and ultimately becomes a vicious killer. ²⁹Before his transformation, he has shown the noblest of feelings. ³⁰He is a vegetarian, believing it immoral to eat animal flesh. ³¹Overhearing an account of how America was discovered, he weeps at the fate of the original inhabitants. ³²Hiding out in a farmhouse, he stops stealing the food for which he desperately hungers when he observes how little food the family has for itself.

³³In an extraordinary finale, anticipating *Moby-Dick* by over thirty years, the doctor pursues the daemon to the ends of the earth, insanely believing, as does Captain Ahab, that once the monster is destroyed all evil will vanish from the earth. ³⁴In the end it is Frankenstein, not the daemon, who dies. ³⁵The daemon is reclaimed by Nature, his true and only parent. ³⁶Dwarfed by the frozen mountains of the polar circle, he sails on a raft of ice into a mist, there to meet who knows what destiny. ³⁷We feel that he belongs in this primordial limbo outside of time, deep within which lie the ultimate secrets glimpsed and even unleashed but never grasped or fully controlled by human intelligence.

—Janaro, Richard and Altschuler, Thelma, *The Art of Being Human: The Humanities as a Technique for Living*, 10th ed., pp. 484–486.

_____ **1.** What is the topic of the passage?
   a. Frankenstein movies
   b. the value of Nature
   c. how science controls Nature
   d. the theme of Mary Shelley's *Frankenstein*

_____ **2.** Which sentence best states the main idea of paragraph 4 (sentences 14–20)?
   a. sentence 15   c. sentence 18
   b. sentence 17   d. sentence 20

_____ **3.** Sentence 22 states a
   a. main idea.   b. supporting detail.

_____ **4.** Which sentence states the central idea of the passage?
   a. sentence 1   c. sentence 6
   b. sentence 3   d. sentence 10

REVIEW TEST 3

Score (number correct) _____ × 25 = _____%

Visit MyReadingLab to take this test online and receive feedback and guidance on your answers.

Topics, Main Ideas, and Supporting Details

Read the following passage from a college anatomy and physiology textbook. Answer the questions that follow.

Skin Cancer

Textbook
Skills

[1]Numerous types of neoplasms (tumors) arise in the skin. [2]Most skin neoplasms are benign and do not spread (metastasize) to other body areas. [3](A wart caused by a virus is one such example.) [4]However, some skin neoplasms are malignant, or cancerous, and they tend to invade other body areas. [5]Indeed, skin cancer is the single most common type of cancer in humans. [6]One in five Americans now develops skin cancer at some point in his or her life. [7]The most important risk factor is overexposure to ultraviolet radiation in sunlight. [8]Frequent irritation of the skin by infections, chemicals, or physical trauma also seems to be a predisposing factor.

Basal Cell Carcinoma [9]Basal cell carcinoma (kar'/sĭno'/mah) is the least malignant and most common skin cancer. [10]Cells of the stratum basale, altered so that they cannot form keratin, no longer honor the boundary between epidermis and dermis. [11]They proliferate, invading the dermis and subcutaneous tissue. [12]The cancer lesions occur most often on sun exposed areas of the face and appear as shiny, dome-shaped nodules that later develop a central ulcer with a "pearly" beaded edge. [13]Basal cell carcinoma is relatively slow-growing, and metastasis seldom occurs before it is noticed. [14]Full cure is the rule in 99 percent of cases in which the lesion is removed surgically.

Squamous Cell Carcinoma [15]Squamous cell carcinoma arises from the cells of the stratum spinosum. [16]The lesion appears as a scaly, reddened papule (small, rounded elevation) that gradually forms a shallow ulcer with a firm, raised border. [17]This variety of skin cancer appears most often on the scalp, ears, dorsum of the hands, and lower lip. [18]It grows rapidly and metastasizes to adjacent lymph nodes if not removed. [19]This epidermal cancer is also believed to be sun-induced. [20]If it is caught early and removed surgically or by radiation therapy, the chance of complete cure is good.

Malignant Melanoma [21]Malignant melanoma (mel"ah-no'mah) is a cancer of melanocytes. [22]It accounts for only about 5 percent of skin cancers, but its incidence is increasing rapidly and it is often deadly. [23]Melanoma can begin wherever there is pigment; most such cancers appear spontane-ously, but some develop from pigmented moles. [24]It arises from accumulated DNA damage in a skin cell and usually appears as a spreading brown to black patch that metastasizes rapidly to surrounding lymph and blood vessels. [25]The chance for survival is about 50 percent, and early detection helps. [26]The American Cancer Society suggests that people who sunbathe frequently or attend tanning parlors examine their skin periodically for new moles or pig-mented spots and apply the **ABCD rule** for recognizing melanoma:

A. **Asymmetry.** [27]The two sides of the pigmented spot or mole do not match.

B. **Border irregularity.** [28]The borders of the lesion are not smooth but exhibit indentations.

C. **Color.** [29]The pigmented spot contains areas of different colors (blacks, browns, tans, and sometimes blues and reds).

D. **Diameter.** [30]The spot is larger than 6 millimeters (mm) in diameter (the size of a pencil eraser).

[31]Some experts have found that adding an **E**, for *elevation* above the skin surface, improves diagnosis. [32]The usual therapy for malignant mela-noma is wide surgical excision along with immunotherapy.

—Marieb, Elaine N., *Essentials of Human Anatomy & Physiology,* 9th ed., pp. 125–126.

VISUAL *VOCABULARY*

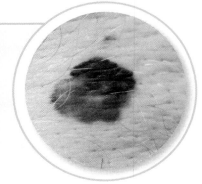

This type of cancer is known as ———.

a. basal cell carcinoma

b. squamous cell carcinoma

c. malignant melanoma

_____ **1.** What is the topic of the passage?
  a. cancer   c. skin cancer
  b. causes of skin cancer   d. three types of skin cancer

_____ **2.** Which sentence states the main idea of paragraph 2 (sentences 9–14)?
  a. sentence 9   c. sentence 12
  b. sentence 10   d. sentence 14

_____ **3.** Sentence 20 states a
  a. main idea.   b. supporting detail.

_____   **4.** Which sentence states the central idea of the passage?
    a. sentence 1   c. sentence 5
    b. sentence 4   d. sentence 26

SUMMARY RESPONSE

Restate the author's most important idea in your own words using some of the words in **bold** print. Begin your summary response with the following: *The most important idea of "Skin Cancer" by Marieb is …*

WHAT DO YOU THINK?

What is the most important risk factor that causes skin cancer? Assume you are a camp counselor or a coach of a youth sports team. Part of your job is to educate your youth group about the risks of developing skin cancer. Write a draft of your speech and create a PowerPoint® presentation in which you:

- State your topic and main idea clearly.
- Support your point with illustrations and clear details.
- Summarize key ideas and details.

REVIEW TEST 4

Score (number correct) _____ × 10 = _____ %

Visit MyReadingLab to take this test online and receive feedback and guidance on your answers.

Topics and Main Ideas

Before reading: Survey the following passage adapted from the college textbook *Psychology and Life*. Skim the passage, noting the words in **bold** print. Answer the Before Reading questions that follow the passage. Then read the passage. Next, answer the After Reading questions. Use the discussion and writing topics as activities to do after reading.

Vocabulary Preview

consistent (1): constant, regular
appreciation (6): admiration, enjoyment, understanding
philosophy (6): viewpoint, way of life
deteriorated (14): declined
maturation (21): growth

What Is Learning?

[1]Learning is a process that results in a relatively **consistent** change in behavior or behavior potential and is based on experience. [2]The three critical parts of this definition deserve careful study.

A Change in Behavior or Behavior Potential

[3]It is obvious that learning has taken place when you are able to demonstrate the results, such as when you drive a car or use a microwave oven. [4]You can't directly observe learning itself, but learning is **apparent** from improvements in your performance. [5]Often, however, your performance doesn't show everything that you have learned. [6]Sometimes, too, you have **acquired** general attitudes, such as an **appreciation** of modern art or an understanding of Eastern **philosophy**, that may not be apparent in your measurable actions. [7]In such cases, you have achieved a potential for behavior change. [8]You have learned attitudes and values that can influence the kinds of books you read or the way you spend your leisure time. [9]This is an example of learning performance distinction; it is the difference between what has been learned and what is expressed, or performed, in **overt** behavior.

A Relatively Consistent Change

[10]To qualify as learned, a change in behavior or behavior potential must be relatively consistent over different occasions. [11]Thus once you learn to swim, you will probably always be able to do so. [12]Note that consistent changes are not always permanent changes. [13]You may, for example, have become quite a consistent dart thrower when you practiced every day. [14]If you gave up the sport, however, your skills might have **deteriorated** toward their original level. [15]But if you have learned once to be a championship dart thrower, it ought to be easier for you to learn a second time. [16]Something has been "saved" from your prior experience. [17]In that sense, the change may be permanent.

A Process Based on Experience

[18]Learning can take place only through experience. [19]Experience includes taking in information and making responses that affect the environment. [20]Learning is made up of a response affected by the lessons of memory. [21]Learned behavior does not include changes that come about because of physical **maturation**, nor does it simply rely on brain development as the organism ages. [22]Some learning requires a combination of experience and **maturity**. [23]For example, think about the timetable that controls when an infant is ready to crawl, stand, walk, run, and be toilet trained. [24]No amount of training or practice will produce those behaviors before the child is mature enough to be ready to learn.

—Adapted from Gerrig, Richard J., and Zimbardo, Philip G.,
Psychology and Life, 16th ed., p. 181.

Before Reading

Vocabulary in Context

_____ **1.** The word **apparent** in sentence 4 means
      a. unseen.   c. reinforced.
      b. obvious.   d. encouraged.

_____ **2.** The word **acquired** in sentence 6 means
      a. rated.   c. rejected.
      b. overcome.   d. gained.

_____ **3.** The word **overt** in sentence 9 means
      a. hidden.   c. visible.
      b. wise.   d. concerned.

_____ **4.** The word **maturity** in sentence 22 means
      a. fully developed.   c. passion.
      b. understanding.   d. inexperience.

Topics and Main Ideas

_____ **5.** What is the topic of the passage?
      a. demonstrating results   c. consistent change
      b. learning   d. change in behavior

After Reading

_____ **6.** Which sentence states the central idea of the passage?
      a. sentence 1   c. sentence 10
      b. sentence 3   d. sentence 24

_____ **7.** What is the topic of the third paragraph (sentences 10–17)?
      a. a change in behavior or behavior potential
      b. a relatively consistent change in behavior or behavior potential
      c. permanent changes in behavior potential
      d. prior experiences of behavior change

_____ **8.** Which sentence states the main idea of the third paragraph?
      a. sentence 10   c. sentence 12
      b. sentence 11   d. sentence 16

9–10. Label each of the following two sentences from the fourth paragraph (sentences 18–24). Use **A** if it states the main idea or **B** if it supplies a supporting detail.

_____ **9.** Learning can take place only through experience.

_____ **10.** Learning is made up of a response affected by the lessons of memory.

SUMMARY RESPONSE

Respond to the passage by restating the topic sentence in your own words. Be sure to identify the topic and the author's attitude about the topic. Begin your summary response with the following: *The most important idea of "What Is Learning?" by Gerrig and Zimbardo is …*

WHAT DO YOU THINK?

Have you or someone you know experienced a change in behavior or behavior potential because of a lesson learned? Assume you are applying for a scholarship to continue your education. The application calls for you to write a short essay that explains the value of learning.

- Explain how learning can shape your attitude.
- Explain how experience leads to learning.
- Describe an important lesson that has changed you or someone you know.

After Reading About Stated Main Ideas

A crucial step in the reading process occurs during the after reading phase when you take time to reflect on what you have learned. Before you move on to the Mastery Tests on stated main ideas, take time to reflect on your learning and performance by answering the following questions. Write your answers in your notebook.

- How has my knowledge base or prior knowledge about stated main ideas changed?
- Based on my studies, how do I think I will perform on the Mastery Test(s)? Why do I think my scores will be above average, average, or below average?
- Would I recommend this chapter to other students who want to learn more about stated main ideas? Why or why not?

Test your understanding of what you have learned about stated main ideas by completing the Chapter 3 Review.

Name _____ Section _____

Date _____ **Score** (number correct) _____ × 20 = _____ %

Visit MyReadingLab to take this test online and receive feedback and guidance on your answers.

A. Skim each of the following paragraphs and circle the topic as it recurs throughout the paragraph. Then identify the idea that correctly states the topic. (*Hint:* one idea is too general to be the topic; another idea is too specific.)

_____ **1.** [1]Did you know that May is Foot Health Awareness Month? [2]The foot is often the most ignored part of our bodies. [3]Yet with its 28 bones, 33 joints, and 19 muscles, the foot deserves year-round pampering. [4]Good foot care begins with shoes that fit properly. [5]Ill-fitting shoes cause many problems, including poor circulation, injury due to lack of proper support, corns, bunions, and calluses. [6]Good foot care also entails keeping the feet clean. [7]Plantar warts are caused by a virus that enters the foot through an open sore or cut. [8]The best activity for the feet is walking. [9]Walking stimulates circulation and keeps the feet strong and limber.

   a. feet
   b. Foot Health Awareness Month
   c. proper foot care

_____ **2.** [1]"Hispanic" is a widely used term for a person of Spanish-language heritage living in the United States. [2]The term was first coined by the government for census-taking purposes. [3]Hispanic, from the Latin word for "Spain," refers generally to all Spanish-speaking peoples. [4]The term emphasizes the common factor of a shared language among groups that may have little else in common. [5]Hispanic can be used in referring to Spain and its history and culture. [6]A native of Spain residing in the United States is a Hispanic. [7]Hispanics are persons of Cuban, Mexican, Puerto Rican, South or Central-American, or other Spanish culture or origin, regardless of race. [8]The federal government considers race and Hispanic origin to be two separate and distinct concepts. [9]Hispanic Americans may be any race. [10]According to the 2000 U.S. Census, Hispanics of all races represent 13.3 percent of the U.S. population, which is about 37.4 million individuals. [11]The Census Bureau projects that by the year 2040 there will be 87.5 million Hispanic individuals, making up 22.3 percent of the population. [12]Though they share many aspects of a common heritage such as language and emphasis on extended family, Hispanic cultures vary greatly by country of origin. [13]Therefore, the broad term "Hispanic" is not an appropriate title for such a diverse people.

—Adapted from United States Centers for Disease Control. "Hispanic or Latino Populations." Office of Minority Health.

    a. the origin of the term "Hispanic"
    b. Latin Americans
    c. the limitations of the term "Hispanic"

B. Read the following group of ideas from a college psychology textbook. Answer the questions that follow.

    a. Basic emotions can combine to produce more complex and subtle ones.
    b. For example, joy and acceptance, which are closely related, can combine to produce love; joy and fear, which are not closely related, can join to produce guilt.
    c. When distant emotions mix, a person typically feels conflicted.

_____ **3.** Statement (a) is
    ● the main idea.   b. a supporting detail.

_____ **4.** Statement (b) is
    a. the main idea.   ●. a supporting detail.

_____ **5.** Statement (c) is
    a. the main idea.   ●. a supporting detail.

VISUAL VOCABULARY

What emotion does Plutchik's palette suggest will be the result of mixing fear and surprise?

_____

Plutchik's "Emotional Palette" ▶

Plutchik proposed a set of emotions that can be combined to form other emotions, much as primary colors can be mixed to create other colors.

—Plutchik, Robert. "Plutchik's 'Emtional Palette'" as appeared in *Emotion* by Robert Plutchik. Copyright © 1980. Reprinted by permission of Anita Plutchik..

Name _____ Section _____

Date _____ **Score** (number correct) _____ × 25 = _____ %

Visit MyReadingLab to take this test online and receive feedback and guidance on your answers.

Identify the topic sentence of each of the following paragraphs from college textbooks.

A. Paragraph from a college psychology textbook

Types of Personality Tests

Textbook
Skills

[1]Think of all the ways in which you differ from your best friend. [2]Psychologists use personality tests to identify the different traits that characterize an individual. [3]They think about what sets one person apart from another; they want to know what distinguishes people in one group from another. [4]For example, certain traits seem to separate shy people from outgoing people. [5]Two beliefs are basic to these attempts to understand and describe human personality. [6]The first is that personal traits of individuals give logic to their behavior. [7]The second belief is that those traits can be measured. [8]Personality tests that represent these two beliefs are known as either *objective* or *projective*.

—Gerrig, Richard J., and Zimbardo, Philip G.,
Psychology and Life, 16th ed., p. 460.

Topic sentence(s): __**2**__

B. Paragraph from a college health textbook

Determining What Triggers an Eating Disorder

Textbook
Skills

[1]Before you can change a behavior, you must first determine what causes it. [2]Many people have found it helpful to keep a chart of their eating patterns: when they feel like eating, the amount of time they spend eating, where they are when they decide to eat, other activities they engage in during the meal (watching television or reading), whether they eat alone or with others, what and how much they consume, and how they felt before they took their first bite. [3]If you keep a detailed daily log of eating triggers for at least a week, you will discover useful clues about what in your environment or emotional makeup causes you to want food. [4]Typically, these dietary triggers center on problems in everyday living rather than on real hunger pangs. [5]Many people find that they eat when stressed or when they have problems in their relationships. [6]For other

people, the same circumstances diminish their appetite, causing them to lose weight.

—Adapted from Donatelle, Rebecca J., *Health: The Basics,* 5th ed., p. 270.

Topic sentence(s): __2__

C. Paragraph from a college accounting textbook

Textbook Skills

Cash Advances

[1]Many credit cards allow cash advances at automated teller machines (ATMs). [2]Since a cash advance represents credit extended by the sponsoring financial institution, interest is charged on this transaction. [3]A transaction fee of 1 to 2 percent of the advance may also be charged. [4]Credit card companies also provide checks that you can use to make purchases that cannot be made by credit card. [5]The interest rate applied to cash advances is often higher than the interest rate charged on credit extended for specific credit card purchases. [6]The interest rate is applied at the time of the cash advance; the grace period that applies to purchases with a credit card does not apply to cash advances. [7]So, although cash advances are convenient, they can also be extremely costly.

—Madura, Jeff, *Personal Finance Update,* p. 196.

Topic sentence(s): __1__

D. Paragraph from a college education textbook

Textbook Skills

[1]Building expectations for student success means encouraging students to see that success can be reached through their own efforts. [2]Helping students realize that they control their fortunes in school by the amount of time and effort they are willing to put into their work is an important task. [3]This control principle can be impressed on students by having them keep track of the time they spend on a unit or project. [4]In addition, students can be shown how to evaluate their work using criteria developed by the teacher or the class. [5]Making students aware of their progress through the use of charts and graphs helps them see that they have control over their achievement. [6]They realize that the grades they receive are not given by the teacher but rather are the result of their own efforts.

—William Wilen, et al., *Dynamics of Effective Teaching,* 4th ed., Upper Saddle River: Pearson Education,. 2000, p. 41.

Topic sentence(s): _____

Name _____ Section _____

Date _____ **Score** (number correct) _____ × 25 = _____ %

Visit MyReadingLab to take this test online and receive feedback and guidance on your answers.

Read the passage. Then answer the questions that follow it.

Tone in a Poem

Textbook
Skills

[1]In old Western movies, when one hombre taunts another, it is customary for the second to drawl, "Smile when you say that, pardner" or "Mister, I don't like your tone of voice." [2]Sometimes in reading a poem, although we can neither see a face nor hear a voice, we can infer the poet's attitude from other evidence.

[3]Like tone of voice, tone in literature often conveys an attitude toward the person addressed. [4]Like the manner of a person, the manner of a poem may be friendly or belligerent toward its reader. [5]Again like tone of voice, the tone of a poem may tell us how the speaker feels about himself or herself: cocksure or humble, sad or glad. [6]But usually when we ask, "What is the tone of a poem?" we mean "What attitude does the poet take toward a theme or subject?" [7]Is the poet being affectionate, hostile, earnest, playful, sarcastic, or what? [8]We may never be able to know, of course, the poet's personal feelings. [9]All we need know is how to feel when we read the poem.

[10]Strictly speaking, tone isn't an attitude; it is whatever in the poem makes an attitude clear to us: the choice of certain words instead of others, the picking out of certain details. [11]In A. E. Houseman's "Loveliest of Trees," for example, the poet communicates his admiration for a cherry tree's beauty by singling out for attention its white blossoms; had he wanted to show his dislike for the tree, he might have concentrated on its broken branches, birdlime, or snails. [12]To perceive the tone of a poem correctly, we need to read the poem carefully, paying attention to whatever suggestions we find in it.

—Kennedy, X. J. and Gioia, Dana, *Literature: An Introduction to Fiction, Poetry, and Drama*, 8th ed., p. 757.

_____ **1.** What is the topic of the passage?
   a. old Western movies
   b. the tone of a poem
   c. tone
   d. A. E. Houseman's "Loveliest of Trees"

_____ **2.** Which sentence or sentences state the central idea of the passage?
   a. sentences 1 and 8   c. sentence 9
   b. sentence 2   d. sentence 11

_____ **3.** Which sentence states the main idea of the second paragraph?
   a. sentence 3   c. sentence 8
   b. sentence 5   d. sentence 9

_____ **4.** Which sentence or sentences state the main idea of the third paragraph?
   a. sentences 10 and 12   c. sentence 11
   b. sentence 10   d. sentence 12

VISUAL *VOCABULARY*

The tone or attitude of the parent portrayed in this photo is _____.

a. compassionate
b. angry
c. joyful

Name _____ Section _____

Date _____ **Score** (number correct) _____ × 20 = _____ %

Visit MyReadingLab to take this test online and receive feedback and guidance on your answers.

A. Each of the following groups of ideas includes one topic, one main idea, and two supporting details. In each group, first identify the topic. Then identify the stated main idea. (*Hint:* circle the topic and underline the author's controlling point in each group.)

Group 1

A. Gardening has emotional and physical benefits.
B. Pulling weeds, raking, digging, and planting while gardening strengthen all of the major muscle groups.
C. The sense of accomplishment and the enjoyment of beautiful surroundings bring many gardeners emotional satisfaction.

_____ **1.** Which of the following best states the topic?
    a. pulling weeds   c. gardening
    b. emotional satisfaction

_____ **2.** Which sentence best states the main idea?

Group 2

A. Also, surprise a child with an unexpected reward, such as a day trip to a special place, for a job well done.
B. Positive reinforcement teaches children the satisfaction and reward of good behavior.
C. One way to offer positive reinforcement is to give sincere praise when it is well deserved; children need to hear statements like "I'm proud of you" or "The way you mow and trim makes the yard look neat and healthy."

_____ **3.** Which of the following best states the topic?
    a. parenting   c. good behavior
    b. positive reinforcement

_____ **4.** Which sentence best states the main idea?

B. Read the following paragraph. Then identify the sentence (or sentences) that state(s) the main idea.

Double Jeopardy

[1]The Fifth Amendment to the U.S. Constitution makes it clear that no person may be tried twice for the same offense, which is known as double jeopardy. [2]In other words, people who have been acquitted or found innocent may not again be "put in jeopardy of life or limb" for the same crime. [3]The same is true of those who have been convicted: They cannot be tried again for the same offense. [4]Cases that are dismissed for a lack of evidence also come under the double jeopardy rule and cannot result in a new trial. [5]The U.S. Supreme Court has ruled that "the Double Jeopardy Clause protects against three distinct abuses: a second prosecution for the same offense after acquittal, a second prosecution for the same offense after conviction, and multiple punishments for the same offense."

—Schmalleger, Frank J., *Criminal Justice: A Brief Introduction*, 9th ed. p. 83.

5. Topic sentence(s): _____

3 Summary of Key Concepts of Stated Main Ideas

 Assess your comprehension of stated main ideas.

- What are the traits of a main idea? _____
  _____

- How does a reader identify a topic of a passage? _____
  _____
  _____

- The topic sentence states _____.
- A central idea is the _____
  _____.

- The thesis statement is a sentence that _____
  _____.

- The stated main idea of a reading selection can be located _____
  _____.

- Deductive thinking is based on the flow of ideas from _____ to
  _____.

- Inductive thinking is based on the flow of ideas from _____ to
  _____.

Test Your Comprehension of Locating Stated Main Ideas

Respond to the following questions and prompts.

 In your own words, what is the difference between deductive and inductive thinking? _____
_____
_____

LO1 LO2 LO3 LO5   In your own words, what is the difference between a topic sentence and a thesis statement? _____

_____

_____

LO4   Draw and label four graphs that show the possible locations of stated main ideas.

LO1 LO2 LO3 LO4 LO5 LO6 LO7   Identify and discuss the two most important ideas in this chapter that will help you improve your reading comprehension.

_____

_____

_____

_____

Implied Main Ideas and Implied Central Ideas

(Suggestion)

CHAPTER 4

LO LEARNING OUTCOMES

After studying this chapter, you should be able to:

LO1 Define the Term *Implied Main Idea*

LO2 Analyze Supporting Details and Thought Patterns to Determine Implied Main Ideas

LO3 Determine the Implied Main Ideas of Paragraphs

LO4 State the Implied Main Idea Based on the Supporting Details

LO5 Determine and State the Implied Central Idea

LO6 Develop Textbook Skills: Use Graphics as Details That Imply a Main Idea

LO7 Apply Information Literacy Skills: Academic, Personal, and Career Applications of Implied Main Ideas

Before Reading About Implied Main Ideas and Implied Central Ideas

Take a moment to study the learning outcomes. Underline key words that refer to ideas you have already studied in previous chapters. Each of these key words represents a great deal of knowledge upon which you will build as you learn about implied main ideas and implied central ideas. Now, circle terms that you need to know more about. Finally, identify your learning goals by completing the following chart:

What I Know and What I Need to Learn About Implied Main Ideas

What I already know that will help me master implied main ideas	_____ _____
What I need to learn to master implied main ideas	_____ _____

After you study this chapter, compare the information you record in this chart with the information you record as you complete the Chapter Review at the end of this chapter.

LO1   Define the Term *Implied Main Idea*

As you learned in Chapter 3, sometimes authors state the main idea of a paragraph in a topic sentence. However, other paragraphs do not include a stated main idea. Even though the main idea is not stated in a single sentence, the paragraph still has a main idea. In these cases, the details clearly suggest or imply the author's main idea.

> An **implied main idea** is a main idea that is not stated directly, but is strongly suggested by the supporting details in the passage.

When the main idea is not stated, you must figure out the author's controlling point about a topic. One approach is to study the facts, examples, descriptions, and explanations given—the supporting details. Another approach is to identify the author's thought pattern. An effective reader often uses both approaches. Learning how to develop a main idea based on the supporting details and thought patterns will help you develop several skills. You will learn how to study information, value the meaning of supporting details, appreciate the relationship between ideas, and use your own words to express an implied main idea.

Many different types of reading material use implied main ideas. For example, many paragraphs in college textbooks do not provide a topic sentence. In these passages, the author uses supporting details to imply the main idea. In addition, you will often need to formulate the implied main idea when you read literature. Short stories, novels, poems, and plays rely heavily on vivid details to suggest the author's point. The following short story is taken from a college literature textbook. Read the story and ask yourself: "What is the main idea?"

Independence

Written by Chuang Tzu and Translated by Herbert Giles

[1]Chuang Tzu was one day fishing, when the Prince of Ch'u sent two high officials to interview him, saying that his highness would be glad of Chuang Tzu's assistance in the administration of his government. [2]The latter quietly fished on, and without looking round, replied, "I have heard that in the State of Ch'u there is a sacred tortoise, which has been dead for

three thousand years, and which the prince keeps packed up in a box on the altar in his ancestral shrine. **3**Now do you think that tortoise would rather be dead and have its remains thus honored, or be alive and wagging its tail in the mud?" **4**The two officials answered that no doubt it would rather be alive and wagging its tail in the mud; whereupon Chuang Tzu cried out, "Begone! I too elect to remain wagging my tail in the mud."

—Chuang Tzu, "Independence." Translated by Herbert Giles. Reprinted in Kennedy, X. J. & Dana Gioia. *Literature: An Introduction to Fiction, Poetry, and Drama*, 8th ed., pp. 6–7.

Did you notice that every sentence in this paragraph is a supporting detail? No single sentence covers all the other ideas. To figure out the implied main idea, ask the following questions.

> **Questions for finding the implied main idea:**
>
> 1. What is the topic, or subject, of the paragraph?
> 2. What are the major supporting details?
> 3. Based on the details about the topic, what point or main idea is the author trying to get across?

Apply these three questions to the passage above by writing your responses to each question in the following blanks.

1. What is the topic of the story? _____

The title of the story gives us a strong clue that the topic is about independence. But each detail in the story also supports this topic.

2. What are the major supporting details?

a. _____

b. _____

c. _____

d. _____

3. What is the main idea the author is trying to get across? _____

_____

In order to formulate this main idea statement, you had to consider each of the details. For example, the author uses a vivid contrast between a dead tortoise that has an "honored" place on the Prince's "ancestral shrine" and a live tortoise

(handwritten margin note: ← What is the author point of view?)

"wagging its tail." In addition, the author has the two officials agree that the tortoise would have been better off alive and living freely. The tortoise serves as an example of independence and helps the reader understand the significance of Chuang Tzu's choice. He did not value power or public honor as much as he valued his own freedom to live simply.

Asking and answering these questions allows you to think about the impact of each detail and how the details fit together to support the author's controlling point. Searching for an implied main idea is like a treasure hunt. You must carefully read the clues provided by the author. This kind of careful reading is a skill that improves dramatically with practice. The following examples and practices are designed to strengthen this important skill.

Analyze Supporting Details and Thought Patterns to Determine Implied Main Ideas

Remember that the main idea of a paragraph is like the frame of a house. Just as a frame includes all the rooms, a main idea must cover all the details in a paragraph. Therefore, the implied main idea will be general enough to cover all the details, but it will not be so broad that it becomes an overgeneralization or a sweeping statement that suggests details not given; nor can it be so narrow that some of the given details are not covered. Instead, the implied main idea must cover *all* the details given.

The skill of identifying a stated main idea will also help you grasp the implied main idea. You learned in Chapter 3 that the stated main idea (the topic sentence) has two parts. A main idea is made up of the topic and the author's controlling point about the topic. One trait of the controlling point is the author's opinion or bias. A second trait is the author's thought pattern. Consider, for example, the topic sentence "Older people benefit from volunteer work for several reasons." "Older people" and "volunteer work" make up the topic. "Benefit" states the opinion, and "several reasons" states the thought pattern. When you read material that implies the main idea, you should mentally create a topic sentence based on the details in the material.

⊘ EXAMPLE Read the following details from a paragraph in a college criminal justice textbook. Circle the topic as it recurs throughout the details. Underline bias or opinion words and transition words. Then choose a statement that best states the author's controlling point about the topic.

- The American frontier was a vast and wild place until late in the nineteenth century.

- The backwoods areas of the frontier proved a natural haven for outlaws and bandits.

- For example, Henry Berry Lowery, a famous outlaw of the Carolinas, the James Gang, and many lesser-known desperadoes felt at home in the frontier's swamps and forests.

- Only the boldest of settlers tried to police the frontier.

- In the late eighteenth century, citizen posses and vigilante groups were often the only law available to settlers on the American frontier.

- Several popular frontier figures of the nineteenth century took it upon themselves to enforce the law on the books as well as the standards of common decency.

- For example, Judge Roy Bean, "Wild Bill" Hickok, Bat Masterson, Wyatt Earp, and Pat Garrett policed the frontier, sometimes in a semiofficial role.

—Adapted from Schmalleger, Frank J., *Criminal Justice Today: An Introductory Text for the 21st Century*, 10th ed., p. 155.

_____ Which statement best expresses the implied main idea?
 a. The American frontier was a dangerous place.
 b. Bold settlers and citizens enforced the law on the American frontier.
 c. By the late nineteenth century, the vast and wild American frontier was policed by bold settlers, citizens, and popular figures who enforced the law.
 d. The American frontier was home to outlaws, bandits, and desperadoes.

VISUAL *VOCABULARY*

A group of _____ hold court on a captured criminal in this sketch from the nineteenth century.

 a. desperadoes
 b. vigilantes

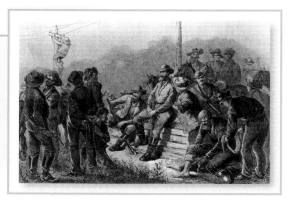

EXPLANATION   Two topics recur throughout these details. The most frequently recurring topic is the *American frontier*. The other topic appears less often and in several forms, such as *police* and *law*. Several biased words characterize the lack of law or the need for law on the American frontier. These words include *wild*, *haven*, *outlaw*, *bandit*, *swamps*, *forests*, *desperadoes*, and *vigilante*. A few other biased words characterize the people who worked to bring law to the frontier. These words include *boldest*, *citizen posse*, *popular figures*, *standards of common decency*, and *semiofficial*. Two transitions give us the time frame about the American frontier and its law: *until late in the nineteenth century* and *in the late eighteenth century*. The only statement that covers all these details is item (c). Item (a) states a general idea, and items (b) and (d) restate supporting details.

Practice 1

Read the following groups of supporting details. Circle the topic as it recurs throughout the list of details. Underline transition words to help you locate the major details. Also underline biased words to determine the author's opinion. Then select the sentence that best expresses the implied main idea.

Group 1

Textbook Skills

- Egypt's pyramids are the oldest existing buildings in the world.
- These ancient tombs are also among the world's largest structures.
- The largest pyramid stands taller than a 40-story building and covers an area greater than that of ten football fields.
- More than 80 pyramids still exist, and their once-smooth limestone surfaces hide secret passageways and rooms.
- The pyramids of ancient Egypt served a vital purpose: to protect the pharaohs' bodies after death.
- Each pyramid held not only the pharaoh's preserved body but also all the goods he would need in his life after death.

—Adapted from Sporre, Dennis J., *The Creative Impulse*, 6th ed., p. 45.

_b_   **1.** Which sentence best states the implied main idea?
  a. Pyramids are large, ancient buildings.
  b. Pyramids are massive structures with several distinctive traits.
  c. Pyramids are tombs that were built for the pharaohs.
  d. Pyramids are remarkable.

Group 2

- Cognitive therapy helps a person deal with negative or painful thoughts and behaviors.
- This therapy, a psychological treatment, was developed by a medical doctor, Aaron T. Beck, in the 1970s.
- First, a person seeks to change thinking patterns such as assumptions and core beliefs.
- Changes in feelings and actions will follow.
- To aid change, a person learns how to replace harmful thoughts and behaviors with positive coping tactics.
- Some of these tactics may include anger management and relaxation training.

_____ **2.** Which sentence best states the implied main idea?
  a. Cognitive therapy is a psychological treatment.
  b. Cognitive therapy is a psychological treatment that helps a person replace negative or painful thoughts and behaviors with positive coping skills.
  c. Cognitive therapy was developed by Aaron T. Beck, M.D., in the 1970s.
  d. Cognitive therapy focuses on negative or painful thoughts and behaviors.

LO3 Determine the Implied Main Ideas of Paragraphs

So far, you have learned to recognize the implied main idea by studying the specific details in a group of sentences. In this next step, the sentences will form a paragraph, but the skill of recognizing the implied main idea is exactly the same. The implied main idea of paragraphs must not be too broad or too narrow, so study the supporting details and look for thought patterns that suggest the main idea.

> **EXAMPLE** Read the following paragraph from a college business textbook. Circle the topic as it recurs throughout the paragraph. Underline transition words to help you locate the major details. Also underline biased words to determine the author's opinion. Then select the sentence that best expresses the implied main idea.

Levels of Management

¹**Top managers** are responsible for the overall performance and effectiveness of a firm. ²Common titles for top managers are *president, vice president, treasurer, chief executive officer* (CEO), and *chief financial officer* (CFO). ³They set general policies, plan strategies, approve all major decisions. ⁴They also represent the company in dealing with other firms and government officials. ⁵Just below the ranks of top managers is another group of managers called **middle managers**. ⁶Middle managers go by titles such as *plant manager, operations manager,* and *division manager.* ⁷In general, middle managers carry out the strategies, policies, and decisions made by top managers. ⁸**First-line managers** have titles such as *supervisor, office manager,* and *group leader.* ⁹First-line managers spend most of their time working with and supervising the employees who report to them.

—Adapted from Griffin, Ricky W. and Ebert, Ronald J., *Business*, 8th ed., pp. 165–166.

_____C_____   The best statement of the implied main idea is:

    a. Top managers have the most responsibility and receive the highest pay.

    b. Managers are known by a variety of titles.

    c. Management of a firm or company can be divided into three levels of managers.

EXPLANATION Clues to the implied main idea are found in both the title and the supporting details of this paragraph. The word *management* appears in the title, and the frequently recurring word *managers* appears in most sentences of the paragraph. In addition, the author uses specific words to distinguish three specific levels of managers: *top, middle,* and *first-line.* Thus, the best statement of the implied main idea is item (c). Item (a) states a supporting detail, and it includes the idea of "the highest pay," which is not mentioned in any of the details. Item (b) remains too general or vague for a main idea statement.

Practice 2

Read the following paragraphs. In each paragraph, circle the topic as it recurs throughout the paragraph. Underline transition words to help you locate the major details. Also underline the biased words to determine the author's opinion. Then select the sentence that best expresses the implied main idea for each.

Overcoming Writer's Block

[1]Countless numbers of college students in first-year composition classes face writer's block. [2]One way to overcome writer's block is to read. [3]Beginning writers may not have enough information or prior knowledge about a topic to generate a paper. [4]Therefore, reading about a topic gives the writer information and ideas on which to draw. [5]Another way to overcome this problem is through discussion. [6]Talking to peers, teachers, and others about ideas and beliefs helps novice writers clarify their own understandings so that they can more easily share them on paper. [7]A third way to overcome writer's block is to brainstorm. [8]Brainstorming is just a way to focus thoughts through listing, freewriting, or making concept maps. [9]Brainstorming also allows a writer to discover what to say without worrying about how to say it. [10]Finally, writer's block can be reduced by the wise use of time management skills. [11]Beginning writers need to understand that writing is an outgrowth of thinking, and thinking takes time. [12]Often writer's block is the result of too much stress and too little time; therefore, to avoid this problem, writers should begin the assignment days before it is due.

 1. Which sentence best states the implied main idea?
   a. Writer's block is a problem for many first-year college students.
   b. Reading is an excellent way to overcome writer's block.
   c. Beginning writers can overcome writer's block in several ways.
   d. The writing process should be broken into three phases: pre-writing, writing, and revising.

Green Tea: The Miracle Drink

[1]Green tea has been used for thousands of years in Asia as both a beverage and an herbal medicine. [2]This herbal tea contains catechin, which is a type of tannin that acts as an astringent. [3]Research suggests that men and women in Japan who drink five to six cups of green tea each day have much lower rates of cancer than people who do not. [4]Green tea is also thought to lower cholesterol and blood sugar, control high blood pressure, stop tooth decay, and fight viruses. [5]Green tea has even been credited with the power to slow down the aging process.

 2. Which sentence best states the implied main idea?
   a. Green tea is an ancient herbal drink.
   b. Green tea has caught the attention of medical researchers.

   c. Green tea lowers cholesterol and blood sugar and controls high
      blood pressure.
   d. Green tea, an ancient Asian herbal drink, is thought to have
      many health benefits.

One Handsome Young Man

¹At 6-foot-4, Van stood taller than most young men. ²The Florida sun tanned his skin to a deep bronze and bleached his dark brown hair to varying shades of sandy blond. ³Endowed with the high cheekbones of his Indian ancestors, sapphire eyes, and a luminous smile, he drew attention. ⁴He moved like an athlete at ease in his own skin. ⁵In neighborhood orange wars, Van could throw an orange farther and more accurately than any of us. ⁶In fact, he could outrun, outswim, outhunt, outfish, outdo all of us, and still we loved him. ⁷Guys felt proud to be his friend; girls clamored to be his sweetheart. ⁸Even now, 30 years later, at our high school reunion, Van looms larger than life to those of us he left behind: an unaging memory, a tragic loss.

___a___   3. Which sentence best states the implied main idea?
      a. Van was a handsome, talented, well-liked young man who died
         young and is still missed.
      b. Van was a tall, good-looking young man.
      c. Van is a tragic figure.
      d. Van is still missed by his high school friends.

State the Implied Main Idea Based on the Supporting Details

You have developed the skill of figuring out main ideas that are not directly stated. This ability to reason from specific details to main ideas will serve you well throughout college. One further step will also prove helpful in your reading and studying: the ability to state the implied main idea in your own words. You must learn to summarize the most important details into a one-sentence statement; in other words, you must create a **topic sentence**. To formulate this one-sentence summary, find the topic, determine the author's opinion by examining the biased words, and use the thought pattern to locate the major details. Then combine these ideas into a single sentence. The summary sentence includes the topic and the author's controlling point, just like a topic sentence. The statement you come up with must not be too narrow, for it must cover all the details given. On the other hand, it must not be too broad or go beyond the supporting details.

Remember that a main idea is always written as a complete sentence.

> **EXAMPLE**   Read the list of specific ideas that follows. Circle the topic as it recurs throughout each group of details. Underline words that reveal thought patterns and bias to discover the controlling point. Then write a sentence that best states the implied main idea.

- According to projections by the U.S. Department of Labor, healthcare and social assistance services rank number one in new jobs projected by the year 2018. About 26 percent of all new jobs created in the U.S. economy will be in this industry, which includes public and private hospitals, nursing and residential care facilities, and individual and family services. It is expected to grow by over 4 million new jobs. This employment growth is expected because of an aging population and longer life expectancies.

- Ranked second in the 2018 projections is the area of professional, scientific, and technical services. Employment in these services is projected to grow by 34 percent, adding about 2.7 million new jobs by 2018. Computer systems design and related services will account for nearly one-fourth of all new jobs in this industry sector.

- Rounding out the top three areas for projected job growth are educational services. Employment in public and private educational services is anticipated to grow by 12 percent, adding about 1.7 million new jobs through 2018. Rising student enrollments at all levels of education will create demand for educational services.

—U.S. Bureau of Labor Statistics, Office of Occupational
Statistics and Employment Projections.
<http://www.bls.gov/oco/oco2003.htm>

1. **Implied main idea:** _____

_____

_____

EXPLANATION To formulate an implied main idea statement, you must learn to summarize the important details into a one-sentence summary. The topic is "Projected Job Growth for the U.S. Labor Force in the Year 2018." The transition phrases include *rank number one, ranked second,* and *rounding out the top three.* To properly formulate a main idea sentence, you should have noticed that the details were organized as a list of job fields. The number of jobs projected in each major field provided the basis for their ranking on the list. The implied main idea could be expressed as follows: "The top three areas of job growth projected by the U.S. Department of Labor for 2018 are all in service industries."

EXAMPLE Read the following paragraph. Circle the topic as it recurs throughout the paragraph. Underline words that reveal thought patterns and bias to discover the controlling point. Then write a sentence that best states the implied main idea. Remember: not too narrow, not too broad—find that perfect fit!

Tourism in Greece

¹Of the millions of tourists who go to Greece, many, after visiting Athens, take a ferry boat ride to the famed Greek Islands in the Aegean Sea. ²Crete, the largest island, is rugged and mountainous with beautiful beaches and a reconstruction of King Minos's Palace, which is the oldest European throne, dating back 3,500 years. ³Santorini, the strikingly beautiful island, is a remaining part of the cone of an extinct volcano that erupted some 3,500 yeas ago. ⁴Some of the picturesque white buildings cling to the rim of the volcano and are among the most photographed in the world. ⁵The best way up to the town on top of the hill is by a donkey ride. ⁶Mikonos is a trendy island with its famed windmills and fabulous beaches, some of them nude beaches. ⁷Other often-visited islands include Rhodes, with plenty of ruins, good beaches, and nightlife; Corfu, off the west coast, is greener than the other islands because of higher rainfall, and it has excellent beaches, a museum, nightlife including a casino, and is favored by package tour groups.

—Walker, John R. and Walker, Josielyn T., *Tourism: Concepts and Practices*, pp. 284–285.

2. **Implied main idea:** _____

_____

VISUAL *VOCABULARY*

Based on your reading of the passage, the best meaning of the term **picturesque** is _____.

 pictorial
b. gaudy

EXPLANATION To formulate an implied main idea statement, you must learn to state the most important details of the paragraph in one sentence. Keep in mind that using your own words to formulate an implied main idea means that everyone's answer will be slightly different. The following sentence is one way to word the main idea of the paragraph: "Popular with tourists, each of the Greek Islands has its own special attractions." The frequent use of the word *island* clearly makes the Greek islands the topic of the paragraph. Notice that the different names of the islands and the descriptive terms that precede the word *island* point out the most important details that explain the topic. ◒

Practice 3

A. Read each group of supporting details. Circle the topic as it recurs throughout each group of details. Underline words that reveal thought patterns and bias to discover the controlling point. Then write a sentence that best states the implied main idea. After writing, check the sentence by asking if all the major details support it.

Group 1

- Recent DNA testing has proved several people on death row innocent of the crimes for which they were sentenced to death.
- The cost to taxpayers for death penalty appeals is staggeringly high.
- Many people believe that the death penalty is morally wrong and a form of legalized homicide.
- Many also believe that the death penalty does not deter crime.
- Finally, many believe that the death penalty unfairly targets the poor and the African American population.

1. **Implied main idea:** _____

_____

Group 2

- Narcotics used to control postsurgery pain cause side effects and don't always provide relief .
- A new technique is to drip a local anesthetic directly into the wound for two to five days while healing begins.
- One version, the ON-Q system, slowly drips the drug from a balloonlike ball into a tiny catheter inserted near the stitches, where it oozes out.
- The direct dose of pain medicine avoids the grogginess and other body-wide effects of narcotics.

—Jennifer Boen, From "On-Q System: A New Method
of Pain Relief", *The News-Sentinel,* April 24, 2009.

2. **Implied main idea:** _____

_____

_____

VISUAL *VOCABULARY*

The best meaning of the word **catheter** is _____.

a. the top layer of skin
b. an incision
c. pain medicine
d. a medical tube

—Line drawing from Associated ▶
Press, May 27, 2003. Reprinted with
permission of the YGS Group.

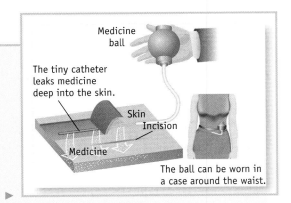

Medicine ball

The tiny catheter leaks medicine deep into the skin.

Skin
Incision

Medicine

The ball can be worn in a case around the waist.

B. Read the following paragraphs. Circle the topic as it recurs throughout each paragraph. Underline words that reveal thought patterns and bias to discover the controlling point. Then write a sentence that states the implied main idea.

Slave Quilts: The Maps to Freedom

[1]Some historians believe that a number of African Americans escaped slavery through a network of supporters called the Underground Railroad. [2]In order for the Underground Railroad to work effectively, it was necessary to relay information to those attempting to make the trip to freedom. [3]Direct communication, however, was not an option. [4]Any overt signal would be quickly discovered. [5]In order to overcome this problem, the principals involved created a system based on designs sewn into quilts that could be conspicuously displayed in appropriate places. [6]Like any good system of subterfuge, the quilts appeared as commonplace items to the adversaries of fugitive slaves. [7]However, to those in flight, the quilts were an encouraging symbol that advised them of the who, what, when, and how of their journey to freedom. [8]Many of the symbols sewn into the patterns are obvious in their meanings, such as the monkey wrench, which denoted that it was time to gather the tools required to make the journey, or sailboats, which indicated the availability of boats for the crossing of crucial bodies of water. [9]Other symbols were more cryptic, such as the star pattern, which had several variations but whose purpose was to point to the North Star. [10]The Drunkard's Path pattern served to remind those on the run to move east to west (in much the way a drunken man staggers) during their journey.

—Adapted from Weadon, "Follow the Drinking Gourd."

3. Implied main idea: _____

_____

Indoor Tanning: The Risks of Ultraviolet Rays

[1]The serious risk of skin cancer is not the only damage caused by tanning. [2]First, tanning causes premature aging. [3]Tanning causes the skin to lose elasticity and wrinkle prematurely. [4]This leathery look may not show up until many years after you've had a tan or sunburn. [5]Second, tanning suppresses the immune system. [6]UV-B radiation may suppress proper functioning of the body's immune system and the skin's natural defenses, leaving you more vulnerable to diseases, including skin cancer. [7]Third, tanning causes eye damage. [8]Exposure to UV radiation can cause irreversible damage to the eyes. [9]Fourth, tanning may develop an allergic reaction. [10]Some people who are especially sensitive to UV radiation may develop an itchy red rash and other adverse effects. [11]Advocates of

tanning devices sometimes argue that using these devices is less danger-ous than sun tanning because the intensity of UV radiation and the time spent tanning can be controlled. [12]But there is no evidence to support these claims. [13]In fact, sunlamps may be more dangerous than the sun be-cause they can be used at the same high intensity every day of the year—unlike the sun whose intensity varies with the time of day, the season, and cloud cover.

—Adapted from FDA Consumer Health Information.
U.S. Food and Drug Administration.

4. **Implied main idea:** _____

_____

LO5 Determine and State the Implied Central Idea

Just as a single paragraph can have an implied main idea, longer passages made up of two or more paragraphs can also have an implied main idea. You encoun-ter these longer passages in articles, essays, and textbooks. As you learned in Chapter 3, the stated main idea or central idea of these longer passages is called the *thesis statement*. When the main idea of several paragraphs is implied, it is called the **implied central idea**. You use the same skills to formulate the im-plied central idea of a longer passage that you use to formulate the implied main idea of a paragraph.

> The **implied central idea** is the main idea suggested by the details of a passage made up of two or more paragraphs.

Annotating the text is a helpful tool in determining the implied central idea. Just as you did to grasp the implied main idea for paragraphs, circle the topic. Underline the signal words for thought patterns. Remember, transition words introduce supporting details. An author often pairs a transition word with a major supporting detail. Consider the following examples: *the first rea-son, a second cause, the final effect, another similarity, an additional difference,* and so on. When you see phrases such as these, your one-sentence summary may include the following kinds of phrases: *several effects, a few differences,* and so on.

A longer passage often contains paragraphs with stated main ideas. The stated main idea of a paragraph is a one-sentence summary of that paragraph and can be used as part of your summary of the implied central idea.

> **EXAMPLE** Read the following passage from a college psychology textbook. Annotate the text. Then select the sentence that summarizes its central idea.

Textbook
Skills

Chunking

¹A chunk is a meaningful unit of information. ²A chunk can be a single letter or number, a group of letters or other items, or even a group of words or an entire sentence. ³For example, the sequence 1-9-8-4 consists of four digits, each of which is a chunk when they are remembered separately. ⁴However, if you see the digits as a year or the title of George Orwell's novel *1984*, they constitute only one chunk, leaving you much more capacity for other chunks of information.

⁵See how many chunks you can find in this sequence of 20 numbers: 19411917186518211776. ⁶You can answer "20" if you see the sequence as a list of unrelated digits or "5" if you break down the sequence into the dates of major wars in U.S. history. ⁷If you do the latter, it's easy for you to recall all the digits in the proper sequence after one quick glance. ⁸It would be impossible for you to remember them from a short exposure if you saw them as 20 unrelated items.

—Gerrig, Richard J.; Zimbardo, Philip G.,
Psychology and Life, 16th ed., p. 225.

_____ The sentence that best summarizes the central idea is:
  a. A chunk is a small part of a larger set of information.
  b. Chunking is a strategy that increases memory by organizing large pieces of information into smaller units of thought.
  c. Chunking is an excellent method of memorizing important dates in history.
  d. Chunking is helpful.

EXPLANATION This passage demonstrates the challenge of grasping the implied central idea. The thought pattern used in the first three sentences is definition. Sentences 1 and 2 introduce and define the term *chunk*, and the transition *or* is used to add details to the definition. Sentence 3 introduces an example by using the signal phrase *for example*. Interestingly, the transition *however* adds a minor supporting detail to the example in sentence 4. Sentences 5 through 8 explain the process of chunking by using an example. The author has mixed patterns (definition and process) to describe a memory strategy called "chunk-ing." The sentence that best summarizes these details and thought patterns is (b) "Chunking is a strategy that increases memory by organizing large pieces of information into smaller units of thought." This sentence presents a definition of the term and indicates that a process is going to be discussed. Sentences (a) and (c) are too narrow; sentence (d) is too broad. ◒

Practice 4

Read the following passage. Annotate the text. Then select the sentence that summarizes its central idea.

The Three Phases of Lyme Disease

¹The first stage of Lyme disease shows up three to 30 days after a person is bitten by an infected tick. ²During this phase, a red-rimmed circular spot or spots emerge, often described as a "bull's-eye" rash. ³The centers of these expanding spots become pale, and the infected person experiences exhaustion, headaches, a fever, and joint and muscle pains.

⁴The second stage of Lyme disease can develop within weeks or take months to appear. ⁵One symptom is Bell's palsy, which causes one side of the face to droop and the eye on that side to stay opened. ⁶In addition, nerve problems can occur, the heart can become inflamed, and the rash seen in stage one can return.

⁷The third stage of Lyme disease, which can occur within weeks or take years to develop, is arthritis, the painful swelling of joints.

⁸Of course, not all cases of Lyme disease exhibit all these symptoms. ⁹Some cases may have only one or two of these signs.

_____ The sentence that best summarizes the central idea is:
   a. Lyme disease can have long-term consequences.
   b. Lyme disease affects different people in different ways.
   c. Lyme disease can attack the nerves and heart.
   d. Lyme disease, a serious illness caused by a tick bite, occurs in three stages.

❯ **EXAMPLE** Read the following passage from a college history textbook. Annotate the text. Write a sentence that summarizes the central idea of the passage.

Textbook
Skills

Why It's Called *Brown v. Board of Education of Topeka, Kansas*

[1]Seven-year-old Linda Brown of Topeka, Kansas, lived close to a good public school, but it was reserved for whites. [2]So every day she had to cross railroad tracks in a nearby switching yard on her way to catch a run-down school bus that would take her across town to a school reserved for African American students. [3]Her father, Oliver Brown, concerned for her safety and the quality of her education, became increasingly frustrated with his youngster's having to travel far from home to get an education.

[4]"The issue came up, and it was decided that Reverend Brown's daughter would be the goat, so to speak," recalled a member of the Topeka NAACP. [5]"He put forth his daughter to test the validity of the law, and we had to raise the money."

[6]The NAACP continued to gather cases from around the nation. [7]The Supreme Court first agreed to hear *Brown* and *Briggs* v. *Elliot* (South Carolina) in 1952. [8]Two days before they were to be heard, the Court issued a postponement and added *Davis* v. *Prince Edward County* (Virginia) to its docket. [9]Just a few weeks later, the Court added *Bolling* v. *Sharpe* from the District of Columbia and *Gebhart* v. *Belton* (Delaware). [10]According to U.S. Supreme Court Justice Tom Clark of Texas, the Court "consolidated them and made *Brown* the first so that the whole question would not smack of being purely a Southern one." [11]Thus the case came to be known as *Brown* v. *Board of Education of Topeka, Kansas*.

> —Larry J. Sabato and Karen O'Connor, *American Government: Continuity and Change.* Upper Saddle River: Pearson Education, Inc., 2000, p. 190.

Implied central idea: _____

_____

_____

_____

EXPLANATION This passage shows the importance of a title or heading. Turn the heading into the question: Why is it called "*Brown v. Board of Education of Topeka, Kansas*"? Reading to find the answer to this question helps you decide what to annotate as you read. The opening two paragraphs use a narrative to give the history of this landmark court case. It is safe to infer that the events in this case are similar to the events in other cases. The problem of racial discrimination was widespread. Instead of underlining the time order transition words, an effective reader might write in the margin the phrase "racial discrimination." This label summarizes the point of the narrative. The third paragraph begins with a topic sentence about bringing in other cases to join *Brown*. The supporting details (the additional cases) that follow are joined by time and addition words. All these details lead up to the final sentence, which restates the title. The transition word *thus* reinforces that this court case was the result of a widespread fight against racial discrimination.

The wording of answers will vary. One possible answer is "The Supreme Court Case *Brown* v. *Board of Education of Topeka, Kansas* was actually four cases brought from different areas of the nation to challenge discrimination against African Americans in public education." This sentence covers all the supporting details but does not go beyond the information given in the passage. For example, this was a landmark case that could be considered the most important civil rights case of the twentieth century. The effect of the ruling dramatically changed our society. However, these details are not included in the passage; thus the thesis statement does not mention them. ◁

Practice 5

Read the following passage from a college geology textbook. Annotate the text. Write a sentence that summarizes the central idea.

The Cenozoic Era

[1]During the Cenozoic, mammals replaced reptiles as the dominant land animal. [2]At nearly the same time, angiosperms (flowering plants with covered seeds) replaced gymnosperms as the dominant plants. [3]The Cenozoic is often called the "Age of Mammals" but can also be considered the "Age of Flowering Plants" because, in the plant world, angiosperms enjoy a status similar to that of mammals in the animal world.

[4]The development of flowering plants strongly influenced the evolution of both birds and mammals that feed on seeds and fruits. [5]During the middle of the Cenozoic, another type of angiosperm, grasses, developed rapidly and spread over the plains. [6]This fostered the emergence of herbivorous (plant-eating) mammals, which, in turn, provided the evolutionary foundation for large, predatory mammals.

[7]During the Cenozoic, the ocean was teaming with modern fish such as tuna, swordfish, and barracuda. [8]In addition some mammals, including seals, whales, and walruses returned to the sea.

—Tarbuck, Frederick K., Edward J. Lutgens and
Dennis G. Tasa. *Essentials of Geology*, 11th ed., p. 487.

Implied central idea: _____

_____

LO6 # Develop Textbook Skills: Use Graphics as Details That Imply a Main Idea

Textbook authors often use pictures, drawings, or graphs to make the relationship between the main idea and supporting details clear.

▷ **EXAMPLE**   Study the following figure from a health textbook. State the main idea suggested by the details in a sentence.

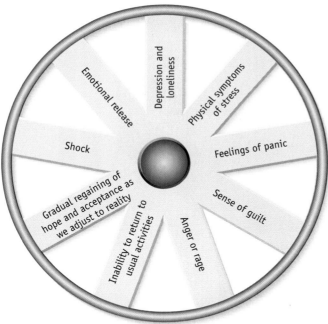

◀ **Stages of Grief**

—Image reprinted from Donatelle, Rebecca J. and Davis, Lorraine G., *Access to Health*, 7th ed., p. 545.

Implied main idea: _____

_____

EXPLANATION   This diagram is a circle graph. Circles often suggest a cycle or process. The caption tells us that each spoke is labeled with a different stage of grief. Each of the nine spokes that radiate from the center of the circle represents a stage of grief. The labels identify each stage. Therefore, by counting the number of spokes and using the caption, we can formulate a possible statement for the main idea: "Grief has nine stages." Since the main idea statement is a summary of the author's main point, it is not necessary to name each stage. Simply stating the number of stages indicates that a list of supporting details is given. <

Practice 6

Study the following figure from a college health textbook. Put the main idea suggested by the details into a sentence.

Psychological Health

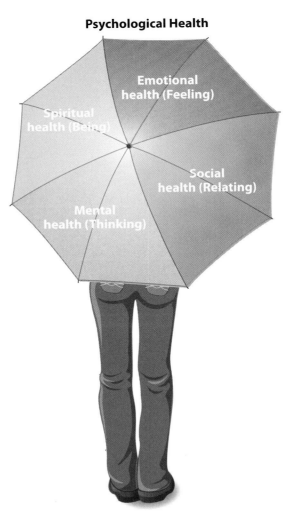

—Figure 2.1 "Psychological Health" from Donatelle, Rebecca J. *Access to Health*, 12th ed., p. 32.

Implied main idea: _____

_____

A Final Note About Experience and Perspective

As you have worked through this chapter, hopefully you have had some lively discussions about the possible answers for activities that asked for implied main ideas to be stated. Often a set of details will suggest many things to many people. Determining main ideas requires that the reader bring personal understandings and experience to the task. Thus people with different perspectives may disagree about what the details suggest. Another complex aspect of determining main ideas is that authors may choose to give a collection of details because the idea suggested is difficult to sum up in one sentence. The author intends several meanings to coexist. The important point to remember is that the main idea you formulate should be strongly supported by the details in the paragraph or longer passage.

Apply Information Literacy Skills

 ## Academic, Personal, and Career Applications of Implied Main Ideas

The ability to identify an implied main idea is another information literacy skill. In addition to locating the stated main idea, being able to determine the implied main idea is an important problem-solving tool that will help you comprehend information. In your academic, personal, and career lives, you will come across many forms of reading material with implied main ideas. Some examples are fiction, poetry, songs, instructions, manuals, non-fiction books, reports, memos, letters, and articles. You will be expected or will want to understand and respond to the implied main idea of these materials. Thus, you will use the skills that you have learned in this chapter in several ways. You will:

- Recognize your own need to know an implied main idea.
- State an implied main idea.
- Apply the implied main idea to your specific situation.

Academic Application

Assume you are taking a college sociology course. As you survey the weekly reading assignment from the textbook, you use graphics and tables to determine important main ideas.

- **Before Reading:** Skim the table from the chapter "World Economic Systems." Create a question based on the title of the table.
- **During Reading:** Underline key words that answer the question based on the title of the table.
- **After Reading:** In the space following the passage, state the implied main idea of the table in a topic sentence.

Question Based on Title: _____

_____

TABLE 14.1 Comparing Capitalism and Socialism	
Capitalism	**Socialism**
1. Individuals own the means of production.	1. The public owns the means of production.
2. Based on competition, the owners determine production and set prices.	2. Central committees plan production and set prices; no competition.
3. The pursuit of profit is the reason for distributing goods and services.	3. No profit motive in the distribution of goods and services.

—Henslin, James M. *Sociology: A-Down-To-Earth Approach*, 9th ed., p. 403.

Topic Sentence Stating Implied Main idea: _____

_____

_____

_____

Personal Application

Assume your grandmother Emma Jones lives in an assisted living facility. She has developed a rash of inflamed and raw pimples on her face, neck, and armpits. You have searched the Internet by using a descriptive list of her symptoms. You found the following article at a government website.

- **Before Reading:** Skim the passage. Create a question based on the title of the article.
- **During Reading:** Underline the symptoms and treatment described in the passage.
- **After Reading:** In the space following the passage, write a sentence that sums up Emma Jones' condition and action to be taken on her behalf, if needed.

Question Based on Title: _____

_____

Definition, Symptoms, and Treatment of MRSA

[1]Methicillin-resistant Staphylococcus Aureus (MRSA) is a type of staph bacteria. [2]MRSA is resistant to certain antibiotics. [3]These antibiotics include methicillin and other more common antibiotics such as oxacillin, penicillin, and amoxicillin. [4]In the community, most MRSA infections are skin infections. [5]More severe or potentially life-threatening MRSA infections occur most frequently among patients in healthcare settings. [6]Most MRSA infections are skin infections that may appear as pustules or boils which often are red, swollen, painful, or have pus or other drainage. [7]They often first look like spider bites or bumps that are red, swollen, and painful. [8]These skin infections commonly occur at sites of visible skin trauma, such as cuts and abrasions, and areas of the body covered by hair (e.g., back of neck, groin, buttock, armpit, beard area of men). [9]Treatment for MRSA skin infections may include having a healthcare professional drain the infection and, in some cases, prescribe an antibiotic. [10]Do not attempt to treat an MRSA skin infection by yourself; doing so could worsen or spread it to others. [11]This includes popping, draining, or using disinfectants on the area. [12]If you think you might have an infection, cover the affected skin, wash your hands, and contact your healthcare provider.

—Centers for Disease Control and Prevention.
"MRSA Infections."

Condition and Action: _____

_____

Career Application

Assume the role of Raul Gomez, who is up for a six-month employee performance review. As Raul, you have an appointment with your supervisor to review your performance. You are eligible for a pay raise based on the length of your employment. Your supervisor gave you a copy of her review of your performance to look over before the meeting.

- **Before Reading:** Skim the passage. Predict Raul's (your) overall performance by circling one of the following: Exceeds Expectations, Meets Expectations, Falls Below Expectations.

- **During Reading:** Underline key details that describe Raul's strengths and needs for improvement.

- **After Reading:** In the space at the end of the passage, write a sentence that states a recommendation based on the details recorded about Raul's (your) performance.

Employee Performance Evaluation: Raul Gomez

General Observations: [1]Raul's performance of many of the expectations is satisfactory. [2]When Raul engages fully, he is a positive contributor to the customer, his work team, the company, and himself. [3]However, his performance falls below several key expectations. [4]When disengaged, which occurs often (see documentation), Raul negatively impacts the quality of his work and his team's work. [5]Improvement in Raul's performance is critical for his success and the success of his work team.

Strengths: [6]Raul demonstrates knowledge of policies and procedures. [7]He is highly skilled in use and care of technology. [8]His turnaround on routine tasks/projects is reasonable. [9]He has low use of sick time.

Opportunities for Professional Development: [10]Develop interpersonal skills with peers and customers. [11]Develop collaboration skills to enhance team work and team effectiveness. [12]Improve communication skills with supervisors, coworkers, and customers. [13]Develop fundamental job skills such as punctuality and completion of special projects in a timely manner without being reminded of due dates.

Recommendation: _____

_____

_____

_____

REVIEW TEST 1

Score (number correct) _____ x 25 = _____ %

Visit MyReadingLab to take this test online and receive feedback and guidance on your answers.

Implied Main Ideas

A. Read each group of supporting details. Annotate the list. Then choose the sentence that best expresses the implied main idea for each group.

1. Supporting details:

- The teenage birth rate declined 8 percent in the United States from 2007 through 2009, reaching a historic low at 39.1 births per 1,000 teens aged 15–19 years.
- Birth rates fell significantly for teenagers in all age groups and for all racial and ethnic groups.
- Teenage birth rates for each age group and for nearly all race and Hispanic origin groups in 2009 were at the lowest levels ever reported in the United States.
- Birth rates for teens aged 15–17 dropped in 31 states from 2007 through 2009; rates for older teenagers aged 18–19 declined significantly in 45 states during this period.

—Data from National Center for Health Statistics, NCHS Data Brief, Number 58. <http://www.cdc.gov/nchs/data/databriefs/db58.htm.>

_____ **Implied main idea:**
  a. The U.S. teenage birthrate declined to the lowest rate ever reported in the early 2000s.
  b. The U.S. teenage birthrate declined 8 percent from 2007 through 2009.
  c. Birthrates dropped more for older teens than for younger teens in 45 states.
  d. There were 39.1 births per 1,000 U.S. teens aged 15–19 years in 2009.

2. Supporting details:

- Maria focused all her attention on the television set even when she was flipping through the channels.
- By the time her husband Jesse entered the room, one of the shows had caught her attention.
- Jesse tried to talk to Maria about an issue that had come up at work.
- Jesse felt anxious and needed to talk.

▪ Although Maria nodded at everything Jesse said, her eyes never left the television set.

▪ In addition, she offered no comments, nor did she ask any questions.

▪ Jesse finally fell silent, then sighed deeply, and quietly left the room.

_____ **Implied main idea:**
a. Jesse and Maria are not happily married.
b. Maria's lack of attention discouraged her husband at a time when he needed her support.
c. Maria and Jesse do not listen to each other.
d. Jesse's rude behavior of interrupting Maria's television show led to the couple's lack of communication.

B. Study the following graph, and examine the details given. In the space provided, write the letter of the sentence that best states the implied main idea of the graph.

   3. Supporting details:

Figure 1. Estimated world population, 1950-2000, and projections: 2000-2050

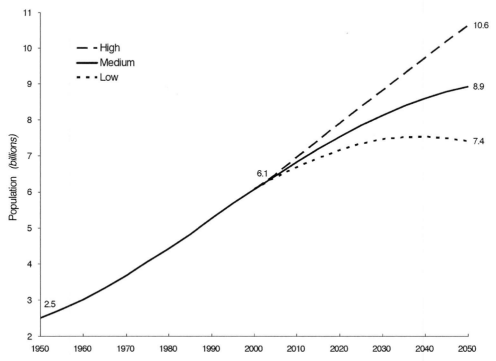

—"Estimated World Population, 1950–2000, and Projections: 2000–2050," *United Nations Department of Economic and Social Affairs Population Division, World Population to 2300*, p. 5. Copyright © United Nations 2004. Reproduced by permission of United Nations Publications Board.

_____   **Implied main idea:**
   a. The low estimate for the world's population in 2050 is 7.4 billion, but the high estimate is 10.6 billion.
   b. The world's population has risen from 1950 and will continue to rise.
   c. It is estimated the world's population will increase from 2.5 billion in 1950 to between 7.4 billion and 10.6 billion in 2050.
   d. The world's population is estimated to increase dramatically, and steps must be taken to limit the increase.

C. Read the following paragraph. Annotate the text. In the space provided, write the letter of the best statement of the implied main idea.

Textbook Skills

> Most people think "Anything worth doing is worth doing well." In contrast, perfectionists think, "Anything worth doing is worth doing perfectly." Nothing less than perfection will do. "Procrastinating perfectionists" find the task so daunting that they wait until too late to prepare. They excuse themselves by thinking they could have done wonderfully, if only they had not procrastinated. "Tedious perfectionists" hone each step of preparation in great detail, but run out of time. For example, while preparing to deliver a speech, this perfectionist will gather volumes of material, write detailed outlines, but never practice delivering the speech.
>
> —Adapted from Kelly, Marilyn, *Communication @ Work*, p. 70.

_____   **4.** The best statement of the implied main idea is
   a. Don't aim for perfection; aim to do a very good job.
   b. Perfection is an excuse.
   c. Two types of perfectionists have unrealistic expectations.
   d. Perfectionists are failures.

REVIEW TEST 2

Score (number correct) _____ x 25 = _____ %

Visit MyReadingLab to take this test online and receive feedback and guidance on your answers.

Implied Main Ideas and Implied Central Ideas

A. Read each group of supporting ideas. Annotate the lists. Then use your own words to write the best statement of the implied main idea for each group.

Group 1

Oil Pollution

- Used engine oil can end up in waterways.

- Coral reefs and mangroves are more likely to be damaged by oil pollution than are sandy beaches or sea-grass beds.

- Oil-covered fur or feathers do not provide the insulation marine mammals and diving birds need in cold water.

- When an animal cleans itself, it also swallows oil.

- Fish exposed to oil pollution such as tanker spills may develop liver disease and reproductive and growth problems.

- Oil pollution occurs through major oil spills, runoff from city and industrial wastes, and exhaust particles from automobiles.

1. **Implied main idea:** _____

   _____

Group 2

A Few Duties for June for Florida Gardeners

- In June, Florida gardeners fertilize blackberries and blueberries.

- They also plant the herbs that thrive in heat, such as basil, chives, and lemongrass.

- Florida gardeners know that June is a good month to spread thick layers of mulch in flowerbeds to smother quickly growing weeds.

- With June come the early days of the hurricane season, so Florida gardeners also take notice of weak or rotting trees or limbs that need pruning.

2. **Implied main idea:** _____

   _____

Group 3

"Do Not Call" Registry to Block Telemarketing Calls.

- Since July 2003, the Federal Trade Commission (FTC) has been registering consumers for the free online "do not call" registry.

- Telemarketers and other sellers have access to the registry.

- They will be required to check their call lists against the national "do not call" registry at least once every 90 days.
- The "do not call" registry accepts home phone numbers and cell phone numbers.
- Violators are subject to a fine of up to $11,000 per violation.

—Federal Trade Commission, "The 'Do Not Call' Registry."

3. **Implied main idea:** _____

   _____

   _____

B. Read the following poem and then write a sentence that states the implied central idea.

Batteries and Bottled Water

by Dustin Weeks

I'm making a list of the things I need
To ride out the storm:
Candles and cans of tuna,
A deck of cards,
Tape for the windows,
Or better yet sheets of plywood
Securely screwed.

I'm still making my list
As the wind begins to rise.
How long will half a jar of peanut butter last
In desperate hours?
I decide to drink the milk
Before it's too late and
A white frown trickles down my chin.

I decide I am good at making lists
While watching the water rising from under the door.
Right here I listed the wet/dry vac,
Just after the chain saw
And before the first aid kit.
The TV says it pays to be prepared
And they will let me know in the event of an actual emergency.

I have almost completed my list
When the roof lifts off

Like a giant Japanese kite
And the list is torn from my hands.
I watch it whipped higher and higher
Into the raging sky
A bottleless message urging evacuation.

4. Implied central idea: _____

_____

_____

REVIEW TEST 3

Score (number correct) _____ x 20 = _____ %

Visit MyReadingLab to take this test online and receive feedback and guidance on your answers.

Textbook
Skills

Read the following passage from a college science textbook. Answer the questions that follow.

Smoking—A Life and Breath Decision

[1]About 440,000 people in the United States die of smoking-related diseases each year. [2]These diseases include lung cancer, emphysema, chronic bronchitis, heart disease, stroke, and other forms of cancer.

[3]In smokers, microscopic smoke particles build up in the alveoli over the years until the lungs of a heavy smoker are literally blackened. [4]Adhering to the particles are about 200 different toxic substances. [5]Of these, more than a dozen are known or probable carcinogens (cancer-causing substances). [6]The longer the delicate tissues of the lungs are exposed to the carcinogens on the trapped particles, the greater the chance that cancer will develop.

[7]Some smokers will develop chronic bronchitis, a persistent lung infection. [8]Bronchitis is characterized by coughing, swelling of the lining of the respiratory tract, an increase in mucous production, and a decrease in the number and activity of cilia. [9]The result is a decrease in air flow to the alveoli. [10]Emphysema develops when toxic substances in cigarette smoke lead to brittle and ruptured alveoli. [11]The loss of the alveoli, where gas exchange occurs, deprives all body tissues of oxygen. [12]In an individual with emphysema, breathing becomes increasingly labored and loss of breath may ultimately be fatal.

[13]Carbon monoxide is present at high levels in cigarette smoke. [14]Carbon monoxide binds to red blood cells in place of oxygen. [15]This binding reduces the blood's oxygen-carrying capacity and thereby increases the work the heart must do. [16]Chronic bronchitis and emphysema compound this problem, making smokers twice as likely as nonsmokers to suffer a heart attack. [17]Smoking also causes atherosclerosis. [18]As a result, smokers are 70% more likely than nonsmokers to die of heart disease. [19]The carbon monoxide in cigarette smoke may also contribute to the reproductive problems of women who smoke during pregnancy. [20]These problems include infertility, miscarriage, lower birth weight of their babies, and, for their children, more learning and behavioral problems.

[21]Children whose parents smoke are more likely to contract bronchitis, pneumonia, ear infections, coughs, and colds. [22]Their lung capacity is often decreased, and they are more likely to develop asthma and allergies as well. [23]For children with asthma, the number and severity of asthma attacks are increased by secondhand smoke. [24]Among adults, nonsmoking spouses of smokers face a 30% higher risk of both heart attack and lung cancer than do spouses of nonsmokers. [25]A recent study links even relatively infrequent exposure to secondhand smoke with atherosclerosis. [26]Government agencies report that secondhand smoke is responsible for an estimated 3,000 lung cancer deaths and at least 35,000 deaths from heart disease in nonsmokers in the United States each year. [27]For smokers who quit, however, healing begins immediately and the chances of heart attack, lung cancer, and numerous other smoking-related illnesses gradually diminish.

—Adapted from Audesirk, Teresa, Audesirk, Gerald, and Byers, Bruce E., *Life on Earth*, 5th ed., p. 389.

_____ 1. Which sentence best states the implied main idea of the second paragraph (sentences 3–6)?
a. Tobacco smoke has a dramatic impact on the human respiratory tract.
b. Tobacco smoke contains hundreds of toxic chemicals.
c. Tobacco smoke can cause lung cancer.
d. Tobacco smoke is deadly.

_____ 2. Which sentence best states the implied main idea of the third paragraph (sentences 7–12)?
a. Smoking causes chronic bronchitis.
b. Smoking causes emphysema.
c. Tobacco smoke harms the cilia and the alveoli of the lungs.
d. Tobacco smoke can cause serious respiratory problems and may lead to death.

_____ **3.** Which sentence best states the implied main idea of the fourth paragraph (sentences 13–20)?
  a. Tobacco smoke contains carbon monoxide.
  b. The carbon monoxide in tobacco smoke causes heart disease.
  c. The carbon monoxide in tobacco smoke is linked to heart problems and contributes to reproductive problems in women who smoke.
  d. The carbon monoxide in tobacco smoke restricts the body's ability to absorb oxygen.

_____ **4.** Which sentence best states the implied main idea of the fifth paragraph (sentences 21–27)?
  a. Children are harmed by breathing secondhand smoke.
  b. Breathing secondhand smoke poses health hazards for both children and adults.
  c. Secondhand smoke causes health problems for adults.
  d. The harmful effects of smoking can be reversed.

_____ **5.** Which sentence best states the central idea of the passage?
  a. Smoking tobacco and breathing secondhand smoke lead to serious health problems and even death.
  b. The harmful effects of smoking are irreversible.
  c. Tobacco smoke has a dramatic impact on the human respiratory system.
  d. Quitting smoking saves lives.

SUMMARY RESPONSE

Respond to the passage by stating the implied main idea in a thesis sentence. Be sure to identify the topic and the author's attitude about the topic. Begin your summary response with the following: _The most important idea of "Smoking— A Life and Breath Decision" by Audesirk, Audesirk, and Byers is…_

WHAT DO YOU THINK?

Given the proven health risks, why do you think so many people choose to smoke? Assume you are taking a college health course, and your professor has assigned a paper to write about an avoidable health hazard. You have chosen to write about the dangers of smoking tobacco. In your paper, discuss the following:

  ▪ Challenge smokers to quite smoking.

  ▪ Explain reasons to stop smoking.

  ▪ Suggest a method to help them quit.

REVIEW TEST 4

Score (number correct) _____ x 10 = _____%

Visit MyReadingLab to take this test online and receive feedback and guidance on your answers.

Implied Main Ideas and Implied Central Ideas

Before you read, skim the following passage from a college social science textbook. Answer the **Before Reading** questions. Read the passage and annotate the text. Then answer the **After Reading** questions.

Two Types of Language: Denotation and Connotation

Textbook
Skills

[1]Consider a word such as *death*. [2]To a doctor, this word might mean the point at which the heart stops beating. [3]This is a denotative meaning, a rather **objective** description of an event. [4]To a mother whose son has just died, however, the word means much more. [5]It recalls the son's youth, his ambitions, his family, his illness, and so on. [6]To her, the word is emotional, subjective, and highly personal. [7]These emotional, subjective, and personal associations are the word's connotative meaning. [8]The denotation of a word is its objective definition; the connotation is its subjective or emotional meaning.

[9]Now consider a simple nod of the head in answer to the question, "Do you agree?" [10]This gesture is largely denotative and simply says yes. [11]What about a wink, a smile, or an overly rapid speech rate? [12]These nonverbal expressions are more connotative; they express your feelings rather than objective information.

[13]The denotative meaning of a message is general or **universal**; most people would agree with the denotative meanings and would give similar definitions. [14]Connotative meanings, however, are extremely personal, and few people would agree on the precise connotative meaning of a word or nonverbal behavior.

[15]"Snarl words" and "purr words" may further clarify the distinction between denotative and connotative meaning. [16]Snarl words are highly negative ("She's an idiot," "He's a pig," "They're a bunch of losers"). [17]Sexist, racist, and heterosexist language and hate speech provide lots of other examples. [18]Purr words are highly positive ("She's a real sweetheart," "He's a dream," "They're the greatest"). [19]Although they may sometimes seem to have denotative meaning and refer to the "real world," snarl and purr words are actually connotative in meaning. [20]They

don't describe people or events, but rather, they reveal the speaker's feelings about these people or events.

—Adapted from DeVito, Joseph A.,
Interpersonal Communication Book, p. 162.

Before Reading

Vocabulary in Context

_____ **1.** The best definition of the word **objective** in sentence 3 is
a. personal.   c. honest.
b. factual.   d. biased.

_____ **2.** The best meaning of the word **universal** in sentence 13 is
a. lofty.   c. common to many people.
b. narrow.   d. exact.

Thought Patterns

_____ **3.** What is the thought pattern suggested by the title of the passage?
a. cause and effect   c. spatial order
b. classification   d. comparison

After Reading

Main Ideas

_____ **4.** Which sentence is the topic sentence for the last paragraph (sentences 15–20)?
a. sentence 15   c. sentence 18
b. sentence 16   d. sentence 19

Supporting Details

_____ **5.** Based on the passage, a simple nod of the head
a. is the only way to communicate agreement with an idea or person.
b. can have many different meanings.
c. is largely denotative and simply says yes.
d. carries connotative meanings.

_____ **6.** Based on the passage, "snarl words" and "purr words"
a. describe people or events.
b. communicate denotative meanings.
c. reveal the speaker's feelings about people or events.
d. are highly positive.

Concept Maps and Charts

7. Complete the concept map with information from the passage.

Two Types of Language	
Denotation	**Connotation**
Objective descriptions	_____ associations
Nod of the head	Wink, smile, rapid rate of speech
Universal meanings	Extremely personal meanings
	Snarl and purr words

Implied Main Ideas and Implied Central Ideas

_____ **8.** Which sentence best states the implied main idea of the second paragraph (sentences 9–12)?
   a. Nonverbal language can also have denotative or connotative meanings.
   b. A nod of the head is an example of denotative language.
   c. A wink is an example of connotative language.
   d. Nonverbal language is powerful.

_____ **9.** Which sentence best states the implied main idea of the third paragraph (sentences 13–14)?
   a. Most people agree with denotative meanings.
   b. Most people disagree over connotative meanings.
   c. Denotative meanings are more widely agreed on than connotative meanings.
   d. Denotative and connotative meanings are very similar.

_____ **10.** Which sentence best states the implied central idea of the passage?
   a. Language has the ability to communicate many meanings.
   b. Verbal and nonverbal language express both denotation and connotation.
   c. Gestures are part of nonverbal language that can express both denotation and connotation.
   d. Racist language is an example of connotative meaning.

SUMMARY RESPONSE

Respond to the passage by stating the implied main idea in a thesis sentence. Be sure to identify the topic and the author's attitude about the topic. Begin your summary response with the following: *The most important idea of "Two Types of Language: Denotation and Connotation" by DeVito is…*

> **WHAT DO YOU THINK?**

Which type of meaning do you think is more powerful: denotative or connotative? When are we most likely to rely on the denotative meanings of words? When are we most likely to rely on connotative meanings of words? Assume you are a reporter for your college newspaper. You are writing an article about the issue of cheating in college. Write a paragraph that uses the denotative meanings of words to discuss how widespread the problem is and to explain why students might cheat. After you have written your paragraph, revise it to use connotative meanings to make your point. Share your work with a peer or small group of classmates. Discuss how the use of connotative and denotative meanings affected your writing.

After Reading About Implied Main Ideas and Implied Central Ideas

Before you move on to the Mastery Tests on implied main ideas and implied central ideas, take time to reflect on your learning and performance by answering the following questions. Write your answers in your notebook.

- What did I learn about implied main ideas and implied central ideas?
- What do I need to remember about implied main ideas and implied central ideas?
- How has my knowledge base or prior knowledge about implied main ideas changed?
- How has my knowledge base or prior knowledge about implied main ideas changed?
- Based on my studies, how do I think I will perform on the Mastery Test(s)? Why do I think my scores will be above average, average, or below average?
- Would I recommend this chapter to other students who want to learn more about implied main ideas? Why or why not?

Test your understanding of what you have learned about implied main ideas and implied central ideas by completing the Chapter 4 Review.

Name _____ Section _____

Date _____ **Score** (number correct) _____ x 25 = _____%

Visit MyReadingLab to take this test online and receive feedback and guidance on your answers.

A. Read and annotate the following paragraphs. In the spaces provided, use your own words to write the best statement of the main idea for each.

[1]Kickboxing as an aerobic exercise uses a bouncing base move. [2]Added to the base move are a variety of self-defense moves such as punches, kicks, and knee strikes. [3]Some cardio-kickboxing classes may also include sparring routines. [4]In addition, some kickboxing classes may incorporate traditional exercises, such as jumping jacks, leg lifts, push-ups, and abdominal crunches.

1. **Implied main idea:** _____

_____

_____

[1]Lassie, one of the most famous animals ever on television, became a beloved symbol of loyalty and courage. [2]The popular sitcom *Friends* featured Marcel the monkey, who came to be regarded by the character Ross as a friend as much as a pet. [3]Another successful sitcom, *Married with Children*, had a dog named Buck—the sole trapping of normality in that dysfunctional family. [4]And who can forget the Taco Bell Chihuahua, who helped sell countless tacos?

2. **Implied main idea:** _____

_____

[1]Mohandas Gandhi was a 20th-century leader of the Indian Nationalist movement. [2]Mahatma, or "great soul," was the name by which he became known later in his life. [3]His use of nonviolent confrontation, or civil disobedience, won freedom for his own people and influenced leaders around the world. [4]Gandhi believed in hard work and humility; he spun his own thread and wove the material for his clothes. [5]Gandhi fought for the rights of the imprisoned and impoverished.

3. **Implied main idea:** _____

_____

B. Read and annotate the following passage from a college health textbook. Write the central idea in the space provided.

Water: The Essential Nutrient

Textbook
Skills

¹Without water, you could live only about one week. ²About 65 to 70 percent of your body weight is made up of water in the form of blood, saliva, urine, cellular fluids, and digestive enzymes. ³In all these various forms, water helps transport nutrients, remove wastes, and control body temperature.

⁴Water carries nutrients along the digestive path and to the cells. ⁵First, it does this by liquefying food and moving it through the stomach, small intestine, and large intestine. ⁶When the food is absorbed into the blood, water plays an important role by regulating the amount of nutrients on both sides of the cell wall.

⁷Water needs vary, depending on the climate and a person's activity level. ⁸In a cold climate, the demand by the body for water is less than in a warm climate. ⁹An active person's demand for water is much greater than an inactive person's demand. ¹⁰Also, more water is needed at higher altitudes than at lower altitudes.

¹¹There are many ways to get liquid from your diet. ¹²The most obvious source is a glass of water. ¹³Most experts agree that six to eight glasses of water per day provide an adequate supply to an average adult. ¹⁴Other healthy beverages are skim or low-fat milk and fruit juices. ¹⁵In addition, many fruits and vegetables are excellent sources of water.

—Adapted from Pruitt, B. E. and Stein, Jane J., *Health Styles: Decisions for Living Well*, 2nd ed., p. 107.

4. **Implied central idea:** _____

_____

Name _____ Section _____

Date _____ **Score** (number correct) _____ x 33.3 = _____%

Read and annotate the following paragraphs. In the spaces provided, write the letter of the sentence that best states the implied main idea for each paragraph.

Paragraph from a college history textbook

Textbook
Skills

Growth of National Feelings

[1]Most modern revolutions have been prompted by strong national feelings, and most have resulted in independence. [2]In the case of the American Revolution, the desire to be free came before any national feeling. [3]The colonies did not enter into a political union because they felt an overwhelming desire to bring all Americans under one rule. [4]Instead they united as the only hope of winning a war against Great Britain. [5]The fact that the colonies chose to stay together after the war shows how much national feeling had developed during the war.

—Adapted from Garraty, John A. and Mark C. Carnes.
American Nation Single Volume Edition, p. 130.

_____ **1.** Which sentence best states the implied main idea?
   a. One result of the American Revolution was the growth of national feelings.
   b. Most wars are caused by national feelings.
   c. The American Revolution was caused by a need for independence.
   d. The fact that the colonies stayed united after the Revolutionary War was a miracle.

Paragraph from a college communications textbook

Textbook
Skills

Gestures

[1]In Texas the raised fist with little finger and index finger held upright is a positive expression of support, because it represents the Texas longhorn steer. [2]But in Italy it's an insult that means "Your spouse is having an affair with someone else." [3]In parts of South America it's a gesture to ward off evil, and in parts of Africa it's a curse: "May you experience bad times."

—DeVito, Joseph A., *Human Communication: The Basic Course*, 12th ed., p. 121.

_____ **2.** Which sentence best states the implied main idea?
   a. In Texas a raised fist with two fingers upright is a positive gesture.
   b. A raised fist with two fingers upright is a gesture found around the world.
   c. Different cultures see things differently.
   d. A raised fist with two fingers upright has different meanings in different cultures.

Paragraph from a college algebra textbook

Textbook
Skills

Three Ways to Study

[1]During systematic study, you begin studying on November 1 for an exam scheduled on November 15, and you continue to study every day until the day of the test. [2]During intense study, you wait until November 14 to begin studying, and you cram all day and through the night. [3]Which of these methods would produce a better result on an exam? [4]Research shows that students who are successful use a third system that combines the first two. [5]They study systematically well ahead of the test, but they also do intense study the day before the test. [6]This works so long as they don't stay up all night.

—Adapted from Bittinger, Marvin L. and Beecher, Judith A.
Introductory and Intermediate Algebra: Combined Approach, p. 805.

_____ **3.** Which sentence best states the implied main idea?
   a. Systematic study requires that a student begin studying weeks before a test.
   b. Intense study drives a student to "cram" the day before the test.
   c. The most effective study system combines systematic and intense study sessions.
   d. There are two basic ways to study for an exam: systematic and intense.

Name _____ Section _____

Date _____ **Score** (number correct) _____ x 25 = _____%

Visit MyReadingLab to take this test online and receive feedback and guidance on your answers.

Read and annotate the following paragraphs. In the spaces provided, use your own words to state the implied main idea.

Poem reprinted in a college literature textbook

To See a World in a Grain of Sand

by William Blake (1803)

Textbook
Skills

To see a world in a grain of sand
And a heaven in a wild flower,
Hold infinity in the palm of your hand
And eternity in an hour.

1. **Implied main idea:** _____

_____

Paragraph from a college social science textbook

Textbook
Skills

Audience Demand in Movie Markets

[1]In the early days, movies catered to the family audience. [2]From the era of the nickelodeon to the age of Panavision, mothers, fathers, and children flocked to neighborhood movie houses and to the theater palaces in the cities. [3]After the advent of television, as couples settled down to raise children in the suburbs, the movies became less attractive. [4]For parents, going to a movie meant paying for a babysitter, tickets, and transportation. [5]So, many chose to stay home and watch television. [6]Slowly, the audience changed. [7]From the late 1960s until the late 1990s, the 17-year-old was the most reliable moviegoer. [8]Now, aging baby boomers far outnumber teenagers in the United States and present a viable group for studios to target.

—Adapted from Jean Folkerts and Stephen Lacy, *The Media in Your Life: An Introduction to Mass Communication*, 2nd ed. Boston: Allyn and Bacon, 2001, p. 141.

2. **Implied main idea:** _____

_____

Paragraph from a college history textbook

America Isolated

Textbook Skills

¹America was isolated from Europe by 3,000 miles of ocean or, as a poet put it, "nine hundred leagues of roaring seas." ²The crossing took anywhere from a few weeks to several months, depending on wind and weather. ³No one undertook an ocean voyage lightly, and few who made the westward crossing ever thought seriously of returning. ⁴The modern mind can scarcely grasp the awful isolation that enveloped settlers. ⁵One had to build a new life or perish—if not of hunger, then of loneliness.

—Adapted from Garraty, John A. and Carnes, Mark C., *American Nation Single Volume Edition*, p. 38.

3. **Implied main idea:** _____

_____

Visual graphic or concept map from a college communications textbook

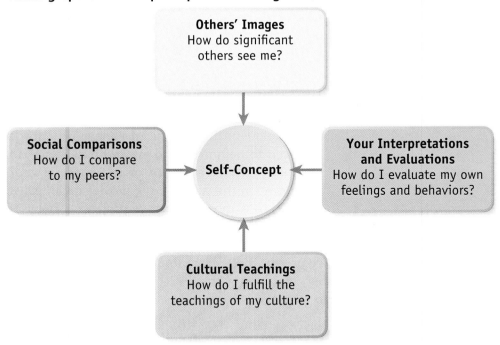

—Adapted from DeVito, Joseph A., *Interpersonal Communication Book*, p. 57.

4. **Implied main idea:** _____

_____

_____

4

Name _____ Section _____

Date _____ **Score** (number correct) _____ × 25 = _____%

Visit MyReadingLab to take this test online and receive feedback and guidance on your answers.

Read the following passage from a college sociology textbook. Answer the questions that follow.

Textbook
Skills

Managing Diversity in the Workplace

¹Times have changed. The San Jose, California, electronic phone book lists ten times more Nguyens than Joneses. ²More than half of U.S. workers are minorities, immigrants, and women. ³Diversity in the workplace is much more than skin color. ⁴Diversity includes ethnicity, gender, age, religion, social class, and sexual orientation.

⁵In our growing global context of life, diversity is increasing. ⁶In the past, the idea was for people to join the "melting pot," to give up their distinctive traits and become like the dominant group. ⁷Today, with the successes of the civil rights and women's movements, people are more likely to prize their distinctive traits. ⁸Realizing that assimilation (being absorbed into the dominant culture) is probably not the wave of the future, most large companies have "diversity training." ⁹They hold lectures and workshops so that employees can learn to work with colleagues of diverse cultures and racial-ethnic backgrounds.

¹⁰Consider the case of Coors Brewery. ¹¹Coors went into a financial tailspin after one of the Coors brothers gave a racially charged speech in the 1980s. ¹²Today, Coors offers diversity workshops, has sponsored a gay dance, and has paid for a corporate-wide mammography program. ¹³In 2004, Coors opposed an amendment to the Colorado constitution that would ban the marriage of homosexuals. ¹⁴The company has even had rabbis certify its suds as kosher. ¹⁵Its proud new slogan: "Coors cares." ¹⁶Now, that's quite a change.

¹⁷What Coors cares about, of course, is the bottom line. ¹⁸It's the same with other corporations.

¹⁹Blatant racism and sexism once made no difference to profitability. ²⁰Today, they do. ²¹To promote profitability, companies must promote diversity—or at least pretend to. ²²The sincerity of corporate leaders is not what's important; diversity in the workplace is.

²³Diversity training has the potential to build bridges. ²⁴However, managers who are chosen to participate can resent it, thinking that it is punishment for some unmentioned insensitivity on their part. ²⁵Some directors of these programs are so incompetent that they create antagonisms and

199

reinforce stereotypes. [26]For example, the leaders of a diversity training session at the U.S. Department of Transportation had women grope men as the men ran by. [27]They encouraged blacks and whites to insult one another and to call each other names. [28]The intention may have been good (understanding the other through role reversal and getting hostilities "out in the open"), but the approach was moronic. [29]Instead of healing, such behaviors wound and leave scars.

—Adapted from Henslin, James M., *Sociology: A Down to Earth Approach*, 9th ed., pp. 192–193.

_____ 1. Which sentence best states the implied main idea of the second paragraph (sentences 5–9)?
  a. Because of increased diversity of the workforce, diversity training in the workplace is becoming more popular.
  b. Diversity has occurred because of increased civil rights for minorities.
  c. Businesses are more diverse today than in the past.
  d. Assimilation no longer occurs.

_____ 2. Which sentence best states the implied main idea of the third paragraph (sentences 10–16)?
  a. Coors Brewery was a racist company at one time.
  b. Coors Brewery only changed to make money.
  c. Coors Brewery is a good example of a company that changed to meet the demands of diversity in the workplace and community.
  d. Coors Brewery produces kosher beer in honor of diversity.

_____ 3. Which sentence best states the implied main idea of the sixth paragraph (sentences 23–29)?
  a. Some managers resent diversity training.
  b. Incompetent managers create problems.
  c. Diversity training gets hostilities out in the open.
  d. Diversity training can backfire.

_____ 4. Which sentence best states the implied central idea of the passage?
  a. Diversity in the workplace is growing.
  b. Managing diversity in the workplace is good for business.
  c. Society has changed dramatically.
  d. Diversity in the workplace goes beyond skin color.

4 Summary of Key Concepts of Implied Main Ideas and Implied Central Ideas

Assess your comprehension of implied main ideas and implied central ideas.

▨ An implied main idea is a main idea that is _____ _____.

▨ To determine an implied main idea, ask three questions:

  ▨ _____?

  ▨ _____?

  ▨ _____?

▨ Implied main ideas must be neither too _____ nor too _____.

▨ To determine a main idea, _____ or mark the _____ and the words that reveal the author's _____ and thought patterns or types of _____ used in the passage.

▨ When the idea of several paragraphs is implied, it is called the _____ _____.

▨ To state an implied main idea of a paragraph, create a _____, a one-sentence summary of the details.

▨ To state an implied central point of a longer passage, create a _____ _____, a one-sentence summary of several paragraphs.

Test Your Comprehension of Implied Main Ideas

Respond to the following questions and prompts.

In your own words, what is an implied main idea? _____ _____ _____

LO1 LO2
LO3 LO4
LO5

Based on the instruction on pages 156 through 160, how can the skills you use to identify the stated main idea help you determine the implied main idea?

_____

_____

_____

_____

LO7

Identify and discuss the two most important ideas in this chapter that will help you improve your reading comprehension. _____

_____

_____

_____

LO2 LO3
LO4 LO6
LO7

Study the following concept map. Then write the implied main idea suggested by the details in the map.

Types of Driver Distractions

Texting	Eating	Petting an animal

Implied main idea: _____

_____

Supporting Details

LO LEARNING OUTCOMES

After studying this chapter, you should be able to:

- **LO1** Create Questions to Locate Supporting Details
- **LO2** Distinguish Between Major and Minor Details
- **LO3** Create a Summary from Annotations
- **LO4** Develop Textbook Skills: Chapter-End Questions in a Textbook
- **LO5** Apply Information Literacy Skills: Academic, Personal, and Career Applications of Supporting Details

Before Reading About Supporting Details

In Chapters 3 and 4, you learned several important ideas that will help you as you work through this chapter. Use the following questions to call up your prior knowledge about supporting details.

What is a main idea? (page 102) _____

_____

_____

What are the three parts of most paragraphs? (page 107) _____,

_____, and _____.

Define supporting details. (page 108) _____

_____

What are the different possible locations of topic sentences? (pages 114–123)

_____

_____

What is a central idea? (page 124) _____

_____

 ## Create Questions to Locate Supporting Details

To locate supporting details, an effective reader turns the main idea into a question by asking one of the following reporter's questions: *who, what, when, where, why,* or *how.* The answer to this question will yield a specific set of supporting details. For example, the question *why* is often answered by listing and explaining reasons or causes. The question *how* is answered by explaining a process. The answer to the question *when* is based on time order. An author strives to answer some or all of these questions with the details in the paragraph. You may want to try out several of the reporter's questions as you turn the main idea into a question. Experiment to discover which question is best answered by the details.

> **Supporting details** explain, develop, and illustrate the main idea.

Take, for example, the topic "dog bites." An author might choose to write about a few of the reasons a dog might bite someone. The main idea of such a paragraph may read as follows:

Main idea: In certain situations, a dog's natural aggression will make it more likely to bite.

Using the word *when* turns the main idea into the following question: "When is a dog likely to bite?" Read the following paragraph for the answers to this question.

A Dog's Natural Aggression

[1]In certain situations, a dog's natural aggression will make it more likely to bite. [2]For example, a dog may react aggressively if its personal space is invaded. [3]Therefore, a dog that is sleeping, eating, or nurturing its puppies may very well react with violence to defend itself, its food, or its offspring. [4]Aggression may also occur when a dog has been fenced in or tethered outside. [5]In these cases, the dog may feel easily frustrated or threatened and thus feel the urge to protect itself or its territory by biting. [6]A final situation that arouses the dog's animal aggression occurs when a person runs away in fear from a dog. [7]A dog's natural desire is to pursue prey; therefore, running past or away from a dog will almost always incite the animal to give chase and perhaps bite.

Controlling Point

Author's thought pattern   Author's attitude   Topic

In certain *situations*, a dog's *natural aggression* will make it more likely to bite.

First situation	Second situation	Third situation
A dog may react aggressively if its personal space is invaded.	Aggression may also occur when a dog has been fenced in or tethered outside.	Animal aggression occurs when a person runs away in fear from a dog.

The supporting details for this main idea answer the question "when?" by listing the situations that are likely to arouse a dog's aggression and lead to biting. Then the paragraph discusses why the dog behaves this way.

Note the relationship between the author's controlling point and the supporting details.

Notice also that the details about situations directly explain the main idea. However, additional supporting details were given in the paragraph that are not listed. Each of the main supporting details needed further explanation. This paragraph shows us that there are two kinds of supporting details: details that explain the main idea and details that explain other details.

▶ **EXAMPLE** Read the paragraph. Turn the topic sentence into a question using one of the reporter's questions (Who? What? When? Where? Why? How?). Write the question in the space provided. Fill in the graph with the answers to the question you have created.

The Healthful Traits of Olive Oil

[1]Olive oil has several traits that benefit our health. [2]First, olive oil is a monounsaturated fat. [3]Monounsaturated fats lower blood cholesterol levels; they keep arteries free of blockages, and they reduce the chances of heart attacks and strokes. [4]Second, olive oil contains antioxidants. [5]Just like rust on a car, oxidation damages our cells. [6]Antioxidants help prevent oxidation. [7]They also may help increase immune function; thus they may decrease risk of infection and cancer. [8]Third, olive oil also has polyphenols. [9]Polyphenols also strengthen the immune system and protect the body from infection. [10]They have been linked to preventing cancer and heart disease.

Question based on topic sentence: _____

_____

Topic sentence: Olive oil has several traits that benefit our health.

First trait/benefit	Second trait/benefit	Third trait/benefit
(1) _____	(2) _____	(3) _____
_____	_____	_____
_____	_____	_____
_____	_____	_____
_____	_____	
_____		

EXPLANATION Using the reporter's question *What?*, you should have turned the topic sentence into the following question: "What are the several traits of olive oil that benefit our health?" The answer to this question yields the supporting details. Compare your answers to the following: (1) Monounsaturated fats, (2) Antioxidants, and (3) Polyphenols.

Practice 1

Read the paragraph. Turn the topic sentence into a question using one of the reporter's questions (Who? What? When? Where? Why? How?). Write the question in the space provided. Fill in the graph with the answers to the question you have created.

Halitosis

[1]Halitosis, more commonly known as bad breath, occurs due to several specific circumstances. [2]As certain foods are digested, they result in bad breath. [3]Foods such as garlic and onions are absorbed into the bloodstream, carried to the lungs and expelled as bad breath through the mouth. [4]When dry mouth occurs and the flow of saliva decreases, bad breath occurs because saliva cleanses the mouth. [5]When oral hygiene is poor, bad breath is the result. [6]Improper brushing and flossing leaves food particles in the mouth. [7]In these instances, bacteria grows and creates sulfur compounds that also result in bad breath. [8]Finally, bad breath occurs when a medical disorder is present. [9]Bad breath may be a warning sign of infections of the sinuses or respiratory tract, liver or kidney problems, and diabetes.

Question based on topic sentence: _____

Topic sentence: Halitosis, more commonly known as bad breath, occurs due to several specific circumstances.

First circumstance	Second circumstance	Third circumstance	Fourth circumstance
(**1**) _____ _____	(**2**) When dry mouth occurs	(**3**) _____ _____	(**4**) When a medical disorder is present

LO2 Distinguish Between Major and Minor Details

A supporting detail will always be one of two types:

> A **major detail** directly explains, develops, or illustrates the *main idea*.
> A **minor detail** explains, develops, or illustrates a *major detail*.

A **major detail** is directly tied to the main idea. Without the major details, the author's main idea would not be clear because the major details are the principal points the author is making about the topic.

In contrast, a **minor detail** explains a major detail. The minor details could be left out, and the main idea would still be clear. Thus minor details are not as important as major details. Minor details are used to add interest and to give further descriptions, examples, testimonies, analysis, illustrations, and reasons for the major details. To better understand the flow of ideas, study the following diagram:

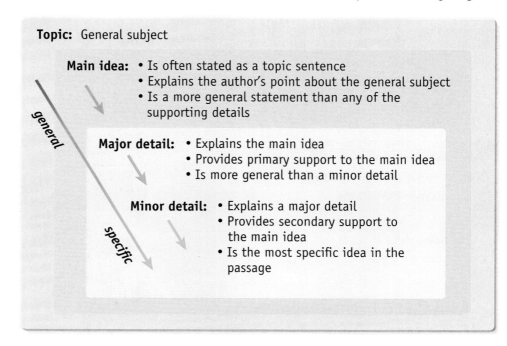

Topic: General subject

Main idea:
- Is often stated as a topic sentence
- Explains the author's point about the general subject
- Is a more general statement than any of the supporting details

Major detail:
- Explains the main idea
- Provides primary support to the main idea
- Is more general than a minor detail

Minor detail:
- Explains a major detail
- Provides secondary support to the main idea
- Is the most specific idea in the passage

general

specific

As ideas move from general to specific details, the author often uses signal words to introduce a new detail. These signal words—such as *first*, *second*, *next*, *in addition*, or *finally*—can help you identify major and minor details.

> **EXAMPLE** See if you can tell the difference between major and minor supporting details. Read the following paragraph from a college science textbook. Then complete the outline with the major and minor details from the paragraph.

What Is Earth Science?

Textbook
Skills

[1]**Earth science** is the name for all the sciences that collectively seek to understand Earth and its neighbors in space. [2]Earth science includes geology, oceanography, meteorology, and astronomy. [3]First, **geology** literally means "study of Earth" and is divided into two broad areas—physical and historical. [4]*Physical geology* examines the materials comprising the Earth and the many processes that operate beneath and upon its surfaces. [5]In contrast to physical geology, the aim of *historical geology* is to understand the origin of Earth and the development of the planet through its 4.5-billion-year history. [6]Another Earth science is oceanography. [7]**Oceanography** includes all the study of the composition and movement of sea water, as well as coastal processes, seafloor topography, and marine life. [8]Oceanography is actually not a separate and distinct science. [9]Rather, it involves the application of all sciences in the study of the ocean. [10]A third Earth science is meteorology. [11]**Meteorology** is the study of the atmosphere and the processes that produce weather and climate. [12]Like oceanography, meteorology involves the application of all other sciences. [13]Finally, because Earth is related to all the other objects in space, the science of **astronomy**

VISUAL *VOCABULARY*

Doppler radar is a tool used by _____ to monitor storms.

a. oceanographers
b. astronomers
c. meteorologists

is very useful. [14]Astronomy is the study of the universe. [15]Indeed, Earth is subject to the same physical laws that govern the many other objects populating the great expanses of space.

—Adapted from Lutgens, Frederick K., Tarbuck, Edward J., and Tasa, Dennis G., *Foundations of Earth Science,* 5th ed., pp. 2–3.

Outline of "What Is Earth Science?"

Stated main idea: **Earth science** is the name for all the sciences that collectively seek to understand Earth and its neighbors in space.

A. _____

   _____

   1. *Physical geology* examines the materials comprising the Earth and the many processes that operate beneath and upon its surfaces.

   2. _____

   _____

   _____

B. _____

   1. Oceanography includes all the study of the composition and movement of sea water, as well as coastal processes, seafloor topography, and marine life.

   2. _____

   3. Rather, it involves the application of all sciences in the study of the ocean.

C. _____

   1. _____

   _____

   2. Like oceanography, meteorology involves the application of all other sciences.

D. _____

   _____

   1. Astronomy is the study of the universe.

   2. _____

   _____

EXPLANATION   The major details are sentences 3, 6, 10, and 13. Note that each of these major details is signaled by a transition: *First* (sentence 3), *Another* (sentence 6), *A third* (sentence 10), and *Finally* (sentence 13). Each of these major details is explained with minor supporting details. For example, the major detail "geology" is further defined by being divided into two subgroups. Thus, sentences 4 and 5 offer minor details about these two subtopics of geology: physical geology and historical geology. The other minor details in this paragraph are sentences 7, 8, 11, 12, 14, and 15. Note that some of these minor details are also introduced with transitions: *In contrast* (sentence 5), *Like* (sentence 12), and *Indeed* (sentence 15).

Practice 2

Read the following passage from a popular online site for health information. Then identify the major and minor details by completing the outline that follows it.

What Is Insomnia?

¹Insomnia (in-SOM-ne-ah) is a common condition in which you have trouble falling or staying asleep. ²This condition can range from mild to severe, depending on how often it occurs and the type of insomnia it is.

³Insomnia can be chronic (ongoing) or acute (short-term). ⁴Chronic insomnia means having symptoms at least 3 nights a week for more than a month. ⁵Acute insomnia lasts for less time. ⁶Some people who have insomnia may have trouble falling asleep. ⁷Other people may fall asleep easily but wake up too soon. ⁸Others may have trouble with both falling asleep and staying asleep. ⁹As a result, insomnia may cause you to get too little sleep or have poor-quality sleep. ¹⁰You may not feel refreshed when you wake up.

¹¹There are two types of insomnia. ¹²The most common type is called secondary or comorbid insomnia. ¹³This type of insomnia is a symptom or side effect of some other problem. ¹⁴More than 8 out of 10 people who have insomnia are believed to have secondary insomnia. ¹⁵Certain medical conditions, medicines, sleep disorders, and substances can cause secondary insomnia. ¹⁶In contrast, primary insomnia isn't due to a medical problem, medicines, or other substances. ¹⁷It is its own disorder. ¹⁸A number of life changes can trigger primary insomnia, including long-lasting stress and emotional upset.

¹⁹Finally, if you have insomnia, you may experience a variety of symptoms. ²⁰Insomnia can cause excessive daytime sleepiness and a lack

of energy. [21]It also can make you feel anxious, depressed, or irritable. [22]You may have trouble focusing on tasks, paying attention, learning, and remembering. [23]This can prevent you from doing your best at work or school. [24]Insomnia also can cause other serious problems. [25]For example, you may feel drowsy while driving, which could lead to an accident.

—U.S. Department of Health and Human Services and
National Institutes of Health. "What Is Insomnia?"
Disease and Conditions Index. March 2009.

Stated main idea: This condition can range from mild to severe, depending on how often it occurs and the type of insomnia it is.

A. _____

1. Chronic insomnia means having symptoms at least 3 nights a week for more than a month.

2. _____

3. Some people who have insomnia may have trouble falling asleep.

4. Other people may fall asleep easily but wake up too soon.

5. Others may have trouble with both falling asleep and staying asleep.

   a. _____

   _____

   b. You may not feel refreshed when you wake up.

B. _____

1. _____

   a. This type of insomnia is a symptom or side effect of some other problem.

   b. More than 8 out of 10 people who have insomnia are believed to have secondary insomnia.

   c. _____

   _____

2. _____

   _____

   a. It is its own disorder.

   b. _____

   _____

C. _____

1. Insomnia can cause excessive daytime sleepiness and a lack of energy.

2. It also can make you feel anxious, depressed, or irritable.

3. You may have trouble focusing on tasks, paying attention, learning, and remembering.

4. This can prevent you from doing your best at work or school.

5. Insomnia also can cause other serious problems.

6. _____

 ## Create a Summary from Annotations

Reading for main ideas and major supporting details is an excellent study technique. After you finish reading, an effective strategy to deepen your understanding and provide study notes for review is to write down main ideas and major supporting details in a summary. (For more reading strategies see Chapter 1.) A **summary** condenses a paragraph or passage to only its primary points by restating the main idea, major supporting details, and important examples. Often you will want to paraphrase, that is, restate the ideas in your own words. Other times, you may need to use the exact language of the text to ensure accuracy. For example, scientific or medical terms have precise meanings that must be memorized; thus your summaries of these types of ideas would include the original language of the text.

Drafting a Summary: Stated Main Ideas

The length of a summary will vary, depending on the length of the original text.

> A **summary** is a brief, clear restatement of the most important points of a paragraph or passage.

For example, a paragraph can be summarized in one sentence or a few sentences. A passage of several paragraphs can be reduced to one paragraph, and a much longer selection such as a chapter in a textbook may require a summary of a page or two.

To create a summary after reading, you can **annotate**, or mark, your text during reading. For example, as you read, circle the main idea and underline the major supporting details and important examples. To learn more about annotating a text, see pages 658–659 in Part Two.

> **EXAMPLE** Read the following paragraph from a college accounting textbook. Circle the main idea, and underline the major supporting details. Then complete the summary.

Liquid Assets

Textbook
Skills

¹Liquid assets are financial assets that can be easily sold without a loss in value. ²They are especially useful for covering upcoming expenses. ³Some of the more common liquid assets are cash, checking accounts, and savings accounts. ⁴Cash is handy to cover small purchases, while a checking account is convenient for large purchases. ⁵Savings accounts are desirable because they pay interest on the money that is deposited. ⁶For example, if your savings account offers an interest rate of 4 percent, you earn annual interest of $4 for every $100 deposited in your account.

—Madura, Jeff, *Personal Finance*, 2nd ed., p. 40.

Summary: Liquid assets are _____

_____

For example, three types are _____

EXPLANATION The main idea about the topic "liquid assets" is stated in the first sentence, which is the topic sentence of the paragraph: "Liquid assets are financial assets that can be easily sold without a loss in value." The paragraph goes on to list the following examples: cash, checking accounts, and savings accounts. Compare your summary to the following: Liquid assets are financial assets that can be easily sold without a loss in value. For example, three types are cash, checking accounts, and savings accounts. <

Practice 3

Read the following paragraph from a college health textbook. Circle the main idea, and underline the major supporting details. Complete the summary by filling in the blanks with information from the passage.

The Body's Response to Stress

Textbook
Skills

¹Whenever we are surprised by a sudden stressor, such as someone swerving into our lane of traffic, the adrenal glands jump into action.

²These two almond-shaped glands sitting atop the kidneys secrete adrenaline and other hormones into the bloodstream. ³As a result, the heart speeds up, breathing rate increases, blood pressure elevates, and the flow of blood to the muscles increases. ⁴This sudden burst of energy and strength is believed to provide the extra edge that has helped generations of humans survive during adversity. ⁵This response is believed to be one of our most basic, innate survival instincts. ⁶Known as the **fight or flight response**, this physiological reaction prepares the body to combat a real or perceived threat. ⁷It is a point at which our bodies go on the alert to either fight or escape.

—Donatelle, Rebecca J., *Health: The Basics,* 5th ed., p. 54.

Summary: The **fight or flight response** is a _____ reaction that prepares the body to combat a real or perceived threat. For example, someone swerving into our lane of traffic triggers the _____ glands to speed up the _____, increase _____ rate, elevate blood pressure, and increase the flow of blood to the _____.

Drafting a Summary: Implied Main Ideas

At times, a textbook author may choose to imply a main idea instead of directly stating it. As you learned in Chapter 4, you can use supporting details to create a topic sentence or thesis statement when the main idea or central point is implied. Annotating your text will also help you create a summary for passages with an implied main idea.

First, identify the topic of the passage. Underline recurring words or phrases. Locate each heading or major supporting detail in the passage. (Remember, minor details explain or support major details. Thus, to create a summary, you can ignore these minor details.) Assign a number or letter to each of the headings or major details you identified. Next, for each piece of information you have marked, ask the question "What controlling point or opinion about the topic does this detail reveal?" Often, a main heading can be turned into a question that will help you determine the implied main idea. Then write a brief answer to each question in the margin next to the detail you marked. After you finish reading, create a topic sentence or thesis statement for the passage. Use only a few brief sentences to create the entire summary.

> **EXAMPLE** Read the following passage taken from a college education textbook. As you read, complete the following steps. Then create a summary of the passage in the space provided after the passage.

Step 1: Annotate the text. Underline the recurring key terms or phrases and label the major supporting details with a number or letter.

Step 2: Turn the main heading into a question in the box below to determine the implied main idea. If needed, turn major details into questions that reveal the author's controlling point.

Step 3: Answer each question in your own words in the box below.

Step 4: Create a thesis statement based on the main heading and/or supporting details.

Step 5: Write a summary that combines the thesis statement and the major supporting details in one or a few brief sentences.

Textbook
Skills

Intelligence

[1]Intelligence has yet to be completely defined. [2]One view is that intelligence is the ability to learn. [3]As David Wechsler, the developer of the most widely used intelligence scales for children and adults, said: "Intelligence, operationally defined, is the aggregate or global capacity to act purposefully, to think rationally, and to deal effectively with the environment." [4]Other views on intelligence include the following:

- [5]It is *adaptive.* [6]It involves modifying and adjusting one's behavior to accomplish new tasks successfully.
- [7]It is related to *learning ability.* [8]Intelligent people learn information more quickly and easily than less intelligent people.
- [9]It involves the *use of prior knowledge* to analyze and understand new situations effectively.
- [10]It involves the complex interaction and coordination of *many different thinking and reasoning processes*.
- [11]It is *culture-specific.* [12]What is "intelligent" behavior in one culture is not necessarily intelligent behavior in another culture.

—Parkay, Forrest, W. and Beverly Stanford.
Becoming a Teacher, p. 300.

Summary: _____

_____

_____

_____

EXPLANATION In this passage, the heading of the passage gives a great clue about the implied main idea. Think about the following question based on the heading, "What is intelligence?" To answer this question, you have to number the major supporting details. The italic print and bullets make locating and numbering these details quite easy. All the supporting details describe intelligence as a mental ability. However, the author states that intelligence is hard to define and offers various views of intelligence. These various views indicate that intelligence is a complex mental ability. So, very quickly, you can answer the question based on the heading: "Intelligence is a complex mental ability." This answer states the central point of the passage. By using your own words to combine the thesis statement and the major supporting details, you create your summary. ◄

Practice 4

Read the following passage based on information from the Centers for Disease Control. As you read, annotate the text by underlining recurring key phrases and numbering the major supporting details. Turn the main heading and major details into questions. Then create a summary of the passage in the space provided after the passage by answering your questions.

_____

_____

The Problem of Distracted Driving

[1]Each day, more than 15 people are killed and more than 1,200 people are injured in crashes that were reported to involve a distracted driver. [2]Distracted driving is driving while doing another activity that takes your attention away from driving. [3]It increases your chances of being involved in a motor vehicle crash.

   [4]There are three main types of distraction:

1. [5]Visual distractions take your eyes off the road. [6]Looking at pretty scenery or gawking at an accident on the side of the road is a visual distraction.

2. [7]Manual distractions take your hands off the wheel. [8]Reaching for something on the passenger seat or in the back seat is a manual distraction.

3. [9]Cognitive distractions take your mind off driving. [10]Daydreaming or thinking about an argument you had with your girlfriend or boyfriend is a cognitive distraction.

[11]All-too-common distracted driving activities include using a cell phone, texting, and eating. [12]Using in-vehicle technologies (such as navigation systems) can also be sources of distraction. [13]While any of these distractions can endanger the driver and others, texting while driving is especially dangerous because it combines all three types of distraction.

<http://www.cdc.gov/Motorvehiclesafety/
Distracted_Driving/index.html>

Summary: _____

_____

_____

_____

LO4 ## Develop Textbook Skills: Chapter-End Questions in a Textbook

Textbook
Skills

Textbooks often provide questions at the end of a chapter or section to help you identify and remember the most important points. In addition, the answers to questions at the end of a section summarize its main idea and major supporting details. Often, to deepen learning, the chapter-end questions will ask you to give some examples of minor details. As you read, annotate your text by marking content words, main ideas, and major supporting details. These key ideas will help you answer the chapter-end questions. Some students look at the chapter-end questions before they read as a guide to finding out what is most important. These students use chapter-end questions before, during, and after reading.

> **EXAMPLE** Read the following section from the college textbook *Introduction to Mass Communications,* 12th ed. Turn the heading into a question. Annotate the text as you read by underlining main ideas, circling content words, and underlining their definitions. Then answer the questions.

What Communication Means

[1]Each of us communicates with another person by directing a message to one or more of the person's senses—sight, sound, touch, taste, or smell. [2]This is known as *interpersonal communication,* in contrast to *intrapersonal communication,* in which one "talks to oneself." [3]When we smile, we communicate a desire for friendliness; the tone in which we say "good morning" can indicate feelings all the way from surliness to warm pleasure; and the words we choose in speaking or writing convey a message we want to "put across" to the other person. [4]The more effectively we select and deliver these words, the better the communication.

[5]In today's complex society, one-to-one communication frequently is inadequate. [6]To be effective, our important messages must reach numerous people at one time. [7]The next step is *group communication,* such as when a homeowner couple invite their neighbors for coffee in order to propose a neighborhood improvement plan. [8]If the sponsoring couple convinces a local television news program to air a story about the project, thousands of people learn about it. [9]This is *mass communication.*

[10]The success of the message, in all phases of communication, depends on the *frame of reference,* that is, the life experience and mind-set of both the sender and receiver of the message. [11]The more these frames of reference overlap, the more likely there will be understanding and possible acceptance of the message. [12]One-to-one communication has heavy overlap when people are close friends or agree wholeheartedly on the subject of interpersonal discussion. [13]As the size of the receiving audience grows, these attributes decline. [14]So does the degree of interpersonal success.

[15]For example, a news story about plans by Congress to increase unemployment benefits raises hope in the mind of a person who fears being laid off a job; the same dispatch may disturb a struggling entrepreneur who sees in it the possibility of higher taxes.

[16]Similarly, when a presidential candidate appears on a national TV talk show he reaches millions of voters, vastly more than he could through handshaking tours. [17]His use of mass communication may be a comparative failure, however, if he is unable to project over the air the same feeling of sincerity and ability that he displays through a handshake and a smile in personal contacts.

[18]The art of mass communication, then, is much more difficult than that of face-to-face discussion. [19]The communicator who is addressing thousands of different personalities simultaneously cannot adjust an appeal to meet their individual reactions. [20]An approach that convinces

one part of the audience may alienate another part. [21]The successful mass communicator is one who finds the right method of expression to establish empathy with the largest possible number of individuals in the audience. [22]Psychological research and knowledge of communication theory help the speaker to "push the right buttons."

—Agee, Warren K. et al., *Introduction to Mass Communications*, pp. 64–65.

1. What is interpersonal communication? _____

   _____

   _____

2. What is intrapersonal communication? _____

   _____

3. When does group communication occur? _____

   _____

4. When does mass communication occur? _____

   _____

5. How and why does "frame of reference" affect communication? _____

   _____

   _____

   _____

EXPLANATION   To answer these questions, you should have circled the following terms and underlined their definitions: *interpersonal communication, intrapersonal communication, group communication, mass communication,* and *frame of reference.* Compare your answers to the chapter-end questions with the following:

1. What is interpersonal communication? Interpersonal communication is directing a message to one or more of another person's senses—sight, sound, touch, taste, or smell.

2. What is intrapersonal communication? Intrapersonal communication occurs when one talks to one self.

3. When does group communication occur? <u>Group communication occurs</u>
   <u>when a message must reach numerous people at one time.</u>

4. When does mass communication occur? <u>Mass communication occurs when</u>
   <u>a message must reach thousands of people.</u>

5. How and why does "frame of reference" affect communication? <u>Frame of</u>
   <u>reference is made up of the life experiences and mind-sets of the people</u>
   <u>communicating. Understanding and accepting a message is more likely if the</u>
   <u>message is based on a shared frame of reference.</u>

Practice 5

Read the following section from a college law textbook. Annotate the text as
you read by underlining the main ideas, circling the content words, and underlining their definitions. Then answer the questions.

The Mental Element of Crime

[1]The mental element is known as the *mens rea*, or mental state, of
the defendant. [2]Sometimes this is referred to as the "guilty mind" of the
defendant, or the defendant's criminal intent. [3]Under the Model Penal
Code, four states of mind fulfill the *mens rea* requirement: purposeful,
knowing, reckless, and negligent.

[4]A purposeful act occurs when the defendant acts with the desire to
cause the result. [5]For example, suppose the defendant shot a gun at the
victim, intending to shoot him. [6]This is a purposeful act.

[7]A knowing act occurs when the defendant acts with the knowledge
that the result is almost certain to occur. [8]The difference between a purposeful act and a knowing act is that the knowing actor is not acting to
cause the result. [9]For example, suppose a defendant fired a gun into a
crowded room. [10]He knew that he would almost certainly shoot a person.
[11]However, he did not intend harm to any specific victim. [12]This is thus a
knowing act rather than a purposeful act.

[13]A reckless act occurs when the defendant acts with a conscious disregard that a substantial and unjustifiable risk will result. [14]For example,
suppose that at a public park on the Fourth of July, the defendant fired
his gun into the air and the bullet struck and injured a child. [15]This is a
reckless act.

[16]A negligent act occurs when the defendant acts with a substantial and unjustifiable risk. [17]However, there is no conscious disregard of

the risk. [18]For example, suppose that a defendant's 1,000-acre ranch was clearly posted with "No Trespassing" signs; no one should have been on the ranch on the Fourth of July. [19]The defendant fired his gun into the air and the bullet struck and injured a trespasser. [20]This is a negligent act.

—Hames, Joanne B. and Ekern, Yvonne, *Introduction to Law,* 4th ed., pp. 346–347.

1. What is *mens rea*? _____
   _____

2. When is the *mens rea* a purposeful act? _____
   _____

3. What is a knowing act and how does it differ from a purposeful act?
   _____
   _____
   _____

4. When does a reckless act occur? _____
   _____

5. When does a negligent act occur? _____
   _____
   _____

Apply Information Literacy Skills

LO5 ### Academic, Personal, and Career Applications of Supporting Details

The ability to identify supporting details is another part of information literacy. Now that you have mastered the ability to locate and determine stated and implied main ideas, you can also use supporting details to access and connect information to the main idea. Understanding how to locate and evaluate supporting details will help in your academic, personal, and career lives. You will come across a wide range of documents such as essays, articles, reports, memos, or e-mails. You will be expected to pay attention to the supporting details in these documents. Thus, you will use the skills that you have learned in this chapter in several ways:

- Identify your own need to know the supporting details.
- Locate key supporting details.
- Restate the key details supporting the author's main idea in your own words.
- Apply key supporting details to your specific situation.

Academic Application

Assume you are taking a college biology course. You are working with several classmates on a group presentation to be given in class. Your group chose the topic "Requirements for Life." You begin your research with information from your textbook.

- **Before Reading:** In the table of contents, highlight the title of the section that relates to your topic. Then skim the passage from that chapter section. Create a pre-reading question to guide your reading.
- **During Reading:** Annotate the text. Underline the topic sentence and major supporting details that answer the pre-reading question.
- **After Reading:** In the notecard following the passage, write a summary of the main idea and major supporting details.

Pre-Reading Question: _____

[1]Earth teems with life. Consider, for example, the lichens on Arctic rocks, the heat-loving algae in the hot springs of Yellowstone National Park, the bacteria thriving under the pressure-cooker conditions of a deep-sea vent, and the great diversity of ocean coral reefs and tropical rain forests. [2]These habitats all share the ability to provide, to varying degrees, four basic, needed requirements for life.

- [3]Nutrients from which to construct living tissue.
- [4]Energy to power metabolic activities.
- [5]Liquid water to serve as a medium in which metabolic activities occur.
- [6]Appropriate temperatures at which to carry out these processes.

[7]These necessities are unevenly distributed over Earth's surface. [8]This unevenness limits the types of life that can exist within the various terrestrial (land) and aquatic ecosystems on Earth.

[9]Communities within the various ecosystems are extraordinarily diverse. [10]However, clear patterns emerge. [11]Variations in temperature and in the availability of light, water, and nutrients shape the adaptations of organisms that inhabit each ecosystem. [12]Desert communities, for example, are dominated by plants adapted to heat and drought. [13]The cacti of the Mojave Desert in the American Southwest are similar to the euphorbias of the Canary Islands off the northwest African coast. [14]However, these plants are only distantly related. [15]Their reduced leaves and thick, water-storing stems are adaptations for dry climates. [16]Likewise, the plants of the arctic tundra and those of the alpine tundra on high mountaintops show growth patterns that are clearly adaptations to a cold, dry, windy climate.

—Adapted from Audesirk, Teresa, Gerald
Audesirk, and Bruce E. Byers, _Biology:
Life on Earth_, 5th ed., pp. 557–558.

Summary Notecard: _____

_____

_____

_____

Personal Application

Assume your (or a family member's) recent lab results indicate a diagnosis of diabetes. To prepare for your next visit with your physician, you have accessed a website for information about diabetes and what to ask the doctor.

- **Before Reading:** Skim the screenshot of the webpage. Circle the topics that link to specific details about which you want more information.

- **During Reading:** Underline the major details in the article that explain diabetes.

- **After Reading:** In the space following the passage, restate the major details. Then create two questions to ask the doctor to learn additional specific details about diabetes.

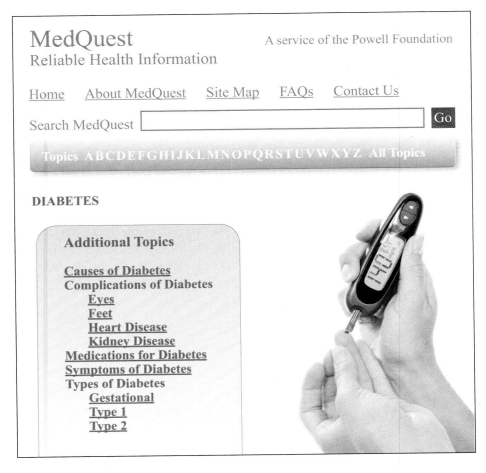

Diabetes

[1]Diabetes is a disease in which your blood glucose, or sugar, levels are too high. [2]Glucose comes from the foods you eat. [3]Insulin is a hormone that helps the glucose get into your cells to give them energy. [4]With type 1 diabetes, your body does not make insulin. [5]With type 2 diabetes, the more common type, your body does not make or use insulin well. [6]Without enough insulin, the glucose stays in your blood.

[7]Over time, having too much glucose in your blood can cause serious problems. [8]It can damage your eyes, kidneys, and nerves. [9]Diabetes can also cause heart disease, stroke and even the need to remove a limb. [10]Pregnant women can also get diabetes, called gestational diabetes. [11]Exercise, weight control and sticking to your meal plan can help control your diabetes. [12]You should also monitor your glucose level and take medicine if prescribed.

—NIH: National Institute of Diabetes and Digestive and Kidney.
<http://www.nlm.nih.gov/medlineplus/diabetes.html>

Major Details: _____

_____

_____

_____

_____

Questions for Doctor: _____

_____

Career Application

Assume you own a local café and catering business. The Occupational Safety and Health Administration dictates the placement of fire extinguishers based on the fire risks. You have accessed the U.S. Government Fire Administration website to learn about equipping your business with fire extinguishers.

- **Before Reading:** Skim the information. Create two pre-reading questions to guide your hunt for details that are relevant to your situation.
- **During Reading:** Underline the details that answer your pre-reading questions.

■ **After Reading:** In the space following the passage, record the type(s) of fire extinguishers you need. State your reasons.

■ **Pre-reading Questions:** _____

_____

Types of Fire Extinguishers

Class A extinguishers put out fires in ordinary combustible materials such as cloth, wood, rubber, paper, and many plastics.

A
Ordinary
Combustibles

Class B extinguishers are used on fires involving flammable liquids, such as grease, gasoline, oil, and oil-based paints.

B
Flammable
Liquids

Class C extinguishers are suitable for use on fires involving appliances, tools, or other equipment that is electrically energized or plugged in.

C
Electrical
Equipment

Class D extinguishers are designed for use on flammable metals and are often specific for the type of metal in question. These are typically found only in factories working with these metals.

D
Combustible
Metals

Class K fire extinguishers are intended for use on fires that involve vegetable oils, animal oils, or fats in cooking appliances. These extinguishers are generally found in commercial kitchens, such as those found in restaurants, cafeterias, and caterers. Class K extinguishers are now finding their way into the residential market for use in kitchens.

K
Combustible
Cooking

There are also multi-purpose fire extinguishers - such as those labeled "B-C" or "A-B-C" - that can be used on two or more of the above type fires.

<www.usfa.fema.gov/citizens/home_fire_prev/
extinguishers.shtm>

Fire Extinguishers Needed: _____

_____

_____

_____

REVIEW TEST 1

Score (number correct) _____ × 20 = _____ %

Visit MyReadingLab to take this test online and receive feedback and guidance on your answers.

Main Ideas, Major and Minor Supporting Details

Read the following passage from a college sociology textbook. Then answer the questions that follow.

Fads

Textbook
Skills

¹A fad is a novel form of behavior that briefly catches people's attention. ²The new behavior appears suddenly and spreads by imitation and identification with people who are already involved. ³Reports by the mass media help to spread the fad, which, after a short life, fades away, although it may reappear from time to time (Best 2006).

⁴Fads come in many forms. ⁵Very short, intense fads are called *crazes.* ⁶They appear suddenly and are gone almost as quickly. ⁷"Tickle Me Elmo" dolls and Beanie Babies were *object crazes.* ⁸There also are *behavior crazes,* such as streaking: As a joke, an individual or a group runs nude in some public place. ⁹This craze lasted only a couple of months in 1974. ¹⁰"Flash mobs" was a behavior craze of 2003; alerted by e-mail messages, individuals would gather at a specified time, do something, such as point toward the ceiling of a mall, and then, without a word, disperse. ¹¹As fads do, this one has reappeared (Urbina 2010b).

¹²Administrators of businesses and colleges also get caught up in fads. ¹³For about ten years, quality circles were a fad. ¹⁴These were supposedly effective in getting workers and management to work together in developing innovative techniques to increase production. ¹⁵Peaking in 1983, this fad quickly dropped from sight (Strang and Macy 2001). ¹⁶There are also fads in child rearing—permissive versus directive, spanking versus nonspanking. ¹⁷Our food is subject to fads as well: tofu, power drinks, herbal supplements. ¹⁸Fads in dieting also come and go, with many seeking the perfect diet, and practically all leaving the fad diet disillusioned.

¹⁹Fads can involve millions of people. ²⁰In the 1950s, the hula hoop was so popular that stores couldn't keep them in stock. ²¹Children cried and pleaded for these brightly colored plastic hoops. ²²Across the nation, children—and even adults—held contests to see who could keep the

hoops up the longest or who could rotate the most hoops at one time. [23]Then, in a matter of months it was over, and parents wondered what to do with these items, which seemed useless for any other purpose. [24]Hula hoops can again be found in toy stores, but now they are just another toy.

[25]When a fad lasts, it is called a fashion. [26]Some fashions, as with clothing and furniture, are the result of a coordinated marketing system that includes designers, manufacturers, advertisers, and retailers. [27]By manipulating the tastes of the public, they sell billions of dollars of products. [28]Fashion, however, also refers to hairstyles, to the design and colors of buildings, and even to the names that parents give their children (Lieberson 2000).

[29]Sociologist John Lofland (1985) pointed out that fashion also applies to common expressions, as demonstrated by these roughly comparable terms: "Neat!" in the 1950s, "Right on!" in the 1960s, "Really!" in the 1970s, "Awesome!" in the 1980s, "Bad!" in the 1990s, "Sweet" and "Tight" in the early 2000s, "Hot" in the middle 2000s, "Sick" in the late 2000s, and, recurringly, "Cool."

—Henslin, James M., *Sociology:
A Down-to-Earth Approach*, 11th ed., p. 614.

_____ 1. Sentence 4 is a
   a. main idea.
   b. major supporting detail.
   c. minor supporting detail.

_____ 2. Sentence 5 is a
   a. main idea.
   b. major supporting detail.
   c. minor supporting detail.

_____ 3. Sentence 19 is a
   a. main idea.
   b. major supporting detail.
   c. minor supporting detail.

_____ 4. Sentence 24 is a
   a. main idea.
   b. major supporting detail.
   c. minor supporting detail.

_____ 5. The central idea is stated in
   a. sentence 1.
   b. sentence 2.
   c. sentence 3.
   d. sentence 25.

REVIEW TEST 2

Score (number correct) _____ × 25 = _____%

Visit MyReadingLab to take this test online and receive feedback and guidance on your answers.

Main Ideas, Major and Minor Supporting Details

Read the following passage from a college film studies textbook. Then answer the questions that follow.

Textbook
Skills

Film Acting

[1]Acting in the cinema is almost totally dependent on the filmmaker's approach to the story materials. [2]In general, the more realistic the director's techniques, the more necessary it is to rely on the abilities of the players. [3]Such directors tend to favor long shots, which keep the performer's entire body within the frame. [4]The realist also tends to favor lengthy takes—thus permitting the actors to sustain performances for relatively long periods without interruption. [5]From the audience's point of view, it's easier to evaluate acting in a realistic movie because we are permitted to see sustained scenes without any apparent directorial interference. [6]The camera remains essentially a recording device.

[7]The more formalistic the director, the less likely he or she is to value the actor's contribution. [8]Some of Hitchcock's most stunning cinematic effects were achieved by minimizing the contributions of actors. [9]During the production of *Sabotage*, Hitchcock's leading lady, Sylvia Sidney, burst into tears on the set because she wasn't permitted to act a crucial scene. [10]The episode involved a murder in which the sympathetic heroine kills her brutish husband in revenge for his murder of her young brother. [11]On stage, of course, the heroine's feelings and thoughts would be communicated by words and the actress's exaggerated facial expression. [12]But in real life, Hitchcock observed, people's faces don't necessarily reveal what they think or feel. [13]The director preferred to convey these ideas and emotions through edited juxtapositions.

[14]The setting for the scene is a dinner table. [15]The heroine looks at her husband, who is eating as usual. [16]Then a close-up shows a dish containing meat and vegetables with a knife and fork lying next to it; the wife's hands are seen behind the dish. [17]Hitchcock then cuts to a medium shot of the wife thoughtfully slicing some meat. [18]Next, a medium shot of the brother's empty chair. [19]Close-up of the wife's hands with knife and fork. [20]Close-up of a bird cage with canaries—a reminder to the heroine

of her dead brother. [21]Close-up of wife's thoughtful face. [22]Close-up of the knife and plate. [23]Suddenly a close-up of the husband's suspicious face: He notices the connection between the knife and her thoughtful expression, for the camera pans, rather than cuts, back to the knife. [24]He gets up next to her. [25]Hitchcock quickly cuts to a close-up of her hand reaching for the knife. [26]Cut to an extreme close-up of the knife entering his body. [27]Cut to a two-shot of their faces, his convulsed with pain, hers in fear. [28]When Sylvia Sidney saw the finished product, she was delighted with the results. [29]The entire scene, of course, required very little acting in the conventional sense of the term.

—Giannetti, Louis, *Understanding Movies*, 12th ed., p. 243.

_____ 1. Which sentence is the thesis statement that states the topic and the author's controlling point about the topic?
a. sentence 1   c. sentence 3
b. sentence 2

_____ 2. In the second paragraph, sentence 7 serves as a _____ for the paragraph.
a. main idea   c. minor supporting detail
b. major supporting detail

_____ 3. In the second paragraph, sentence 8 serves as a _____ for the paragraph.
a. main idea   c. minor supporting detail
b. major supporting detail

_____ 4. Sentence 9 is a
a. main idea.   c. minor supporting detail.
b. major supporting detail.

REVIEW TEST 3

Score (number correct) _____ × 20 = _____%

Visit MyReadingLab to take this test online and receive feedback and guidance on your answers.

Main Ideas and Supporting Details

Read the following passage from a college business textbook. Answer the questions that follow.

Capitalism: Competing in a Free Market

[1]Competition doesn't suddenly disappear from your life when you finish the marathon, quit the football team, or refuse to play another game of Rock Band. [2]You can't even go out for fast food without running into competition: McDonald's competes with Burger King, Coca Cola competes with PepsiCo. [3]Whether you're ordering a chicken sandwich or working in the back flipping burgers, those companies' competitive relationships shape your fast food experience by affecting how much customers pay for their meals, how much the burger-flipper is paid, which items are on the menu, what the quality of the food is, and many other details. [4]If you live in a capitalistic economy—an economic system in which the means to produce goods and services are owned by private interests—you can't avoid competition.

[5]So the United States is a capitalist economy, right? [6]Well, not exactly. [7]It's more of a mixed market economy. [8]This just means that the United States borrows elements from different economic systems, like capitalism or socialism, to create an ideal system. [9]In both capitalistic and mixed market economies, competition plays a very big role.

[10]For example, let's say you decide to open a business installing swimming pools. [11]You'll get the materials you need, hire employees, and prepare advertising. [12]In return, any profits you make belong to you. [13]But can you charge as much as you want to install a new pool? [14]Of course not. [15]If your prices are too high, nobody will buy your product. [16]If your prices are too low, you won't earn a profit. [17]In a capitalistic economy, the types of goods and services produced, the prices charged, and the amount of income received are all determined through the operation of the free market.

[18]Of course, the free market doesn't mean that everything is free of cost. [19]In this case, the word free refers to people's freedom to choose what they buy and sell. [20]For example, when you buy a DVD, you voluntarily exchange your money for a copy of the latest Oscar-winning film; no one is forcing you to buy that particular movie from that particular store. [21]An employee voluntarily exchanges his or her time and labor for money. [22]In return, a company voluntarily exchanges money for employees' time and labor. [23]Both parties take part in an exchange because they have something to gain. [24]If they didn't expect to gain, they wouldn't agree to the exchange.

[25]Think about that swimming pool company you started in the last section. [26]You're competing with other swimming pool builders for customers and money in order to make your business a financial success. [27]But how, exactly, do you measure success? [28]Is a company successful if it earns a profit for six months, one year, or maybe 10 years?

[29]Often, if people see profits early on for a new company, they may call the company a success. [30]However, focusing on short-term profitability doesn't give you the big picture. [31]Today, a better measure of success is sustainability. [32]In 1987, the World Commission on Environment and Development defined sustainable development as meeting "the needs of the present without compromising the ability of future generations to meet their own needs."

[33]What does that mean exactly? [34]**Sustainability** is the capacity for an organization to create profit for its shareholders today while making sure that its business interests are also in the best interests of the environment and other stakeholders for the future. [35]Stakeholders are all people who have an interest in an organization. [36]This may include employees, suppliers, and the community. [37]Shareholders are the people who actually own a company and directly benefit from its profits. [38]The good news about a sustainable business is that it stands an excellent chance of beating out the competition, being more successful tomorrow, and remaining successful for generations.

—Adapted from Van Syckle, Barbara and Brian Tietje. *Anybody's Business*, pp. 56–57.

VISUAL *VOCABULARY*

Striking and locked-out grocery workers rally outside a Pavilions supermarket in the Hollywood section of Los Angeles. These _____ want better health insurance and wages for new union employees.

a. shareholders
b. stakeholders

_____ **1.** The central idea or thesis statement is
    a. sentence 1.   c. sentence 6.
    b. sentence 2.   d. sentence 9.

_____ **2.** Sentence 10 is a
    a. main idea.   c. minor supporting detail.
    b. major supporting detail.

_____ **3.** Sentence 18 is a
    a. main idea.   c. minor supporting detail.
    b. major supporting detail.

_____ **4.** Sentence 34 is a
    a. main idea.   c. minor supporting detail.
    b. major supporting detail.

_____ **5.** Sentence 37 is a
    a. main idea.   c. minor supporting detail.
    b. major supporting detail.

SUMMARY RESPONSE

Restate the author's central idea in your own words. Include key major details in your summary. Begin your summary response with the following: *The central idea of "Capitalism: Competing in a Free Market" by Van Syckle and Tietje is...*

WHAT DO YOU THINK?

Do you think competition in the marketplace is good for customers? Is capitalism good for businesses? Why or why not? Assume you are taking a college business class, and you are studying to become a business owner. An upcoming exam in your business class gives you an opportunity to test your understanding. Write a short-answer response of one or two paragraphs for the following essay exam questions:

- Describe why and how companies compete in a capitalist economy.
- Explain how a focus on sustainability keeps companies competitive.

Score (number correct) _____ × 10 = _____%

Visit MyReadingLab to take this test online and receive feedback and guidance on your answers.

Main Ideas, Major and Minor Supporting Details

Before you read the following passage from a college sociology textbook, skim the material and answer the Before Reading questions. Read the passage. Then answer the After Reading questions.

Vocabulary Preview

subtly (2) indirectly
cohesion (3) unity
autonomy (5) independence, self-reliance
regulation (8) control
enmeshed (9) entangled, tangled

Textbook
Skills

Family Cohesion

¹From the moment you were born, you have been learning how to handle distance or closeness within your family system. ²You were taught directly or **subtly** how to be connected to, or separated from, other family members. ³**Cohesion** occurs on two levels. ⁴First, cohesion deals with the levels of emotional bonding between family members. ⁵In addition, cohesion considers the amount of **autonomy** a person achieves within the family system. ⁶In other words, every family attempts to deal with the level of closeness that is encouraged or discouraged.

⁷Although different terms are used, cohesion has been identified by scholars from various fields as central to the understanding of family life. ⁸Family researchers Kantor and Lehr (1976) view "distance **regulation**" as a major family function. ⁹Family therapist Minuchin et al. (1967) talks about "**enmeshed** and disengaged" families. ¹⁰Sociologists Hess and Handel (1959) describe the family's need to "establish a pattern of separateness and connectedness." ¹¹There are four levels of cohesion ranging from extremely low cohesion to extremely high cohesion. ¹²These levels are as follows:

¹³**Disengaged:** Family members maintain extreme separateness and little family belonging or loyalty.

[14]**Separated:** Family members are emotionally independent with some joint involvement and belonging.

[15]**Connected:** Family members strive for emotional closeness, loyalty, and joint involvement with some individuality.

[16]**Enmeshed:** Family members are extremely close and loyal, and they express almost no individuality (Carnes, 1989).

[17]It is through communication that family members are able to develop and maintain or change their patterns of cohesion. [18]A father may decide that it is inappropriate to continue the physical closeness he has experienced with his daughter now that she has become a teenager, and he may limit his touching or playful roughhousing. [19]These nonverbal messages may be confusing or hurtful to his daughter. [20]She may become angry, find new ways of being close, develop more outside friendships, or attempt to force her father back into the old patterns. [21]A husband may demand more intimacy from his wife as he ages. [22]He asks for more serious conversation, makes more sexual advances, or shares more of his feelings. [23]His wife may ignore this new behavior or engage in more intimate behaviors herself.

[24]Families with extremely high cohesion are often referred to as "enmeshed." [25]Members are so closely bonded and over-involved that individuals experience little autonomy or fulfillment of personal needs and goals. [26]Family members appear fused or joined so tightly that personal identities do not develop appropriately. [27]Enmeshed persons do not experience life as individuals, as indicated by the following example:

[28]*My mother and I are the same person.* [29]*She was always protective of me, knew everything about me, told me how to act, and how to answer questions.* [30]*None of this was done in a bad way or had* **detrimental** *effects, but the reality is that she was and still is somewhat overbearing.* [31]*If someone asked me a question, I typically answered, "Please direct all questions to my mother.* [32]*She knows what to say."*

[33]"Disengaged" refers to families at the other end of the continuum in which members experience very little closeness or family **solidarity**, yet each member has high autonomy and individuality. [34]There is a strong sense of emotional separation or divorce. [35]Members experience little or no sense of connectedness to each other.

[36]As you examine cohesion in families, you may want to look at factors such as "emotional bonding, independence, boundaries, time, space, friends, decision making, and interests and recreation" (Olson, Sprenkle, & Russell, p. 6). [37]Families do not remain permanently at one point on the

cohesion scale. [38]Members do not come together and stay the same, as is evident from the previous examples. [39]Because there are widely varying cultural norms, what seems balanced for one family may be quite distant for another. [40]For example, Latino families may find balanced cohesion at a point that is too close for families with a Northern European background.

—Adapted from Kathleen M.Galvin and Bernard J. Brommel. *Family Communication: Cohesion and Change,* 5th ed. Boston: Allyn and Bacon, 2000, pp. 31–32.

Before Reading

Vocabulary in Context

_____ **1.** In sentence 30 of the passage, the word **detrimental** means
          a. helpful.
          b. injurious.
          c. long lasting.
          d. short term.

_____ **2.** In sentence 33 of the passage, the word **solidarity** means
          a. disengagement.
          b. independence.
          c. understanding.
          d. unity.

After Reading

Main Ideas

_____ **3.** Which of the following best states the topic and the author's controlling point about the topic?
          a. levels of family cohesion
          b. causes of family cohesion
          c. ways to achieve family cohesion
          d. dangers of family cohesion

_____ **4.** Which sentence is the thesis statement for the passage?
          a. sentence 1
          b. sentence 6
          c. sentence 11
          d. sentence 40

Supporting Details

_____ **5.** Sentences 13 through 16 are
          a. major supporting details.
          b. minor supporting details.

_____ **6.** Sentences 28 through 32 are
  a. major supporting details.
  b. minor supporting details.

7–10. Complete the summary notes with information from the passage. The four levels of family cohesion, which range from extremely low to high, include the following: _____ (family members are separate, with little loyalty or sense of belonging), _____ (family members are independent, with some involvement and sense of belonging), _____ (family members work to remain close, loyal, and involved, with some individuality), and _____ (members are extremely close and loyal, with almost no individuality).

SUMMARY RESPONSE

Restate the author's central idea in your own words. Include key major details in your summary. Begin your summary response with the following: *The central idea of "Family Cohesion" by Galvin and Brommel is...*

WHAT DO YOU THINK?

How would you describe most American families in terms of family cohesion? Does family cohesion differ among cultures? Why or why not? Assume you are taking a college sociology course. Your professor has assigned a one-page report about family cohesion. In your own words, define family cohesion and its four levels. Give examples based on your observations of everyday life. Consider the following ideas when writing your essay:

- Define family cohesion and its four levels.
- Give examples based on your observations of everyday life.

After Reading About Supporting Details

Before you move on to the Mastery Tests on supporting details, take time to reflect on your learning and performance by answering the following questions. Write your answers in your notebook.

- How has my knowledge base or prior knowledge about supporting details changed?
- Based on my studies, how do I think I will perform on the Mastery Test(s)? Why do I think my scores will be above average, average, or below average?
- Would I recommend this chapter to other students who want to learn more about supporting details? Why or why not?

Test your understanding of what you have learned about supporting details by completing the Chapter 5 Review.

Name _____ Section _____

Date _____ **Score** (number correct) _____ × 20 = _____%

Visit MyReadingLab to take this test online and receive feedback and guidance on your answers.

Read the following passage from a college literature textbook and answer the questions.

Textbook
Skills

Character in Fiction

[1]A character is presumably an imagined person who inhabits a story. [2]However, that simple definition may admit to a few exceptions. [3]In George Stewart's novel *Storm,* the central character is the wind; in Richard Adams's *Watership Down,* the main characters are rabbits. [4]But usually we recognize, in the main characters of a story, human personalities that become familiar to us. [5]If the story seems "true to life," we generally find that its characters act in a reasonably consistent manner, and that the author has provided them with motivation. [6]The author gives the characters sufficient reason to behave as they do. [7]Should a character behave in a sudden and unexpected way, we trust that he had a reason, and sooner or later we will discover it. [8]Characters may seem flat or round, depending on whether a writer sketches or sculpts them.

[9]A **flat** character has only one outstanding trait or feature, or at most a few distinguishing marks. [10]For example, one familiar stock character is the mad scientist, with his lust for absolute power and his crazily gleaming eyes. [11]Flat characters, however, need not be stock characters. [12]For instance, in all of literature there is probably only one Tiny Tim, though his functions in *A Christmas Carol* are mainly to invoke blessings and to remind others of their Christian duties. [13]Some writers try to distinguish the flat ones by giving each a single odd physical feature or mannerism—a nervous twitch, a piercing gaze, an obsessive fondness for oysters. [14]**Round** characters, however, present us with more facets—that is, their authors portray them in greater depth and in more generous detail. [15]Such a round character may appear to us only as he appears to the other characters in the story. [16]If their views of him differ, we will see him from more than one side. [17]In other stories, we enter a character's mind and come to know him through his own thoughts, feelings, and perceptions. [18]By the time we finish reading Katherine Mansfield's "Miss Brill," we are well acquainted with the central character and find her amply three-dimensional.

[19]Flat characters tend to stay the same throughout a story, but round characters often change—learn or become enlightened, grow or

deteriorate. [20]In William Faulkner's "Barn Burning," the boy Sarty Snopes, driven to defy his proud and violent father, becomes at the story's end more knowing and more mature. [21](Some critics call a fixed character **static**; a changing one, **dynamic**.) [22]This is not to damn a flat character as an inferior work of art. [23]In most fiction—even the greatest—minor characters tend to be flat instead of round. [24]Why? [25]Rounding them would cost time and space; and so enlarged, they might only distract us from the main characters.

—Adapted from Kennedy, X. J. and Gioia, Dana, *Literature: An Introduction to Fiction, Poetry, and Drama*, 3rd Compact Ed., p. 61.

_____ **1.** Which sentence is the thesis sentence that states the topic and the author's controlling point about the topic?
   a. sentence 1
   b. sentence 2
   c. sentence 8

_____ **2.** Sentence 9 is a _____ of the paragraph.
   a. main idea
   b. major supporting detail
   c. minor supporting detail

_____ **3.** Sentence 19 is a _____ of the paragraph.
   a. main idea
   b. major supporting detail
   c. minor supporting detail

_____ **4.** Sentence 20 is a _____ of the paragraph.
   a. main idea
   b. major supporting detail
   c. minor supporting detail

_____ **5.** Sentence 21 is a _____ of the paragraph.
   a. main idea
   b. major supporting detail
   c. minor supporting detail

Name _____ Section _____

Date _____ **Score** (number correct) _____ × 20 = _____%

Visit MyReadingLab to take this test online and receive feedback and guidance on your answers.

Read the following passage from a college psychology textbook. Then answer the questions and complete the summary.

Textbook
Skills

**Extrasensory Perception (ESP):
Is There Scientific Evidence?**

[1]The real-world implications of ESP are mind-boggling. [2]Imagine that we could forecast catastrophic events, like the terrorist attacks of September 11, 2001, or figure out whether a romantic partner is cheating by viewing his actions at a distance or reading his mind.

[3]In the 1930s, Joseph B. Rhine, who coined the term *extrasensory perception,* launched the full-scale study of ESP in the United States. [4]Rhine used a set of stimuli called *Zener cards,* which consist of five standard symbols: squiggly lines, star, circle, plus sign, and square. [5]He presented these cards to subjects in random order and asked them to guess which card would appear (precognition), which card another subject had in mind (telepathy), and which card was hidden from view (clairvoyance). [6]Rhine (1934) initially reported positive results, as his subjects averaged about 7 correct Zener card identifications per deck of 25, where 5 would be chance performance.

[7]But there was a problem, one that has dogged ESP research for well over a century: Try as they might, other investigators couldn't replicate Rhine's findings. [8]Moreover, scientists later pointed out serious flaws in Rhine's methods. [9]For example, some of the Zener cards were so worn down or poorly manufactured that subjects could see the imprint of the symbols through the backs of the cards (Alcock, 1990; Gilovich, 1991).

[10]Other attempts to document ESP have proven equally disappointing (Bern & Honorton, 1994; Lilienfeld, 1999c; Milton & Wiseman, 1999; Moulton & Kosslyn, 2008). [11]For example, research conducted over three decades ago suggested that people could mentally transmit images to dreaming subjects (Ullman, Krippner, & Vaughn, 1973). [12]Yet later investigators couldn't replicate these results.

[13]The negative findings we've reviewed suggest that the extraordinary claim of ESP isn't matched by equally extraordinary evidence. [14]But these findings don't demonstrate that ESP doesn't exist. [15]In science, it's

exceedingly difficult to prove a negative. [16]But more than 150 years of failed replications suggest that the research evidence for it is awfully weak.

—Lilienfield, Scott O. Lynn, Steven J. Namy, Laura L., and Woolf, Nancy J., *Psychology: A Framework for Everyday Thinking*, pp. 138–139.

_____ 1. Sentence 3 is a
   a. main idea.
   b. major supporting detail.
   c. minor supporting detail.

_____ 2. Sentence 6 is a
   a. main idea.
   b. major supporting detail.
   c. minor supporting detail.

_____ 3. Sentence 10 is a
   a. main idea.
   b. major supporting detail.
   c. minor supporting detail.

4–5. Complete the summary with information from the passage.

Joseph B. Rhine launched a full-scale study of _____ in the United States in the 1930s. Rhine tested three areas of ESP by asking subjects to identify Zener cards and initially reported positive results. However, neither his nor later attempts to document ESP could be replicated. There is no research _____ that ESP exists.

Name _____ Section _____

Date _____ **Score** (number correct) _____ × 20 = _____ %

Visit MyReadingLab to take this test online and receive feedback and guidance on your answers.

Read the following passage from a college communications textbook. Then complete the summary.

Touch Communication

1Touch communication (known technically as **haptics**) is perhaps the most primitive form of communication. **2**Touch develops before the other senses; even in the womb the child is stimulated by touch. **3**Soon after birth the child is fondled, caressed, patted, and stroked. **4**In turn, the child explores its world through touch and quickly learns to communicate a variety of meanings through touch. **5**Nonverbal researchers have identified the major meanings of touch:

- **6Positive emotion:** Touch may communicate such positive feelings as support, appreciation, inclusion, sexual interest or intent, and affection.
- **7Playfulness:** Touch often speaks of our intention to play. **8**This kind of touch can be either affectionate or aggressive.
- **9Control:** Touch may also direct the behaviors, attitudes, or feelings of the other person. **10**In attention-getting, for example, you touch the person to gain his or her attention. **11**This kind of touch says "look at me" or "look over here."
- **12Ritual:** Ritualistic touching centers on greetings and departures. **13**For example, shaking hands to say "hello" or "goodbye" or hugging, kissing, or putting your arm around another's shoulder when greeting or saying farewell are rituals.
- **14Task-relatedness:** Task-related touching occurs while you're performing some function. **15**Removing a speck of dust from another person's face or helping someone out of a car are two examples.

16Different cultures will view these types of touching differently. **17**For example, some task-related touching is viewed as acceptable in much of the United States. **18**However, this same touch would be viewed negatively in some cultures. **19**Among Koreans, for example, it's considered rude for a store owner to touch a customer while handing back change. **20**It's considered too intimate a gesture. **21**Members of other cultures, expecting some touching, may consider the Korean's behavior cold and insulting.

—Adapted from DeVito, Joseph A., *Messages: Building Interpersonal Communication Skills*, pp. 152–153.

243

The people in this picture illustrate _____ touch.

   a. playful
   b. task-related
   c. ritualistic

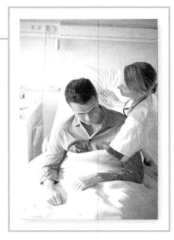

1–5. Complete the summary with information from the paragraph.

Researchers of touch communication, which is also known as (**1**) _____, have identified several major meanings of touch. Touch can convey positive emotion, (**2**) _____, (**3**) _____, (**4**) _____, and task-relatedness. Different (**5**) _____ view these types of touch differently.

Name _____ Section _____

Date _____ **Score** (number correct) _____ × 20 = _____%

Visit MyReadingLab to take this test online and receive feedback and guidance on your answers.

Read the following news release published by the Federal Trade Commission. Answer the questions, and complete the summary.

Cigars: No Such Thing As a Safe Smoke

[1]Since 2000, cigar packages and ads have been required to warn smokers about the serious health risks of cigar smoking. [2]Whether you buy Coronas or Churchills, Panatelas, Robustos, Lonsdales, or any other kind of cigar, you will see five new federally mandated health warnings. [3]The messages should sound familiar: Cigarette companies have been required to give similar health warnings since the mid-1960's and smokeless tobacco manufacturers since the mid-1980's.

[4]The warnings came about as a result of a report by the National Cancer Institute detailing the health risks of cigar smoking. [5]Specifically, cigar smoking can cause cancers of the mouth, esophagus, pharynx, larynx, and lungs. [6]For smokers who inhale, the health risks increase dramatically. [7]Cigar smoking also can cause heart disease and emphysema.

SURGEON GENERAL WARNING:	Cigar Smoking Can Cause Cancers Of The Mouth And Throat, Even If You Do Not Inhale.
SURGEON GENERAL WARNING:	Cigar Smoking Can Cause Lung Cancer And Heart Disease.
SURGEON GENERAL WARNING:	Tobacco Use Increases The Risk Of Infertility, Stillbirth And Low Birth Weight.
SURGEON GENERAL WARNING:	Cigars Are Not A Safe Alternative To Cigarettes.
SURGEON GENERAL WARNING:	Tobacco Smoke Increases The Risk Of Lung Cancer And Heart Disease, Even In Nonsmokers.

[8]The warnings, which cigar companies are required to rotate, are shown on the previous page.

[9]Cigar companies must display these warnings clearly and prominently on packages, in print ads, on audio and video ads, on the Internet, and on point-of-purchase displays. [10]The point, say federal consumer protection and health officials, is to make sure that companies disclose the health risks of cigar smoking and that consumers understand that there's no such thing as a safe smoke.

—Adapted from "Cigars: No Such Thing As a Safe Smoke." Federal Trade Commission.

_____ **1.** Sentence 1 is a
    a. main idea.   c. minor supporting detail.
    b. major supporting detail.

_____ **2.** Sentence 3 is a
    a. main idea.   c. minor supporting detail.
    b. major supporting detail.

_____ **3.** Sentence 10 is a
    a. main idea.   c. minor supporting detail.
    b. major supporting detail.

4–5. Complete the summary.

Cigar packages and advertisements are required _____

_____

Cigar smoking can cause _____

_____

_____

5 Summary of Key Concepts of Supporting Details

(LO1) (LO2)   Assess your comprehension of supporting details.

▪ To locate supporting details in a passage, an effective reader turns the
_____ into a _____.

▪ A major supporting detail _____
_____.

▪ A minor supporting detail _____
_____.

▪ A _____ is a _____
_____.

▪ Often you will want to _____ or restate the ideas in your own
words.

▪ _____ or marking your text _____ reading will help
you create a _____ after you read.

▪ To create a summary for a passage with a stated main idea, _____
_____.

▪ To create a summary for a passage with an implied main idea, _____
_____.

Test Your Comprehension of Supporting Details

Respond to the following questions and prompts.

(LO1) (LO2)   In your own words, how do major and minor supporting details differ? _____
_____
_____

_____

_____

LO1 **LO2**
LO4 **LO5**
In the space below, outline the steps for creating a summary for stated and implied main ideas. See pages 212–214.

Topic:

Main Idea: _____

_____

    A.   **Major Supporting Details: Stated Main Ideas**

         _____

         _____

         _____

         _____

         _____

    B.   **Major Supporting Details: Implied Main Ideas**

         _____

         _____

         _____

         _____

         _____

         _____

         _____

         _____

LO1 **LO2**
LO3 **LO4**
LO5
Summarize the two most important ideas in this chapter that will help you improve your reading comprehension. _____

_____

_____

Outlines and Concept Maps

LO LEARNING OUTCOMES

After studying this chapter, you should be able to:

LO1 Create Outlines

LO2 Create Concept Maps

LO3 Develop Textbook Skills: The Table of Contents

LO4 Apply Literacy Information Skills: Academic, Personal, and Career Applications of Outlines and Concept Maps

Before Reading About Outlines and Concept Maps

In Chapter 5, you learned several important ideas that will help you use outlines and concept maps effectively. To review, reread the diagram about the flow of ideas on page 207 in Chapter 5. Next, skim this chapter for key ideas in boxes about outlines, concept maps, and the table of contents in a textbook. Refer to the diagrams and boxes and create at least three questions that you can answer as you read the chapter. Write your questions in the following spaces (record the page number for the key term in each question):

_____

_____? (page _____)

_____

_____? (pages _____)

_____

_____? (page _____)

    Compare the questions you created with the following questions. Then write the ones that seem most helpful in your notebook, leaving enough space between each question to record the answers you find as you read and study the chapter.

How does an outline show the relationship among the main idea, major supporting details, and minor supporting details? Where are main ideas used in an outline, concept map, and table of contents? Where are major supporting details used in an outline, concept map, and table of contents? Where are minor supporting details used in an outline, concept map, and table of contents? What is the difference between a formal outline and an informal outline?

LO1 Create Outlines

An outline shows how a paragraph moves from a general idea to specific supporting details; thus it helps you make sense of the ways ideas relate to one another. An effective reader uses an outline to see the main idea, major supporting details, and minor supporting details.

> An **outline** shows the relationship among the main idea, major supporting details, and minor supporting details.

An author often uses signal words or phrases such as *a few causes*, *a number of reasons*, *several steps*, or *several kinds of* to introduce a main idea; in addition, an author often uses signal words such as *first, second, furthermore, moreover, next,* or *finally* to indicate that a supporting detail is coming. You will learn more about signal words, also called transitions, and their relationship to ideas in Chapters 7 and 8.

Outlines can be formal or informal. A **formal** or **traditional outline** uses Roman numerals to indicate the main idea, capital letters to indicate the major details, and Arabic numbers to indicate minor details. A formal outline is particularly useful for studying complex reading material. Sometimes, you may choose to use an **informal outline** and record only the main ideas and the major supporting details. Because these outlines are informal, their format may vary according to each student's notetaking style. Elements may or may not be capitalized. One person might label the main idea with the number 1 and the major supporting details with letters *a, b, c, d,* and so on. Another person might not label the main idea at all and identify each major supporting detail with letters or numbers.

> **EXAMPLE** Read the following paragraph from a college geography textbook. Fill in the details to complete the outline. Then answer the questions that follow it.

Textbook
Skills

Two Natural Processes That Shape Earth's Landforms

[1]Geographers studying the shape of Earth's surface—its topography—recognize that it includes many features that seem to have distinctive characteristics. [2]Elements of Earth's surface that have such identifiable

form—its mountains, valleys, hills, and depressions—are called **landforms**. [3]Landforms are built through a combination of endogenic and exogenic processes. [4]First, **endogenic** processes are forces that cause movements beneath or at Earth's surface, such as mountain building and earthquakes. [5]These internal mechanisms move portions of Earth's surface horizontally and vertically. [6]Endogenic forces raise some parts and lower others. [7]Second, **exogenic** processes are forces from the atmosphere aided by gravity. [8]Even as endogenic forces are building Earth's features, these features are simultaneously attacked by exogenic processes, which are forces of erosion, such as running water, wind, and chemical action. [9]Endogenic and exogenic forces continually move and shape Earth's crust. [10]Endogenic processes form rocks and move them to produce mountain ranges, ocean basins, and other topographic features. [11]As these rocks become exposed, exogenic activities go to work. [12]They erode materials, move them down hill slopes, and deposit them in lakes, oceans, and other low-lying areas.

—Adapted from Bergman, Edward and William H. Renwick. *Introduction to Geography: People, Places and Environment*, 4th ed., pp. 96–97.

VISUAL *VOCABULARY*

The devastation caused by the high winds and heavy flooding in the greater New Orleans area due to Hurricane Katrina, August 30, 2005, is an example of _____ forces.

   a. endogenic
   b. exogenic

Outline

Main Idea: _____

_____

A. Elements of Earth's surface that have such identifiable form—its mountains, valleys, hills, and depressions—are called **landforms**.

B. _____

_____

C. _____

Questions

1. What word or phrase in the title signals the major details in the paragraph?

_____

_____ 2. Sentence 12 is a
    a. main idea.   c. minor supporting detail.
    b. major supporting detail.

3–5. How does the author signal each major supporting detail?

Major detail 1: _____

Major detail 2: _____

Major detail 3: _____

_____ 6. The outline used in this activity is an example of
    a. an informal outline.   b. a formal outline.

EXPLANATION The main idea of this passage is located in two places: near the beginning (sentence 3) and in the middle (sentence 9). Although these two sentences differ in wording, they state the same main idea. The reason for stating the main idea twice might be due to the way the author organized the details. Sentences 1 through 8 introduce and define the terms *landform*, *endogenic forces*, and *exogenic forces*. Then sentences 9 through 12 summarize how these two forces work together to affect landforms. The author previews each of the major details in the title by using the words "two natural processes" and "landforms." All three major details are signaled for the reader by the use of bold print. However, two major details are also introduced with the signal words "First" in sentence 4 and "Second" in sentence 7. Sentence 12 is a minor supporting detail that illustrates "exogenic forces," the third major supporting detail. This outline is an example of an informal outline that includes only the main idea and the major supporting details.

Notice how an outline of the main idea and major supporting details—without the minor details—condenses the material into a summary of the author's primary points.

A formal outline of the information looks like the following:

Stated Main Idea: Endogenic and exogenic forces continually move and shape Earth's crust.

    I. Elements of Earth's surface that have such identifiable form—its mountains, valleys, hills, and depressions—are called landforms.

II. Endogenic processes are forces that cause movements beneath or at Earth's surface, such as mountain building and earthquakes.

    A. These internal mechanisms move portions of Earth's surface horizontally and vertically.

    B. Endogenic forces raise some parts and lower others.

III. Exogenic processes are forces from the atmosphere aided by gravity.

    A. Even as endogenic forces are building Earth's features, these features are simultaneously attacked by exogenic processes, which are forces of erosion, such as running water, wind, and chemical action.

IV. Endogenic and exogenic forces continually move and shape Earth's crust.

    A. Endogenic processes form rocks and move them to produce mountain ranges, ocean basins, and other topographic features.

    B. As these rocks become exposed, exogenic activities go to work.

    C. They erode materials, move them down hill slopes, and deposit them in lakes, oceans, and other low-lying areas.

Note that in a formal outline of one paragraph, the first major supporting detail is labeled with the Roman numeral I, and the minor supporting details are labeled A and B. This pattern continues: the second and third major supporting details are labeled Roman numerals II and III, and each of the minor supporting details is labeled A, B, C, and so on. ◀

Practice 1

Read the following paragraph from a college communications textbook. Then answer the questions that follow it.

Eye Contact

Textbook Skills

[1]You use eye contact to serve several important functions. [2]First, you can use eye contact to monitor feedback. [3]For example, when you talk with someone, you look at the person intently as if to say, "Well, what do you think?" or "React to what I have just said." [4]You also look at speakers to let them know you are listening. [5]Another important use of eye contact is to gain the attention and interest of your listeners. [6]When someone fails to pay the attention you want, you may increase your eye contact, hoping your focus on this person will increase attention. [7]When making an especially important point, maintaining close eye contact with your listeners may prevent them from giving attention to anything but what you are saying. [8]A third important function of eye contact is control of the conversation.

[9]Eye movements inform the other person that the channel of communication is open and that she or he should now speak. [10]A clear example of controlling the conversation occurs in the college classroom, where the instructor asks a question and then locks eyes with a student. [11]Without any verbal message, it is known that the student should answer the question.

—Adapted from DeVito, Joseph A., *Interpersonal Communication Book*, p. 187.

1–5. Complete the following outline.

Stated Main Idea: You use eye contact to serve several important functions.

I. _____

   A. _____

   B. Eye contact also lets speakers know you are listening.

II. _____

   _____

   A. Increased eye contact will increase attention.

   B. Close eye contact prevents listeners from giving attention to anything but what you are saying.

III. _____

   A. Eye movements inform the other person that the channel of communication is open.

   B. _____

   _____

6. What word or phrase in the topic sentence signals that a list of details will follow? _____

_____ **7.** Sentence 3, "For example, when you talk with someone, you look at the person intently as if to say, 'Well, what do you think?' or 'React to what I have just said,'" is a
   a. major supporting detail.   b. minor supporting detail.

8–10. What word or phrase introduces the first, second, and third major detail?

Major detail 1: _____

Major detail 2: _____

Major detail 3: _____

L02 Create Concept Maps

An outline is one way to see the details that support a main idea. Another way to see details is through the use of a concept map. A **concept map** is a diagram that shows the flow of ideas from the main idea to the supporting details. Think of what you already know about a map. Someone can tell you how to get somewhere, but it is much easier to understand the directions if you can see how each road connects to the other by studying a map. Likewise, a concept map shows how ideas connect to one another.

> A **concept map** is a diagram that shows the flow of ideas from the main idea to the supporting details.

To make a concept map, an effective reader places the main idea in a box or circle as a heading and then places the major supporting details in boxes or circles beneath the main idea. Often arrows or lines are used to show the flow of ideas.

EXAMPLE Read the following paragraph. Then complete the concept map by filling in the four major supporting details from the paragraph.

A Brief History of Armor

[1]From the earliest civilizations to current times, humans have used armor to protect themselves from injury. [2]The earliest armor was most likely a shield made of wood and animal hide used to deflect rocks and spears during the Neolithic era. [3]Eventually, the Greeks fashioned a set of armor that consisted of a large round shield, a bronze helmet, and shin guards. [4]Later, body armor advanced with the development of scale armor, made of metal plates that overlap each other and chain mail, made up of thousands of iron rings that interlocked to form an entire suit. [5]Currently, armor is still used to protect soldiers in combat, but its use has been expanded to include athletes and workers. [6]Modern soldiers still use helmets and now have flak jackets or bullet proof vests made of Kevlar. [7]In addition, athletes use helmets, pads, and shin guards to protect themselves as they compete in various sports such as football and baseball. [8]Similarly, construction workers don hard hats and boots with reinforced steel toes to protect themselves from on-the-job injuries.

1. _____
_____

2. _____   3. _____   4. _____   5. _____
_____   _____   _____   _____
_____   _____   _____   _____

EXPLANATION   Compare your answers to the following: (1) From the earliest civilizations to current times, humans have used armor to protect themselves from injury; (2) earliest, a shield; (3) Eventually, helmets; (4) Later, body armor; (5) Currently, soldiers, athletes, workers. Note that the main idea is in the top box. The phrase "From the earliest civilizations to current times" in the topic sentence indicates that the major details follow a time order. The signal words "earliest," "eventually," "later," and "currently" indicate the major supporting details. As you can see, a concept map presents ideas in a highly visual manner, making it easy for the reader to grasp the author's primary points. This particular concept map includes only the major supporting details. However, mapping can include the minor supporting details as well. Look at the concept map below that follows the flow of ideas for the third major supporting detail, "Currently, armor is still used . . . " Concept maps, like outlines, can show all three levels of thought: the main idea, the major supporting details, and the minor supporting details. ◀

Stated main idea

From the earliest civilizations to current times, humans have used armor
to protect themselves from injury.

Major supporting detail

Currently, soldiers, athletes, workers

Minor supporting details

Soldiers use helmets
and bullet proof vests

Athletes use helmets,
pads, and shin guards

Workers use hard
hats and boots

Practice 2

Read the following paragraphs. Fill in the concept maps with the missing information from each paragraph.

Paragraph A

Keeping a Personal Journal

[1]Many people find that keeping a personal journal has several benefits. [2]The first benefit of a personal journal is the opportunity the act of writing gives to vent emotions in private; instead of allowing them to build up over time and then explode, writing acts as a release. [3]The second benefit of keeping a journal is the level of self-reflection it demands; the act of putting experiences and emotions into words forces one to think about what is and what is not important enough to record. [4]Another benefit is the personal historical record the writer compiles over time; instead of fading away, memories are in a lasting record that can be revisited at any time.

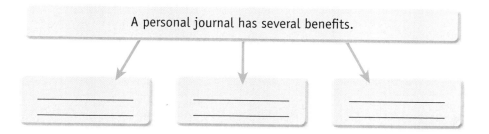

A personal journal has several benefits.

Paragraph B from a College Textbook on Workplace Skills

Textbook
Skills

Interview Questions

[1]The three general types of interview questions are structured, unstructured, and behavioral. [2]Structured interview questions address job-related issues where each applicant is asked the same question(s). [3]An example of a structured question is, "How long have you worked in the retail industry?" [4]An unstructured interview question is a probing, open-ended question. [5]An example of an unstructured interview question is, "Tell me about yourself." [6]Behavioral interview questions are questions that ask candidates to share a past experience related to a workplace

situation. [7]An example of a behavioral question is: "Describe a time you motivated others."

—Adapted from Anderson, Lydia E. and Bolt, Sandra B., *Professionalism: Skills for Workplace Success*, 2nd ed., p. 246.

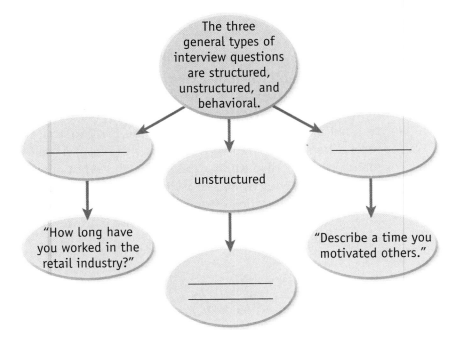

LO3 Develop Textbook Skills: The Table of Contents

Textbook Skills

The table of contents of a textbook is a special kind of outline that is based on topics and subtopics. A **topic** is the *general subject*, so a **subtopic** is a *smaller part* of the topic. The general subject of the textbook is stated in the textbook's title. For example, the title *Health in America: A Multicultural Perspective* tells us that the book is about health concerns from the view of different cultures.

Textbooks divide the general subject into smaller sections or subtopics. These subtopics form the chapters of the textbook. Because a textbook looks deeply into the general subject, a large amount of information is found in each chapter. Thus, a chapter is further divided into smaller parts or subtopics, and each subtopic is labeled with a heading.

The table of contents lists the general subjects and subtopics of each chapter. Most textbooks provide a brief table of contents that divides the textbook into sections and lists the chapter titles for each section. A separate detailed table of contents may also be provided that lists the subtopics for each chapter.

An effective reader examines the table of contents of a textbook to understand how the author has organized the information and where specific information can be found.

> **EXAMPLE** Survey, or look over, the following brief table of contents from the college textbook *Business* by Griffin and Ebert. Then answer the questions.

1. What is the general topic of this textbook? _____

_____

2. How many chapters did the author use to divide Part 1? _____

v

3. What is the topic of Part 1? _____

What is the approximate length of Chapter 2? _____ pages

4. Create two questions based on two of the chapter titles.

_____

_____

EXPLANATION The general topic of this textbook is stated as its title: *Business*. The author divided the textbook into parts and then divided Part 1 into five chapters. The topic of Part 1 is "Understanding the Contemporary Business Environment." Knowing the length of each chapter helps you set aside the proper amount of time needed to read and study. In this textbook, each chapter is about 30 pages in length. One way to set a purpose for reading is to create questions from chapter titles. Compare your questions to the following: "What is the U.S. business system?"(Chapter 1) and "How does one conduct business ethically and responsibly?" (Chapter 3). ◀

Practice 3

Study the following detailed table of contents for Chapter 1 of *Business*, 8th ed. Answer the questions that follow.

1. What is the topic of the chapter? _____

2. How many subtopics are listed for the section "Economic Systems Around the World"? _____

3. On what page does the discussion about demand and supply begin?

_____

4. What are the major supporting details of this chapter? _____

_____

_____

_____

_____

_____

Contents

Apply Information Literacy Skills

 ## Academic, Personal, and Career Applications of Outlines and Concept Maps

The use of outlines and concept maps is an information literacy skill that you can apply to your academic, personal, and career lives. Now that you have learned how to locate and identify supporting details, you can apply that skill to help create outlines and concept maps. Outlines and concept maps enable you to organize and visualize information. For example, in your academic life, outlines and concept maps are useful study and writing tools. In your personal life, the ability to outline or create a concept map will help you in many aspects, such as weighing the pros and cons of an important decision, even down to small events like making a grocery list. In your career life, outlines and concept maps become tools to sum up or illustrate business plans, project timelines, or flow of resources. Thus, you will use the skills that you learned in this chapter in several ways:

- First, you will recognize your own need for the use of an outline or concept map.
- Then, you will evaluate information to determine main ideas and key supports.
- Finally, you will depict the flow of information from main ides to supporting details for a specific purpose.

Academic Application

Assume you are taking a college course in sociology. You are studying for a unit exam on Social Interactions. The following paragraph is a chapter summary from the unit in your textbook.

- **Before Reading:** Skim the paragraph. Identify key terms you need to know for the exam.
- **During Reading:** Underline the key details related to each key term you need to know.
- **After Reading:** In the space following the paragraph, create an outline or concept map of the main ideas and supporting details of the passage.

How does social structure influence our behavior?

[1]The term **social structure** refers to the social envelope that surrounds us and establishes limits on our behavior. [2]Social structure consists of culture, social class, social statuses, roles, groups, and social institutions. [3]Our location in the social structure underlies our perceptions, attitudes, and

behaviors. [4]Culture lays the broadest framework, while **social class** divides people according to income, education, and occupational prestige. [5]Each of us receives **ascribed statuses** at birth. [6]An ascribed status is involuntary such as son or daughter. [7]Later we add **achieved statuses**. [8]An achieved status is voluntary such as student or friend. [9]Our behaviors and orientations are further influenced by the roles we play, the groups to which we belong, and our experiences with social institutions. [10]These components of society work together to help maintain social order.

—Henslin, James M., *Sociology: A Down-to-Earth Approach*, 9th ed., p. 122.

Outline or Concept Map of How Social Structure Influences Our Behavior

I. Social Structure

    A. _____

    B. _____

       _____

    C. _____

II. Social Class Divides

    A. _____

    B. _____

    C. _____

III. Statuses

    A. Ascribed status

        1. _____

        2. _____

    B. _____

        1. _____

        2. _____

IV. Further Influences

    A. _____

B. _____

C. _____

Personal Application

Assume you are shopping for a tablet. You have a good friend who is a computer expert and who keeps up with all the new technology. You asked for her advice, and she sent you the following e-mail in response.

- **Before Reading:** Skim the passage. Identify key features you need to compare among the three tablets to decide which one best meets your needs.

- **During Reading:** Underline features and the details of comparison for the tablets.

- **After Reading:** In the space following the passage, complete the concept map that compares key features among the three tablets. Identify the tablet with the best features for you. Explain what additional information you need to know before you make a purchase.

iPad Versus Kindle Fire HDX Versus Microsoft Surface 2

[1]At one time, the Apple iPad was the unchallenged best-selling tablet on the market. [2]However, recently, Kindle Fire HDX and Microsoft Surface 2 tablets have entered the market and offer serious competition to the iPad. [3]The following discussion of the similarities and differences among these three popular tablets should help you make a decision. [4]The sizes of the three tablets vary enough to give you a significant choice. [5]For example, the iPad screen measures 9.7 inches diagonally, weighs approximately 1.46 pounds, and is around .045 inch thick. [6]In contrast, the Kindle Fire HDX is a little smaller with a screen of 8.9 inches diagonally, a weight of 13.5 ounces, and a thickness of 0.31 inch. [7]The largest of the three is the Surface. [8]Its screen is 10.6 inches diagonally; it weighs 1.49 pounds, and is 0.35 inch thick. [9]All three tablets feature cameras, but they do vary. [10]First, the iPad has a 5-megapixel camera on the back and a low–resolution camera on its front, for videoconferencing. [11]Likewise, the Kindle Fire HDX offers front and rear cameras with an 8-megapixel rear camera and a low-resolution front camera. [12]In contrast, the Surface 2 is equipped with two 720p HD LifeCams, front and rear facing. [13]The screen resolutions of the three tablets also vary. [14]iPad's screen resolution is 2048 by 1536 pixels (264 pixels per inch). [15]Kindle Fire HDX's is 2560 by 1600 pixels (339 pixels per inch). [16]Surface 2's screen resolution is 1920 by 1080 pixels (208 pixels per inch).

[17]Finally, perhaps the most important difference among these three tablets is the price, which ranges based on the amount of storage you want. [18]Apple's iPad price varies from $499 with 16 gigabytes of storage, $599 with 32 GB, $699 with 64 GB, and $799 with 128 GB. [19]The Kindle Fire HDX price begins at $379 with 16 gigabytes of storage, rises to $429 with 32 GB, and $479 with 64 GB. [20]The Surface 2 ranges from $449 with 32 gigabytes of storage to $549 with 64 GB.

Comparison Shopping: iPad, Kindle Fire HDX, Microsoft Surface 2			
Features	iPad	Kindle Fire HDX	Surface 2
Screen Measurement			
Weight			
Thickness:			
Back Camera			
Front Camera			
Screen resolution			
Price			

Decision and Explanation:

_____

_____

_____

Career Application

Assume you want to start a home business. Your business could be handicrafts, mail-order items, seasonal products, party goods, or personal services such as house cleaning, tutoring, or childcare. In your research about how to start a home business, you found the following information on a government website.

- **Before Reading:** Skim the passage. Identify three topics you need to know more about as you read.
- **During Reading:** Underline key words about the three topics.
- **After Reading:** In the space following the passage, complete the concept map that identifies elements of your home-based business based on what you read. Then identify topics about which you want more information.

Home-Based Businesses

[1]Starting a home-based business has many rewards as well as challenges. [2]This guide provides resources that will help you learn more about working out of your house, starting a home-based business and managing your business within the law.

Before You Begin: Work Space and Life Style

[3]Can you live and work in the same area? [4]Find the answer by asking yourself the following questions:
- [5]Where in the home will the business be located?
- [6]Will you need to meet with clients in your home?
- [7]What adjustments to living arrangements will be required?
- [8]How will your home business affect your family's daily routine?
- [9]What will be the cost of changes?
- [10]How will your family react?
- [11]What will the neighbors think? Where will you work?
- [12]Can you work without supervision?
- [13]What equipment do you need such as phones, computers, etc.?

Start a Home-Based Business

[14]For additional guidance on how to start your business, use the resources listed below.
- [15]Check out the first steps for starting any small business.
- [16]Obtain a checklist of things to do at How to Set Up a Home-Based Business.
- [17]Get planning ideas by reading an article that provides a comprehensive approach to developing a business plan for a home-based business.

Promote Your Business

[18]Decide how to advertise your home-based business. [19]The following list offers several forms of promotion. [20]Choose the ones best suited to your business.

Word-of-mouth
Business cards

Social media, such as Facebook or a blog
Newspaper advertisements

—Adapted from SBA.gov "Home-Based Businesses."
<http://www.sba.gov/content/home-based-business>

I want to learn more about _____

_____

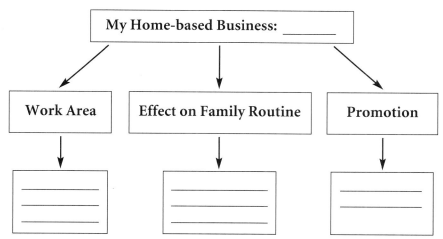

Score (number correct) _____ × 10 = _____%

Visit MyReadingLab to take this test online and receive feedback and guidance on your answers.

Main Ideas, Major and Minor Supporting Details, and Outlines

A. **(1–5.)** Read the paragraph. Then complete the outline of the paragraph by giving the main idea and inserting the missing major and minor details.

Types of Strength Training

¹Building muscle mass has several advantages and can be accomplished through a variety of strength-training activities. ²First, well-defined

muscles give the body a pleasing aesthetic quality. [3]Second, muscle mass increases the body's metabolism, burning more calories than fat, thus making weight control by dieting less of an issue. [4]In addition, strength training builds bone mass, which helps protect against fractures, "shrinking," and osteoporosis. [5]Several types of strength-training exercises bring effective results. [6]One of the most common methods is lifting weights using either free weights or machines. [7]A second method is the use of resistance bands, which are rubberized strips or cables of varying tensions. [8]A third method consists of doing exercises that bear the body's weight, such as push-ups and pull-ups.

Stated Main Idea: _____

_____

   I. Muscle mass

      A. _____

      B. _____

         _____

      C. In addition, strength training builds bone mass, which helps protect against fractures, "shrinking," and osteoporosis.

  II. _____

      A. One of the most common methods is lifting weights using either free weights or machines.

      B. A second method is the use of resistance bands, which are rubberized strips or cables of varying tensions.

      C. _____

         _____

B. **(6–10.)** Read the following paragraph. Then complete the outline with major and minor details from the paragraph.

What Is Love?

    [1]Many social scientists maintain that love may be of two kinds: *companionate* and *passionate.* [2]Companionate love is a secure, affectionate, and trusting attachment. [3]It is similar to what we may feel for

family members or close friends. [4]In companionate love, two people are attracted, have much in common, care about each other's well-being, and express reciprocal liking and respect. [5]*Passionate love* is an intense state of wanting to bond with another person. [6]It has three components: cognitive, emotional, and behavioral. [7]In the cognitive component, someone has a preoccupation with another person, idealizes that person, and has an intense desire to know that person. [8]The emotional component includes strong feelings about another person, physiological arousal and attraction, including sexual attraction, and a desire for sexual intimacy with the other person. [9]The behavioral component encompasses actions to know the other person's feelings and to maintain physical closeness and be helpful to the other person.

—Adapted from Donatelle, Rebecca J.,
Access to Health, 12th ed., p. 120.

Stated Main Idea: Many social scientists maintain that love may be of two kinds: companionate and passionate.

   I. Companionate love is a secure, affectionate, and trusting attachment.

      A. _____

      B. In companionate love, two people are attracted, have much in common, care about each other's well-being, and express reciprocal liking and respect.

  II. _____

      A. _____

         1. _____

            _____

            _____

         2. The emotional component includes strong feelings about another person, physiological arousal and attraction, including sexual attraction, and a desire for sexual intimacy with the other person.

         3. _____

            _____

            _____

REVIEW TEST 2

Score (number correct) _____ × 10 = _____%

Visit MyReadingLab to take this test online and receive feedback and guidance on your answers.

Main Ideas, Supporting Details, Signal Words, and Concept Maps

A. Read the following paragraph from a college health textbook.

Healthy Eating

[1]Healthy eating involves several key principles. [2]A balanced diet includes healthy proportions of all nutrients. [3]For instance, a student subsisting largely on bread, bagels, muffins, crackers, chips, and cookies might be eating too much carbohydrate and fat but too little protein, vitamins, and minerals. [4]A varied diet includes many different foods. [5]A student who habitually chooses the same foods for breakfast, lunch, and dinner is not likely to be consuming the wide range of phytochemicals, fiber, and other benefits that a more varied diet could provide. [6]Finally, a moderate diet provides adequate amounts of nutrients and energy. [7]Both crash diets and overconsumption are immoderate.

—Adapted from Blake, Joan. *Nutrition and You*,
2nd ed., pp. 346–347.

Fill in the concept map with the main idea and the missing major supporting details from the paragraph.

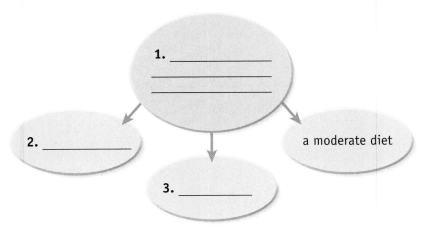

1. _____
   _____
   _____

2. _____

3. _____

a moderate diet

4. What signal word or phrase introduces the third major supporting detail?

_____

B. Read the following paragraph from a college political science textbook.

Traditional Democratic Theory

Textbook
Skills

[1]Democracy depends on a number of key values. [2]The first value is equality in voting. [3]The ideal of "one person, one vote" is basic to democracy. [4]Another principle of a self-ruling people is effective participation. [5]Citizens must be able to express their desires and wishes during the decision-making process. [6]A third value is enlightened understanding. [7]A self-governing society must be a marketplace of ideas with a free press and free speech. [8]Fourth, citizens must control the agenda. [9]Citizens should have the collective right to control the government's policy agenda. [10]Finally, inclusion is key. [11]The government must include, and extend rights to, all who are subject to its laws.

—Adapted from George C. Edwards III, Martin P. Wattenberg, and Robert L. Lineberry, *Government in America: People, Politics, and Policy, Brief version,* 5th ed. Addison-Wesley Educational Publishers Inc., 2000, pg. 10.

Fill in the concept map with the main idea and major supporting details from the paragraph.

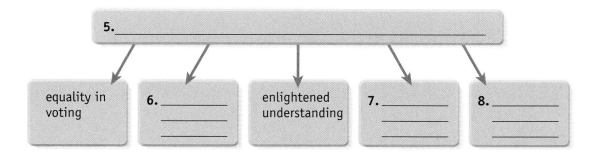

5. _____

equality in voting

6. _____

enlightened understanding

7. _____

8. _____

9. What word or phrase in the topic sentence indicates that a list of supporting details will follow? _____

10. What word or phrase introduces the second major supporting detail?

_____

REVIEW TEST 3

Score (number correct) _____ × 10 = _____%

Visit MyReadingLab to take this test online and receive feedback and guidance on your answers.

Read the following passage from a college communications textbook. Then complete the informal outline with details from the passage.

Beware of Groupthink

Textbook Skills

[1]Groupthink is a way of thinking that people use when agreement among members has become excessively important. [2]Groupthink is most likely to occur when there is high stress, when like-minded individuals are isolated from others, and when there is an especially strong and opinionated leader. [3]Overemphasis on agreement among members tends to shut out realistic and logical analysis of a problem or of possible alternatives (Ganis, 1983; Mullen, Tara, Salas, & Driskell, 1994). [4]The term *groupthink* itself is meant to signal a "deterioration of mental efficiency, reality testing, and moral judgment that results from ingroup pressures" (Ganis, 1983).

[5]The following symptoms should help you recognize groupthink in groups you observe or participate in (Ganis, 1983; Richmond, McCroskey, & McCroskey, 2005; Schafer & Crichlow, 1996).

- [6]Illusion of invulnerability. [7]Group members think the group and its members are invulnerable, that they are virtually beyond being harmed.
- [8]Avoidance. [9]Members create rationalizations to avoid dealing with warnings or threats.
- [10]Assumption of morality. [11]Members believe their group is moral and, often, that any opposition is immoral.
- [12]Intolerance of differences of opinion. [13]Those opposed to the group are perceived in simplistic, stereotyped ways, and group pressure is applied to any member who expresses doubts or questions the group's arguments or proposals.
- [14]Self-censorship. [15]Members censor their own doubts.
- [16]Assumption of unanimity. [17]Group members believe that all members are in unanimous agreement, whether this is stated or not. [18]This belief is encouraged, of course, by members censoring their own doubts and not allowing differences of opinion to be discussed.

- [19]Gatekeeping. [20]Group members emerge whose function it is to guard the information that gets to other members, especially when it may create diversity of opinion.
- [21]Peer pressure. [22]Groupthinkers pressure others to go along with the group and not to express any disagreement.

[23]Here are three suggestions for combating groupthink.

1. [24]When too-simple solutions are offered to problems, try to illustrate (with specific examples, if possible) for the group members how the complexity of the problem is not going to yield to the solutions offered.

2. [25]When you feel that members are not expressing their doubts about the group or its decisions, encourage members to voice disagreement. [26]Ask members to play devil's advocate, to test the adequacy of the solution. [27]Or, if members resist, do it yourself. [28]Similarly, if you feel there is unexpressed disagreement, ask specifically if anyone disagrees. [29]If you still get no response, it may be helpful to ask everyone to write his or her comments anonymously, then read them aloud to the group.

3. [30]To combat the group pressure toward agreement, reward members who do voice disagreement or doubt. [31]Say, for example. "That's a good argument; we need to hear more about the potential problems of this proposal. [32]Does anyone else see any problems?"

DeVito, Joseph A. *Human Communication: The Basic Course*, 12th ed., p. 229.

VISUAL *VOCABULARY*

Bullying is an example of which symptom of groupthink? _____

   a. avoidance
   b. self-censorship
   c. peer pressure

Stated main idea: _____

_____

    I. Symptoms of Groupthink

        A. _____

        B. _____

        C. _____

        D. _____

        E. _____

        F. _____

        G. _____

        H. _____

    II. _____

        A. Illustrate that the problem is too complex for the solutions.

        B. _____

        C. _____

SUMMARY RESPONSE

Restate the author's central idea in your own words. Include key major details in your summary. Begin your summary response with the following: *The central idea of "Beware of Groupthink" by DeVito is …*

WHAT DO YOU THINK?

Have you ever witnessed groupthink or been a member of a group where it occurred? Why do you think groupthink happens? What might be some negative consequences of it? Assume you are applying for a job in a management position for a local company. It is looking for someone who can lead his or her team to create innovative solutions. Include the following ideas in your cover letter:

- Explain how you would help your team avoid groupthink.
- Use an example of how you might motivate others to think innovatively.

REVIEW TEST 4

Score (number correct) _____ × 10 = _____%

Visit MyReadingLab to take this test online and receive feedback and guidance on your answers.

Supporting Details and Outlines

Before you read the following passage, skim the material and answer the Before Reading questions. Read the passage. Then answer the After Reading questions.

Vocabulary Preview

prevalence (4): frequency of occurrence
adolescence (5): teenage years
surveyed (9): studied, questioned
symptoms (16): warning signs
compulsiveness (24): urgent desire or driven behavior
deviant (24): abnormal, strange

Binge Drinking

[1]Despite laws that make it illegal for anyone under the age of 21 to purchase or possess alcohol, young people report that alcohol is easy to obtain and that many drink with one goal in mind—to get drunk. [2]Binge drinking is defined as consuming five or more drinks in a row for males and four or more in a row for females. [3]The alarming aspects of binge drinking cannot be overlooked or underestimated.

[4]One troubling aspect of binge drinking is its **prevalence** among youth. [5]Often starting as young as age 13, binge drinking tends to increase during **adolescence**. [6]The behavior peaks in young adulthood, from the ages of 18 to 20. [7]After age 22, this **perilous** conduct slowly decreases. [8]One study on youth risk behavior reported that 24% of high school students binge drank. [9]Numerous studies consistently indicate that about 40% of college students **surveyed** engage in binge drinking. [10]More than 80% of American youth consume alcohol before their twenty-first birthday. [11]About 90% of the alcohol consumed by them is in the form of binge drinks.

[12]Binge drinking is risky behavior that has serious **consequences**. [13]The most grave effect is **alcohol poisoning**, which is an **acute** physical reaction to an overdose of the alcohol. [14]During bingeing, the brain is deprived of oxygen. [15]This lack of oxygen eventually causes the brain to shut down the heart and lungs. [16]Alcohol poisoning has several

symptoms. [17]They include vomiting and unconsciousness. [18]In addition, the skin becomes cold, clammy, pale or bluish in color. [19]Breathing becomes slow or irregular.

[20]Binge drinking brings about other disturbing behaviors or effects as well. [21]In schools with high binge drinking rates, binge drinkers are likely to insult, **humiliate**, push, or hit their peers. [22]Frequent binge drinkers were eight times more likely than nonbinge drinkers to miss a class, fall behind in schoolwork, get hurt or injured, and damage property. [23]Binge drinking during college may be linked with mental health disorders. [24]These disorders include **compulsiveness**, depression or anxiety, or early **deviant** behavior. [25]Alarmingly, nearly one out of every five teenagers has experienced "blackout" spells. [26]During these spells, they could not remember what happened the previous evening because of heavy binge drinking. [27]Finally, many who are frequent binge drinkers also drink and drive.

—Adapted from U.S. Department of Health and
Human Services, "Binge Drinking in Adolescents
and College Students," and the Centers
for Disease Control and Prevention.

Before Reading

Vocabulary in Context

_____ **1.** In sentence 7 of the passage, the word **perilous** means
   a. adventurous.   c. fun-loving.
   b. dangerous.   d. disgusting.

_____ **2.** In sentence 13 of the passage, the word **acute** means
   a. unavoidable.   c. invisible.
   b. short-term.   d. severe.

After Reading

Main Ideas

_____ **3.** Which sentence states the central idea of the passage?
   a. sentence 1   c. sentence 3
   b. sentence 2   d. sentence 4

_____ **4.** Which sentence is the topic sentence of the fourth paragraph?
   a. sentence 20   c. sentence 26
   b. sentence 21   d. sentence 27

Supporting Details

5–7. Complete the summary with information from the passage.

Alcohol poisoning is _____.

Symptoms include vomiting; _____; cold, clammy, pale or bluish skin; slow or irregular _____.

8–10. Complete the following informal outline of the fourth paragraph by filling in the blanks.

Stated Main Idea: Binge drinking brings about other disturbing behaviors or effects.

A. _____

B. Binge drinkers are more likely to do poorly in school, get hurt, cause damage.

C. _____

D. Binge drinkers may have blackout spells.

E. _____

SUMMARY RESPONSE

Restate the author's central idea in your own words. Include key major details in your summary. Begin your summary response with the following: *The central idea of "Binge Drinking" by the Centers for Disease Control is …*

WHAT DO YOU THINK?

Why is binge drinking so prevalent among youth and college students? Why do you think binge drinking is related to mental disorders? Should colleges address the problem of binge drinking? If so, how? Write a letter to a college or school newspaper explaining the dangers of binge drinking. Include real-life examples if you know of any.

After Reading About Outlines and Concept Maps

Before you move on to the Mastery Tests on outlines and concept maps, take time to reflect on your learning and performance by answering the following questions. Write your answers in your notebook.

- How has my knowledge base or prior knowledge about outlines and concept maps changed?

- Based on my studies, how do I think I will perform on the Mastery Test(s)? Why do I think my scores will be above average, average, or below average?

- Would I recommend this chapter to other students who want to learn more about outlines and concept maps? Why or why not?

Test your understanding on what you have learned about outlines and concept maps by completing the Chapter 6 Review.

Name _____ Section _____

Date _____ **Score** (number correct) _____ × 20 = _____ %

Visit MyReadingLab to take this test online and receive feedback and guidance on your answers.

Read the following passage from a college textbook about gender and communication. Complete the activities that follow with information from the passage.

Self-Concept

Textbook
Skills

[1]Self-concept is comprised of everything one thinks and knows about oneself. [2]It is the relatively stable set of views one attributes to oneself. [3]As a personal assessment of yourself, your self-concept can be summed up by what you think of yourself in relationship to others. [4]Your self-concept didn't form overnight. [5]Like your gender identity, your self-concept developed in early childhood. [6]And, once established, self-concept is fairly resistant to change. [7]The first day you said "I," or "me," you recognized yourself as separate from your surroundings. [8]You distinguished yourself from others around you. [9]The idea *self-concept* is sometimes broken into two components: *self-image* and *self-esteem.*

Self-Image and Self-Esteem

[10]Self-image is the sort of person you believe yourself to be. [11]Self-image is made up of physical and emotional descriptions of the self and the roles you play. [12]**Self-esteem** is a measure of the value you place on the images you have of yourself. [13]Self-esteem includes your attitudes and feelings about yourself including how well you like and value yourself. [14]It is your judgment of how you are doing in life (your perceived self) compared to how you think you should be doing (your ideal self).

[15]According to researcher Chris Mruk, self-esteem is composed of five dimensions:

- [16]*competence* (your beliefs about your ability to be effective),
- [17]*worthiness* (your beliefs about the extent to which others value you),
- [18]*cognition* (your beliefs about your character and personality),
- [19]*affect* (how you evaluate yourself and the feelings generated by this evaluation), and
- [20]*stability* or change (which greatly affects your communication with others).

[21]A number of social forces come together to help create and feed your self-concept. [22]First, the image people have of you guides what they

expect of you, how they relate to you, and how they interact with you. [23]Second, as you learn about and understand their images, your self-concept affects the way you think about yourself. [24]For example, if people who are important to you have a positive image of you, they are apt to make you feel accepted, valued, worthwhile, loved, and significant. [25]If, on the other hand, they have a negative image of you, more than likely they will contribute to your feeling small, worthless, unloved, or insignificant. [26]Whatever its nature, you never stop receiving information about yourself.

—Adapted from Teri Kwal Gamble and Michael W. Gamble, *The Gender Communication Connection.* Boston: Houghton Mifflin, 2002, pp. 43–44.

1–5. Complete the concept map by filling in the main idea and the missing major and minor supporting details.

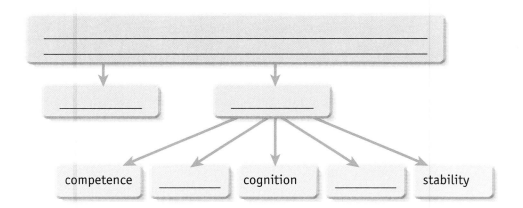

Name _____ Section _____

Date _____ **Score** (number correct) _____ × 20 = _____ %

Visit MyReadingLab to take this test online and receive feedback and guidance on your answers.

A. Read the following paragraph from a college textbook on marriage and family. Then complete the questions that follow.

Dating

[1]Did you know that dating is not a common practice in most countries? [2]In general, when we speak of dating we are referring to a process of pairing off. [3]It involves the open choice of mates and engagement in activities that allow people to get to know each other and progress toward coupling and mate selection. [4]In places such as China, India, South America, and most countries in Africa, dating is very rare. [5]In addition, it is forbidden in most Muslim countries, including Iraq, Egypt, Iran, and Saudi Arabia. [6]Only in Western countries such as the United States, Great Britain, Australia, and Canada is dating a common form of mate selection.

—Adapted from Schwartz, Mary Ann A. and Scott, Barbara Marliene, *Marriage and Families: Diversity and Change*, 6th ed., p. 112.

_____ **1.** Which sentence contains the main idea of the paragraph?
   a. sentence 1   c. sentence 3
   b. sentence 2   d. sentence 6

_____ **2.** In general, the major details of this paragraph are
   a. the reasons for dating.
   b. the effects of dating.
   c. different definitions of dating.
   d. facts about where dating is practiced.

_____ **3.** Dating is forbidden in
   a. South America.
   b. most African countries.
   c. most Muslim countries.
   d. Western countries.

_____ **4.** How many major details does the author give in this paragraph?
   a. two   c. four
   b. three   d. five

_____ **5.** The second major detail is signaled by the word or phrase
   a. in general.   c. in addition.
   b. in places.   d. only.

B. Read the following paragraph from a college geography textbook and complete the concept map that illustrates the hydraulic cycle.

[1]The hydrologic cycle is a continual worldwide flow of water among the four spheres: Water in the atmosphere condenses as clouds, falls as precipitation, runs off into the ocean or is stored in the ground, and returns to the atmosphere through transpiration by plants or evaporation. [2]Humans play major roles in all major biogeochemical cycles.

— Bergman, Edward and Renwick, William H., *Introduction to Geography: People, Places, and Environment*, 4th ed., p. 130.

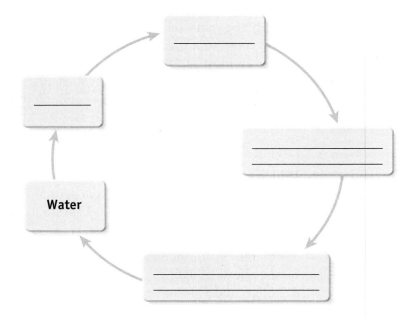

Name _____ Section _____

Date _____ **Score** (number correct) _____ × 10 = _____ %

Visit MyReadingLab to take this test online and receive feedback and guidance on your answers.

Read the following passage. Then complete the questions that follow.

Work Addiction

Textbook Skills

[1]Work addiction is a serious problem for two reasons: lack of understanding about the addiction and the effects of the addiction on the addicts and those around them.

[2]First, in order to understand work addiction, we need to understand the concept of healthy work and how it differs from work addiction. [3]Healthy work provides a sense of identity, helps develop our strengths, and is a means of satisfaction, accomplishment, and mastery of problems. [4]Healthy workers may work for long hours. [5]Although they have occasional projects that keep them away from friends, family, and personal interests for short periods, they generally maintain balance in their lives and are in full control of their schedules. [6]Healthy work does not consume the worker. [7]In contrast, work addiction is the compulsive use of work to fulfill needs of intimacy, power, and success. [8]It is characterized by obsession, rigidity, fear, anxiety, low self-esteem, isolation, and the need to be perfect. [9]Work addiction is more than being unable to relax when not doing something thought of as "productive." [10]It is the pursuit of the "work persona," an image that work addicts wish to project onto others.

[11]In addition to understanding the basic traits of work addiction, we must also understand the dangerous effects it has on individuals and those around them. [12]One area that is deeply affected is family life. [13]Work addiction is a major source of marital problems and family breakups. [14]In fact, most work addicts come from homes that were alcoholic, rigid, violent, or otherwise unhealthy. [15]In addition to harming the family, work addiction takes a toll on people's emotional and physical health. [16]They may become emotionally crippled. [17]They lose the ability to connect with other people. [18]They are often riddled with guilt and fear; they fear failure, and they fear their shortcomings will be discovered. [19]Work addicts may also suffer several physical effects. [20]For example, because they are unable to relax and play, they often suffer from chronic fatigue syndrome. [21]Work addicts suffer as well from digestive problems, and they often report feeling pressure in the chest, difficulty breathing, dizziness, and lightheadedness.

—Adapted from Donatelle, Rebecca J. and Davis, Lorraine G., *Access to Health*, 7th ed., p. 318.

_____ 1. In the overall passage, sentence 2 is a
    a. thesis statement.   c. minor supporting detail.
    b. major supporting detail.

_____ 2. How many major supporting details support the thesis statement in this passage?
    a. two   c. four
    b. three   d. five

_____ 3. What word or phrase signals the first major supporting detail?
    a. first   c. for example
    b. one   d. during

_____ 4. What word or phrase signals the second major supporting detail?
    a. and   c. in addition
    b. next   d. also

_____ 5. In general, the supporting details of the second paragraph
    a. explain the differences between healthy work and work addiction.
    b. offer ways to cope with work addiction.
    c. explain the term *work persona*.
    d. list situations in which workers become addicted to their work.

_____ 6. Overall, the supporting details of the third paragraph
    a. list the physical effects of work addiction.
    b. list the emotional effects of work addiction.
    c. explain the causes of work addiction.
    d. explain the emotional and physical effects of work addiction.

7–10. Complete the concept map with supporting details from the second paragraph.

provides sense of identity | _____ | is a means of satisfaction, accomplishment, mastery | obsession and rigidity | fear, anxiety, isolation | low self-esteem, need to be perfect

Name _____ Section _____

Date _____ **Score** (number correct) _____ × 10 = _____ %

Visit MyReadingLab to take this test online and receive feedback and guidance on your answers.

Read the following passage from a college textbook for a course in criminal justice. Then complete the outline that follows.

Types of Evidence

Textbook
Skills

1The crux of the criminal trial is the presentation of evidence. **2**First, the state is given the opportunity to present evidence intended to prove the defendant's guilt. **3**After prosecutors have rested their case, the defense is afforded the opportunity to provide evidence favorable to the defendant.

4Evidence can be either direct or circumstantial. **5**Direct evidence, if believed, proves a fact without requiring the judge or jury to draw inferences. **6**For example, direct evidence may consist of the information contained in a photograph or a videotape. **7**It might also consist of testimonial evidence provided by a witness on the stand. **8**A straightforward statement by a witness ("I saw him do it!") is a form of direct evidence.

9Circumstantial evidence is indirect. **10**It requires the judge or jury to make inferences and to draw conclusions. **11**At a murder trial, for example, a person who heard gunshots and moments later saw someone run by with a smoking gun in hand might testify to those facts. **12**Even without an eyewitness to the actual homicide, the jury might conclude that the person seen with the gun was the one who pulled the trigger and committed the crime. **13**Circumstantial evidence is sufficient to produce a conviction in a criminal trial. **14**In fact, some prosecuting attorneys prefer to work entirely with circumstantial evidence, weaving a tapestry of the criminal act into their arguments to the jury.

15Real evidence, which may be either direct or circumstantial, consists of physical material, traces of physical activity. **16**Weapons, tire tracks, ransom notes, and fingerprints all fall into the category of real evidence. **17**Real evidence, sometimes called physical evidence, is introduced at the trial by means of exhibits. **18**Exhibits are objects or displays that, after having been formally accepted as evidence by the judge, may be shown to members of the jury. **19**Documentary evidence, one type of real evidence, includes written evidence like business records, journals, written confessions, and letters. **20**Documentary evidence can extend beyond paper and ink to include stored computer data and video and audio recordings.

—Schmalleger, Frank J.Criminal Justice Today: An Introductory
Text for the *21st Century*, 10th ed., p. 367.

Stated Main Idea: _____

   I. _____

      A. _____

      B. Photograph

      C. Video

      D. Statement by a witness

  II. _____

      A. _____

      B. Is sufficient to produce a conviction in a criminal trial

 III. _____

      A. May be either direct or circumstantial; consists of _____

                                        _____

          1. Weapons

          2. Tire tracks

          3. Ransom notes

          4. _____

      B. Is introduced at the trial by means of exhibits

      C. _____

          1. Business records, journals, written confessions, and letters

          2. _____

VISUAL *VOCABULARY*

The detective interviews witnesses to gather _____ evidence.

  a. direct

  b. indirect

6 Summary of Key Concepts of Outlines and Concept Maps

LO1 LO2 Assess your comprehension of concept maps and outlines.

▪ An outline shows _____

_____ .

▪ An author often uses _____ such as *a few causes, a number of reasons, several steps,* or *several kinds of* to introduce a _____ .

▪ An author often uses signal words such as *first, second, furthermore, moreover, next,* or *finally* to introduce a _____ .

▪ A formal outline uses _____ to indicate the _____ , _____ to indicate the _____ , and _____ to indicate the _____ .

▪ A concept map is a _____

_____ .

Test Your Comprehension of Outlines and Concept Maps

Respond to the following questions and prompts.

LO1 In your own words, what is an outline? _____

_____

_____

_____

_____

LO2 In your own words, what is a concept map? _____

_____

_____

_____

_____

LO1 LO2 LO4   In the space below, create an outline and a concept map for the following terms: Anxiety, Causes, Effects, Stress at work, Stress from school, Stress in personal life, Overwhelming fear, Shortness of breath, Chest pain.

Outline: Anxiety

    I. _____

       A. _____

       B. _____

       C. _____

   II. _____

       A. _____

       B. _____

       C. _____

Concept Map:

LO1 LO4   Outline the three most important ideas in this chapter that will help you improve your reading comprehension.

    I. _____

   II. _____

  III. _____

Transitions and Thought Patterns

7 CHAPTER

(LO) LEARNING OUTCOMES

After studying this chapter, you should be able to:

(LO1) Recognize Transition Words to Determine Relationships Within a Sentence

(LO2) Recognize Thought Patterns to Determine Relationships Between Sentences

(LO3) Develop Textbook Skills: Thought Patterns in Textbooks

(LO4) Apply Information Literacy Skills: Academic, Personal, and Career Applications of Transitions and Thought Patterns

Before Reading About Transitions and Thought Patterns

Using the reporter's questions (Who? What? When? Where? Why? and How?), refer to the learning outcomes and create at least three questions that you can answer as you study the chapter. Write your questions in the following spaces:

_____?

_____?

_____?

Now take a few minutes to skim the chapter for ideas and terms that you have studied in previous chapters. List those ideas in the following spaces:

_____

_____

Compare the questions you created based on the learning outcomes with the following questions. Then write the ones that seem the most helpful in your notebook, leaving enough space between each question to record the answers as you read and study the chapter.

What are transitions? What are thought patterns? What is the relationship between transition words and thought patterns? How do thought patterns use transition words?

On page 297, the terms main idea, minor details, and major details are discussed in relationship to transitions and thought patterns. Consider the following study questions based on these ideas: How can transitions help me understand the author's main idea? How can transitions help me create an outline?

 ## Recognize Transition Words to Determine Relationships Within a Sentence

Read the following set of ideas. Which word makes the relationship within the second sentence clear?

> In 1998, Major League Baseball player Mark McGwire broke the single-season home run record by hitting 70 home runs. In 2010, McGwire cast doubt on his record _____ he admitted to taking steroids during his record-breaking season.
>
> a. when   b. for example   c. however

The word that makes the relationship between the two ideas clear in the second sentence is (a) "when." Mark McGwire's record of hitting 70 home runs was quite a feat, even for a natural and talented athlete like McGwire. His accomplishment was tarnished the moment he admitted to using performance-enhancing drugs. Until he admitted drug use, his record stood as evidence of his natural ability. Thus the transition *when* best expresses the relationship between ideas in the second sentence.

Transitions are key pattern words and phrases that signal the logical relationships within and between sentences. **Transitions** help you make sense of an author's idea in two basic ways. First, transitions join ideas within a sentence.

> **Transitions** are words and phrases that signal thought patterns by showing the logical relationships within a sentence and between sentences.
>
> A **thought pattern** (or **pattern of organization**) is established by using transitions to show the logical relationship between ideas in a paragraph or passage.

Second, transitions establish **thought patterns** so readers can understand the logical flow of ideas between sentences.

Read the following sentence. Which word makes the relationship of ideas within the sentence clear?

> Fernando deserves to be recognized for his public service _____
>
> he has worked faithfully for twenty years with the Boy Scouts and the
>
> youth soccer league.
>
> a. before   b. in addition   c. because

All three of these choices are transitions; however, the word that best clarifies the relationship of ideas within this sentence is (c) "because." Fernando's work with youth is the reason he deserves to be recognized. The relationship is one of cause and effect. Transition (a) "before" reveals time order, and transition (b) "in addition" indicates that the author is adding to the first idea. In the next section, you will learn more about these transitions and thought patterns. First, it is helpful to see how transitions serve a vital function in building ideas within a sentence.

> **EXAMPLE** Complete the following with a transition that shows the relationship of ideas within each sentence. Fill in each blank with a word or phrase from the box. Use each transition once.

> also   as a result   inside   such as

1. Not only does academic cheating rob the cheating student of knowledge, it can ____1____ severely damage that student's reputation.

2. One kind of effective foot warmer is a soft, lightweight insole that generates its own heat with exposure to air and can be slipped ____3____ a shoe or boot.

3. Travis eliminated unhealthy eating habits, diligently worked out at the gym three times a week, and walked vigorously for 30 minutes every day; ____2____, after six months he attained his ideal weight.

4. Olivia invests in a variety of financial assets ____4____ stocks, bonds, and real estate.

EXPLANATION

1. The topic of this sentence is cheating. The author makes two points about cheating. "Also" indicates the addition of the second point.

2. The topic of this sentence is one kind of foot warmer. The author is describing its traits. One trait is where it is used; it is placed *inside* the shoe or boot.

3. This sentence brings two topics or ideas together. The first part of the sentence deals with Travis' healthy lifestyle (this topic is suggested by the list of details). The topic of the second part of the sentence is "ideal weight." The second idea is the result of the first. The correct answer is *as a result*.

4. The topic of this sentence is the variety of Olivia's assets. The phrase *such as* indicates that a list of examples follows.

Note that to determine the correct transition for each of the sentences, you had to rely upon context clues to first determine the relationship of ideas. Understanding relationships and thought patterns is closely related to a clear understanding of vocabulary. ◁

Practice 1

Textbook
Skills

Study the following list of scientific terms from a college textbook. Complete each item with a transition that shows the relationship of ideas within each sentence. Fill in each blank with a word from the box. Use each word once.

as	or	when	while

1. *Predation* occurs ____3____ members of one species, a *predator*, hunt, capture, kill, and consume members of another species, the *prey*.

2. In *parasitism*, one organism, the *parasite*, depends on another, the *host*, for food or some other benefit ____4____ doing the host harm.

3. In *mutualism*, species benefit from one another ____1____ they interact.

4. Mutualism and parasitism occur between organisms that live in close physical contact __2__ *symbiosis*.

—Adapted from Jay Withgott and Scott Brennan, *Essential Environment: The Science Behind the Stories,* 3rd ed. Upper Saddle River: Pearson Education, p. 95.

VISUAL *VOCABULARY*

The relationship between this Green sea turtle and the Yellow Tang fish

is _____.

   a. predatory

   b. parasitic

   . symbiotic

Transitions express a variety of relationships between ideas. You must therefore look carefully at the meaning of each transitional word or phrase. Some transition words have similar meanings. For example, *also*, *too*, and *furthermore* all signal the relationship of addition or listing. Sometimes a single word can serve as two different types of transitions, depending on how it is used. For example, the word *since* can reveal time order, or it can signal a cause. Notice the difference in the following two sentences.

> *Since* I began working, I have saved several thousand dollars.
>
> *Since* you are familiar with the assignment, Janice, please lead the group discussion.

The relationship between the ideas in the first sentence is based on time order. The relationship between the ideas in the second sentence is based on cause and effect.

Effective readers look for transition words, study their meaning in context, and use them as keys to unlock the author's thought patterns.

Practice 2

Read the following paragraph from a government website. Fill in each blank with a transition that shows the relationship between ideas. Choose your answers from the words in the box. Use each word or phrase once.

although	as well as	for example	than	until
and	besides	such as	then	while

**A Call to Action: Changing the Culture
of Drinking at U.S. Colleges**

(1) _Besides_ the damage and injuries that occur during spring break each year, the only consequences of college drinking that usually come to the public's attention are occasional student deaths from alcohol overuse, (2) _Such as_ alcohol poisoning. They prompt a brief flurry of media attention; (3) ___then___, the topic disappears (4) ___until___ the next incident. In fact, the consequences of college drinking are much more than occasional; (5) _4 example_, at least 1,400 college student deaths a year are linked to alcohol. In addition, high-risk drinking results in serious injuries and assaults, (6) _as well as_ other health and academic problems. Alcohol is a major factor in damage to college property. The relative lack of headlines about college drinking denies the facts. The consequences of excessive college drinking are more widespread and destructive (7) ___than___ most people realize. (8) ___While___ only isolated incidents tend to make news, many school presidents conclude that these pervasive, (9) _although_ less obvious, problems are occurring on their campuses at the same time. It is a persistent and costly problem, (10) ___and___ it affects nearly all residential colleges, college communities, and college students, whether they drink or not.

—Adapted from "A Call to Action: Changing the Culture of
Drinking at U.S. Colleges." *College Drinking: Changing the Culture.*
National Institute on Alcohol Abuse and Alcoholism.

LO2 Recognize Thought Patterns to Determine Relationships Between Sentences

Not only do transitions reveal the relationships of ideas *within* a sentence, they also show the relationship *between* sentences. Read the following sentences and choose the word that best states the relationship between the sentences.

Resistance training, such as weightlifting, offers several benefits.

_____, it tones the muscles and increases bone density.

    a. As a result   b. However   c. For example

The transition that best states the relationship between these sentences is (c) "For example." The first sentence is a generalization. It contains a topic and a controlling point about the topic. The topic is "resistance training"; the point is "several benefits." The second sentence offers an example as a supporting detail for the general point. Transition (a) "As a result" signals cause and effect. And (b) "However" indicates a contrast. In this chapter and Chapter 8, you will study the ways in which authors use these and other thought patterns in paragraphs and longer passages. First, it is important to learn to find the relationship between sentences.

⊘ **EXAMPLE** Complete the following with transitions that make the relationship between the sentences clear. Fill in each blank with a word from the box. Use each word once.

            after   above   furthermore

1. Simon Cowell became well known in the United States as a judge on the popular TV show *American Idol*. __*After*__ eight seasons on the show, Cowell left *American Idol* to star on the American version of *X-factor*.

2. A frustrated father talking to his son said, "You are going to make several major changes. You will come home at a decent hour. You will keep your room orderly. You will speak respectfully to your mother and me. __*3*__, you will get a job."

3. Airplanes offer two storage places for carry-on luggage. Small bags can be placed under the seat in front of a passenger. Larger bags must be stored in compartments located __*2*__ the seat.

EXPLANATION

1. The relationship between the sentences is based on time. The words "eight seasons" serve as a clue that the correct transition is *after*.

2. The father states a list of behaviors he expects from his son. The word *furthermore* signals an additional behavior that is expected.

3. The first sentence establishes the relationship between these sentences as space order with the use of the word *places*. The correct transition is *above*. ◁

Practice 3

Complete the following with transitions. Fill in each blank with a word or phrase from the box. Use each transition once.

as a result	before	during	in contrast	when

Kaleigh learned that equipment makes a significant difference in the success and enjoyment of a sport or exercise when she traded her old bike in for a new comfort bike. Her old bike was equipped with aerodynamic handle bars, a hard, narrow seat, and no shock absorbers. **(1)** _____, she endured bumpy, uncomfortable rides that left her sore, and she dreaded cycling as an activity. **(2)** _____, her comfort bike is equipped with upright handle bars, a plush gel seat, and state-of-the-art shock absorbers. Now Kaleigh loves long-distance cycling. Every morning, long **(3)** _____ most people are up, Kaleigh already has on her helmet, pads, and gloves. **(4)** _____ she first begins a ride, she considers how long the ride will be so that she can set a pace and conserve her energy. **(5)** _____ the ride, Kaleigh varies her pace to maximize her workout. After a long ride, Kaleigh feels a sense of satisfaction and strength.

Practice 4

Complete the following paragraph by inserting transitions. Fill in each blank with a word or phrase from the box. Use each transition once.

although	as with	in addition
as well	however	whereas

Eco-Tourism

What often comes to mind when people think about eco-tourism is the vision of a middle-aged couple in flannel shirts and hiking boots strolling around the wilderness with a pair of binoculars, hoping to spot a rare bird. **(1)** _____ a number of tourists engage in that stereotypical activity, there are many other opportunities for fun and action. These opportunities include a guided tour through a rain forest, witnessing the magical world under the sea, rafting roaring rapids, or participating in a cultural event. **(2)** _____ all tourism, the types of available activities depend on the destination. If traveling in Norway, visitors have the opportunity to go on a whale or elk safari, **(3)** _____ in Kenya they will encounter giraffes or elephants or zebras. In Brazil, they can explore the rain forest, and in the Middle East, a lush oasis. Travelers encounter plenty of photo opportunities while on an eco-tourism trip **(4)** _____. Pictures can be taken in just about every location and of just about anything that comes into view. **(5)** _____, if eco-tourists plan to photograph animals, they need to be very patient because wild animals tend to hide or move along rather quickly. **(6)** _____, eco-tourists must be aware of the host community's norms for photographs; some cultures are against photos, and others might charge tourists for the opportunity to photograph community members.

—Adapted from John R. Walker and Josielyn T. Walker,
Tourism: Concepts and Practices. Upper Saddle River:
Pearson Education, 2011, pp. 387–388, 389.

You will recall that a paragraph is made up of a group of ideas. Major details support the main idea, and minor details support the major details. Transitions make the relationship between these three levels of ideas clear, smooth, and easy to follow.

Before beginning to write, an author must ask, "What thought pattern best expresses these ideas?" or "How should these ideas be organized so that the reader can follow and understand my point?" A **thought pattern** (also called a **pattern of organization**) allows the author to arrange the supporting details in a clear and smooth flow by using transition words.

> **Thought patterns** (or **patterns of organization**) are signaled by using transitions to show the logical relationship between ideas in a paragraph, passage, or textbook chapter.

As you learned in Chapter 3, a main idea is made up of a topic and the author's controlling point about the topic. One way an author controls the topic is by using a specific thought pattern. Read the following paragraph. Identify the topic sentence by circling the topic and underlining the controlling point.

The Traits of Olfaction

The sense of smell, also known as olfaction, has two interesting traits. First, people have difficulty describing odors in words. Second, odors have a powerful ability to call to mind old memories and feelings, even many years after an event.

—Carlson/Buskist, *Psychology: Science of Behavior*, Text Excerpt from p. 191 © 1997. Reproduced by permission of Pearson Education, Inc.

The topic is the "sense of smell" and the controlling point is the phrase "two interesting traits." The word "interesting" states the author's opinion. The words "two traits" state the author's thought pattern. The author's controlling point limits the supporting details to listing and describing two interesting traits of smell. The transition words *first* and *second* signal each of the supporting details. Authors often introduce supporting details with transition words based on the controlling point. Creating an outline using transition words is an excellent way to grasp an author's thought pattern.

⊙ **EXAMPLE** Read the following paragraph. Complete the informal outline, then answer the question.

The Landscape of Taste

Moving from front to back, the surface of the tongue is differentially sensitive to taste. The front or tip is most sensitive to sweet and salty substances. Next, the sides are most sensitive to sour substances. Finally, the back of the tongue, the back of the throat, and the soft palate overhanging the back of the tongue are sensitive to bitter substances.

—Carlson, Neil, and William Buskist. *Psychology: Science of Behavior*, 5th ed., p. 190.

Topic sentence: _____

_____

a. _____

b. _____

c. _____

_____

_____ What is the author's thought pattern?
   a. time order   b. space order

EXPLANATION Compare your outline to the following:

Topic sentence: Moving from front to back, the surface of the tongue is differentially sensitive to taste.

A. The front or tip is most sensitive to sweet and salty substances.

B. Next, the sides are most sensitive to sour substances.

C. Finally, the back of the tongue, the back of the throat, and the soft palate overhanging the back of the tongue are sensitive to bitter substances.

   The topic is "the surface of the tongue." The thought pattern is expressed in the words "moving from front to back" and "differentially sensitive." The transitions clearly carry out the thought pattern by beginning with the *front* of the tongue, next the *sides*, and finally the *back* of the tongue. In this paragraph, the transitions establish the (b) space order thought pattern.

Practice 5

Read the following paragraph. Then complete the informal outline.

Taste Versus Flavor

Textbook
Skills

   Taste is different from flavor. On the one hand, taste is the simple ability to sense four sensations: sourness, sweetness, saltiness, and bitterness. On the other hand, the flavor of a food includes its odor as well as its taste. For example, you have probably noticed that the flavors of foods are diminished when you have a head cold. Mucus makes it difficult for odor-laden air to reach your receptors for the sense of smell.

—Carlson, Neil, and William Buskist. *Psychology:
Science of Behavior*, 5th ed., p. 189.

Topic sentence: _____

a. _____

_____

b. _____

1. _____

_____

2. Mucus makes it difficult for odor-laden air to reach your receptors for the sense of smell.

Note how the headings for the paragraphs you just read show the close connection between the topic and the author's thought pattern used to present the main idea and organize the supporting details. For example, the title "The Landscape of Taste" uses the word *landscape* to clue the reader to the space order thought pattern. An excellent activity to do before reading is to read the heading and skim ahead for transition words to get the gist of the author's thought pattern.

In this chapter, we discuss four common thought patterns and the transition words and phrases used to signal each:

- The time order pattern
- The space order pattern
- The listing pattern
- The classification pattern

Some additional common thought patterns are covered in Chapter 8.

The Time Order Pattern

The **time order** thought pattern generally shows a chain of events. The actions or events are listed in the order in which they occur. This is called *chronological order*. Two types of chronological order are narration and process. An author will use narration to tell about the important events in the life of a famous person or a significant event in history. Narration is also used to organize a piece of fiction. The second type of chronological order is process. Process is used to give directions to a task in time order. In summary, there are two basic uses of time order: (1) narration: a chain of events and (2) process: steps, stages, or directions.

Narration: A Chain of Events

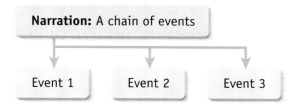

Transitions of **time** signal that the writer is describing *when* things occurred and *in what order*. The writer presents an event and then shows when each of the additional details or events flowed from the first event. Thus the details follow a logical order based on time.

> John Wilkes Booth, who led a very prominent life as an actor in the years before he assassinated Abraham Lincoln, ultimately died a traitor's death.

Notice that this sentence lays out three events. The transition words *before* and *ultimately* tell the order in which the events occurred.

Transitions Used in the Time Order Pattern for Narration				
after	during	later	previously	ultimately
afterward	eventually	meanwhile	second	until
as	finally	next	since	when
before	first	now	soon	while
currently	last	often	then	

> **EXAMPLE** Determine the logical order of the following sentences. Write **1** by the sentence that should come first, **2** by the sentence that should come second, **3** by the sentence that should come third, and **4** by the sentence that should come last. (*Hint:* Circle the time transition words.)

_____ Eventually, his passion for learning earned him a master's degree and a doctorate.

_____ During those early years as a teacher, he found that the more he learned, the more excited he was about teaching, and he loved studying under the guidance of professional teachers.

_____ His first notions of wanting only a four-year bachelor's degree were quickly dispelled.

_____ When Corbin decided to become a teacher, he had no idea that he was also deciding to become a career student.

EXPLANATION Compare your answers to the sentences arranged in the proper order in the following paragraph. The transitions are in **bold** print.

> [1]**When** Corbin decided to become a teacher, he had no idea that he was also deciding to become a career student. [2]His **first** notions of wanting only a four-year bachelor's degree were quickly dispelled. [3]**During** those early years as a teacher, he found that the more he learned, the more excited he was about teaching, and he loved studying under the guidance of professional teachers. [4]**Eventually**, his passion for learning earned him a master's degree and a doctorate.

Practice 6

Determine the logical order for the following sentences. Write **1** by the sentence that should come first, **2** by the sentence that should come second, **3** by the sentence that should come third, **4** by the sentence that should come fourth, and **5** by the sentence that should come fifth. (*Hint:* Circle the time transition words.)

Battling Emotional Eating

_____ Clara constantly struggles with the cycle of emotional eating.

_____ At the first sign of a stressor, she resists the urge to eat the foods that bring her comfort, such as fast-food hamburgers and fries, cookies, ice cream, or anything else high in fat and carbohydrates.

_____ Eventually, she gains enough unwanted weight to shock her into self-control.

_____ Then she begins to eat a balanced diet and lose the weight—until the next stressful time.

_____ As the stress stretches into days, she finds her resolve weakened and heads for the junk food.

Process: Steps, Stages, or Directions

The time order thought pattern for steps, stages, or directions shows actions that can be repeated at any time with similar results. This pattern is used to give steps or directions for completing a task.

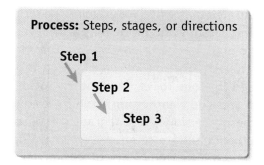

Read the following topic sentences. Underline the words that signal process time order.

1. Follow five simple steps to develop and deepen your friendships.

2. Procrastination recurs in a cycle of self-destruction.

3. Grief moves through several stages.

Sentence 1 uses the word *steps* to introduce directions for the reader to follow. Sentence 2 signals that procrastination occurs as part of a pattern of self-destruction with the word *cycle*. Sentence 3 uses the process signal word *stages* to convey the time order of grief. In paragraphs that developed these topic sentences, transitions of time order would likely signal the supporting details.

Transitions Used in the Time Order Pattern for Process

after	during	later	previously	ultimately
afterward	eventually	meanwhile	second	until
as	finally	next	since	when
before	first	now	soon	while
currently	last	often	then	

EXAMPLE The following paragraph from a college ecology textbook uses the time order pattern for process to organize its ideas. Complete the concept map that follows it by giving the missing details in their proper order. (*Hint:* Circle the time order transition words.)

Textbook
Skills

Earth as a System: The Rock Cycle

¹Earth is a system. ²This means that our planet consists of many interacting parts that form a complex whole. ³Nowhere is this idea better

illustrated than when we examine the rock cycle. [4]To begin, magma is molten material that forms inside the Earth. [5]Eventually magma cools and solidifies. [6]This process is called **crystallization**. [7]It may occur either beneath the surface or, following a volcanic eruption, at the surface. [8]The resulting rocks are called **igneous rocks**. [9]As igneous rocks are exposed at the surface, they will undergo weathering, in which the day-in and day-out influences of the atmosphere slowly disintegrate and decompose rocks. [10]Then, the materials that result are often moved downslope by gravity before being picked up and transported by any of a number of erosional agents, such as running water, glaciers, wind, or waves. [11]Eventually, these particles and dissolved substances, called **sediment**, are deposited. [12]Although most sediment ultimately comes to rest in the ocean, other sites of deposition include river floodplains, desert basins, swamps, and sand dunes. [13]Next, the sediments undergo **lithification**, a term meaning "conversion into rock." [14]Sediment is usually lithified into **sedimentary rock** when compacted by the weight of overlying layers or when cemented as percolating groundwater fills the pores with mineral matter. [15]When the resulting sedimentary rock is buried deep within Earth and involved in the dynamics of mountain building or intruded by a mass of magma, it will be subjected to great pressures and/or intense heat. [16]This phase is called **metamorphism**. [17]The sedimentary rock will react to the changing environment and turn into the third rock type, **metamorphic rock**. [18]Finally, if metamorphic rock is subjected to still higher temperatures, it will melt, creating magma, which will eventually crystallize into igneous rock, starting the cycle all over again.

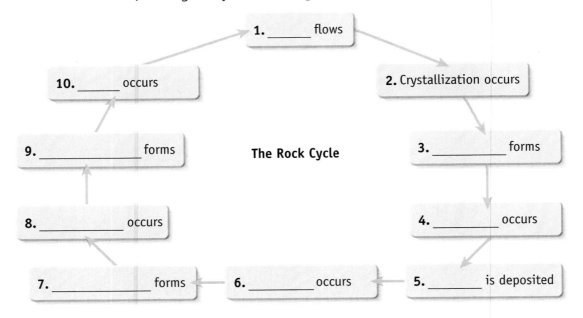

1. _____ flows

2. Crystallization occurs

10. _____ occurs

3. _____ forms

9. _____ forms

The Rock Cycle

4. _____ occurs

8. _____ occurs

5. _____ is deposited

7. _____ forms

6. _____ occurs

VISUAL *VOCABULARY*

The Devil's Tower in Wyoming is an example of _____ rock.

    a. igneous
    b. sedimentary
    c. metamorphic

EXPLANATION Compare your answers to the following: (1) Magma flows; (2) Crystallization occurs; (3) Igneous rock forms; (4) Weathering occurs; (5) Sediment is deposited; (6) Lithification occurs; (7) Sedimentary rock forms; (8) Metamorphism occurs; (9) Metamorphic rock forms; (10) Melting occurs; and the cycle begins again, (1) Magma flows.

Practice 7

The following paragraph uses the time order pattern for process to organize its ideas. Complete the list of steps that follows it by giving the missing details in their proper order. (*Hint:* Circle the time order transition words.)

How to Change Your Car's Oil

¹First, warm up your car's engine. ²Next, before getting under your car, turn off the engine, block the wheels, and set the parking brake. ³Third, remove the drain plug on the bottom of the engine's oil pan, and allow the used oil to drain from your car into a drip pan. ⁴Fourth, tightly replace the drain plug. ⁵Fifth, carefully add the new engine oil. ⁶Do not overfill. ⁷Sixth, with the parking brake still set, and in a well-ventilated area, start the car, and allow the engine to run for a few minutes. ⁸Seventh, turn off the engine and check the oil level. ⁹Also check around the oil filter and drain plug for leaks. ¹⁰Eighth, so you know when to change your oil next, write down the date, mileage, grade, and brand of the motor oil you installed. ¹¹Next, carefully pour the used oil from the drip pan into a suitable recycling container. ¹²Finally, protect the environment and conserve resources by taking your used oil to the nearest public used-oil collection center, such as a service station or lube center. ¹³Also look for

the "oil drop." **14**This is a petroleum industry symbol indicating that used oil is collected for recycling or reuse.

—U.S. Environmental Protection Agency, "Collecting Used Oil for Recycling/Reuse."

How to Change Your Car's Oil

Step 1: _____.

Step 2: _____.

Step 3: Remove the drain plug on the bottom of the engine's oil pan, and drain oil into a drip pan.

Step 4: _____.

Step 5: Add the new engine oil.

Step 6: Start the car, and run the engine for a few minutes.

Step 7: Turn off the engine, check the oil level, and check the oil filter and drain plug for leaks.

Step 8: _____.

Step 9: Pour the used oil from the drip pan into a suitable recycling container.

Step 10: _____.

Practice 8

The following paragraph uses time order to describe the stages of development that teams in the workplace go through. Complete the following paragraph by inserting transitions. Fill in each blank with a word from the box. Use each word once.

during	first	second	when
final	once	then	

Workplace Teams

Teams go through five stages of team development: forming, storming, norming, performing, and adjourning. **(1)** _____, in the forming stage, you are getting to know and forming initial opinions about your team members. Assumptions are based on first impressions. Sometimes these impressions are right; other times, they are wrong. In the (2) _____ stage, the storming stage, some team members begin to have conflict with each other. (3) _____ team members accept other members for who they are (i.e., overcome the conflict), the team has moved into the norming stage. It is only (4) _____ that the team is able to enter the performing stage, (5) _____ which they work on the task. (6) _____ the team has completed its task, it is in the adjourning stage. This (7) _____ stage brings closure to the project. Note that it is normal for a team to go through these phases. Some teams successfully and rapidly move through the forming, storming, and norming phases and get right to work (performing), while other teams cannot get beyond the initial phases of forming or storming. Make every effort to move your team along to the performing stage, and recognize that minor conflicts are a part of team development.

—Adapted from Anderson, Lydia E. and Bolt, Sandra B.,
Professionalism: Skills for Workplace Success, 2nd ed., p. 158.

The Space Order Pattern

The **space order pattern** allows authors to describe a person, place, or thing based on its location or the way it is arranged in space. In the space order pattern, also known as spatial order, the writer often uses descriptive details to help readers create vivid mental pictures of what the writer is describing. An author may choose to describe an object from top to bottom, from bottom to top, from right to left, from left to right, from near to far, from far to near, from inside to outside, or from outside to inside.

> **Space Order: Descriptive Details**
>
> Descriptive detail 1 → Descriptive detail 2 → Descriptive detail 3

Transition words of **space order** signal that the details follow a logical order based on two elements: (1) how the object, place, or person is arranged in space, and (2) the starting point from which the author chooses to begin the description.

Transition Words Used in the Space Order Pattern

above	at the side	beneath	close to	here	nearby	right
across	at the top	beside	down	in	next to	there
adjacent	back	beyond	far away	inside	on	under
around	behind	by	farther	left	outside	underneath
at the bottom	below	center	front	middle	over	within

▶ **EXAMPLE**   Study the following paragraph from a college anatomy and physiology textbook. Choose a word or phrase from the box to fill in each blank with a signal word or phrase that shows the relationship between ideas. Use each word or phrase once.

away from	erect	in	on	side
between	forward	left	right	sides

The Language of Anatomy

Textbook
Skills

Anatomy and physiology is the study of the structures and functions of the human body. To accurately describe body parts and positions, we must have an initial reference point and use directional terms. To avoid confusion, it is always assumed that the body is (**1**) _____ the standard position called the anatomical position. In the **anatomical position**, the body is (**2**) _____ with the feet parallel and the arms hanging at the (**3**) _____ with palms facing (**4**) _____ and the thumbs pointing (**5**) _____ the body. **Directional terms** allow us to explain exactly where one body structure is in relation to another. For example, we can describe the relationship (**6**) _____ the ears and the nose informally by saying, "The ears are located (**7**) _____ each (**8**) _____ of the head to the (**9**) _____ and (**10**) _____ of the nose." Using anatomical terminology, this shortens to "The ears are lateral to the nose." Anatomical terms save a good deal of description and, once learned, are much clearer.

—Adapted from Marieb, Elaine N. *Essentials of Human Anatomy* and Physiology, 9th ed., p. 15.

EXPLANATION Compare your answers to the following: (1) in, (2) erect, (3) sides, (4) forward, (5) away from, (6) between, (7) on, (8) side, (9) right, and (10) left.

Practice 9

Study the following paragraph from a college anatomy and physiology textbook. Choose a word or phrase from the box to fill in each blank with a signal word that shows the relationship between ideas. Use each word or phrase once.

| above | at the level | internal | lengthwise | planes |
| along | front | into | middle | through |

Textbook
Skills

Body Planes and Sections

When preparing to look at the (**1**) _____ structures of the body, medical students make a section, or cut. When the section is made (**2**) _____ the body wall or an organ, it is made (**3**) _____ an imaginary line called a plane. Because the body is three-dimensional, we can refer to three types of planes or sections that lie at right angles to one another.

A sagittal (saj'i-tal) section is a cut along the (**4**) _____, or longitudinal, plane of the body, dividing the body (**5**) _____ right and left parts. If the cut is down the median or (**6**) _____ plane of the body and the right and left parts are equal in size, it is called a median, or midsagittal, section.

A frontal section is a cut along a lengthwise plane that divides the body or an organ into anterior or (**7**) _____ and posterior or back parts. It is also called a coronal (ko-ro' nal) section.

A transverse section is a cut along a horizontal plane, dividing the body or organ into superior or (**8**) _____ and inferior or below parts. It is also called a cross section.

Sectioning a body or one of its organs along different (**9**) _____ often results in very different views. For example, a transverse section of the body trunk **(10)** _____ of the kidneys would show kidney structure in cross section very nicely; a frontal section of the body trunk would show a different view of kidney anatomy; and a midsagittal section would miss the kidneys completely.

—Adapted from Marieb, Elaine N., *Essentials of Human Anatomy and Physiology*, 9th ed., p. 17.

VISUAL *VOCABULARY*

This image shows the _____ view of the nerve supply of the upper body. The surface anatomy of the body is semi-transparent and tinted red.

a. median
b. anterior
c. transverse

—From Marieb, Elaine N., *Essentials of Human Anatomy and Physiology*, 9th ed.

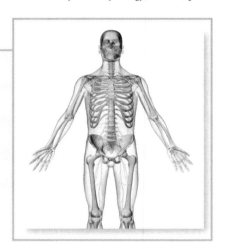

Practice 10

The following paragraph uses space order to discuss satellites in space. Complete the paragraph by inserting transitions. Fill in each blank with a word from the box. Use each word once.

above	from	high	into	over

Engineers design satellites to support instruments flown in space. Satellites must be light enough to be carried **(1)** _____ space on rockets, yet strong enough to withstand the forces of launching. Earth-observing satellites observe our planet **(2)** _____ paths called orbits, many of which are greater than 400 miles **(3)** _____ the ground. That distance is at least as far as Washington, D.C., to Boston, Massachusetts. Satellites are so **(4)** _____ above Earth and travel so quickly that, in the right orbit, a satellite can pass **(5)** _____ every part of Earth once every few days. Such orbits allow satellites to study and take pictures of all of Earth's features: land, plant life, oceans, clouds, and polar ice. Some satellites, such as those used for weather forecasting, are placed in fixed orbits to look at Earth continuously.

—Adapted from NASA, *Our Mission to Planet Earth: A Guide to Teaching Earth System Science*. NASA.

The Listing Pattern

Often authors want to list a series or set of reasons, details, or points. These details are listed in an order that the author has chosen. Changing the order of the details does not change their meaning. Transitions of addition, such as *and, also,* and *furthermore,* are generally used to indicate a *listing pattern.*

Listing pattern

Idea 1
Idea 2
Idea 3

Weightlifting builds *and* tones muscles; it *also* builds bone density.

Notice that in this statement, two words signal the addition of ideas: *and* and *also.* Transitions of addition signal that the writer is using a second idea along with the first one. The writer presents an idea and then adds other ideas to deepen or clarify the first idea.

Addition Transitions Used in the Listing Pattern

also	final	for one thing	last of all	second
and	finally	furthermore	moreover	third
another	first	in addition	next	
besides	first of all	last	one	

▷ EXAMPLE Refer to the box of addition transitions used in the listing pattern. Complete the following paragraph with transitions that show the appropriate relationship between sentences.

Preventing Childhood Obesity: A Community Checklist

Today, more than 12.5 million children—17 percent of children and adolescents ages 2 to 19—are overweight. Communities can hold events and create places that help kids stay active and encourage healthy eating habits. **(1)** _____, a community can help kids stay active. **(2)** _____, community leaders can work with schools to increase physical activity. **(3)** _____, a community can create and maintain community recreation areas, **(4)** _____ city planners can increase the "walkability" of the community. **(5)** _____, a community can encourage healthy eating habits. **(6)** _____ supporting the places people can get healthy food they can afford, community members can **(7)** _____ work with grocery stores and businesses to limit displays and ads of junk foods and candy aimed at children. **(8)** _____, faith-based community organizations can help promote healthy eating habits. Churches or other places of worship can encourage members of the congregation to bring healthier meal options such as more fruits and vegetables to functions. **(9)** _____, they can eliminate junk food in children's worship and fellowship programs. **(10)** _____, a community can promote healthy choices. Businesses, schools, and parents can create community groups to address childhood overweight and obesity.

—Adapted from Office of the Surgeon General, "Childhood Obesity Prevention: Community Checklist." U.S. Department of Health and Human Services.

EXPLANATION   Compare your answers to the following: (1) First, (2) For one thing, (3) In addition, (4) and, (5) Next, (6) Besides, (7) also, (8) Furthermore, (9) Moreover, and (10) Finally.

This paragraph begins with a general idea that is then followed by three major supporting details. Not only is each major detail introduced with a transition to show addition, but also many of the minor supporting details are also signaled by transitions that show addition.

Practice 11

The following paragraph uses the listing thought pattern. Finish the outline that follows it by listing the major supporting details in their proper order. (*Hint:* Circle the addition transition words.)

The Value of Artifacts

[1]Artifacts reveal much about the people who made them and the time period in which they were made. [2]Studying artifacts is important for several reasons. [3]First, artifacts tell a story. [4]By thinking about the purpose and need of the particular object, we can learn about the nature of the humans who created the object. [5]Studying the great pyramids teaches us to appreciate the human drive and sacrifice that went into building such mammoth structures. [6]Second, artifacts connect us to the people who used them. [7]By thinking about the ways in which the objects were used, we begin to understand more about the people who used them. [8]Consider children's lunchboxes popular from 1950 to 1980. [9]These lunchboxes, decorated with images from popular children's television shows, reflect the profound influence television has had on young children. [10]Finally, artifacts reflect and cause change. [11]Think of a typewriter and a computer. [12]Both are used for many of the same purposes; both reflect the change of their times, and both caused great change as well.

—Adapted from Lubar & Kendrick, "Looking at Artifacts, Thinking About History." *Artifact & Analysis.* Smithsonian Center for Education and Museum Studies.

The Value of Artifacts

Studying artifacts is important for several reasons.

1. _____

2. _____

3. _____

Practice 12

Determine the logical order of the following sentences. Write **1** by the sentence that should come first, **2** by the sentence that should come second, **3** by the sentence that should come third, and so on. (*Hint:* Circle the classification listing words.)

Textbook
Skills

Avoiding Ageism

_____ Third, avoid implying that relationships are no longer important. Older people continue to be interested in relationships.

_____ To avoid ageism, be on guard against the following:

_____ Ageism signifies discrimination against the old.

_____ Next, don't assume you have to refresh an older person's memory each time you see the person.

_____ Finally, don't speak in an abnormally high volume; don't maintain an overly close physical distance.

_____ First, avoid talking down to a person because he or she is older. Older people are not slow; most people remain mentally alert well into old age.

—Adapted from DeVito, Joseph A., *Essentials of Human Communication*, pp. 93–94.

The Classification Pattern

Authors use the **classification pattern** to sort ideas into smaller groups and describe the traits of each group. Each smaller group, called a *subgroup*, is based on shared traits or characteristics. The author lists each subgroup and describes its traits.

Because groups and subgroups are listed, transitions of addition are used in this thought pattern. These transitions are coupled with words that indicate classes or groups. Examples of classification signal words are *first type, second kind*, and *another group*.

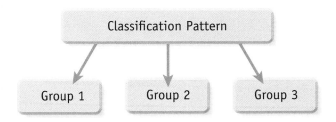

Transitions Used in the Classification Pattern		
another (group, kind, type)	first (group, categories, kind, type)	order
characteristics	second (group, class, kind, type)	traits

> **EXAMPLE** Determine the logical order for the following sentences. Write **1** by the sentence that should come first, **2** by the sentence that should come second, **3** by the sentence that should come third, and **4** by the sentence that should come last. (*Hint:* Circle the classification transition words.)

Types of Wetlands

_____ Another type of wetland is the marsh, which is frequently or continually swamped with water; it is characterized by soft-stemmed vegetation adapted to saturated soil conditions.

_____ One type of wetland is a bog, one of North America's most distinctive wetlands; it is characterized by spongy peat deposits, acidic waters, and a floor covered by a thick carpet of sphagnum moss.

_____ Finally, a swamp is a type of wetland dominated by woody plants.

_____ *Wetlands* is a general term that includes several types of vital links between water and land.

—Adapted from U.S. Environmental Protection Agency, "America's Wetlands."

EXPLANATION Compare your answers to the sentences arranged in the proper order in the following paragraph. The transition words are in **bold** print.

Types of Wetlands

[1]*Wetlands* is a general term that includes **several types** of vital links between water and land. [2]**One type** of wetland is a bog, one of North America's most distinctive wetlands; it is characterized by spongy peat deposits, acidic waters, and a floor covered by a thick carpet of sphagnum moss. [3]**Another type** of wetland is the marsh, which is frequently or continually swamped with water; it is characterized by soft-stemmed vegetation adapted to saturated soil conditions. [4]**Finally**, a swamp is **a type** of wetland dominated by woody plants.

In this paragraph, transitions of addition work with the classification signal words. In this case, *another* and *finally* convey the order of the types listed. ◀

Practice 13

The following paragraph uses the classification thought pattern. Fill in the outline that follows by giving the missing details in their proper order. (*Hint:* Circle the classification transition words.)

Types of Volcanic Eruptions

[1]During an episode of activity, a volcano commonly displays a distinctive pattern or type of behavior. [2]One type of eruption is a Vesuvian eruption; during this type of eruption, great quantities of ash-laden gas are violently discharged. [3]These gases form a cauliflower-shaped cloud high above the volcano. [4]A second kind of eruption is the Strombolian. [5]In a Strombolian-type eruption, huge clots of molten lava burst from the summit crater to form luminous arcs through the sky. [6]The lava collects on the flanks of the cone, and then lava clots combine to stream down the slopes in fiery rivulets. [7]Another kind of eruption is the Vulcanian type. [8]In this eruption, a dense cloud of ash-laden gas explodes from the crater and rises high above the peak. [9]Steaming ash forms a whitish cloud near the upper level of the cone. [10]A fourth kind of eruption is a Peléan or Nuée Ardente (glowing cloud) eruption. [11]A large amount of gas, dust, ash, and incandescent lava fragments are blown out of a central crater, fall back, and form tongue-like glowing avalanches. [12]These avalanches move down slope at speeds as great as 100 miles per hour.

—Adapted from U.S. Geological Survey,
"Types of Volcanic Eruptions."

Types of Volcanic Eruptions

1. _____

2. _____

3. _____

4. _____

VISUAL *VOCABULARY*

This volcano is experiencing a
_____ eruption.

a. Vesuvian
b. Strombolian
c. Vulcanian
d. Peléan

Practice 14

The following passage uses the classification thought pattern. Complete the concept map by giving the missing details in their proper order. (*Hint:* Circle the classification transition words.)

General Categories of Crime

[1]Violations of criminal law can be of many different types and vary in severity. [2]Five general categories of criminal law violations can be identified.

[3]Felonies are serious crimes; they include murder, rape, aggravated assault, robbery, burglary, and arson. [4]Today, many felons receive prison sentences, although the range of potential penalties includes everything from probation and a fine to capital punishment. [5]Following common law tradition, people who are convicted of felonies today usually lose certain privileges. [6]Some states, for example, make a felony conviction and incarceration grounds for uncontested divorce. [7]Others prohibit offenders from voting, running for public office, or owning a firearm and exclude them from some professions, such as medicine, law, and police work.

[8]Misdemeanors are relatively minor crimes, consisting of offenses such as petty theft, simple assault, breaking and entering; possessing burglary tools; being disorderly in public, disturbing the peace; filing a false crime report; and writing bad checks. [9]In general, misdemeanors are any crime punishable by a year or less in prison. [10]In fact, most misdemeanants receive suspended sentences involving a fine and supervised probation.

[11]A third category of crime is the offense. [12]Although, strictly speaking, all violations of the criminal law can be called criminal offenses, the term *offense* is used specifically to refer to minor violations of the law that are less serious than misdemeanors. [13]When the term is used in that sense, it refers to such things as jaywalking, spitting on the sidewalk, littering, and committing certain traffic violations, including the failure to wear a seat belt. [14]Another word used to describe such minor law violations is *infractions*. [15]People committing infractions are typically ticketed and released, usually on a promise to appear later in court. [16]Court appearances may often be waived through payment of a small fine that can be mailed to the court.

[17]Felonies, misdemeanors, offenses, and the people who commit them constitute the daily work of the justice system. [18]However, special categories of crime do exist and should be recognized. [19]One such category is treason and espionage, two crimes that are often regarded as the most serious of felonies.

[20]Another special category of crime is called *inchoate*. [21]The word *inchoate* means "incomplete or partial," and inchoate offenses are those that have not been fully carried out. [22]Conspiracies are an example. [23]When a person conspires to commit a crime, any action undertaken in furtherance of the conspiracy is generally regarded as a sufficient basis for arrest and prosecution. [24]For instance, a woman who intends to kill her husband may make a phone call or conduct an Internet search to find a hit man to carry out her plan. [25]The call and search are themselves evidence of her intent and can result in her imprisonment for conspiracy to commit murder.

—Condensed from Schmalleger, Frank J., *Criminal Justice: A Brief Introduction*, 9th ed., pp. 63, 65.

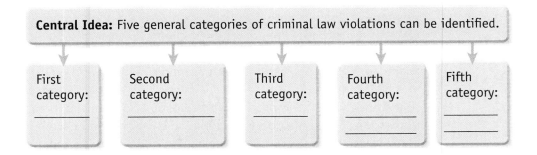

Central Idea: Five general categories of criminal law violations can be identified.

| First category: | Second category: | Third category: | Fourth category: | Fifth category: |

LO3 Develop Textbook Skills: Thought Patterns in Textbooks

Textbook Skills

Textbook authors often use transitions to make relationships between ideas clear and easy to understand. However, often an author will use more than one type of transition. For example, classification combines words that indicate addition and types. Sometimes addition and time words are used in the same paragraph or passage for a specific purpose. Furthermore, authors may mix thought patterns in the same paragraph or passage. Finally, be aware that relationships between ideas still exist even when transition words are not explicitly stated. The effective reader looks for the author's primary thought pattern.

►EXAMPLE Read the following paragraphs from college textbooks. Circle the transitions or signal words used in each paragraph. Then identify the primary thought pattern used in the paragraph.

A.

Textbook
Skills

A Dangerous Diet

Depriving the body of food for prolonged periods forces it to make adjustments to prevent the shutdown of organs. The body depletes its energy reserves to obtain the necessary fuels. The body first turns to protein tissue in order to maintain its supply of glucose. As this occurs, weight is lost rapidly because protein contains only half as many calories per pound as fat. At the same time, significant water stores are lost. Over time, the body begins to run out of liver tissue, heart muscle, blood, and so on, as these readily available substances are burned to supply energy.

—Adapted from Donatelle, Rebecca J.
Access to Health 12th ed., p. 271.

_____ The primary thought pattern of the paragraph is
   a. time order.
   b. classification.

B.

Textbook
Skills

Clothing

Clothing serves a variety of purposes. First, it protects you from the weather and, in sports like football, from injury. In addition, it helps you conceal parts of your body and so serves a modesty function. Clothing also serves as a cultural display. It communicates your cultural and subcultural affiliations. In the United States, where there are so many different ethnic groups, you can see examples of dress that indicate what country the wearers are from.

—Adapted from DeVito, Joseph A., *The Interpersonal Communication Book*, 10th ed., p. 204.

_____ The primary thought pattern of the paragraph is
   a. time order.
   b. listing.

C.

Textbook
Skills

Types of Interest Groups

Whether they are lobbying politicians or appealing to the public, interest groups are everywhere in the American political system. As with other aspects of American politics and policymaking, political scientists loosely categorize interest groups into clusters. Among the most important clusters are those that deal with economic issues, environmental concerns, equality issues, and the interests of consumers. A study of these four distinct types of interest groups will give you a good picture of the American interest group system.

—Adapted from George C. Edwards III, Martin P. Wattenberg,
and Robert L. Lineberry. *Government in America: People,
Politics, and Policy, Brief version,* 5th ed. Addison-Wesley
Educational Publishers Inc., 2000, p. 10.

_____ The primary thought pattern of the paragraph is
   a. time order.   b. classification.

Practice 15

Read the following paragraph from a college communications textbook. Circle the transitions or signal words used in the paragraph. Then identify the primary thought pattern used.

Culture Shock

Textbook
Skills

Culture shock refers to the psychological reaction you experience when you're in a culture very different from your own. Anthropologist Kalervo Oberg, who first used the term, notes that it occurs in stages. Stage one is the honeymoon. At first you experience fascination with the new culture and its people. This stage is characterized by cordiality and friendship in these early and superficial relationships. Stage two is the crisis. Here the differences between your own culture and the new one create problems. This is the stage at which you experience the actual shock of a new culture. Stage three is the recovery. During this period, you gain the skills necessary to function. You learn the language and ways of the new culture. Stage four is the adjustment. At this final stage, you adjust to and come to enjoy the new culture and experiences. You may still experience periodic difficulties and strains, but on the whole, the experience is pleasant.

—Adapted from DeVito, Joseph A., *The Interpersonal
Communication Book*, 10th ed., p. 59.

_____ The primary thought pattern of the paragraph is
   a. time order.
   b. classification.

Apply Information Literacy Skills

 Academic, Personal, and Career Applications of Transitions and Thought Patterns

As you learned in Chapter 6, understanding how knowledge is organized is a basic information literacy skill. Transitions and thought patterns also help organize information and ideas by focusing attention on key concepts and relationships. Transitions and thought patterns connect specific details to logically support a main idea. The transitions, or signal words, of a thought pattern help you predict what's to come. When you understand the structure of an idea, you can monitor your comprehension as you read. Transitions and thought patterns show how ideas are connected in academic, personal, and career situations. Therefore, you will use the skills that you learned in this chapter in several ways:

- You will recognize your own need to identify transitions and thought patterns.
- You will analyze information to see the relationships among ideas.
- You will determine the author's use of a thought pattern to develop a main idea.

Academic Application

Assume you are taking a college course in communication. You are required to give an in-class speech about a communication topic of your choice. You have chosen to speak about the steps in the listening process. You want to focus on how listeners take in information.

- **Before Reading:** Skim the table of contents and identify the page numbers you need to read to learn about the steps in the listening process and how listeners take in information. Use the topic and thought pattern to create a pre-reading question to guide your reading.
- **During Reading:** Annotate the details in the passage that answer your pre-reading question.
- **After Reading:** In the space following the passage, create an outline or concept map that captures the details you will use in your speech.

—DeVito, Joseph A. *Interpersonal Communication Book.* © 2009.

Before Reading: Page numbers of relevant information: _____

_____

Pre-Reading Question: _____

_____

The Stages of Listening

[1]Listening is a five-stage process of (1) receiving, (2) understanding, (3) remembering, (4) evaluating, and (5) responding to oral messages. [2]As you'll see from the following discussion, listening involves a collection of skills that work together at each of these five stages. [3]Listening can go wrong at any stage; by the same token, you can enhance your listening ability by strengthening the skills needed for each step of the process.

[4]All five stages overlap. [5]When you listen, you're performing all five processes at essentially the same time. [6]For example, when listening in conversation, you're not only processing what you hear for understanding, but you're also putting it into memory storage, critically evaluating what was said, and responding (nonverbally and perhaps with verbal messages as well).

Receiving

[7]Unlike listening, hearing begins and ends with this first stage—receiving. [8]Hearing is something that just happens when you get within earshot of auditory stimuli. [9]Listening is quite different. [10]Listening begins, but does not end, with receiving messages the speaker sends. [11]In listening, you receive both the verbal and the nonverbal messages—not only the words but also the gestures, facial expressions, variations in volume and rate, and lots more. [12]The following suggestions should help you receive messages more effectively:

- [13]Focus attention on the speaker's verbal and nonverbal messages, on both what is said and what is not said, rather than on what you'll say next.
- [14]Maintain your role as listener and avoid interrupting the speaker until he or she is finished.

- [15]Avoid assuming you understand what the speaker is going to say before he or she actually says it.

After Reading Outline or Concept Map of Key Ideas:

Five-Stage Process of Listening   **How to Receive Messages**

1. _____   a. _____

2. _____   b. _____

3. _____   _____

4. _____   c. _____

5. Responding   d. _____

Personal Application

Assume you live in an area prone to a specific type of natural disaster such as flooding, tornados, hurricanes, or wildfires. You have decided to prepare before a disaster occurs. To locate information, use key transition words of specific thought patterns along with a specific natural disaster to create search terms for an Internet search box.

Search Terms: _____

_____

- **Before Reading:** First, skim the homepage *Ready: Prepare, Plan, Stay Informed,* hosted by the U.S. Federal Emergency Management Agency (FEMA). Circle the term(s) you would click on to learn more about a specific type of disaster. Second, skim the passage about earthquakes. Create a pre-reading question using a key transition of a thought pattern.
- **During Reading:** Annotate the details in the passage that answer your pre-reading question.
- **After Reading:** In the space following the passage, create a poster, visual chart, or illustration of the key ideas in the passage to post in your home as part of your preparation plan.

Ready: Prepare, Plan, Stay Informed

Get To Know Ready	Resources & Polices	Participate	Languages	Follow Us	Disaster Types
About Us	FEMA Website	National Preparedness Month	Español	Facebook	Hurricanes
Contact Us	DHS Website		Français	Twitter	Floods
FAQS	Disaster Assistance	Community & State Info	Kreyòl Ayisyen	Email Sign-up	Earthquakes
Press & News	Citizen Corps	Resolve to be Ready	Русский	FEMA YouTube	Wildfires
Publications	USA.gov		Tagalog	FEMA Blog	Tornadoes
Ready.gov Mobile Site	Freedom of Information Act		TiếngViệt		Home Fires
PSA & Multimedia	No FEAR Act Data		한국어		Blackouts
Important Notices	Equal Opportunity Data		日本語		Biological Threats
Localized Ready Programs	Privacy Policy		中文		
Testimonials	Accessibility		العربية		
	Download Plugins		☐☐☐☐☐☐		
			اردو,		

http://www.ready.gov/natural-disasters

Pre-Reading Question: _____

_____

What to Do During an Earthquake

^{1}Drop, cover and hold on. ^{2}Minimize your movements to a few steps to a nearby safe place.

If Indoors

^{3}First, **Drop** to the ground; take **cover** by getting under a sturdy table or other piece of furniture; and **hold on** until the shaking stops. ^{4}If there isn't a table or desk near you, cover your face and head with your arms and crouch in an inside corner of the building. ^{5}Stay away from glass, windows, outside doors and walls, and anything that could fall, such as lighting fixtures or furniture. ^{6}Second, stay in bed if you are there when the earthquake strikes. ^{7}Hold on and protect your head with a pillow, unless you are under a heavy light fixture that could fall. ^{8}In that case, move to the nearest safe place. ^{9}Third, do not use a doorway except if you know it is a strongly supported, load-bearing doorway and it is close to you. ^{10}Many inside doorways are lightly constructed and do not offer protection. ^{11}Fourth, stay inside until the shaking stops and it is safe to go outside. ^{12}Do not exit a building during the shaking. ^{13}Research has shown that most injuries occur when people inside buildings attempt to move to a different location inside the building or try to leave. ^{14}Finally, _do not_ use the elevators.

If Outdoors

[15]First, stay there. [16]Next, move away from buildings, streetlights, and utility wires. [17]Then, once in the open, stay there until the shaking stops. [18]The greatest danger exists directly outside buildings, at exits and alongside exterior walls. [19]Many of the 120 fatalities from the 1933 Long Beach earthquake occurred when people ran outside of buildings only to be killed by falling debris from collapsing walls. [20]Ground movement during an earthquake is seldom the direct cause of death or injury. [21]Most earthquake-related casualties result from collapsing walls, flying glass, and falling objects.

—"Earthquakes: During." <http://www.ready.gov/earthquakes>

Poster, Chart, or Visual Illustration: _____

Career Application

Assume you work in the human resources department of an independent hotel in your area. You are on a search committee for a lodging manager to run the day-to-day operations of the hotel. The committee has received dozens of letters of application. You are in the process of reading and evaluating the letters of each applicant before you meet with the committee to discuss your recommendations.

- **Before Reading:** Skim the following letter. In the space provided after the passage, create a list of the desirable traits of the applicant. Leave room to list examples after reading the letter.
- **During Reading:** Annotate the details in the letter that illustrate each desirable trait.
- **After Reading:** Make a recommendation about hiring the individual. State your reasons.

Dear Ms. Holmes

[1]I read in the March 3, 2012, *News Journal* employment section that The Lotus Inn is hiring a lodging manager, and I would like to speak with you about this job. [2]My skills, education, experience, and work ethic make me an excellent candidate for the position. [3]I am able to get along with many different types of people, even in stressful situations. [4]I am able to solve problems quickly and concentrate on details. [5]Initiative, self-discipline, effective communication skills, and the ability to organize and direct the work of others are skills I bring to the job.

[6]Before earning an associate's degree in hospitality management from Central State College, I gained hands-on experience as a work-study front desk clerk for Mango Inn, an intern in the public relations department at Good Knight Suites, and a part-time employee for five summers on the janitorial staff at Home Suites, all in East Beach. [7]My experience gives me a solid knowledge of hotel operations, including safety and security measures, repair and maintenance, and personnel practices. [8]I have learned firsthand that hotels are open 24/7, and lodging managers work more than 40 hours per week and are often on call. [9]My strong work ethic makes me ideal for the hotel industry.

[10]I look forward to meeting with you to discuss the lodging manager position. [11]I am confident that my skills, education, experience, and work ethic will enable me to contribute to the success of The Lotus Inn. [12]If you have any questions, please call me at 840-676-4987. [13]For your reference I have included my resume. [14]Thank you for taking time to review my documents.

Sincerely,

Jean H. Nance

Desirable Traits of Applicant

Skills
_____

_____

_____

_____

_____

Education _____

Experience _____

_____

_____

Work Ethic _____

Recommendation: _____

_____

_____

REVIEW TEST 1

Score (number correct) _____ × 10 = _____%

Visit MyReadingLab to take this test online and receive feedback and guidance on your answers.

Transition Words and Thought Patterns

Match each of the thought patterns to the appropriate group of transition words. Thought patterns will be used more than once.

a. time order
b. space order
c. listing
d. classification

___d___ **1.** one type, several kinds, another group

___c___ **2.** first, second, third, fourth

___a___ **3.** before, after, while, during

___b___ **4.** behind, below, above, over

___a___ **5.** currently, eventually, previously

___c___ **6.** furthermore, moreover, besides

___d___ **7.** characteristics, traits, order

___b___ **8.** beneath, nearby, within

___b___ **9.** here, there

___c___ **10.** and, also, for one thing

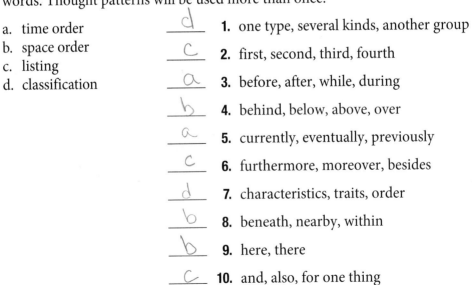

REVIEW TEST 2

Score (number correct) _____ × 10 = _____ %

Visit MyReadingLab to take this test online and receive feedback and guidance on your answers.

Transition Words

Select a transition word for each of the blanks. Then identify the type of transition you chose.

A. Pilates develops a strong and supple spine by extending the space _____ each vertebra.

_____ **1.** The best transition word for the sentence is
   a. between.   c. before.
   b. after.

_____ **2.** The relationship between the ideas is one of
   a. classification.   b. space order.

B. Proper posture is a matter of correctly positioning your body; place the joints between your big and second toes under your knees; pull your abdominals _____ your spine, relax your shoulders down, and lengthen your body through the crown of your head.

_____ **3.** The best transition word for the sentence is
   a. toward.   c. one.
   b. eventually.

_____ **4.** The relationship between the ideas is one of
   a. space order.   b. addition.

C. The best course of action to take _____ one has made a mistake is to admit it, learn from it, and avoid making it again.

_____ **5.** The best transition word for the sentence is
   a. when.   c. since.
   b. before.

_____ **6.** The relationship between the ideas is one of
   a. listing.   b. time order.

D. A character in a work of fiction is often studied on the basis of two groups of traits. The first group identifies whether the character is dynamic and changes or is static and stays the same. The _____ identifies whether the character is round and fully developed or remains flat with only one main personality feature.

_____ **7.** The best transition word or phrase for the sentence above is
a. additional part.   c. later time.
b. second group.

_____ **8.** The relationship between the ideas is one of
a. classification.   b. time order.

E. A monarch butterfly has four stages in its life cycle. The first stage begins _____ a female monarch mates and lays eggs on leaves. The second stage occurs when a tiny larva hatches and begins to eat its eggshell and the leaves of the plant. The larva changes into the pupa or chrysalis, the third major stage of the monarch's life cycle. The final stage involves the adult monarch emerging from its chrysalis to dry its wings.

VISUAL VOCABULARY

This insect is in what stage of its life cycle? _____

a. egg
b. larva
c. chrysalis

_____ **9.** The best transition word for the sentence is
a. before.   c. as.
b. and.

_____ **10.** The relationship between the ideas is one of
a. time order.   b. addition.

REVIEW TEST 3

Score (number correct) _____ × 25 = _____%

Visit MyReadingLab to take this test online and receive feedback and guidance on your answers.

Transitions and Thought Patterns

Textbook Skills

Read the following passage from a college psychology textbook.

Where Are You in the Career Development Process?

[1]Have you ever wondered what type of work you are best suited for? [2]If so, you may want to begin your quest for an answer by looking at two models of career development, the process of choosing and adjusting to a particular career. [3]Recommendations about what you might do to enhance your search for the ideal career can be derived from both. [4]Ultimately, though, the degree to which you are satisfied with your career may depend on how you integrate your work into your life as a whole.

Holland's Personality Types

[5]The work of John Holland has been very influential in shaping psychologists' ideas about personality and career. [6]Holland proposes six basic personality types: realistic, investigative, artistic, social, enterprising, and conventional. [7]His research shows that each of the six types is associated with work preferences. [8]First, realistic types are aggressive, masculine, and physically strong, often with low verbal or interpersonal skills. [9]The work preferences of this type include mechanical activities and tool use. [10]They often choose jobs such as mechanic, electrician, or surveyor. [11]Second, investigative types are oriented toward thinking (particularly abstract thinking), organizing, and planning. [12]They are often low in social skills. [13]Their work presences include ambiguous, challenging tasks. [14]They often choose to become a scientist or engineer. [15]Third, artistic types are asocial. [16]They prefer unstructured, highly individual activity; often they become artists. [17]Fourth, the social types are extraverted, people-oriented, sociable, and need attention; additionally, they avoid intellectual activity and dislike highly ordered activity. [18]The social type likes working with people in service jobs like nursing and education. [19]Fifth, the enterprising type is highly verbal and dominating; they enjoy organizing and directing others. [20]They are persuasive and strong leaders.

[21]They often choose a career in sales. [22]Finally, the conventional type prefers structured activities and subordinate roles; likes clear guidelines; accurate and precise. [23]They may choose an occupation such as book-keeping or filing.

[24]As Holland's theory predicts, people whose personality matches their job are also more likely to be satisfied with their work. [25]Thus, a personality assessment may help you make an appropriate occupational choice and give you confidence about the decision.

Super's Career Development Stages

[26]Psychologist Donald Super proposed that career development happens in stages that begin in infancy. [27]First comes the growth stage (from birth to 14 years), in which you learn about your abilities and interests. [28]Next is the exploratory stage, roughly between the ages of 15 and 24. [29]According to Super, there's a lot of trial and error in this stage, so job changes happen frequently. [30]Next is the establishment stage (also called the stabilization stage), from 25 to 45. [31]This stage begins with learning how things work in your career, the culture of your organization, and progression through the early steps of the career ladder. [32]Sometimes, additional formal training is required during this stage. [33]Setting goals is also important in this stage. [34]You must decide how far you want to go and how you intend to get there. [35]Mentoring by an experienced co-worker often helps you negotiate this stage successfully. [36]Once an individual has become well established in a career, she or he enters the maintenance phase (age 45 through retirement), in which the goal is to protect and maintain the gains made in earlier years. [37]Of course, in today's rapidly changing economy, people are often required to change careers. [38]Thus, an individual may reenter the exploratory stage at any time. [39]As with most stage theories, the ages associated with Super's stages of career development are less important than the sequence of the stages.

—Adapted from Wood, Samuel E., Wood, Ellen
Green, and Boyd, Denise G., *Mastering the World
of Psychology*, 3rd ed., p. 275.

_____ **1.** The thought pattern of the second paragraph (sentences 5–23) is
   a. process.   c. narration.
   b. classification.   d. space order.

_____ **2.** The thought pattern of the third paragraph (sentences 26–39) is
a. process.   c. narration.
b. classification.   d. space order.

_____ **3.** The relationship of ideas within sentence 17 is
a. time order.   c. space order.
b. addition.

_____ **4.** The relationship of ideas between sentences 27 and 28 is
a. time order.   c. space order.
b. addition.

VISUAL *VOCABULARY*

Based on the work she has chosen, this woman represents the _____ type of personality.

a. artistic
b. investigative
c. realistic

SUMMARY RESPONSE

Restate the author's central idea in your own words. Include the two major thought patterns used by the authors in your summary. Begin your summary response with the following: *The central idea of "Where Are You in the Career Developmental Process?" by Wood, Wood, and Boyd, is …*

WHAT DO YOU THINK?

Write a brief essay that includes the following ideas:

■ Describe your career goals based on your personality.

■ Describe your current state of career development.

■ Predict how your current state of career development will affect your career goals.

REVIEW TEST 4

Score (number correct) _____ × 10 = _____%

Visit MyReadingLab to take this test online and receive feedback and guidance on your answers.

Transition Words and Thought Patterns

The following passage is from a college textbook on professionalism. Before you read, skim the passage and answer the Before Reading questions. Read the passage. Then answer the After Reading questions.

Making Ethical Choices

[1]As you attempt to make ethical choices at work, use the three levels of ethical decisions. [2]The first level of ethics is the law. [3]When **confronted** with an ethical issue, first ask if the action is legal. [4]If the action is illegal, it is unethical.

[5]The second level of ethics is fairness. [6]Your actions/behavior should be fair to all parties involved. [7]If, when making a decision, someone is clearly going to be harmed or is unable to defend himself or herself, the decision is probably not ethical. [8]Note that the concept of "fairness" does not mean that everyone is happy with the outcome. [9]It only means that the decision has been made in an impartial and unbiased manner. [10]Sometimes, a behavior is legal but may be considered unethical. [11]Just because a behavior is legal does not mean it is right. [12]Take the case of an individual who has a romantic relationship with someone who is married to someone else. [13]There is no law that says having an extramarital affair is illegal.[14]_____, many consider this behavior unethical.

[15]It is understandable that not everyone agrees on what is right and fair. [16]This is where the third level of ethics—one's conscience—must be considered. [17]This is also when an ethical decision gets personal. [18]In the classic Disney movie, *Pinocchio*, there was a character named Jiminy Cricket. [19]He was Pinocchio's conscience. [20]He made Pinocchio feel bad when Pinocchio behaved inappropriately. [21]Just like Pinocchio, each individual has a conscience. [22]When one knowingly behaves inappropriately, most will eventually feel bad about his poor behavior. [23]Some people take a bit longer to feel bad than others, but most everyone at some point feels bad when they have wronged another. [24]Sometimes a behavior may be legal and it may be fair to others, but it still may make us feel guilty or bad. [25]If it does, the behavior is probably unethical.

²⁶What should you do when others are not behaving ethically? ²⁷Let us go back to the three levels of ethical decision making. ²⁸Everyone must abide by the law. ²⁹If someone at work is breaking the law, you have an obligation to inform your employer immediately. ³⁰This can be done confidentially to either your supervisor or the human resources department. ³¹Whenever you accuse anyone of wrongdoing, have documented facts and solid evidence. ³²Keep track of important dates, events, and copies of evidence. ³³Your **credibility** is at stake. ³⁴Remember, depending on the **enormity** of the situation, you, as an employee, have three choices: (1) alert outside officials if the offense is illegal and extreme; (2) if the offense is not extreme and is accepted by management, accept management's decision; or (3) if the inappropriate behavior is accepted by management and you are still bothered, decide whether you want to continue working for the company.

³⁵Another common ethical issue at work occurs in the area of company theft. ³⁶Company theft is not always large items such as computers or equipment. ³⁷More often, it is smaller items such as office supplies. ³⁸Time can also be stolen from a company. ³⁹If you use company time to surf the Internet, make personal calls, or take extra long breaks, you are stealing from the company. ⁴⁰You may not realize that taking a pen or pencil home is stealing from your company. ⁴¹Office supplies should only be used for business purposes. ⁴²Although it is heavily influenced by the company and how others view right behavior from wrong, ethical behavior starts with the individual.

—Adapted from Anderson, Lydia E. and Bolt, Sandra B., *Professionalism: Skills for Workplace Success*, 2nd ed., pp. 60, 62.

Before Reading

Vocabulary in Context

_____ **1.** The word **confronted** in 3 sentence means
    a. puzzled.   c. faced.
    b. surprised.   d. stopped.

_____ **2.** The word **credibility** in sentence 33 means
    a. believability.   c. honor.
    b. position.   d. status.

_____ **3.** The word **enormity** in sentence 34 means
    a. understanding.   c. size.
    b. occurrence.   d. seriousness.

After Reading

Concept Maps

4. Finish the concept map by filling in the missing idea with information from the passage.

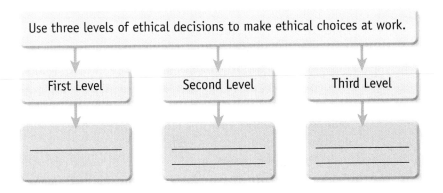

Use three levels of ethical decisions to make ethical choices at work.

First Level ▸ _____

Second Level ▸ _____

Third Level ▸ _____

Central Idea and Main Idea

_____ **5.** Which sentence states the central idea of the passage?
   a. sentence 1   c. sentence 35
   b. sentence 3   d. sentence 42

Supporting Details

_____ **6.** What type of supporting detail is sentence 11?
   a. major supporting detail   b. minor supporting detail

Transitions and Thought Patterns

_____ **7.** The word **as** in sentence 1 is a transition that shows
   a. space order.   b. time order.

_____ **8.** What thought pattern is suggested by sentence 35?
   a. listing   b. time order

_____ **9.** What is the relationship between sentence 16 and sentence 17?
   a. time order   b. addition

_____ **10.** Which is the best transition for the blank in sentence 14?
   a. However   c. Finally
   b. In addition   d. Thus

SUMMARY RESPONSE

Restate the author's central idea in your own words. Include the two major thought patterns used by the authors in your summary. Begin your summary response with the following: *The central idea of "Making Ethical Choices" by Anderson and Bolt is …*

WHAT DO YOU THINK?

Do you agree with the author's analysis of the levels of ethical decisions? How do you make ethical choices? In general, do you think people today are as concerned with personal ethics as they were in the past? What about college students? Assume you are a columnist for your college newspaper. Write a column on making ethical choices at school. Consider the following ideas to help guide your writing:

- Use examples that college students may be faced with.
- Use the concept map to help organize your writing.

After Reading About Transitions and Thought Patterns

Before you move on to the Mastery Tests on transitions and thought patterns, take time to reflect on your learning and performance by answering the following questions. Write your answers in your notebook.

- How has my knowledge base or prior knowledge about transitions and thought patterns changed?
- Based on my studies, how do I think I will perform on the Mastery Test(s)? Why do I think my scores will be above average, average, or below average?
- Would I recommend this chapter to other students who want to learn more about transitions and thought patterns? Why or why not?

Test your understanding of what you have learned about thought patterns by completing the Chapter 7 Review.

Name _____ Section _____

Date _____ **Score** (number correct) _____ × 10 = _____%

Visit MyReadingLab to take this test online and receive feedback and guidance on your answers.

A. The following items are from a college math textbook. Fill in the blanks with the correct transition word from the box. Use each word once.

before	during	in	then	when

Textbook Skills

1–2. Reading and highlighting a section of your textbook _____ your instructor lectures on it allows you to maximize your learning and understanding _____ the lecture.

3–4. Try to keep one section ahead of your syllabus. _____ you study ahead of your lectures, you can _____ concentrate on what is being explained in them instead of trying to write everything down.

5. Highlight key points _____ your textbook as you study.

—Adapted from Bittinger, Marvin L. and Beecher, Judith A., *Introductory and Intermediate Algebra*, 2nd ed., p. 43.

B. Read the following paragraph from a college communications textbook. Fill in each blank with the correct transition word from the box. Use each word once.

frequently	immediate	past	then	when

Gunnysacking

Textbook Skills

A gunnysack is a large bag, usually made of burlap. As a conflict strategy, gunnysacking refers to the practice of storing up grievances to unload them at another time. The **(6)** _____ occasion may be relatively simple (or so it may seem at first), such as someone's coming home late without calling. Instead of arguing about this, the gunnysacker unloads all **(7)** _____ grievances: the birthday you forgot two years ago, the time you arrived late for dinner last month, and the hotel reservations you forgot to make. As you probably know from experience, gunnysacking leads to more gunnysacking. (**8**) _____ one person gunnysacks, the other person often does so as well. (**9**) _____ two people end up dumping their stored up grievances on one another. (**10**) _____, the original problem never gets addressed. Instead, resentment and hostility build up.

—Adapted from DeVito, Joseph A.,
Essentials of Human Communication, p. 177.

Name _____ Section _____

Date _____ **Score** (number correct) _____ × 10 = _____%

Visit My ReadingLab to take this test online and receive feedback and guidance on your answers.

A. Fill in each blank with the correct transition word from the box. Use each word once.

another   during   in   occasionally   often

1. Although it doesn't happen frequently, American society has _____ been gripped by fear, and its responses have not done credit to the nature of freedom.

2. The Red Scare, the hunt for communist traitors living in America, is one

   example of a fear that occurred following World War I. _____ this time, hundreds of innocent immigrants were rounded up, imprisoned, and deported, for no reason other than fear of their allegedly radical ideas.

3. Even though the great fears of the first Red Scare were unfounded, the conflict between the United States and its allies and the Soviet Union and

   its allies, known as the Cold War, unleashed _____ Red Scare in the late 1940s and early 1950s.

4. The hunt for alleged traitors started during World War II and was furthered

   by congressional committees. These committees _____ abused their powers and harassed people who did not share their political views.

5. In February 1950, Senator Joseph McCarthy of Wisconsin began a witch hunt for so-called traitors; he claimed that communists were working

   _____ the State Department. For four years, he used his power improperly as he led a senate investigation. He and his aides made wild accusations, browbeat witnesses, ruined reputations, and threw mud at harmless people. Moreover, even the president of the United States was afraid to stand up to him.

   —Adapted from U.S. Department of State,
   "Censure of Senator Joseph McCarthy."

B. Read the following paragraph from a college social science textbook. Fill in each blank with the correct transition from the box. Then answer the question that follows it.

finally   one   second   third

Textbook
Skills

Relax and Listen

¹Learning to relax is among the best ways to improve concentration during listening. ²A variety of physical and mental exercises will help you sustain attention as you listen. ³**(6)** _____ activity is relaxing your muscles. ⁴Tighten a single muscle group such as your neck, your lower arm, or your foot for five or six seconds, and then completely relax it. ⁵Begin at the extremities of your body and work inward. ⁶You will realize that you were experiencing muscle stress as normal. ⁷**(7)** A _____ exercise is imagery. ⁸To relax before the listening session, vividly recall a positive experience; relive all of the sights, smells, and sounds. ⁹Your mind will relax as it focuses on these memories. ¹⁰This effect can also be reached through fantasy by calling up imaginary events or images. ¹¹A **(8)** _____ exercise is mental rehearsal, trying out in your mind various solutions to a stressful problem; when athletes have rehearsed mentally and see themselves winning, they have gone on to be highly successful. ¹²**(9)** _____, deep breathing clears your mind and enables you to relax; this technique is helpful for any stressful listening event.

—Adapted from Brownell, Judi, *Listening: Attitudes, Principles, and Skills*, p. 88.

_____ **10.** The thought pattern of the paragraph is
   a. time order.   b. listing.

Name _____ Section _____

Date _____ **Score** (number correct) _____ × 10 = _____%

Visit MyReadingLab to take this test online and receive feedback and guidance on your answers.

A. Read the following paragraph from a college mathematics textbook.

Textbook
Skills

A Five-Step Strategy for Solving Problems

[1]Many students fear solving mathematical problems so much that their thinking freezes with anxiety. [2]A five-step strategy can be very helpful in solving problems. [3]First, familiarize yourself with the problem situation; read it out loud or make and label a drawing, and assign a letter or variable to the unknown. [4]Second, translate the problem into an equation; use mathematical expressions and symbols and the letter or variable. [5]Third, solve the equation. [6]_____, check the answer in the original wording of the problem. [7]Finally, clearly state the answer to the problem with the appropriate units, such as dollars and cents or inches.

—Adapted from Bittinger, Marvin L., Beecher and
Judith A., *Introductory and Intermediate Algebra:
Combined Approach*, p. 387.

_____ **1.** The transition word that best fits the blank in sentence 6 is
   a. First.
   b. Third.
   c. Next.

_____ **2.** The thought pattern used in the paragraph is
   a. classification.
   b. time order.

3–8. Fill in the concept map with the topic sentence and major supporting details from the passage.

B. Read the following paragraph on self health care.

When the Doctor Is Not Necessary

[1]Many trips to the doctor's office and especially the hospital emergency room are not necessary. [2]While seeking a doctor's expertise is often wise or even essential, people can take care of many minor health problems themselves. [3]Self health care requires knowing one's body and recognizing the signs of common ailments. [4]These include colds and allergy symptoms as well as minor injuries such as abrasions. [5]Simple ways to care for oneself when ill or injured include taking over-the-counter medicines as directed, knowing first aid for minor injuries, and using doctor-recommended home remedies such as gargling with salt water for a sore throat. [6]_____, sometimes just plain rest can go a long way to helping cure an ailment.

_____ 9. In this paragraph, the author's thought pattern involves
   a. listing ways to cure minor ailments.
   b. explaining step by step how to cure oneself.

_____ 10. The transition that best fits the blank in sentence 6 is
   a. First.
   b. For one thing.
   c. Furthermore.

Name _____ Section _____

Date _____ **Score** (number correct) _____ × 10 = _____%

Visit MyReadingLab to take this test online and receive feedback and guidance on your answers.

Read the following passage from a college textbook about the environment. Fill in each blank with a transition from the box. Use each transition once. Then complete the concept map with information from the passage.

first   fourth type   one example   second type   third type

Textbook
Skills

Toxicants Come in Different Types

Toxicants can be classified based on their particular effects on health. **(1)** _____ are carcinogens, the best known. These are chemicals or types of radiation that cause cancer. In cancer, malignant cells grow uncontrollably, creating tumors, damaging the body's functioning, and often leading to death. In our society today, the greatest number of cancer cases is thought to result from carcinogens contained in cigarette smoke. Carcinogens can be difficult to identify because there may be a long lag time between exposure to the agent and the detectable onset of cancer.

Mutagens, a **(2)** _____, are chemicals that cause mutations in the DNA of organisms. Although most mutations have little or no effect, some can lead to severe problems, including cancer and other disorders. If mutations occur in an individual's sperm or egg cells, then the individual's offspring suffer the effects.

The **(3)** _____ of chemicals that cause harm to the unborn are called teratogens. Teratogens that affect the development of human embryos in the womb can cause birth defects. **(4)** _____ involves the drug thalidomide, developed in the 1950s as a sleeping pill and to prevent nausea during pregnancy. Tragically, the drug turned out to be a

345

powerful teratogen, and caused birth defects in thousands of babies. Thalidomide was banned in the 1960s once scientists recognized this connection.

The (5) _____ of chemical toxicants, neurotoxins, assaults the nervous system. Neurotoxins include various heavy metals such as lead, mercury, and cadmium, as well as pesticides and some chemical weapons developed for use in war. A famous case of neurotoxin poisoning occurred in Japan, where a chemical factory dumped mercury waste into Minamata Bay between the 1930s and 1960s. Thousands of people there ate fish contaminated with the mercury and soon began suffering from slurred speech, loss of muscle control, sudden fits of laughter, and in some cases death. The company and the government eventually paid out about $5,000 in compensation to each poisoned resident.

—Adapted from Withgott, Jay H. and Scott R. Brennan, *Essential Environment: The Science Behind the Stories*, 3rd ed., p. 218.

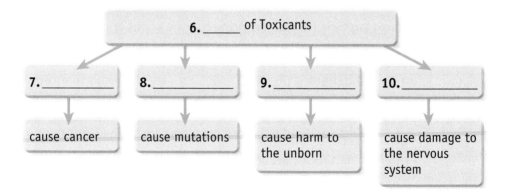

6. _____ of Toxicants

7. _____ → cause cancer

8. _____ → cause mutations

9. _____ → cause harm to the unborn

10. _____ → cause damage to the nervous system

7 Summary of Key Concepts of Transitions and Thought Patterns

 LO1 LO2 LO3   Assess your comprehension of transitions and thought patterns.

▪ Transitions are _____

_____.

▪ A thought pattern is established by using _____ to show the logical relationship among ideas in a paragraph or passage.

▪ _____ and process are two uses of the _____ order thought pattern.

▪ In addition to showing a chain of events, the time order pattern is used to show _____, _____, or _____ that can be repeated at any time with similar results.

▪ The space order pattern allows authors to _____

_____.

▪ Some of the words used to establish the space order pattern include *adjacent*,

_____, and _____.

▪ Transitions of addition, such as _____, _____, and *furthermore*, are generally used to indicate a _____ pattern.

▪ Authors use the classification pattern to _____

_____.

▪ Examples of classification signal words are _____, *second type*, and *another group*.

Test Your Comprehension of Transitions and Thought Patterns

Respond to the following questions and prompts.

LO1 LO2 In your own words, what is a transition? _____

_____

_____

LO1 LO2
LO3 In your own words, what is a thought pattern? _____

_____

LO2 LO3
LO4 In the space below, organize the following ideas from a college earth science textbook into a logical thought pattern. Create an outline or concept map.

> The Earth can be thought of as having four major spheres. First, the hydrosphere is a dynamic mass of water that is always on the move, evaporating from the oceans to the atmosphere, precipitating to the land, and flowing back to the ocean again. Additionally, Earth is surrounded by a life-giving gaseous envelope called the atmosphere. This thin blanket of the atmosphere provides the air we breathe and protects us from the sun's rays. Next, lying beneath the atmosphere and the ocean is the solid Earth or the geosphere. The fourth sphere, the biosphere, includes all life on Earth.

> —Adapted from Lutgens, Frederick K., Tarbuck, Edward J., and Tasa, Dennis G., *Foundations of Earth Science*, 5th ed., pp. 4–6.

LO1 LO2
LO3 LO4 Summarize the two most important ideas in this chapter that will help you improve your reading comprehension. _____

_____

_____

More Thought Patterns

After studying this chapter, you should be able to do:

LO1 Recognize the Comparison-and-Contrast Pattern and Signal Words

LO2 Recognize the Cause-and-Effect Pattern and Signal Words

LO3 Recognize the Generalization-and-Example Pattern and Signal Words

LO4 Recognize the Definition-and-Example Pattern and Signal Words

LO5 Develop Textbook Skills: Thought Patterns in Textbooks

LO6 Apply Information Literacy Skills: Academic, Personal, and Career Applications of More Thought Patterns

Before Reading About More Thought Patterns

In Chapter 7, you learned several important ideas that will help you as you work through this chapter. Use the following questions to call up your prior knowledge about transitions and thought patterns.

What are transitions? (Refer to page 290.) _____

_____

_____

What are thought patterns? (Refer to page 290.) _____

_____

_____

What is important to know about mixed thought patterns? Give an example

from Chapter 7. (Refer to page 318.) _____

_____

_____

_____

You have learned that transitions and thought patterns show the relationships of ideas within sentences as well as between sentences and paragraphs, and you studied four common types: time order, space order, listing, and classification. In this chapter, we will explore some other common thought patterns:

- The comparison-and-contrast pattern
- The cause-and-effect pattern
- The generalization-and-example pattern
- The definition-and-example pattern

Recognize the Comparison-and-Contrast Pattern and Signal Words

Many ideas become clearer when they are thought of in relation to one another. For example, comparing the prices different grocery stores charge makes us smarter shoppers. Likewise, noting the difference between loving and selfish behavior helps us choose partners in life. The comparison-and-contrast pattern enables us to see these relationships. This section discusses both comparison and contrast, starting with comparison. The discussion then turns to the important and effective comparison-and-contrast pattern, in which these two basic ways of organizing ideas are combined when writing an explanation, a description, or an analysis.

Comparison

Comparison points out the ways in which two or more ideas are alike. Sample signal words are *similar, like,* and *just as.*

Words and Phrases of Comparison				
alike	in a similar fashion	just as	resemble	similarly
as	in a similar manner	just like	same	
as well as	in like manner	like	similar	
equally	in the same way	likewise	similarity	

Here are some examples:

Just as we relate to others based on their personality traits, we tend to interact with our personal computers based on their performance.

Writing, **like** farming, follows a cycle of planting, growing, and reaping.
African and European artists use many of the **same** subjects in their art.

Each of these sentences has two topics that are similar in some way. The similarity is the author's main point. For example, the first sentence compares human personality traits to the way a personal computer performs. The comparison is introduced by the phrase *just as*. The second sentence compares the writing process to the farming process using the signal word *like*. And the third sentence compares the subjects African artists choose for their art to the subjects European artists choose.

When comparison is used to organize an entire paragraph, the pattern looks like the following chart.

Comparison Pattern		
Idea 1		**Idea 2**
Idea 1	*like*	Idea 2
Idea 1	*like*	Idea 2
Idea 1	*like*	Idea 2

⊘ **EXAMPLE** Determine a logical order for the following four sentences. Write **1** by the sentence that should come first, **2** by the sentence that should come second, **3** by the sentence that should come third, and **4** by the sentence that should come last. Then use the information to fill in the chart.

_____ Humans and mice both have about 30,000 genes.

_____ The genetic similarities between humans and mice support the use of mice in scientific research.

_____ Another important similarity is that 90 percent of genes linked to diseases are identical in the human and the mouse.

_____ In addition, 99 percent of the 30,000 genes in humans and mice are the same.

Genetic Similarities Between Humans and Mice	
Humans	**Mice**
1. _____	1. _____
2. _____	2. _____
_____	_____
3. _____	3. _____
_____	_____

EXPLANATION Here are the sentences arranged in proper order. The organization and transition words are in bold type.

> The genetic **similarities** between humans and mice support the use of mice in scientific research. Humans and mice **both** have about 30,000 genes. **In addition**, 99 percent of the 30,000 genes in humans and mice are the same. **Another** important **similarity** is that 90 percent of genes linked to diseases are **identical** in the human and the mouse.

The addition signal words *in addition* and *another* provided important context clues for understanding the proper order of ideas. Compare your completed chart to the one that follows.

Genetic Similarities Between Humans and Mice

Humans	Mice
1. have 30,000 genes	1. have 30,000 genes
2. share 99 percent of genes with mice	2. share 99 percent of genes with humans
3. have 90 percent of the same genes linked to diseases as mice	3. have 90 percent of the same genes linked to diseases as humans

---

Practice 1

Complete the following ideas with a transition that shows comparison. Use each expression only once.

1. Physical fatigue affects the body; _____, mental stress affects the mind.

2. Jealousy destroys a relationship _____ thoroughly as a wildfire consumes a forest.

3. Compulsive gambling is an addiction _____ in some ways to drug addiction.

4. The toddler and the teenager often behave _____.

5. In her poem "Because I Could Not Stop for Death," Emily Dickinson writes that death _____ a gentleman.

Practice 2

Read the following paragraph. Complete the ideas with transitions from the box that show comparisons. Use each transition once.

both	likewise	similarities
in the same way	similar	

The Similarities Between Christianity and Islam

Two of the most influential religions, Christianity and Islam, actually share many (**1**) _____. Both religions are monotheistic, worshipping one God, and the God of both religions is an all-powerful and all-knowing being. (**2**) _____ Islam and Christianity believe God has a special relationship with humans. Muslims and Christians have a (**3**) _____ view of God as the creator to whom they submit in obedience. Islam and Christianity share a moral code based on a Covenant, or agreement, established by God. Both religions view Satan (**4**) _____, as an enemy of God and humanity. (**5**) _____, Muslims and Christians agree that humans have free will and are going to face a final judgment based on their actions in light of God's moral code. In a similar fashion, both believe in the return of Jesus Christ at the end of this age to defeat Satan and judge humanity.

Contrast

Contrast points out the ways in which two or more ideas are different. Sample signal words are *different*, *but*, and *yet*.

Words and Phrases of Contrast

although	conversely	different from	in spite of	on the other hand
as opposed to	despite	differently	instead	still
at the same time	differ	even though	nevertheless	to the contrary
but	difference	however	on the contrary	unlike
by contrast	different	in contrast	on the one hand	yet

Here are some examples:

> Capitalism and socialism are two very **different** worldviews.
> Women **differ** from men in their styles of communication.
> Weather refers to the current atmospheric conditions, such as rain or sunshine. Climate, **on the other hand**, describes the general weather conditions in a particular place during a particular season or all year round.

Each of these sentences has two topics that differ from each other in some way. The difference is the author's main point. For example, the first sentence sets up a contrast between two points of view: capitalism and socialism. The contrast is introduced by the word *different*. The second sentence states that the communication styles of women *differ* from the communication styles of men. And the third sentence contrasts the definitions of *weather* and *climate*; the author connects the definitions with the signal phrase *on the other hand*.

When contrast is used to organize an entire paragraph, the pattern looks like this.

Contrast Pattern		
Idea 1		**Idea 2**
Idea 1	*differs from*	Idea 2
Idea 1	*differs from*	Idea 2
Idea 1	*differs from*	Idea 2

⊙ **EXAMPLE** Determine a logical order for the following five sentences. Write **1** by the sentence that should come first, **2** by the sentence that should come second, **3** by the sentence that should come third, and so on. Then use the information to fill in the chart.

_____ Even though Alec had rarely spoken to others in the hallways, he had often interrupted coworkers who were speaking during meetings.

_____ In contrast, after counseling, he listened politely to others as they spoke during meetings.

_____ Quiet and withdrawn before counseling, Alec rarely spoke, smiled, or made eye contact with his coworkers as he passed them in the hallways or at their desks.

_____ However, after counseling, he became more friendly and outgoing, taking time to make eye contact and speak with colleagues.

_____ Alec behaved very differently after attending a series of counseling sessions aimed at improving his communication skills.

Changes in Alec's Communication Skills	
Alec Before Counseling	**Alec After Counseling**
1. quiet and withdrawn in hallways	1. _____
2. interrupted others during meetings	2. _____
	_____

EXPLANATION Here are the sentences arranged in the proper order. The transition and signal words are in **bold** type.

[1]Alec behaved very **differently after** attending a series of counseling sessions aimed at improving his communication skills. [2]Quiet and withdrawn **before** counseling, Alec rarely spoke, smiled, or made eye contact with his coworkers as he passed them in the hallways or at their desks. [3]**However, after** counseling, he became more friendly and outgoing, taking time to make eye contact and speak with colleagues. [4]**Even though** Alec had rarely spoken to others in the hallways, he had often interrupted coworkers who were speaking during meetings. [5]**In contrast, after** counseling, he listened politely to others as they spoke during meetings.

The time signal words *before* and *after* provided important context clues for understanding the proper order of the ideas. You should have filled in the chart with the following information. ◐

Alec Before Counseling	**Alec After Counseling**
1. quiet and withdrawn in hallways	1. friendly and outgoing
2. interrupted others during meetings	2. listened politely to others during meetings

Practice 3

Complete the following sentences with a transition that shows contrast. Use each expression only once.

1. _____ his family is originally from Mexico, Juan does not speak Spanish.

2. Some people such as Oprah Winfrey choose to work _____ the fact that they no longer need the money.

3. Marie knows that she needs to take her allergy medicine every day; _____, she forgets unless she is reminded.

4. _____ of cramming for the test the night before, Jordan and his study group started studying two weeks before the scheduled exam date.

5. Every member of the study group performed well on the exam, _____ the students who waited and crammed.

Practice 4

Read the following paragraph. Complete the ideas with transitions from the box that show contrasts. Use each word once.

contrast	difference	distinction	less	more
differ	differently	however	lower	than

Global Discrimination Against Women

Textbook Skills

  In his textbook *Sociology: A Down-to-Earth Approach*, James Henslin points out four ways in which men and women are treated (**1**) _____ worldwide. The first (**2**) _____ is the global gap in education. World-wide, more men (**3**) _____ women are literate. Almost 1 billion adults around the world cannot read; (**4**) _____, two-thirds are women (UNESCO 2006). The second (**5**) _____ between the treatment of men and women is the global gap in politics; around the world, men have (**6**) _____ access than women to national decision making. Except for Rwanda (at 49 percent), no national legislature of any country has as many women as men. A third way in which men and women (**7**) _____ is the global gap in pay. In every nation, women average (**8**) _____ pay than men. In the United States, full-time working women average only 70 percent of what men make. In some countries, the earnings of women are much **(9)** _____ than this. The fourth **(10)** _____ between men and women is related to violence. A global human rights issue is violence against women. Historical examples are foot binding in China, witch burning in Europe, and *suttee* (burning the living widow with the body of her dead husband) in India.

—Adapted from Henslin, James M., *Sociology:
A Down-to-Earth Approach*, 9th ed., p. 309.

Comparison and Contrast

The **comparison-and-contrast pattern** shows how two things are similar and also how they are different.

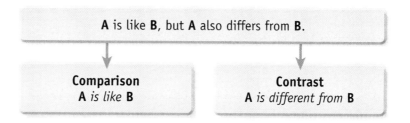

Yoga and Pilates: The Similarities and Differences

[1]Although yoga and Pilates share **similar** characteristics, an important **difference** exists. [2]**Both** yoga and Pilates are low-impact forms of exercise that improve posture, flexibility, and concentration. [3]**In addition**, *both* emphasize that a balance between body and mind is important. [4]**However**, the primary goal of Pilates is to strengthen the midsection and buttocks. [5]Pilates calls this area of the body the "powerhouse." [6]**On the other hand**, yoga does not focus on any one part of the body. [7]**Rather**, yoga works the opposing muscles of the entire body.

In the paragraph, two kinds of exercise are being compared and contrasted: yoga and Pilates. Remember, a topic sentence contains the topic and the author's controlling point about the topic. In this topic sentence, the author uses the words *similar* and *difference* to set up the points of comparison and contrast. The author's supporting details are a list of similarities introduced by the word *both.* The second similarity is introduced with the addition transition phrase *in addition.* The shift in the paragraph from similarities to differences is introduced in sentence 4 with the word *however.* The supporting details that explain these differences are introduced with the expressions *on the other hand* and *rather.*

⊙ **EXAMPLE**   Determine a logical order for the following four sentences. Write **1** by the sentence that should come first, **2** by the sentence that should come second, **3** by the sentence that should come third, and **4** by the sentence that should come fourth.

_____ Yet anorexia and bulimia are two different eating disorders.

_____ Although anorexia and bulimia share certain similarities, they are very different.

_____ Bulimia occurs when a person binges on large amounts of food and then induces vomiting; in contrast, anorexia occurs when a person refuses to eat much of anything.

_____ Both arise out of a perceived need to be thin and lose weight, and both have devastating effects on the body.

Read the following paragraph from a college education textbook. Underline the comparison-and-contrast words, and answer the questions that follow the paragraph.

What's the Difference?

Textbook
Skills

¹Those with a disability and those with a handicap often face similar reactions from others. ²They are often misunderstood. ³And both are often given the same labels. ⁴However, the two conditions have a distinct difference. ⁵The distinction between the two is important. ⁶A disability is an inability to do something specific, such as see or walk. ⁷On the contrary, a handicap is a disadvantage only in certain situations. ⁸Sometimes a disability leads to a handicap, but not always. ⁹For example, being blind (a visual disability) is a handicap if you want to drive. ¹⁰But blindness is not a handicap when you are creating music or talking on the telephone.

—Adapted from Anita Woolfolk, *Educational Psychology*,
8th ed., Boston: Allyn and Bacon, 2001, pp. 107–108.

1. What two ideas are being compared and contrasted? _____

_____

2. List four different comparison-and-contrast words or phrases in the paragraph. _____

_____

EXPLANATION Here are the four sentences about eating disorders arranged in the proper order. The transition words are in **bold** type.

[1]**Although** anorexia and bulimia share certain **similarities**, they are very **different**. [2]**Both** arise out of a perceived need to be thin and lose weight, and **both** have devastating effects on the body. [3]Yet anorexia and bulimia are two **different** eating disorders. [4]Bulimia occurs when a person binges on large amounts of food and then induces vomiting; **in contrast**, anorexia occurs when a person refuses to eat much of anything.

Here are the answers to the questions about the paragraph from an education textbook: The paragraph compares and contrasts a disability and a handicap. You were correct to choose any four of the following comparison-and-contrast words or phrases: *similar, both, same, however, difference, distinction, on the contrary, but.* ◀

Practice 5

The following paragraph is from a college geology textbook. Read the paragraph and circle any words or phrases that show comparison or contrast. Then answer the questions that follow the paragraph.

Types of Lava Flows

[1]Both aa (pronounced ah-ah) and pahoehoe (pronounced pah-hoy-hoy) are types of lava flow known by their Hawaiian names. [2]The more common of the two, aa flows have surfaces of rough jagged blocks with dangerously sharp edges and spiny projections. [3]Crossing an aa flow can be a trying and miserable experience. [4]By contrast, pahoehoe flows exhibit smooth surfaces that often resemble the twisted braids of ropes. [5]*Pahoehoe* means "on which one can walk." [6]Aa and pahoehoe lavas can erupt from the same vent. [7]However, pahoehoe lavas form at higher temperatures and are more fluid than aa flows. [8]In addition, pahoehoe lavas can change into aa lava flows, although the reverse (aa to pahoehoe) does not occur.

—Adapted from Tarbuck, Frederick K., Edward J. Lutgens,
and Dennis G. Tasa. *Essentials of Geology*, 11th ed., p. 96.

_____   **1.** What pattern is used in this passage?
          a. comparison only
          b. contrast only
          c. comparison and contrast

  2. What two ideas are being discussed? _____ and _____

Practice 6

Read the following paragraph. Complete the ideas with transitions from the box. Use each transition once.

conversely	different	even though	in contrast	same
despite	differs	however	just as	similar

       The similarities between high school and college are numerous and even obvious. Both levels teach many of the **(1)** _____ subject areas: English, history, algebra, physics, and so on. Often the physical environment is **(2)** _____, with the same kinds of classroom configurations, desks, chalkboards, and technology. **(3)** _____ high school students can participate in various extra-curricular activities such as student government, sports, and clubs, so too can college students. However, **(4)** _____ these apparent similarities, the college experience **(5)** _____ significantly from the high school experience. First, high school is required and free; **(6)** _____, college is voluntary and expensive. Second, high school students must obtain parental permission to participate in extracurricular activities; **(7)** _____, college students only have to volunteer to participate. Finally, high school students often expect to be reminded about deadlines or guided through assignments. **(8)** _____, college students are expected to take full responsibility and to think independently. Overall, **(9)** _____ high school and college seem to be similar experiences, they are very **(10)** _____ indeed.

Recognize the Cause-and-Effect Pattern and Signal Words

Sometimes an author talks about *why* something happened or *what* results came from an event. A **cause** states why something happens. An **effect** states a result or outcome. Sample signal words include *because* and *consequently*.

Cause-and-Effect Words			
accordingly	consequently	leads to	therefore
affect	due to	outcome	thus
as a result	if . . . then	results in	
because	impact	since	
because of	influence	so	

Here are some examples:

> **Because** Selena memorized the algebra formulas and practiced using them, she did well on the chapter test.
>
> Lance seeks out personal and sensitive details in a conversation; he often repeats this information to others. **As a result**, those who know Lance have come to distrust him.
>
> **Due to** the amount of snow on the streets and highways, schools and businesses have shut down.

Each of these sentences has two topics: one topic causes or has an effect on the second topic. The cause or effect is the author's controlling point. For example, the two topics in the first sentence are memorizing formulas and doing well on the test. This main idea states that memorizing is the cause of doing well. The cause is introduced by the word *because*. The two topics of the second sentence are Lance's behavior and the effect of that behavior. The effect is introduced by the signal phrase *as a result*. And the two topics in the third sentence are the amount of snow and the closing of schools and businesses; the author focuses on the cause by using the signal phrase *due to*. Note that cause and effect has a strong connection to time, and many of the transitions for this thought pattern therefore have a time element. Although many of these transition words have similar meanings and may be interchangeable, authors must carefully choose the transition that best fits the context.

The writer using cause and effect introduces an idea or event and then provides supporting details to show how that idea *results in* or *leads to* another idea. Many times, the second idea comes about because of the first idea. Thus the first idea is the cause, and the following ideas are the effects.

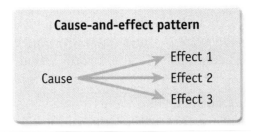

For example, read the following topic sentence:

> Over time, the eating disorder bulimia may damage the digestive system and the heart.

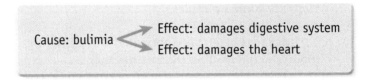

Often an author will begin with an effect and then give the causes.

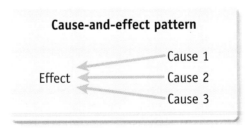

For example, read the following topic sentence:

> The eating disorder bulimia may be the result of poor self-esteem and cultural values.

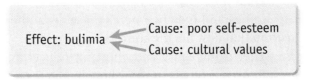

Sometimes the author may wish to emphasize a chain reaction.

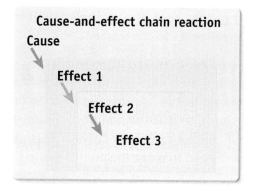

Cause-and-effect chain reaction
Cause
　　Effect 1
　　　　Effect 2
　　　　　　Effect 3

For example, read the following topic sentence.

Low self-esteem leads to dissatisfaction with one's appearance, which leads to control issues and can ultimately result in bulimia.

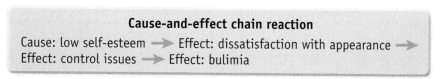

Cause-and-effect chain reaction
Cause: low self-esteem ➡ Effect: dissatisfaction with appearance ➡
Effect: control issues ➡ Effect: bulimia

⊘ **EXAMPLE** Determine a logical order for the following three sentences. Write **1** by the sentence that should come first, **2** by the sentence that should come second, and **3** by the sentence that should come last.

_____ For example, a character may change due to an inner conflict such as the struggle between ambition and honor.

_____ In a piece of fiction, a change in a dynamic character is usually the result of conflict.

_____ In addition, a character may change because of a conflict with another person or group of people, such as a struggle between a father and a son or between a citizen and the government.

EXPLANATION Here are the sentences arranged in the proper order. The transition and signal words are in **bold** type.

What Causes a Character to Change?

[1]In a piece of fiction, a change in a dynamic character is usually the **result of** conflict. [2]**For example**, a character may change **due to** an inner

conflict **such as** the struggle between ambition and honor. [3]**In addition**, a character may change **because of** a conflict with another person or group of people, **such as** a struggle between a father and a son or between a citizen and the government.

In this paragraph, two addition words combine with the cause-and-effect signal words. The cause-and-effect signal words are *result of*, *due to*, and *because of*. *For example* and *in addition* indicate the order of the cause-and-effect discussion. Also note that the addition phrase *such as* introduces examples of the kinds of conflict that cause change. This paragraph actually uses two patterns of organization to make the point—the listing pattern is used to add the cause-and-effect details. Even though two patterns are used, the cause-and-effect pattern is the primary pattern of organization.

Practice 7

Complete each sentence with a cause-and-effect word or phrase from the box. Use each word only once.

consequently	if . . . then	leads to	results in	thereby

1. Reading magazines, newspapers, and books _____ a large vocabulary.

2. Over the summer, Molly grows to be several inches taller than all her peers. Her additional height _____ better performance and more playing time on the basketball court.

3. Maurice surfed the Internet and bought an essay for his history class. His teacher, who suspected that Maurice didn't write the essay he submitted, surfed the Internet and found the essay Maurice had bought. _____, Maurice received a failing grade for the assignment.

4. The American dream is based on the premise that _____ you work hard, _____ you will succeed.

5. On January 12, 2010, a 7.0 magnitude quake rocked Haiti, _____ killing thousands of people as it toppled both the presidential palace and hillside shanties and leaving the poor Caribbean nation appealing for international help.

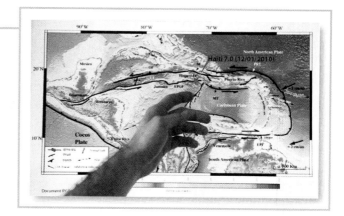

VISUAL *VOCABULARY*

A technician at the French National Seismic Survey Institute points at a map showing the **epicenter** of a major earthquake that hit Haiti.

The best meaning of **epicenter** is _____.

a. focal point
b. large area
c. area of destruction

Practice 8

The following paragraph from a college tourism textbook uses the cause-and-effect pattern of organization. Read the paragraph, underline the cause-and-effect signal words in it, and complete the concept map that follows it.

Textbook
Skills

Route 66

[1]Route 66 is still the most famous in the States and attracts many tourists every year. [2]Route 66 was decommissioned in 1985. [3]By then, it had been replaced by the quicker and more efficient interstate highway system. [4]Because many people opted for the convenience of the interstates, Route 66 was neglected. [5]As a result, the towns that spanned along Route 66 faded away with the setting of the sun. [6]Without tourist dollars to support their economies, many people closed shop and headed elsewhere. [7]Those who have stayed have faced tough times. [8]Today there is, however, an increase in the number of Route 66 devotees and seekers of nostalgia. [9]The combination of history, culture, scenic views, and the fact that it might be the most famous stretch of American highway make it an excellent choice for a road trip.

—Walker, John R. and Walker, Josielyn T.,
Tourism: Concepts and Practices, p. 449.

Cause-and-effect chain reaction

Cause: quicker, more efficient _____ →
Effect: people opt for interstates → Effect: _____
→ Effect: towns along it faded; _____ ; people close shop and move away

Practice 9

Read the following paragraph. Complete the ideas with transitions from the box. Use each transition once.

affects	consequence	effects	impacts	lead to
cause	due to	impact	influence	result

Alcohol's Damaging Effect on the Brain

Difficulty walking, blurred vision, slurred speech, slowed reaction times, impaired memory—clearly, alcohol **(1)** _____ the brain. Some of these **(2)** _____ are noticeable after only one or two drinks and quickly resolve when drinking stops. On the other hand, a person who drinks heavily over a long period of time may have brain deficits that persist well after he or she achieves sobriety. Exactly how alcohol affects the brain and the likelihood of reversing the **(3)** _____ of heavy drinking on the brain remain hot topics in alcohol research today. A number of factors **(4)** _____ how and to what extent alcohol **(5)** _____ the brain. For example, how much and how often a person drinks is one factor. Other factors include the age at which he or she first began drinking, and how long he or she has been drinking; the person's age, level of education, gender, genetic background, and family history of alcoholism; whether he or she is at risk **(6)** _____ prenatal alcohol exposure; and his or her general health status. Alcohol can **(7)** _____ obvious impairments in memory after only a few drinks and, as the amount of alcohol increases, so does the degree of impairment. Large quantities of alcohol, especially when consumed quickly and on an empty stomach, can **(8)** _____ a blackout, or an interval of time for which the intoxicated person cannot recall key details of events, or even entire events. People who have been drinking large amounts of alcohol for long periods of time risk the **(9)** _____ of serious and persistent changes in the brain. Damage may be a **(10)** _____ of the direct effects of alcohol on the brain or may result indirectly, from a poor general health status or from severe liver disease.

—Adapted from National Institute on Alcohol Abuse and Alcoholism, "Alcohol's Damaging Effect on the Brain." *Alcohol Alert.*

LO3 Recognize the Generalization-and-Example Pattern and Signal Words

As technology evolves, it saves time; broadband Internet access cuts down on the time needed to access information on the World Wide Web.

Some people may read this sentence and think that the author's focus is on the topic of broadband Internet access. But evolving technology saves time in many other areas of our lives, such as in traveling, cooking, or cleaning. Adding an **example word or phrase** makes it clear that broadband Internet access is only one instance in which technology saves time.

Read the sentence about technology and the Internet again. Note how the use of the example phrase makes the relationship between ideas clear.

As technology evolves, it saves time; *for example*, broadband Internet access cuts down on the time needed to access information on the World Wide Web.

In the generalization-and-example thought pattern, the author makes a general statement and then offers an example or a series of examples to clarify the generalization.

The Generalization-and-Example Pattern

Statement of a general idea
    Example
    Example

Example words signal that a writer is giving an instance of a general idea.

Words and Phrases That Introduce Examples

an illustration	for instance	once	to illustrate
for example	including	such as	typically

⊙ **EXAMPLE** Read each of the following items and fill in the blanks with an appropriate example word or phrase.

1. Food labels provide important information. _____, the label on Rich Harvest Sweet Dark Whole Grain bread states that one slice has 120 calories.

2. Fatigue can interfere with performance. _____, Carla was so tired after working straight through two shifts at the restaurant that she made careless mistakes on her math exam.

3. Tyler's intelligence and energy allow him to excel in a variety of areas _____ sports, academics, and community service.

EXPLANATION Many words and phrases that introduce examples are easily interchanged. Notice that in the first two examples, the phrases *for example* and *for instance* are similar in meaning. In the third example, the use of the transition phrase *such as* signals a list. Even though transition words or phrases have similar meanings, authors carefully choose transitions based on style and meaning. ◁

Practice 10

Complete each selection with an example word or phrase. Fill in the blanks with words from the box.

1. Luis is a gracious host ready for an instant party; he always keeps his pantry stocked with items _____ soft drinks, bottled water, wine, and a variety of crackers, chips, and nuts.

2. Although Gene and Paula love each other deeply, they face significant problems in their relationship. _____, Paula wants to continue her education, yet Gene wants to have children right away.

3. Leigh seems to have a number of allergy symptoms, _____ extreme itching, scaly patches on her skin, watery eyes, and headaches.

4. Hunter will go to great lengths to have fun; _____ he drove for 22 hours round trip to attend a Saturday afternoon beach party with a group of friends.

5. Watching television can have a soothing effect. _____, when Jean has trouble falling asleep after a long, difficult day at the office, she turns the television volume down low, turns off all the lights, and lies down; the rhythm of the flickering images and low tones puts her right to sleep.

Practice 11

Read the following passage. Complete the ideas with transitions from the box. Use each transition once.

for example	illustrates	such as
for instance	including	

Freedom of Speech

[1]One of the most important rights enjoyed by citizens of the United States is the right of free speech. [2]By allowing citizens to speak out freely about important issues and political leaders, this right plays a vital role in shaping U.S. government and its political system. [3]This right, however, is not limited to the political arena. [4]It extends to other areas, **(1)** _____ artistic and literary works. [5]It also extends to conduct that expresses ideas. [6]**(2)** _____, if a person burns a flag as a political protest, this is considered a type of speech and is protected by the First Amendment. [7]Although the Constitution includes no express limitation to this right, the Supreme Court held that limits must apply. [8]As the famous Justice Oliver Wendell Holmes once commented, a person cannot yell "Fire!" in a crowded theater. [9]This **(3)** _____ that the right to free speech is sometimes limited when it injures others. [10]Speech or expressive conduct can injure others in various ways. [11]**(4)** _____, yelling "Fire!" in a

crowded theater can result in physical injury to the occupants of the building. **12**Advertising of tobacco products results in more tobacco use, especially by young people, and leads to health problems. **13**Burning a cross on a person's property may carry with it implicit threats of violence and certainly poses a threat to the property owner's piece of mind. **14**Publishing trade secret information **(5)** (_____ source codes) can damage a person's business.

—Adapted from Hames, Joanne B. and Ekern, Yvonne,
Introduction to Law, 4th ed., pp. 112, 116.

Recognize the Definition-and-Example Pattern and Signal Words

Textbooks are full of new words and special terms. Even if a word is common, it can take on a special meaning in a specific course. To help students understand ideas, authors often include a definition of each new or special term. Then, to make sure the meaning of the word or concept is clear, authors also give examples.

Textbook Skills

> **Emblems** are body gestures that directly translate into words or phrases—for example, the OK sign, the thumbs-up for "good job," and the V for victory.
>
> —Adapted from DeVito, Joseph A. *Human Communication: The Basic Course*, 12th ed., p. 141.

In this sentence, the term *emblem* is defined first. Then the author gives three examples to make the term clear to the reader.

The Definition Pattern

Term and definition
    Example
    Example

---

 * The **definition** explains the meaning of new, difficult, or special terms. Definitions include words like *is, are,* and *means*: "Emblems *are* body gestures that directly translate into words or phrases . . ."

 * The **examples** follow a definition to show how the word is used or applied in the content. Examples are signaled by words like *for example* and *such as*: "for example, the OK sign, the thumbs-up for 'good job,' and the V for victory."

> **EXAMPLES**

A. Determine a logical order for the following three sentences. Write **1** by the sentence that should come first, **2** by the sentence that should come second, and **3** by the sentence that should come last. Then read the explanation.

_____ For example, a person may give up a high-paying job in the city to take a lower-paying job in a small town.

_____ Downshifting is a deliberate effort to reduce stress by choosing to live more simply.

_____ Some people who choose to downshift may also avoid the use of televisions, computers, and cell phones.

B. Read the following paragraph from a college communications textbook. Annotate the paragraph: Circle the term being defined, and underline the key words in the definition. Then answer the questions that follow it.

Paralanguage

Textbook
Skills

[1]**Paralanguage** is the meaning that is perceived along with the actual words used to deliver a message. [2]It is how we say something. [3]This is a broad category that includes a number of traits such as dialects, accents, pitch, rate, vocal qualities, pauses, and silence. [4]A pleasing voice, for example, will make people more likely to listen to us. [5]And a modulated voice indicates higher social status and educational levels.

—Adapted from Thomas E. Harris and John C. Sherblom,
Small Groups and Team Communication, 2nd ed.
Boston: Allyn and Bacon, 2002, p. 112.

1. What are the two examples that illustrate the term being defined?

_____ and _____.

2. Which words signal each example? _____ and _____.

A. The sentences have been arranged in the proper order in the following paragraph. The definition, example, and transition words are in **bold** type.

Downshifting

Downshifting **is** a deliberate effort to reduce stress by choosing to live more simply. **For example**, a person may give up a high-paying job in the city to take a lower-paying job in a small town. Some people who choose to downshift may **also** avoid the use of televisions, computers, and cell phones.

This sequence of ideas begins by introducing the term *downshifting*. The term is linked to its definition with the verb *is*. The author provides two examples of behaviors common to people who downshift. The sentence that contains *for example* would logically follow the definition. The example that contains the addition transition *also* would come last.

B. By circling and underlining only key terms, you highlight the most important information for easy review. Compare your annotations to the following:

Paralanguage

Textbook Skills

¹Paralanguage is the meaning that is perceived along with the actual words used to deliver a message. ²It is how we say something. ³This is a broad category that includes a number of traits such as dialects, accents, pitch, rate, vocal qualities, pauses, and silence. ⁴A pleasing voice, for example, will make people more likely to listen to us. ⁵And a modulated voice indicates higher social status and educational levels.

—Adapted from Thomas E. Harris and John C. Sherblom,
Small Groups and Team Communication, 2nd ed. Boston:
Allyn and Bacon, 2002, p. 112.

1. The two examples are *a pleasing voice* and *a modulated voice*.

2. The signal words that introduce the examples are for *example* and *and*.

Practice 12

Read the paragraph from a college science textbook. Finish the definition concept map that follows it by adding the missing details in the proper order.

What Are Fossils?

[1]**Fossils** are the remains or traces of prehistoric life found in sediment and sedimentary rocks. [2]Many types of fossils exist and are important basic tools for interpreting the geologic past. [3]One example is the petrified fossil. [4]*Petrified* literally means "turned into stone." [5]Another example of a fossil is the mold or cast fossil. [6]When a shell or other structure is buried in sediment and then dissolved by underground water, a *mold* of the organism's outer structure is created; if the hollow spaces of inside the organism are filled with mineral matter, then a *cast* is created. [7]Fossils are also made by *carbonization*. [8]In this case, fine sediment encases the remains of the organism. [9]As time passes, pressure squeezes out the liquid and gases and leaves behind a thin residue of carbon. [10]If the film of carbon is lost from a fossil preserved in fine-grained sediment, a replica on the surface, called an *impression*, may still show considerable detail. [11]Finally, delicate organisms, such as insects, have been preserved in *amber*, the hardened resin of trees. [12]After being trapped in the sticky resin, the remains of the organism are protected from damage by water and air.

—Adapted from Lutgens, Frederick K., Tarbuck, Edward J., and Tasa, Dennis G., *Foundations of Earth Science*, 5th ed., pp. 230–234.

Term: _____

Definition: _____

Example: _____

Example: _____

Example: _____

Example: _____

VISUAL *VOCABULARY*

This collection of fossilized wood is an example of _____ fossils.

   a. amber

   b. carbonized

   c. petrified

Practice 13

Read the following passage. Finish the definition concept map that follows it by adding the missing details in proper order.

Choosing a Marriage Partner

[1]Finding someone to marry can be a daunting prospect, but in the United States the options are relatively open. [2]There are only a few rules: potential mates cannot already be married, must be of legal age, must not be closely related, and, in most states, must be of a different sex. [3]In fact, most cultures have similar restrictions regarding age and other social issues.

[4]Despite this relative freedom in choosing marital partners, many people practice **homogamy**, or marriage between people with the same characteristics. [5]This occurs when people choose a partner with a similar background: religion, race, class, geographic location, or age. [6]Partners of similar backgrounds are likely to socialize their children the same way, which avoids conflict. [7]Also, coming from similar backgrounds increases the likelihood that the couple will have things in common, which can increase the longevity of the relationship.

[8]Some cultures and groups strive to enforce marrying within a group, which is a practice known as **endogamy**. [9]If, for example, your race or religion requires you to marry a person of the same faith, endogamy becomes a primary predictor of who you might marry. [10]For example, a Native American student often talked about how important it was to her and her tribe that she marry someone from within the tribe. [11]Although this was not a "rule" to which she had to adhere, the attitude of her family and friends provided a clear directive that she needed to marry a tribal member. [12]On the other hand, **exogamy** is the practice marrying someone from a different group. [13]European royalty used this method by marrying royalty from different nations to strengthen bonds with other groups and form alliances.

—Carl, John D., *Think Sociology*, 2nd ed., p. 252.

Term: _____

Definition: marriage between people with the same characteristics

Examples: people choose partners of similar religion, race, class, geographic location, or age

Term: _____

Definition: marrying within a group

Example: _____

_____

Term: exogamy

Definition: _____

Example: _____

LO5 Develop Textbook Skills: Thought Patterns in Textbooks

Textbook authors rely heavily on the use of transitions and thought patterns to make information clear and easier to understand.

> **EXAMPLES** The following topic sentences have been taken from college textbooks. Identify the _primary_ thought pattern that each sentence suggests.

Textbook Skills

_____ **1.** Issuing orders or making it clear that we have the power to control the behavior of others results in others' defensiveness.
   a. cause and effect   c. definition
   b. comparison and contrast

_____ **2.** Distress is stress that brings about negative mental or physical responses such as having trouble relaxing.
   a. cause and effect   c. definition
   b. comparison and contrast

_____ **3.** When stock prices fully reflect information that is available to investors, the stock market is efficient; in contrast, when stock prices do not reflect all information, the stock market is inefficient.
   a. cause and effect   c. definition
   b. comparison and contrast

EXPLANATIONS Topic sentence 1, from a psychology textbook, uses (a) cause and effect, signaled by the phrase _results in_. Topic sentence 2, from a health textbook, is organized according to (c) definition, using the verb _is_ and the phrase _such as_ to signal examples. Note that the sentence includes the phrase _brings about_, which suggests cause and effect; however, the sentence is set up in the form of a definition. Therefore, definition is the _primary_ thought pattern. Topic sentence 3, from an economics textbook, uses (b) comparison and contrast as the primary thought pattern. Some readers may pick up on the author's use of time order, signaled by the word *when*. The use of time order can suggest cause and effect. However, in this sentence, *when* is used to describe two instances or events. The signal phrase *in contrast* joins these two events to point out the differences between them.

Practice 14

Textbook Skills

The following sentences are from college textbooks. Identify the thought pattern that each topic sentence suggests. (The type of textbook is identified after each topic sentence.)

_____ **1.** Creativity is the result of looking at things in a new way. (social science)
   a. cause and effect
   b. comparison and contrast
   c. generalization and example

_____ **2.** The occasional drinker differs slightly from the social drinker. (health)
   a. cause and effect
   b. comparison and contrast
   c. generalization and example

_____ **3.** Some pressed for war because they were suffering an agricultural depression. (history)
   a. cause and effect
   b. comparison and contrast
   c. definition and example

_____ **4.** Several factors influence the way we relate to and use space in communicating. (communication)
   a. cause and effect
   b. comparison and contrast
   c. generalization and example

_____ **5.** Analgesics, such as aspirin and ibuprofen, are pain relievers. (health)
   a. cause and effect
   b. comparison and contrast
   c. definition and example

Apply Information Literacy Skills

 LO6 ## Academic, Personal, and Career Applications of More Thought Patterns

As you learned in Chapter 7, transitions and thought patterns organize information by directing your attention to key concepts and relationships of ideas.

Transitions and thought patterns connect specific details to logically support a main idea. The signal words of a thought pattern help you predict what's to come. When you understand the structure of an idea, you can monitor your comprehension as you read. Transitions and thought patterns show how ideas are connected in academic, personal, and career situations. Therefore, you will use the skills that you learned in this chapter in several ways:

- You will recognize your own need to identify transitions and thought patterns.
- You will analyze information to see the relationships among ideas.
- You will determine the author's use of a thought pattern to develop a main idea.

Academic Application

Assume you are taking a college course in biology. You are creating a vocabulary journal of key scientific terms you are learning.

- **Before Reading:** Skim the passage. Determine which thought pattern to use to record the scientific term and key details about the term. Visualize the pattern.
- **During Reading:** Highlight the term and key details to record in your vocabulary journal entry.
- **After Reading:** In the space following the passage, create a vocabulary journal entry for the scientific term.

Living Things Maintain Relatively Constant Internal Conditions Through Homeostasis

[1]Complex, organized structures are not easy to maintain. [2]Consider the molecules of your body or the books and papers on your desk; organization tends to crumble into chaos unless energy is used to sustain it. [3]To stay alive and function effectively, living things must keep the conditions within their bodies fairly constant. [4]In other words, they must maintain **homeostasis** (from Greek words meaning "to stay the same"). [5]For example, organisms must precisely regulate the amount of water and salts within their cells. [6]Their bodies must also be kept at suitable temperatures for biological functions to occur. [7]Among warm-blooded animals, vital organs such as the brain and heart are kept at a warm, constant temperature despite wide changes in outside temperature. [8]Homeostasis is maintained by a variety of means. [9]In the case of temperature control, these include sweating during hot weather and exercise, dousing oneself

with cool water, metabolizing more food in cold weather, basking in the sun, or even adjusting a thermostat.

—Adapted from Audesirk, Teresa, Audesirk, Gerald, and Byers, Bruce E., *Biology: Life on Earth with Physiology*, 9th ed., p. 13.

Vocabulary Journal Entry:

Term	Definition	Examples

Personal Application

Assume you want to buy a video game console, and you are going to research the Internet for information to guide your choice. To find the information you need, think about how information about video game consoles would be organized on the Internet. Use key transition words of specific thought patterns to create search terms to use in an Internet search box.

Key search terms: _____

_____

Now, assume your search led you to the chart "Comparison Shopping: Video Game Consoles."

- **Before Reading:** Skim the chart to identify what is available in the video game consoles.
- **During Reading:** Annotate the information to highlight details that will help you decide which console to buy.
- **After Reading:** Complete the following sentence:

I would buy the _____ because _____

_____

Career Application

Assume you are a supervisor of a group of mechanics at The Auto Mall.

- **Before Reading:** Skim the memo. Write a pre-reading question to guide your thinking.
- **During Reading:** Annotate the details that answer your pre-reading question.

Comparison Shopping: Video Game Consoles

	XBOX 360 (250 GB)	PlayStation 3 (250 GB)	Nintendo Wii U
Features			
Game Media	DVD	Blu-Ray Disc	Wii U Optical Disc
Memory Upgrade	Yes	Yes	Yes
Backward Compatibility (plays older games)	Xbox	PlayStation	Wii
Online Service	Xbox Live	PlayStation Network	Nintendo Network
Number of Controllers	4	7	2 (game pad) + 4 (Wii)
Video			
Netflix	✓ Yes	✓ Yes	✓ Yes
Hulu Plus			
YouTube			
Video Store			
Connectivity			
Multi AV Output Ports	✓ Yes	✓ Yes	✓ Yes
HDMI Ports			
USB Ports			
VGA			
Headphone			
Ethernet Port	✓ Yes	✗ No	✓ Yes
Flash Card	✗ No	✗ No	✓ Yes
SD Memory Card	✗ No	✓ Yes	✓ Yes
Memory Stick	✗ No	✓ Yes	✓ Yes
Camera	Kinect (optional)	GamePad	PlayStation Eye (optional)
Community and Support			
Social Networking	✓ Yes	✓ Yes	✓ Yes
Text Messaging			
Voice Chat			
Video Chat			
User Forum			
Phone			
Email			
FAQs			
Online Chat	✓ Yes	✗ No	✓ Yes
Warranty	1 year	1 year	1 year
Price (estimated)	$200–$300	$250	$250

—<http://www.consumersearch.com/video-game-consoles/compare>

- **After Reading:** In the space following the passage, draft an answer to your pre-reading question.

Pre-Reading Question: _____

_____

To: Managers and Supervisors
From: Pam Glower, Director Human Resources
RE: Workplace Stress Committee Assignment

The Human Resources Department surveyed our employees about their perception of workplace stress here at the Auto Mall. The following list itemizes their concerns and experiences. Please review this information. Bring to our meeting next Wednesday any ideas or suggestions you have to reduce workplace stress at The Auto Mall.

Causes of Workplace Stress	Symptoms of Workplace Stress
Fear of being laid off	Apathy, loss of interest in work
More overtime due to staff cutbacks	Problems sleeping
Pressure to perform to meet rising expectations but with no increase in job satisfaction	Fatigue
	Trouble concentrating
	Using alcohol or drugs to cope
Pressure to work at peak levels—all the time	Anxiety or depression
	Muscle tension or headaches
Lack of rewards or recognition for good job performance	Stomach problems
	Social withdrawal

Answer to pre-reading question: _____

_____

_____

_____

_____

_____

_____

_____

Score (number correct) _____ × 10 = _____%

Visit MyReadingLab to take this test online and receive feedback and guidance on your answers.

Transition Words and Thought Patterns

A. Based on the thought pattern used to state each idea, fill in the blanks with the transition words from the box. Use each choice only once.

because	even though	for example	on the other hand	so

1. _____ Chloe is afraid of heights, she went bungee jumping to celebrate her birthday.

2. Distance education is learning that takes place when the student is in a location apart from the classroom, building, or site; _____, online courses and telecourses are distance learning courses.

3. As a student, Armando likes distance education _____ he works a full-time job, and online courses offer a more flexible schedule.

4. Isabella wanted to become a professional stage actress, _____ she moved to New York City.

5. A person who takes too much of a group's time may be poorly perceived; _____, a person in an influential position may be granted more leeway in bending expectations regarding the use of time.

B. Underline the signal words. Then identify the thought pattern used in each short passage, as follows:

   a. cause and effect
   b. comparison and contrast
   c. generalization and example

_____ 6. The purpose of a documentary is to give depth and context for important public issues. One memorable example is *Harvest of Shame*, which exposed the mistreatment of migrant workers.

_____ 7. Assertive communicators speak calmly, directly, and clearly to those around them; in contrast, nonassertive communicators may speak too rapidly, use a tone too low to be heard easily, or fail to say directly what is on their minds.

_____ **8.** Research shows that low doses of aspirin are beneficial to heart patients due to the blood-thinning properties of the drug.

_____ **9.** Rebekah overeats when she is under stress. Rebekah is overeating; therefore, she must be experiencing stress.

_____ **10.** The eureka experience is a sudden rush of understanding. I can recall one early instance of a eureka experience when the meaning of the word *frown* suddenly dawned on me. In that moment, by understanding one simple word, I became aware of the value of words.

REVIEW TEST 2

Score (number correct) _____ × 10 = _____%

Visit MyReadingLab to take this test online and receive feedback and guidance on your answers.

Thought Patterns

A. 1–5. Arrange the following sentences from a college health textbook in their proper order. Write **1** by the sentence that should come first, write **2** by the sentence that should come second, and so on. Use the transitions to figure out the proper order.

Textbook
Skills

_____ In contrast, Gilligan believes that men have an ethic based on justice.

_____ According to Harvard Professor Carol Gilligan, men and women make very different decisions when facing moral choices.

_____ Gilligan believes that women have an ethic based on care.

_____ For example, men are more interested in fair play and individual rights.

_____ For example, women value loyalty, self-sacrifice, and peacemaking.

—Adapted from Donatelle, Rebecca J. and Davis, Lorraine G., *Access to Health*, 7th ed., p. 135.

_____ **6.** What is the primary thought pattern used here?
a. generalization and example   c. comparison and contrast
b. cause and effect

B. Identify the thought pattern used in the following paragraphs, as follows:
a. cause and effect   c. definition
b. comparison and contrast

Textbook
Skills

_____ **7.** Parenting style is the blend of attitudes and behaviors toward a child that creates an emotional climate. For example, a parent's style includes the parent's tone, a parent's body language, and signs of affection or hostility toward the child.

—Adapted from Michael L. Jaffe, *Understanding Parenting*,
2nd ed. Boston: Allyn and Bacon, 1997, pp. 163–164.

_____ **8.** Marijuana has several short-term effects. First, physically, it speeds up the heart and reddens the eyes. In addition, psychologically, it may cause feelings of giddiness and increased hunger or sexual desire.

_____ **9.** Even though Gary and Tony are identical twins, their personalities differ greatly. On the one hand, Gary is outspoken, outgoing, and overcommitted. He serves on several service clubs, volunteers, and leads study sessions. On the other hand, Tony is shy and withdrawn and has few commitments. He enjoys reading, creating music, and drawing and prefers to study alone.

_____ **10.** Cassie suffered several long-term effects from the constant teasing she endured during her childhood. Because her peers ridiculed her for being too heavy, Cassie felt embarrassed about her body even as an adult and became unrealistic about what her ideal weight should be. In addition, the teasing caused Cassie to fear rejection; as a result, she often gave in to her children's demands in order to win their affection. Another impact of the teasing showed in Cassie's inability to trust people; she always had a vague feeling that others were judging her or saying negative things about her behind her back.

REVIEW TEST 3

Score (number correct) _____ × 25 = _____%

Visit MyReadingLab to take this test online and receive feedback and guidance on your answers.

Thought Patterns

Read the following passage from a college political science textbook. Then, answer the questions that follow.

Textbook
Skills

The Media's Influence on the Public

[1]There are many important questions concerning the media's influence on the public. [2]For instance, how much influence do the media

actually have on public opinion? [3]Do the media have an obvious point of view or bias, as some people suggest? [4]Are people able to resist information that challenges their preexisting beliefs?

[5]In most cases, the press has surprisingly little effect on what people believe. [6]To put it bluntly, people tend to see what they want to see. [7]That is, human beings will focus on parts of a report that reinforce their own attitudes. [8]And they ignore parts that challenge their core beliefs. [9]Most people also selectively tune out or ignore reports that contradict their preferences in politics and other fields. [10]Therefore, a committed Democrat will remember certain parts of a televised news program about a current campaign—primarily the parts that reinforce his or her own choice. [11]And an equally committed Republican will recall very different sections of the report or remember the material in a way that supports the GOP position. [12]In other words, most voters are not empty vessels into which the media can pour their own beliefs. [13]Indeed, many studies were done from the 1940s and 1950s. [14]This was an era when partisan identification was very strong. [15]These studies suggested that the media had no effect at all on public opinion. [16]During the last forty years, however, the decline in political identification has opened the door to greater media influence. [17]On the one hand, research had indicated for some time that the media have little effect on changing public opinion. [18]On the other hand, more recent studies show that the media have a definite effect on shaping public opinion, especially during elections.

[19]Some experts argue that the content of network television news accounts for a large portion of the volatility and change in policy preferences of Americans, when measured over relatively short periods of time. [20]These changes are called **media effects**. [21]Let's examine how these media-influenced changes might occur.

[22]First, reporting can sway people who have no strong opinion in the first place. [23]So, for example, the media have a greater influence on political independents than on strong partisans. [24]That said, the politically unmotivated individual who is subject to media effects may not vote in a given election. [25]In that case, the media influence may be of little particular consequence.

[26]Second, it is likely that the media have a greater impact on topics far removed from the lives and experiences of readers and viewers. [27]News reports can probably shape public opinion about events in foreign countries fairly easily. [28]Yet, what the media say about domestic issues such as rising prices, neighborhood crime, or child rearing may have relatively little effect, because most citizens have personal experience of and well-formed ideas about these subjects.

[29]Third, in a process often referred to as agenda setting, news organizations can help tell us what to think about, even if they cannot determine what we think. [30]Indeed, the press often sets the agenda for a campaign or for government action by focusing on certain issues or concerns. [31]For example, nationwide in 2003, the media reported the abduction and recovery of fifteen-year-old Utah resident Elizabeth Smart. [32]Many in the press and in the Utah government attributed the success in finding Smart to the use of the state's Amber alert. [33]Due to the Amber alert system, the law enforcement uses the media to notify the public of a kidnapping. [34]Soon after, there were calls for a national Amber alert system. [35]Thus, Congress quickly passed as law the Protection Act of 2003, and the president just as quickly signed. [36]Before the Smart story, child kidnapping had not been a national issue. [37]It was only after sustained media coverage put Smart and the Amber alert system in headlines that the problem received national attention.

[38]Fourth, the media influence public opinion through a subtle process referred to as framing. [39]*Framing* is the process by which a news organization defines a political issue and consequently affects opinion about the issue. [40]For example, an experiment conducted by one group of scholars found that if a news story about a Ku Klux Klan rally was framed as a civil rights story, then viewers were generally tolerant of the rally. [41]In this case, the story was about the right of a group to express their ideas, even if they are unpopular ideas. [42]However, when the same story was framed as a law and order issue, then public tolerance for the rally decreased. [43]In this case, the story was about how the actions of one group disrupted a community and threatened public safety. [44]In either case, the media exert subtle influence over the way people respond to the same information.

[45]Fifth, the media have the power to indirectly impact the way the public sees politicians and government. [46]For example, choices voters make in presidential elections are often related to their view of the economy. [47]In general, a healthy economy causes voters to reelect the sitting president. [48]In contrast, a weak economy causes voters to choose the challenger. [49]Hence, if the media paint a consistently dismal picture of the economy, then that picture may well hurt the sitting president seeking reelection. [50]In fact, one study convincingly proves this point. [51]The media's relentlessly negative coverage of the economy in 1992 shaped voters' view of the economy. [52]Thus, negative media helped lead to George Bush's defeat in the 1992 presidential election.

—Adapted from O'Connor, Karen and Larry J. Sabato, *American Government: Continuity and Change*, pp. 571–572.

_____ **1.** The overall thought pattern for the passage is
   a. comparison.
   b. contrast.
   c. definition and example.
   d. cause and effect.

_____ **2.** The relationship of ideas between sentences 9 and 10 is
   a. comparison.
   b. contrast.
   c. cause and effect.
   d. generalization and example.

_____ **3.** The relationship of ideas between sentences 17 and 18 is
   a. comparison.
   b. contrast.
   c. definition and example.
   d. cause and effect.

_____ **4.** The relationship of ideas between sentences 39 and 40 is
   a. comparison.
   b. contrast.
   c. definition and example.
   d. cause and effect.

SUMMARY RESPONSE

Restate the authors' central idea in your own words. In your summary, follow the thought pattern used by the authors. Begin your summary response with the following: *The central idea of "The Media's Influence on the Public" by O'Connor and Sabato is . . .*

WHAT DO YOU THINK?

Do you think media influences the way people think or the choices they make? Do you think *framing* is a fair practice in the media? Assume you are a reporter for your college newspaper. The administration has just made two announcements. Tuition is going up by 10%, and the college is going to build a multimillion dollar sports complex. Write an article that frames the story to either favor or oppose the administration's decisions.

Consider the following points for how you will frame your article:

* Should students have to pay for a sports complex to earn an education at this particular college?

* What are some advantages of having a sports complex at your (assumed) college?

REVIEW TEST 4

Score (number correct) _____ × 10 = _____%

Visit MyReadingLab to take this test online and receive feedback and guidance on your answers.

Transitions and Thought Patterns

Before you read the following essay from the college textbook *Encyclopedia of Stress,* skim the passage and answer the Before Reading questions. Read the essay. Then answer the After Reading questions.

Vocabulary Preview

provokes (4): causes, stirs up
phobia (5): deep, irrational fear
interacting with (13): relating to, working with
inflammation (21): swelling

Technostress

[1]The computer revolution has created a new form of stress that is threatening the physical and mental health of many workers. [2]"Technostress" is a modern disorder caused by an inability to cope in a healthy manner with the new computer technology.

[3]Technostress reveals itself in several distinct ways. [4]It can surface as a person struggles to learn how to use computers in the workplace, which often **provokes** anxiety. [5]Some people develop a **phobia** about modern technology and need professional help to deal with their fears.

[6]Technostress can also surface as overidentification with computers. [7]Some people develop a machinelike **mind-set** that reflects the traits of the computer itself. [8]Some who were once warm and sensitive people become cold, lose their friends, and have no patience for the easy give-and-take of conversation. [9]In addition, they watch television as their major or only leisure activity.

[10]Further, *technostress* is the term used for such physical stress reactions as computer-related eyestrain, headaches, neck and shoulder

tension, and backache. [11]Also, many people who use computer keyboards often develop carpal tunnel syndrome.

[12]These various reactions to technostress arise from long-term use of computers. [13]If someone spends most of their working hours **interacting with** only a computer screen and a keyboard, then that person may develop a number of the following symptoms.

[14]Eyestrain is caused by focusing continuously on a screen at close range. [15]The person who focuses for a long time on one specific colored screen may see the **complementary** color when looking up at a blank wall or ceiling. [16]This color reversal is normal and quickly lessens. [17]Headaches, though sometimes caused by eyestrain, are most often due to tension involving muscles of the brow, temples, jaw, upper neck, and base of the skull. [18]These headaches can be affected by improper height of the chair and screen. [19]Even the lack of an armrest can contribute. [20]Lack of an armrest causes the arms to pull down on the shoulders, creating, in turn, tension at the shoulder tip and base of the skull and spasms radiating up into the head. [21]Carpal tunnel syndrome, a numbness, tingling, or burning sensation in the fingers or wrists, may be induced by **inflammation** of the ligaments and tendons in fingers and wrists.

—Adapted from McGuigan, F. J.,
Encyclopedia of Stress, pp. 237–238.

VISUAL *VOCABULARY*

The best meaning of **ergonomic**
is _____.

a. poorly designed
b. well designed
c. cheaply produced

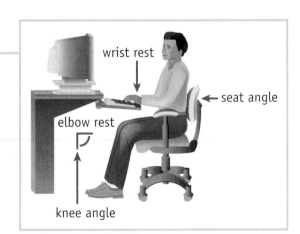

wrist rest

seat angle

elbow rest

knee angle

▲ An ergonomic chair will provide appropriate support to the back, legs, buttocks, and arms. This support can reduce contact stress, overexertion, and fatigue. It will also promote proper circulation to the extremities.

"Ergonomic Solutions: Workstation Chair." Occupational Safety and Health Administration, U.S. Department of Labor.

Before Reading

Vocabulary in Context

_____ **1.** The term **mind-set** in sentence 7 means
a. stubbornness.   c. attitude.
b. decision.   d. opinion.

_____ **2.** The best synonym for **complementary** in sentence 15 is
a. beautiful.   c. praise.
b. opposite.   d. similar.

After Reading

Concept Map

3–4. Finish the concept map by filling in the missing idea with information from the passage.

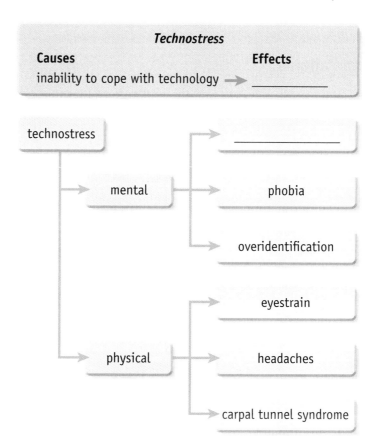

Technostress

Causes   Effects
inability to cope with technology ⟶ _____

technostress

mental ⟶ _____

mental ⟶ phobia

⟶ overidentification

physical ⟶ eyestrain

physical ⟶ headaches

⟶ carpal tunnel syndrome

Central Idea and Main Idea

_____ **5.** Which sentence states the central idea of the passage?
  a. sentence 1
  b. sentence 2
  c. sentence 12
  d. sentence 13

Supporting Details

_____ **6.** Sentence 19 is a
  a. major supporting detail.
  b. minor supporting detail.

Transitions

_____ **7.** The word **further** in sentence 10 is a signal word that shows
  a. comparison.
  b. cause.
  c. addition.

_____ **8.** The word **though** in sentence 17 signals
  a. cause and effect.
  b. contrast.
  c. addition.

Thought Patterns

_____ **9.** The primary thought pattern for the entire passage is
  a. cause and effect.
  b. generalization and example.
  c. comparison and contrast.

_____ **10.** The thought pattern for the fourth paragraph (sentences 10–11) is
  a. cause and effect.
  b. generalization and example.
  c. listing.

SUMMARY RESPONSE

Restate the author's central idea in your own words. In your summary, follow the thought pattern used by the author. Begin your summary response with the following: *The central idea of "Technostress" from the* Encyclopedia of Stress *by McGuigan is …*

WHAT DO YOU THINK?

Do you or someone you know suffer from technostress? Although this selection discusses the negative effects of technology, what are some of the benefits of technology? Do the advantages outweigh the disadvantages? What other tech-nology besides computers could lead to technostress? How could a person lessen the stress associated with technostress? Assume you are an office manager, and you are giving a presentation about technostress at a training session for new employees. Write a draft of your presentation and include the following ideas:

- Warn new employees about the dangers of technostress.
- Explain how to avoid or reduce technostress.

After Reading About More Thought Patterns

Before you move on to the Mastery Tests on thought patterns, take time to reflect on your learning and performance by answering the following questions. Write your answers in your notebook.

- How has my knowledge base or prior knowledge about thought patterns changed?
- Based on my studies, how do I think I will perform on the Mastery Test(s)? Why do I think my scores will be above average, average, or below average?
- Would I recommend this chapter to other students who want to learn about more thought patterns? Why or why not?

Test your understanding of what you have learned about thought patterns by completing the Chapter 8 Review.

Name _____ Section _____

Date _____ Score (number correct) _____ × 5 = _____%

Visit MyReadingLab to take this test online and receive feedback and guidance on your answers.

A. **1–9.** Write the numbers **1** to **9** in the spaces provided to show the correct order of the ideas. Then answer the question that follows the list.

Expected Effects of Cocaine

Textbook Skills

_2_ The first effect the user can expect is a powerful burst of energy.

_5_ However, if snorted through the nose, the effect begins in about three to five minutes; it peaks after fifteen to twenty minutes and wears off in sixty to ninety minutes.

_4_ If the cocaine is injected through the veins, the effect is immediate and intense; it peaks in three to five minutes and wears off in thirty to forty minutes.

_1_ Cocaine users can expect certain effects.

_3_ The time it takes to feel the effects varies, based on whether the cocaine is injected or snorted.

_6_ Users can also expect to experience a general sense of well-being.

_7_ However, in some instances, cocaine may cause a panic attack.

_9_ Finally, these uncomfortable aftereffects create a powerful craving for another dose.

_8_ Once the cocaine wears off, the user becomes irritable and depressed.

—Adapted from Charles F. Levinthal, *Drugs, Behavior, and Modern Society,* 3rd ed. Boston: Allyn and Bacon, 2002, p. 81.

_____ **10.** The primary thought pattern is
   a. generalization and example.
   b. comparison and contrast.
   c. cause and effect.

B. Fill in the blanks with the correct transition word or phrase from the box. Use each transition once.

for example   in contrast   leads to   result in   subsequently

Rest Well

Adequate rest **(11)** _____ improved performance. **(12)** _____, sleep deprivation causes a host of problems. **(13)** _____, lack of rest may **(14)** _____ loss of concentration and loss of energy. **(15)** _____, poor concentration and lack of energy could lead to slow and flawed work.

C. Write the letter of the appropriate thought pattern before each item, as follows:

a. generalization and example
b. comparison and contrast
c. cause and effect

_____ **16.** Marcel began to practice yoga because of a shoulder injury.

_____ **17.** Marcel compared several types of yoga to determine which method was best for him.

_____ **18.** For example, he considered Iyengar yoga, a style of yoga emphasizing body placement and alignment.

_____ **19.** In addition, he thought about Ashtanga yoga, also known as power yoga, which focuses on high-energy, free-flowing movement.

_____ **20.** Marcel chose Ashtanga because he enjoys an intense workout.

Name _____ Section _____

Date _____ Score (number correct) _____ × 10 = _____%

Visit MyReadingLab to take this test online and receive feedback and guidance on your answers.

Read the paragraphs from college textbooks. Then answer the questions and complete the concept maps.

Public Speaking Anxiety

[1]Fear of public speaking causes major anxiety for a number of Americans. [2]Understanding some of its causes and effects often helps relieve public speaking anxiety. [3]This anxiety is triggered by the anticipation of performing in front of an audience. [4]Many fear public speaking because they fear they will make a mistake and look foolish. [5]In some instances, lack of preparation contributes to the problem. [6]A few obvious physical effects are a quavering voice, stuttering, vomiting, cold and sweaty hands, dry mouth, and even fainting. [7]This fear can also have mental effects, such as blocked ideas or short-term memory loss.

—Adapted from McGuigan, F. J., *Encyclopedia of Stress*, p. 210.

_____ 1. The relationship between sentence 4 and sentence 5 is
    a. cause and effect.
    b. addition.
    c. comparison.

Causes and Effects of Public Speaking Anxiety

Main idea: Understanding some of its causes and effects often helps lessen the fear of speaking in public.

Causes

Effects

2. _____

3. _____

4. _____

Public speaking anxiety

5. _____

6. _____

Different Perspectives

¹The same event in a family has a different meaning for each of its family members, based on age and cognitive ability. ²This difference in perspectives can be clearly seen in studies on the effects of parents' divorce on their children. ³Children who are 5 years old when parents divorce respond in predictable ways that are different from the predictable ways that 11-year-olds respond. ⁴Five-year-olds assume the divorce is a result of something they did, whereas 11-year-olds can reason and understand that the divorce may be caused by other factors.

—Adapted from Kosslyn, Stephen M. and Robin S. Rosenberg.
Psychology: The Brain, The Person, The World, p. 378.

_____ **7.** The relationship between sentence 1 and sentence 2 is
   a. definition.
   b. comparison and contrast.
   c. cause and effect.

_____ **8.** The thought patterns used in the paragraph are comparison and contrast and
   a. generalization and example.
   b. time order.
   c. cause and effect.

The same event in a family has a different meaning for each of its family members, based on age and cognitive ability.

9. 5-year-olds _____

10. 11-year-olds _____

Name _____ Section _____

Date _____ Score (number correct) _____ × 10 = _____%

Visit MyReadingLab to take this test online and receive feedback and guidance on your answers.

A. Read the following paragraph from a college finance textbook. Then answer the question and complete the concept map.

Textbook
Skills

Buying a Car Online Versus Buying a Car on a Lot

[1]Buying a new car online is still not as efficient as buying a car off a dealer's lot. [2]The personal options of a car make online buying difficult. [3]First, at a dealership, a customer can actually see the difference in the design of the two models of a particular car. [4]It is not as easy to detect the differences on a Web site. [5]Second, unlike a Web site, a dealer can also anticipate your questions and arrange for a test drive. [6]It is also more difficult to communicate with an online service. [7]For example, it is difficult to force an online service to meet its delivery promise to you because you have limited access to them through email and phone messages. [8]However, you can place pressure on a local dealership to meet its promise by showing up at the dealership to express your concerns in person.

—Adapted from Madura, Jeff, *Personal Finance*, 2nd ed., p. 235.

_____ 1. The thought patterns used in the paragraph are listing and
  a. definition.
  b. comparison and contrast.
  c. cause and effect.

Buying a Car Online Versus Buying a Car on a Lot

Main idea: Buying a new car online is still not as efficient as buying a car off a dealer's lot.

	Online	Dealership
First difference	Customer can't see differences in cars.	Customer can see differences in cars.
Second difference	(2) _____	(3) _____
Third difference	(4) _____	(5) _____

B. Read the following paragraph from a college psychology textbook. Then answer the question and complete the outline with the major supporting details.

Effects of Sleep Deprivation

Textbook
Skills

¹If you have ever stayed up late, say, studying or partying, and then awakened early the next morning, you have probably experienced sleep deprivation. ²In fact, you may be sleep-deprived right now. ³What happens as a result of sleep deprivation? ⁴Young adults who volunteered for a sleep deprivation study were allowed to sleep for only five hours each night, for a total of seven nights. ⁵After three nights of restricted sleep, volunteers complained of mental, emotional, and physical difficulties. ⁶Moreover, their abilities to perform visual motor tasks declined after only two nights. ⁷Hormones are also affected by sleep deprivation. ⁸For example, the loss of even one night's sleep can lead to increases in the next day's level of cortisol. ⁹Cortisol helps the body meet the demands imposed by stress. ¹⁰Finally, going without sleep for long stretches of time, such as 4 to 11 days, causes profound psychological effects. ¹¹Long-term sleep deprivation can lead to feelings of losing control and anxiety.

—Adapted from Kosslyn, Stephen M. and Robin S. Rosenberg.
Psychology: The Brain, The Person, The World, p. 138.

_____ 6. The thought patterns used in the paragraph are listing and
    a. generalization and example.
    b. comparison and contrast.
    c. cause and effect.

Effects of Sleep Deprivation

(7) _____

(8) _____

(9) _____

(10) _____

Name _____ Section _____

Date _____ Score (number correct) _____ × 10 = _____%

Visit MyReadingLab to take this test online and receive feedback and guidance on your answers.

Read the passage and answer the questions that follow. Then complete the study notes with information from the passage.

Textbook
Skills

Dreams Vary

[1]The influence of culture on dream content reveals itself in a variety of ways. [2]For example, reports from the West African nation of Ghana tell us dreams in that region often feature attacks by cows (Barnouw, 1963). [3]Americans frequently find themselves embarrassed by public nudity in their dreams, although such reports rarely occur in cultures where people customarily wear few clothes. [4]Images of death appear more often in dreams of Mexican American college students than in dreams of Anglo American students, probably because concerns about death are a more important feature of life in Latin American cultures (Roll et al., 1974). [5]In general, cross-cultural research lends support to Rosalind Cartwright's (1977) hypothesis that dreams reflect life events that are important to the dreamer.

[6]Sleep scientists now know that the content of dreams also varies by age and gender (Domhoff, 1996). [7]Children are more likely to dream about animals than adults are, and the animals in their dreams are more likely to be large, threatening, and wild. [8]In contrast, college students dream more often of small animals, pets, and tame creatures. [9]This may mean children feel less in control of their world than adults do and thus see the world depicted in scarier imagery while they sleep (Van de Castle, 1983, 1994).

[10]Women everywhere more commonly dream of children, while men more often dream of aggression, weapons, and tools (Murray, 1995). [11]And American women may be more equal-opportunity dreamers than their male counterparts: In a sample of more than 1,800 dreams collected by dream researcher Calvin Hall, women dreamed about both men and women, while men more often dreamed about men—twice as often, in fact, as they dreamed about women. [12]Hall also found that hostile interactions between characters outnumbered friendly exchanges, and that two-thirds of emotional dreams had a negative complexion, such as anger and sadness (Hall, 1951, 1984).

—Adapted from Zimbardo, Philip G., Johnson, Robert L., and Hamilton, Vivian McCann, *Psychology: Core Concepts*, 7th ed., pp. 339–340.

_____ **1.** The relationship of ideas between sentences 1 and 2 is
  a. comparison.   c. generalization and example.
  b. contrast.   d. definition and example.

_____ **2.** The relationship of ideas within sentence 3 is
  a. comparison.   c. definition and example.
  b. contrast.   d. generalization and example.

_____ **3.** The relationship of ideas within sentence 4 is first contrast and then
  a. comparison.   c. generalization and example.
  b. cause and effect.   d. definition and example.

_____ **4.** The relationship of ideas between sentences 6 and 7 is
  a. comparison.   c. cause and effect.
  b. contrast.   d. generalization and example.

_____ **5.** The title implies that the thought pattern of the passage is
  a. comparison.   c. cause and effect.
  b. contrast.   d. generalization and example.

Differences in dreams reported from different countries are evidence that dream content is influenced by (**6**) _____. Differences in dream content between college students and (**7**) _____ show the influence of age, while differences in the dreams of women and men reveal the effect of (**8**) _____. For example, (**9**) _____ dream more about men than they do about women. In addition, one researcher found that people are more likely to dream of (**10**) _____ interactions and negative emotions.

8 Summary of Key Concepts of More Thought Patterns

 Assess your comprehension of thought patterns.

- Comparison points out _____.
- Contrast points out _____.
- The words *like, similarly,* and *likewise* signal the _____ pattern.
- A cause states _____.
- An effect states _____.
- An author will often begin with the _____ and then give the effects.
- The phrases *as a result, leads to,* and *therefore* signal the _____ pattern.
- _____ words signal that a writer is giving an instance of a general idea to clarify a point.
- Definition explains the _____.
- Examples often follow a definition to show _____.

Test Your Comprehension of More Thought Patterns

Respond to the following questions and prompts.

LO1 LO2 In your own words, what is the difference between comparison and contrast?

_____

_____

LO1 LO3 In your own words, what is the difference between a cause and an effect?

_____

_____

In the space below create a concept map based on the information in the paragraph.

> Carbon dioxide (CO_2) absorbs some of the radiation emitted by Earth and thus contributes to the greenhouse effect. Because CO_2 is a heat absorber, a change in CO_2 levels in Earth's atmosphere influences air temperature. Two main factors cause the increase of CO_2 and greenhouse warming. The use of coal and other fossil fuels is the most prominent means by which humans add CO_2 to the atmosphere, but it is not the only cause. The clearing of forests called deforestation also contributes substantially because CO_2 is released as vegetation is burned or decays.
>
> —Adapted from Lutgens, Frederick K.; Tarbuck, Edward J.; Tasa, Dennis G., *Foundations of Earth Science*, 5th ed., pp. 309–310.

LO1 Summarize the two most important ideas in this chapter that will help you improve your reading comprehension. _____

_____

_____

_____

Fact and Opinion

LEARNING OUTCOMES

After studying this chapter, you should be able to:

LO1 Define the Terms *Fact* and *Opinion*

LO2 Ask Questions to Identify Facts

LO3 Analyze Biased Words to Identify Opinions

LO4 Analyze Qualifiers to Identify Opinions

LO5 Analyze Supposed Facts

LO6 Read Critically: Evaluate Details as Fact or Opinion in Context

LO7 Develop Textbook Skills: Fact and Opinion in Textbooks

LO8 Apply Information Literacy Skills: Academic, Personal, and Career Applications of Fact and Opinion

Before Reading About Fact and Opinion

You are most likely already familiar with the commonly used words *fact* and *opinion*, and you probably already have an idea about what each one means. Take a moment to clarify your current understanding about fact and opinion by writing a definition for each one in the spaces below:

Fact: _____

_____

Opinion: _____

_____

_____

As you work through this chapter, compare what you already know about fact and opinion to new information that you learn about each one using the following method.

On a blank page in your notebook, draw a line down the middle of the page to form two columns. Label one side "Fact" and the other side "Opinion." Just below each heading, copy the definition you wrote for each one. As you work through the chapter, record new information you learn about facts and opinions in their corresponding column.

LO1 ## Define the Terms *Fact* and *Opinion*

Fact: Eva Longoria is known for her role as Gabrielle Solis on ABC's *Desperate Housewives*.

Opinion: Eva Longoria is one of the most influential Hispanics in Hollywood.

Effective readers must sort fact from opinion to properly understand and evaluate the information they are reading.

> A **fact** is a specific detail that is true based on objective proof. A fact is discovered.
> An **opinion** is an interpretation, value judgment, or belief that cannot be proved or disproved. An opinion is created.
> **Objective proof** can be physical evidence, an eyewitness account, or the result of an accepted scientific method.

Most people's points of view and beliefs are based on a blend of fact and opinion. Striving to remain objective, many authors rely mainly on facts. The main purpose of using facts is to inform. For example, textbooks, news articles, and medical research rely on facts. In contrast, editorials, advertisements, and fiction often mix fact and opinion. The main purpose of these types of writing is to persuade or entertain.

Separating fact from opinion requires you to think critically because opinion is often presented as fact. The following clues will help you separate fact from opinion.

Fact	Opinion
Is objective	Is subjective
Is discovered	Is created
States reality	Interprets reality
Can be verified	Cannot be verified
Is presented with unbiased words	Is presented with biased words
Example of a fact	*Example of an opinion*
Spinach is a source of iron.	Spinach tastes awful.

A fact is a specific, objective, and verifiable detail; in contrast, an opinion is a biased, personal view created from feelings and beliefs.

> **EXAMPLE** Read the following statements, and mark each one **F** if it states a fact or **O** if it expresses an opinion.

_____ **1.** *Avatar* is a 3D science fiction movie written and directed by James Cameron.

_____ **2.** James Cameron's films are always too predictable, with worn-out stories and stereotypical characters.

_____ **3.** Within three weeks of its release, earning over $1 billion, *Avatar* became the second highest-grossing film of all time worldwide, exceeded only by Cameron's previous film, *Titanic*.

_____ **4.** *Avatar* takes us to a spectacular world beyond imagination.

EXPLANATION Sentences 1 and 3 state facts that can be verified through research. Sentences 2 and 4 express opinions, personal reactions to James Cameron's work as a filmmaker. Sentence 2 expresses a negative personal opinion; sentence 4 expresses a positive personal opinion.

Practice 1

Read the following statements and mark each one **F** if it states a fact or **O** if it expresses an opinion.

_____ **1.** Michelangelo is the greatest painter of all time.

_____ **2.** The Sistine Chapel is the private chapel of the popes in Rome.

_____ **3.** Between 1508 and 1512, Michelangelo produced frescos for the chapel's ceiling; the murals depict scenes from the Book of Genesis, from the Creation to the Flood.

_____ **4.** One cannot really understand what a human is capable of producing until one sees Michelangelo's work in the Sistine Chapel.

LO2 Ask Questions to Identify Facts

To test whether a statement is a fact, ask these three questions:

- Can the statement be proved or demonstrated to be true?
- Can the statement be observed in practice or operation?
- Can the statement be verified by witnesses, manuscripts, or documents?

If the answer to any of these questions is no, the statement is not a fact. Instead, it is an opinion. Keep in mind, however, that many statements blend both fact and opinion.

> **EXAMPLE** Read the following statements, and mark each one **F** if it states a fact or **O** if it expresses an opinion.

_____ **1.** Lady Gaga collapsed and passed out before a show in West Lafayette, Indiana.

_____ **2.** Lady Gaga wears outlandish costumes just to get attention.

_____ **3.** Lady Gaga combines music, fashion, art, and technology in her body of work.

_____ **4.** Lady Gaga's stage name is based on the song "Radio Ga Ga" by Freddie Mercury and his band Queen.

EXPLANATION

1. **F:** This statement can be easily verified in newspapers.

2. **O:** This is a statement of personal opinion. Some critics and fans may think her costumes are innovative and fun.

3. **F:** This statement can be verified through research and eyewitness experiences.

4. **F:** This statement can be easily verified through research. <

Practice 2

Read the following statements, and mark each one **F** if it states a fact or **O** if it expresses an opinion.

_____ **1.** In 2012, reality shows like *American Idol, Survivor,* and *America's Next Top Model* still appealed to the American television market.

_____ **2.** Small dogs make the best house pets.

_____ **3.** The chemicals in marijuana smoke can cause cancer.

_____ **4.** Florida, with its mild winters, is the ideal place to retire.

_____ **5.** The poet Emily Dickinson composed over 1,000 poems.

_____ **6.** Spanking of any kind is a form of child abuse.

_____ **7.** The Harry Potter books and films have stimulated many children's interest in reading.

_____ **8.** Television reduces the intelligence of viewers.

_____ **9.** Within the next decade, as the "baby boom" generation retires, a significant number of teachers will leave the workplace.

_____ **10.** The mass production of the automobile changed the way people and goods moved from one place to another.

L03 Analyze Biased Words to Identify Opinions

Be on the lookout for biased words. **Biased words** express opinions, value judgments, and interpretations. They are often loaded with emotion. The box below contains a small sample of this type of words.

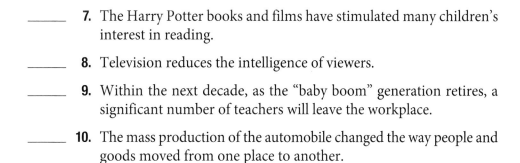

Biased Words

amazing	best	favorite	great	miserable	stupid
awful	better	frightful	greatest	more	ugly
bad	disgusting	fun	handsome	most	unbelievable
beautiful	exciting	good	horrible	smart	very

Realize that a sentence can include both facts and opinions. The part of the sentence that includes a biased word may be an opinion about another part of the sentence that is a fact.

EXAMPLE Read the following sentences. Underline the biased words.

1. Even though actor George Clooney is in his fifties, he is still very handsome.

2. The grasslands of the American West were tragically plowed under for crops.

EXPLANATION In the first sentence, "George Clooney is in his fifties" is a fact that can be proved by research. However, the second part of the sentence, "he is still very handsome," is an opinion about his appearance. In the second sentence, the grasslands of the American West _were_ plowed under to make way for crops, but whether that fact is tragic is a matter of opinion.

Practice 3

Read the following sentences. Underline the biased words.

1. Even though spinach is low in calories and rich in fiber, iron, folate, and vitamin A, its bitter taste makes it a less desirable food.

2. A Labrador retriever is a medium-sized dog with a distinctive double coat that requires brushing; loyal and friendly, this breed makes an excellent pet for a family.

Analyze Qualifiers to Identify Opinions

Be on the lookout for words that qualify an idea. Sometimes a qualifier may express an absolute, unwavering opinion using words such as *always* or *never*. Other times a qualifier may express an opinion in the form of a command as in *must*, or the desirability of an action with a word such as *should*. Qualifiers may indicate different degrees of doubt with words such as *seems* or *might*. The box below contains a few examples of this type of words.

Words That Qualify Ideas					
all	could	likely	never	possibly, possible	sometimes
always	every	may	often	probably, probable	think
appear	has/have to	might	only	seem	usually
believe	it is believed	must	ought to	should	

Remember that a sentence can include both fact and opinion. Authors use qualifiers to express opinions about facts.

EXAMPLE   Read the following sentences. Underline the qualifiers.

1. Every citizen who wants to be informed about current events should subscribe to at least two newspapers and never miss the nightly news.

2. Amber, fossilized tree resin, was one of the first substances used for decoration; it is believed to exert a healthful influence on the endocrine system, spleen, and heart.

1. The qualifiers in this sentence are *every*, *should*, and *never*. The fact is that newspapers and the nightly news do cover current events, but these qualifiers express a personal opinion about this fact.

2. The qualifier in this sentence is the phrase *it is believed*. The author has signaled that what follows is not a proven fact, only a belief. ◀

Practice 4

Read the following sentences. Underline the qualifiers.

1. While swimming, the woman suddenly disappeared from sight, possibly pulled underwater by an alligator.

2. You have to let me go to the annual New Year's Eve celebration in Times Square; everybody is going. I will be the only one who can't go.

L05 Analyze Supposed Facts

Beware of **false facts**, or statements presented as facts that are actually untrue. At times, an author may mislead the reader with a false impression of the facts. Political and commercial advertisements often present facts out of context, exaggerate the facts, or give only some of the facts. For example, a retailer publishes the following claim in a local newspaper: "Batteries for $.10 each." However, the batteries are sold in packets of one hundred; they are not sold individually. Even though the advertisement told a partial truth, it misled consumers by leaving out an important fact. A truthful advertisement of the same situation states, "Batteries for $.10 each, sold only in packages of 100 for $10.00 per package."

Sometimes an author deliberately presents false information. Janet Cooke, a reporter for the *Washington Post,* concocted a false story about a boy named Jimmy, whom she described as "8 years old and a third-generation heroin addict," and whose ambition was to be a heroin dealer when he grew up. After she won a Pulitzer Prize for this story, it was learned that she had never met Jimmy and most of the details were simply not true. The *Washington Post* also learned that she had falsified facts on her résumé. She was fired, and the *Washington Post* returned the Pulitzer Prize. Cooke's use of false facts ruined her career and embarrassed the prestigious newspaper.

Read the following two examples of false facts:

1. The earliest humans lived at the same time as the dinosaurs.

2. The virus that causes mononucleosis, also known as the kissing disease, can be spread through the air.

Fossil records and scientific research have proved that the first statement is a false fact. The second statement is a false fact because the virus that causes mononucleosis can be spread only through contact with saliva. Often some prior knowledge of the topic is needed to identify false facts. The more you read, the more effective you will become at evaluating facts as true or false.

Sometimes a statement may describe a factual event but use words that slant the meaning toward a particular opinion. For example, read these statements:

1. The U.S. government **pours** millions of dollars **into** the space program.

2. The U.S. government **spends** millions of dollars **on** the space program.

The slanted term *pours into* creates an impression that the money is not being spent wisely, which is an opinion. The term *spends on* does not create such a bias.

In which of the following statements do you sense a negative opinion about the protesters?

1. On their way to the Capitol, the protesters walked through the park.

2. On their way to the Capitol, the protesters traipsed through the park.

VISUAL *VOCABULARY*

A bull wapiti (elk) **traipses** into a residential neighborhood in Banff, Alberta, disrupting traffic.

The best synonym for **traipses**

is _____.

   a. wanders

   b. runs

   c. stumbles

In addition to thinking carefully about false facts, beware of opinions stated to sound like facts. Remember that facts are specific details that can be researched and verified as true. However, opinions may be introduced as facts with phrases like "in truth," "the truth of the matter," or "in fact." Read the following two statements:

1. In truth, computers make life miserable.

2. Computers make life miserable; in point of fact, viruses and worms are just two of the problems that can infect a computer, possibly damaging it and even causing it to crash.

The first statement is a general opinion that uses the value word *miserable*. The second statement is a blend of fact and opinion. It begins with a biased statement, but then uses the phrase "in point of fact" to introduce factual details.

> EXAMPLE Read the following statements, and mark each one as follows:

F if it states a fact

O if it expresses an opinion

F/O if it combines fact and opinion

_____ 1. *Glee* is an American musical comedy-drama television series that focuses on a high school glee club.

_____ 2. *Glee* is America's favorite comedy, winning several major awards; for example, the show won a Golden Globe for "Best Television Series—Musical Comedy" in 2011.

_____ 3. So far, the show's highest ratings occurred during its second season, with 10.1 million viewers.

_____ 4. In addition to dealing with relationships, sexuality, and social issues, the show offers elaborate and beautiful choreography.

_____ 5. Everyone should watch *Glee*.

EXPLANATION Items 1 and 3 are facts that can be verified through research. Item 5 states an opinion by using the phrasing "Everyone should." Item 2 is a mixture of fact and opinion. Research verifies that *Glee* has won several awards, but the word "favorite" is a value word, and the use of "America" implies that everyone in America favors this show—an idea that cannot be verified. Item 4 also blends fact and opinion. The facts are that the show deals with relationships, sexuality, and social issues. However, the words "elaborate" and "beautiful" are statements of opinion about which people will disagree.

> **EXAMPLE** Study the following editorial cartoon. Then write one fact and one opinion based on the issue as expressed in the cartoon.

Fact: _____

_____

Opinion: _____

_____

EXPLANATION Answers will vary. Compare your answers to the following:

Fact: Texting while driving distracts drivers and causes accidents.

Opinion: Texting while driving should be illegal.

Practice 5

A. Read the following statements. Circle biased words and qualifiers as needed. Then mark each one as follows:

F if it states a fact

O if it expresses an opinion

F/O if it combines fact and opinion

_____ **1.** Unhealthy diets and lack of exercise are serious national problems; in fact, 300,000 deaths each year are linked to these two problems.

_____ **2.** Tobacco use kills more Americans than motor vehicle crashes, AIDS, cocaine use, heroin use, homicide, and suicide combined.

_____ **3.** Tobacco products should be outlawed.

_____ **4.** Diets high in fruits, vegetables, and fiber lower the risk for some types of cancer.

_____ **5.** Public schools ought to serve fruits and vegetables instead of pizza and hamburgers.

_____ **6.** Exercise is the only sure way to lose weight.

_____ **7.** Executives of tobacco companies murder millions of people with their products.

_____ **8.** All cancers caused by cigarette smoking could be prevented.

_____ **9.** The sugar glider, which is a small opossum, is smaller than a gerbil, larger than a mouse, and more adorable than a teddy bear.

_____ **10.** Pot-bellied pigs make great pets.

B. Read the following short reviews of destinations, restaurants, movies, and plays. Circle biased words and qualifiers as needed. Then mark each one as follows:

F if it states a fact

O if it expresses an opinion

F/O if it combines fact and opinion

_____ **11.** The Palms Casino Resort in Las Vegas is the absolute best tourist destination.

_____ **12.** Russell Crowe starred in a thrilling movie version of the story of Robin Hood, the legendary hero who fought against injustice by robbing from the rich to give to the poor.

_____ **13.** The Nine Steakhouse, which serves prime aged steaks and imported spirits, is Chicago's most popular night spot.

_____ **14.** Set at the edge of Texas Hill Country on the Colorado River, Austin, the capital of Texas, offers many unexpected pleasures to the visitor.

_____ **15.** After pirates, hurricanes, and wars, Key West, Florida, survives as a great tourist town, with superb sunsets, informal living, wonderful festivals, relaxing beaches, top fishing possibilities, and all the services that a visitor could want.

_____ **16.** Come on in to Steve's Diner for a mouth-watering selection of home-cooked comfort food. Selections on the menu range from Italian, Greek, and American, with an old-fashioned breakfast menu served all day. Come enjoy the excellent service, the comfortable atmosphere, and the reasonable prices.

_____ **17.** Peter Jackson's Oscar-winning film of the *Lord of the Rings* epic by J. R. R. Tolkien remains one of the greatest achievements in cinema history.

_____ **18.** *Phantom of the Opera* is the longest-running production in Broadway history.

_____ **19.** Half of the land on Sanibel Island, Florida, is designated as natural areas, with two preserves protecting the island ecosystem and wildlife.

_____ **20.** The *Internet Movie Database* remains the ultimate source for movie and movie star information.

LO6 Read Critically: Evaluate Details as Fact or Opinion in Context

Because the printed word seems to give authority to an idea, many of us accept what we read as fact. Yet much of what is published is actually opinion. Effective readers question what they read. Reading critically is noting the use of fact and opinion in the context of a paragraph or passage, the author, and the type of source in which the passage is printed.

Evaluate the Context of the Passage

Much of what you read in print and electronic media is a mixture of factual details and the author's opinion. Often, an author words an opinion as a fact in an effort to make a point more believable. One way to distinguish between fact and opinion is to evaluate the context. The language used by an author helps us to decide whether a statement can be backed up with evidence and proven in some way. Language also indicates whether the statement is someone's point of view, judgement, or belief. You have already studied biased words and qualifiers that signal an opinion. Also consider the following examples of language that expresses facts and opinions.

Examples of Language Expressing Facts	Examples of Language Expressing Opinions
According to the results of the latest poll	The prosecution **argues** that
The latest studies **confirm**	The defense **claims** that
The research has **demonstrated**	In the President's **view**
Researchers have recently **discovered**	Most experts in this field **suspect** that

In addition to the wording of an idea, relationships between ideas and thought patterns may also signal a fact or an opinion. For example, facts are often stated as examples or details that can be verified.

Examples of Thought Patterns for Facts	Examples of Thought Patterns for Opinions
Definition	Comparisons
Causes and Effects	Reasons (explanations and interpretations)
Examples	Quality, Traits, Attributes
Details	

Of course, some comparisons and traits are factual. And authors can present possible or probable causes and effects that haven't been proven. So an effective reader must analyze the context of each statement.

The mixture of fact and opinion occurs when an author interprets or evaluates a fact. Look at the following three statements in which the facts are highlighted in red and the opinions are highlighted in green.

Fact:	**A constitution is a document establishing the structure, function, and limitations of a government.**
Opinion:	**The United States Constitution is far superior to other forms of government.**
Fact and **Opinion:**	**The fifty-five delegates who attended the Constitutional Convention** labored long and hard that hot **summer of 1787.**

The first statement is a definition, a fact that can be verified. The second statement begins like a definition but really only offers an opinion based on a comparison. The third statement offers factual historical details. However, the author has also characterized the work of the delegates with biased language that describes traits of the work and the environment. The phrase "labored long and hard" may have different meanings to different people. The questions "how hard and how long" remain unverified. Likewise, what is "hot" to one person may not be "hot" to another. Thus, the trait "hot" is a statement of opinion.

⊙ **EXAMPLE** Read the passage, and identify each sentence as follows:

F if it states a fact

O if it expresses an opinion

F/O if it combines fact and opinion

Alexander the Great

[1]Alexander III, more commonly known as Alexander the Great, was one of the greatest military leaders in world history. [2]He was born in Pella, Macedonia. [3]The exact date of his birth was probably July 20 or 26, 356 B.C. [4]Shortly before his 33rd birthday, Alexander the Great died. [5]The cause of his death remains unknown.

1. _____   2. _____   3. _____   4. _____   5. _____

EXPLANATION

1. **F/O:** His name and title are factual, but the value word *greatest* is an opinion with which some people may disagree.

2. **F:** This statement can be verified in historical records.

3. **O:** The word *probably* makes this a statement of opinion.

4. **F:** This statement can be checked and verified as true.

5. **F:** This is a factual statement that something isn't known. ◄

Practice 6

A. Read the passage, and identify each sentence as follows:

F if it states a fact

O if it expresses an opinion

F/O if it combines fact and opinion

Tough Little Robot

[1]The United States government sponsors research projects to advance traditional military roles and missions. [2]One such project is the Tactical Mobile Robot program and one advanced robot created under this program is called Packbot. [3]Packbot is a tough little robot developed by iRobot of Somerville, MA, for The Defense Advanced Research Projects Agency, or DARPA. [4]Small in size, but durable and versatile, Packbot was designed to venture into areas too dangerous for people. [5]The value of robots in real-world situations was demonstrated after the collapse of the World Trade Centers. [6]Drew Bennent of iRobot helped deploy Packbots supporting search and rescue operations. [7]Packbots went where it was just too dangerous for the human crews. [8]Right now the robot is equipped with a video camera and the operator can "see" on a computer screen what the robot sees. [9]Researchers working with a special response team are exploring its existing capabilities. [10]They are developing scenarios where Packbot could gather intelligence, create a diversion, or act as a force multiplier.

—Gatens, Kathy. "Science Fiction becomes Science Reality."
Robotics and Intelligence Systems. Idaho National Laboratory,
U.S. Department of Energy.

1. _____ 2. _____ 3. _____ 4. _____ 5. _____

6. _____ 7. _____ 8. _____ 9. _____ 10. _____

Packbot, a tactical mobile robot, searches dangerous areas.

The best meaning of the word **tactical** is _____.

    a. moving
    b. strategic
    c. landmark

Evaluate the Context of the Author

Even though opinions can't be proved true like facts can, many opinions are still sound and valuable. To judge the accuracy of the opinion, you must consider the source, the author of the opinion. Authors offer two types of valid opinions: informed opinions and expert opinions.

> An author develops an **informed opinion** by gathering and analyzing evidence.
>
> An author develops an **expert opinion** through much training and extensive knowledge in a given field.

❯ EXAMPLE Read the topic and study the list of authors who have written their opinions about the topic. Identify each person as **IO** if he or she is more likely to offer an informed opinion and **EO** if he or she is more likely to offer an expert opinion.

How to Parent a Teen

_____ **1.** Dr. Lisa Boesky, a leading child psychologist, television guest expert, national speaker, and author of several books such as *When to Worry: How to Tell If Your Teen Needs Help—and What to Do About It*

_____ **2.** An advice columnist such as Ann Landers or Dear Abby responding to a reader's question

_____   **3.** A pediatrician giving advice to the parents of one of his patients

_____   **4.** A high school science teacher who writes a lesson plan about disciplining children for a unit on human development in a health class

EXPLANATION

1. Dr. Boesky is considered to be an expert opinion in the field of childrearing. One way to identify an expert opinion is to note if the person giving the opinion holds an advanced degree or title or has published articles or books about the topic being discussed. Boesky has both the education and the achievement of being a successful author about this topic.

2. Advice columnists offer informed opinions on a wide range of topics. They often cite experts in their advice.

3. A pediatrician is a medical doctor for children. A pediatrician has had extensive training in child development.

4. A health teacher offers an informed opinion based on research to prepare the lesson. The teacher's main field is not child development, but science. ◐

Evaluate the Context of the Source

Often people turn to factual sources to find the factual details needed to form informed opinions and expert opinions. A medical dictionary, an English handbook, and a world atlas are a few excellent examples of factual sources.

> **EXAMPLE**   Read the passage, and then answer the questions that follow it.

Message from the Surgeon General

[1]Our nation stands at a crossroads. [2]Today's epidemic of overweight and obesity threatens the historic progress we have made in increasing Americans' quality and years of healthy life. [3]Two-thirds of adults and nearly one in three children are overweight or obese [according to the _Journal of the American Medical Association_]. [4]In addition, many racial and ethnic groups and geographic regions of the United States are disproportionately affected [according to the Centers for Disease Control]. [5]The sobering impact of these numbers is reflected in the nation's concurrent epidemics of diabetes, heart disease, and other chronic diseases. [6]If we do not reverse these trends, researchers warn that many of our children—our most precious resource—will be seriously afflicted in early adulthood with

medical conditions such as diabetes and heart disease. [7]This future is unacceptable. [8]I ask you to join me in combating this crisis.

> —Regina M. Benjamin, Surgeon General of the United States. U.S. Department of Health and Human Services. The Surgeon General's Vision for a Healthy and Fit Nation. Rockville, MD: U.S. Department of Health and Human Services, Office of the Surgeon General, January 2010.

_____ **1.** Sentence 3 is
  a. a fact.   b. an opinion.

_____ **2.** The Centers for Disease Control cited in sentence 4 serves as
  a. an informed opinion.   b. a factual source.

_____ **3.** Sentence 6 states
  a. a fact.   b. an expert opinion.

EXPLANATION

1. Sentence 3 is a statement of fact.

2. In sentence 4, the Centers for Disease Control serves as a factual source for the information given in the statement. It provides facts on which expert and informed opinions can be based.

3. Sentence 6 is the author's expert opinion backed up by facts. As Surgeon General of the United States, Benjamin has a medical background and cites current statistics and researchers' warnings that support her opinion. ◀

Practice 7

Read the passage, and then answer the questions that follow it.

[1]Dreams, those mysterious worlds we enter once we fall asleep, have fascinated humankind for generations. [2]According to the *Grolier Encyclopedia of Knowledge*, dream interpretation dates back to 2000 B.C. [3]People in ancient Greece, Rome, Egypt, and China recorded and studied their dreams. [4]Views on dreams have been as varied and as vivid as the cultures of the people who have studied them. [5]Some believed dreams to be messages from God. [6]Others thought them to be signs of indigestion. [7]Neil Carlson and William Buskist, authors of the textbook *Psychology: The Science of Behavior*, state that people have long used dreams to wage war, predict the future, or detect the guilt or innocence of people accused of a crime. [8]Sigmund Freud, noted psychiatrist, believed that dreams are connected to our subconscious; he believed that our dreams are the result

of emotions and desires we cannot express while awake. ⁹Carl Jung, a widely published psychologist who studied under Freud, thought dreams were a way to work out problems we face in our waking lives. ¹⁰No matter what the truth is, one-third of our life is spent dreaming, which adds up to a total of 27 years of our lifetime. ¹¹And everybody dreams!

_____ **1.** Sentence 1 is
      a. a fact.   b. an opinion.

_____ **2.** In sentence 2, the *Grolier Encyclopedia of Knowledge* offers
      a. a factual source.   b. an opinion.

_____ **3.** Sentence 2 is
      a. a fact.   b. an opinion.

_____ **4.** In sentence 8, Sigmund Freud's ideas are
      a. fact.   b. expert opinion.

_____ **5.** In sentence 9, Carl Jung's ideas are
      a. fact.   b. expert opinion.

VISUAL *VOCABULARY*

The names of Freud's and Jung's professions share a prefix and a suffix. What are they? The names also have word parts that differ. What are they? What does each word part mean? Use your dictionary if necessary to complete the chart:

Shared Prefix: _____   Meaning: _____

Shared Suffix: _____   Meaning: _____

Other word parts: iatreia   Meaning: _____

               ology   Meaning: _____

A **psychiatrist** is one who heals the mind. A **psychologist** is one who studies the mind.

LO7 Develop Textbook Skills: Fact and Opinion in Textbooks

Textbook
Skills

Most textbook authors are careful to present only ideas based on observation, research, and expert opinion. Read the following passage from a college health textbook, and identify each sentence as follows:

F if it states a fact

O if it expresses an opinion

F/O if it combines fact and opinion

Textbook
Skills

> **EXAMPLE** **Safety Guidelines During Weight Training**

¹During a weight training program, the following guidelines should be followed. ²First, when you use free weights (like barbells), spotters or helpers should assist you as you perform an exercise. ³They help when you are unable to complete a lift. ⁴Second, tightening the collars on the end of the bars of free weights prevents the weights from falling off. ⁵Dropping weight plates on toes and feet results in serious injuries. ⁶Third, warming up before weightlifting protects muscles from injuries. ⁷Finally, using slow movements during weightlifting is a wise approach. ⁸Some experts argue that high-speed weightlifting is superior to slow-speed lifting in terms of strength gains. ⁹However, slow movements may reduce the risk of injury. ¹⁰And slow movement during weightlifting does increase muscle size and strength.

—Adapted from Powers, Scott K. and Stephen L. Dodd.
Total Fitness and Wellness, 3rd ed., p. 111.

1. _____ 2. _____ 3. _____ 4. _____ 5. _____

6. _____ 7. _____ 8. _____ 9. _____ 10. _____

EXPLANATION Compare your answers to the ones below.

1. **O:** The word *should* indicates that this is an opinion or a suggestion. However, keep in mind that textbook authors offer information based on a great deal of research. This particular textbook lists the resources the authors used to form their opinions. This statement is therefore an expert opinion.

2. **O:** The word *should* indicates an opinion.

3. **F:** This is a statement of fact about what spotters can do.

4. **F:** This is a statement of fact that is supported by observation.

5. **F:** This is a statement of fact that can be verified by research and observation.

6. **F:** This is a statement of fact that can be verified through research. In fact, this textbook offers a list of expert and factual sources at the end of the chapter so that students can research the ideas for themselves.

7. **O:** This is an expert opinion based on research. The following sentences state facts to support this opinion.

8. **F:** This is a statement of fact. Experts do debate which method is best. This sentence does not favor one method over the other; it notes there is a debate and states both sides.

9. **F/O:** This is a statement that qualifies the facts. The facts can be verified through research and observation; however, the verb "may" indicates that results can vary.

10. **F:** This is a statement of fact that can be verified through research and observation. ◄

Practice 8

A. Read the following passage from a college history textbook. Then identify each sentence as follows:

F if it states a fact

O if it expresses an opinion

F/O if it combines fact and opinion

Textbook
Skills

The TV President

¹John Fitzgerald Kennedy was made for television. ²His tall, lean body gave him the strong vertical line that cameras love, and his weather-beaten good looks appealed to women without intimidating men. ³He had a full head of hair, and even in the winter he maintained a tan. ⁴Complementing his appearance was his attitude. ⁵He was always "cool" in public. ⁶This too was tailor-made for the "cool medium," television. ⁷Wit, irony, and understatement, all delivered with a studied ease, translate

well on television. [8]Table-thumping, impassioned speech, and even earnest sincerity often just do not work on television.

[9]The first presidential debate was held in Chicago on September 26, 1960, only a little more than a month before the election. [10]Richard Nixon arrived looking ill and weak. [11]During the previous six weeks, he had banged his kneecap, which became infected, and he had spent several weeks in the hospital. [12]Then he caught a bad cold that left him hoarse and weak. [13]By the day of the debate, he looked like a nervous corpse. [14]He was pale, 20 pounds underweight, and haggard. [15]Makeup experts offered to hide his heavy beard and soften his jaw line, but Nixon accepted only a thin coat of Max Factor's "Lazy Shave," a pancake makeup base.

[16]Kennedy looked better, very much better. [17]He didn't need any makeup to appear healthy, nor did he need special lighting to hide a weak profile. [18]He did, however, change suits. [19]He believed that a dark blue suit rather than a gray suit would look better under the bright lights. [20]Kennedy was right, of course, as anyone who watches a nightly news program realizes.

[21]When the debate started, Kennedy spoke first. [22]Although he was nervous, he slowed down his delivery. [23]His face was controlled and smooth. [24]He smiled with his eyes and perhaps the corners of his mouth, and his laugh was a mere suggestion of a laugh. [25]His body language was perfect.

[26]Nixon fought back. [27]He perspired, scored debating points, gave memorized facts, and struggled to win. [28]But his efforts were "hot"—bad for television. [29]Viewers saw a nervous, uncertain man, one whose clothes did not fit and whose face looked pasty and white.

[30]After the debate, Kennedy inched ahead of Nixon in a Gallup poll. [31]Most of the people who were undecided before watching the debate ended up voting for Kennedy.

—Adapted from Martin, James Kirby, Randy J. Roberts,
Steven Mintz, Linda O. McMurry, and James H. Jones.
America and Its People: Volume II: A Mosaic in the Making,
3rd ed., pp. 1001–1002.

_____ **1.** His tall, lean body gave him the strong vertical line that cameras love, and his weather-beaten good looks appealed to women without intimidating men.

_____ **2.** The first presidential debate was held in Chicago on September 26, 1960, only a little more than a month before the election.

_____ **3.** During the previous six weeks, he had banged his kneecap, which became infected, and he had spent several weeks in the hospital.

_____ **4.** By the day of the debate, he looked like a nervous corpse.

_____ **5.** He was pale, 20 pounds underweight, and haggard.

_____ **6.** Kennedy looked better, very much better.

_____ **7.** He did, however, change suits.

B. Study the two pictures, and read the caption below them. Then identify each sentence based on the pictures as follows:

F if it states a fact

O if it expresses an opinion

F/O if it combines fact and opinion

▲ Tom Torlino, a Navajo Indian, photographed before and after his "assimilation." Torlino attended the Carlisle Indian School in Pennsylvania.

_____ **8.** Some Native Americans gave up their traditional dress to fit into white society.

_____ **9.** Native American men wore long hair and jewelry.

_____ **10.** Tom Torlino was more handsome dressed in his native attire than in white attire.

Apply Information Literacy Skills

 ### Academic, Personal, and Career Applications of Fact and Opinion

The ability to separate fact from opinion is a key information literacy skill. For example, the Internet has become a major resource for academic, personal, and career information. However, the nature of the Internet means that anyone can publish anything at any time. Knowing the difference between fact and opinion improves your ability to find, evaluate, and use information. In all areas of your life, you need to determine the facts. You need to recognize bias. You need to determine the accuracy of information. And you need to judge the trustworthiness of a source. Thus, you will use the skills that you learned in this chapter in academic, personal, and career situations:

- Recognize your own need to identify fact and opinion.
- Analyze a source to determine its reliability.
- Determine an author's use of fact and opinion to develop a main idea.

Academic Application

Assume you are taking a college course in health. You are currently studying the unit on preventing violence and injury. The passage that follows is part of your required textbook reading. In addition, you have chosen to research and write about gun control. You have found the following four sources on the Internet. In the spaces given, identify each source as P = Pro (for) gun control; C = Con (against) gun control; or O = Objective about gun control.

_____ Brady Campaign to Prevent Gun Violence. "4 Victories for Strong Gun Laws." Jan 2012. Web.

_____ Children's Defense Fund, *Protect Children Not Guns 2009*, September 2009. Web.

_____ National Rifle Association. "Firearms Fact Card 2012." NRA Institute for Legislative Action: Gun Laws. 9 Jan. 2012. Web.

_____ U.S. Department of Justice. *Federal Firearms Regulations Reference Guide 2005*. Jan. 2012. Web.

- **Before Reading:** Skim the passage. Predict the author's stand as pro, con, or neutral in the gun debate.

- **During Reading:** Underline the key facts. Enclose statements of opinion in (parentheses).

- **After Reading:** In the space following the passage, state the author's stand as pro, con, or neutral in the gun debate. Give reasons for your judgment.

Health Headlines: The Gun Debate

[1]According to the most recent statistics, more than 100,000 people in the United States were shot in murders, assaults, suicides, accidents, or by police intervention in 2007. [2]Nearly 31,000 died from gun violence. [3]Many who survived experienced major physical and emotional effects.

- [4]In 2007, firearm homicide was the second leading cause of injury or death for men and women aged 10 to 24, second only to motor vehicle crashes.
- [5]Today, 35 percent of American homes have a gun on the premises. [6]More than 283 million privately owned guns are registered. [7]40 percent of those registered are handguns.
- [8]The presence of a gun in the home triples the risk of a homicide there. [9]The presence of a gun in the home increases suicide risk by more than five times.

[10]What factors contribute to excessive gun deaths in the United States? [11] Of course, by sheer numbers, if you have more guns, the likelihood of people using them in inappropriate ways increases. [12]Critics of gun control argue that guns don't murder people. [13]It's the person pulling the trigger on the gun who is ultimately the problem. [14]In addition the argument about the "right to bear arms" as a constitutional right is a difficult area of debate.

—Adapted from Donatelle, Rebecca J.
Health: The Basics, Green Edition, p. 105.

Author's Stand on Gun Control: _____

_____

_____

_____

_____

Personal Application

Assume you are in the market to buy a used car. You begin your search on the Internet, and you come across a site with the following information.

- **Before Reading:** Skim the page. Then rate it on the following scale for trustworthiness.
- **During Reading:** Highlight facts useful to you as a consumer looking to buy a used car.
- **After Reading:** Complete the company's customer service survey that follows the information.

Evaluation of Source:	Untrustworthy				Trustworthy
BargainCarsEveryday.com	1	2	3	4	5

To improve our service, please tell us what about our page convinced you to shop with us. What can we do to improve our page? What information do you need? _____

_____

_____

_____

Career Application

Assume you are a supervisor of the receiving department in an electronics retail store. One of your employees has reported an incident to which you must respond.

- **Before Reading:** Use the reporter's questions *who, what, when, where, why,* and *how* to get an idea of the incident.
- **During Reading:** Highlight the relevant facts.
- **After Reading:** In the space following the passage, make a recommendation for action to respond to the incident.

Employee Incident Report

Name: Jamal Odum
Age: 28
Position: Forklift Operator
Employee ID #: 33358

Date of Accident: December 12
Time: 6 a.m.
Location: Loading dock 3
Witnesses: Amy Presser, John Hall

Description of Event: Jamal Odum drove the forklift at Dock 3 at the store on Beeville Road. The routine job involved unloading and storing cardboard containers delivered by truck from another store in the chain. Each bale of cardboard weighed 700 pounds, and the bales were stacked double. As Odum lifted a stack off a truck, the top bail slid off and into Carl Jones, the truck driver. The accident caused severe injury to Jones. Odum stated that he had not stabilized the load before beginning to move it. He claimed there was not room at the top of the truck. He admitted that he had previously dropped loads off his forklift and blamed the accidents on the driving surface. He said that the handling of the forklift truck was very unstable. He used his hands to describe the motion of the truck—it floated.

Comments from Witnesses: Amy Presser stated that Odum is an ideal worker who had to put up with unsafe job conditions. The surface of the floor/road at the loading dock was uneven and soft, often causing heavy loads to shift and the forklift to sink into the surface. John Hall stated that the top bale was too high, making it unsafe to lift with a forklift. John Hall stated that Odum was careless as a forklift driver.

Supervisor's Recommendation for Action: _____

_____

_____

_____

_____

_____

REVIEW TEST 1

Score (number correct) _____ × 10 = _____%

Visit MyReadingLab to take this test online and receive feedback and guidance on your answers.

Fact and Opinion

A. Read the following statements, and mark each one as follows:

F if it states a fact

O if it expresses an opinion

F/O if it combines fact and opinion

_____ **1.** Government should do more to help the poor and needy.

_____ **2.** Affirmative action programs give preference to qualified minorities.

_____ **3.** Denying welfare benefits to unwed mothers is not likely to affect the number of children born out of wedlock.

_____ **4.** In 2009, the percentage of births to unwed mothers was 41.0.

_____ **5.** By 2020, more than one in five children in the United States will be of Hispanic origin; Spanish should therefore be a required subject for all schoolchildren.

B. Study the graph and its accompanying text. Then read the statements that follow it, based on the given information. Mark each statement as follows:

F if it states a fact

O if it expresses an opinion

F/O if it combines fact and opinion

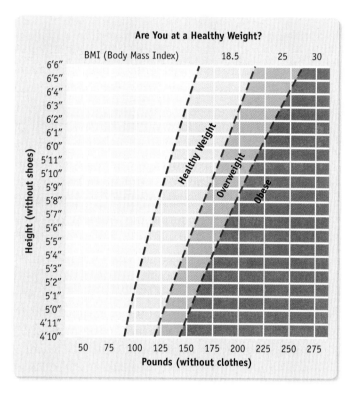

—Bren, Linda. "Losing Weight: Start By Counting Calories."
FDA Consumer. U.S. Food and Drug Administration.

_____ **6.** The higher a person's BMI, the greater the risks for health problems.

_____ **7.** A 5'7" person who weighs 175 lbs. is overweight.

_____ **8.** A 5'10" person who weighs 225 lbs. is obese due to bad eating habits.

_____ **9.** Obesity is the result of moral choices.

_____ **10.** A BMI of 30 or above indicates obesity.

REVIEW TEST 2

Score (number correct) _____ × 20 = _____%

Visit MyReadingLab to take this test online and receive feedback and guidance on your answers.

Fact and Opinion

Read the following passage from a college film study textbook. Complete the items that follow.

Two Actors, Two Ideologies

[1]Personality stars frequently convey a ready-made ideology—a set of values that are associated with a given star because of his or her previous film roles. [2]Their personas often incorporate elements from their actual lives as well. [3]For example, John Wayne was associated in the public mind with a **right-wing** ideology. [4]Most of his roles were military commanders, western heroes, law-and-order advocates, and authoritarian patriarchs. [5]In private life, he was a political activist and an outspoken conservative, an America-first patriot who championed respect for authority, family values, and military supremacy. [6]Even during the Vietnam War era, when most Americans had grown disenchanted with war, Wayne remained a champion of the military, incurring considerable flak from the political left and center. [7]He also put his money where his mouth was, producing, directing, and starring in *The Green Berets* (1968), a nationalistic salute to the Special Forces in Vietnam.

[8]At the opposite end of the ideological spectrum, Gregory Peck conveyed a left-wing ideology in most of his movies. [9]His most celebrated performance was as the small-town Southern lawyer, Atticus Finch, in *To Kill a Mockingbird*. [10]Like most ambitious actors, Peck didn't like to be typecast, and he occasionally attempted to play morally flawed characters and even outright villains. [11]But audiences loved Peck in a more heroic mold—heroic, that is, without making a big deal about it. [12]It's tough to embody such sterling virtues as compassion, decency, and tolerance without coming off as a sanctimonious prig, yet Peck managed to play variations of the good liberal for most of his career, combining strength with gentleness, principle with flexibility. [13]In real life too, he was an outspoken champion of liberal values and a political activist. [14]Himself a father of five, the actor was often at his best playing fathers, and the strong emotional rapport between him and his screen children was probably based on life: "Love and marriage and kids, those are the moments of all happiness and fulfillment," he once remarked. [15]In an American Film Institute poll taken in 2003, Atticus Finch was named the most admired hero of the American cinema.

[16]Said Harper Lee, the writer of the Pulitzer Prize-winning novel that the movie is based on: "Gregory Peck was a beautiful man. Atticus Finch gave him the opportunity to play himself."

—From Giannetti, Louis, *Understanding Movies*, 12th ed., p. 427.

_____ **1.** Sentence 4 is
    a. a fact.
    b. an opinion.
                    c. a mixture of fact and opinion.

_____ **2.** Sentence 9 is
    a. a fact.
    b. an opinion.
                    c. a mixture of fact and opinion.

_____ **3.** Sentence 12 is
    a. a fact.
    b. an opinion.
                    c. a mixture of fact and opinion.

_____ **4.** Sentence 14 is
    a. a fact.
    b. an opinion.
                    c. a mixture of fact and opinion.

_____ **5.** In sentence 15 the American Film Institute serves to give
    a. a factual detail.
    b. an informed opinion.
                    c. an expert opinion.

REVIEW TEST 3

Score (number correct) _____ × 20 = _____ %

Visit MyReadingLab to take this test online and receive feedback and guidance on your answers.

Fact and Opinion

Textbook
Skills

Read the following passage from a college sociology textbook. Complete the items that follow.

Culture

[1]In his book *Amusing Ourselves to Death* professor and social commentator Neil Postman sounds a sociological alarm, warning readers that a culture based purely on technology and TV is not necessarily a culture worth enjoying.

[2]We are rapidly becoming a society that focuses on trivia. [3]We all know who's dating who in Hollywood and which TV star recently got arrested, but can we name the vice president? [4]If we become caught up in a culture of mindless entertainment, he argues, we spend our time thinking about insignificant trivia and ignoring important issues. [5]We are at risk of killing our culture because people are too busy focusing on the insignificant.

[6]Is Postman's warning nothing more than hyperbole? [7]Not necessarily. [8]Recently, I watched a family sitting at a table eating frozen custard. [9]The mother listened to her iPod as a Nintendo DS game hypnotized her son. [10]The father talked on his cell phone, and the five-years-old daughter seemed totally bored because she had no electronic toy or anyone to talk to. [11]This technophilic family was clearly caught up in our country's culture of instant, constant entertainment. [12]Entertainment is not all bad, as Postman points out, but pursuing entertainment at all costs affects our relationships and our nation. [13]Of course, there's more to culture than movies, slot machines, and electronic gizmos. [14]In fact, culture forms the foundation of society and frames our perception of life.

[15]One category of culture is material culture: items within a society that you can taste, touch, or feel. [16]The jewelry, art, music, clothing, architecture, and crafts a society creates are all examples of material culture. [17]Of course, the natural resources available to a culture can influence that culture's creations. [18]For example, while seven countries (the United States, Japan, Russia, Canada, Germany, France, and the United Kingdom) use more than 46 percent of the world's electricity and oil, these countries combined hold only about 12 percent of the world's population. [19]What do these statistics tell you about material culture? [20]On a tour of these countries, you'd be likely to stumble across plenty of cars, air conditioners, heaters, blow dryers, and a host of other modem conveniences. [21]If you took a trip to Nigeria, though, you'd notice that a lack of access to energy also influences material culture. [22]Nigeria is the ninth largest country in the world, yet it ranks 71st in the world's electricity use and 42nd in the world's use of oil. [23]Few people own a car, and many live without regular access to electricity.

[24]Not all elements of culture are items you can touch, see, or buy at your local mall. [25]Nonmaterial culture consists of the nonphysical products of society, including our symbols, values, rules, and sanctions. [26]Symbols represent, suggest, or stand for something else. [27]They can be words, gestures, or even objects, and they often represent abstract or complex concepts. [28]Values, part of society's nonmaterial culture, represent cultural standards by which we determine what is good, bad, right, or wrong.

²⁹How can people uphold and enforce their values in everyday life? ³⁰They develop rules for appropriate behavior based on those values. ³¹We call these rules norms. ³²Norms provide the justification for sanctions. ³³A sanction is a prize or punishment you receive when you either abide by a norm or violate it. ³⁴If you do what you are supposed to do, you get a positive sanction; if you break the rules, you earn a negative sanction.

—Adapted from Carl, John D., *Think Sociology*,
2nd ed., pp. 48–49.

A. Complete the following items.

_____ **1.** Sentence 1 is
     a. a fact.   c. a mixture of fact and opinion.
     b. an opinion.

_____ **2.** Sentence 2 is
     a. a fact.   c. a mixture of fact and opinion.
     b. an opinion.

_____ **3.** Sentence 18 is
     a. a fact.   c. a mixture of fact and opinion.
     b. an opinion.

_____ **4.** In this passage, Neil Postman's ideas are
     a. factual details.   c. expert opinions.
     b. informed opinions.

B. Complete the concept map with ideas from the passage.

(5) _____	(6) _____
Items within a society that you can taste, touch, feel, see, or hear	Nonphysical products of society
	(7) _____: represent, suggest, or stand for something (words, gestures)
	(8) _____: standards to determine what is good, bad, right, or wrong
	Norms: (9) _____
	(10) _____: prizes for abiding by norms; punishment for violating them

SUMMARY RESPONSE

Restate the author's central idea in your own words. In your summary, follow the thought pattern used by the author. Begin your summary response with the following: *The central idea of "Culture" from the textbook* Think Sociology *is …*

WHAT DO YOU THINK?

Do you agree with Neil Postman that people focus too much on entertainment technology and insignificant things in our society today? The author cites a personal experience as an example that appears to support Postman's claim. Assume you are writing a paper for a sociology class. State your position—whether you agree or disagree with Postman.

- Cite personal experience to support your view.
- Use one detail from a factual source.

REVIEW TEST 4

Score (number correct) _____ x 10 = _____%

Visit MyReadingLab to take this test online and receive feedback and guidance on your answers.

Fact and Opinion

Textbook
Skills

Before you read the following passage from a psychology textbook, skim the passage and answer the Before Reading questions. Read the passage. Then answer the After Reading questions.

Vocabulary Preview

ritual (4): formal process or procedure
charismatic (6): appealing, fascinating
dictates (8): orders, commands
celibate (11): refraining from sex
omnipotence (19): state of being all-powerful
omniscience (19): state of being all-knowing
coercive (21): using force
litany (28): long list

Why Do People Join Cults?

[1]Cults have no doubt forced themselves into your awareness in recent years. [2]Their extreme, often bizarre behaviors are widely covered in the media. [3]In the United States, 39 members of Heaven's Gate committed suicide in March 1997. [4]They did so in an orderly **ritual** that was planned by their leader. [5]Nearly 20 years earlier, more than 900 American citizens committed mass suicide-murder in a jungle compound in Guyana. [6]They did so at the urging of their **charismatic** leader, Reverend Jim Jones. [7]In France, Canada, and Switzerland, members of The Order of the Solar Temple also took their lives in **ritualized** cult deaths. [8]Meanwhile, in Japan, members of Aum Shin Rikyo gased subway riders, and they had planned mass destruction to fulfill the **dictates** of their cult leader. [9]Beyond these clearly dramatic examples, there are members of literally thousands of groups that qualify as cults. [10]They give total loyalty to their groups and leaders. [11]Members obey every command: they marry a partner they have never met in mass ceremonies; beg, recruit, work long hours for no pay; give all their money and possessions to the group; or become **celibate**.

[12]Can you imagine doing such things? [13]Are there any circumstances under which you would join a cult and become subject to the pressures that cults bring to bear on their members? [14]Obviously, most of you would say, "No way!" [15]But as psychologists, our task is to understand how such groups and leaders develop their coercive power and to recognize the conditions that make many people at risk to their persuasive message.

[16]So what exactly are cults? [17]Cults vary widely in their activities, but they typically are nontraditional religious groups led by a strict, controlling leader who is the sole source of the group's thoughts, beliefs, and actions. [18]This leader is often charismatic, filled with energy and intense dedication. [19]And sometimes he or she claims special godlike powers of **omnipotence, omniscience,** and immortality. [20]Despite differences in the traits of particular cult groups, what is common are the recruiting promises. [21]The group's **coercive** power undercuts the personal exercise of free will and critical thinking of its members.

[22]Why, then, would people want to join a cult? [23]First of all, no one ever joins a *cult*, as such. [24]People join interesting groups to fulfill their pressing needs. [25]The groups are known as cults later on when they are seen as deceptive, dangerous, or opposing society's basic values. [26]Cults become appealing when they promise to fulfill an individual's personal needs. [27]The need may be for instant friendship, an identity, or an

organized daily agenda. [28]Cults also promise to make up for a **litany** of societal failures. [29]By eliminating people's feelings of isolation and alienation, cults make their slice of the world safe, healthy, caring, predictable, and controllable. [30]Cult leaders offer simple solutions to a complex world by offering a path to happiness, success, and salvation.

[31]Although the mass suicides of cult members make media headlines, most cults operate quietly to achieve their goals. [32]When they deliver on their promises, they can serve a valuable function for some people by helping fill voids in their lives. [33]But when they are deceptive, coercive, and distort basic values of freedom, independence, and critical thinking, they become dangerous to members and to society. [34]One question worth raising is, Can society provide what most cults promise so they need not become an alternate lifestyle for so many people throughout the world?

—Gerrig, Richard J. and Zimbardo, Philip G.,
Psychology and Life, 16th ed., p. 588.

Before Reading

Vocabulary in Context

_____ **1.** What does the word **ritualized** mean in sentence 7?
   a. violent
   b. senseless
   c. organized
   d. dramatic

Topic

_____ **2.** The topic of this passage is
   a. the benefits of joining a cult.
   b. reasons to legally ban cults.
   c. cults, what they are and why people join.
   d. cults, freedom of religious expression.

After Reading

Central Idea

_____ **3.** The central idea of the article is stated in paragraph
   a. 1 (sentences 1–11).
   b. 2 (sentences 12–15).
   c. 4 (sentences 22–30).
   d. 5 (sentences 31–34).

Supporting Details

_____ **4.** According to the authors, people join cults when
a. they want to commit suicide.
b. they are in need.
c. they are deceptive.
d. they need to control others.

Transitions

_____ **5.** The relationship of ideas between sentence 27 and sentence 28 is one of
a. cause and effect.   c. contrast.
b. time order.   d. addition.

Thought Patterns

_____ **6.** The thought pattern for the first paragraph of the passage (sentences 1–11) is one of
a. cause and effect.   c. examples.
b. time order.   d. contrast.

Implied Main Ideas

_____ **7.** Which of the following best states the implied main idea of paragraph 4 (sentences 22–30)?
a. Cults offer security.
b. People join cults for a variety of reasons.
c. Loneliness is the major reason people join cults.
d. People who fail at life join cults.

Fact and Opinion

_____ **8.** Sentence 1 of the article is
a. fact.   c. a mixture of fact and opinion.
b. opinion.

_____ **9.** Sentence 5 is
a. fact.   c. a mixture of fact and opinion.
b. opinion.

_____ **10.** Sentence 23 is
a. fact.   c. a mixture of fact and opinion.
b. opinion.

SUMMARY RESPONSE

Restate the author's central idea in your own words. Begin your summary response with the following: *The central idea of the textbook excerpt "Why Do People Join Cults?" by Gerrig and Zimbardo is …*

WHAT DO YOU THINK?

Why do you think people seek out cults? Assume you are a peer counselor at your college. Several students have approached you about joining a cult. Write an article for your college newspaper that warns against the dangers of cults.

After Reading About Fact and Opinion

Before you move on to the Mastery Tests on fact and opinion, take time to reflect on your learning and performance by answering the following questions. Write your answers in your notebook.

- How has my knowledge base or prior knowledge about fact and opinion changed?
- Based on my studies, how do I think I will perform on the Mastery Test(s)? Why do I think my scores will be above average, average, or below average?
- Would I recommend this chapter to other students who want to learn about fact and opinion? Why or why not?

Test your understanding of what you have learned about fact and opinion by completing the Chapter 9 Review.

Name _____ Section _____

Date _____ **Score** (number correct) _____ x 5 = _____%

Visit MyReadingLab to take this test online and receive feedback and guidance on your answers.

A. Read the following statements, and mark each one as follows:

F if it states a fact

O if it expresses an opinion

F/O if it combines fact and opinion

_____ 1. Hydrogen is a perfect fuel and is undoubtedly the best that will be available for future use.

_____ 2. In the United States, 39 states run lotteries to raise funds; this practice is immoral and should be stopped.

_____ 3. Over 50 percent of Americans participate in state lotteries.

_____ 4. State lotteries lure people who are poor and uneducated into playing by promising a quick way to get rich.

_____ 5. Lotteries, which raise billions of dollars, are the only way for state governments to raise money for education and other services.

_____ 6. Many of the people who play state lotteries have average to above-average levels of income and education.

_____ 7. Road traffic is a growing source of pollution in Europe.

_____ 8. Gas-guzzling cars account for half the oil consumed in the United States.

_____ 9. Funding for electric cars should be supported by taxes.

_____ 10. The drawbacks of automobiles far outweigh their benefits.

B. Read the following short reviews. Mark each one as follows:

F if it states only facts

O if it expresses opinions

F/O if it combines fact and opinion

_____ 11. Three times the danger! Three times the drama! Three times the enjoyment! Fast-paced and action-packed, *Driving Dangerous* will air for the first time on television Thursday night at 9 P.M. and run for three nights in a row, same time, same channel.

_____ **12.** Outrageously fun and funny, don't miss _Bridesmaids_, co-written by and starring Kristen Wiig of _Saturday Night Live_ fame.

_____ **13.** _Meet the Press_ is the longest running United States television series.

_____ **14.** _American Idol_ exploits people who have no talent for the sake of high ratings.

_____ **15.** Adam Lambert is the most talented and successful singer to have appeared on _American Idol_.

C. Study the advertisement for a lost dog prepared to run in a local newspaper and fliers. Then identify each item from the ad as follows:

F if it states a fact

O if it expresses an opinion

F/O if it combines fact and opinion

Our Dog, Brutus, is missing!

[16]Our dog, Brutus, is missing! [17]Brutus weighs four pounds and is a tan-colored Chihuahua. [18]Although he is a swift-moving little dog with a saucy personality, he has been well-trained. [19]Therefore, he should obey the command "come." [20]We are offering a $100 reward for his safe return.

_____ **16.** Our dog, Brutus, is missing!

_____ **17.** Brutus weighs four pounds and is a tan-colored Chihuahua.

_____ **18.** Although he is a swift-moving little dog with a saucy personality, he has been well-trained.

_____ **19.** Therefore, he should obey the command "come."

_____ **20.** We are offering a generous reward for his safe return.

Name _____ Section _____

Date _____ **Score** (number correct) _____ x 5 = _____%

Visit MyReadingLab to take this test online and receive feedback and guidance on your answers.

A. Read the following statements, and mark each one **F** (states a fact); **O** (states an opinion); or **F/O** (combines fact and opinion).

_____ **1.** Don't take Math 101 from Dr. Harvey; it is too hard.

_____ **2.** The college catalog states that two semesters of English and math are required.

_____ **3.** Small dogs such as toy poodles make annoying pets.

_____ **4.** Animals have improved the physical and emotional well-being of shut-ins such as the elderly in nursing homes.

_____ **5.** Hip-hop music is the voice of people oppressed by social injustice.

_____ **6.** Oprah Winfrey and Michelle Obama are the two most influential African American women of this generation.

_____ **7.** African American scientists have impacted society through their inventions and discoveries.

_____ **8.** It is not wise to get medical advice from online sources.

_____ **9.** Several types of cancer have been linked to diet.

_____ **10.** To be safe, airlines should weigh everyone who travels by air.

B. Read the following advertisements for used cars. Mark each one **F** (states a fact); **O** (states an opinion); or **F/O** (combines fact and opinion).

_____ **11.** 2012 Kia Sedona LX, *** 1 FLORIDA OWNER *** CLEAN VEHICLE HISTORY REPORT *** BACKUP CAMERA *** BLUETOOTH *** So clean, it looks like it just rolled off the showroom floor. Platinum Graphite w/Gray Cloth Interior, Automatic 6-Speed Transmission, ONLY 18,625 Miles! Exterior Features Include: 18 Inch Alloy Wheels, Dual Power Sliding Side Doors, Rear Parking Assist, Roof Rack, Electronic Stability Control, Rear Window Wiper & Defroster, and More! Interior Features Include: In Dash MP3 CD Player, Automatic Dimming Rear View Mirror w/Compass & Backup Camera, Side Impact Airbags, Front & Rear Side Curtain Airbags, Remote Keyless Entry, Bluetooth, 4 Captains Chairs, 3rd Row Seat, Auxiliary/USB Outlets, Rear A/C w/Climate Controls, Power Windows/Locks/Mirrors, Tilt Steering Wheel w/Audio & Cruise Controls, and Much More! Free Vehicle History Report Available! $19,100.

443

_____ **12.** Well kept SUV, Aztec Red. Mostly highway miles. Still has plastic under floor mats—A MUST SEE! 29,300 miles. $21,500.

_____ **13.** Chevy Silverado 1500 LT Crew Cab 6 Inch Lift Monster 4X4* with $5,500 in upgrades, only 23K miles and Balance of Factory warranty good thru 2/1/15! Also comes with a powertrain warranty from the manufacturer good thru 2/1/17 or 100K miles! Do not make a $3K+ mistake, B4 you buy a used truck demand to see shop bills & have the truck inspected by a 3rd party! Riding high on $5,500 of 6 inch RCX lift kit with a like new set of 35 inch tires and 20 inch Mayhem wheels, CD player with aux line in, nerf bars, tilt steering, cruise control, keyless entry, alarm, bed liner, towing package, power windows, power mirrors and power door locks. *STILL UNDER FACTORY WARRANTY. **Repair Description: Total Invested =$615.25*10 Mile Road Test, 135 Point Inspection, Lube, Oil & Filter, Alignment, Balanced & Rotated Tires, Battery Condition Test: Good, Alternator Condition Test Good*Labor time quoted by All Data Universal ShopKey* $34,995.

_____ **14.** 1994 Corvette. White with tan leather seats, automatic, A/C, 80,500 miles. $18,500.

_____ **15.** Lexus LS 430. In the pursuit of perfection, this car exceeds expectations and offers an unmatchable experience in luxury, comfort, and power. The interior is serene, inviting, even cozy. The ride is sure and smooth. The look is sleek and sophisticated. Often, automakers claim their cars are "revolutionary" or the "benchmark of excellence," only to be proven false on the road. In contrast, even used, the Lexus LS 430 is indeed revolutionary and the benchmark of excellence.

C. Following is a list of sources from which information can be obtained. Label each source **IO** (offers an informed opinion); **EO** (offers an expert opinion); or **FS** (is a factual source).

_____ **16.** The National Aeronautics and Space Administration (NASA) at http://www.nasa.gov

_____ **17.** Nicholas D. Kristof, columnist on human rights for the _New York Times_, winner of the Pulitzer Prize for Commentary, the George Polk Award, and the Dayton Literary Peace Prize's 2009 Lifetime Achievement Award

_____ **18.** A news article on the front page of the _New York Times_

_____ **19.** _The Encyclopedia of Indians of the Americas_, Scholarly Publications, 1974

_____ **20.** A letter to the editor of a local paper from a concerned citizen

Name _____ Section _____

Date _____ **Score** (number correct) _____ x 10 = _____%

Visit MyReadingLab to take this test online and receive feedback and guidance on your answers.

Read the following passage from a history textbook. Then identify each excerpt from the passage as follows:

F if it states a fact

O if it expresses an opinion

F/O if it combines fact and opinion

Textbook
Skills

A Nation Divided

¹To the delight of the media, the race for the White House in 2000 proved to be close and exciting. ²George Bush led in the polls until Al Gore moved ahead after the Democratic Convention in August. ³Gore's running mate, Joe Lieberman, proved popular. ⁴In contrast, Bush's choice of running mate, former defense secretary Dick Cheney, failed to excite the public. ⁵But Gore's surprisingly uneven performance in three televised debates allowed Bush to regain a narrow lead in the polls in October. ⁶Then, in the final week of the campaign, Gore began to draw even with Bush.

⁷The early returns on election night proved that the polls were right in stressing the closeness of the presidential race. ⁸Gore seemed the likely winner when the networks mistakenly predicted a Democratic victory in Florida. ⁹When the TV analysts put Florida back in the undecided column, Bush began to forge ahead, sweeping the rest of the South. ¹⁰After midnight, when the networks again mistakenly called Florida, this time for Bush, Gore telephoned Bush to concede. ¹¹An hour later, however, he recanted when it became clear that the Bush margin in Florida was paper thin.

¹²For the next five weeks, all eyes were on the outcome in Florida. ¹³Gore had a lead of more than 200,000 nationwide in the popular vote and 267 electoral votes. ¹⁴Yet Bush, with 246 votes in the electoral college, could win the presidency with Florida's 25 electoral votes. ¹⁵Both sides sent phalanxes of lawyers to Florida. ¹⁶Bush's team sought to certify the results that showed him with a lead of 930 votes out of nearly six million cast. ¹⁷Citing many voting problems disclosed by the media, Gore asked for a recount in three heavily Democratic counties in south Florida. ¹⁸All three used old-fashioned punch card machines that resulted in some ballots not being clearly marked for any presidential candidate.

¹⁹The decision finally came in the courts. ²⁰Democrats appealed the first attempt to certify Bush as the victor to the Florida Supreme Court, where most of the judges had been appointed by Democrats. ²¹The Florida court ordered recounts two times, but the Bush team appealed to the United States Supreme Court. ²²On December 12, five weeks after the election, the Supreme Court overturned the state's call for recounts. ²³The Supreme Court ruling was a 5–4 decision that reflected a long-standing divide in thought among the nine judges. ²⁴The next day, Gore gracefully conceded, and Bush finally became the president-elect. ²⁵Although the rule of law prevailed, neither the winner nor the loser could take much pride in his party's behavior.

—Adapted from Divine, Robert A., T. H. H. Breen, George M. Frederickson, and R. Hal Williams. *The American Story*, 16th ed., pp. 1116–1117.

_____ 1. To the delight of the media, the race for the White House in 2000 proved to be close and exciting.

_____ 2. But Gore's surprisingly uneven performance in three televised debates allowed Bush to regain a narrow lead in the polls in October.

_____ 3. In the final week of the campaign, Gore began to draw even with Bush.

_____ 4. After midnight, when the networks again mistakenly called Florida, this time for Bush, Gore telephoned Bush to concede.

_____ 5. An hour later, however, he recanted when it became clear that the Bush margin in Florida was paper thin.

_____ 6. For the next five weeks, all eyes were on the outcome in Florida.

_____ 7. Gore had a lead of more than 200,000 nationwide in the popular vote and 267 electoral votes.

_____ 8. Bush's team sought to certify the results that showed him with a lead of 930 votes out of nearly six million cast.

_____ 9. The next day, Gore gracefully conceded, and Bush finally became the president-elect.

_____ 10. Although the rule of law prevailed, neither the winner nor the loser could take much pride in his party's behavior.

Name _____ Section _____

Date _____ **Score** (number correct) _____ x 5 = _____%

Visit MyReadingLab to take this test online and receive feedback and guidance on your answers.

A. Read the following statements, and mark each one as follows:

F if it states a fact

O if it expresses an opinion

F/O if it combines fact and opinion

_____ **1.** The Super Bowl is the most watched show on television.

_____ **2.** The Super Bowl is America's favorite sporting event.

_____ **3.** In an open society such as the United States, secrecy in government is difficult to maintain, or should be.

_____ **4.** Hollywood exports movies to all parts of the world.

_____ **5.** Hollywood is to blame for the worldwide view that Americans are immoral and selfish.

_____ **6.** *Letter to My Mother* by Edith Bruck is an extraordinary incisive retelling of her life in wartime Auschwitz. It is one of the most important and impressive works of its kind. This book is a necessary and urgent read.

_____ **7.** In 1837, Michigan became the 26th state.

_____ **8.** The Hispanic population is one of the fastest-growing groups in America.

_____ **9.** Doctors fear that they will not be able to offer quality services due to the looming crisis caused by the rising costs of malpractice insurance.

_____ **10.** Doctors should not strike because of insurance malpractice issues.

B. Following is a list of sources from which information can be obtained. Label each source as follows:

IO if it offers an informed opinion

EO if it offers an expert opinion

FS if it is a factual source

_____ **11.** "Dr. Phil" McGraw. (2009) *Real Life: Preparing for the 7 Most Challenging Days of Your Life*, Free Press

_____ **12.** A college mathematics textbook

_____ **13.** A friend who has recently researched the best bargain for a flat-screen television

_____ **14.** Internal Revenue Service. (2011). *Your Federal Income Tax* (Publication 17). Washington, D.C.: U.S. Government Printing Office.

_____ **15.** A college history teacher with 25 years of experience

_____ **16.** The Modern Language Association's *Handbook for Writers of Research Papers*, 7th ed., 2009.

_____ **17.** A student research paper on the collapse of communism

_____ **18.** Randolph, J. (1992). "Recycling of Materials." In *The New Grolier Multimedia Encyclopedia*. [CD-ROM]. Danbury, Conn.: Grolier Electronic.

_____ **19.** A syllabus for a college course

_____ **20.** Peter Travers, film critic for *Rolling Stone* and host of an interview-based movie show called *Popcorn* on ABC

9 Summary of Key Concepts of Fact and Opinion

(LO1) Assess your comprehension of identifying facts and opinions.

- A fact is _____.

- An opinion is _____

  _____.

- Objective proof can be _____

  _____.

- An informed opinion is developed _____.

- An expert opinion is developed _____

  _____.

- A fact _____ reality and uses _____ words.

- An opinion _____ reality and uses _____ words.

- Biased words express _____.

- A qualifier may express _____

  _____.

Test Your Comprehension of Fact and Opinion

Respond to the following questions and prompts.

(LO1) (LO6) In your own words, what is the difference between a fact and an opinion?

_____

_____

_____

LO2 LO3 LO4 In your own words, what is the difference between an informed opinion and an expert opinion? _____

_____

_____

_____

_____

_____

LO1 LO2 LO3 LO4 LO5 In your own words, describe how to distinguish between fact and opinion.

_____

_____

_____

_____

_____

_____

LO6 LO7 Describe how you will use what you have learned about fact and opinion in your reading process to comprehend textbook material. _____

_____

_____

_____

LO6 LO8 Summarize the two most important ideas in this chapter that will help you improve your reading comprehension. _____

_____

_____

Tone and Purpose

LO LEARNING OUTCOMES

After studying this chapter, you should be able to:

LO1 Define the Terms *Tone* and *Purpose*

LO2 Understand How Tone Is Established

LO3 Identify Subjective and Objective Tone Words

LO4 Determine the General Purpose in the Main Idea

LO5 Determine the Primary Purpose of a Passage

LO6 Evaluate Passages for the Use of Irony

LO7 Develop Textbook Skills: Recognize an Author's Tone and Purpose

LO8 Apply Information Literacy Skills: Academic, Personal, and Career Applications of Tone and Purpose

Before Reading About Tone and Purpose

Study the learning outcomes and underline words that relate to ideas you have already studied. Did you underline the following terms: *subjective, objective,* and *main idea?* What you already know about these topics will help you learn about tone and purpose. Use the blanks that follow to write a short one- or two-sentence summary about each topic.

Subjective words: _____

_____.

Objective words: _____

_____.

Main idea: _____

_____.

Refer to the learning outcomes and draw upon your prior knowledge to create at least five questions that you can answer as you study about tone and purpose:

_____?

_____?

_____?

_____?

_____?

Compare the questions you created with the following questions. Then write the ones that seem the most helpful in your notebook, leaving enough space between each question to record the answers as you read and study the chapter.

What are tone and purpose? How is tone established? How will objective facts and subjective opinions help me identify tone? Will fact and opinion help me identify purpose? How will the main idea help me discover the general purpose? What is the primary purpose, and how do I figure it out? How is irony used for special effects?

LO1   Define the Terms *Tone* and *Purpose*

Every piece of information is created by an author who has a specific attitude toward the chosen topic and a specific reason for writing and sharing that attitude. The author's attitude is conveyed by the tone. **Tone** is the emotion or mood of the author's written voice. Understanding tone is closely related to understanding the author's reason for writing about the topic. This reason for writing is known as the author's **purpose**.

Tone and purpose are established with word choice. Effective readers read to understand the author's tone and purpose. To identify tone and purpose, you need to build on several skills you have already studied: vocabulary, fact and opinion, and main ideas.

> **Tone** is the author's attitude toward the topic.
> **Purpose** is the reason the author writes about a topic.

Read the following two passages. As you read, think about the difference in the tone and purpose of each one.

What Is Distracted Driving?

There are three main types of distraction. The first type is visual—taking your eyes off the road. The second is manual—taking your hands off the wheel. The third is cognitive—taking your mind off what you're doing. Distracted driving is any non-driving activity a person engages in that has the potential to distract him or her from the primary task of driving and increase the risk of crashing. While all distractions can endanger drivers' safety, texting is the most alarming because it involves all three types of distraction. Other distracting activities include the following: using a cell phone, eating and drinking, talking to passengers, grooming, reading, including maps, using a PDA or navigation system, watching a video, or changing the radio station, CD, or Mp3 player.

Research on distracted driving reveals some surprising facts. Using a cell phone while driving, whether it's hand-held or hands-free, delays a driver's reactions as much as having a blood alcohol concentration at the legal limit of .08 percent. Driving while using a cell phone reduces the amount of brain activity associated with driving by 37 percent. 80 percent of all crashes and 65 percent of near crashes involve some type of distraction. Nearly 6,000 people died in 2008 in crashes involving a distracted or inattentive driver, and more than half a million were injured. The worst offenders are the youngest and least-experienced drivers: men and women under 20 years of age. Drivers who use hand-held devices are four times as likely to get into crashes serious enough to injure themselves.

—United States Department of Transportation. "Statistics and
Facts about Distracted Driving." *Distraction.gov.*

I will never forget that nightmarish moment when my entire world shattered. It was the moment the police officer told me that my 18-year-old son Marcus had died as the result of an automobile accident. In the fog of grief, I learned he had caused the fatal accident that took his life and the life of a young family. Four people alive one moment, dead the next.

Early that morning, running late for school, he had dashed out of the house without his backpack with his books and homework and his sports bag with his baseball gear. His phone revealed that he was texting me to bring his stuff to him. I never got the message. If only he had waited until he got to school to call me. If only he had pulled off the road to text me. If only he had turned around and come back for his gear. So what if he was tardy for school!

Evidently, distracted by his texting, Marcus never saw the light change to red. Evidently, he applied no brakes. There were no skid marks. As a result, he broadsided a sedan. Plowed into it so hard that both vehicles became airborne and flipped off the road. The sedan carried a mother and her two daughters, both under the age of five. Their names are Mary, Christine, and Teresa.

One preventable moment changed the lives of so many. I have since dedicated my life to educating others about the dangers of distracted driving. At first, friends and family advised me to move on, to get on with my life. However, I couldn't; I can't. People need to hear our story. I have to spread the word. Distracted driving kills. It can happen to anyone.

The differences in the tone and purpose of these two passages are obvious. The first passage was written and published by the government to inform the public about the dangers of distracted driving. The passage uses unbiased words and an objective, formal tone. The second passage approaches the same subject with a different purpose—to persuade people to avoid distracted driving. The second passage conveys a painful personal experience using biased words and a subjective, informal tone.

As the two passages demonstrate, tone and purpose work together to convey the author's meaning.

LO2 Understand How Tone Is Established

The author's attitude is expressed by the tone of voice he or she assumes in the passage. An author chooses carefully the words that will make an impact on the reader. Sometimes an author wants to appeal to reason and just gives facts and factual explanations. At other times, an author wants to appeal to emotions and stir the reader to feel deeply.

For example, in an effort to share reliable information, textbooks strive for an objective tone. An objective tone includes facts and reasonable explanations. It is matter-of-fact and neutral. The details given in an objective tone are likely to be facts. In contrast, sharing an author's personal worldview through fiction and personal essays often calls for a subjective tone. A subjective tone uses words that describe feelings, judgments, or opinions. The details given in a subjective tone are likely to include experiences, senses, feelings, and thoughts. Study the following list of words that describe the characteristics of tone.

Characteristics of Tone Words	
Objective Tone impartial	**Subjective Tone** personal
unbiased	biased
neutral	emotional
formal	informal

An *unbiased* or *neutral* tone does not show any feelings for or against a topic. Instead, it focuses on facts. A *formal* tone chooses higher-level words and avoids using the pronouns *I* and *you,* thereby creating a sense of distance between the writer and the reader. An *objective* tone is thus impartial, unbiased, neutral, and most often formal. In contrast, a *biased* tone does show favor for or against a particular topic. A biased tone uses *emotional* words that focus on feelings. Finally, an *informal* tone uses the pronouns *I* and *you* to create a connection between the writer and the reader. A *subjective* tone is thus personal, biased, emotional, and often informal. In summary, to grasp the author's tone, you need to carefully note the author's choice of vocabulary and details.

> **EXAMPLES** Look at the following list of statements. Based on word choice, choose the tone word that best describes each statement.

_____ **1.** In January of 2010, an earthquake devastated Port-au-Prince, Haiti.
   a. biased   b. unbiased

_____ **2.** The magnitude-7 quake killed an estimated 200,000, left 250,000 injured, and made 1.5 million homeless.
   a. objective   b. subjective

_____ **3.** Unless you saw it for yourself, you can't imagine the horror caused by the earthquake.
   a. formal   b. informal

_____ **4.** Reports of children crying for parents and parents digging with their fingers for children are heart-rending images of human suffering caused by the quake.
   a. neutral   b. emotional

_____ **5.** The United States government mobilized resources and manpower to aid in the relief effort.
   a. objective   b. subjective

EXPLANATION Compare your answers to the following: **1.** The word "devastated" may seem like a value judgment, but it is actually a factual description so the correct answer is (b) unbiased; **2.** This sentence states facts so the answer is (a) objective; **3.** The use of "you" is informal and is used to state an opinion so the answer is (b) informal; **4.** The sentence creates a vivid image that taps into human emotions so the answer is (b) emotional; **5.** The sentence states facts and does not evaluate or judge the government's effort, so the answer is (a).

Practice 1

Read the following statements from a college biology textbook. Based on the word choice, choose a tone word that best describes each statement.

> Many fruits and vegetables contain vitamins C and E as well as other antioxidants. But did you know that chocolate also contains antioxidants, and so might actually be a type of health food?
> Now, amazingly, researchers have given us an excuse to eat chocolate and feel good about it! Cocoa powder (the dark, bitter powder made from the seeds inside cacao pods) contains high concentrations of flavonoids, which are powerful antioxidants.
>
> —Audesirk, Teresa, Gerald Audesirk, and Bruce E. Byers.
> *Biology: Life on Earth*, 5th ed., p. 26.

_____ **1.** Many fruits and vegetables contain vitamins C and E as well as other antioxidants.
   a. objective   b. subjective

_____ **2.** But did you know that chocolate also contains antioxidants, and so might actually be a type of health food?
   a. formal   b. informal

_____ **3.** Now, amazingly, researchers have given us an excuse to eat chocolate and feel good about it!
   a. objective   b. subjective

_____ **4.** Cocoa powder (the dark, bitter powder made from the seeds inside the cacao pods) contains high concentrations of flavonoids, which are powerful antioxidants.
   a. neutral   b. emotional

Identify Subjective and Objective Tone Words

Recognizing tone and describing an author's attitude deepens your comprehension and helps you become a more effective reader. A small sample of words used to describe tone are listed here. Look up the meanings of any words you do not know. Developing your vocabulary helps you better understand an author's word choice to establish tone.

Subjective			Objective
admiring	disbelieving	persuasive	accurate
angry	discouraged	pleading	factual
annoyed	disdainful	poetic	impartial
anxious	dramatic	reverent	matter-of-fact
approving	earnest	rude	straightforward
argumentative	elated	sad	truthful
arrogant	entertaining	sarcastic	
assured	fearful	self-pitying	
belligerent	friendly	serious	
biting	funny	sincere	
bitter	gloomy	supportive	
bored	happy	suspenseful	
bubbly	hostile	sympathetic	
calm	humorous	tender	
candid	idealistic	tense	
cold	informal	thoughtful	
comic	informative	threatening	
complaining	irritated	timid	
confident	joking	urgent	
cynical	jovial	warning	
demanding	joyful	wistful	
direct	lively	wry	
disappointed	loving		

> **EXAMPLES** Read the following items. Choose a word that best describes the tone of each statement. Use each word once.

anxious   encouraging   persuasive
elated   gloomy

1. "If you care about saving lives, you should vote for gun control."

   Tone: _____

2. "You can do anything if you put your mind to it. Come on! You can do it!"

   Tone: _____

3. "I hope I do all right on this test. Even though I studied all night, I might forget important information."

   Tone: _____

4. "I won! I won!" Snively shouted as he realized he held the winning lottery ticket.

   Tone: _____

5. Thick, heavy clouds hung low in the sky, like a soggy gray blanket. The trees were winter bare, and the ground was brown and wet. Though it was only 2 o'clock in the afternoon, a dusky shroud covered the neighborhood.

   Tone: _____

VISUAL *VOCABULARY*

The tone of the message in this photo

and its caption is _____.

   a. despairing
   b. celebratory
   c. neutral

▲ We did it! We never gave up hope that she would be alive in the rubble even though it was 6 days after the earthquake.

EXPLANATIONS   Compare your answers to these:

1. persuasive. As you learned when you studied fact and opinion, the words "should," "ought," and "must" are opinion words. They suggest a persuasive tone.

2. encouraging

3. anxious

4. elated

5. gloomy ◁

Practice 2

Read the following items. Based on word choice, choose a word from the box that best describes the tone of each statement. Use each word once.

admiring	arrogant	factual	informative	warm
angry	bitter	happy	sad	wistful

1. "It is with sorrow that I must submit my resignation."

    Tone: _____

2. "The best days were growing up on the farm before life became so fast-paced."

    Tone: _____

3. "It is so good to see you again after such a long time. How is your wonderful family?"

    Tone: _____

4. Manny shoots for the basket at an awkward angle. He hesitates. The ball is knocked out of his hands. The lost points may have just cost his team the win.

    Tone: _____

5. "Animals can be divided into three groups based on the way they maintain body temperature."

    Tone: _____

6. A quiet yet thrilling feeling of peace swept over her. Her children were healthy, she was successful in her job, and she was in love with her husband. It seemed she had all a person could want.

    Tone: _____

7. "It isn't enough to say you are sorry after years of doing wrong. You just can't say you are sorry! How dare you think you can! Don't expect forgiveness, either!"

   Tone: _____

8. "It is with pleasure and pride that I offer this recommendation on behalf of Kareem Smith. He is hardworking, intelligent, and honest."

   Tone: _____

9. "Who broke the vase in the foyer? When I find out who did it, that person is going to be so sorry. Do you know how much that vase cost?"

   Tone: _____

10. "I am the best there is, and don't you forget it. There is no one who beats me."

    Tone: _____

LO4 Determine the General Purpose in the Main Idea

Many reasons can motivate a writer. These can range from the need to take a stand on a hotly debated issue to the desire to entertain an audience with an amusing story. Basically, an author writes to share a main idea about a topic. An author's main idea, whether stated or implied, and the author's purpose are directly related. One of the following three general purposes will drive a main idea: to inform, to entertain, and to persuade.

In Chapter 3, you learned that a main idea is made up of a topic and the author's controlling point. You identified the controlling point by looking for thought patterns and biased (tone) words. The next two sections will build on what you have learned. First, you will study the relationship between the three general purposes and the author's main idea. You will practice using the main idea to discover the general purpose. Then you will apply what you have learned to figure out an author's primary purpose.

> ■ **To inform.** When a writer sets out to inform, he or she shares knowledge and information or offers instruction about a particular topic. A few of the tone words often used to describe this purpose include *objective*, *matter-of-fact*, and *straightforward*. Authors use facts to explain or describe the main idea to readers. Most textbook passages are written

to inform. The following topic sentences reflect the writer's desire to inform.

1. The main causes of road rage are stress and anxiety.

2. A healthful diet includes several daily servings from each of the major food groups.

In sentence 1, the topic is *road rage*, and the words that reveal the controlling point are *main causes, stress,* and *anxiety*. The author uses a tone that is unbiased and objective, so the focus is on the information. In sentence 2, the topic is *diet*, and the words that reveal the controlling point are *healthful, several daily servings,* and *major food groups*. Again, the author chooses words that are matter-of-fact and that suggest factual details will follow. Both topic sentences indicate that the author's purpose is to provide helpful information.

- **To persuade.** A writer who sets out to persuade tries to bring the reader into agreement with his or her view on the topic. A few of the tone words often used to describe this purpose include *argumentative, persuasive, forceful, controversial, positive, supportive, negative,* and *critical*. Authors combine facts with emotional appeals to sway the reader to their point of view. Politicians and advertisers often write and speak to persuade. The following topic sentences reflect the writer's desire to persuade.

3. Violence that arises from road rage must be harshly and swiftly punished.

4. How to achieve should be a part of public school education from elementary through high school.

In sentence 3, the topic is *violence*. The words that reveal the author's controlling point include *arises from, must be, harshly,* and *swiftly punished*. This sentence deals with the same general topic as sentence 1. Notice the difference in the treatments of this topic. Sentence 3 refocuses the topic from the causes of road rage to the effect of road rage: the *violence* that *arises from* road rage. The author then introduces a forceful, biased viewpoint.

In sentence 4, the topic is *public school education*. The author uses the process thought pattern to limit the topic with the phrase *how to achieve*. Additional words that reveal the controlling point are *should be,* which are followed by a recommendation for action. The author is offering a controversial personal opinion about how children should be educated. In both of these sentences, the authors want to convince others to agree with them about taking a specific course of action.

- **To entertain.** A writer whose purpose is to entertain sets out to captivate or interest the audience. A few of the tone words often used to describe this purpose include *amusing, entertaining, lively, humorous,* and *suspenseful.* To entertain, authors frequently use expressive language and creative thinking. Most readers are entertained by material that stirs an emotional reaction such as laughter, sympathy, or fear. Thus, authors engage readers creatively through vivid images, strong feelings, or sensory details (such as sights, sounds, tastes, textures, and smells). Both fiction and nonfiction writers seek to entertain. The following topic sentences reflect the writer's desire to entertain.

5. Think of our highways as a place to study how operating a powerful machine can turn normal people into four types of maniacs: the bully, the loudmouth, the speed-demon, and the exterminator.

6. I am zealously committed to eating a balanced diet from the four basic food groups: low-calorie, low-carbohydrate, low-fat, and low-taste.

You may have found identifying the topic and controlling point a little more challenging in these two sentences. Often, when writers entertain, they imply the main idea. And when they use an implied main idea, they rely much more heavily on tone words. Sentence 5, like sentences 1 and 3, deals with the topic of the stresses of driving. In this sentence, the author focuses the topic on the drivers with the phrase *four types of maniacs.* The use of *maniacs* (a biased word) offers a strong clue that the author's purpose is to entertain. Other words that reveal tone include *powerful, normal, bully, loudmouth, speed-demon,* and *exterminator.* The author seeks to amuse the reader with the contrast between "normal people" and what they become behind the wheel of a vehicle.

Sentence 6, like sentence 2, deals with the topic of a *diet.* In this case, the words that reveal the author's controlling point are *balanced* (which suggests healthful) and *four basic food groups* (which indicates the classification thought pattern). However, the main idea is not really about a balanced diet. The point seems to be about dieting. Clearly, the author is trying to make us smile by setting up an unexpected contrast. In most cases, the words *four food groups* are followed by a very different list of details. Surprising contrasts often set up an ironic tone. And irony often amuses the reader. You will learn more about irony later in this chapter. Authors also use other methods to entertain such as exaggerations, vivid details, and dramatic descriptions.

These six sentences show that a topic can be approached in a variety of ways. The author chooses a topic and a purpose. The purpose shapes the focus of the main idea. The author carefully chooses tone words to express the main idea in light of the purpose. Each of these choices then controls the choices of supporting details and the thought pattern used to organize them.

> **EXAMPLES** Read each of the following paragraphs. Annotate them for main idea and tone.

I = to inform   **P** = to persuade   **E** = to entertain

_____ **1.**   A young woman suffering from anxiety was constantly biting her nails. Worried about her habit of biting her fingernails down to the quick, she asked her doctor for some advice. To her surprise, her doctor advised her to take up yoga. She did, and soon her fingernails were growing normally. During her next scheduled appointment, her doctor noticed her healthy nails asked her if yoga had totally cured her nervousness. "No," she replied, "but now I can reach my toe-nails so I bite them instead."

_____ **2.**   Yoga exercises benefit a person in three ways. Yoga leads to physical balance, mental alertness, and fewer injuries. The practice of yoga uses slow, steady motions to enter and hold poses that stretch and strengthen the body's muscles. Because each pose is held for at least 10 seconds, the body learns to adjust and find its natural balance. To find this balance, the mind must be actively involved. And as the muscles are stretched and strengthened, injuries are less likely to occur.

_____ **3.**   Yoga is a much healthier practice than simple stretching. Stretching relies on a jerky movement that forces the body into a certain position. Often stretching is dynamic, using a bouncing motion, and the stretch is only held for a moment or two. Such stretching can lead to injuries. In contrast, yoga uses a static stretch that relies on inner balance to hold the pose for at least 10 to 15 seconds. To successfully enter and hold a yoga pose, the mind must focus on what the body needs to stay balanced. By holding a stretch, the body becomes strong and flexible, and the connection between the mind and body is strengthened more so than with simple stretching.

VISUAL *VOCABULARY*

The purpose of the lawyer is to

_____.

a. entertain
b. inform
c. persuade

EXPLANATIONS

1. The topic of this paragraph is presented in the middle of the paragraph—yoga. The author uses the narrative thought pattern to set up a personal experience as the basis of a joke about yoga. Throughout the narrative, the author uses vivid details, descriptions, and a surprise ending—a punch line—(E) to entertain the reader.

2. This paragraph opens with the main idea stated in a topic sentence. The topic is yoga exercises, and the words that reveal the author's controlling points are *benefit* and *three ways.* The details consist of a list and explanations of these benefits. The author's purpose here is simply (I) to inform the reader about three benefits of yoga.

3. This paragraph also opens with the main idea stated in a topic sentence. Again, the topic is yoga, and the words that reveal the controlling point are *much healthier* (which is an opinion) and *than simple stretching* (which indicates the contrast thought pattern). The author clearly believes that yoga is better than simple stretching and gives details (P) to persuade the reader that this view is correct.

Practice 3

Read the following topic sentences. Label each according to its purpose:

I = to inform   **P** = to persuade   **E** = to entertain

_____ 1. Cloning human beings should be banned.

_____ 2. The National Hurricane Center predicts a record number of hurricanes in the upcoming months.

_____ **3.** Friends don't let friends drive drunk.

_____ **4.** Bulimia and anorexia are two serious eating disorders.

_____ **5.** A celebrity is a person who works hard all his life to become well known, then wears dark glasses to avoid being recognized.

—Fred Allen, *Simpson's Contemporary Quotations*,
Houghton Mifflin Harcourt Publishing Company, 1988.

_____ **6.** Spanking as a way to discipline a child has a long history in many cultures.

_____ **7.** Age is strictly a case of mind over matter. If you don't mind, it doesn't matter.

—Jack Benny, *Simpson's Contemporary Quotations*,
Houghton Mifflin Harcourt Publishing Company, 1988.

_____ **8.** Kwanzaa is an African American tradition that is based on the African celebration of the "first fruits" of the harvest.

_____ **9.** When I was a boy of fourteen, my father was so ignorant I could hardly stand to have the old man around. But when I got to be twenty-one, I was astonished at how much he had learned in seven years.

—Mark Twain

_____ **10.** Rely on Denta-Fresh toothpaste to stop bad breath just as millions of others have.

L05 ## Determine the Primary Purpose of a Passage

In addition to the three general purposes, authors often write to fulfill a more specific purpose. The following table offers several examples of specific purposes.

General and Specific Purposes

To inform	To entertain	To persuade
to analyze	to amuse	to argue against
to clarify	to delight	to argue for
to discuss	to frighten	to convince
to establish		to criticize
to explain		to inspire (motivate a change)

Often a writer has two or more purposes in one piece of writing. Blending purposes adds interest and power to a piece of writing. Take, for example, the award-winning documentary *Fahrenheit 9/11*. This film attempts to inform and entertain, but its primary purpose is to argue. The film uses facts, personal bias, and humor to take a strong stand for or against political issues. Comics like Jon Stewart and Jimmy Fallon use facts from daily events to entertain their audiences. In these cases, when an author has more than one purpose, only one purpose is in control overall. This controlling purpose is called the **primary purpose**.

You have studied several reading skills that will help you grasp the author's primary purpose. For example, the author's primary purpose is often suggested by the main idea, the thought pattern, and the tone of the passage. Read the following topic sentence. Identify the author's primary purpose by considering the main idea, thought pattern, and tone.

_____ Spanking must be avoided as a way to discipline due to its long-term negative effects on the child.
   a. to discuss the disadvantages of spanking
   b. to argue against spanking as a means of discipline
   c. to make fun of those who use spanking as a means of discipline

This topic sentence clearly states a main idea "against spanking" using the tone words *must* and *negative*. The details will be organized using the thought pattern *long-term effects*. Based on the topic sentence, the author's primary purpose is (b) to argue against spanking as a means of discipline. Even when the main idea is implied, tone and thought patterns point to the author's primary purpose.

You should also take into account titles, headings, and prior knowledge about the author. For example, it's easy to see that Jay Leno's primary purpose is to entertain us with his book *If Roast Beef Could Fly*. The title is funny, and we know Jay Leno is a comedian. An effective reader studies the general context of the passage to find out the author's primary purpose.

> **Primary purpose** is the author's main reason for writing the passage.

⊙ **EXAMPLES** Read the following paragraphs. Identify the primary purpose of each paragraph.

1.   **On the Decay of the Art of Lying**
                      by Mark Twain [Samuel Clemens]

   Observe, I do not mean to suggest that the "custom" of lying has suffered any decay or interruption—no, for the Lie, as a Virtue, A Principle, is eternal; the Lie, as a recreation, a solace, a refuge in time of need, the fourth Grace, the tenth Muse, man's best and surest friend, is immortal, and cannot perish from the earth while this club remains. My complaint simply concerns the decay of the "art" of lying. No high-minded man, no man of right feeling, can contemplate the lumbering and slovenly lying of the present day without grieving to see a noble art so prostituted. … No fact is more firmly established than that lying is a necessity of our circumstances—the deduction that it is then a Virtue goes without saying. No virtue can reach its highest usefulness without careful and diligent cultivation—therefore, it goes without saying that this one ought to be taught in the public schools—even in the newspapers. What chance has the ignorant uncultivated liar against the educated expert? What chance have I against Mr. Per—against a lawyer?

—Excerpt from Mark Twain, "On the Decay of the Art of Lying." *Classic Literature Library.* <http://mark-twain.classic-literature.co.uk/on-the-decay-of-the-art-of-lying>

_____ The main purpose of this passage is to
   a. explain the virtue of lying.
   b. amuse the reader by poking fun at the human act of lying.
   c. convince the reader that lying is a virtue.

2. ## Letter from Birmingham Jail
by Martin Luther King, Jr.

We know through painful experience that freedom is never voluntarily given by the oppressor; it must be demanded by the oppressed. Frankly, I have yet to engage in a direct-action campaign that was "well timed" in the view of those who have not suffered unduly from the disease of segregation. For years now I have heard the word "Wait!" It rings in the ear of every Negro with piercing familiarity. This "Wait" has almost always meant "Never." We must come to see, with one of our distinguished jurists, that "justice too long delayed is justice denied."

—Martin Luther King Jr., From "Letter from Birmingham Jail" Copyright © 1963 Dr. Martin Luther King Jr., copyright renewed 1991 by Coretta Scott King.

_____ The main purpose of this paragraph is
   a. to entertain the reader with details from the civil rights movement.
   b. to convince the reader that the Negro deserves justice now.
   c. to explain why the Negro has been treated unfairly.

3.   **Long-Term Memory**

Think of long-term memory as a "data bank" or warehouse for all of your feelings and ideas. Information you heard hours, days, weeks, even years ago is stored in long-term memory. Long-term memory differs from short-term memory in several ways. Long-term memory can handle large amounts of information; short-term memory has less space for storage. Putting information in and getting it out again is a slow process in long-term memory. On the other hand, short-term memory is a rapid process.

—Adapted from Brownell, Judi, *Listening: Attitudes,
Principles, and Skills*, p. 150.

_____ The main purpose of this paragraph is
   a. to argue against poor memory skills.
   b. to amuse the reader with humorous details about long-term memory.
   c. to inform the reader about the differences between long-term and short-term memory.

EXPLANATIONS

1. Mark Twain, also known as Samuel Clemens, is a well-known American humorist. Thus, a reader can expect his primary purpose to be (b) to amuse the reader by poking fun at the human act of lying. Notice how his use of tone words makes this piece amusing, as in calling lying an "art" and "grieving to see a noble art so prostituted." His unexpected praise of a dishonest behavior is meant to make us smile.

2. It is common knowledge that Dr. Martin Luther King, Jr., is a beloved martyr of the civil rights movement. He is famous for his stand against injustice. The title tells us that this piece was written from the Birmingham jail. He was jailed for his stand against segregation. His main purpose is (b) to convince the reader that the Negro deserves justice now.

3. Based on the source note, you know that this paragraph comes from a textbook, and the primary purpose of a textbook is to inform. In addition, the tone of the title and details is factual and objective. Its main purpose is (c) to inform the reader about the differences between long-term and short-term memory. ◄

Practice 4

Read each of the following paragraphs. Identify the primary purpose of each.

1.   **Gender Differences in Defining the Self**

Is there any truth to the stereotype that when women get together they talk about interpersonal problems and relationships, whereas men talk about anything but their feelings (usually sports)? Although this stereotype is clearly an exaggeration, it does have a grain of truth and reflects a difference in women's and men's self-concept. Women have more relational interdependence. They focus more on their close relationships, such as how they feel about their spouse or their child. Men have more collective interdependence. They focus on their memberships in large groups, such as the fact that they are Americans or that they belong to a fraternity. Starting in early childhood, American girls are more likely to develop intimate relationships, cooperate with others, and focus their attention on social relationships. In contrast, boys are more likely to focus on their group memberships. These differences persist into adulthood.

—Adapted from Aronson, Elliot, *Social Psychology*,
8th ed., pp. 108–109.

_____ The main purpose of this paragraph is
  a. to entertain with amusing details about gender differences in defining the self.
  b. to explain that there appear to be differences in the way women and men define themselves.
  c. to argue that women are better than men at creating social relationships.

Textbook
Skills

2.   **Human Impact on Lakes**

Wakes created by motorboating disturb vegetation and the birds that nest in it. Motorboats discharge an oily mixture with gas exhausts beneath the surface of the water. This mixture escapes notice. One gallon of oil per million gallons of water imparts an odor to lake water. Eight gallons per million taints fish. These oily discharges can lower oxygen levels and hurt the growth and life span of fish.

—Adapted from Robert L. Smith and Thomas M. Smith. *Elements
of Ecology*, 4th ed., p. 462. Upper Saddle River: Addison Wesley
Longman, Inc., Benjamin Cummings imprint.

_____ The main purpose of this paragraph is
  a. to inform the reader about the impact of human motorboating activity on lakes.
  b. to argue against the use of boats in lakes.
  c. to entertain the reader with interesting details about boating.

Textbook
Skills

3. **The Metamorphosis**
by Franz Kafka

As Gregor Samsa awoke one morning from uneasy dreams he found himself transformed in his bed into a gigantic insect. He was lying on his hard, as it were armor-plated, back and when he lifted his head a little he could see his dome-like brown belly divided into stiff arched segments on top of which the bed quilt could hardly keep in position and was about to slide off completely. His numerous legs, which were pitifully thin compared to the rest of his bulk, waved helplessly before his eyes.

—Franz Kafka, *Metamorphosis*. New York: Random House, 1946.

_____ The main purpose of this paragraph is
   a. to explain to the reader that a human has turned into a bug.
   b. to convince the reader that a human has turned into a bug.
   c. to engage the reader with an absurd story.

VISUAL *VOCABULARY*

The purpose of this poster is to

.

   a. inform
   b. entertain
   c. persuade

LO6 Evaluate Passages for the Use of Irony

Irony is a tone often used in both conversation and written text. An author uses **irony** when he or she says one thing but means something else. Irony is the contrast between what is stated and what is implied, or between actual events and expectations.

Irony is often used to entertain and enlighten. For example, in the novel *Huckleberry Finn* by Mark Twain, the boy Huckleberry Finn believes he has done something wrong when he helps his older friend Jim escape slavery. The ironic contrast lies between what Huckleberry Finn thinks is wrong and what really is wrong: slavery itself. Twain set up this ironic situation to reveal the shortcomings of society.

Irony is also used to persuade. In her essay "I Want a Wife," Judy Brady seems to be saying she wants a wife to take care of the children, do the household chores, and perform all the other countless duties expected of a wife in the mid-twentieth century. However, she doesn't really want a wife; she wants equality with men. As she describes the role of a wife as a submissive servant, she argues against the limitations that society placed on women.

Due to its powerful special effects, authors use irony in many types of writings. For example, you will come across irony in fiction, essays, poetry, comedy routines, and cartoons. When authors use irony, they imply their main ideas and rely heavily on tone. Thus you need to understand two common types of irony so that you can see and enjoy their effects: verbal irony and situational irony.

> **Verbal irony** occurs when the author's words state one thing but imply the opposite.

During a violent storm, your friend says, "Nice weather, eh?"

At the finish line of a marathon, a tired runner says, "Why, I'm ready to run another 26 miles."

A father reviews his son's straight A report card and says, "Well, you have certainly made a mess of things!"

> **Situational irony** occurs when the events of a situation differ from what is expected.

A high school dropout eventually becomes a medical doctor.
An Olympic swimmer drowns.
A multimillionaire clips grocery coupons.

> **EXAMPLES** Read the items, and identify the type of irony used in each.

_____ **1.** Martha and Charlotte, who can't stand each other, show up at the prom wearing the exact same dress.
  a. verbal irony   c. no irony
  b. situational irony

_____ **2.** The burglar who had robbed the neighborhood garages of golf clubs and bicycles turned out to be a grandmother of six.
  a. verbal irony   c. no irony
  b. situational irony

_____ **3.** After getting stuck babysitting for her younger brothers and sisters, Kerry said, "This must be my lucky day."
 a. verbal irony   c. no irony
 b. situational irony

_____ **4.** Dark- or bright-colored foods are the healthiest because of their nutrients.
 a. verbal irony   c. no irony
 b. situational irony

EXPLANATIONS

1. (b) situational irony: The fact that people who can't stand each other have similar taste in fashion is unexpected.

2. (b) situational irony: Most would not suspect a grandmother to be a thief.

3. (a) verbal irony: The author provides a clue to the tone by using the phrase "getting stuck babysitting." These words let us know that Kerry is not pleased and doesn't mean what she is saying.

4. (c) no irony: The author provides facts without emotion.

Practice 5

Read the items, and identify the type of irony used in each.

_____ **1.** Looking out the window at the gray skies and wind-blown trees, Robert said, "Great day for a picnic."
 a. verbal irony   c. no irony
 b. situational irony

_____ **2.** On opening night, the beautiful, talented, and famous actress stood frozen with stage fright as the curtain rose.
 a. verbal irony   c. no irony
 b. situational irony

_____ **3.** "Driving while under the influence of drugs or alcohol is really smart."
 a. verbal irony   c. no irony
 b. situational irony

_____ **4.** Kim stayed up all night typing the paper that was due the next day. Just as she was ready to print, her computer crashed, and she lost

all her information. She had failed to save her work as she wrote. It was the best paper she had ever written.
   a. verbal irony
   b. situational irony
   c. no irony

_____ **5.** Algebra is a challenging course for many college students.
   a. verbal irony
   b. situational irony
   c. no irony

LO7 Develop Textbook Skills: Recognize an Author's Tone and Purpose

Read the excerpt from the textbook *Messages: Building Interpersonal Communication Skills*. Then answer these questions about the author's purpose and tone.

264   PART 3: Messages in Context

How would you explain the cartoon to the right in terms of social exchange theory?

Intimacy

At the intimacy stage you commit yourself still further to the other person and, in fact, establish a kind of relationship in which this individual becomes your best or closest friend, lover, or companion. Usually the intimacy stage divides itself quite neatly into two phases: an *interpersonal commitment* phase in which you commit yourselves to each other in a kind of private way and a *social bonding* phase in which the commitment is made public—perhaps to family and friends, perhaps to the public at large through formal marriage. Here the two of you become a unit, a pair.

Commitment may take many forms; it may be an engagement or a marriage; it may be a commitment to help the person or to be with the person, or a commitment to reveal your deepest secrets. It may consist of living together or an agreement to become lovers. The type of commitment varies with the relationship and with the individuals. The important characteristic is that the commitment made is a special one; it's a commitment that you do not make lightly or to everyone. This intimacy stage is reserved for very few people at any given time—sometimes just one, sometimes two, three, or perhaps four. Rarely do people have more than four intimates, except in a family situation.

True love comes quietly, without banners or flashing lights. If you hear bells, get your ears checked.
   —*Erich Segal*

Immature love says: "I love you because I need you."
Mature love says: "I need you because I love you."
   —*Erich Fromm*

—DeVito, Joseph A. *Messages: Building Interpersonal Communication Skills.*, p. 264.

_____ **1.** The author's primary purpose for this section of the text is
   a. to inform.   c. to persuade.
   b. to entertain.

_____ **2.** The tone of the main text is
   a. biased.   b. objective.

_____ **3.** The purpose of the cartoon "Accountants in Love" is
   a. to inform.   c. to persuade.
   b. to entertain.

_____ **4.** The tone of the quote by Erich Segal is
   a. earnest.   c. irritated.
   b. loving.   d. sarcastic.

_____ **5.** The tone of the quote by Erich Fromm is
   a. biting.   c. poetic.
   b. cheerful.   d. insulting.

Apply Information Literacy Skills

 ## Academic, Personal, and Career Applications of Tone and Purpose

The ability to determine the tone and purpose of information is a key information literacy skill. Considering the tone and purpose of information improves your ability to find, evaluate, and use relevant ideas. For example, think about the topic of health care. We view the claim of a politician differently than we view a joke by a comedian or an expert opinion of a medical doctor. Tone and purpose affect meaning. As a student, consumer, citizen, and worker, you may come across materials such as textbook passages, advertisements, reports, or memos. Skimming for the purpose of the information helps you know where to focus your attention and how to react. Also, you may access or create specific types of documents for specific purposes such as brochures, journals, letters, recordings, or videos. Or you may think about how to use a part of a text, such as a quotation, in your own writings or speech.

Therefore, you will use the skills that you have learned in academic, personal, and career situations:

- Recognize your own need to identify tone and purpose.
- Analyze tone and purpose to determine the relevance of an idea.
- Determine the use of tone and purpose to develop a main idea.

Academic Application

Assume you are taking the college course Student Success. One of the course requirements is for each student to give a five-minute speech about a topic to ensure student success. You have chosen to speak about using time management skills. You would like to use a quotation to either introduce or conclude your speech.

- **Before Reading:** Skim the quotes to identify the types of speakers who are being quoted and to note the tone of each quote.
- **During Reading:** Label the quotes to indicate your ranking of each one's usability.
- **After Reading:** In the space following the passage, indicate which quote you will use to make your point. Explain your choice.

Quote 1: "I am definitely going to take a course on time management . . . just as soon as I can work it into my schedule."—Louis E. Boone, Emeritus Professor of Business at the University of South Alabama

Source: Louis E. Boone, *Simpson's Contemporary Quotations*, Houghton Mifflin Harcourt Publishing Company, 1988.

Quote 2: "Dost thou love life? Then do not squander time, for that is the stuff life is made of. If you have time, don't wait for time."—Benjamin Franklin, American

Source: *Poor Richard's Almanack*. U. S. C Publishing Co. Waterloo, Iowa. 1914, pages 20, 31.

Quote 3: "The bad news is time flies. The good news is you're the pilot." —Michael Altshuler, Motivational Speaker, Expert in Sales and Communication

Source: Altshuler, Michael L. From" The Management Quotes: Recognizing the Importance of Time Management", Time-Management-Central.net. Reprinted by permission of the author.

_____

_____

_____

Personal Application

Assume you are interested in buying a large-screen television for your home. You have found the following three sources of information about large-screen TVs on the Internet.

- **Before Reading:** Skim the information about each source to get an overview of the differences among the sites.
- **During Reading:** Highlight details that identify the purpose of the source.
- **After Reading:** In the space following the passage, describe the usefulness of each site as a source of information for purchasing a large-screen television.

Source 1: "TV Buying Guide" and "TV Recommendations and Ratings," ConsumerReports.org

About: Consumer Reports (CR) is an expert, independent nonprofit organization. CR's mission is to work for a fair, just, and safe marketplace for all consumers and to empower consumers to protect themselves. The organization was founded in 1936 when advertising first flooded the mass media. Consumers lacked a reliable source of information they could depend on to help them distinguish hype from fact and good products from bad ones. Since then, CR has filled that vacuum with a broad range of consumer information. To maintain its independence and impartiality, CR accepts no outside advertising and no free samples and employs several hundred mystery shoppers and technical experts to buy and test the products it evaluates.

Source 2: "Buying Guide: Choosing a Big TV," WIRED

About: WIRED is the first word on how ideas and innovation are changing the world. Each month in the magazine and every day online, our editors deliver a glimpse into the future of business, culture, innovation, and science.

Source 3: "Shop TV & Video," Best Buy

About: Best Buy is a multinational retailer of technology and entertainment products and services with a commitment to growth and innovation.

_____

_____

_____

_____

_____

Career Application

Assume you are the office manager of a company that is changing its policy about employee work schedules. You have asked the human resource department to draft a memo to introduce the new policy to all employees. The human resource department has submitted two drafts for you to consider.

- **Before Reading:** Skim both drafts to determine if the tone is appropriate and the purpose is clear.
- **During Reading:** Underline words that need to be revised to improve tone or to clarify purpose.
- **After Reading:** In the space following the passage, discuss which memo is more effective and why.

Draft 1:

To: All Employees

From: Human Resources

RE: Good News!

Soon, you can choose your own work hours! Of course, you can't work just any time. You do have to be here certain core hours, but everything else is up to you. No doubt this is going to make life easier for all of you, but especially parents. This will help with the hassle of juggling work life with home life. Just think, you can shop, exercise, or whatever whenever. Be sure to check with your supervisor. Not everybody can be gone at once. Someone has to work the floor and phones between 8 A.M. to 6 P.M.

Draft 2:

To: All Employees

From: Human Resources

RE: Flextime

In accordance with company policy, management is announcing changes to procedures. On June 1, the company is initiating Flextime. Employee attendance at work is required for the core five hours between 11 A.M. and 4 P.M. However, employees will determine their hours of arrival and departure, subject to approval of their supervisors, to create an 8-hour work day. Supervisors must ensure that personnel are on duty at all times to meet customer needs.

_____

_____

_____

REVIEW TEST 1

Score (number correct) _____ × 10 = _____%

Visit MyReadingLab to take this test online and receive feedback and guidance on your answers.

Tone

Read the following items, and choose a tone word from the box that best describes each.

angry	encouraging	pessimistic	sympathetic
confident	joking	pleading	timid
disbelieving	joyful	~~sarcastic~~	warning

joking **1.** "Quitting smoking is easy; I quit two or three times a day."

Sarcastic **2.** "Very funny, Joe, I can hardly stop laughing. I mean, risking cancer is just so funny."

confident **3.** "I am not going to get cancer because I can kick the smoking habit any time I choose to."

warning **4.** "You'd better think again, Joe. That's what my uncle thought, too."

simpatlet **5.** "Oh, yeah, I'm sorry, how is he doing? I know you must be worried."

Pessaut r **6.** "Not so good. The chemotherapy is making him really sick. I'm afraid he might not make it."

encouraging **7.** "Don't worry, Sue, the treatment is going to work. The doctors said he had an 80 percent chance of beating the cancer."

angry **8.** "Well, those odds don't mean anything when you act as stupidly as my uncle. He still smokes at least a pack a day!"

disbelieving **9.** "You have to be kidding! Still smoking? That's hard to believe!"

pleading **10.** "Please, Joe, don't end up like my uncle. Please, stop smoking now before it becomes impossible for you to quit, too."

REVIEW TEST 2

Score (number correct) _____ × 10 = _____%

Visit MyReadingLab to take this test online and receive feedback and guidance on your answers.

Tone and Purpose

A. Read the following topic sentences. Label each according to its purpose:

I = to inform

P = to persuade

E = to entertain

_E_ **1.** The best way to survive babysitting a set of triplets is to come armed with plenty of energy, lots of patience, and a first-aid kit.

_I_ **2.** The Trail of Tears is the name of the journey that more than 70,000 Indians took when they were forced to give up their homes and move to Oklahoma.

_P_ **3.** According to fitness specialist Jack Tremagne, a long-term weight-lifting program is the only effective method for losing and keeping off unhealthy body fat.

_I_ **4.** The northbound lane of State Road 17 will be shut down for several days this week due to road construction.

_P_ **5.** The death penalty is unfair and cruel and should be abolished.

_____ E **6.** The sound of a thousand motorcycles fills the night air as leather-clad, tough-looking, party-minded bikers roar into the sleepy coastal town for one wild, crazy, unforgettable week.

B. Read the following items, and identify the primary purpose of each.

Editorial Cartoon Published in a Newspaper

_____ **7.** The primary purpose of this cartoon is
   a. to inform the reader about the need to ban smoking.
   b. to entertain the reader with a funny situation about smoking bans.
   c. to persuade the reader to ban smoking outside.

Literary Passage Published in a Book

Central Park at Dusk

Buildings above the leafless trees
Loom high as castles in a dream,

While one by one the lamps come out
To thread the twilight with a dream.

There is no sign of leaf or bud,
A hush is over everything—

Silent as women wait for love,
The world is waiting for the spring.

—Sara Teasdale

_____ **8.** The tone of this poem could best be described as
    a. reflective.   c. ironic.
    b. humorous.   d. loving.

_____ **9.** The primary purpose of this poem is
    a. to inform what Central Park looks like.
    b. to entertain the reader with its poetic language and emotion.
    c. to persuade the reader that winter can be as beautiful as spring.

Paragraph from a Health Textbook

Smokeless Tobacco

Textbook
Skills

    Smokeless tobacco is used by approximately 5 million U.S. adults. Most users are teenage (20 percent of male high school students) and young adult males, who are often emulating a professional sports figure or family member. There are two types of smokeless tobacco—chewing tobacco and snuff. Chewing tobacco contains tobacco leaves treated with molasses and other flavorings. The user places a "quid" of tobacco in the mouth between the teeth and gums and then sucks or chews the quid to release the nicotine. Once the quid becomes ineffective, the user spits it out and inserts another. Dipping is another method of using chewing tobacco. The dipper takes a small amount of tobacco and places it between the lower lip and teeth to stimulate the flow of saliva and release the nicotine. Dipping rapidly releases the nicotine into the bloodstream.

    Snuff can come in either dry or moist powdered form or sachets (teabaglike pouches) of tobacco. The most common placement of snuff is inside the cheek. In European countries, inhaling dry snuff is more common than in the United States.

—Donatelle, Rebecca J. and Davis, Lorraine G.,
Access to Health, 7th ed., p. 365.

_____ **10.** The primary purpose of this passage is
    a. to inform the reader about smokeless tobacco.
    b. to entertain the reader with graphic details about smokeless tobacco.
    c. to persuade the reader to avoid using smokeless tobacco.

Score (number correct) _____ × 25 = _____ %

Visit MyReadingLab to take this test online and receive feedback and guidance on your answers.

Tone and Purpose

Read the following passage from a college sociology textbook. Answer the questions that follow.

Textbook
Skills

Is Big Brother Knocking on the Door?
Civil Liberties and Homeland Security

[1]See if you can guess which country this is. [2]Government agents can break into your home while you are at work, copy the files on your computer, and leave a "bug" that records every keystroke from then on, all this without a search warrant. [3]Government agents can also check with the local library and make a list of every book, record, or movie that you've ever checked out.

[4]Is this Russia? [5]Albania? [6]Maybe there, too, but this is now how it is in the United States.

[7]We have had fundamental changes since 9/11. [8]There is no question that we must have security. [9]Our nation cannot be at risk, and we cannot live in peril. [10]But does security have to come at the price of our civil liberties?

[11]Balancing security and civil liberties has always been a sensitive issue in U.S. history. [12]In times of war, the U.S. government has curtailed freedoms. [13]During the War Between the States, as the Civil War is called in the South, Abraham Lincoln even banned the right of habeas corpus (Neely 1992). [14]This took away people's right to appear in court and ask judges to determine whether they had been unlawfully arrested and imprisoned.

[15]After the terrorist attacks on New York City and Washington, D.C. in 2001, Congress authorized the formation of the Department of Homeland Security. [16]Other than beefed-up security at airports, few citizens noticed a difference. [17]People who were suspected of terrorism, however, felt a major impact. [18]They were imprisoned without charges being lodged against them in a court, and they were denied the right to consult lawyers or to have a hearing in court.

[19]People shrugged this off. [20]"Terrorists deserve whatever they get," they said. [21]What ordinary citizens didn't realize was that behind the scenes, their own liberties were being curtailed. [22]FBI agents placed

listening devices on cars, in buildings, and on streets. [23]They used Night Stalkers (aircraft outfitted with electronic surveillance equipment) to listen to conversations (Hentoff 2003). [24]No longer does the FBI need a judge's order to search your e-mails, telephone records, travel records, or credit and bank transactions. [25]The FBI can simply demand that telephone and Internet access companies, colleges, libraries, banks, and credit companies produce them—and be punished as criminals if they reveal that the FBI has demanded these records ("FBI Director . . . " 2007).

[26]Then there is the "no-fly list" of the Transportation Security Agency. [27]Anyone who might have some kind of connection with some kind of terrorist is not allowed to board an airplane. [28]This agency has also developed CAPPS II (Computer Assisted Passenger Pre-Screening System). [29]Each traveler is labeled as a "green," "yellow," or "red" security risk. [30]Green means you're fine, and red is reserved for known terrorists.

[31]But what about the yellow code? [32]These people are "suspects." [33]The American Civil Liberties Union points out that anyone can get stamped yellow—with no way to know it or to change it. [34](For all I know, I could be coded yellow for criticizing Homeland Security in this essay.) [35]Agents in "government intelligence"—an oxymoron, if ever there was one—are known for being humorless, suspicious, and almost downright paranoid. [36]You could get stamped yellow simply for reading the wrong books—because agents of the Department of Homeland Security now have the right to track the books we buy or those we check out at libraries. [37]They can even record the Internet sites we visit at libraries. [38]This is all done in secret. [39]When librarians receive orders to reveal who has checked out certain books, they can be arrested if they even tell anyone that they received such an order (Lichtblau 2005).

[40]If such surveillance continues, our government will become like the former police state of East Germany and eventually keep secret files on almost all of us. [41]If you get coded yellow, that information could be shared with other government agencies. [42]This, in turn, could affect your chances of getting a job or even a college scholarship.

[43]Security we must have. [44]But at what cost? [45]Government watch-dogs looking over our shoulders, writing down the names of our friends and associates, even the books and magazines we read? [46]Microphones planted to eavesdrop on our conversations? [47]Will they eventually install a computer chip in our right hand or in our forehead?

— Adapted from Henslin, James M., *Sociology: A Down-to-Earth Approach*, 9th ed., p. 453.

_____ **1.** The tone of sentence 20 is
        a. cynical.   c. hateful.
        b. objective.   d. resigned.

_____ **2.** The tone of sentence 47 is
        a. neutral.   c. sarcastic.
        b. timid.   d. supportive.

_____ **3.** The overall tone of the passage is
        a. objective.   b. biased.

_____ **4.** The main purpose of this essay is to
        a. explain the relationship between civil rights and homeland security.
        b. amuse the reader with details about civil rights and homeland security.
        c. warn the reader about the dangers posed to civil rights for the sake of homeland security.

VISUAL _VOCABULARY_

This humor in this cartoon relies

on _____.

    a. situational irony
    b. verbal irony

"Look, you've got to accept some curtailment of your freedom
in exchange for increased security."

SUMMARY RESPONSE

Restate the author's central idea in your own words. In your summary, state the author's tone and purpose. Begin your summary response with the following: _The central idea of "Is Big Brother Knocking on the Door? Civil Liberties and Homeland Security" by James M. Henslin is …_

WHAT DO YOU THINK?

What civil liberties do you think we should give up to help our nation be secure? Are you willing to have the government keep track of your everyday affairs in the name of homeland security? Write a letter to your senator that expresses your support for or against government surveillance for security. In your letter discuss the following point:

- Discuss the effects of the government keeping a list of the books you check out at the library, listening to your conversations on the phone, or keeping track of the people you associate with.
- Use historical examples to support your point.

REVIEW TEST 4

Score (number correct) _____ × 10 = _____ %

Visit MyReadingLab to take this test online and receive feedback and guidance on your answers.

Combined Skills Test

Before you read the following passage by a college sociology professor, read the Vocabulary Preview, skim the passage, and answer the Before Reading questions. Then read the passage carefully and answer the After Reading questions that follow.

Vocabulary Preview

haggard (8): looking wasted and worn
abject (12): of the lowest degree; miserable
fitful (14): irregular; restless
juxtaposing (20): placing side by side

Social Class in the United States

¹Ah, New Orleans, that fabled city on the Mississippi Delta. ²Images from its rich past floated through my head—pirates, treasure, intrigue. ³Memories from a pleasant vacation stirred my thoughts—the exotic French Quarter with its enticing aroma of Creole food and sounds of earthy jazz drifting through the air.

⁴The shelter for the homeless, however, forced me back to an unwelcome reality. ⁵The shelter was like those I had visited in the North,

West, and East—only dirtier. ⁶The dirt, in fact, was the worst that I had encountered during my research. ⁷On top of that, this was the only shelter to insist on payment in exchange for sleeping in one of its filthy beds.

⁸The men here looked the same as the homeless anywhere in the country—**disheveled** and **haggard**, wearing that unmistakable expression of sorrow and of despair. ⁹Except for the accent, you wouldn't know what region you were in. ¹⁰Poverty wears the same tired face wherever you are, I realized. ¹¹The accent may differ, but the look remains the same.

¹²I had grown used to the sights and smells of **abject** poverty. ¹³Those no longer surprised me. ¹⁴But after my **fitful** sleep with the homeless night, I saw something that did. ¹⁵Just a block or so from the shelter, I was startled by a sight so out of step with the misery and despair I had just experienced that I stopped and stared. ¹⁶I felt indignation swelling within me. ¹⁷Confronting me were life-size, full-color photos mounted on the transparent Plexiglas shelter of a bus stop. ¹⁸Staring back at me were images of finely dressed men and women, proudly strutting about as they modeled elegant suits, dresses, diamonds, and furs. ¹⁹A wave of disgust swept over me. ²⁰"Something is cockeyed in this society," I thought, as my mind refused to stop **juxtaposing** these images of extravagance with the suffering I had just witnessed.

—Henslin, James M., *Sociology: A Down-to-Earth Approach*, 9th ed., p. 249.

Before Reading

Vocabulary in Context

_____   **1.** What does the word **disheveled** mean in sentence 8?
   a. comfortable   c. frightening
   b. rumpled   d. serious

Purpose

_____   **2.** The primary purpose of this passage is to
   a. illustrate homelessness and inequality in our society.
   b. entertain readers with an anecdote about New Orleans.
   c. persuade readers to volunteer in homeless shelters.

After Reading

Central Idea and Main Idea

_____ **3.** Which sentence best states the central idea of the passage?
- a. sentence 1
- b. sentence 4
- c. sentence 16
- d. sentence 20

Supporting Details

_____ **4.** Sentence 6 is a
- a. major supporting detail for the central idea.
- b. minor supporting detail for the central idea.

Transitions

_____ **5.** The relationship between sentences 6 and 7 is
- a. cause and effect.
- b. time order.
- c. contrast.
- d. addition.

Thought Patterns

_____ **6.** The overall thought pattern of the passage is
- a. cause and effect.
- b. time order.
- c. contrast.
- d. definition and example.

Fact and Opinion

_____ **7.** Sentence 17 is a statement of
- a. fact.
- b. opinion.
- c. fact and opinion.

_____ **8.** Sentence 18 is a statement of
- a. fact.
- b. opinion.
- c. fact and opinion.

Tone

_____ **9.** Sentence 20 contains an example of
- a. verbal irony.
- b. situational irony.

_____ **10.** The tone of sentence 10 is
- a. serious.
- b. objective.
- c. humble.
- d. defiant.

SUMMARY RESPONSE

Restate the author's central idea in your own words. In your summary, state the author's tone and purpose. Begin your summary response with the following: *The central idea of "Social Class in the United States" by Henslin is ...*

WHAT DO YOU THINK?

What are your views on poverty and homelessness in this country? Do you agree with the author that it is unjust to have such extreme poverty and wealth existing side by side? Write a letter to the editor of your local newspaper expressing your opinion on this matter. Include the following points:

- Describe a personal experience or an experience of someone you know to illustrate your opinion.
- Evaluate if or why homelessness and poverty should or should not be considered civic responsibilities.

After Reading About Tone and Purpose

Before you move on to the Mastery Tests on tone and purpose, take time to reflect on your learning and performance by answering the following questions. Write your answers in your notebook.

- How has my knowledge base or prior knowledge about tone and purpose changed?
- Based on my studies, how do I think I will perform on the Mastery Test(s)? Why do I think my scores will be above average, average, or below average?
- Would I recommend this chapter to other students who want to learn about tone and purpose? Why or why not?

Test your understanding of what you have learned about tone and purpose by completing the Chapter 10 Review.

Name _____ Section _____

Date **Score** (number correct) _____ × 10 = _____%

Visit MyReadingLab to take this test online and receive feedback and guidance on your answers.

A. Read the following items. Choose a tone word from the list below that best describes each item.

a. amazed   d. logical
b. argumentative   e. reflective
c. factual

_____ **1.**   Those of us who shout the loudest about Americanism in making character assassinations are all too frequently those who, by our own words and acts, ignore some of the basic principles of Americanism: the right to criticize, the right to hold unpopular beliefs, the right to protest, the right of independent thought. The exercise of these rights should not cost one single American citizen his reputation or his right to a livelihood. Nor should he be in danger of losing his reputation or livelihood merely because he happens to know someone who holds unpopular beliefs. Who of us doesn't? Otherwise none of us could call our souls our own.

—Margaret Chase Smith, *Declaration of Conscience.* <http://www.americanrhetoric.com/speeches/margaretchasesmithconscience.html>

_____ **2.**   The sky was as full of motion and change as the desert beneath it was monotonous and still,—and there was so much sky, more than at sea, more than anywhere else in the world. The plain was there, under one's feet, but what one saw when one looked about was that brilliant blue world of stinging air and moving cloud. Even the mountains were mere ant-hills under it. Elsewhere the sky is the roof of the world; but here the earth was the floor of the sky. The landscape one longed for when one was away, the thing all about one, the world one actually lived in, was the sky, the sky!—Willa Cather, *Death Comes for the Archbishop.*

—*The Columbia World of Quotations.* New York: Columbia University Press, 1996. <www.bartleby.com/66/>

_____ **3.**   When things are investigated, then true knowledge is achieved; when true knowledge is achieved, then the will becomes sincere; when the will is sincere, then the heart is set right (or then the mind sees right); when the heart is set right, then the personal life is cultivated; when the personal life is cultivated, then the family life is regulated; when the family life is regulated, then the national life is orderly;

and when the national life is orderly, then there is peace in this world.—
Confucius

> —*Liki* (*Record of Rites*), Chapter 42.—*The Wisdom of Confucius,* ed. and trans. Lin
> Yutang, Chapter 4, pp. 139–40 (1938). *Respectfully Quoted: A Dictionary of Quotations
> Requested from the Congressional Research Service.* Washington, D.C.: Library of
> Congress, 1989; Bartleby.com, 2003. <www.bartleby.com/73/>

_____ **4.** We are all citizens of one world; we are all of one blood. To hate
a man because he was born in another country, because he speaks a
different language, or because he takes a different view on this subject or that, is a great folly. Desist, I implore you, for we are all equally
human.... Let us have but one end in view, the welfare of humanity.
—John Amos Comenius

> —*Respectfully Quoted: A Dictionary of Quotations Requested from the Congressional
> Research Service.* Washington, D.C.: Library of Congress, 1989; Bartleby.com, 2003.
> <www.bartleby.com/73/>

_____ **5.** The United Arab Emirates is a federation of sheikhdoms (1995
est. pop. 2,925,000), c.30,000 sq mi (77,700 sq km), SE Arabia, on the
Persian Gulf and the Gulf of Oman. The federation, commonly known
as the UAE, consists of seven sheikhdoms: Abu Dhabi (territorially the
largest of the sheikhdoms), Ajman, Dubai, Fujairah, Ras al-Khaimah,
Sharjah, and Umm al-Qaiwain. The city of Abu Dhabi (1991 est. pop.
798,000) in Abu Dhabi is the capital.—World Factbook, 2003.

> —*The World Factbook.* Washington, D.C.: Central Intelligence Agency, 2003;
> Bartleby.com, 2003. <www.bartleby.com/151/>

B. Read the following topic sentences. Label each one according to its purpose:

> **I** = to inform   **P** = to persuade   **E** = to entertain

_____ **6.** Florida offers a wide variety of fun vacation activities, from traditional tourist attractions to pristine natural retreats.

_____ **7.** Paris never sleeps; at night, the River Seine glistens as the City of
Light comes alive.

_____ **8.** Explore the nature of Armada—with our all natural hair care products, offering the purest of ingredients designed to bring out the
shine and body of healthy hair.

_____ **9.** The number of teenagers who are choosing to not have sex is growing for a variety of reasons.

_____ **10.** Congress must act quickly to head off the looming health care crisis.

Name _____ Section _____

Date _____ **Score** (number correct) _____ × 25 = _____%

Visit MyReadingLab to take this test online and receive feedback and guidance on your answers.

Read each item; then answer the questions that follow it.

Poem

Richard Cory

by *Edwin Arlington Robinson*

Whenever Richard Cory went down town,
We people on the pavement looked at him:
He was a gentleman from sole to crown,
Clean favored, and imperially slim.

And he was always quietly arrayed,
And he was always human when he talked;
But still he fluttered pulses when he said,
"Good-morning," and he glittered when he walked.

And he was rich—yes, richer than a king—
And admirably schooled in every grace:
In fine, we thought he was everything
To make us wish that we were in his place.

So on we worked, and waited for the light,
And went without the meat, and cursed the bread;
And Richard Cory, one calm summer night,
Went home and put a bullet through his head.

_____ **1.** The primary purpose of this poem is to
  a. inform.   c. entertain.
  b. persuade.

_____ **2.** The overall tone of this poem can be described as
  a. ironic.   c. disbelieving.
  b. humorous.   d. excited.

Passage from a Health Textbook

Eating for Health

Americans consume more calories per person than any other group of people in the world. A *calorie* is a unit of measure that indicates the amount of energy we get from a particular food. Calories are eaten in the

Textbook
Skills

form of protein, fats, and carbohydrates. These are three basic nutrients needed for life. Three other nutrients—vitamins, minerals, and water— are necessary for bodily function but do not add any calories to our diets.

Taking in too many calories is a major factor in our tendency to be over-weight. However, it is not the amount of food we eat that is likely to cause weight problems and related diseases. It is the relative amount of nutrients in our diets and lack of exercise. Most Americans get about 38 percent of their calories from fat, 15 percent from proteins, 22 percent from complex carbohydrates, and 24 percent from simple sugars. Experts recommend that complex carbohydrates be increased to make up 48 percent of our total calo-ries. They also suggest that we reduce proteins to 12 percent, simple sugars to 10 percent, and fats to no more than 30 percent of our total diets.

—Adapted from Donatelle, Rebecca J. and Davis, Lorraine G. *Access to Health*, 7th ed., p. 217.

_____ **3.** The primary purpose of this passage is to
   a. convince students to lose weight.
   b. condemn the typical American diet.
   c. share useful information that will lead to a healthy lifestyle.

_____ **4.** The overall tone of this passage can be described as
   a. critical.   c. cynical.
   b. bossy.   d. neutral.

VISUAL *VOCABULARY*

The power of this image relies on

_____.

a. situational irony
b. verbal irony

Name _____ Section _____

Date _____ **Score** (number correct) _____ × 25 = _____%

Visit MyReadingLab to take this test online and receive feedback and guidance on your answers.

Read each passage; then answer the questions that follow it.

Textbook
Skills

Paragraph from a Science Textbook

The caffeine people ingest comes from various natural sources, including coffee beans, teas, kolanuts, and cocoa beans. Kolanut extracts are used for making cola drinks, and cocoa beans (not to be confused with the cocaine-producing coca plant) are roasted and then ground to a paste used for making chocolate. Caffeine is relatively easy to remove from these natural products. This allows for the economical production of "decaffeinated" beverages, many of which, however, still contain small amounts of caffeine. Interestingly, cola drink manufacturers use decaffeinated kolanut extract in their beverages. The caffeine is added in a separate step to guarantee a particular caffeine concentration. In the United States, about 2 million pounds of caffeine is added to soft drinks each year.

—Adapted from Hewitt, Paul G. *Conceptual Physical Science*, 2nd ed., p. 568.

_____ **1.** The primary purpose of this passage is to
   a. explain the side effects of caffeine.
   b. inform readers where the caffeine in drinks comes from.
   c. persuade readers to limit the caffeine they take in.

_____ **2.** The tone of this paragraph is
   a. accusing.   c. objective.
   b. depressing.   d. harsh.

Passage from an American History Textbook

Textbook
Skills

The Question of Slavery

Early on the evening of January 21, 1850, Senator Henry Clay of Kentucky trudged through knee-deep snowdrifts to visit Senator Daniel Webster of Massachusetts. Clay, 73 years old, was a sick man, wracked by a severe cough. But he braved the snowstorm. He feared for the Union's future.

For four years, Congress had bitterly debated the issue of the expansion of slavery in new territories. Ever since Daniel Wilmot had proposed that slavery be banned from any territory acquired from Mexico, those against slavery had argued that Congress had the right to ban slavery in all of the territories. Southerners who were for slavery strongly disagreed.

Politicians had been unable to work out a compromise. One simple proposal had been to extend the Missouri Compromise line to the Pacific Ocean. Thus slavery would have been outlawed north of 36'30" north latitude, but it would have been allowed south of that line. Moderate southerners supported this proposal, but few others agreed. Another proposal was known as "squatter sovereignty." It stated that the people who lived in a territory should decide whether or not to allow slavery.

Neither idea offered a solution to the whole range of issues dividing the North and the South. It was up to Henry Clay, who had just returned to Congress after a seven-year absence, to work out a solution. For an hour on the evening of January 21, Clay outlined the following plan to save the Union:

- California be admitted as a free state.
- Mexico and Utah have no restrictions on slavery.
- Texas give up land in exchange for unpaid debts.
- Congress enact a strict Fugitive Slave Law.
- Slave trade, but not slavery, be banned in the District of Columbia.

Clay's proposal set off an eight-month debate in Congress and led to threats of southern succession. Eventually parts of Clay's compromise were accepted. The compromise gave the false sense that the issue had been resolved. Hostility was defused, and calm returned. But as one southern editor correctly noted, it was "the calm of preparation, and not of peace."

—Adapted from Martin et al., *America and Its Peoples:*
A Mosaic in the Making, 3rd ed., pp. 455–457.

_____ **3.** The primary purpose of this passage is to
    a. inform.   c. persuade.
    b. entertain.

_____ **4.** The overall tone of this passage can be described as
    a. argumentative.   c. bitter.
    b. factual.   d. stern.

Name _____ Section _____

Date _____ **Score** (number correct) _____ × 10 = _____%

Visit MyReadingLab to take this test online and receive feedback and guidance on your answers.

Read the following items. Choose a tone word from the box below that best describes each.

admiring	factual	humble	ironic	pleading
cautionary	hopeful	humorous	persuasive	prayerful

_____ **1.** When you become senile, you won't know it.—Bill Cosby

—Bill Cosby, *Simpson's Contemporary Quotations,* Houghton Mifflin Harcourt Publishing Company, 1988.

_____ **2.** I believe that unarmed truth and unconditional love will have the final word in reality. This is why right, temporarily defeated, is stronger than evil triumphant.—Martin Luther King, Jr., accepting Nobel Peace Prize 10 Dec 64

—Martin Luther King, Jr., *Simpson's Contemporary Quotations,* Houghton Mifflin Harcourt Publishing Company, 1988.

_____ **3.** Tennis is a perfect combination of violent action taking place in an atmosphere of total tranquillity.—Billie Jean King, tennis player

—Billie Jean King, *Simpson's Contemporary Quotations,* Houghton Mifflin Harcourt Publishing Company, 1988.

_____ **4.** Let every nation know, whether it wishes us well or ill, that we shall pay any price, bear any burden, meet any hardship, support any friend, oppose any foe to assure the survival and the success of liberty.—John F. Kennedy, 35th U.S. President

—John F. Kennedy, *Simpson's Contemporary Quotations,* Houghton Mifflin Harcourt Publishing Company, 1988.

5. Tell him, if he doesn't mind, we'll shake hands.—John F. Kennedy, 35th U.S. President, on meeting Soviet Premier Nikita S. Khrushchev

> —John F. Kennedy, *Simpson's Contemporary Quotations,* Houghton Mifflin Harcourt Publishing Company, 1988.

6. Mama and Daddy King represent the best in manhood and womanhood, the best in a marriage, the kind of people we are trying to become.—Coretta Scott King

> —Coretta Scott King, *Simpson's Contemporary Quotations,* Houghton Mifflin Harcourt Publishing Company, 1988.

7. God give me the serenity to accept things which cannot be changed; Give me courage to change things which must be changed; And the wisdom to distinguish one from the other.

> —*Respectfully Quoted: A Dictionary of Quotations Requested from the Congressional Research Service.* Washington, D.C.: Library of Congress, 1989; Bartleby.com, 2003. <www.bartleby.com/73/>

8. The term embryology, in its widest sense, is applied to the various changes which take place during the growth of an animal from the egg to the adult condition.

> —Henry Gray, *Anatomy of the Human Body.* Philadelphia: Lea.& Febiger, 1918; Bartleby.com, 2000. <www.bartleby.com/107/>

9. A novel everyone should read is H. G. Wells's *Invisible Man,* a tale of psychological terror. Wells created a gripping masterpiece on the destructive effects the invisibility has on the scientist and the insane and murderous chaos left in his malicious wake.

> —Wells, H. G. "Introduction, The Invisible Man, A Grotesque Romance" by H. G. Wells, Bartleby.com.

10. "Yet, I implore you, pause! Yield to my advice, do not do this deed."—Jocasta, *Oedipus the King*

10 Summary of Key Concepts of Tone and Purpose

L01 L02   Assess your comprehension of tone and purpose.

- Tone is _____.

- Objective tone words _____.

- Subjective tone words _____.

- The author's purpose is _____.

- The primary purpose is _____.

- A writer whose purpose is _____ uses facts to teach or explain a main idea.

- A writer whose purpose is _____ sets out to amuse or interest the audience.

- A writer whose purpose is _____ combines facts with emotional appeals to sway readers to a particular point of view.

- Verbal irony occurs when _____
  _____.

- Situational irony occurs _____
  _____.

Test Your Comprehension of Tone and Purpose

Respond to the following questions and prompts.

L01 L02   In your own words, what is the relationship between tone and purpose?

_____

_____

_____

_____

L02 L06 In your own words, what is the difference between verbal and situational irony?

_____

_____

_____

L02 L04
L05 In your own words, describe how to determine tone and purpose.

_____

_____

_____

_____

L03 L04
L05 L06
L07 Use a checklist to help determine the tone and purpose of passages. Select a passage to analyze; then complete the following checklist with information from the passage.

Title of Passage:	Yes	No	Examples (words or phrases)/Explanations
Subjective Tone			
Objective Tone			
Irony			
Primary Purpose			
To Inform			
To Persuade			
To Entertain			

L07 L08 Summarize the two most important ideas in this chapter that will help you improve your reading comprehension. _____

_____

_____

_____

Inferences

LO LEARNING OUTCOMES

After studying this chapter, you should be able to:

- **LO1** Describe Inferences as Educated Guesses
- **LO2** Define a Valid Inference
- **LO3** Apply the VALID Approach to Make Inferences and Avoid Invalid Conclusions
- **LO4** Make Inferences Based on Creative Expressions
- **LO5** Develop Textbook Skills: Inferences and Visual Aids in Textbooks
- **LO6** Apply Information Literacy Skills: Academic, Personal, and Career Applications of Inferences

 Before Reading About Inferences

Predict what you need to learn based on the learning outcomes for this chapter by completing the following chart.

What I already know: _____

_____

_____

_____ .

What I need to know: _____

_____

_____

_____

_____ .

Now, skim the chapter to find three additional topics that you have already studied. List those topics. _____

_____

Copy the following study outline in your notebook. Leave ample blank spaces between each topic. Use your own words to fill in the outline with information about each topic as you study about inferences.

Reading Skills Needed to Make VALID Inferences

    I. Verify facts.

  II. Assess prior knowledge.

III. Learn from text.

       A. Context clues

       B. Thought patterns

       C. Implied main ideas

 IV. Investigate bias.

  V. Detect contradictions.

LO1 Describe Inferences as Educated Guesses

Read the following passage.

> The air in the darkened movie theater felt chilly on Crystal's bare shoulders and arms. Her best friend, Julie, who had seen the movie three times already, had been smart to wear layered shirts, even if they were short-sleeved. Crystal placed the icy soft drink she had been holding in her chair's cup holder. Her right hand was freezing cold. She shivered as she watched the shark's fin, larger than life on the big screen, approaching the pretty young woman swimming in the ocean. As the music became faster and louder and the shark moved closer, a tingle ran up her spine. The shark struck. The victim screamed. At the same time, Crystal's right hand suddenly grabbed Julie's arm. Julie screamed too.

Which of the following statements might be true, based on the ideas in the passage?

_____ Crystal shivered because she was cold.

_____ Crystal shivered because she felt fear.

_____ Julie screamed because Crystal's cold hand surprised her.

_____ Julie screamed because she was afraid.

Did you choose the first three statements? Congratulations! You just made a set of educated guesses or **inferences**. An author suggests or **implies** an idea, and the reader comes to a conclusion and makes an inference about what the author means.

In the paragraph about Crystal and Julie, the first three statements are all firmly based on the information in the passage. However, the last statement is not backed by the supporting details. The facts point to Crystal's being cold and afraid, yet there is no hint of any fear on Julie's part. The only evidence given that could explain Julie's scream is Crystal's cold hand suddenly grabbing her.

 ## Define a Valid Inference

People constantly draw conclusions about what they notice. We observe, gather information, and make inferences all the time.

For example, as we communicate with other people, we read their body language and facial expressions to determine their moods, their comprehension, or their acceptance of what is being said. In general, we assume a frown means that someone is unhappy or puzzled. And we assume a smile means someone is pleased. Of course, these inferences have to be confirmed with all the evidence in context.

> An **inference** or **conclusion** is an idea that is suggested by the facts or details in a passage.

Just as we rely on inferences to make sense of our everyday life, we also rely on inferences in our work and academic lives. For example, scientists make inferences based on clues they gather from photographs, fossils, artifacts, and their own prior knowledge. Study the photo on the next page. Then make inferences to fill in the blanks in the caption.

A **valid inference** is a rational judgment based on details and evidence. The ability to make a valid inference is a vital life skill. Making valid inferences aids us in our efforts to care for our families, succeed in our jobs, and even guard our health.

VISUAL *VOCABULARY*

Based on the skull and teeth of this animal, the traits of its mouth include

(1) _____

_____.

Based on the traits of the mouth, this animal eats

(2) _____. This is the skull and teeth of a

(3) _____.

For example, doctors strive to make inferences about our health based on our symptoms. A red throat and swollen glands may lead a doctor to conclude that a patient has a strep infection. The doctor then orders a strep test to find out if her educated guess (a guess based on evidence) is correct. If it is correct, she prescribes an antibiotic to treat the infection.

> A **valid inference** is a logical conclusion based on evidence.

▶ **EXAMPLE**   Read the following passage. Write **V** beside the three valid inferences. (*Hint:* valid inferences are firmly supported by the details in the passage.)

¹At 15 years old, José is the oldest child in a family of five brothers and one sister. ²His family came to the United States from Mexico when José was 6 years old. ³His parents are still unable to speak much English. ⁴The only work his father and mother have been able to find is picking crops. ⁵They are migrant workers. ⁶To earn a living, the family constantly moves to find new crops to help harvest. ⁷Because their pay is based on how much they pick, often the older children join their parents in the fields and work from dawn to dusk. ⁸Over the years, José and his siblings have attended more than a dozen different schools. ⁹All of the children receive low scores and are several grade levels behind other children their age. ¹⁰José has learned to speak English fairly well, and he reads whenever he can find discarded newspapers, magazines, or books. ¹¹His mother and father always take José with them when they buy food or clothes.

_____ **1.** José and his family work hard and sacrifice to make a living.

_____ **2.** José's parents don't care about their children's education.

_____ **3.** Migrant work does not provide a stable lifestyle.

_____ **4.** José is not very smart.

_____ **5.** José's ability to speak English is a help to his parents.

EXPLANATION Statements 1, 3, and 5 are valid inferences firmly based on the information in the passage. It is valid to infer that picking crops is hard work. It is also valid to infer that the family's need to move around to follow the work demands sacrificing friends and stability. Finally, it is valid to infer that José's parents take him shopping because he speaks English better than they do, so he is a help to them.

Statements 2 and 4 are not based on the information in the passage. It is invalid to assume that José's parents don't care about education. The facts only support the idea that the family's need to move interferes with the children's education. It is also wrong to infer that José is not smart. In fact, his desire to read is a sign of intelligence.

Practice 1

Each of the following items contains a short passage and three inferences. In each item, only one inference is valid. In the space provided, write the letter of the inference that is clearly supported by each passage.

_____ **1.** Randall took great notes in class and from his textbooks. He studied every night for a week before the test. Of all the students in his class, Randall earned the highest grade on the test.
a. Randall is smarter than his classmates.
b. Randall is the teacher's favorite student.
c. Randall worked hard for his grade.

_____ **2.** Sandra was 20 pounds overweight, so she decided to cut out all carbohydrates (such as cereal, rice, potatoes, and bread) from her diet. Instead, she ate a bowl of fruit every morning and extra helpings of meat, colorful vegetables, and salads for lunch and dinner. Sandra lost the 20 pounds in four months.
a. Sandra did not look good before she changed her diet.
b. Eating too many carbohydrates may cause weight gain.
c. Sandra enjoyed her new diet.

_____ **3.** Mark takes charge of the TV's remote control every night. He watches three or four different sports events at the same time. During the commercials or when the sportscasters are talking, he switches to the other games. By doing this, Mark is able to follow racing, basketball, tennis, and golf.

    a. There is nothing else good on television, so Mark watches only sports.

    b. Mark is rude to his family.

    c. Mark is a dedicated sports fan.

LO3 Apply the VALID Approach to Make Inferences and Avoid Invalid Conclusions

Two of the most common pitfalls of making inferences are ignoring the facts and relying too much on personal opinions and bias. Often we are tempted to read too much into a passage because of our own prior experiences or beliefs. Of course, to make a valid inference, we must use clues based on logic and our experience. However, the most important resource must be the written text. As effective readers, our main goal is to find out what the author is saying, stating, or implying. Sound inferences come from orderly thinking. Effective readers learn to use the VALID thinking process to make valid inferences. The VALID approach avoids drawing false inferences or coming to invalid conclusions.

> An **invalid conclusion** is a false inference that is not based on the details, or facts in the text, or on reasonable thinking.

The VALID approach is made up of 5 steps:

Step 1: **V**erify and value the facts.
Step 2: **A**ssess prior knowledge.
Step 3: **L**earn from the text.
Step 4: **I**nvestigate for bias.
Step 5: **D**etect contradictions.

Step 1: Verify and Value the Facts

Develop a devotion to finding the facts. In Chapter 9, you learned to identify facts and to beware of false facts. You learned that authors may mix fact with opinion or use false information for their own purposes. Just as authors may make this kind of mistake, readers may, too. Readers may draw false inferences by mixing the author's facts with their own opinions or by misreading the facts. So it is important to find, verify, and stick to factual details. Once you have all the facts, only then can you begin to interpret the facts by making inferences.

> **EXAMPLE**   Read the following short passage. Then write **V** next to the two valid inferences firmly supported by the facts.

> [1]Korea has long been known as the "Eastern Land of Courtesy." [2]When happy, a Korean simply smiles or gently touches the one who brings the happiness. [3]When angry, a Korean simply stares directly at the person, and that person's humble smile is a powerful apology.

_____ **1.** Koreans are quiet and reserved people.

_____ **2.** Koreans show their emotions.

_____ **3.** Koreans are afraid of hurting the feelings of other people.

EXPLANATION   The first two statements are correct inferences based on the facts. However, there is no hint or clue that Koreans are afraid of hurting anyone's feelings. In fact, directly staring at someone when angry is a bold act in this Asian culture. The third statement goes beyond the facts without any reason to do so. Effective readers draw conclusions that are supported by the facts. <

VISUAL *VOCABULARY*

These protestors are members of _____.

a. a scientific research team
b. an animal rights group
c. a farmer's union

Step 2: Assess Prior Knowledge

Once you are sure of the facts, the next step is to draw on your prior knowledge. What you have already learned and experienced can help you make accurate inferences.

⊙ **EXAMPLE** Read the following excerpt of an article posted on a government website. Identify the facts. Check those facts against your own experience and understanding. Write **V** next to the three inferences firmly supported by the facts in the passage.

Chronic Media Multi-tasking Makes
It Harder to Focus

[1]You may think e-mailing, texting, talking on the phone and listening to music all at once is making you more efficient. [2]But new research suggests the opposite is true.

[3]Processing multiple streams of information from different sources of media is a challenge for the human brain, according to a recent study.

[4]New research shows that students who did the most multi-tasking were less able to focus and concentrate—even when they were trying to do only one task at a time.

[5]"The human mind is not really built for processing multiple streams of information," said study author Eyal Ophir. [6]Ophir is a researcher at Stanford University's Communication Between Humans and Interactive Media Lab. [7]"The ability to process a second stream of information is really limited."

[8]Researchers had 262 college students fill out a questionnaire about how often they multi-tasked. [9]Students then completed a series of tests that measured cognitive control. [10]Cognitive control is a mental process. [11]In this process, the brain directs attention, decides where to assign mental resources at a given moment, and determines what's important from the many bits of information being received.

[12]Students who were at the upper end of the media multi-tasking spectrum performed more poorly on all the tests than those who multi-tasked the least. [13]Interestingly, the students had similar overall intelligence and SAT scores.

[14]Computers are well-equipped to switch rapidly from one task to another. [15]But the human brain struggles with such demands.

_____ **1.** Eyal Ophir offers an expert opinion.

_____ **2.** People with short attention spans tend to multi-task.

_____ **3.** The reasons for the decreased cognitive control are clear.

_____ **4.** Multi-tasking damages cognitive control.

_____ **5.** People should multi-task less and instead build periods of time to focus on one thing.

_____ **6.** Multi-tasking involves doing one or more activities at once, including e-mailing, surfing the Web, writing on a computer, watching TV, texting, playing video games, listening to music, or talking on the phone.

EXPLANATION Items 1, 5, and 6 are valid inferences based on the information in the passage. However, the article offers no evidence or discussion about items 2, 3, or 4. For example, the article does not give any data about short attention spans as a cause for multi-tasking. Likewise, the article only discusses the decrease in cognitive control. It does not explain the reasons for the decrease. Finally, the article asserts that cognitive control is decreased, not damaged. The term "damaged" has long-term implications not addressed in the article. ◀

VISUAL *VOCABULARY*

Write a caption that states the cartoonist's message:

_____

_____

Step 3: Learn from the Text

When you value and verify facts, you are learning from the text. A valid inference is always based on what is stated or implied by the details in the text; in contrast, an invalid inference goes beyond the evidence. Thus, to make a valid inference, you must learn to rely on the information in the text. Many of the skills you have studied from previous chapters work together to enable you to learn from the text. For example, context clues unlock the meaning of an author's use of vocabulary. Becoming aware of thought patterns teaches you to look for the logical relationship between ideas. Learning about stated and implied main ideas trains you to examine supporting details. (In fact, you use inference skills to find the implied main idea.) In addition, tone and purpose reveal the author's bias and intent. (Again, you often use inference skills to grasp the author's tone and purpose.) As you apply these skills to your reading process, you are carefully listening to what the author has to say. You are learning from the text. Once you learn from the text, only then can you make a valid inference. The following examples show you how you learn from the text.

> ⊙ **EXAMPLE**   Read the following paragraph from a psychology textbook. Answer the questions that follow.

Textbook
Skills

¹Motives can arise from something inside yourself, such as when you keep studying because you find the subject matter interesting. ²Such activities are pursued as ends in themselves, simply because they are enjoyable, not because any external reward is attached. ³This type of motivation is known as **intrinsic motivation**. ⁴Other motives originate from outside. ⁵Some external stimulus, or **incentive**, pulls or entices you to act. ⁶When the desire to get a good grade—or to avoid a bad grade—causes you to study, the grade is serving as this kind of external incentive. ⁷When we act so as to gain some external reward or to avoid some undesirable consequence, we are pulled by **extrinsic motivation**. ⁸According to B. F. Skinner, a **reinforcer** is a result that increases the frequency of a behavior. ⁹Once the link between a behavior and a reinforcer has been established, the prospect of receiving the reinforcer again serves as an incentive to perform the behavior. ¹⁰For example, the prospect of getting a generous tip serves as an incentive for restaurant servers to serve their customers promptly and courteously.

—Adapted from Wood, Samuel E.; Wood, Ellen Green; Boyd, Denise G., *Mastering the World of Psychology*, 3rd ed., p. 289.

_____ **1.** The best synonym for the word *intrinsic* is
     a. enjoyable.   c. hidden.
     b. basic.   d. learned.

_____ **2.** The best synonym for the word *extrinsic* is
     a. profitable.   c. inessential.
     b. accidental.   d. essential.

_____ **3.** The overall thought pattern of the paragraph is
     a. listing.   c. definition and example.
     b. time order.   d. comparison and contrast.

_____ **4.** The author's tone is
     a. emotional.   b. neutral.

_____ **5.** The author's purpose is
     a. to inform the reader about the basic terms used to discuss motivation.
     b. to persuade the reader to analyze his or her own motivations.
     c. to entertain the reader with interesting details about motivation.

_____ **6.** Which of the following is a valid inference?
     a. An example of intrinsic motivation is a person donating money to a college to build a library, provided the library bears the name of the donor.
     b. An example of extrinsic motivation is a child reading one book a week to avoid losing television privileges.
     c. An example of intrinsic motivation is a person secretly donating money to Haiti to help the survivors of the earthquake.

EXPLANATION Compare your answers to the following: **1.** Something that comes from within or "inside" is basic or inherent. It is the very nature of the being; thus the correct answer is (b) basic. **2.** Because the paragraph makes it clear that extrinsic is the opposite of intrinsic, we can infer that anything extrinsic is (c) inessential. **3.** The overall thought pattern is (c) definition and example as indicated by the bold print, the details, and the phrase "for example." **4.** The author's tone is (b) neutral. **5.** The author's purpose is (a) to inform. **6.** Based on the definitions and examples in the paragraph, (c) is the only valid inference. ◐

A food treat is _____ that taps into a dog's _____ motivation to perform a trick.

   a. an incentive
   b. a reinforcer
   c. intrinsic
   d. extrinsic

Step 4: Investigate for Bias

One of the most important steps in making a valid inference is confronting your biases. Each of us possesses strong personal views that influence the way we process information. Often our personal views are based on prior experiences. For example, if we have had a negative prior experience with a used car salesperson, we may become suspicious and stereotype all used car salespeople as dishonest. Sometimes, our biases are based on the way in which we were raised. Some people register as Democrats or Republicans and vote for only Democratic or Republican candidates simply because their parents were members of either the Democratic or Republican party. To make a valid inference, we must investigate our responses for bias. Our bias can shape our reading of the author's meaning. To investigate for bias, note biased words and replace them with factual details as you form your conclusions.

> **EXAMPLE** Read the following paragraph. Investigate the list of inferences that follow for bias. Underline biased words. Mark each item as follows: **V** if the inference is valid or **I** if the inference is invalid due to bias.

The Five Pillars of Islam

¹The guiding principles of the Islamic faith are known as the Five Pillars of Islam. ²Muslims, the believers of Islam, devote their lives to these principles. ³The first principle is called *shahadah* (shah-HAH-dah). ⁴*Shahadah* is the prayer of faith that says, "There is no God but Allah, and Muhammad is his messenger." ⁵The second rule is known as *salat* (sah-LAHT); *salat* is

the act of praying five times a day to Allah. ⁶Prayer occurs at dawn, noon, afternoon, dusk, and night. ⁷The third principle is *saum* (sah-OHM); *saum* is a fast from food or drink that lasts 30 days during the holy month of Ramadan. ⁸The fourth pillar is called *zakat* (zeh-KAHT); this is the act of giving money to the poor and needy. ⁹The final principle of Islam is *haj* (HAHDJ); this is the journey of pilgrimage that Muslims all over the world must make to the holy city of Mecca in Saudi Arabia at least once in their lifetime.

_____ **1.** *Shahadah* is the word for a very specific prayer that is always worded the same way.

_____ **2.** Islam teaches one to seek God and to help others.

_____ **3.** Islam takes discipline to practice.

_____ **4.** Islam is a radical belief that teaches people to think selfishly of themselves first.

EXPLANATION Items 1, 2, and 3 are (**V**) valid inferences based on the details in the paragraph. Item 1 includes the qualifier *always,* which usually indicates a bias. However, based on the fact that the paragraph gives the name and exact wording of the prayer, it is reasonable to infer that the exact wording is the unique trait of the prayer and always used. Item 4 is an (**I**) invalid inference. This sentence includes two biased words: *radical* and *selfishly*. This biased statement is not grounded in the details. ◁

VISUAL *VOCABULARY*

A crowd of poor people in Bangladesh gather near the house of a rich man in anticipation. Muslims pay _____ (two and a half percent of their savings) to the poor according to Islamic law.

a. shahadah
b. salat
c. zakat
d. haj

Step 5: Detect Contradictions

Have you ever misjudged a situation or had a wrong first impression? For example, have you ever assumed a person was conceited or rude, only to find out later that he or she was acutely shy? Many times, there may be a better explanation for a set of facts than the first one that comes to mind. The effective reader hunts for the most reasonable explanation. The best way to do this is to consider other explanations that could logically contradict your first impression.

⊘ **EXAMPLE** Read the following list of behaviors. Then write as many explanations for the behaviors as you can think of on the lines below.

- Slurred words
- Poor balance
- Slow movement
- Uncontrolled shaking in limbs

- Rigid muscles and stooped posture
- Fatigue or tiredness
- Depression

_____

_____

EXPLANATION Some people may think the behaviors in this list describe an alcoholic or a drug addict. But the list is actually a list of symptoms for Parkinson's disease, a brain disease that affects body movement. Often, people with this disease, like actor Michael J. Fox, also suffer from depression. Alcoholics and drug addicts do share most of the listed symptoms, except for rigid muscles and stooped posture. People with Parkinson's disease struggle with muscles that become stiff and even freeze into place.

A reader who does not think about other possible views can easily jump to a wrong conclusion. Effective readers consider all the facts and all the possible explanations for those facts. Effective readers look for contradictions.

Use the 5 VALID steps to think your way through to logical conclusions based on sound inferences: (1) verify and value the facts, (2) assess prior knowledge, (3) learn from the text, (4) investigate for bias, and (5) detect contradictions. ◉

Based on the details in the image, we can reasonably come to the conclusion that this is a photo of _____.

    a. sea fan coral

    b. a pygmy seahorse

    c. a tree in autumn

Practice 2

Read the following passage from a college textbook about nursing. Investigate the list of inferences that follow for bias. Underline biased words. Mark each inference as follows: **V** for a valid inference firmly supported by the facts, **I** for an invalid inference.

Textbook
Skills

Definitions of Nursing

[1]Florence Nightingale defined nursing nearly 150 years ago as "the act of utilizing the environment of the patient to assist him in his recovery." [2]Nightingale considered a clean, well-ventilated, and quiet environment essential for recovery. [3]Often considered the first nurse theorist, Nightingale raised the status of nursing through education. [4]Nurses were no longer untrained housekeepers. [5]Instead they were people educated in the care of the sick.

[6]Virginia Henderson was one of the first modern nurses to define nursing. [7]She wrote, "The unique function of the nurse is to assist the individual, sick or well, in the performance of those activities contributing to health or its recovery (or to peaceful death) that he would perform unaided if he had the necessary strength, will, or knowledge, and to do this in such a way as to help him gain independence as rapidly as possible." [8]Like Nightingale, Henderson described nursing in relation to

the client and the client's environment. [9]Unlike Nightingale, Henderson saw the nurse as concerned with both healthy and ill individuals. [10]She acknowledged that nurses interact with clients even when recovery may not be feasible. [11]She also mentioned the teaching and advocacy roles of the nurse.

[12]In the latter half of the 20th century, a number of nurse theorists developed their own theoretical definitions of nursing. [13]Theoretical definitions are important. [14]They go beyond simplistic common definitions. [15]They describe what nursing is and the interrelationship among nurses, nursing, the client, the environment, and the intended client outcome: health.

—Adapted from Berman, Audrey J., Snyder, Shirlee,
Kozier, Barbara J., and Erb, Glenora, *Kozier & Erb's
Fundamentals of Nursing*, 8th ed., p. 11.

_____ **1.** Florence Nightingale never focused on preventing illness, just treating illness.

_____ **2.** Nursing focuses only on the sick.

_____ **3.** Nursing should include assisted suicide for the terminally ill to promote a peaceful death.

_____ **4.** A theoretical definition of nursing serves as a mission statement for nurses.

_____ **5.** Nursing involves treating the whole person, not just the symptoms of an illness.

(LO4) Make Inferences Based on Creative Expressions

As you have learned, nonfiction writing, such as in textbooks and news articles, directly states the author's point. Everything is done to make sure that the meanings are clear and unambiguous (not open to different interpretations). However, in many other types of writing, both fiction and nonfiction, authors use creative expression to suggest layers of meaning. Creative expressions are also known as literary devices. The following chart is made up of a few common literary devices, their meanings, and an example of each.

Creative Expression: Literary Devices

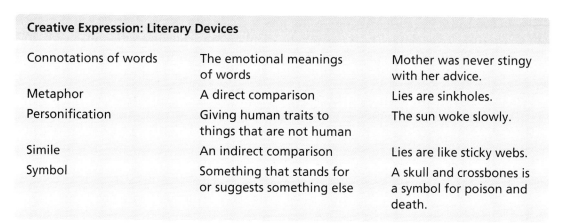

Connotations of words	The emotional meanings of words	Mother was never stingy with her advice.
Metaphor	A direct comparison	Lies are sinkholes.
Personification	Giving human traits to things that are not human	The sun woke slowly.
Simile	An indirect comparison	Lies are like sticky webs.
Symbol	Something that stands for or suggests something else	A skull and crossbones is a symbol for poison and death.

By using these devices, a writer creates a vivid mental picture in the reader's mind. When a creative expression is used, a reader must infer the point the writer is making from the effects of the image. The following paragraph is the introduction to an essay about alcoholism. Notice its use of literary devices. After you read, write a one-sentence statement of the author's main idea for this paragraph.

Trapped in the Darkness

[1]Jean squeezed her eyes tight against the painful light that poured into the room with daybreak. [2]She groaned, rolled over, and buried her head in her pillow. [3]Hiding was useless; her misery followed her. [4]As she lay there, fighting the jumping nausea, she tried to recall the night before, but the events seemed shrouded in a dense fog. [5]She lifted her fingers to press on her temples; she had her usual tequila headache. [6]Her stomach twisted with familiar shame. [7]I *am* going to quit, she promised herself—again. [8]She groaned and curled into the darkness of her blanket.

This paragraph uses several creative expressions. Darkness is often used as a symbol of death, pain and suffering, or denial. All of these meanings could apply to Jean's situation. Light is often used as a symbol for wisdom and truth. The use of contrast between dark and light suggests many meanings. The painful light (sentence 1) could represent Jean's inability to face the truth or act wisely. The phrase "jumping nausea" (sentence 4) is the use of personification. Live beings jump, so to give such an action to nausea is to give it lifelike qualities. The phrase "events seemed shrouded in a dense fog" (sentence 4) is a simile.

Perhaps the author is comparing Jean's memory to a fog. Or maybe the author is referring to Jean being drunk the night before. The phrase "tequila headache" (sentence 5) is a metaphor for a hangover. Based on all the details, it is valid to infer that Jean has a drinking problem. The author could have simply stated "Jean suffers from a serious drinking problem." But the creative expressions intensify the meaning. And they suggest many levels of meaning. Therefore, as an effective reader, carefully consider the shades and levels of meaning while reading examples of creative writing.

> **EXAMPLE**   A fable is a short story that makes a pointed statement. Read the following short fable written by Aesop in the sixth century B.C.E. Then answer the questions that follow it.

The North Wind and the Sun

¹A dispute arose between the North Wind and the Sun, each claiming that he was stronger than the other. ²At last they agreed to try their powers on a traveler, to see which could strip him of his cloak the fastest. ³The North Wind had the first try; gathering up all his force for the attack, he came whirling furiously down upon the man and caught up the man's cloak as though he would **wrest** it from the man in a single effort. ⁴But the harder he blew, the more closely the man wrapped the cloak around himself. ⁵Then came the turn of the Sun. ⁶At first, he beamed gently upon the traveler, who soon unclasped his cloak and walked on with it hanging loosely about his shoulders. ⁷Then the Sun shone forth in full strength, and the man, before he had gone many steps, was glad to throw his cloak right off and complete his journey lightly clad.

1. Choose the three valid inferences that are firmly based on the information in the passage by writing a **V** next to each one.

    _____   a. The North Wind and the Sun are given human traits.

    _____   b. The traveler is not very smart.

    _____   c. The North Wind uses force to try to make the man take off his cloak.

    _____   d. The Sun uses heat to influence the man to take off his cloak.

_____ 2. Based on context clues, we can infer that the meaning of the word *wrest* in sentence 3 is

    a. wrap.   b. rip.   c. give.

_____ **3.** Based on the details in the passage, we can conclude that the implied main idea of the passage is
   a. persuasion is better than force.
   b. the Sun is harsher than the North Wind.
   c. humans are easily controlled by nature.

EXPLANATION

1. The correct inferences are (a), (c), and (d). Often creative writers give human traits to things that are not human. In this fable, the wind and the sun, like some humans, are in competition with one another, each wanting to be the stronger one. The text clearly implies the North Wind's use of force in words such as *force, attack, whirling,* and *wrest.* However, the Sun's efforts are described with words such as *gently* and *shone forth.* There is nothing to suggest that the traveler is not smart. Instead, he acts very logically.

2. The words *force* and *attack* indicate that the best meaning of the word *wrest* is (b) "rip."

3. The main idea suggested by the details is (a) persuasion is better than force. To make logical inferences, we must use our common sense and life experiences. Based on our own experiences, we know that the wind and the sun are both strong, but they are harsh in different ways. Although humans are influenced by nature, that point is a supporting detail and not the main idea.

Practice 3

Read the following poem by D. H. Lawrence. Choose the inferences that are most logical, based on the details in the poem.

Vocabulary Preview

verge (4): edge; border

A Winter's Tale

Yesterday the fields were only grey with scattered snow,
And now the longest grass-leaves hardly emerge;
Yet her deep footsteps mark the snow, and go
On towards the pines at the hills' white verge.

5   I cannot see her, since the mist's white scarf
      Obscures the dark wood and the dull orange sky;
      But she's waiting, I know, impatient and cold, half
      Sobs struggling into her frosty sigh.

      Why does she come so promptly, when she must know
10   That she's only the nearer to the inevitable farewell;
      The hill is steep, on the snow my steps are slow—
      Why does she come, when she knows what I have to tell?

—<http://www.publicdomainpoems.com/winterstale.html>

_____ **1.** What has happened between yesterday and today?
      a. The grassy field has been mowed.
      b. It has turned wintry cold.
      c. It has snowed.

_____ **2.** Who is the speaker referring to by "she" and "her"?
      a. Mother Earth
      b. a woman with whom he has a romantic relationship
      c. a woman with whom he has fought

_____ **3.** Which line helps you infer that two people have arranged to meet?
      a. "Yet her deep footsteps mark the snow"
      b. "Sobs struggling into her frosty sigh"
      c. "Why does she come so promptly"

_____ **4.** What does the speaker "have to tell" (line 12)?
      a. He is breaking up with the woman.
      b. He must go far away.
      c. He has become ill and is near the end of his life.

_____ **5.** Why do you think the poem is set during winter?
      a. A snowy hill and woods create a beautiful setting.
      b. The speaker is thus able to see footsteps in the snow.
      c. Winter is a cold, lifeless time.

LO5 Develop Textbook Skills: Inferences and Visual Aids in Textbooks

Textbook authors often use pictures, photos, and graphs to imply an idea. These visuals are used to reinforce the information in that section of the textbook.

▲ Dilbert @ 1997 Reprinted by permission of United Features Syndicate, Inc.

> EXAMPLE This "Dilbert" cartoon was reprinted in a textbook. Based on the cartoon, what was the topic of the chapter?

_____ marriage and communication in intimate relationships

_____ women and low self-esteem

_____ effects of nonverbal communication

EXPLANATION The woman in the cartoon is obviously self-confident and outspoken about what she wants, so the chapter is not about women and low self-esteem. In addition, the artist did not include any gestures in the cartoon, so the chapter is not about the effect of nonverbal communication. Indeed, the humor is based on the kind of communication the woman expects. The cartoon was in a chapter about marriage and communication in intimate relationships. **<**

Practice 4

Study the figure on page 520, taken from the textbook *Access to Health*. Then answer the questions.

_____ **1.** What is the topic of the chapter?
   a. benefits of exercise
   b. overall health of a man
   c. causes of cancer

2. Write a caption in a complete sentence that best states the implied main idea of the figure.

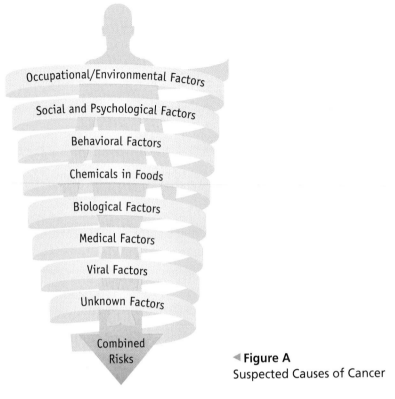

Occupational/Environmental Factors

Social and Psychological Factors

Behavioral Factors

Chemicals in Foods

Biological Factors

Medical Factors

Viral Factors

Unknown Factors

Combined
Risks

◀ **Figure A**
Suspected Causes of Cancer

—Rebecca J. Donatelle. *Access to Health,* 7th ed., p. 432.

Apply Information Literacy Skills

 Academic, Personal, and Career Applications of Inferences

Information literacy relies upon the ability to make inferences. For example, think about how to find information about a specific topic, such as bullying. First, you rely on what you need to know to direct your search. Do you need to know the traits of a bully, the ways to cope with a bully, or the causes of bullying? Next, you make an educated guess about the key words related to bullying that would help you find the information you need. Then once you locate information, you infer the reliability of the source. You look for clues to determine if the source is biased or factual. As you read the information, you infer the importance and relevance of details based on what you need to know. Ultimately,

you decide the best way to apply or use what you have learned. You will use the skills that you learned in this chapter in academic, personal, and career situations. For example, you will:

- Recognize your own need to make an inference.
- Determine if a conclusion is valid.
- Use inferences to create meaning.

Academic Application

Assume you are taking the college course Interpersonal Communication. Your professor has assigned the following passage and skill building exercise from your textbook.

- **Before Reading:** Skim the passage. Read the instructions for the Skill Building Exercise: Nonverbal Impression Management.
- **During Reading:** Highlight the details in the passage that will help you complete the skill building exercise.
- **After Reading:** In the space following the passage, complete the skill building exercise.

Forming Impressions

[1]Nonverbal communication is communication without words.

[2]It is, in part, through the nonverbal communications of others that you form impressions of them. [3]Based on a person's body size, skin color, and dress, as well as on the way the person smiles, maintains eye contact, and expresses himself or herself facially, you form impressions—you judge who the person is and what the person is like.

[4]And, at the same time that you form impressions of others, you are also managing the impressions they form of you. [5]As explained in the discussion of impression management, in Chapter 3 you use different strategies to achieve different impressions. [6]And of course many of these strategies involve nonverbal messages. [7]Also, as noted earlier, each of these strategies may be used to present a false self and to deceive others. [8]For example:

- [9]*To be liked* you might smile, pat another on the back, and shake hands warmly.
- [10]*To be believed* you might use focused eye contact, a firm stance, and open gestures.
- [11]*To excuse failure* you might look sad, cover your face with your hands, and shake your head.

- [12]*To secure help* while indicating helplessness, you might use open hand gestures, a puzzled look, and inept movements.
- [13]*To hide faults* you might avoid self-touching gestures that might reveal doubts or lack of confidence.
- [14]*To be followed* you might dress the part of a leader or put your diploma or awards where others can see them.
- [15]*To confirm self-image and to communicate it to others*, you might dress in certain ways or decorate your apartment with things that reflect your personality.

Skill Building Exercise: Nonverbal Impression Management

[16]Impression management is one of the major functions nonverbal communication serves. [17]Consider how you would manage yourself nonverbally in the following situations. [18]Choose one of these situations. [19]Indicate the nonverbal cues you'd use to create these impressions as well as the nonverbal cues you'd be especially careful to avoid.

1. [20]You want a job at a conservative, prestigious law firm.
2. [21]You want a part in a movie in which you'd play a homeless drug addict.
3. [22]You're single, and you're applying to adopt a child.
4. [23]You want to ask another student to go out with you.
5. [24]You want to convince your romantic partner that you did not see your ex last night; you were working.

[25]*Interpersonal messages are a combination of verbal and nonverbal signals; even subtle variations in eye movements or intonation can drastically change the impression communicated.*

—Adapted from DeVito, Joseph A., *The Interpersonal Communication Book*, 10th ed., pp. 132–133.

Nonverbal Impression Management: _____

_____

_____

_____

_____

Personal Application

Assume you are a parent of a student attending high school. The Board of Education is considering creating a new policy that will require all students in all schools to wear school uniforms. You are not sure what stand to take on this issue, so you have searched the Internet for information and found the following article.

- **Before Reading:** Skim the passage. Note the information about the source. Rate the reliability of the information by circling one of the following: Very Reliable, Somewhat Reliable, or Not Reliable. Be prepared to explain your reasons.

- **During Reading:** Underline the key details.

- **After Reading:** In the space following the passage, take a stand for or against school uniforms. State your reasons.

Source information: GreatSchools is a national nonprofit whose mission is to inspire and guide parents to become effective champions of their children's education at home and in their communities.

Do Uniforms Make Schools Better?

[1]Researchers are divided over how much of an impact, if any, dress policies have upon student learning. [2]A 2004 book makes the case that uniforms do not improve school safety or academic discipline. [3]A 2005 study, on the other hand, indicates that in some Ohio high schools uniforms may have improved graduation and attendance rates, although no improvements were observed in academic performance.

The Pros and Cons of School Uniforms

According to proponents, school uniforms:

- Help prevent gangs from forming on campus
- Encourage discipline
- Help students resist peer pressure to buy trendy clothes
- Help identify intruders in the school
- Diminish economic and social barriers between students
- Increase a sense of belonging and school pride
- Improve attendance

Opponents contend that school uniforms:

- Violate a student's right to freedom of expression
- Are simply a Band-Aid on the issue of school violence

- Make students a target for bullies from other schools
- Are a financial burden for poor families
- Are an unfair additional expense for parents who pay taxes for a free public education
- Are difficult to enforce in public schools

—Wilde, Marian. "Do Uniforms Make Schools Better?"
by Marian Wilde, www.greatschools.org. Reprinted
by permission of GreatSchools, Inc.

Career Application

Assume you have been offered two jobs, one in a candy factory and one at a retail clothing store. As you think about which job to take, consider the following facts about your personal situation: You do not own a car; thus you must take the bus or walk to work. The factory job requires an hour bus ride, including transfers. The retail clothing store is at a local strip plaza within walking distance to your home. The factory job site has a cafeteria on site. The strip plaza is near several fast food restaurants.

- **Before Reading:** Skim the job descriptions to get an overview of pay, job requirements, transportation needs, and personal expenses.

- **During Reading:** Complete a comparison-contrast chart of the details for both jobs. Be sure to include the "facts about your personal situation."

- **After Reading:** In the space following the passage, indicate which job you will take. State your reasons.

Candy Factory Job Description: Worker is responsible for a wide range of activities such as candy processing, packaging, and operating machines. Work hours are 12-hour shifts with 4 shifts scheduled per week. Factory provides uniform and hard hat. Worker provides steel-toed boots. Rate of pay is $12.00 per hour.

Retail Clothing Store: Employee is responsible for a wide range of activities such as helping customers find what they want, operating cash registers, bagging purchases, arranging displays of products, restocking shelves. Work hours are 8-hour shifts, with 5 scheduled shifts per week. Shifts may include evenings, weekends, holidays, and other peak sales periods. Employee is required to wear one article of the store's clothing per shift. Employees get 50% off the price of the store's clothing. Rate of pay is $8.50 per hour.

	Candy Factory	Retail Clothing Store

My Decision: _____

_____

_____

_____

_____

Score (number correct) _____ × 10 = _____%

Visit MyReadingLab to take this test online and receive feedback and guidance on your answers.

Making Inferences

A. Study the cartoon. Then answer the questions.

"Because my genetic programming prevents me from stopping to ask directions—that's why!"

_____ **1.** The cartoon is about
          a. communication.   c. differences between men and women.
          b. cars.

2–4. Write **V** for valid by the three inferences that are firmly supported by the details in the cartoon.

_____ The couple is getting along well.

_____ The couple is lost in the country.

_____ The woman has asked the man why he doesn't ask for directions.

_____ The woman knows where they are.

_____ The cartoon suggests that most men do not ask for directions when they are lost.

B. Read the following textbook passage. Write **V** for valid by two inferences firmly supported by details in the passage.

5–6.   [1]The U.S. Constitution's opening line, "We the people," ended, at least for the time being, the question of the source of the government's power. [2]It came directly from the people. [3]The Constitution then explained the need for the new outline of government. [4]The words "in Order to form a more perfect Union" indirectly acknowledges the weakness of the Articles of Confederation (a loose "league of friendship" among the thirteen independent colonies) in governing a growing nation. [5]Next, the optimistic goals of the Framers for the new nation were set out to "establish Welfare, and secure the Blessing of Liberty to ourselves and our Posterity."

[6]The structure of the new national government owed much to the writings of the French philosopher Montesquieu (1689–1755). [7]He advocated distinct functions for each branch of government, called separation of powers, with a system of checks and balances between each branch. [8]Separation of powers is simply a way of parceling out power among the three branches of government. [9]Its three key features are:

- [10]Three distinct branches of government: the legislative, the executive, and the judicial.
- [11]Three separately staffed branches of government to exercise their function.
- [12]Constitutional equality and independence of each branch.

[13]The legislative branch, Congress, passes all federal laws. [14]Passes the federal budget. [15]Declares war. [16]Establish lower federal courts and the number of judges. [17]The executive branch enforces federal laws and court orders. [18]Proposes laws to Congress. [19]Makes foreign treaties. [20]Nominates officers of the U.S. government and federal judges. [21]Serves as commander in chief of the armed forces. [22]Pardons people convicted in federal courts or grants reprieves. [23]The Judicial Branch interprets federal law and U.S. Constitution. [24]Reviews the decisions of lower state and federal courts.

—Adapted from O'Connor, Karen, et al., *American Government: Roots and Reform*, pp. 45–46.

_____   The French philosopher Montesquieu was one of the writers of the U.S. Constitution.

_____   The President of the United States represents the executive branch of government.

_____   Congress may refuse to pass or fund a law suggested by the President.

_____   The judges of the Supreme Court are elected into office.

C. **7–10.** Write **V** for valid by the four inferences that are firmly based on the information in the label that follows the paragraph.

Reading Nutritional Labels

[1]The first place to start when you look at the Nutrition Facts panel is the serving size and the number of servings in the package. [2]Serving sizes are given in familiar units, such as cups or pieces, followed by the metric amount, such as the number of grams. [3]Serving sizes are based on the amount of food people typically eat, which makes them realistic and easy to compare to similar foods. [4]Calories are a measure of how much energy you get from a serving of this food. [5]The nutrients listed first are the ones Americans generally eat in adequate amounts, or even too much. [6]Eating too much fat or too much sodium may increase your risk of certain chronic diseases, like heart disease, some cancers, or high blood pressure. [7]Eating too many calories is linked to being overweight and obesity. [8]Americans often don't get enough dietary fiber, vitamin A, vitamin C, calcium, and iron in their diets. [9]Eating enough of these nutrients can improve your health, and they help reduce the risk of some diseases. [10]For example, getting enough calcium can reduce the risk of osteoporosis. [11]This disease causes bones to become brittle and break as one ages. [12]The Percent Daily Value section of the Nutrition Facts panel tells you whether the nutrient (fat, sodium, fiber, etc.) in a serving of food adds a lot or a little to your total daily diet.

—"Guidance on How to Understand and Use the Nutrition Facts Panel on Food Labels," U.S. Food and Drug Administration: Center for Food Safety and Applied Nutrition, June 2000.

▼Sample Label for
Macaroni and Cheese

Nutrition Facts

Serving Size 1 cup (228g)
Serving Per Container 2

Amount Per Serving	
Calories 250	Calories from Fat 110

	% Daily Value*
Total Fat 12g	18%
Saturated Fat 3g	15%
Cholesterol 30mg	10%
Sodium 470mg	20%
Total Carbohydrate 31g	10%
Dietary Fiber 0g	0%
Sugars 5g	
Protein 5g	

Vitamin A	4%
Vitamin C	2%
Calcium	20%
Iron	4%

*Percent Daily Values are based on a 2000 calorie diet. Your Daily Values may be higher or lower depending on your calorie needs:

	Calories:	2,000	2,500
Total Fat	Less than	85g	80g
Sat Fat	Less than	20g	25g
Cholesterol	Less than	300mg	300mg
Sodium	Less than	2,400mg	2,400mg
Total Carbohydrate		300g	375g
Dietary Fiber		25g	30g

_____ Food labels are designed to make it easier for you to use nutrition facts to make quick, informed food choices that contribute to a healthy diet.

_____ Macaroni and cheese is not a healthy food.

_____ An entire package of macaroni and cheese has a total fat of 24g.

_____ Macaroni and cheese does not contain enough iron to be of value in a healthy diet.

_____ Macaroni and cheese has 20% of the recommended daily amount of calcium for a healthy diet.

_____ Macaroni and cheese is a good food to eat to reduce the risk of osteoporosis.

_____ A person who eats macaroni and cheese runs the risk of becoming obese.

REVIEW TEST 2

Score (number correct) _____ × 20 = _____%

Visit MyReadingLab to take this test online and receive feedback and guidance on your answers.

Making Inferences

Read the poem from *Spoon River Anthology* by Edgar Lee Masters. Then answer the questions that follow it.

Mrs. Charles Bliss

REVEREND WILEY advised me not to divorce him
For the sake of the children,
And Judge Somers advised him the same.
So we stuck to the end of the path.
5   But two of the children thought he was right,
And two of the children thought I was right.
And the two who sided with him blamed me,
And the two who sided with me blamed him,
And they grieved for the one they sided with.
10   And all were torn with the guilt of judging,
And tortured in soul because they could not admire
Equally him and me.
Now every gardener knows that plants grown in cellars
Or under stones are twisted and yellow and weak.
15   And no mother would let her baby suck
Diseased milk from her breast.
Yet preachers and judges advise the raising of souls
Where there is no sunlight, but only twilight,
No warmth, but only dampness and cold—
20   Preachers and judges!

—<http://www.bartleby.com/84/88.html>

_____   **1.** The overall tone of the poem is one of
a. guilt.
b. bitterness.
c. acceptance.

_____   **2.** The path referred to in line 4, "end of the path," is
a. marriage.
b. life.
c. a road.

_____   **3.** The metaphor "where there is no sunlight, but only twilight" in line 18 refers to
a. an unhappy home.
b. a poor home.
c. a dark home.

_____   **4.** Based on the meaning of the poem, which implies irony?
a. the name "Mrs. Charles Bliss"
b. "But two of the children thought he was right"
c. "Preachers and judges!"

_____   **5.** What is the main idea of the poem?
a. Marriage is difficult and requires hard work.
b. Preachers and judges never offer good advice.
c. Staying married for the sake of the children may not be to their benefit.

REVIEW TEST 3

Score (number correct) _____ × 25 = _____ %

Visit MyReadingLab to take this test online and receive feedback and guidance on your answers.

Read the following feature about DNA testing from a college biology textbook. Then write **V** for valid by the four inferences that are firmly supported by the details in the passage.

Guilty or Innocent?

[1]"IT'S OK TO CRY," Innocence Project attorney Aliza Kaplan told Dennis Maher, on his way to court for his release from prison in 2003. [2]Maher seemed calm as District Attorney Martha Coakley asked the judge to dismiss all of the charges for which Maher had been imprisoned for

19 years, 2 months, and 29 days. [3]The judge ordered Maher's immediate release. [4]Although outwardly composed in court, Maher and his family hugged and wept in the hall outside. [5]"We're a bunch of crybabies," said his father, Donat. [6]Nineteen years earlier, Maher had been convicted of two counts of rape and one of attempted rape. [7]As it turned out, his only crimes were to live in the vicinity of the rapes, to wear a red sweatshirt, and to look like the real assailant. [8]All three victims picked Maher out of lineups. [9]How can three people all identify the wrong man? [10]It was dark, the assaults were swift, and, obviously, the women were tremendously stressed. [11]In fact, contrary to popular belief, eyewitness testimony is really very unreliable. [12]Various studies have found error rates for eyewitness identification from about 35% to 80%, depending on the conditions used in the experiments.

[13]You have probably already guessed what led to Maher's eventual exoneration—DNA evidence. [14]In 1993, while watching the *Phil Donahue Show* in prison, Maher heard about the Innocence Project, founded in 1992 by Barry Scheck and Peter Neufeld of the Benjamin Cardozo School of Law at Yeshiva University. [15]He wrote to Scheck asking for help. [16]Scheck agreed, but the Innocence Project hit a brick wall—no biological evidence was available for any of the cases.

[17]Finally, 7 years later, an Innocence Project law student found the semen-stained underwear of one of the rape victims, lost in a box in a courthouse storage room. [18]A few months later, a semen specimen from the second rape turned up as well. [19]DNA profiling proved that Maher was not the assailant in either case. [20]DNA profiling is often considered the gold standard of evidence, because of its extremely low error rate. [21]Thanks to the power of DNA profiling, Dennis Maher is now a free man. [22]Many people exonerated after years in prison have a hard time adjusting to life "outside." [23]Maher, however, is a real success story. [24]Soon after his release, he got a job servicing trucks for Waste Management, a trash pickup and recycling company. [25]He met his wife, Melissa, through an online dating service, using the name DNADennis. [26]They have two children, one named Aliza after his Innocence Project attorney. [27]He's even a movie star of sorts, having been featured in *After Innocence*, an award-winning film following the lives of eight exonerated men. [28]Does Maher harbor any resentment against the system that cost him 19 years of his life? [29]Sure. [30]As he puts it, "I lost what I can never get back." [31]But he also says, "I don't have time to be angry. [32]If I'm an angry person, I won't have the things I have in my life."

—Audesirk, Teresa; Audesirk, Gerald; Byers, Bruce E., *Biology: Life on Earth with Physiology*, 9th ed., pp. 240, 261.

_____   **1.** Police and prosecutors knew Dennis Maher was innocent.

_____   **2.** The tone of sentence 7 is slightly sarcastic.

_____   **3.** Stress can affect what people think they saw.

_____   **4.** The tone of sentence 12 is subjective.

_____   **5.** Biological evidence is necessary in order to run DNA tests.

_____   **6.** The author believes that Maher should be angry about his false conviction and imprisonment.

_____   **7.** One purpose of this passage is to explain how DNA testing works.

_____   **8.** One purpose of this passage is to inform readers of how the science of DNA has aided the criminal justice system.

VISUAL *VOCABULARY*

The best meaning of the word **exonerated** in sentence 21 of the passage is: _____.

a. examined
b. freed

SUMMARY RESPONSE

Restate the author's central idea in your own words. Begin your summary response with the following: *The central idea of "Guilty or Innocent?" by Auder-sirk and Byers is …*

WHAT DO YOU THINK?

How did Dennis Maher's story affect you? Did you put yourself in his place and consider how you would feel if you were convicted of a crime you did not commit? Assume you live in a state that enforces capital punishment. Write a letter to your state representative that argues the importance of including DNA based evidence, in addition to eyewitness testimony. Use details from the passage the support your argument. Consider the following points:

- Explain why eyewitness testimony is considered unreliable.
- Describe the benefits of DNA profiling.

REVIEW TEST 4

Score (number correct) _____ × 10 = _____%

Visit MyReadingLab to take this test online and receive feedback and guidance on your answers.

Making Inferences

Before you read the following passage from a college history textbook, skim the passage. Answer the Before Reading questions. Then read the passage and answer the After Reading questions.

Textbook
Skills

The Great Depression

[1]The **prosperity** of the 1920s came to an abrupt halt in October 1929. [2]The stock market, which had boomed during the decade, suddenly faltered. [3]Investors who had borrowed heavily to take part in the buying **mania** that had swept Wall Street were suddenly forced to sell their securities to cover their loans. [4]The wave of selling triggered an avalanche of trading.

[5]On October 24, later known as Black Thursday, nearly 13 million shares were traded as **high-fliers** such as RCA and Westinghouse lost nearly half their value. [6]The stock market rallied for the next two days, but on Tuesday, October 29, the downslide resumed. [7]Frightened sellers dumped more than 16 million shares, and the industrial stock price average fell by 43 points. [8]The panic ended in November, with stocks at 1927 levels. [9]For the next four years, there was a steady drift downward. [10]By 1932, prices were at only 20 percent of their 1920 highs.

[11]The Great Depression that followed the crash of 1929 was the most devastating economic blow ever suffered by the nation. [12]It lasted

Vocabulary Preview

prosperity (1): wealth

mania (3): craze

deprivation (15): lack

optimistic (20): hopeful

vagrants (32): homeless persons

for more than ten years, and it dominated every aspect of American life during the 1930s. [13]Unemployment rose to 12 million by 1932. [14]Though it dipped midway through the decade, it still stood at 10 million by 1939. [15]Children grew up thinking that economic **deprivation** was the norm rather than the exception in America. [16]Year after year, people kept looking for a return to wealth. [17]But the outlook remained **dismal**. [18]The Depression loosened its grip on the nation only after the outbreak of World War II in 1939. [19]Even then, it left lasting mental and emotional scars. [20]The Americans who lived through it would never again be so **optimistic** about their economic future.

[21]It is difficult to measure the human cost of the Great Depression. [22]The material hardships were bad enough. [23]Men and women lived in lean-tos made of scrap wood and metal. [24]Families went without meat and fresh vegetables for months. [25]They existed on a diet of soup and beans. [26]The emotional burden was even greater: Americans suffered through year after year of grinding poverty with no relief in sight. [27]The unemployed stood in lines for hours waiting for relief checks. [28]Veterans sold apples or pencils on street corners.

[29]Many Americans sought escape in movement. [30]Men, boys, and some women rode the rails in search of jobs. [31]They hopped freight trains to move south in the winter or west in the summer. [32]One town in the Southwest hired special police to keep **vagrants** from leaving the boxcars. [33]Those who became tramps had to keep on the move, but they did find a sense of community in the hobo jungles that sprang up along the major railroad routes. [34]Here the unfortunate could find a place to eat and sleep and people with whom to share their misery. [35]Louis Banks told interviewer Studs Terkel what the informal camps were like:

> [36]Black and white, it didn't make any difference who you were, 'cause everybody was poor. [37]All friendly, sleep in a jungle. [38]We used to take a big pot and cook food, cabbage, meat, and beans all together. [39]We all set together, we made a tent. [40]Twenty-five or thirty would be out on the side of the rail, white and colored. [41]They didn't have no mothers or sisters, they didn't have no home, they were dirty, they had overalls on, they didn't have no food, they didn't have anything.

—Adapted from Divine, Robert A., T. H. H. Breen, George M. Frederickson, and R. Hal Williams, *The American Story*, 16th ed., pp. 834–839.

Before Reading

Vocabulary in Context

_____ **1.** The word **highflier** in sentence 5 means
    a. stocks usually sold at a higher price than other stocks.
    b. stocks usually sold at a lower price than other stocks.
    c. stocks usually sold at the same price as most stocks.

Tone and Purpose

_____ **2.** Which of the following best describes the author's tone and purpose?
    a. to delight the reader with entertaining details
    b. to inform the reader with factual details
    c. to persuade the reader with emotional details

After Reading

Concept Maps

Finish the timeline with information from the passage.

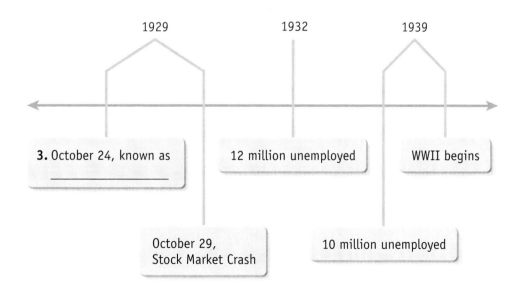

1929

1932

1939

3. October 24, known as _____

12 million unemployed

WWII begins

October 29, Stock Market Crash

10 million unemployed

Central Idea and Main Idea

_____ **4.** Choose the best statement of the central idea of the passage.
  a. The Great Depression was a devastating economic and emotional blow to the United States.
  b. The Great Depression put millions of people out of work.
  c. The Great Depression lasted for more than ten years.

Supporting Details

_____ **5.** Sentence 6, "The stock market rallied for the next two days, but on Tuesday, October 29, the downslide resumed," is a
  a. major supporting detail.   b. minor supporting detail.

Transitions

_____ **6.** "Year after year, people kept looking for a return to wealth. But the outlook remained dismal." (sentences 16–17)

  The relationship between the ideas in these two sentences is one of
  a. cause and effect.   c. contrast.
  b. time order.

Thought Patterns

_____ **7.** The thought pattern used in the second paragraph (sentences 5–10) is
  a. cause and effect.   c. classification.
  b. time order.   d. definition.

Fact and Opinion

_____ **8.** Sentence 11 is a statement that expresses
  a. a fact.   c. a mixture of fact and opinion.
  b. an opinion.

Inferences

9–10. Write **V** for valid by the two inferences that are firmly based on the information in the passage.

_____ Fear was a factor in causing the stock market crash in October 1929.

_____ The outbreak of World War II created jobs for Americans.

_____ Many Americans made their fortunes during the Great Depression.

_____ Racial tensions between whites and blacks were common in the "hobo jungles."

SUMMARY RESPONSE

Restate the author's central idea in your own words. Begin your summary response with the following: *The central idea of "The Great Depression" by Divine, Breen, Frederickson, & Williams is . . .*

WHAT DO YOU THINK?

Based on the details in the passage, what were the major causes and effects of the Great Depression? In 2008, the economy experienced another downturn that many have called the "Great Recession." Assume you are taking a college course in history, and your professor has asked you to make a connection between a recent event and a historic event. Write an essay that compares and contrasts the causes and effects of the Great Depression with the "Great Recession" of 2008. Include the following details in your essay:

- Compare the similarities between the Great Depression and the recession of 2008.
- Contrast the ways the 2008 recession differs from the Great Depression.

After Reading About Inferences

Before you move on to the Mastery Tests on inferences, take time to reflect on your learning and performance by answering the following questions. Write your answers in your notebook.

- How has my knowledge base or prior knowledge about inferences changed?
- Based on my studies, how do I think I will perform on the Mastery Test(s)? Why do I think my scores will be above average, average, or below average?
- Would I recommend this chapter to other students who want to learn more about inferences? Why or why not?

Test your understanding of what you have learned about inferences by completing the Chapter 11 Review.

Name _____ Section _____

Date _____ **Score** (number correct) _____ × 20 = _____%

Visit MyReadingLab to take this test online and receive feedback and guidance on your answers.

A. Read the passage. Then answer the questions that follow it.

Diagnosing Alcoholism

Textbook
Skills

_____ [1]Alcoholism involves the development of certain harmful behaviors associated with long-term use of great amounts of alcohol. [2]It is a **chronic** illness with medical and social effects. [3]Alcoholism advances slowly as tolerance and dependence develop. [4]Although there is some disagreement about what alcoholism is, the following eight symptoms usually aid in its diagnosis:

1. Being drunk frequently in ways that are obvious and destructive

2. Failing in marriage and increasing absences from work

3. Being fired

4. Seeking medical treatment for drinking

5. Suffering physical injury

6. Being arrested for driving under the influence

7. Being arrested for drunkenness

8. Being hospitalized for cirrhosis of the liver or DTs [delirium tremens, or mental confusion that may include hallucinations]

—Adapted from Diana H. Fishbein and Susan E. Pease, *The Dynamics of Drug Abuse*. Boston: Allyn and Bacon, 1996. p. 116.

1. Write **V** for valid by the inference that is firmly supported by the passage.

_____ Alcoholism can be difficult to diagnose.

_____ Most people who drink become alcoholics.

_____ Alcoholism is not a life-threatening disease.

_____ **2.** The word **chronic** in sentence 2 implies
  a. short-term.   b. curable.   c. constant.

B. Read the following passage from a college business textbook.

Business with an Ethical Focus

[1]How can firms create business by acting ethically? [2]By examining the world with an eye toward social responsibility, many firms have created opportunities with new types of products and services.

[3]Topia Energy, an energy company in Canada, has opened the first chain of alternative fuel stations, named GreenStop. [4]They offer only renewable fuel blends, such as gasoline combined with corn ethanol. [5]The gasoline products can be used in regular cars, and

the stations themselves are constructed from renewable, chemical-free products. [6]Inside you won't see the same lineup of cigarettes and candy, but you will have your choice of organic veggie wraps and coffee roasted using solar energy.

[7]Other companies have created business opportunities by addressing the world's most serious medical needs. [8]Malaria kills up to three million people a year, mostly children. [9]It is the leading cause of death in children worldwide, mostly in Africa. [10]The disease is transmitted very easily, whereas the drugs currently used to treat it are becoming increasingly ineffective. [11]Many businesses haven't found a way to balance the tremendous cost of research for creating a malaria vaccine with the anticipated meager profits. [12]Enter Sanaria, a new pharmaceutical company founded by Dr. Stephen Hoffman, whose mission is to create a malaria vaccine. [13]Hoffman remarks, "I haven't spent 25 years working on diseases of the most disadvantaged and neglected people in the world to start a company that's just here to make money." [14]Already the company has secured government grants and a $29.3 million Gates Foundation grant. [15]A malaria vaccine, long considered to be impossible, is now about to enter clinical trials.

[16]Still other companies are creating business opportunities by fighting censorship. [17]The Chinese government maintains a tight rein on the flow of information to its citizens, including controlling the accessibility of certain Internet sites. [18]This censorship left Dynamic Internet Technology (DIT) company founder Bill Xia with a very skewed view of the world when he arrived in the United States from China. [19]"I was a believer of the propaganda," he says. [20]DIT and similar companies provide a service to their clients in an effort to counteract the impact of censorship. [21]When a site is placed on the list of censored sites by the Chinese government, DIT quickly creates a new, uncensored Web address that points users to the same material. [22]A list of the new accessible sites is then emailed to Web surfers who want full Internet access. [23]Chinese censors often stamp out the new site within a few days, at which point DIT starts the process again. [24]It is determined to override censorship through its business. [25]DIT and other companies are showing there are ways to fight censorship and profit from it.

—Adapted from Solomon, Michael R., Poatsy, Mary Anne, and Martin, Kendall, *Better Business*, 2nd ed., pp. 80–81.

3–5. Write **V** for valid by the three inferences that are firmly supported by details in the passage.

_____ Fuel stations are all going "green" and will sell only alternative fuels.

_____ Customers interested in alternative fuels are also likely to be interested in healthful eating choices.

_____ Most companies try to develop medicines only if they can make a good profit on them.

_____ Pharmaceutical companies are headed by doctors.

_____ Dynamic Internet Technology charges customers for its censorship-evading technology.

_____ A socially responsible business is almost guaranteed to be successful.

Name _____ Section _____

Date _____ **Score** (number correct) _____ × 20 = _____%

Visit MyReadingLab to take this test online and receive feedback and guidance on your answers.

Read the following passage from a college psychology textbook. Then choose the four inferences that are firmly supported by the details in the passage. Write **V** for valid by your choices.

Textbook
Skills

[1]One of the foremost tasks that needs to be accomplished in the early stages of marriage, and one that is often negotiated and renegotiated throughout marriage, is the establishment of a mutually acceptable division of labor. [2]Marital couples, often for the first time in their relationship, must decide how they will meet their mutual instrumental and emotional needs. [3]They need to decide who will do the shopping, cooking, washing up, housecleaning, yard care, car maintenance, finances, and so on. [4]They also have to make decisions about who will work for pay outside the home and, if they choose to have children, who will be primarily responsible for childcare and child rearing. [5]These decisions are not easy ones because individual choices have implications for societal functioning, the conflict between interest groups, individual identity, and levels of costs and rewards in the marriage.

[6]Traditionally, few roles of women have held a higher priority than that of wife and homemaker. [7]In contrast, for men, work generally is defined in terms of labor force employment, not in terms of housework and childcare. [8]Traditionally, husbands and fathers were not responsible for any substantial amount of housework or childcare. [9]The husband's responsibility to the family was to provide economic support through paid employment. [10]In terms of role differentiation, the male held primary responsibility for relationships and needs external to the family. [11]The female held responsibility for relationships and needs internal to the family. [12]In terms of exchange, the husband exchanged his work and economic services for the wife's companionship and household services.

[13]Are these traditional ideas changing? Some observers would say "yes, but not much." [14]In 2007, 38.4 percent of married women with a husband present did not work outside the home. [15]However, rates of employment were higher for married women with older children in the home. [16]There is also, as you will see, little question that wives continue to hold the primary responsibility for housework and childcare. [17]And the pace of change has been both slow and minimal.

¹⁸Nevertheless, men's behavior appears to be changing. ¹⁹There is currently no major trend toward full-time male homemakers. ²⁰ But studies reveal an increased participation of men in household and childcare tasks.

—Eshleman, J. Ross and Richard A. Bulcroft.
The Family, 12th ed., p. 344.

_____   **1.** Women are better at housework than men are.

_____   **2.** Marriages function best when women are homemakers and men are wage earners.

_____   **3.** Throughout a marriage, the roles and division of labor within a marriage may change.

_____   **4.** The word *traditionally* (sentences 6 and 9) suggests "an ongoing social practice."

_____   **5.** The author's tone is unbiased.

_____   **6.** The author's tone is resentful.

_____   **7.** The author's purpose is to inform the reader about the division of labor in marriage.

_____   **8.** The author's purpose is to argue against the unfair division of labor in marriage.

_____   **9.** The traditional roles and division of labor within marriage will never change.

_____   **10.** Many women who work outside the home also do most of the housework and childcare.

VISUAL *VOCABULARY*

The differentiation of a key creates an exact fit to a specific lock because of the key's _____ shape.

a. individual
b. uniform
c. random

Name _____ Section _____

Date _____ **Score** (number correct) _____ × 20 = _____%

Visit MyReadingLab to take this test online and receive feedback and guidance on your answers.

Read the passage below. Then answer the questions that follow it.

Textbook
Skills

Social Class and Health

[1]In 2005, a team of *New York Times* reporters published a series of articles based on their year of exploring ways that social class influences a person's destiny. [2]The articles, "Life at the Top in America Isn't Just Better, It's Longer," followed three New York City residents—Mr. Miele, Mr. Wilson, and Ms. Gora—from different social classes—the upper middle class, the middle class, and the working class. [3]Although each of the three residents experienced a heart attack around the same time, each had very different outcomes. [4]Mr. Miele, who was with friends at the time of his attack, was rushed to the hospital of his choice in an ambulance. [5]Minutes after his arrival, a doctor assessed his condition and Mr. Miele was quickly given the treatment he needed. [6]In another part of town, Mr. Wilson was also taken to a hospital in an ambulance, but his hospital was not able to perform the surgery he needed. [7]After suffering through a painful night, Mr. Wilson was taken to a different facility that could treat his condition. [8]Ms. Gora had to be persuaded to let an ambulance take her to a city-run hospital, known for its busy emergency room. [9]She had to wait for two hours to see a doctor. [10]In the end, Ms. Gora was finally released without ever receiving the angiogram treatment that she needed. [11]Based on these stories, can you figure out to which social classes Mr. Miele, Mr. Wilson, and Ms. Gora belong?

[12]Sociologists believe that one's social class has a direct effect on his or her health, particularly in the United States, where health care availability is connected to your ability to pay for it. [13]Studies show that a higher socioeconomic status leads to longer, healthier, and happier lives. [14]When asked to rate their health, only 23.4 percent of people with an income of $20,000 or less reported excellent health compared to 46.3 percent of people making $55,000 or more. [15]Sociologist Jason Schnittker argues that income improves health because more money means that affordable health care and basic needs are met.

—Carl, John D., *Think Sociology,* 2nd ed., p. 212.

A. Match each patient with the class to which he or she most likely belongs.

1. _____ Mr. Miele   a. working class

2. _____ Mr. Wilson   b. middle class

3. _____ Ms. Gora   c. upper middle class

B. **4–5.** Write **V** for valid by the two inferences that are firmly supported by details in the passage.

_____ Ms. Gora likely had heart problems in the future.

_____ Mr. Miele probably had no heart problems in the future.

_____ Hospitals are not equal in the quality of care they can offer.

_____ If health care were free, there would be no class difference in health.

Name _____ Section _____

Date _____ **Score** (number correct) _____ × 25 = _____%

Visit MyReadingLab to take this test online and receive feedback and guidance on your answers.

Read the following passage from a college psychology textbook. Then choose the four inferences that are firmly supported by the details in the passage. Write **V** for valid by your choices.

Textbook
Skills

Learning Styles: Different Strokes for Different Folks

[1]Life would be so much easier, if everyone learned new information in exactly the same way. [2]Teachers would know exactly how to present material so that all students would have an equal opportunity to learn. [3]Unfortunately, that just is not the way it works—people are different in many ways, and one of the ways they differ is in the style of learning that works best for each person.

[4]What exactly is a learning style? [5]In general, a learning style is the particular way in which a person takes in information (Dunn et al., 1989, 2001; Felder, 1993, 1996; Felder & Spurlin, 2005). [6]People take in information in several ways: through the eyes, by reading text or looking at charts, diagrams, and maps; through the ears, by listening, talking things out, and discussing things with others; and through the sense of touch and the movement of the body, by touching things, writing things down, drawing pictures and diagrams, and learning by doing (Barsch, 1996).

Types of Learning Styles

[7]Learning styles are often classified based on personality theories or theories of intelligence. [8]The number of different learning styles varies with the theory, but most theories of learning styles include visual learners, who learn best by seeing, reading, and looking at images; **auditory learners**, who learn best by hearing and saying things out loud; **tactile learners**, who need to touch things; **kinesthetic learners**, who prefer to learn by doing and being active; and **social learners**, who prefer to learn with other people or in groups (Dunn et al., 1989). [9]Most people will find that they have one dominant, or most powerful, learning style along with one or two secondary styles. [10]Notice that several of the learning styles described would work well together: Auditory learners and social learners, for example, work well together, as do tactile and kinesthetic learners, because they are both hands-on kinds of learners. [11]Many theories simply divide people into four basic styles of learning (Barsch, 1996; Dunn et al., 1989; Jester, 2000):

545

Visual/Verbal. [12]These people learn best when looking at material, particularly things that are written down. [13]Reading the textbook, using classroom notes, and having an instructor who uses overhead projections, writes on the board, or uses visual multimedia presentations are very helpful. [14]Visual/verbal learners, because they focus on reading and taking notes, tend to learn best when studying alone rather than in a group.

Visual/Nonverbal. [15]These visual learners learn best through the use of diagrams, pictures, charts, videos, and other image-oriented material rather than printed text. [16]This type of learner, like the visual/verbal learner, also prefers to study alone.

Auditory/Verbal. [17]Auditory/verbal learners take in information best by listening. [18]Group discussions and a lecture format in which the instructor talks about the subject are of the most benefit to this style of learning.

Tactile/Kinesthetic. [19]This style of learner needs a "hands-on" opportunity to learn. [20]Lab classes are very good ways for this type of learner to absorb material. [21]Instructors who do lots of demonstrations and use field experiences outside of the classroom are good for this style of learner. [22]Some kinesthetic learners benefit from writing notes during a lecture or from writing a summary of their lecture notes afterward.

—Ciccarelli, Saundra K.; White, J. Noland, *Psychology: An Exploration*, pp. 1, 2.

_____ Knowing one's learning style guarantees higher grades.

_____ Most professors create lessons based on their students' learning styles.

_____ Visual learners are less likely to be social learners.

_____ Creating and studying flash cards only helps visual learners.

_____ Auditory learners most likely benefit from participation in study groups outside of class.

_____ Visiting museums and historical sites promotes learning for kinesthetic/tactile learners.

_____ All types of learners benefit from taking notes.

_____ All four of these learning styles make use of similar methods.

11 Summary of Key Concepts about Inferences

LO1 **LO2** Assess your comprehension of inferences.

- An inference is an _____

  _____.

- An effective reader must sort _____ from _____ to infer the author's meaning.

- Biased words express _____.

- A qualifier signals _____

  _____.

- A valid inference is _____.

- An invalid conclusion is _____

  _____.

- The VALID approach consists of 5 thinking steps to take to make a valid inference.

  - Step 1: Verify _____.

  - Step 2: Assess _____.

  - Step 3: Learn _____.

  - Step 4: Investigate _____.

  - Step 5: Detect _____.

Test Your Comprehension of Inferences

Respond to the following questions and prompts.

(LO1) (LO2) In your own words, what is the difference between a valid and an invalid inference? _____

_____

_____

_____

(LO3) (LO4)
(LO6) Study the following examples of creative expressions. Identify the literary device each one represents.

Literary Device	Example
1. _____	"My love is like a red, red, rose."
2. _____	A gold cross on a necklace
3. _____	"We can make the sun run."
4. _____	The Earth wept.
5. _____	home, shanty, palace

(LO5) (LO6) Describe how you will use what you have learned about inferences in your reading process to comprehend textbook material. _____

_____

_____

_____

(LO1) (LO2)
(LO3) (LO4)
(LO5) (LO6) Summarize the two most important ideas in this chapter that will help you improve your reading comprehension. _____

_____

_____

The Basics of Argument

12

CHAPTER

LEARNING OUTCOMES

After studying this chapter, you should be able to:

LO1 Define the Terms *Argument, Claim,* and *Supports*

LO2 Identify the Author's Claim and Supports

LO3 Determine Whether the Supports Are Relevant

LO4 Determine Whether the Supports Are Adequate

LO5 Analyze the Argument for Bias

LO6 Develop Textbook Skills: The Logic of Argument in Textbooks

LO7 Apply Information Literacy Skills: Academic, Personal, and Career Applications of the Basics of Argument

Before Reading About the Basics of Argument

Many of the same skills you learned to make valid inferences will help you master the basics of argument. Take a moment to review the five steps in the VALID approach to making sound inferences. Fill in the following blanks with each of the steps.

Step 1: _____

Step 2: _____

Step 3: _____

Step 4: _____

Step 5: _____

Skim the chapter and list any other reading skills you have studied from prior chapters that seem to apply to the basics of argument: _____

_____

Copyright © 2015 Pearson Education, Inc.

549

Use your prior knowledge about valid inferences, other reading skills, and the learning outcomes to create at least three questions that you can answer as you study:

1. _____

   _____?

2. _____

   _____?

                                                                  ?
3. _____

Reading skills you have studied in prior chapters that will help you master the basics of argument are main ideas, supporting details, fact and opinion, and tone and purpose (to persuade). Compare the questions you created based on your prior knowledge and the learning outcomes with the following questions. Then write the ones that seem the most helpful in your notebook, leaving enough space between questions to record your answers as you read and study the chapter.

How will verifying and valuing the facts help me decide if supports in an argument are relevant? How will learning from the text help me decide if supports in an argument are adequate? How does an argument use bias? What is the relationship between main ideas and the author's claim? How does opinion affect an argument? What is the connection between tone, purpose, and the basics of argument?

LO1   Define the Terms *Argument*, *Claim*, and *Supports*

Have you noticed how many of us enjoy debating ideas and winning arguments? You can see this on television, where many shows thrive on conflict and debate. For example, the *Jerry Springer* show uses the conflicts between guests to amuse the audience. Programs such as *Meet the Press,* hosted by David Gregory, or *The O'Reilly Factor* with Bill O'Reilly debate political and social issues. Likewise, talk radio fills hours of air time with debate about issues related to culture and politics. Two examples are *The Rush Limbaugh Show* and *The Diane Rehm Show.*

Some people are so committed to their ideas that they become emotional, even angry. However, effective **argument** is reasoned: is a process during which a claim is made and logical details are offered to support that claim.

> An **argument** is made up of two types of statements:
> 1. The author's claim—the main point of the argument
> 2. The supports—the evidence or reasons that support the author's claim

The purpose of an argument is to persuade the reader that the claim is valid. To decide if a claim is valid, you must analyze the argument in four basic steps.

1. Identify the author's claim and supports.

2. Decide whether the supports are relevant.

3. Decide whether the supports are adequate.

4. Check the argument for bias.

Step 1: Identify the Author's Claim and Supports

Read the following claim.

Psycho is a movie worth seeing.

The claim certainly states the speaker's point clearly. But it probably wouldn't inspire most of us to see the movie. Instead, our first response to the claim is likely to be "Why?" We need reasons before we can decide if we think a claim is valid. Notice that a claim, like any main idea, is made up of a topic and a controlling point. Here, *Psycho* is the topic, and the controlling point is "worth seeing." Notice that the details that follow answer a question about the controlling point: "Why is *Psycho* a movie worth seeing?"

1. It is a classic—the first "slasher" movie that inspired hundreds of slasher movies, none of which come close to it in style or substance.

2. It is suspenseful and shocking, with a haunting score by Bernard Hermann.

3. It contains the notorious "shower scene"—one of the most famous scenes in movie history.

These three sentences offer the supports for the author's claim. We are now able to understand the basis of the argument, and we now have details about which we can agree or disagree.

Writers frequently make claims that they want us to accept as valid. To assess whether the claim is valid, an effective reader first identifies the claim and the supports. Identifying the author's claim and supports for that claim is the first step in analyzing an argument.

> **EXAMPLES**

A. Read the following groups of ideas. Identify the claim and supports in each group. Write **C** if the sentence states the author's claim or **S** if the sentence offers support for the claim.

Group 1

[1]Dog bites pose a serious national problem. [2]Dogs bite an estimated 4.7 million people each year, with 800,000 individuals needing medical treatment.

_____   **1.** Sentence 1

_____   **2.** Sentence 2

Group 2

[1]They never wave or say hello. [2]Our neighbors are unfriendly people.

_____   **3.** Sentence 1

_____   **4.** Sentence 2

Group 3

[1]Popcorn contains only 15 calories per cup when it is air-popped. [2]Popcorn is a good snack. [3]Popcorn is a good source of fiber.

_____   **5.** Sentence 1

_____   **6.** Sentence 2

_____   **7.** Sentence 3

Group 4

[1]Mrs. Overby takes time to explain difficult ideas in class. [2]Mrs. Overby is always available for student conferences. [3]Mrs. Overby's students have a high passing rate. [4]Mrs. Overby is a good teacher.

_____   **8.** Sentence 1

_____   **9.** Sentence 2

_____ **10.** Sentence 3

_____ **11.** Sentence 4

B. Editorial cartoons offer arguments through the use of humor. The cartoonist has a claim to make and uses the situation, actions, and words in the cartoon as supporting details. Study the cartoon reprinted here. Then write a claim based on the supports in the cartoon.

—*The Detroit News,* Larry Wright © 2002

_____

_____

_____

_____

EXPLANATIONS

A.

Group 1

1. Sentence 1 states the author's claim (C). **2.** Sentence 2 offers support for the claim (S).

Group 2

3. Sentence 1 offers support for the claim (S). **4.** Sentence 2 states the author's claim (C).

Group 3

5. Sentence 1 offers support for the claim (S). **6.** Sentence 2 states the author's claim (C). **7.** Sentence 3 offers support for the claim(s).

Group 4

8–10. Sentences 1, 2, and 3 offer support for the claim (S). **11.** Sentence 4 states the author's claim (C).

B. The note from school came from the school's administration. The horrible spelling is a sign that the people running the school do not have basic writing or thinking skills. Several claims can be suggested by the details in the cartoon. The following are a few possibilities.

> Students must not be receiving a good education.
>
> School administrators should not allow teachers to teach outside their fields.
>
> School administrators are the main problem in education.
>
> School administrators are not smart.
>
> School administrators must not care about education. ◀

Practice 1

Read the following groups of ideas. Identify the claim and supports in each group. Write **C** if the sentence states the author's claim or **S** if the sentence offers support for the claim.

Group 1

^{1}Everyone needs to wear sunglasses while outdoors. ^{2}The sun contains UV rays that damage the eyes by causing cataracts, skin cancer on the eyelids, and macular degeneration.

_____   **1.** Sentence 1

_____   **2.** Sentence 2

Group 2

[1]Spaying or neutering a pet reduces the animal's chance of suffering from diseases, and spaying or neutering reduces the pet's urge to roam or mark its territory. [2]Spaying or neutering a pet is the action of a responsible pet owner.

_____ **3.** Sentence 1

_____ **4.** Sentence 2

Group 3

[1]In the past 60 years, researchers have conducted more than 21,000 studies on the effects of caffeine. [2]Caffeine has several benefits. [3]Caffeine produces feelings of well-being, improves memory, speeds the metabolism, and may reduce diseases such as cancer and Parkinson's disease.

_____ **5.** Sentence 1

_____ **6.** Sentence 2

_____ **7.** Sentence 3

Group 4

[1]Fish is a protein source rich in omega 3 fatty acids. [2]These healthy fats have amazing brain power: higher dietary omega 3 fatty acids are linked to lower dementia and stroke risks; slower mental decline. [3]Omega 3 fatty acids may also play a vital role in enhancing memory, especially as we get older. [4]For brain health, you should eat fish two times a week.

_____ **8.** Sentence 1

_____ **9.** Sentence 2

_____ **10.** Sentence 3

_____ **11.** Sentence 4

Group 5

[1]"Sexting" usually refers to teens sharing nude photos or sexually explicit messages via cell phone, but "sexting" also occurs through the use of other devices and the Web. [2]A recent survey said a third of young adults and 20% of teens had posted or sent nude or semi-nude photos or videos of themselves. [3]Sexting violates current child pornography laws and can lead to serious legal consequences. [4]Sexting is a disturbing trend among young people.

_____ **12.** Sentence 1

_____ **13.** Sentence 2

_____ **14.** Sentence 3

_____ **15.** Sentence 4

Group 6

[1]School vouchers are government cash grants or tax credits for parents, equal to all or part of the cost of educating their child at an elementary or secondary school of their choice. [2]School vouchers are not the best ways to improve education. [3]The greatest gains in student achievement have occurred in places where vouchers do not exist. [4]Private schools who receive money from school vouchers are not required to adopt the academic standards, hire highly qualified teachers, or administer the assessments required of public schools. [5]School vouchers require taxpayers to fund both public and private schools.

_____ **16.** Sentence 1

_____ **17.** Sentence 2

_____ **18.** Sentence 3

_____ **19.** Sentence 4

_____ **20.** Sentence 5

LO3 Step 2: Determine Whether the Supports Are Relevant

In Step 1, you learned to identify the author's claim and supports. The next step is to decide whether the supports are relevant to the claim. Remember, a claim, like any main idea, is made up of a topic and a controlling point. Irrelevant supports change the topic or ignore the controlling point. Relevant supports will answer the reporter's questions (*Who? What? When? Where? Why? How?*). Use these questions to decide whether the supports for a claim are relevant.

For example, read the following argument a teenager makes about her curfew. Identify the support that is irrelevant to her claim.

[1]"I am mature enough to make my own decisions about my curfew. [2]When I work the closing shift at McDonald's, I am out until 2 A.M., and no matter where I am, I always make sure to stick with a group of people. [3]And I am not just out roaming the streets; I only want to stay out late

for specific events like a concert or a late movie. ⁴None of my friends even have curfews. ⁵Just like always, I will tell you ahead of time where I will be and when I will be home, and I do have my cell phone in case you get worried and want to call me. ⁶Or I can call you if I need help."

By turning this teenager's claim into a question, she and her parents can test her ability to offer valid reasons: "How have I shown I am mature enough to make my own decisions about my curfew?" Sentences 2, 3, 5, and 6 offer relevant examples of her maturity. However, sentence 4 states an irrelevant support that changes the topic. The argument is about *her* curfew based on *her* maturity, not her friends' curfews.

When evaluating an argument, it is important to test each piece of supporting evidence to determine whether it is relevant.

> **EXAMPLES**

A. Read the following lists of claims and supports. Mark each support **R** if it is relevant to the claim or **N** if it is not relevant to the claim.

1. Claim: Online shopping offers a lot of benefits.

   Supports

   _____ a. You can shop at any time of the day or night.

   _____ b. You don't have to leave your house.

   _____ c. You can't try on clothes to see if they fit.

   _____ d. You may have to pay postage to return items.

   _____ e. You can save money because comparison shopping takes less time.

2. Claim: Water supplies should have fluoride added to prevent tooth decay.

   Supports

   _____ a. Research shows that drinking fluoride from birth reduces tooth decay by as much as 65 percent.

   _____ b. Fluoride is a safe, natural mineral that makes bones and teeth stronger.

   _____ c. Drinking eight glasses of water every day promotes good health.

   _____ d. Although fluoride is present in plants, animals, and water, the amount is too low to offer protection against tooth decay.

   _____ e. Fluoride is tasteless and odorless.

3. Claim: Gun ownership by citizens reduces crime in the United States.

Supports

_____ a. Since 1991, the number of guns in the U.S. has risen by more than four million annually, to an all-time high.

_____ b. Since 1991, federal and state gun control laws have been eliminated or made less restrictive.

_____ c. Citizens of the United States own more than half of all guns owned worldwide.

_____ d. Most school shooters used guns taken from their homes.

_____ e. Nationwide, the rate of violent crime has decreased to about a 30-year low, and the murder rate has decreased to about a 40-year low.

B. Argument is also used in advertisements. It is important for you to be able to understand the claims and supports of ads. Many times advertisers appeal to emotions, make false claims, or give supports that are not relevant because their main aim is to persuade you to buy their product. Study the advertisement for milk put out by America's Dairy Farmers and Milk Processors. Mark each support **R** if it is relevant to the claim or **N** if it is not relevant to the claim.

4. Claim: Drinking milk is good for your health.

Supports

_____ a. Taylor Swift drinks milk.

_____ b. Exercise leads to physical fitness.

_____ c. Taylor Swift pours herself into her music.

_____ d. Taylor Swift is a popular entertainer.

_____ e. The protein and nutrients in lowfat milk build muscles.

EXPLANATIONS

1. Items (a), (b), and (e) are relevant to the claim. Items (c) and (d) are not relevant because they point out drawbacks to online shopping instead of supporting the claim that online shopping offers a lot of benefits.

2. Items (a), (b), and (d) are relevant to the claim. Items (c) and (e) are not relevant. The benefits of drinking water are not the issue. The taste and odor of fluoride are not directly tied to its ability to prevent tooth decay.

3. Items (a), (b), and (e) are relevant to the claim. Items (c) and (d) are not relevant. The claim focuses on reducing crime in the United States, so any information about worldwide gun ownership is not relevant.

4. Only item (e) is relevant to the claim that drinking milk is good for your health. Advertisers often use celebrities as spokespeople, but personal remarks or information about Taylor Swift are not relevant to the healthfulness of milk. Item (b) states a fact, but this detail has nothing to do with the claim about milk.

Practice 2

A. Read the following lists of claims and supports. Mark each support **R** if it is relevant to the claim or **N** if it is not relevant to the claim.

1. Claim: Use of steroids is harmful and should be avoided.

    Supports

    _____ a. Excessive use of steroids can cause rage.

    _____ b. One short-term effect of steroid use is acne.

    _____ c. One long-term effect of steroid use is stunted growth in teenagers.

    _____ d. Other long-term effects of steroid use may be liver damage, prostate cancer, and a higher risk of heart disease.

    _____ e. Drinking alcohol poses greater risks than using steroids.

2. Claim: Left-handed people face obstacles in the classroom and in school activities.

    Supports

    _____ a. In school sports, standard equipment (for example, hockey sticks and baseball gloves) is designed for right-handed players.

    _____ b. Musician Kurt Cobain, who dropped out of high school, was left-handed.

_____ c. The word *left* comes from an old Anglo-Saxon word that means "weak."

_____ d. In schools, colleges, and universities, the standard desk has a small top attached to the right side of the desk, which makes it difficult for left-handed students to write.

_____ e. School supplies such as scissors, three-ring binders, and keyboards are mostly made for right-handed writers.

3. Claim: Migrant farmworkers boost the economy.

   Supports

   _____ a. Most migrant farmworkers are legal residents or U.S. citizens.

   _____ b. The efforts of migrant workers support the multibillion-dollar farming business.

   _____ c. Most of the vegetables and fruits in this country are grown and picked with the aid of migrant workers.

   _____ d. Without migrant workers, farmers would not be able to produce and harvest their crops.

   _____ e. Farming is ranked as one of the three most dangerous jobs in the nation.

4. Claim: Easter Seals is a nonprofit organization worthy of support in terms of time and money.

   Supports

   _____ a. Easter Seals provides adult and senior service programs across the country.

   _____ b. Easter Seals runs hundreds of camping and recreation programs nationwide for children and adults with disabilities.

   _____ c. Easter Seals offers job training and employment programs.

   _____ d. Dr Pepper/Seven Up is a corporate sponsor of Easter Seals.

   _____ e. Easter Seals uses the lily as its official logo.

B. Study the mock advertisement that encourages viewers to consume a soy product. Read the claim, and then mark each support **R** if it is relevant to the claim
or **N** if it is not relevant to the claim.

Soy-Sublime

◆ **Reduces the risks of certain types of cancer**
◆ **Promotes strong bones**
◆ **Alleviates symptoms of menopause**
◆ **Contains cancer-fighting isoflavones**

Soybeans grow abundantly and actually
replenish the soil they grow in. Consuming
25 grams of soy protein per day, as part of a
diet that is low in saturated fat and cholesterol,
may reduce the risk of heart disease. Good
cooks use soy. Organic and pesticide free.
Made with 100% natural whole soy beans.

Stay Healthy with Soy-Sublime

5. Claim: Soy-Sublime is a healthful food that you should buy.

Supports

_____ a. Soy reduces the risks of certain types of cancer.

_____ b. Soy alleviates symptoms of menopause.

_____ c. Soybeans grow abundantly and actually replenish the soil they
grow in.

_____ d. Consuming 25 grams of soy protein per day, as part of a diet
that is low in saturated fat and cholesterol, may reduce the risk
of heart disease.

_____ e. Good cooks use soy.

Now that you have practiced identifying relevant supports in a list format,
you are ready to isolate relevant supports in reading passages. In a paragraph,
the topic sentence states the author's claim. Each of the supporting details must
be evaluated as relevant or irrelevant supports for the topic sentence.

> **EXAMPLE**   Read the following paragraph.

> [1]A culture of drug abuse permeates many of the college campuses in the United States of America. [2]This chronic problem must be immediately addressed by the proper authorities. [3]According to government statistics, nearly one fourth of full-time college students display the medical symptoms of substance dependence and abuse. [4]The government studies show that the number of college students who abuse drugs—nearly 2 million—is more than double the number of those who abuse drugs in the public as a whole. [5]Alcohol, illegal drugs, and prescription drugs are widely available, easy to get, and frequently abused by college students across the country. [6]First, the age-old problem of alcohol abuse has not abated. [7]Not only do around 70 percent of current students drink alcohol, but also many more than ever before are frequent drinkers and binge drinkers, drinking for the sole purpose of getting drunk. [8]While alcohol use has remained constant since the 1990s, according to experts, students' daily use of marijuana has risen to alarming levels. [9]Likewise in recent years, college students have turned to abuse of prescription drugs. [10]Adderall and Ritalin are taken to stay alert while studying while OxyContin is used to create an intense feeling of euphoria. [11]Parents, students, and educators must come together and take a firm stand against this plague. [12]Fortunately, more and more students are choosing to live in substance-free housing.

1. Underline the topic sentence (the sentence that states the author's claim).

_____   2. Which sentence is *not* relevant to the author's point?
     a. sentence 2
     b. sentence 5
     c. sentence 11
     d. sentence 12

EXPLANATIONS

1. Sentence 2 is the topic sentence that states the author's claim.

2. The sentence that is *not* relevant to the author's point is (d), sentence 12. The author's claim is that the chronic problem of drug abuse must be addressed by the proper authorities. The fact that more students are choosing to live in substance-free housing is good news. However, the fact does not support the author's claim. <

Practice 3

Read the following paragraphs.

"At Risk" with AD/HD

[1]Attention Deficit-Hyperactivity Disorder (ADHD) is one of the most common neurobehavioral disorders of childhood. [2]Usually first diagnosed in childhood, it often lasts into adulthood. [3]People with ADHD have trouble paying attention, controlling impulsive behaviors, or being overly active. [4]People with ADHD have difficulty organizing or finishing a task, paying attention to details, or following instructions or conversations. [5]Often, the person fidgets and finds it hard to sit still for long, interrupts others a lot, grabs things from people, or speaks at inappropriate times. [6]ADHD is a serious condition with long-term effects. [7]Those with ADHD may experience troubled relationships, higher risk of injuries, failure at school or on the job. [8]Even so, many who suffer from ADHD can be very successful.

—"Attention-Deficit/Hyperactivity Disorder (ADHD)."
Centers for Disease Control and Prevention.

1. Underline the topic sentence (the sentence that states the author's claim).

_____ 2. Which sentence is *not* relevant to the author's point?

    a. sentence 3   c. sentence 7

    b. sentence 4   d. sentence 8

Intimate Partner Violence

[1]Intimate partner violence (IPV) occurs between two people in a close relationship. [2]The term "intimate partner" includes current and former spouses and dating partners. [3]IPV exists as a range of behaviors—from a single episode of violence to ongoing battering. [4]IPV is a serious problem in the United States. [5]Each year, women experience about 4.8 million intimate partner related physical assaults and rapes. [6]Of course, rape is also committed by complete strangers. [7]Men are the victims of about 2.9 million intimate partner related physical assaults. [8]IPV resulted in 1,510 deaths in 2005. [9]Of these deaths, 78% were females and 22% were males. [10]The medical care, mental health services, and lost productivity (e.g., time away from work) cost of IPV was an estimated $5.8 billion in 1995. [11]Updated to today's dollars, that's more than $8.3 billion.

—Adapted from National Center for Injury Prevention and Control. "Understanding Intimate Partner Violence: Fact Sheet 2009." CDC

3. Underline the topic sentence (the sentence that states the author's claim).

_____ **4.** Which sentence is *not* relevant to the author's point?

      a. sentence 3   c. sentence 6

      b. sentence 4   d. sentence 7

Step 3: Determine Whether the Supports Are Adequate

In Step 1 you learned to identify the author's claim and supports. In Step 2 you learned to make sure the supports are relevant. In Step 3 you must decide whether the supports are adequate. A valid argument is based not only on a claim and relevant support but also on the amount and quality of the support given. That is, supports must give enough evidence for the author's claim to be convincing. Just as you use the reporter's questions to decide whether supports are relevant, you also can use them to test whether supports are adequate. Supporting details fully explain the author's controlling point about a topic. Remember, those questions are *Who? What? When? Where? Why? How?*

For example, you may argue, "A vegetarian diet is a more healthful diet. I feel much better since I became a vegetarian." However, the reporter's question "Why?" reveals that the support is inadequate. The answer to "Why is a vegetarian diet a more healthful diet?" should include expert opinions and facts, not just personal opinion. Often in the quest to support a claim, people oversimplify their reasons. Thus, they do not offer enough information to prove the claim. Instead of logical details, they may offer false causes, false comparisons, or forced choices, or leave out facts that hurt the claim. You will learn more about inadequate argument in Chapter 13.

In Chapter 11, you studied how to avoid invalid conclusions and make valid inferences (see pages 500–514). The same thinking steps you use to make valid inferences help you identify valid claims: consider the facts, don't infer anything that is not there, and make sure nothing contradicts your conclusion.

◉ **EXAMPLE** Read the list of supports.

Supports

    ▪ One pound of muscle burns 50 calories a day.

    ▪ One pound of fat burns 2 calories a day.

- Two pounds of muscle can burn up 10 pounds of fat in one year.
- Lean muscle mass weighs more than fat.

Write **V** for valid by the claim that is adequately supported by the evidence in the list.

_____ a. Building muscles will help one lose weight.

_____ b. Muscles burn more calories than fat.

_____ c. It is hard to lose weight.

_____ d. Weight training is the best way to lose weight.

EXPLANATION Choices (a), (c), and (d) use the evidence to jump to false conclusions about losing weight. However, none of the evidence mentions weight loss. In fact, since muscle weighs more than fat, adding muscle can cause a weight gain. The only logical conclusion based on the evidence is (b), "muscles burn more calories than fat."

Practice 4

A. Read the list of supports.

Supports

- When a couple fights, name-calling creates distrust, anger, and a sense of helplessness.
- Assigning blame makes others defensive during a fight.
- When two people fight, words like _never_ or _always_ are usually not true and create more anger.
- Exaggerating or making up a complaint can keep the couple's real issues hidden during a fight.
- A couple bringing up gripes and hurt feelings stockpiled over time can lead to explosive anger in a fight.

Write **V** for valid by the claim that is adequately supported by the evidence.

_____ a. Fighting leads to violence.

_____ b. Using unfair methods during a fight makes the situation worse.

_____ c. Everyone uses unfair fighting methods.

_____ d. Fighting cannot be avoided.

B. Study the graph.

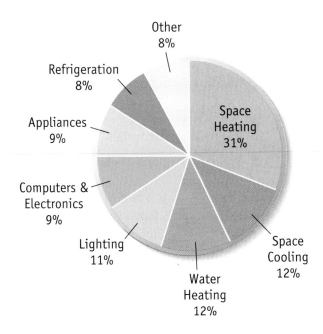

How We Use Energy in Our Homes

> —*2007 Buildings Energy Data Book, Table 4.2.1., 2005 Energy Cost Data.* 29 Jan. 2010
> https://www1.eere.energy.gov/consumer/tips/printable_versions/home_energy.html.

Write **V** for valid by the claim that is adequately supported by the evidence.

_____ a. Our homes are not energy efficient.

_____ b. We use too much energy.

_____ c. Our homes are energy efficient.

_____ d. Home heating systems use the most energy.

LO5 Step 4: Analyze the Argument for Bias

In Step 1, you learned to identify the author's claim and supports. In Step 2, you learned to make sure the supports are relevant to the claim. In Step 3, you learned to avoid false inferences and identify valid claims based on adequate supports. Again, the skills you use to make sound inferences help you determine whether an argument is valid. In Step 4, you must also check for the author's bias for or against the topic. Authors may use emotionally slanted language or biased words to present either a favorable or a negative view of the topic under debate. In addition, authors may include only the details that favor the stances they have taken. A valid argument relies on objective, factual details. As you evaluate the argument for the author's bias, ask the following questions:

- Does the author provide mostly positive or negative supports?
- Does the author provide mostly factual details or rely on biased language?
- Does the author include or omit opposing views?

❯ **EXAMPLE** Read the following information.

Underage Drinking

[1]Alcohol use by persons under age 21 years is a major public health problem. [2]Alcohol is the most commonly used and abused drug among youth in the United States, more than tobacco and illicit drugs. [3]And alcohol use is responsible for more than 4,700 annual deaths among underage youth. [4]Although drinking by persons under the age of 21 is illegal, people aged 12 to 20 years drink 11% of all alcohol consumed in the United States. [5]More than 90% of this alcohol is consumed in the form of binge drinks. [6]In 2010, persons under age 21 made approximately 189,000 emergency rooms visits for injuries and other conditions linked to alcohol. [7]The 2011 Youth Risk Behavior Survey tracked the drinking levels of high school students, during the past 30 days. [8]According to the survey, 39% drank some amount of alcohol; 22% binge drank; 8% drove after drinking alcohol, and 24% rode with a driver who had been drinking alcohol.

[9]Underage drinkers face alarming social problems, such as fighting, and school problems, such as higher absence and poor or failing grades. [10]Underage drinkers are more often arrested for driving or physically hurting someone while drunk. [11]They are more vulnerable to physical and sexual assault. [12]They are at a higher risk for suicide and homicide. [13]They are apt to engage in unwanted, unplanned, and unprotected sexual activity. [14]At the same time, alcohol use disrupts normal growth and sexual development and causes changes in brain development that may have life-long effects. [15]Underage drinkers also endure more illnesses, loss of memory, alcohol-related, car crashes and other unintentional injuries, such as burns, falls, and drowning, and death from alcohol

poisoning. [16]They also abuse other drugs. [17]Underage drinking has disastrous consequences.

—"Fact Sheets—Underage Drinking." Centers for Disease
Control and Prevention.

_____ **1.** Overall, the passage mostly relies on
   a. factual details.
   b. emotionally slanted language.

_____ **2.** Which of the following statements is true?
   a. Sentence 1 offers an opposing view.
   b. Sentence 8 offers an opposing view.
   c. Sentence 11 offers an opposing view.
   d. No opposing view is offered.

_____ **3.** In this passage, the author expresses a biased attitude
   a. in favor of lowering the drinking age.
   b. in favor of raising the drinking age.
   c. against underage drinking.
   d. against all alcohol consumption.

EXPLANATION **1.** Although the passage contains some emotionally slanted language such as *alarming* and *disastrous*, overall, the author relies on (a) factual details that can be verified through research. **2.** The author offers no opposing view. **3.** In the passage, the author expresses a biased attitude (c) against underage drinking. In fact, this biased attitude is the author's main idea. ◀

Practice 5

Read the following argument for lowering the legal drinking age to 18. Answer the questions that follow.

Grant Full Adult Rights:
Lower the Legal Drinking Age to 18

[1]An 18-year-old has the same legal rights as a 21-year-old—except the right to drink alcohol. [2]Just like a 21-year-old, an 18-year-old can serve on a jury, vote, sign contracts, hold public office, marry, and buy cigarettes. [3]This discrimination was established in the National Minimum Drinking Act of 1984. [4]The National Minimal Legal Drinking Age (MLDA) should be lowered to 18.

⁵One of the main arguments for lowering MLDA is that citizens officially receive the rights of adulthood (as listed above) at 18. ⁶Two additional rights and responsibilities afforded 18-year-olds support their right to drink alcohol. ⁷First, an 18-year-old can be prosecuted as an adult. ⁸If a person is old enough to be held accountable for criminal behavior, then the person is old enough to make sound judgments—such as about drinking alcohol. ⁹Second, an 18-year-old can volunteer or be drafted to serve in the military. ¹⁰If a person is adult enough to die for his or her country, then that person is adult enough to have a drink. ¹¹Opponents to this view argue that the brain of an 18-year-old has not yet fully developed. ¹²Furthermore, alcohol interferes with brain development. ¹³However, 18-year-olds are given the right to consume tobacco with its addictive and medical dangers. ¹⁴They are also deemed able to endure the psychological and physical horrors of war.

¹⁵Lower the legal drinking age to 18. ¹⁶It's the right thing to do.

_____ **1.** Overall, the passage relies on
  a. factual details.
  b. emotionally slanted language.

_____ **2.** Which of the following statements is true?
  a. Sentence 5 offers an opposing view.
  b. Sentence 7 offers an opposing view.
  c. Sentence 11 offers an opposing view.
  d. No opposing view is offered.

_____ **3.** In this passage, the author expresses a biased attitude
  a. in favor of lowering the drinking age.
  b. in favor of raising the drinking age.
  c. against 18-year-olds going to war.
  d. against alcohol consumption.

LO6 Develop Textbook Skills: The Logic of Argument in Textbooks

Textbook
Skills

Most of the subjects you will study in college rely on research by experts, and these experts may have differing views on the same topic. Often textbooks spell out these arguments. Sometimes textbook authors will give several experts' views. But occasionally only one view will be presented. In this case, be aware that there may be other sides to the story.

Textbook arguments are usually well developed with supports that are relevant and adequate. These supports may be studies, surveys, expert opinions, experiments, theories, examples, or reasons. Textbooks may also offer graphs, charts, and photos as supports. An effective reader tests passages in textbooks for the logic of the arguments they present. The exercises that follow are designed to give you practice evaluating the logic of arguments in textbooks.

Practice 6

A. Read the following paragraph from a college psychology textbook, and study the figure that accompanies it. Mark each statement in the passage and the figure **C** if it is an author's claim or **S** if it provides support for the claim.

Textbook
Skills

Locus of Control

¹Locus of control is the most important trait of a person's personality. ²**Locus of control** is a person's belief about who or what controls the consequences of actions. ³A person who expects to control his or her own fate has an *internal* locus of control. ⁴This person thinks that rewards come through effort. ⁵A person who sees his or her life as being controlled by forces outside himself or herself has an *external* locus of control. ⁶This person thinks that his or her own behavior has no effect on outcomes.

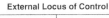

—Carlson, Neil, and William Buskist. *Psychology: Science of Behavior*, 5th ed., pp. 460–461.

_____ **1.** sentence 1   _____ **4.** sentence 4

_____ **2.** sentence 2   _____ **5.** sentence 5

_____ **3.** sentence 3   _____ **6.** sentence 6

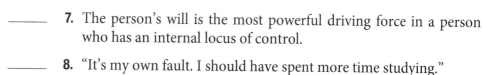

———— **7.** The person's will is the most powerful driving force in a person who has an internal locus of control.

———— **8.** "It's my own fault. I should have spent more time studying."

———— **9.** The environment is the most powerful driving force in a person who has an external locus of control.

———— **10.** "Did I get lucky or what? The teacher must really have gone easy on the grading."

B. Read the following paragraph from a college sociology textbook.

Textbook
Skills

Age and Crime

[1]Essentially, crime is a young person's game. [2]This idea is supported by the relationship between age and crime. [3]It indicates that the majority of arrests peak between the ages of 15 to 25. [4]After that point, they follow a slow but steady decrease throughout life. [5]Arrest data from other cultures and times in history also support this claim. [6]The link between age and crime is very clear in criminology. [7]According to Steffensmeier and Harer, a 60 percent decrease in crime rates in the 1980s is attributable to a decrease in the total number of 15- to 24-year-olds. [8]Clearly, age matters when discussing crime. [9]Social class and gender are also linked to criminal arrest.

—Carl, John D., *Think Sociology*, 2nd ed., p. 230.

11. Underline the topic sentence that states the claim of the author's argument.

———— **12.** Which sentence is *not* relevant to the author's point?
a. sentence 2   c. sentence 7
b. sentence 4   d. sentence 9

C. The following information comes from a college health textbook. Read each list of supports. Choose the claim that is adequately supported by the evidence in the list.

13. Supports

■ People who chronically skip breakfast burn an average of 150 fewer calories per day than regular breakfast eaters.

■ Breakfast eaters awaken with a souped-up metabolism.

■ Breakfast skippers greet each day cold and tired with the "metabolic furnace" set on low until lunch.

Textbook
Skills

Write **V** for valid by the claim that is adequately supported by the evidence.

    _____ a. People who skip breakfast lose more weight than people who eat breakfast.

    _____ b. People who skip breakfast use less energy.

    _____ c. Breakfast is the most important meal of the day.

    _____ d. People who skip breakfast are more hungry than people who eat breakfast.

14. Supports

- Eat a juicy apple or a cup of soup instead of a dry granola bar or a bag of popcorn.
- Dehydration stimulates the appetite.
- Foods with high water content will make you feel even more full than drinking water to wash down dry foods with the same calorie count.

Write **V** for valid by the claim that is adequately supported by the evidence.

    _____ a. Wet foods are healthier than dry foods.

    _____ b. Dry foods are not appropriate diet foods.

    _____ c. The water content of foods plays an important role in weight control.

    _____ d. Water intake is the most important part of a diet aimed at weight control.

VISUAL *VOCABULARY*

The context given in the three supports, along with this photo, suggests that **dehydrated** means _____. The word **dehydrated** is composed of three word parts: a prefix, a root, and a suffix. What is the root, and what does it mean?

Root: _____
Meaning: _____

▶ Dehydrated food

15. Supports

- A Tufts University study of women who took up moderate weightlifting found that they increased their strength by 35 to 75 percent.
- The women increased their balance by 14 percent.
- And they increased their bone density by 1 percent.
- The greater your muscle mass, the greater your metabolic rate and hence the more calories you burn.

Write **V** for valid by the claim that is adequately supported by the evidence.

_____ a. Women who lift moderate weights develop large muscle mass.

_____ b. Beginning a moderate weightlifting program demands time and dedication.

_____ c. Weightlifting is the best way to lose weight.

_____ d. A moderate weightlifting program has several health benefits in addition to burning calories.

—Adapted from Donatelle, Rebecca J.,
Health: The Basics, 5th ed., p. 271.

Apply Information Literacy Skills

 ## Academic, Personal, and Career Applications of the Basics of Argument

Learning the basics of argument is an important information literacy skill. In every area of your life you make and hear claims that may or may not be based on solid evidence. In your academic life, you sharpen your thinking skills as you examine the logic of specific claims and seek evidence for them in content courses. For example, historians may offer opposing views on the causes or effects of the war in Iraq. Psychologists may differ in their views of human development. In your personal life, you need to determine which claims are valid as you make decisions about everyday issues such as child care, products to purchase, or investments to make. In your career life, you will seek information to test claims raised by supervisors, coworkers, or customers. Thus, you will use the skills that you have learned in this chapter in academic, personal, and career situations. For example, you will:

■ Recognize your own need to make or evaluate a claim.

■ Determine if a claim is supported by sound evidence.

■ Support or reject a claim based on the validity of the evidence.

Academic Application

Assume you are taking a college course in sociology. The following passage is part of your weekly reading assignment from your textbook. Your professor has given you the following question based on your reading. "Although Freud was one of the most influential theorists of the twentieth century, most of his ideas have been discarded. What may have caused the rejection of Freud's ideas?"

■ **Before Reading**: Skim the passage. Underline the major claims made by Freud in his theory of personality.

■ **During Reading**: Double underline the opposing views of other sociologists in the passage.

■ **After Reading**: In the space following the passage, answer the question posed by the professor.

Freud and the Development of Personality

[1]As the mind and the self develop, so does the personality. [2]Sigmund Freud (1856–1939) developed a theory of the origin of personality that has had a major impact on Western thought. [3]Freud, a physician in Vienna in the early 1900s, founded psychoanalysis, a technique for treating emotional problems through long-term exploration of the subconscious mind. [4]Let's look at his theory. [5]Freud believed that personality consists of three elements. [6]Each child is born with the first element, an **id**, Freud's term for inborn drives that cause us to seek self-gratification. [7]The id of the newborn is evident in its cries of hunger or pain. [8]The pleasure-seeking id operates throughout life. [9]It demands the immediate fulfillment of basic needs: food, safety, attention, sex, and so on.

[10]The id's drive for immediate gratification, however, runs into a roadblock: primarily the needs of other people, especially those of the parents. [11]To adapt to these constraints, a second component of the personality emerges, which Freud called the ego. [12]The **ego** is the balancing force between the id and the demands of society that suppress it. [13]The ego also serves to balance the id and the **superego**, the third component of the personality, more commonly called the conscience. [14]The superego represents culture within us, the norms and values we have internalized from our social groups. [15]As the moral component of the personality, the

superego provokes feelings of guilt or shame when we break social rules, or pride and self-satisfaction when we follow them. [16]According to Freud, when the id gets out of hand, we follow our desires for pleasure and break society's norms.

[17]When the superego gets out of hand, we become overly rigid in following those norms and end up wearing a straitjacket of rules that inhibit our lives. [18]The ego, the balancing force, tries to prevent either the superego or the id from dominating. [19]In the emotionally healthy individual, the ego succeeds in balancing these conflicting demands of the id and the superego. [20]In the maladjusted individual, the ego fails to control the conflict between the id and the superego. [21]Either the id or the superego dominates this person, leading to internal confusion and problem behaviors.

Sociological Evaluation [22]Sociologists appreciate Freud's emphasis on socialization—his assertion that the social group into which we are born transmits norms and values that restrain our biological drives. [23]Sociologists, however, object to the view that inborn and subconscious motivations are the primary reasons for human behavior. [24]This denies the central principle of sociology: that factors such as social class (income, education, and occupation) and people's roles in groups underlie their behavior (Epstein 1988; Bush and Simmons 1990).

[25]Feminist sociologists have been especially critical of Freud. [26]Although what I just summarized applies to both females and males, Freud assumed that "male" is "normal." [27]He even referred to females as inferior, castrated males (Chodorow 1990; Gerhard 2000). [28]It is obvious that sociologists need to continue to research how we develop personality.

—Adapted from Henslin, James M., *Sociology: A Down-to-Earth Approach*, 9th ed., p. 67.

What may have caused the rejection of Freud's ideas? _____

_____

_____

_____

_____

Personal Application

Assume your doctor has strongly suggested that you change your diet to address health issues such as high cholesterol and inflamed arteries. You are reading labels and analyzing claims about foods before you consume them.

- **Before Reading**: Skim the advertisement for Sunshine Sweet Potato Sticks. Write at least one question you need answered to determine if this is a food you should add to your diet.

- **During Reading**: Highlight the facts that support the claim made by the advertisement.

- **After Reading**: In the space following the advertisement, record any additional questions you need answered to accept the claim made by the advertisement. Rate the product from 1 for unhealthful food to 5 for healthful food. Explain your rating.

Before Reading Questions: _____

_____

_____

Nature made it sweet.
Nature made it a superfood.
We make it fresh and easy!

Loaded with Vitamin A,
Vitamin B6, Vitamin C,
Calcium, and Potassium.
Great source of fiber.
Super anti-inflammatory.
Sunshine Sweet Potato Sticks–
Superfood for the super busy!

Low in sodium, saturated fat, and cholesterol, *Sunshine Sweet Potato Sticks*, made from sweet potatoes picked fresh from the farm, a healthy addition to any meal!

After Reading Evaluation of Advertisement: _____

_____

_____

_____

_____

_____

Career Application

Assume you are a supervisor of a department in a local business. One of your employees has made a claim that she is being sexually harassed. To evaluate the claim, you have the employee handbook as a resource.

- **Before Reading**: Skim the handbook. Skim the incident report.

- **During Reading**: Underline key details in the handbook that you can use to evaluate the incident report. Underline details in the incident report that support the claim of sexual harassment. Put question marks by the details in the report that raise questions. Double underline details in the report that refute sexual harassment.

- **After Reading**: In the space following the passage, record your conclusion about the incident report.

Employee Handbook: Workplace Harassment

[1]Unlawful harassment is a form of discrimination. Harassment violates Title VII of the Civil Rights Act of 1964 and other federal authority.

[2]Harassment is the unwelcome verbal or physical conduct based on race, color, religion, sex (whether or not of a sexual nature and including same-gender harassment and gender identity harassment), national origin, age (40 and over), disability (mental or physical), sexual orientation, or retaliation. [3]Harassment may occur in one of two ways or both.

1. [4]The conduct is severe or pervasive to create a hostile work environment.
2. [5]A supervisor's harassing conduct results in a tangible change in an employee's employment status or benefits (for example, demotion, termination, failure to promote, etc.).

[6]**Hostile work environment harassment** has several traits. [7]This harassment is the unwelcome comments or conduct based on sex, race, or

other legally protected characteristics. [8]The harassment interferes with an employee's work performance. [9]Or the harassment creates an intimidating, hostile, or offensive work environment. [10]Anyone in the workplace might commit this type of harassment. [11]A harasser could be a manager, co-worker, or non-employee. [12]Examples of non-employees are a contractor, vendor, or guest. [13]The victim can be anyone affected by the conduct, not just the individual at whom the offensive conduct is directed. [14]The following are examples of actions that may create sexual hostile environment harassment.

- [15]Leering—staring in a sexually suggestive manner.
- [16]Making offensive remarks about looks, clothing, or body parts.
- [17]Touching in a way that may make an employee feel uncomfortable. [18]Patting, pinching, or intentional brushing against another's body are examples.
- [19]Telling sexual or lewd jokes, hanging sexual posters, making sexual gestures, etc.
- [20]Sending, forwarding or asking for sexually suggestive letters, notes, emails, or images.

What Is Not Harassment? [21]Federal law does not prohibit simple teasing, offhand comments, or minor isolated incidents. [22]Rather, the conduct must be so offensive as to alter the conditions of one's employment. [23]Immediately report any case of harassment to your supervisor, any member of management, or the Human Resource Department.

—Adapted from Federal Communications Commission.
"Understanding Workplace Harassment."
FCC Encyclopedia. FCC.gov.

Harassment Incident Report Form

Background Information

Date of Incident: September 24   **Victim Name:** Rosa Smythe

Alleged Harasser: Clint Edwards   **Incident location:** in office, email

Type of Harassment ___Age ___Disability ___Gender ___Marital Status

___National Origin ___Physical Attributes ___Race ___ Religion _x_ Sexual

Brief Description of Incident: Ms. Smythe alleges that Mr. Edwards has continually sexually harassed her over the past several months both in the office and by email. On September 24, Mr. Edwards sent Ms. Smythe an email congratulating her on her sales figures. The content of the message complimented Ms. Smythe on her "sexy good looks and flirty ways" to which he credited her success. Shortly before receiving the email, Mr. Edwards and Ms. Smythe were in the employee break room. As Ms. Smythe was pouring her coffee, Mr. Edwards approached from behind and leaned up against her as he reached for a cup on the shelf beside the coffee pot. When Ms. Smythe objected, Mr. Edwards patted her lower back, winked, and said, "Oh, I'm sorry. You know you like it." Ms. Smythe states that this incident is only one of many similar in nature. Email sent from Edwards to Smythe on September 24 is in attachment.

List of Names of Witness(es) People in the break room during the incident: Doug Webb, Kim Majors, and Juan Rejos.

Response/Recommendation to Harassment Incident Report: _____

_____

_____

_____

_____

_____

_____

REVIEW TEST 1

Score (number correct) _____ x 5 = _____%

Visit MyReadingLab to take this test online and receive feedback and guidance on your answers.

Argument

A. Read the following groups of ideas. Mark each statement **C** if it is an author's claim or **S** if it provides support for the claim.

   Group 1

   _____   **1.** Julie has a high fever.

   _____   **2.** Julie has the flu, not just a common cold.

   _____   **3.** Julie's symptoms came on suddenly.

   _____   **4.** Julie also has a cough, chills, and muscle aches.

   Group 2

   _____   **5.** Veterinary pet insurance is a good investment for a pet owner.

   _____   **6.** A good insurance policy can cost as little as $15 a month for cats and $18 a month for dogs.

   _____   **7.** Benefits cover the cost of tests, treatments, and medicine.

   _____   **8.** After a $50 deductible, all the pet's medical bills are covered.

B. Read the following lists of claims and supports. Mark each support **R** if it is relevant to the claim or **N** if it is not relevant to the claim.

   Claim: A negative outlook on life is a key barrier to success.

   Supports

   _____   **9.** Many people play a "tape" of negative messages in their heads, and these negative messages control their thoughts.

   _____   **10.** Messages like "I can't do this" or "No one cares what I do" are often untrue statements that block positive action.

   _____   **11.** Most actions begin as thoughts or beliefs.

   _____   **12.** Success begins with the belief or thought that the goal is attainable.

_____ **13.** Everybody fails sometimes.

_____ **14.** Success leads to more success.

Claim: The study of mathematics is essential to becoming a well-educated person with a large number of career options.

Supports

_____ **15.** Knowledge of mathematics makes one a smarter, better-informed consumer.

_____ **16.** The study of mathematics is difficult for many people.

_____ **17.** Solving mathematical problems helps develop critical thinking skills.

_____ **18.** Mathematics has always been a part of a good education.

_____ **19.** Understanding mathematical concepts helps one understand and use technology better.

_____ **20.** Mathematical skills are the basis of hundreds of good-paying jobs in accounting, engineering, and computer programming.

REVIEW TEST 2

Score (number correct) _____ x 5 = _____%

Visit MyReadingLab to take this test online and receive feedback and guidance on your answers.

Argument

A. Read the following groups of ideas. Mark each statement **C** if it is an author's claim or **S** if it provides support for the claim.

_____ **1.** In California, Senator Deborah Ortiz proposed a law that would ban soft drinks from all public schools in the state.

_____ **2.** In Maine, State Representative Sean Faircloth sponsored the "Maine Obesity Package"; this law would force fast-food chains to place nutritional information on menus.

_____ **3.** The obesity bill would also set aside dollars for walking trails, bike lanes, and cross-country ski trails in Maine.

_____ **4.** Lawmakers in several states believe that Americans should become more active and eat healthier fare.

B. Study the following mock advertisement for gun locks. Read the claim and the list of supports. Mark each support **R** if it is relevant to the claim or **N** if it is not relevant to the claim.

An Unlocked Gun is an Open Door to Disaster

Most often, you do not leave home without locking your front door in order to ensure your personal safety. Locking the door just makes sense. Use common sense also when you own and use firearms. A gun lock ensures personal safety. When not in use, a gun should be kept unloaded, in a gun safe, and equipped with a gun lock.

Shut the door on disaster. Lock your firearms.

Claim: Gun owners should use gun locks on their firearms to ensure safety.

Supports

_____ **5.** Most often, you do not leave home without locking your front door in order to ensure your personal safety.

_____ **6.** Locking the door just makes sense.

_____ **7.** Use common sense also when you own and use firearms.

_____ **8.** A gun lock ensures personal safety.

_____ **9.** When not in use, a gun should be kept unloaded, in a gun safe, and equipped with a gun lock.

_____ **10.** Responsible gun ownership is just common sense.

C. Read the following lists of claims and supports. Mark each support **R** if it is relevant to the claim or **N** if it is not relevant to the claim.

Claim: Anger can be controlled.

Supports

_____ **11.** Relaxation skills such as deep breathing and slowly repeating words like *relax* can ease angry feelings.

_____ **12.** Avoiding situations that cause anger can help prevent anger; for example, a person who is angered by traffic should take less traveled roads when possible.

_____ **13.** Anger is healthy and normal.

_____ **14.** Some people are hotheads and just can't help themselves.

Claim: Some websites sell medicine that may not be safe to use and could put your health at risk.

_____ **15.** Some websites that sell medicine aren't U.S. state-licensed pharmacies or aren't pharmacies at all.

_____ **16.** Some websites may give a diagnosis that is not correct and sell medicine that is not right for you or your condition.

_____ **17.** Some medicines sold online are fake (counterfeit or "copycat" medicines); they are too strong or too weak, or they are made with dangerous ingredients.

_____ **18.** Identity theft is always a concern when buying from online sources.

D. Study the following table.

College Students' Top Ten Reasons for Cheating

1. The instructor gave too much material.
2. The instructor left the room.
2.* A friend asked me to cheat, and I couldn't say no.
4. The instructor doesn't seem to care if I learn the material.
5. The course information is useless.
6. The course material is too hard.
6.* Everyone else seems to be cheating.
8. I'm in danger of losing a scholarship due to low grades.
9. I don't have time to study because I'm working to pay for school.
10. People sitting around me made no effort to protect their work.

* = tied

—Haines, Valerie J., et al., from "College Cheating," *Research in Higher Education*, p. 52.

19–20. Choose the *two* claims that are *not* adequately supported by the evidence.

_____ a. Instructors are unfair in their expectations.

_____ b. Students blame their actions on teachers and other students.

_____ c. Students may cheat because of grades and time concerns.

_____ d. Most students take responsibility for their own cheating.

REVIEW TEST 3

Score (number correct) _____ x 10 = _____ %

Visit MyReadingLab to take this test online and receive feedback and guidance on your answers.

Read the following passage from a textbook for a college business course. Answer the questions that follow.

High Seas Dumping

Textbook
Skills

¹Cruising has become a very popular vacation. ²More than eight million passengers take an ocean voyage each year, cruising many areas of the world's oceans in search of pristine beaches and clear tropical waters. ³The Caribbean Sea, the Mediterranean Sea, and the coast of Alaska are among the most popular destinations. ⁴The coasts of Europe and Asia are also growing in popularity. ⁵While tourists and the giant ships that carry them are usually welcome for the revenues that they bring, unfortunately, the ships also bring something much less desirable—pollution.

⁶A modern cruise ship carries an average of 2,000 passengers and 1,000 crew members. ⁷This many people, of course, generate a lot of waste. ⁸On a typical day, a ship will produce seven tons of solid garbage, which is incinerated and then dumped; fifteen gallons of highly toxic chemical waste; 30,000 gallons of sewage; 7,000 gallons of bilge water containing oil; and 225,000 gallons of "gray" water from sinks and laundries. ⁹Cruise ships also pick up ballast water whenever and wherever it's needed and then discharge it later, releasing animals and pollution from other parts of the world. ¹⁰Multiply this problem by more than 167 ships worldwide, cruising 50 weeks per year, and the scope of the environmental damage is staggering.

¹¹Environmental groups see the top pollution-related problem as death of marine life, including extinction. ¹²Foreign animals bring parasites

and diseases, and in some cases, replace native species entirely. [13]Bacteria that are harmless to human beings can kill corals that provide food and habitat for many species. [14]Oil and toxic chemicals are deadly to wildlife even in minute quantities.

[15]Turtles swallow plastic bags, thinking they are jellyfish, and starve. [16]Seals and birds become entangled in the plastic rings that hold beverage cans and drown.

[17]Other problems include the habitat destruction or disease that affects U.S. industries, costing $137 billion each year. [18]For example, cholera, picked up in ships' ballast water off the coast of Peru, caused a devastating loss to fish and shrimp harvesters in the Gulf of Mexico in the 1990s when infected catches had to be destroyed. [19]Heavy metal poisoning of fish is rising. [20]And concern is on the rise that the poisons are moving up the food chain from microscopic animals, to fish, and ultimately to humans. [21]Phosphorus, found in detergents, causes an overgrowth of algae, which then consume all the available oxygen in the water, making it incapable of supporting any flora or fauna. [22]One such "dead zone" occurs each summer in the Gulf of Mexico at the mouth of the Mississippi River. [23]The area, caused by pollution and warm water, is about the size of Massachusetts—8,000 square miles of lifelessness.

[24]Lack of regulation is the biggest obstacle to solving the problem. [25]By international law, countries may regulate oceans for three miles off their shores. [26]International treaties provide some additional regulation up to 25 miles offshore. [27]Beyond the 25-mile point, however, ships are allowed free rein. [28]Also, each country's laws and enforcement policies vary considerably. [29]And even when laws are strict, enforcement may be limited. [30]The U.S. Coast Guard enforces regulations off the U.S. coast, but it is spread thinly. [31]Only about 1 percent of the Coast Guard's annual budget is spent.

[32]While some polluting by cruise ships can be expected, intentional illegal dumping may also be growing in scope. [33]Over the last decade, for instance, as enforcement has tightened, 10 cruise lines have collectively paid $48.5 million in fines related to illegal dumping. [34]In the largest settlement to date, Royal Caribbean (www.royalcaribbean.com) paid $27 million for making illegal alterations to facilities, falsifying records, lying to the Coast Guard, and deliberately destroying evidence. [35]The fine may seem high, but it covers 30 different charges and 10 years of violations and seems small compared to the firm's 2001 profits of almost $1 billion. [36]Observers agree that Royal Caribbean's fine was less than

what the firm would have paid to dispose of the waste properly over a decade. [37]In addition, a lawsuit is pending regarding the firing of a whistle-blower, the firm's former vice president for safety and environment. [38]"This [case] is like the Enron of the seas," says attorney William Arnlong, who represents the whistle-blower.

[39]Many feel that the fines haven't been steep enough. [40]Norwegian Cruise Lines (www.ncl.com) recently paid just $1 million for falsifying records in a case that included "some of the worst [violations] we've ever seen," according to Rick Langlois, an EPA investigator. [41]Langlois and others are outspoken against the cruise lines profiteering from an environment that they are destroying. [42]But the critics note that the companies won't stop as long as the profits continue. [43]Technology exists to make the waste safe. [44]But industry experts estimate that dumping can save a firm millions of dollars annually. [45]From that perspective, Norwegian's actions were just a "brilliant business decision," says Langlois.

—Adapted from Griffin, Ricky W. and Ebert,
Ronald J., *Business*, 8th ed., pp. 57–58, 83.

_____ **1.** The main claim asserted by the author is stated in
    a. sentence 1.   c. sentence 10.
    b. sentence 5.   d. sentence 11.

_____ **2.** In paragraph 6, sentence 20 states
    a. a claim.
    b. evidence supporting a claim.

_____ **3.** In paragraph 7, sentence 27 states
    a. a claim.
    b. evidence supporting a claim.

_____ **4.** In paragraph 8, sentence 32 states
    a. a claim.
    b. evidence supporting a claim.

_____ **5.** The author expresses a bias
    a. in favor of the cruise lines' waste management systems.
    b. in favor of high fines against cruise lines for acts against the environment.
    c. against tourists who enjoy cruising.
    d. against regulations of cruise lines.

6–10. Complete the following outline with the series of claims asserted by the author in the passage.

Main claim: Multiply this problem by more than 167 ships worldwide, cruising 50 weeks per year, and the scope of the environmental damage is staggering.

I. _____

_____

II. _____

_____

III. _____

IV. _____

_____

V. _____

SUMMARY RESPONSE

Restate the author's central idea in your own words. In your summary, state the author's claim. Begin your summary response with the following: *The central idea of "High Seas Dumping" by Griffin and Ebert is . . .*

WHAT DO YOU THINK?

Is taking a cruise the kind of vacation you would enjoy? Why or why not? Has reading this passage affected your views about cruising? Assume you are a representative of one side of this issue—either as an environmental activist or as a spokesperson for the cruising industry. Write a letter to the editor of your local newspaper in which you take a stand on this issue. In your letter discuss the following points:

- Summarize how cruising is harmful.
- Suggest ways to improve cruising regulations.

REVIEW TEST 4

Score (number correct) _____ x 10 = _____%

Visit MyReadingLab to take this test online and receive feedback and guidance on your answers.

Combined Skills Test

Before you read the following passage from a college textbook on marriage and families, read the Vocabulary Preview, skim the passage, and answer the Before Reading questions. Then read the passage carefully and answer the After Reading questions that follow.

Vocabulary Preview

intervened (19): came between two people or things in order to exert influence

Helicopter Parents

¹Every summer across the United States children gather on playgrounds to board buses that will carry them away to summer camp. ²And, every summer one or more of these children cry, having trouble saying good-bye to Mom and Dad. ³However, according to camp counselors, the camp crybabies are now the parents who are having trouble letting go. ⁴Some experts call it "kid-sickness," a condition attributed in large part to today's involved style of parenting aided by the ever-present cell phones, email, and text message (Irvine, 2008). ⁵Others, who deal with young people, including college administrators, refer to many of today's parents as hovering or helicopter parents (Fortin, 2008). ⁶Even employers are finding that "helicopter parenting" extends into the workplace. ⁷Parents accompany their children to job fairs and then contact employers to discuss their child's salary, benefits, and working conditions (Armour, 2007).

⁸The process is much the same regardless of the child's age. ⁹These parents, though well meaning, are ever-present, making sure that the children are OK, but often preventing their children from learning to solve problems on their own. ¹⁰Many camp counselors, college administrators, and employers see this as too much parental involvement and are taking steps to limit it. ¹¹Many summer camps now spend as much time preparing parents for camp as they do the campers themselves. ¹²They restrict the timing and number of faxes, emails, or calls between parents and campers. ¹³Camp owners have even hired full-time parent **liaisons** to parental concerns (Kelley, 2008). ¹⁴They also insist that the camp staff, not parents, handle routine issues like homesickness and disputes

between campers. [15]Similarly, college administrators are telling parents to step back and allow their children to become independent. [16]Employers, too, say that too much parental involvement can backfire. [17]An adult child may lose a job opportunity because the employer doesn't want to deal with their parents.

[18]However, the news is not all bad. [19]Data gathered for the National Survey of Student Engagement found that students whose parents were in frequent contact with them and often **intervened** on their behalf reported higher levels of engagement. [20]They also more frequently used deep learning activities such as after-class discussion with professors, intensive writing exercises, and independent research than students with less-involved parents. [21]According to the survey, children of helicopter parents were more satisfied with their college experience than were other students. [22]However, students with very involved parents had lower grades than those whose parents were not as involved (Mathews, 2007).

—Adapted from Schwartz, Mary Ann A. and Scott, Barbara Marliene, *Marriage and Families: Diversity and Change*, 6th ed., pp. 249–250.

Before Reading

Vocabulary in Context

_____ **1.** The word **liaisons** in sentence 13 refers to people who
a. counsel.   c. lead.
b. train.   d. communicate.

Tone and Purpose

_____ **2.** The overall tone of the passage is
a. objective.   b. biased.

_____ **3.** The primary purpose of the passage is to
a. inform.   c. persuade.
b. entertain.

After Reading

Central Idea and Main Idea

_____ **4.** Which sentence best states the central idea of the passage?
a. sentence 1   c. sentence 8
b. sentence 3   d. sentence 9

Supporting Details

_____ **5.** Sentence 6 is a
  a. major supporting detail for the central idea.
  b. minor supporting detail for the central idea.

Transitions

_____ **6.** The relationship between sentences 14 and 15 is
  a. contrast.   c. cause and effect.
  b. comparison.   d. time order.

Thought Patterns

_____ **7.** The overall thought pattern of the passage is
  a. contrast.   c. cause and effect.
  b. time order.   d. definition and example.

Fact and Opinion

_____ **8.** Sentence 18 is a statement of
  a. fact.   c. fact and opinion.
  b. opinion.

Inferences

_____ **9.** Based on the details in the passage, we can infer that
  a. children resent helicopter parents.
  b. children of helicopter parents never solve problems on their own.
  c. separation from parents is a necessary step toward adulthood.
  d. helicopter parents have only their children's interests in mind.

Argument

_____ **10.** Which statement is not relevant to the following claim?

  Claim: There are some positive effects of heavy parental involvement.

  a. Students with heavily involved parents reported higher levels of engagement in school.
  b. Students with heavily involved parents were more frequently involved in deep learning activities.

c. Students with heavily involved parents were more satisfied with their college experience.

d. Students with heavily involved parents tended to have lower grades.

SUMMARY RESPONSE

Restate the author's central idea in your own words. In your summary, state the author's claim. Begin your summary response with the following: *The central idea of "Helicopter Parents" by Schwartz and Scott is . . .*

WHAT DO YOU THINK?

Have you experienced or witnessed helicopter parenting? Do you agree with the author that parents may hinder their children's success by overparenting? Assume you are a summer camp counselor and you are writing a welcome letter to prepare participating families to transition their children from home to camp. In your letter discuss the following points:

- Explain how campers will develop independence and problem solving skills.
- List some of the benefits of separating parents from their children.
- Explain when and why parents will be contacted if needed.

 ## After Reading About the Basics of Argument

Before you move on to the Mastery Tests on the basics of argument, take time to reflect on your learning and performance by answering the following questions. Write your answers in your notebook.

- How has my knowledge base or prior knowledge about the basics of argument changed?
- Based on my studies, how do I think I will perform on the Mastery Test(s)? Why do I think my scores will be above average, average, or below average?

- Would I recommend this to other students who want to learn more about the basics of argument? Why or why not?

Test your understanding of what you have learned about the basics of argument by completing the Chapter 12 Review.

Name _____ Section _____

Date _____ **Score** (number correct) _____ x 10 = _____%

Visit MyReadingLab to take this test online and receive feedback and guidance on your answers.

A. Read the following group of ideas. Mark each statement **C** if it is an author's claim or **S** if it provides support for the claim.

_____ **1.** Our groundwater is being withdrawn to be packaged in plastic bottles and sold on supermarket shelves.

_____ **2.** The energy costs of bottled water have been estimated to be 1,000–2,000 times greater than the energy costs of tap water.

_____ **3.** Most energy was used in manufacturing the bottle and transporting the product.

_____ **4.** Since at least three out of four bottles in the United States are thrown away after use, we must dispose of 30–40 billion containers per year.

_____ **5.** Bottled water has substantial environmental impact.

—Jay Withgott and Matthew Laposata, *Essential Environment: The Science Behind the Stories, 3rd ed.* Upper Saddle River: Pearson Education, 2012.

B. Read the author's claim and the list of supports. Then mark each support **R** if it is relevant to the claim or **N** if it is not relevant to the claim.

Claim: Standardized testing improves student learning in the United States.

_____ **6.** A 100-year study of standardized testing by assessment expert Richard P. Phelps reveals the positive effect standardized testing has on student learning.

_____ **7.** Standardized tests make sure all students are taught the same information and receive the same opportunities to learn.

_____ **8.** Standardized tests focus on the essential basic skills all students need to master.

_____ **9.** Teaching to the test destroys creativity and promotes rote learning based on skill and drill teaching strategies.

_____ **10.** Standardized tests are too stressful; in many cases students' test anxiety is the cause for poor performance on the test, not lack of knowledge.

A woman holds a sign during a protest to demand climate action in central Sydney.

The maps in this protest sign state _____.

   a. a claim
   b. evidence for a claim

Name _____ Section _____

Date _____ **Score** (number correct) _____ x 10 = _____%

Visit MyReadingLab to take this test online and receive feedback and guidance on your answers.

A. Read the following groups of ideas. Each group contains the author's claim and supports for that claim. Identify the author's claim in each group.

_____ **1.** a. Reading short stories allows us to experience times and places other than our own.
b. Reading short stories stimulates our imagination.
c. Short stories should be read for a number of reasons.
d. Reading short stories helps us connect with the experiences and feelings of others.

_____ **2.** a. Space tourism will someday be a money-making business.
b. Businessman Dennis Tito was the first space tourist.
c. Tito flew aboard a Russian rocket to the international space station on April 30, 2001.
d. In a survey of over 1,000 households, 60 percent of those surveyed said they were interested in traveling to space for a vacation.

_____ **3.** a. Daytona Beach plays host to hundreds of thousands of race fans during the world-famous Daytona 500 NASCAR race every February.
b. Year-round mild climate and beautiful beaches make Daytona a perfect family vacation spot.
c. Every October and March, thousands of motorcycles thunder into Daytona Beach for Oktoberfest and Bike Week, respectively.
d. Daytona Beach appeals to a wide array of tourists.

_____ **4.** a. Some computer users complain about the amount of time their service provider is down and inaccessible.
b. Computers have some disadvantages.
c. Many computer users are discouraged by the amount of e-mail they must deal with on a daily basis.
d. A growing concern among parents is the access children have to unsuitable material on the Internet.

B. Read the following claim and its supports. Mark each support **R** if it is relevant to the claim or **N** if it is not relevant to the claim.

Claim: Animals become extinct mainly as a result of human action.

Supports

_____ **5.** Humans destroy the natural environment of a species by damming rivers, filling in swamps and marshes, and cutting down trees to build homes, roads, and other developments.

_____ **6.** Many species of fish and birds have been damaged by oil spills, acid rain, and water pollution created by industry.

_____ **7.** Many animals are hunted to extinction for their meat, furs, or other valuable parts.

_____ **8.** Some people have taken positive steps to protect endangered species.

_____ **9.** New species introduced into a habitat by humans can bring diseases that destroy the native species.

C. Read the following paragraph, which consists of supports.

[1]As early as 1900, Frank Lloyd Wright (1867–1959) advocated an "organic" approach that integrated architecture with nature. [2]The best-known expression of Wright's conviction that buildings ought to be not only on the landscape, but in it, is Fallingwater, in rural Pennsylvania, commissioned by Edgar Kaufmann, a Pittsburgh department store owner, to replace a family summer cottage on a site that featured a waterfall into a pool where the Kaufmann children played. [3]Wright decided to build the house into the cliff over the pool, allowing the water to flow around and under the house. [4]In a daring engineering move, he designed a series of broad concrete terraces out from the house, echoing the great slabs of natural rock. [5]The rocks on which the family had once sunbathed by the waterfall became the hearthstone of their fireplace. [6]Long bands of windows and glass doors offer spectacular views, uniting woods, water, and house. [7]Such houses do not simply testify to the ideal of living in harmony with nature; they declare war on the modern industrial city. [8]When asked what could be done to improve the city, Wright responded bluntly, "Tear it down."

—Adapted from Marilyn Stokstad and Michael Cothren, From *Art: A Brief History*, 5th ed., Upper Saddle River: Pearson Education, Inc., 2012, p. 546.

_____ **10.** In this paragraph, the author expresses a bias
   a. against Frank Lloyd Wright for building a house over a waterfall.
   b. against Frank Lloyd Wright for advocating that we tear down cities.
   c. toward Frank Lloyd Wright for a daring design integrating architecture with nature.
   d. toward Frank Lloyd Wright for his dislike of the modern industrial city.

Name _____ Section _____

Date _____ **Score** (number correct) _____ x 20 = _____%

Visit My ReadingLab to take this test online and receive feedback and guidance on your answers.

A. Read each list of supports. Choose the claim that is adequately supported by the evidence in each list.

Supports

Textbook Skills

▪ The push to create public schools began in earnest in the 1820s.

▪ Many people saw public education as the answer to poverty.

▪ Others saw public education as a way to fight crime and help immigrants fit into society.

▪ At first, many thought Sunday schools were the way "to reclaim the vicious, to instruct the ignorant, and to raise the standard of morals among the lower classes of society."

▪ But soon these religious reformers called for public schools, too.

—Adapted from James Kirby Martin, et al., From *America and Its People: Volume II: A Mosaic in the Making*, 3rd ed. Upper Saddle River: Pearson Education, Inc., 1999, p. 340.

_____ **1.** Which claim is adequately supported by the evidence?
   a. Public schools were created for the good of both the individual and the country.
   b. Public schools were created so that everyone in the country could have free education.
   c. Education is the only way a person can become successful.
   d. Education is a basic right owed to everyone.

Supports

Textbook Skills

▪ Whole grains are packed with vitamins, minerals, and fiber that you just don't find in plain white bread, processed cereals, white rice, or even many healthful-looking enriched "multigrain" breads.

▪ Researchers have found disease-fighting properties in the nutrients in whole grains.

▪ In addition to being nutritious, whole grains are loaded with flavor and texture, adding interest to meals.

—Rebecca J. Donatelle, *Health: The Basics,* 5th ed., Upper Saddle River: Pearson Education, Inc., 2002, p. 231.

_____ **2.** Which claim is adequately supported by the evidence?
   a. Whole grains are the most healthful food available.
   b. Multigrain breads are not good for you.
   c. Whole-grain foods are hard to beat for nutrition, taste, and texture.
   d. The easiest way to get whole grain in the diet is by eating whole-wheat bread.

597

Supports

- Infant mortality rates are higher for boys, and women live an average of seven years longer than men.
- Females have a more acute sense of smell and taste than males, and women's hearing is better and lasts longer than men's.
- While alcoholism is twice as common in men as in women, alcoholic women are at much greater risk for death from drinking.
- Women have a higher risk than men of developing diabetes, and a heart attack is more likely to be fatal for a woman than for a man.

—Adapted from Benokraitis, Nijoke. *Marriage and Families: Changes, Choices and Constraints*, p. 75.

_____ **3.** Which claim is adequately supported by the evidence?
   a. Women are stronger than men.
   b. Men are stronger than women.
   c. Women live longer than men.
   d. Men and women are different from each other.

B. Read the following paragraph. Then answer the questions that follow it.

Power Goes to the Less Interested

[1]If you can walk away from the rewards that your partner controls or can suffer the punishment your partner gives, then you control the relationship. [2]If, on the other hand, you need the rewards that your partner controls or are unable or unwilling to suffer the punishments that your partner can give, then your partner has the power and controls the relationship. [3]Power corrupts people. [4]In a love relationship, for example, the person who maintains the greater power is the one who would find it easier to break up the relationship. [5]The person who is unwilling or unable to break up has little power. [6]This lack of power is due to the fact that he or she is dependent on the relationship and the rewards provided by the other person.

—Adapted from DeVito, Joseph A. *Messages: Building Interpersonal Communication Skills*, p. 328.

_____ **4.** Which sentence states the author's claim?
   a. In any interpersonal relationship, the person who holds the power is the one who is less interested in and less dependent on the other person.
   b. Some people like to be controlled by others.
   c. Some people like to control others.
   d. Powerful people do not make lasting commitments to others.

_____ **5.** Which sentence is *not* relevant to the argument?
   a. sentence 1   c. sentence 3
   b. sentence 2   d. sentence 6

Name _____ Section _____

Date _____ **Score** (number correct) _____ x 25 = _____%

Visit MyReadingLab to take this test online and receive feedback and guidance on your answers.

Read the following passage from a college psychology textbook. Answer the questions that follow.

Issues in Animal Research

Textbook
Skills

[1]Should animals be used in psychological and medical research? [2]This question has often produced very polarized responses. [3]On one side are researchers who point to the very important breakthroughs research with animals has allowed in several areas of behavioral science. [4]The benefits of animal research have included discovery and testing of drugs that treat anxiety and mental illnesses. [5]Research with animals has also yielded important knowledge about drug addiction. [6]Animal research benefits animals as well. [7]For example, psychological researchers have shown how to ease the stresses of confinement experienced by zoo animals. [8]Their studies of animal learning and social organization have led to the improved design of enclosures. [9]Their research has brought about animal facilities that promote good health.

[10]For defenders of animal rights "ethical concerns about compromised animal welfare cannot be eased by human benefits alone." [11]Specialists in ethics encourage researchers to adhere to the 3 *Rs*: reduce, replace, and refine. [12]Researchers should use tests of their hypothesis that *reduce* the number of animals they require. [13]Or researchers should *replace* the use of animals altogether. [14]They should *refine* their tests to minimize pain and distress. [15]Each animal researcher must judge his or her work with heightened scrutiny. [16]The American Psychological Association provides firm ethical guidelines for researchers who use nonhuman animals in their research.

[17]Surveys of 1,188 psychology students and 3,982 American Psychological Association members on their attitudes toward animal research support a standard of heightened scrutiny.

[18]Roughly 80 percent of the people surveyed believed that animals should be observed in naturalistic settings. [19]Smaller numbers (30 to 70 percent) supported studies involving caging or confinement. [20]Support of caging depended in part on the type of animal (for example, rats, pigeons, dogs, or primates). [21]Both students and their professors disapproved of studies involving physical pain or death.

[22]A majority of both groups (roughly 60 percent) supported the use of animals in undergraduate psychology courses. [23]But only about a third of each group felt that laboratory work with animals should be a required part of an undergraduate psychology major.

—Adapted from Gerrig, Richard J.; Zimbardo, Philip G., *Psychology and Life*, 16th ed., pp. 37, 58 © 2010 Pearson Education, Inc. Reproduced by permission of Pearson Education, Inc.

_____ 1. The author expresses
   a. a bias for use of animals in testing.
   b. a bias against use of animals in testing.
   c. a balanced view of the issues in animal research.

_____ 2. Sentence 6 states
   a. a claim.   b. evidence in support of a claim.

_____ 3. The main claim of the passage is stated in
   a. sentence 1.   c. sentence 3.
   b. sentence 2.   d. sentence 16.

_____ 4. Which statement is not relevant to the following claim?

   Claim: Use of animals in psychological and medical testing should be banned.
   a. Confined animals experience stress.
   b. Use of animals in research compromises animal welfare to benefit humans.
   c. Researchers should replace the use of animals in research altogether.
   d. Use of animals in research benefits animals as well.

VISUAL *VOCABULARY*

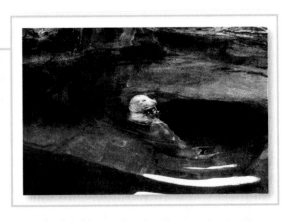

Sea lion in a naturalistic habitat of Seward SeaLife Center, Seward, Alaska, USA. The best meaning of the word **naturalistic** is _____.

   a. real life
   b. safe
   c. ideal

12 Summary of Key Concepts about the Basics of Argument

 Assess your comprehension of the basics of argument.

▫ Effective argument is a _____

_____.

▫ An argument is made up of two types of statements:

▫ _____.

▫ _____.

▫ An invalid conclusion is _____

_____.

▫ The four steps to analyze an argument are as follows:

▫ Step 1: _____.

▫ Step 2: _____.

▫ Step 3: _____.

▫ Step 4: _____.

▫ An invalid conclusion is making a claim without _____

_____.

Test Your Comprehension of the Basics of Argument

Respond to the following questions and prompts.

 In your own words, explain the relationship between making an inference and

analyzing an argument. _____

_____

_____

_____

LO2 LO3
LO4 LO5
LO7

Create a valid argument. Study the photograph. Then, based on the details in the photo, write a claim and two supports that clearly support the claim.

▲ The Impact of Marine Debris

Claim: _____

Support 1: _____

Support 2: _____

LO1 LO2
LO3 LO4
LO5 LO6
LO7

Summarize the two most important ideas in this chapter that will help you improve your reading comprehension.

_____

_____

_____

Advanced Argument: Persuasive Techniques

13

LO LEARNING OUTCOMES

After studying this chapter, you should be able to:

LO1 Identify Biased Arguments

LO2 Detect Fallacies Based on Irrelevant Arguments

LO3 Detect Propaganda Techniques Based on Irrelevant Arguments

LO4 Detect Fallacies Based on Inadequate Arguments

LO5 Detect Propaganda Techniques Based on Inadequate Arguments

LO6 Develop Textbook Skills: Examining Biased Arguments in Textbooks

LO7 Apply Information Literacy Skills: Academic, Personal, and Career Applications of Advanced Argument: Persuasive Techniques

Before Reading About Advanced Argument: Persuasive Techniques

In this chapter, you will build on the concepts you studied about the basics of argument. Take a moment to review the four steps in analyzing an argument. Fill in the following blanks with each of the steps.

Step 1: _____

Step 2: _____

Step 3: _____

Step 4: _____

Based on the learning outcomes and what you learned about the basics of argument, complete the following idea:

A valid argument is made up of relevant and adequate supports.

Biased arguments that use logical fallacies and propaganda techniques are

composed of _____ and _____ supports.

To help you master the material in the chapter, create a three-column chart in your notebook. In the left column write the headings from the learning outcomes, as in the example that follows. Leave enough room between each heading to fill in definitions and examples as you work through the chapter.

General definition: A fallacy is

Fallacy	**Definition**	**Example**
Personal attack		
Straw man		

General definition: Propaganda is

Propaganda technique	**Definition**	**Example**
Name-calling		
Testimonials		

LO1 Identify Biased Arguments

Much of the information that we come in contact with on a daily basis is designed to influence our thoughts and behaviors. Advertisements, editorials, and political campaigns constantly offer one-sided, biased information designed to sway public opinion.

This biased information is based on two types of reasoning: the use of **fallacies** in logical thought and the use of **propaganda**. An effective reader identifies and understands the use of these persuasion techniques in biased arguments.

What Is a Fallacy in Logical Thought?

You have already studied logical thought in Chapter 12, "The Basics of Argument." Logical thought or argument is a process that includes an author's claim, relevant support, and a valid conclusion. A **fallacy** is an error in the process of logical thought. A fallacy leads to an invalid conclusion. You have also studied two general types of fallacies: irrelevant details and inadequate details. By its nature, a fallacy is not persuasive because it weakens an argument. However, fallacies are often used to convince readers to accept an author's claim. In fact, the word *fallacy* comes from a Latin word that means "to deceive" or "trick." You will learn more about irrelevant and inadequate arguments in the next two sections of this chapter.

Fallacies are not to be confused with false facts. A fact, true or false, is stated without bias, and facts can be proven true or false by objective evidence. In contrast, a fallacy is an invalid inference or biased opinion about a fact or set of facts. Sometimes the word *fallacy* is used to refer to a false belief or the reasons for a false belief.

A **fallacy** is an error in logical thought.

> **EXAMPLE**   Read the following sets of ideas. Mark each statement as follows:

> **UB** for unbiased statements
> **B** for biased arguments

_____   **1.** Thomas Edison invented the light bulb.

_____   **2.** Every time Ralph has worn his New York Mets t-shirt, he has passed his math exams; therefore, to pass the next exam he will wear it again.

_____   **3.** Lashonda trusts the news story because it's printed in the newspaper.

_____   **4.** Randall attended classes regularly, took detailed notes during classes and from his textbooks, reviewed his notes daily, asked questions during classes, and, as a result, earned a high grade point average.

_____   **5.** Even though sunlight travels approximately 93 million miles to reach earth, its ultraviolet rays cause premature aging of the skin, cataracts, and skin cancer.

EXPLANATION

1. This is an unbiased statement (UB); however, it is a false fact. Thomas Edison did not invent the light bulb. Research reveals that several men had produced various types of electrical lights before Edison. Edison improved upon a 50-year-old idea based on a patent he bought from inventors Henry Woodward and Matthew Evans. This idea is not a fallacy; it does not represen an error in thinking. The detail is simply incorrect information. Logical thinking begins with verifying the facts.

2. This is a biased argument (B) based on a fallacy in logical thought. Ralph has jumped to the wrong conclusion about why he did well on his math exams. By not considering other reasons for his success, he has identified a false cause and made an invalid inference. You will learn more about the fallacy of false cause later in this chapter.

3. This is also a biased argument (B) based on a fallacy in logical thought. Lashonda is arguing in a circle. She has a favorable bias toward words in print. She trusts the news because it is in the paper. Unfortunately, publication does not guarantee accuracy. You will learn more about the fallacy of circular reasoning later in this chapter.

4. This is an unbiased statement (UB). Every detail can be verified through testimony or eyewitness accounts of Randall's classmates, teachers, and transcripts.

5. This is an unbiased statement (UB). This statement is factual and can be proven with objective evidence, case histories, and expert opinions.

Practice 1

Read the following sets of ideas. Mark each statement as follows:

> **UB** for unbiased statements
> **B** for biased arguments

_____ 1. Birds evolved from dinosaurs.

_____ 2. Teenager to his friend, "You are jealous because I have my own car."

_____ 3. People under the age of 18 should not be allowed to vote because they are too young.

_____ 4. British soldiers fired in self-defense on American colonists in the Boston Massacre.

What Is Propaganda?

Propaganda is a means by which an idea is widely spread. The word *propaganda,* first used by Pope Gregory XV, comes from a Latin term that means to "propagate" or "spread." In 1612, the Pope created a department within the church to spread the Christian faith throughout the world by missionary work. Centuries later, President Woodrow Wilson used propaganda to sway the American people to enter World War I. **Propaganda** is a biased argument that advances or damages a cause. Propaganda is often used in politics and advertising.

Read the following two descriptions of a fictitious version of a common product used in daily life by millions. The first description is a mock advertisement. The second description includes withheld details about the fictitious product—information not included in the advertisement.

> **Mock Advertisement:** Sweet has changed the world of sweeteners by offering a healthy, no-calorie, sugar-based option. Sweet measures and pours just like sugar. Sweet is the brand name of glucralose. Glucralose comes from sugar, so Sweet tastes like sugar. For the natural taste of sugar without the guilt of added calories and carbohydrates, sweeten your life with Sweet. Made from sugar—tastes like sugar. Use Sweet instead of sugar in all your favorite recipes. Life is sweet with Sweet.

> **Withheld Details:** Glucralose is not a natural product. Instead, it is a chlorinated artificial sweetener. Glucralose is a chemical compound derived from sugar in a laboratory. A significant number of scientific tests reveal that glucralose may weaken the human immune system.

Notice how many times the mock advertisement repeats the word *sugar*. This repetition creates a false comparison between the natural substance sugar and the synthetic compound glucralose. This direct comparison to sugar is misleading and may confuse consumers into thinking glucralose is as natural as sugar because it's "made from sugar and tastes like sugar." In addition to its misleading wording, the advertisement also may also be making a false claim by using the term *healthy*. The advertisement withholds information about scientific tests that raise concerns about the harmful effects of glucralose on the human immune system. The mock advertisement offers only a positive view of the artificial sweetener. Thus, this advertisement is an example of **propaganda**.

> **Propaganda** is an act of persuasion that systematically spreads biased information that is designed to support or oppose a person, product, cause, or organization.

Propaganda uses a variety of techniques that are based on **emotional appeal**. If you are not aware of these techniques, you may be misled by the way information is presented and come to invalid conclusions. Understanding propaganda techniques will enable you to separate factual information from emotional appeals so that you can come to valid conclusions.

For example, the mock advertisement of the product Sweet uses emotional appeals with phrases such as *healthy, without guilt, favorite recipes,* and "Life is sweet with Sweet." Often advertisements like this one appeal to the readers' personal values; in contrast, the withheld details report only facts.

> **Emotional appeal** is the arousal of emotions to give a biased meaning or power to an idea.

> **EXAMPLE**   Read the following sets of ideas. Mark each statement as follows:

> **UB** for unbiased statements
> **B** for biased arguments

_____ **1.** A healthful diet includes a variety of foods including grain, fresh fruits and vegetables, fats, and protein.

_____ **2.** Use your vote to put Grace McKinney in the Senate because, like you and me, she comes from a hardworking, middle-class family and wants to give control of government back to the people.

_____ **3.** Spicy foods and stress cause stomach ulcers.

_____ **4.** Don't buy your insurance from DealState; that outfit is a bunch of crooks. Instead trust us, TruState, to meet your insurance needs.

_____ **5.** To avoid identity theft, do not give out personal information, periodically obtain a copy of your credit report, and keep detailed records of your banking and financial accounts.

EXPLANATION

1. This is an unbiased statement (UB). It is factual and can be proven with objective evidence, research studies, and expert opinions.

2. This is a biased argument (B) using the emotional appeal of propaganda. The statement uses the "plain folks" appeal. Grace McKinney is described as an everyday person with the same values of everyday people. You will learn more about this propaganda technique later in this chapter.

3. This is an unbiased statement (UB); however, it is a false fact. Research reveals that stomach ulcers are caused by an infection from a bacterium or by use of pain medications such as aspirin or ibuprofen. Cancer can also cause stomach ulcers. Stress and spicy food can aggravate an ulcer, but they do not cause one to occur.

4. This is a biased argument (B) using the emotional appeal of the propaganda technique of "name-calling." You will learn more about this propaganda technique later in this chapter.

5. This is an unbiased statement (UB). This statement offers factual advice, based on research, about how to respond to the crime of identity theft. ◁

Practice 2

Read the following sets of ideas. Mark each statement as follows:

UB for unbiased statements
B for biased arguments

_____ 1. Buy Gold Plus Jeans; they are made in America by Americans.

_____ 2. Advertisement: "This beautiful and famous actress wears Gold Plus Jeans."

_____ 3. Cortisol is a hormone triggered by stress that causes fat to collect in the abdomen.

_____ 4. Charles Darwin is respected by many in the scientific community for his theory of evolution.

Often the emotional appeal of propaganda is found in the supporting details, which are either irrelevant or inadequate (for more information on irrelevant and inadequate details, see Chapter 12, "The Basics of Argument"). The following sections of this chapter offer in-depth discussions and practices to help you identify irrelevant and inadequate arguments that use fallacies in logical thought and propaganda techniques.

LO2 Detect Fallacies Based on Irrelevant Arguments

Writing based in logical thought offers an author's claim and relevant supporting details, and it arrives at a valid conclusion. Fallacies and propaganda offer irrelevant arguments based on irrelevant details. Irrelevant details draw attention away from logical thought by ignoring the issue or changing the subject.

Personal Attack

Personal attack is the use of abusive remarks in place of evidence for a point or argument. Also known as an *ad hominem* attack, a personal attack attempts to discredit the point by discrediting the person making the point.

For example, Sam, a convicted felon, takes a stand against smoking in public places and calls for a law to ban smoking in restaurants. Those who disagree with the law focus attention on Sam's criminal record and ignore his reasons for opposing smoking in restaurants with statements like "Now the lawbreakers want to make the laws" or "Don't listen to a loser who can't stay out of jail." However, Sam's criminal past has nothing to do with smoking laws; making it a part of the argument is a personal attack.

> **EXAMPLE**   Read the following paragraph. Underline two uses of the logical fallacy of *personal attack*.

> [1]Teenager Tyrone is trying to persuade his father that he, Tyrone, should have a motorcycle. [2]Tyrone points out that he has held a steady part-time job for three years and has saved enough money to pay for the motorcycle. [3]Tyrone's father asks, "What about the cost of insurance?" [4]Tyrone replies that he has checked with several insurance companies and found a reasonable rate. [5]He added that he has enough money in his budget to cover the costs. [6]When his father still hesitates, Tyrone says, "You don't like this because it wasn't your idea; you would rather be the one in control." [7]His father retorts, "Well, it's hard to trust your judgment when you have a dozen piercings in your face."

> **EXPLANATION**   Tyrone is trying to assert that he is mature enough to handle the responsibility of owning a motorcycle. He begins with logical reasons to support this claim. He works, saves, and budgets his own money. In addition, he took the initiative to shop for the best price for insurance. These are impressive supports for his argument. However, when his father resists his logic, Tyrone falls into the use of personal attack in sentence 6. Tyrone accuses his father of selfishly trying to stay in control of his life. Tyrone's father responds in sentence 7 with his own personal attack on the way Tyrone looks. The issue of the motorcycle is no longer the focus of their discussion. <

Straw Man

A **straw man** is a weak argument substituted for a stronger one to make the argument easier to challenge. A straw man fallacy distorts, misrepresents, or falsifies an opponent's position. The name of the fallacy comes from the idea that it is easier to knock down a straw man than a real man who will fight back. The purpose of this kind of attack is to shift attention away from a strong argument to a weaker one that can be more easily overcome. Study the following example:

> Governor Goodfeeling opposes drilling for oil in Alaska. But the United States is too dependent on foreign oil supplies, and the American economy would benefit from having an American supply of oil. Governor Good-feeling is opposed to American-based oil drilling and wants to keep us dependent on foreign oil cartels.

This passage doesn't mention Governor Goodfeeling's reasons for opposing drilling for oil in Alaska. Instead, the writer restates the governor's position in ways that are easy to attack: continued dependence on foreign supplies and the implied economic hardships this might bring.

⊙ **EXAMPLE** Read the following paragraph. Underline the *straw man* fallacy in it.

> *Candidate Manuel Cortez:* [1]"We must protect our natural environment. [2]Unique and irreplaceable habitats are being devoured by uncontrolled growth. [3]I propose that we set the area known as the Loop aside as a natural reserve. [4]The Loop is a 30-mile stretch of road that cuts through a section of the vanishing Florida forests and marshes. [5]Let us work together to halt McRay's Building Corporation's plans for a new housing development in the Loop once and for all."
>
> *Candidate Rory Smith:* [6]"New construction is a sign of healthy economic development. [7]Candidate Cortez is against economic development."

EXPLANATION Candidate Rory Smith uses the straw man fallacy when he accuses his opponent of being against economic development in sentence 7. Candidate Manuel Cortez has not said he is against economic development. He is against this particular development in this one specific area known as the Loop. He is for protecting the environment. ⊙

Begging the Question

Begging the question restates the point of an argument as the support and conclusion. Also known as *circular reasoning*, begging the question assumes that an unproven or unsupported point is true. For example, the argument "Spinach is an awful tasting food because it tastes bad" begs the question. The point "Spinach is an awful tasting food" is assumed to be true because it is restated in the phrase "tastes bad" without specific supports that give logical reasons or explanations. Compare the same idea stated without begging the question: "I never eat spinach because it has a bitter taste, and I don't like foods that taste bitter."

> **EXAMPLE** Read the following paragraph. Underline the irrelevant argument of *begging the question*.

King Cameron

¹*Avatar* reigns supreme at the box office worldwide. ²In 2010, *Avatar*, directed by James Cameron, passed *Titanic*, also directed by Cameron, as the highest grossing film of all time. ³*Avatar* made $1.859 billion globally—after only 37 days in theaters. ⁴*Titanic*, released in 1997, held the previous record with $1.843 billion. ⁵The public embraced *Avatar*'s themes of "protecting the environment, respecting life, and yearning for a peaceful planet." ⁶But the true power of *Avatar* comes from its visually stunning special effects. ⁷Cameron created a fantastical and beautiful world on screen and became king of the movie world. ⁸James Cameron is the best director of his generation because he is better than all the other directors.

EXPLANATION Sentence 8 begs the question. To say that James Cameron is *better than all the other directors* is simply restating the idea that he is *the best director of his generation* without giving any concrete evidence or reasons to back up the claim. If he is the best, then naturally he is better than the others. As an effective reader, you want to know the reasons that explain why he is the best director or better than other directors. <

Practice 3

Identify the fallacy in each of the following items. Write **A** if the statement begs the question, **B** if it constitutes a personal attack, or **C** if it is a straw man.

_____   **1.** Big Red chewing gum is my favorite gum because I like it.

_____   **2.** Don't re-elect the senator; she is a dishonest anti-American liberal posing as a patriot.

_____   **3.** Alfred Simmons should not hold a public office because he admitted to experimenting with drugs when he was a teenager.

_____   **4.** Biology is a difficult subject because the concepts are hard to understand.

_____ **5.** We should not fund the construction of more roads because more roads will increase driving for pleasure.

LO3 Detect Propaganda Techniques Based on Irrelevant Arguments

Name-Calling

Name-calling uses negative labels for a product, idea, or cause. The labels are made up of emotionally loaded words and suggest false or irrelevant details that cannot be verified. Name-calling is an expression of personal opinion. For example, a bill for gun control may be labeled "anti-American" to stir up opposition to the bill. The "anti-American" label suggests that any restriction to the ownership of guns is against basic American values.

> EXAMPLE Read the following paragraph. Underline the irrelevant details that use *name-calling*.

From Good Girl to Diva

¹Christina Singer has veered a long way from the bubblegum pop music and teeny-bop image that made her famous. ²In her newest album, *Taunt and Tease*, she has the air of a raunchy diva. ³Even though her voice delivers a decent mix of pop, rock, soul, and R&B, her vampire-in-leather costume and wicked-witch makeup make her act scary to watch.

EXPLANATION The first sentence uses two labels to name the kind of appeal of this fictitious singer: *bubblegum pop* is a kind of music aimed at the preteen market, and *teeny-bop image* is usually linked to this market. Sentence 2 calls Christina Singer a *raunchy diva*. The word *raunchy* means "crude" or "vulgar," and the word *diva* suggests the large ego of a star. So saying she has the air of a raunchy diva is calling her rude and full of herself. Sentence 3 includes three negative labels: *vampire-in-leather costume, wicked-witch,* and *scary*. These names evoke images of the singer's evil and dark side.

Testimonials

Testimonials use irrelevant personal opinions to support a product, idea, or cause. Most often the testimonial is provided by a celebrity whose only qualification as a spokesperson is fame. For example, a famous actor promotes a certain brand of potato chips as his favorite, or a radio talk show host endorses a certain type of mattress.

> **EXAMPLE** Read the following paragraph. Underline the irrelevant details that use a *testimonial*.

The Benefits of Milk

¹Milk and milk products are important dietary sources of calcium. ²Milk and milk products are also good sources of other vital nutrients, including high-quality protein for building and repairing body tissues and vitamin A for better eyesight and healthy skin. ³They are also rich in riboflavin, vitamin B_{12}, and phosphorus. ⁴Famous athlete Jerome High-Jumper says, "Drinking milk every day makes me the athlete I am."

EXPLANATION Sentences 1 through 3 offer factual details about milk and milk products. However, sentence 4 uses the testimonial of a famous athlete. Being a famous athlete doesn't make the spokesperson an expert about the nutritional value of milk. A doctor, nurse, or nutritionist could offer a relevant expert opinion.

Practice 4

Identify the propaganda technique used in each of the following items. Write **A** if the sentence is an example of name-calling or **B** if it is a testimonial.

_____ 1. I have used Dr. Smith as our pets' veterinarian for over 25 years. He is knowledgeable and compassionate. You should make an appointment with him when you adopt your puppy from the pound.

_____ 2. Winfield Scott was "the Peacock of American politics, all fuss and feathers and fireworks."

_____ 3. Marie Osmond and Dan Marino claim that Nutrisystem helped them lose weight because Nutrisystem is easy to follow and easy to stay on.

_____ 4. Supreme Court Chief Justice John G. Roberts is a conservative judicial activist whose rulings are robbing citizens of basic freedoms.

_____ 5. I write this letter to inform you about the impact of your gift on the lives of the children in Haiti. Your donation is supplying lifegiving food, and we have seen amazing results. On average we have seen a weight increase of at least 10% in the first two to four weeks of placing the children on our food program. The food we provide due to your support is reversing the starvation process for hundreds of children. –Thank you on behalf of these children, Martha Dugall, CEO, Helping Hands for Children

Bandwagon

The **bandwagon** appeal uses or suggests the irrelevant detail that "everyone is doing it." This message plays on the natural desire of most individuals to conform to group norms for acceptance. The term *bandwagon* comes from the 19th-century use of a horse-drawn wagon that carried a musical band to lead circus parades and political rallies. To *jump on the bandwagon* meant to follow the crowd, usually out of excitement and emotion stirred up by the event rather than out of thoughtful reason or deep conviction.

> **EXAMPLE** Read the following paragraph. Underline the irrelevant details that use the *bandwagon* appeal.

Prom Curfew

[1]Alissa, a sophomore, has been asked to the senior prom by a popular football player. [2]Her parents are protective and strict, so she has a curfew that will force her to come home long before the after-prom parties are over. [3]As she is talking over her plans with her parents, she offers to pay for her dress with her own money, and she reassures them that her date is trustworthy and comes from a family that her parents know and respect. [4]She also tells them that all her friends' parents are letting them stay out until 3 A.M. [5]She reminds them that she has a cell phone and can call if she needs to for any reason. [6]When her parents resist, she says, "I'm the only one who isn't allowed to stay out late on prom night."

EXPLANATION Alissa uses the bandwagon appeal in two sentences. In sentence 4, she implies that her parents should jump on the bandwagon and conform to what other parents are doing when she says all her friends' parents are letting them stay out until 3 A.M. She then follows this argument in sentence 6 with "I am the only one who isn't allowed," a statement that shows she has already jumped on the bandwagon and wants to do what everyone else is doing. Read the paragraph with the bandwagon details removed.

Prom Curfew

Alissa, a sophomore, has been asked to the senior prom by a popular football player. Her parents are protective and strict, so she has a curfew that will force her to come home long before the after-prom parties are over. As she is talking over her plans with her parents, she offers to pay for her dress with her own money, and she reassures them that her date is trustworthy and comes from a family that her parents know and respect. She reminds them that she has a cell phone and can call if she needs to for any reason. ◀

Plain Folks

The **plain folks** appeal uses irrelevant details to build trust based on commonly shared values. Many people distrust the wealthy and powerful, such as politicians and the heads of large corporations. Many assume that the wealthy and powerful cannot relate to the everyday concerns of plain people. Therefore, the person or organization of power puts forth an image to which everyday people can more easily relate. For example, a candidate may dress in simple clothes, pose for pictures doing everyday chores like shopping for groceries, or talk about his or her own humble beginnings to make a connection with "plain folks." These details strongly suggest that "you can trust me because I am just like you." The appeal is to the simple, everyday experience, and often the emphasis is on a practical or no-nonsense approach to life.

▶ **EXAMPLE** Read the following paragraph. Underline the irrelevant details that appeal to *plain folks*.

Cooking with Helen

[1]A woman dressed in everyday casual clothes, wearing a sleeveless blue-collared shirt and khaki slacks, is busy preparing food in a television studio that has been created to look like a cozy kitchen. [2]She says, "Hello, my name is Helen. [3]Welcome to my kitchen. [4]For the next hour, I will share with you a few of the family-secret, down-home cooking techniques that have put my book, *Helen's Favorite Southern Recipes,* on the national best-seller list for the past three years."

EXPLANATION The woman, Helen, is described as wearing clothes that many plain folks also wear: She is *dressed in everyday casual clothes, wearing a sleeveless blue-collared shirt and khaki slacks.* So plain folks can relate to the woman based on her style of clothing. The kitchen is described as *cozy,* which suggests basic or simple values common to many people. Helen sets a friendly tone with the use of her first name, and the word *my* in *my kitchen* suggests that she is inviting the audience into her home. She then taps into everyday family values with the phrases *family-secret* and *down-home*. All of these details suggest that this best-selling author and television spokesperson is just one of the "plain folks." Once you identify these irrelevant details, you can come to a conclusion based on the relevant details. Read the paragraph with the appeals to plain folks removed; the remaining details are facts that can be verified.

Cooking with Helen

A woman is busy preparing food in a television studio that has been created to look like a kitchen. She says, "Hello, my name is Helen. Welcome to this kitchen. For the next hour, I will share with you a few of the cooking techniques that have put my book, *Helen's Favorite Southern Recipes,* on the national best-seller list for the past three years." ‹

Practice 5

Label each of the following items according to the propaganda techniques they employ:

A. plain folks
B. bandwagon

C. testimonial
D. name-calling

_____ **1.** People who support health care reform are socialists who favor big government.

_____ **2.** The President of the United States, wearing a collarless shirt and casual sports jacket, goes on late night talk shows such as *David Letterman* and *Jimmy Kimmel* to talk about his plans for education and jobs.

_____ **3.** Over three million people can't be wrong—buy Stay Trim now.

VISUAL *VOCABULARY*

This protestor uses the propaganda technique of _____ during a protest organized by a group called "Moratorium Now" in front of the Bank of America building in downtown Detroit, Michigan.

a. bandwagon
b. plain folks
c. testimonial

_____ **4.** "I suffered with acne all through high school. It robbed me of any self-confidence and made it really hard for me to make friends. Then my college roommate told me about AcuClear. Within three months, my skin was smooth and healthy. If you suffer from acne, I recommend AcuClear," Melinda, college student.

_____ **5.** If you think government can reform health care and education, then you really are naïve.

LO4 Detect Fallacies Based on Inadequate Arguments

In addition to offering relevant supporting details, logical thought relies on adequate supporting details. A valid conclusion must be based on adequate support. Fallacies and propaganda offer inadequate arguments that lack details. Inadequate arguments oversimplify the issue and do not give a person enough information to draw a proper conclusion.

Either-Or

Either-or assumes that only two sides of an issue exist. Also known as the *black-and-white fallacy*, either-or offers a false dilemma because more than two options are usually available. For example, the statement "If you don't give to the toy drive, you don't care about children" uses the either-or fallacy. The statement assumes there is only one reason for not giving to the toy drive—not caring about children. Yet it may be that a person doesn't have the money to buy a toy for the drive, or the person may help children in other ways. Either-or leaves no room for the middle ground or other options.

> **EXAMPLE** Read the following paragraph. Underline the *either-or* fallacy in it.

Peer Pressure

[1]Clay, Chad, Diego, and Stefan are spending the night together at Chad's house. [2]Around 3 A.M., Chad suggests that they sneak out, take his father's car, and go for a ride around town.

[3]Diego says, "I don't know. [4]What if we get caught?"

[5]"We won't," Chad says. [6]"Don't be such a wuss. [7]It will be fun."

[8]"Yeah," Clay chimes in. [9]"Everyone sneaks out at least once in their life—no big deal."

[10]"Listen, Diego," Chad says in a low, serious voice, "either you're with us or you're not. [11]What's it going to be?"

¹²Diego is still not sure and says, "I don't know, guys, we will be grounded for life if we get caught. ¹³Why can't we just stay here and watch movies like we planned?"

¹⁴"Fine," Stefan says, "you just stay home like a good little boy."

EXPLANATION Sentence 10 asserts the either-or fallacy "either you're with us or you're not." Chad makes it sound like Diego will be an enemy if he doesn't go along with the plans. Diego is actually looking out for their best interests. He reminds them of the punishment they will face if they are caught.

False Comparison

False comparison assumes that two things are similar when they are not. This fallacy is also known as a *false analogy*. An analogy is a point-by-point comparison that is used to explain an unfamiliar concept by comparing it to a more familiar one.

For example, an author may draw an analogy between a computer and the human anatomy. The computer's motherboard is like the human nervous system; the computer's processor is like the part of the human brain that tells the other parts of the body what to do. Just like a human brain, a computer's brain also has memory. However, the analogy breaks down when one considers all the differences between a computer and the human anatomy. The human body can repair itself, and the human brain can think creatively and critically. A false comparison occurs when the differences outweigh the similarities.

EXAMPLE Read the following paragraph. Underline the logical fallacy of *false comparison*.

¹A community college president is giving a speech at a local gathering of business professionals. ²He says, "The community college is just like your own business. ³We charge fees for our services. ⁴We worry about public relations. ⁵We have to pay for buildings, water, and electricity. ⁶We hire, train, and promote employees. ⁷And we both have the same bottom line."

EXPLANATION Sentences 1 through 6 state traits that community colleges do have in common with businesses. However, sentence 7 draws a false analogy. Businesses do not receive public funding from tax dollars. And the primary purpose of a community college is to educate the public, not make large profits. So in significant ways, a community college's bottom line is very different from the bottom line of a business.

False Cause

False cause, also known as **Post Hoc**, assumes that because events occurred around the same time, they have a cause-and-effect relationship. For example, Tyrell wears a blue baseball cap and hits a record number of home runs. To continue hitting home runs, he feels he must wear his blue baseball cap. Tyrell has made the mistake of believing that his blue baseball cap has something to do with his ability to hit a record number of home runs. What are the other possible causes? The Post Hoc fallacy is the false assumption that because event B *follows* event A, event B *was caused by* event A. An effective reader does not assume a cause without thinking about other possible causes.

> **EXAMPLE** Read the following paragraph. Underline the logical fallacy of *false cause.*

> ¹Haley's family moved from the small town in which she was born and had lived her entire 16 years to a large city. ²At first, the separation from her lifelong friends caused her to feel lonely and depressed. ³Eventually she made new friends. ⁴They were very different from any friends she had before. ⁵They wore body art in the form of tattoos and piercings, and they loved heavy metal music. ⁶Around the same time, her parents noticed that Haley was drinking alcohol frequently and heavily. ⁷Her parents blamed her new bad habits on her new friends and forbade Haley to see them anymore.

EXPLANATION Haley's parents jumped to a false conclusion based on a false cause in sentence 7. Because Haley made new friends around the same time they noticed her drinking habits, her parents blamed her new friends. Instead, they should consider other explanations. Perhaps Haley is still depressed and is using alcohol as a means of self-medication. Or maybe Haley began drinking long before they moved, but her parents just now noticed the behavior.

Practice 6

Identify the fallacy in each of the following items. Write **A** if the sentence states a false cause, **B** if it makes a false comparison, or **C** if it employs the either-or fallacy.

_____ **1.** A true patriot serves in the military.

_____ **2.** Animals deserve the same legal rights as humans.

_____ **3.** I shouldn't have gone to bed with my hair wet; now I have a cold.

_____ **4.** If you don't vote, you have no right to complain.

_____ **5.** Corbin smoked marijuana before he became addicted to heroin. Marijuana use leads to addiction to hard drugs.

_____ **6.** Which logical fallacy does this World War II poster use?
a. false cause
b. false comparison
c. either-or

LO5 Detect Propaganda Techniques Based on Inadequate Arguments

Card Stacking

Card stacking omits factual details in order to misrepresent a product, idea, or cause. Card stacking intentionally gives only part of the truth. For example, a commercial for a snack food advertises that it is "low in fat," which suggests that it is healthier and lower in calories than a product that is not low in fat. However, the commercial does not mention that the snack is loaded with sugar and calories.

▶ **EXAMPLE** Read the following paragraph and the list of details used to create the paragraph. Place a check beside the details that were omitted by *card stacking*.

BriteTeeth

[1]BriteTeeth will turn yellow teeth into a dazzling smile. [2]Recent research revealed that 9 out of 10 people who used BriteTeeth had noticeably whiter teeth. [3]Apply BriteTeeth to your teeth every night before you go to sleep. [4]Then in the morning, brush your teeth as you normally do. [5]Results should be apparent in two applications.

Omitted Details:

_____   BriteTeeth is made of a special mix of baking soda and carbamide peroxide.

_____   BriteTeeth has been used by more than 300,000 people.

_____   BriteTeeth has a temporary effect and must be used on a daily basis.

_____   BriteTeeth was linked in the research to softer teeth and higher rates of tooth decay.

EXPLANATION The detail that should not have been left out but was omitted as a method of card stacking is the last detail in the list: *BriteTeeth was linked in the research to softer teeth and higher rates of tooth decay.* Consumers who are truly concerned about their teeth will not want a product that is likely to cause softening and tooth decay.

Transfer

Transfer creates an association between a product, idea, or cause with a symbol or image that has positive or negative values. This technique carries the strong feelings we may have for something over to something else.

Symbols stir strong emotions, opinions, or loyalties. For example, a cross represents the Christian faith; a flag represents a nation; a white lab coat represents science and medicine; and a beautiful woman or a handsome man represents acceptance, success, or sex appeal. Politicians and advertisers use symbols like these to win our support. For example, a political candidate may end a speech with a prayer or the phrase "God bless America," to suggest that God approves of the speech. Another example of transfer is the television spokesperson who wears a white lab coat and quotes studies about the health product she is advertising.

Transfers can also be negative. For example, a skull and crossbones together serve as a symbol for death. Therefore, placing a skull and crossbones on a bottle transfers the dangers of death to the contents of the bottle.

EXAMPLE Read the following paragraph. Underline the irrelevant details that use *transfer*.

Governor Edith Public

[1]Governor Edith Public, who is appearing at a campaign rally in her bid for reelection, says, "Let me begin by saying thank you to the president of the United States for being here today. [2]Your support is deeply appreciated, particularly now that your numbers in the public opinion polls are soaring again." [3]The president, the governor, and the audience laugh good-naturedly. [4]"Good people," the governor continues, "examine my record. [5]Like the president, I have vetoed every bill that attempted to raise your taxes. [6]At the same time, I have carried out new legislation designed to lower the rising cost of living and still provide good health care."

EXPLANATION Governor Public opens her remarks with a statement that creates a strong link between the president of the United States and her campaign. The weight, authority, and grandeur of the presidency are carried in the physical presence of the president. Thus his mere appearance transforms any occasion into a powerful event. However, Governor Public's thank-you to the president lays claim to his personal and official support. The phrase "particularly now that your numbers in the public opinion polls are soaring again" combines bandwagon appeal with transfer by suggesting that many people in a poll support the president. If many support the president and the governor has the same values as the president, then many support the governor as well. Governor Public uses transfer again when she says, "Like the president," in sentence 5. ◄

Glittering Generalities

Glittering generalities offer general positive statements that cannot be verified. A glittering generality is the opposite of name-calling. Often words of virtue and high ideals are used, and the details are inadequate to support the claim. For example, words like *truth, freedom, peace,* and *honor* suggest shining ideals and appeal to feelings of love, courage, and goodness.

> EXAMPLE Read the following paragraph. Underline the irrelevant details that use *glittering generalities.*

A Vote for Education

[1]A candidate for political office has been asked about her views on education. [2]She responds, "Our democracy is based on the rights of all individuals to be educated. [3]The ability to read and write allows citizens to express their views to those who represent them in government. [4]A society that is uneducated is less likely to enjoy the right to pursue happiness and

is less able to protect hard-won freedoms. [5]Research indicates that those with at least a two-year college education are better able to make a good living and pay taxes. [6]And I applaud those teachers who hold their students to standards of moral and academic excellence. [7]I propose that we raise the beginning salaries of teachers and limit class size."

EXPLANATION Most of the glittering generalities used by the candidate call to mind American virtues. Sentence 2 includes *democracy* and *rights.* Sentence 4 includes *right to pursue happiness,* which is a paraphrase from the U.S. Constitution, and *freedoms.* Sentence 6 includes *applaud* which is a glittering generality that expresses a feeling, not an action, and *standards of moral and academic excellence.* These are all noble ideals that few people would argue against; however, they do not add any substance to her ideas. Read the paragraph with the glittering generalities removed.

A Vote for Education

A candidate for political office has been asked about her views on education. She responds, "The ability to read and write allows citizens to express their views to those who represent them in government. Research indicates that those with at least a two-year college education are better able to make a living and pay taxes. I propose that we raise the beginning salaries of teachers and limit class size."

Practice 7

For **1–4**, label each of the following items according to the propaganda techniques they employ:

A. transfer C. card stacking
B. glittering generality

_____ 1. A candidate campaigning to be a United States senator is photographed in front of an American flag with a group of decorated soldiers who served in Afghanistan.

_____ 2. A new dawn is breaking in America. Fight for freedom. Cast your vote. A vote for me is a vote for liberty.

_____ 3. Health care is a human right.

_____ 4. A law firm looking for clients hires actors for a series of television commercials. The male and female actors dress and behave as middle class workers who are worried about what to do if they are injured in a car accident or on the job. In a typical commercial, the actor is driving a car and talking to the camera as if talking to a passenger in the car, using the following script: "An auto accident can change your life in an instant. Suddenly, you may find yourself disabled, in pain, and out of work. Get the help you need and deserve. Call today. We're on your side."

_____ 5. Identify the detail from this list of details that was **omitted** from the paragraph for purposes of card stacking.

Clinical tests prove that AcuClear stops acne breakouts for 8 out of 10 women. Made with green tea oil and aloe to soothe irritated skin, AcuClear kills bacteria and soothes irritated skin.

a. The clinical tests only included 40 women, and over 50% of these women complained of redness and skin peeling.

b. AcuClear is made up of all natural products.

c. AcuClear is carried in drugstores nationwide.

VISUAL *VOCABULARY*

This billboard uses the propaganda technique known as _____.

a. transfer
b. glittering generality
c. card stacking

▲ A Billboard displayed by the North Iowa Tea Party in downtown Mason Iowa, July 2010.

LO6 Textbook Skills

Develop Textbook Skills: Examining Biased Arguments in Textbooks

Textbooks strive to present information in a factual, objective manner with relevant and adequate support, in keeping with their purpose to inform. However, textbook authors may choose to present biased arguments for your examination. As an effective reader, you are expected to evaluate the nature of the biased argument and the author's purpose for including the biased argument.

> **EXAMPLE** The following passage appears in a college mass communication textbook. It serves as an introduction for the chapter "Radio." As you read the passage, underline biased information. After you read, answer the questions.

Limbaugh Speaks: His Listeners Act

Textbook
Skills

[1]His program is unabashedly biased. [2]He sneers at liberals as "dittoheads" and worse. [3]He calls other members of the media liars. [4]He brags about himself on the air.

[5]Millions of his fans love it. [6]They devour his liberal-bashing and accept his statements as political gospel.

[7]That is Rush Limbaugh, the glib commentator who has been called the "800 pound gorilla of talk radio." [8]He is heard on more than 600 radio stations.

[9]Limbaugh's influence on his listeners is enormous. [10]Claiming that the media were distorting the Republican plan in Congress to transfer the federal school lunch program to the states, he urged listeners to call their newspapers, the national networks, and the news magazines to protest.

[11]"All you say is, 'Stop lying about the school lunch program' and hang up," he told them.

[12]Thousands from coast to coast immediately did so, many using his exact words. [13]Typically, Cable News Network in Atlanta received more than 300 calls.

[14]Critics of Limbaugh's bombastic style recognize his power but contend that he is preaching to the converted. [15]William Rentschler observed in *Editor & Publisher:* "His program is largely a love feast of like-minded listeners massaging the giant ego of their hero."

—Agee, Warren K., et al., *Introduction to Mass
Communications,* p. 213

_____ 1. Overall, the tone of the passage is
  a. positive about Rush Limbaugh.
  b. negative about Rush Limbaugh.
  c. neutral toward Rush Limbaugh.

_____ 2. The primary purpose of the passage is
  a. to encourage readers to condemn Rush Limbaugh.
  b. to inform the reader about the power of radio, using Rush Limbaugh as an example.
  c. to persuade readers to listen to Rush Limbaugh by giving entertaining details about his show.

_____ **3.** In sentence 2, Rush Limbaugh uses the propaganda technique
    a. name-calling.   c. bandwagon.
    b. testimonial.   d. false cause.

_____ **4.** The words "gospel," "preaching," and "converted" are examples of the fallacy
    a. begging the question.   c. false comparison.
    b. personal attacks.   d. straw man.

_____ **5.** Sentences 11–13 illustrate the effect of the propaganda technique
    a. card stacking.   c. plain folks.
    b. bandwagon.   d. testimonial.

EXPLANATION The biased information includes the following words: *unabashedly, sneers, liberals, "dittoheads," liars, brags, devour, liberal-bashing, gospel, glib, 800 pound gorilla, enormous, distorting, bombastic, preaching, converted, love feast,* and *giant ego.*

1. This list of biased words indicates the negative tone (b) used in the discussion about Rush Limbaugh.

2. The primary purpose of the passage is (b) to inform the reader about the power of radio by using Rush Limbaugh as an example. As a well-known and controversial radio talk show host, Rush Limbaugh is an excellent example with which to open a chapter about radio and its influence on society. The authors' purpose was not to condemn or endorse Rush Limbaugh, but to make a point about the power of radio. Radio is a medium of mass communication, and Rush Limbaugh uses propaganda and fallacies in logical thought successfully in his daily broadcast. The authors of this mass communication textbook highlight the powerful relationship between radio and persuasion by using Rush Limbaugh as an example.

3. In sentence 2, Rush Limbaugh uses the propaganda technique (a) name-calling.

4. The words "gospel," "preaching," and "converted" are examples of the fallacy (c) false comparison. These words compare Limbaugh and his listeners to a religious leader and followers.

5. Sentences 11–13 illustrate the effect of the propaganda technique (b) bandwagon. Rush Limbaugh has earned the loyalty of a large audience that he can get to jump on the bandwagon of his choice. ◀

Practice 8

The following passage appears in a college history textbook. As you read the passage, underline biased words. After you read, answer the questions.

"Uncle Tom's Cabin"

Textbook
Skills

[1]Tremendously important in increasing sectional tensions and bringing home the evils of slavery to still more people in the North was Harriet Beecher Stowe's novel *Uncle Tom's Cabin* (1852). [2]Stowe was neither a professional writer nor an abolitionist, and she had almost no firsthand knowledge of slavery. [3]But her conscience had been roused by the Fugitive Slave Act. [4]In gathering material for the book, she depended heavily on abolitionist writers, many of whom she knew. [5]She dashed it off quickly; as she later recalled, it seemed to write itself. [6]Nevertheless, *Uncle Tom's Cabin* was an enormous success: 10,000 copies were sold in a week; 300,000 in a year. [7]It was translated into dozens of languages. [8]Dramatized versions were staged in countries throughout the world.

[9]Harriet Beecher Stowe was hardly a distinguished writer; it was her approach to the subject that explains the book's success. [10]Her tale of the pious, patient slave Uncle Tom, the saintly white child Eva, and the callous slave driver Simon Legree appealed to an audience far wider than that reached by the abolitionists. [11]She avoided the self-righteous, accusatory tone of most abolitionist tracts and did not seek to convert readers to belief in racial equality. [12]Many of her southern white characters were fine, sensitive people, while the cruel Simon Legree was a transplanted Connecticut Yankee. [13]There were many heart-rending scenes of pain, self-sacrifice, and heroism. [14]The story proved especially effective on the stage: The slave Eliza crossing the frozen Ohio River to freedom, the death of Little Eva, Eva and Tom ascending to Heaven—these scenes left audiences in tears.

[15]Southern critics pointed out, correctly enough, that Stowe's picture of plantation life was distorted, her slaves atypical. [16]They called her a "coarse, ugly, long-tongued woman" and accused her of trying to "awaken rancorous hatred and malignant jealousies" that would undermine national unity. [17]Most Northerners, having little basis on which to judge the accuracy of the book, tended to discount southern criticism as biased. [18]In any case, *Uncle Tom's Cabin* raised questions that transcended the issue of accuracy. [19]Did it matter if every slave was not as kindly as Uncle Tom, as determined as George Harris? [20]What if only one white master was as evil as Simon Legree? [21]No earlier white American writer had looked at slaves as people.

²²*Uncle Tom's Cabin* touched the hearts of millions. ²³Some became abolitionists; others, still hesitating to step forward, asked themselves as they put the book down: Is slavery just?

—Garraty, John A. and Mark C. Carnes. *American Nation Single Volume Edition*, pp. 378–379

_____ **1.** Overall the tone of the passage
  a. is positive about *Uncle Tom's Cabin*.
  b. is negative about *Uncle Tom's Cabin*.
  c. remains neutral toward *Uncle Tom's Cabin*.

_____ **2.** The author's purpose is
  a. to argue against the injustices of slavery.
  b. to inform the reader about the importance of *Uncle Tom's Cabin*.
  c. to delight the reader by sharing the success of a nineteenth-century woman writer.

_____ **3.** The "heart-rending scenes of pain, self-sacrifice, and heroism" included in *Uncle Tom's Cabin* were most likely examples of the propaganda technique
  a. bandwagon.   c. transfer.
  b. testimonials.   d. name-calling.

_____ **4.** In sentence 16, Stowe's critics use the propaganda technique
  a. bandwagon.   c. transfer.
  b. testimonials.   d. name-calling.

Apply Information Literacy Skills

 L07 **Academic, Personal, and Career Applications of Advanced Argument: Persuasive Techniques**

Learning the techniques of persuasion is an important literacy information skill. Information is often used to sway you to believe or do something. Examining persuasive techniques empowers your thinking. You are better able to form valid conclusions in your academic life. And you are better able to make valid decisions in your personal and career lives. As a college student, you evaluate the use of persuasive techniques in areas such as history, art, and literature. In your personal life, you sift through the everyday uses of persuasive techniques. Family, friends, advertisers, or politicians may use these techniques to influence your thoughts and actions. In your career life, you may confront persuasive techniques in the workplace. Job applicants, proposals, marketing strategies, or sales reports may tap into the power of persuasive techniques to achieve goals. Thus, you will use the skills that you have learned in this chapter in your academic, personal, and career lives to:

- Identify persuasive techniques.
- Evaluate a claim and its supports to determine use of persuasive techniques or sound logic.
- Support or reject a claim based on the use of persuasive techniques.

Academic Application

Assume you are taking a college course in American government. The following image is part of your textbook reading assignment.

- **Before Reading**: Skim this chapter to review the various persuasive techniques. Predict how the information in this chapter may help you analyze the images in this political ad from the 1960s.
- **During Reading**: Label each image with an emotional word that sums up the impact of that image.
- **After Reading**: In the space below, identify and explain the use of persuasive techniques in the ad. You may use the questions in the excerpt to guide your analysis of the images. You may refer to the learning outcomes on page 603 for a list of persuasive techniques.

Analysis of "Peace Little Girl" for Persuasive Techniques: _____

_____

_____

_____

_____

_____

ANALYZING VISUALS

Peace Little Girl

In the 1964 election, President Lyndon B. Johnson's campaign produced a television ad that showed a young girl counting the petals she was picking off a daisy. Once she said the number nine, a voice-over started counting down a missile launch that ended in images of a nuclear explosion and a mushroom cloud. The viewer then heard the president's voice saying, "These are the stakes." Examine the still images taken from the ad and then answer the questions.

- What was this ad trying to imply?
- Why do you think this ad was considered so shocking and unfair?
- What types of ads would generate similar controversy today? Explain your answer.

—O'Connor, Karen, et al. *American Government: Roots and Reform,* p. 468.

Personal Application

Assume you or someone in your family has been diagnosed with diabetes. To learn more, you have found the following sources on the Internet.

- **Before Reading**: Become familiar with the Guide for Evaluating Websites. Skim the sources.

- **During Reading**: Underline the key details about each source that will help you evaluate the source as reliable and useful.

- **After Reading**: In the space following the passage, evaluate the reliability of the information from each site. Rate each source on a scale of 1 to 3, with 1 being least useful or reliable and 3 being most useful or reliable. Refer to the Guide for Evaluating Websites as needed.

> ### Guide for Evaluating Websites
>
> To determine the reliability of the information contained in a website, consider the answers to the following questions about three basic traits of a reliable source or site on the Internet.
>
> **Timely:** Is the information current? How recently has the information been updated? Is the history or background information given as needed? Are all the links within the site active?
>
> **Authoritative:** Does the site disclose the sponsor, creator, or contributors? Are the contributors experts in the field?
>
> **Objective:** What is the purpose of the site? Does the site seek to sell a product or idea? Does the site seek to inform the public for the greater good? Is the information based on facts, research, or bias and opinion?

A. "Diabetes Mellitus." *Wikipedia.org.* http://en.wikipedia.org/wiki/Diabetes_mellitus

> **About:** *Wikipedia* is an encyclopedia written collaboratively by largely anonymous Internet volunteers. These volunteers write without pay. Anyone with Internet access can write and make changes to Wikipedia articles. In certain cases editing is restricted to prevent disruption or vandalism. Users can contribute anonymously, under an assumed name. Or they may use their real identity, if they choose.

B. U.S. National Library of Medicine. "Diabetes." *PubMed Health.* http://www.ncbi.nlm.nih.gov/pubmedhealth/PMH0002194/

> **About:** *PubMed Health* specializes in reviews of clinical effectiveness research. The site offers easy-to-read summaries for consumers as well as full technical reports. Clinical effectiveness research finds answers to the question "What works?" in medical and health care. PubMed Health is a service provided by the National Center for Biotechnology Information (NCBI) at the U.S. National Library of Medicine. The U.S. National Library of Medicine (NLM) is the world's largest medical library. The NLM was founded in 1836 and is part of the National Institutes of Health in Bethesda, Maryland.

C. "Managing Diabetes Long-Term." *Diabetes.com.* http://www.diabetes.com/managing-diabetes-long-term/managing-diabetes.html

> **About:** The content in the diabetes.com program was developed by GlaxoSmithKline. This information is not a substitute for your doctor's

medical advice, nor is your doctor responsible for its content. You should promptly consult a medical professional if you have concerns about your health. GlaxoSmithKline is one of the world's leading research-based pharmaceutical and healthcare companies.

Evaluation of Internet Sources: _____

_____

_____

_____

_____

_____

_____

Career Application

Assume you are an employee in a highly successful chain of retail stores. You and your fellow workers have received the following letter from Sandra Elias, CEO of the company.

- **Before Reading**: Skim this chapter to review the various persuasive techniques. Skim the letter. Predict the purpose of the letter.

- **During Reading**: Underline the persuasive techniques used by the writer of the letter.

- **After Reading**: In the space following the letter, record your response to the letter. Do you agree or disagree with Sandra Elias' claims? In your response, discuss how her use of persuasive techniques influenced you.

[1]Hi. [2]I'm Sandra. [3]Welcome to BigBoxValue, a great place to work! [4]You are part of an important team and a terrific store. [5]That's right. [6]Whether you are a new employee or a seasoned veteran, you were chosen to work with us because you have what it takes to help us achieve our vision of being the best in the business. [7]The leadership team and your fellow team members are eager to help you and to make working at BigBoxValue a rewarding experience. [8]If you ever have a question, all you have to do is ask it. [9]Your success is our success! [10]And we are proud of our open door policy. [11]Not only do you have the right to approach any manager or team member with your ideas or concerns, but you and your ideas are valued and welcomed.

[12]BigBoxValue competes with many other businesses, so we offer high quality products at low prices. [13]And we have the friendliest, most efficient guest services in the business.

[14]Recently, union representatives have approached many of our team members by phone, email, and fliers. [15]As our chain of stores has grown and spread across the globe, we have taken business from other stores which use unionized workers. [16]That's right, and these unionized stores now need fewer employees. [17]And fewer employees means fewer union members. [18]And fewer members means less money for union organizers. [19]The bottom line is that a union must generate money to operate. [20]And the way a union generates money is by charging a membership fee—and dues—and fines—and assessments. [21]You can see how costly a union really is. [22]Really, a union is nothing more than big business—out to make a profit off of you.

[23]Unions might have been needed at one time. [24]Unions played an important part in establishing fair labor laws for work hours and pay. [25]But now with fair labor laws in place, do you really want to pay extra for rights you already have?

[26]Keep in mind that BigBoxValue values you. [27]Your hard work and loyalty will be rewarded. [28]Yes! [29]BigBoxValue values your rights as a worker. [30]That's right! [31]So if you have a question, just ask. [32]If you have a concern, just say so. [33]The leadership team and your fellow team members will work with you to solve problems, keep you motivated, and ensure your success. [34]Your success is our success!

[35]So, keep your hard-earned money in your pocket. [36]Don't give it to a union organizer who cares more about generating money for the union than you or BigBoxValue.

Response to Ms. Elias' letter: _____

_____

_____

_____

_____

_____

_____

REVIEW TEST 1

Score (number correct) _____ x 20 = _____%

Visit MyReadingLab to take this test online and receive feedback and guidance on your answers.

Biased Arguments

Read the following sets of ideas. Write **UB** if the statement is unbiased, or **B** if the idea is a biased argument.

_____ **1.** Joe E. Jones, nationally known film critic, wrote, "*The Descendants*, starring George Clooney, is a must-see movie. It is clearly Clooney's best performance of his career."

_____ **2.** Orange juice contains potassium and vitamins A and C, and it lowers blood pressure.

_____ **3.** A study released by the National Academy on an Aging Society found that care for people with Alzheimer's Disease can be costly. The average cost for a person with Alzheimer's who is still living at home is $12,572 a year.

_____ **4.** Obviously a politician cannot wear his heart on his sleeve when he is working for the success of his country. Only hypocrites and innocent dreamers would demand that he speak openly about his plans. Just as a businessman does not divulge his secrets to his rival, so also in politics, with even greater justification, much must remain a secret.

—Ernst Herbert Lehmann, *How They Lie*, 1940.

_____ **5.** A college sophomore says to her parents, "I can't believe you won't let me go to Cancun for spring break. Everyone I know is going. Not only do their parents let them go, but their parents pay for the trip, too. At least I am willing to pay my own expenses."

REVIEW TEST 2

Score (number correct) _____ x 25 = _____%

Visit MyReadingLab to take this test online and receive feedback and guidance on your answers.

Biased Arguments: Fallacies in Logical Thought and Propaganda Techniques

Read the following feature essay from a college sociology textbook. Answer the questions that follow.

The Coming Star Wars

[1]Star Wars is on its way.

[2]The Predator is an unmanned plane that flies thousands of feet above enemy lines. [3]Operators at a base search the streaming video it emits, looking for targets. [4]When they identify one, they press a button. [5]At this signal, the Predator beams a laser onto the target and launches guided bombs. [6]The enemy doesn't know what hit them. [7]They see neither the Predator nor the laser. [8]Perhaps, however, just before they are blown to bits, they do hear the sound of an incoming bomb (Barry 2001). [9]The Pentagon's plans to "weaponize" space go far beyond the Predator. [10]The Pentagon has built a "space plane," the X-37B, which has an airplane's agility and a spacecraft's capacity to travel five miles per second in space (Cooper 2010).

[11]The Pentagon is also building its own Internet, the Global Information Grid (GIG), with the grandiose goal of encircling the globe to give the Pentagon a "God's eye view" of every enemy everywhere (Weiner 2004). [12]Then they can unleash a variety of weapons: microsatellites the size of a suitcase that can pull alongside an enemy satellite and, using a microwave gun, fry its electronic system; a laser whose beam will bounce off a mirror in space, making the night battlefield visible to ground soldiers who are wearing special goggles—and whatever else the feverish imaginations of military planners can devise.

[13]The Air Force has nicknamed one of its space programs "Rods from God," tungsten cylinders to be hurled from space at targets on the ground. [14]Striking at speeds of 7,000 miles an hour, the rods would have the force of a small nuclear weapon. [15]In another program, radio waves would be directed to targets on the Earth. [16]As the Air Force explains it, the power of the radio waves could be "just a tap on the shoulder—or they could turn you into toast" (Weiner 2005).

¹⁷As the United States has spent much of its national treasure on policing the world and enforcing its ideas, little nations with primitive technology have made easy targets. ¹⁸The Pentagon can fly the Predator over Afghanistan and Pakistan, unleashing guided bombs at will, with no fear of counter missiles being launched against the United States.

¹⁹But what happens if enemy, or even rival, nations develop similar capacities—or even greater ones? ²⁰We are beginning to see an ominous transition in international technological expertise. ²¹Already there is the Pterodactyl, China's answer to the Predator. ²²To the amazement of the Pentagon, China has advanced its technology to the point that its unmanned aerial vehicles (UAVs) have begun to rival those of the United States (Page 2010; Wall 2010). ²³China has even begun to flaunt its space weapons in the face of the Pentagon, a not too subtle warning not to mess with China as its leaders expand their territorial ambitions. ²⁴Weapons are made to be used—despite the constant polite rhetoric about their defensive purposes. ²⁵On both sides are itchy fingers, and now that China has become an ominous threat to U.S. space superiority, the Pentagon faces a new challenge. ²⁶How will it be able to contain China's political ambitions if Star Wars looms?

—Henslin, James M. *Sociology: Down to Earth Approach*, 9th ed.

_____ **1.** Sentence 1 is an example of
    a. straw man.   c. false comparison.
    b. begging the question.   d. glittering generalities.

_____ **2.** The phrase "grandiose goal of encircling the globe to give the Pentagon a 'God's eye view'" in sentence 11 is an example of
    a. straw man.   c. either-or.
    b. personal attack.   d. bandwagon.

_____ **3.** The Pentagon's name of "Rods from God" for a weapon in sentence 13 is an example of
    a. card stacking.   c. transfer.
    b. false comparison.   d. glittering generalities.

_____ **4.** Sentence 24 is an example of
    a. either-or.   c. false comparison.
    b. begging the question.   d. glittering generalities.

REVIEW TEST 3

Score (number correct) _____ x 25 = _____%

Visit MyReadingLab to take this test online and receive feedback and guidance on your answers.

Biased Arguments: Propaganda

Nostalgia Merchants

[1]Why did Reuben Harley think that throwbacks—replicas of old sports jerseys—would catch on?

[2]Call it instinct, street smarts, observing the reactions of others, or whatever you will, he trusted his personal tastes. [3]While making a living doing odd jobs in his West Philly neighborhood, he saved money to buy classic jerseys of legendary players such as Julius Irving, Nolan Ryan, and Jackie Robinson, from century-old Mitchell & Ness's retail store. [4]When people would ask where he got the Hank Aaron jersey he was wearing, the 300-pound-plus Reuben wouldn't tell them. [5]He wanted them all as his own. [6]"But just seeing the cat's reaction, I knew this could really catch on," he says. [7]And so it began for this high school graduate who had even started his own catering business, getting up at 3:00 A.M. to cook chicken, lasagna, and desserts in his grandmother's kitchen before eventually teaming up with Peter Capolino. [8]Capolino was the then 58-year-old owner of Mitchell & Ness Nostalgia Company (M&N). [9]Harley went to Capolino and offered to help him sell 1950s baseball jerseys to inner-city youths. [10]Together, in just two years' time they changed M&N (www.mitchellandness .com) into the nation's best-known marketer of clothing for urban teen African-Americans. [11]Sales jumped from $2.8 million in 2000 to $25 million in 2002, then to an estimated $40 million in 2003. [12]And there's no doubting who the prime mover is for M&N's success: "I consider it a miracle that Reuben fell into my lap. [13]He deserves all the credit," says Capolino.

[14]Reuben started by focusing on celebrities—rappers and pro athletes—who could afford the $250 to $470 price tag for these intricately stitched designs with authentic team colors. [15]He began meeting them by going uninvited to their parties in New York and Philadelphia nightclubs. [16]He soon became a trusted acquaintance with his charming and unassuming personality. [17]When shown samples of M&N's jerseys, hip-hop great Sean (P. Diddy) Combs immediately bought them, as did rapper Fabulous, whose album *Street Dreams* contains a track named "Throwback," dedicated to M&N. [18]Building on these initial successes, Harley—now M&N's new marketing director—targeted major music and sporting

events. [19]He also targeted the celebrity consumers performing at them. [20]During the NBA All-Star weekend, for example, Rap star Eve wore an oversized Michael Jordan Chicago Bulls Jersey. [21]Throughout Super Bowl week, then-Tampa Bay football star Warren Sapp wore M&N throwbacks, including a bright green 1980s Philadelphia Eagles model, in various public appearances. [22]Indiana Pacers basketball star Jermaine O'Neal, who owns 150 throwbacks, says, "Acquiring the hottest model is a competitive sport among teammates." [23]The jerseys are so popular you'll find entertainment stars wearing them most any day in action movies, on MTV, and Black Entertainment Television.

Why All the Popularity?

[24]"The materials, the colors are just a little different, a little special," says rapper Fabulous. [25]"If I wear a Dr. J jersey at a show in Philly or a Jerry West at a joint in L.A., I know the crowd will go crazy." [26]Adds rap star Eve, "Reuben's just a cool guy, and he delivers what you need on time." [27]With so much brand visibility, then, it's little wonder that suburban kids and adults of all races are eagerly imitating what Reuben Harley and Peter Capolino started a few short years ago in inner city Philadelphia. [28]Mitchell & Ness was once the longtime maker of tennis and golf equipment. [29]It now has been turned into the industry's most imitated manufacturer and marketer of authentic old sports jerseys.

Is Nostalgia Just a Fad?

[30]Reuben Harley was 17 years old in 1991 when he bought his first throwback—a 1983 Andre Thornton Cleveland Indians jersey—at Mitchell & Ness (M&N), a tiny retail shop with few young black customers in city-center Philadelphia. [31]In 2001, while watching an Outkast music video, Big Rube realized he owned (bought over the years on layaway) the same throwback jerseys the performers were wearing. [32]Soon thereafter, an Oprah Winfrey TV show about "following your dreams" inspired him to pursue selling, not just buying, vintage jerseys. [33]In joining Peter Capolino at M&N, Reuben came on board for $500 a month and received one of every jersey in the M&N line. [34]Today, most of M&N's jerseys are wholesaled to some 220 retailers around the country.

[35]The potential market as seen by Reuben was worlds apart from Capolino's pre-2001 vision for M&N. [36]Reuben envisioned an urban, largely African-American youth segment that idolizes basketball players with baggy shorts and bigger brightly colored jerseys with striking patterns in double-knits and mesh. [37]Capolino, in contrast, was aiming for middle-aged collectors of sports items, mostly from its retro-baseball line with

body-hugging gray flannels. [38]At an age in life when established business-people might take a safer path, Capolino made a gutsy call in deciding to go along with Reuben. [39]"It's an all-sport thing, but guys identify with basketball players more than anybody," says Harley. [40]Now basketball, instead of baseball, accounts for the largest share of M&N's business.

[41]Because it holds exclusive licenses from the NFL, Major League Baseball, the National Basketball Association, and the National Hockey League, M&N can reproduce authentic jerseys that have been out of circulation for at least five years. [42]The fabric, the stitching, and the lettering are all accurate duplicates of the originals the players wore years ago. [43]Therein, according to Reuben, lies the staying power of M&N's throwbacks. [44]"This isn't a fad. [45]These uniforms are the history of sports. [46]Styles come and go, but you can't change the '79 Magic Johnson jersey." [47]That's why they captured an enthusiastic audience, even at such hefty prices as $325 for a 1979 Willie Stargell Pirates, $450 for the 1963 Lance Alworth Chargers, $300 for the 1983–84 Sidney Moncrief Bucks, and $250 for the 1966–67 Dave Bing Pistons.

[48]Today, Harley is vice president of marketing with a lofty salary and lots of size XXXXL jerseys. [49]His duties include everything from hitting the road as traveling salesman to serving as M&N's public face to clothes designers. [50]With many of his clients, the conversations aren't just about the latest in jerseys but also personal matters and plain talk. [51]And he takes time to be there to help. [52]Backstage when P. Diddy hosted ABC's American Music Awards, Reuben took charge of the star's costume changes during commercial breaks. [53]Eleven different jerseys were worn throughout the performance, including a '73 George McGinnis Pacers and a '74 Hank Aaron Braves. [54]"Shaq called the next day; he wanted every piece that Puff wore," says Harley. [55]The success in his personal approach for marketing is aided by encouragement from the clients he serves. [56]In his album *Street Dreams*, Fabolous yells out a message to the duo at M&N: "Rube, tell Pete to keep it comin'."

—Adapted from Griffin, Ricky W. and
Ebert, Ronald J., *Business*, 8th ed., pp.
351–352, 375.

_____ **1.** Sentences 20 and 21 are examples of
　　　a. bandwagon.　　　　　　　c. testimonials.
　　　b. transfer.　　　　　　　　d. glittering generalities.

_____ **2.** Sentences 24–26 are examples of
　　　a. bandwagon.　　　　　　　c. testimonials.
　　　b. transfer.　　　　　　　　d. glittering generalities.

_____ **3.** The phrase "follow your dreams" in sentence 32 is an example of
   a. card stacking.
   b. bandwagon.
   c. glittering generalities.
   d. bandwagon.

_____ **4.** Sentence 39 is an example of
   a. transfer.
   b. glittering generalities.
   c. testimonial.
   d. bandwagon.

SUMMARY RESPONSE

Restate the author's central idea in your own words. In your summary, state the author's claim. Begin your summary response with the following: _The central idea of "Nostalgia Merchants" by Griffin and Ebert is . . ._

WHAT DO YOU THINK?

Have you ever thought about starting your own business or creating a product to sell? Assume you are an entrepreneur who is starting up your own business or product line. Also assume some investors are interested in your ideas and have asked you to write up a proposal for their consideration. Write a one-page description of your business or product. Consider the following ideas to help you write your business or product proposal:

- State what your product or business claims to accomplish.
- Use persuasion techniques to gain support for your ideas.

REVIEW TEST 4

Score (number correct) _____ x 20 = _____ %

Visit MyReadingLab to take this test online and receive feedback and guidance on your answers.

Advanced Argument

Before you read, skim the following excerpts from a speech by Geraldine Ferraro. With this speech at the Democratic National Convention, Ms. Ferraro was accepting the nomination to be the Democratic vice-presidential candidate in the 1984 election—the first woman to be nominated by either of the two major political parties. Answer the Before Reading questions. Then read the passage and answer the After Reading questions.

Vocabulary Preview

inaudible (5): cannot be heard
austerity (23): a tightened economy, marked by spending cuts
impoverishes (45): makes poor; deprives

Vice Presidential Nomination Acceptance Address

¹My name is Geraldine Ferraro. ²I stand before you to proclaim tonight: America is the land where dreams can come true for all of us. ³As I stand before the American people and think of the honor this great convention has bestowed upon me, I recall the words of Dr. Martin Luther King Jr., who made America stronger by making America more free. ⁴He said, "Occasionally in life there are moments which cannot be completely explained by words. ⁵Their meaning can only be **articulated** by the **inaudible** language of the heart." ⁶Tonight is such a moment for me. ⁷My heart is filled with pride. ⁸My fellow citizens, I proudly accept your nomination for Vice President of the United States. . . .

⁹Tonight, the daughter of a woman whose highest goal was a future for her children talks to our nation's oldest party about a future for us all; tonight, the daughter of working Americans tells all Americans that the future is within our reach, if we're willing to reach for it. ¹⁰Tonight, the daughter of an immigrant from Italy has been chosen to run for Vice President in the new land my father came to love.

¹¹Our faith that we can shape a better future is what the American dream is all about. ¹²The promise of our country is that the rules are fair. ¹³If you work hard and play by the rules, you can earn your share of America's blessings. . . .

¹⁴Americans want to live by the same set of rules. ¹⁵But under this administration, the rules are rigged against too many of our people. ¹⁶It isn't right that every year the share of taxes paid by individual citizens is going up, while the share paid by large corporations is getting smaller and smaller. ¹⁷The rules say: Everyone in our society should contribute their fair share. ¹⁸It isn't right that this year Ronald Reagan will hand the American people a bill for interest on the national debt larger than the entire cost of the federal government under John F. Kennedy. ¹⁹Our parents left us a growing economy. ²⁰The rules say: We must not leave our kids a mountain of debt.

²¹It isn't right that a woman should get paid 59 cents on the dollar for the same work as a man. ²²If you play by the rules, you deserve a fair day's pay for a fair day's work. ²³It isn't right that, if trends continue, by the year 2000 nearly all of the poor people in America will be women and

children. The rules of a decent society say: When you distribute sacrifice in times of **austerity**, you don't put women and children first. [24]It isn't right that young people today fear they won't get the Social Security they paid for, and that older Americans fear that they will lose what they have already earned. [25]Social Security is a contract between the last generation and the next, and the rules say: You don't break contracts. . . .

[26]By choosing a woman to run for our nation's second highest office, you send a powerful signal to all Americans: There are no doors we cannot unlock. [27]We will place no limits on achievement. [28]If we can do this, we can do anything.

[29]Tonight, we reclaim our dream. [30]We're going to make the rules of American life work fairly for all Americans again.

[31]To an Administration that would have us debate all over again whether the Voting Rights Act should be renewed and whether segregated schools should be tax exempt, we say: Mr. President, those debates are over. [32]On the issue of civil rights, voting rights, and affirmative action for minorities, we must not go backwards. [33]We must—and we will—move forward to open the doors of opportunity.

[34]To those who understand that our country cannot prosper unless we draw on the talents of all Americans, we say: We will pass the Equal Rights Amendment. [35]The issue is not what America can do for women, but what women can do for America.

[36]To the Americans who will lead our country into the 21st century, we say: We will not have a Supreme Court that turns the clock back to the 19th century.

[37]To those concerned about the strength of American and family values, as I am, I say: We are going to restore those values—love, caring, partnership—by including, and not excluding, those whose beliefs differ from our own. [38]Because our own faith is strong, we will fight to preserve the freedom of faith for others.

[39]To those working Americans who fear that banks, utilities, and large special interests have a lock on the White House, we say: Join us. [40]Let's elect the people's President; and let's have government by and for the American people again.

[41]To an Administration that would savage student loans and education at the dawn of a new technological age, we say: You fit the classic definition of a cynic; you know the price of everything, but the value of nothing.

[42]To our students and their parents, we say: We will insist on the highest standards of excellence, because the jobs of the future require skilled minds.

⁴³To young Americans who may be called to our country's service, we say: We know your generation will proudly answer our country's call, as each generation before you. . . .

⁴⁴A wise man once said, "Every one of us is given the gift of life, and what a strange gift it is. ⁴⁵If it is preserved jealously and selfishly, it **impoverishes** and saddens. ⁴⁶But if it is spent for others, it enriches and beautifies." ⁴⁷My fellow Americans: We can debate policies and programs, but in the end what separates the two parties in this election campaign is whether we use the gift of life for others or only ourselves.

Source: <http://www.americanrhetoric.com/
speeches/gferraroacceptanceaddress.html>

Before Reading

Vocabulary in Context

_____ **1.** What is the best meaning of the word **articulated** in sentence 4?

    a. expressed   c. hidden

    b. understood   d. confused

Tone and Purpose

_____ **2.** The author's tone and purpose are to

    a. inform with objective evidence.

    b. entertain with heartwarming stories.

    c. persuade with inspiring details.

After Reading

Central Idea and Main Idea

_____ **3.** Which sentence best states the speaker's central idea?

    a. sentence 1   c. sentence 8

    b. sentence 2   d. sentence 11

Supporting Details

_____ **4.** About what issue does the speaker say: "Mr. President, those debates are over"?

    a. Social Security

    b. voting rights and segregation

    c. equal rights for women

    d. student loans and education

Thought Patterns

_____ **5.** The relationship of ideas within sentence 16 is
    a. time order.
    b. cause and effect.
    c. generalization and example.
    d. contrast.

Fact and Opinion

_____ **6.** Overall this passage relies on
    a. fact.
    b. opinion.
    c. fact and opinion.

Inferences

_____ **7.** Based on the details in the passage, which of the following is a valid inference?
    a. The national debt increased during Reagan's term.
    b. Women won important rights in the early 1980s.
    c. The Voting Rights Act was not renewed in the 1980s.
    d. Student loans were easier to get during the Reagan administration.

Argument

_____ **8.** In sentence 2 the speaker uses the propaganda technique of
    a. transfer.
    b. bandwagon.
    c. testimonial.
    d. glittering generality.

_____ **9.** In sentences 9 and 10, the speaker uses
    a. testimonials.
    b. transfer.
    c. plain folks.
    d. card stacking.

_____ **10.** In sentence 47 the speaker uses the fallacy of
    a. either-or.
    b. straw man.
    c. begging the question.
    d. false comparison.

SUMMARY RESPONSE

Restate the author's central idea in your own words. In your summary, state the author's claim. Begin your summary response with the following: *The central idea of "Vice Presidential Nomination Acceptance Address" by Geraldine Ferraro is . . .*

WHAT DO YOU THINK?

Assume you are taking a college course in Political Science. Your professor has assigned an essay that compares or contrasts at least three issues brought up by Ferraro in her 1984 Vice Presidential Nomination Acceptance Address to issues we are facing today. Use the following ideas to help guide your writing:

- Identify persuasion techniques used by the speaker.
- Evaluate whether supports are valid or biased.
- Determine if the issues you choose to write about are still relevant or if they have been resolved.

After Reading About Advanced Argument: Persuasive Techniques

Before you move on to the Mastery Tests on advanced argument, take time to reflect on your learning and performance by answering the following questions. Write your answers in your notebook.

- How has my knowledge base or prior knowledge about advanced argument and persuasive techniques changed?
- Based on my studies, how do I think I will perform on the Mastery Test(s)? Why do I think my scores will be above average, average, or below average?
- Would I recommend this chapter to other students who want to learn more about advanced argument and persuasive techniques? Why or why not?

Test your understanding of what you have learned about advanced argument and persuasive techniques by completing the Chapter 13 Review.

Name _____ Section _____

Date _____ **Score** (number correct) _____ x 10 = _____ %

Visit MyReadingLab to take this test online and receive feedback and guidance on your answers.

Write the letter of the fallacy used in each of the following items.

_____ **1.** Love America or leave it.
- a. begging the question
- b. either-or
- c. personal attack
- d. straw man

_____ **2.** The senator doesn't care about the environment because it doesn't win him any votes to care.
- a. false cause
- b. either-or
- c. begging the question
- d. personal attack

_____ **3.** Being in school is like being in a concentration camp.
- a. false comparison
- b. straw man
- c. begging the question
- d. false cause

_____ **4.** I have won the football lottery at work three times. Every time I won, my boyfriend and I had a fight the night before. I am going to pick a fight with him tonight because I want to win the lottery tomorrow.
- a. straw man
- b. either-or
- c. false cause
- d. personal attack

_____ **5.** The government should continue research in the area of human cloning. Just as space research has brought us useful byproducts such as Teflon, research in human cloning will lead to unexpected discoveries that will benefit humanity.
- a. false comparison
- b. begging the question
- c. straw man
- d. false cause

_____ **6.** The candidate for city commission says, "We need lower taxes because the current taxes are too high."
- a. straw man
- b. personal attack
- c. begging the question
- d. either-or

_____ **7.** I touched a toad. Now I have a wart.
- a. false cause
- b. straw man
- c. either-or
- d. personal attack

_____ **8.** Speaker 1: Our prisons are overcrowded, and we don't have the money to build additional prisons. We need to find other solutions. Many of those in prison for lesser, non-violent crimes could be placed on house arrest and equipped with technology that tracks their whereabouts.

Speaker 2: My opponent wants to set prisoners free to live in the comfort of their own homes.

   a. begging the question   c. personal attack
   b. false comparison   d. straw man

_____ **9.** The charges against the police for brutality are untrue because police are officers of the law.

   a. straw man   c. personal attack
   b. begging the question   d. either-or

_____ **10.** I could never date Samantha; she looks like a horse.

   a. personal attack   c. straw man
   b. false cause   d. either-or

Name _____ Section _____

Date _____ **Score** (number correct) _____ x 10 = _____%

Visit MyReadingLab to take this test online and receive feedback and guidance on your answers.

A. Identify the propaganda technique used in each of the following items. Some techniques are used more than once.

   a. plain folks   d. transfer
   b. bandwagon   e. name-calling
   c. testimonial   f. glittering generality

_____ **1.** A candidate promises, "Elect me, and I will serve the land of the free and the home of the brave with courage and humility."

_____ **2.** I would never listen to, much less buy, Fergie's music; she is an immoral person and a horrible role model.

_____ **3.** A commercial advertising ice cream shows a series of preschool children in settings that look like their homes reading the list of natural ingredients on the ice cream carton as they happily eat the ice cream.

_____ **4.** Michael Jordan, a famous basketball player, recommends Hanes T-shirts because they are comfortable.

_____ **5.** In a television commercial for a breath mint, a young woman is dripping with sweat. She pops a breath mint in her mouth; immediately a breeze begins to blow, she stops sweating, and she breathes out an icy cloud of air that turns the whole scene a refreshing blue color.

_____ **6.** Don't take classes with that professor; he's a tough grader and a boring lecturer.

_____ **7.** I am going to vote for gun control because all my friends and family are voting for gun control.

_____ **8.** If you want a good, old-fashioned home-cooked meal, come into Andy's. We make the meals mom used to make.

_____ **9.** Identify the propaganda technique used in this poster.

    a. plain folks

    b. bandwagon

    c. testimonial

    d. transfer

    e. name-calling

    f. glittering generality

B. Read the following fictitious advertisement. Identify the detail that was **omitted** from the advertisement for the purpose of card stacking.

_____ **10.** House for sale: Built in 2003, this four-bedroom, three-bath pool home with a total living space of 1,800 square feet is located close to shopping and in an excellent school district. All appliances are included.

    a. The house is underpriced for a quick move because the owner received a job transfer.

    b. The appliances are still under warranty.

    c. The house is sitting on a recently filled sinkhole.

Name _____ Section _____

Date _____ **Score** (number correct) _____ × 10 = _____%

Visit MyReadingLab to take this test online and receive feedback and guidance on your answers.

A. Identify the propaganda technique used in each of the following items. Some techniques are used more than once.

a. plain folks   d. transfer
b. bandwagon   e. name-calling
c. testimonial   f. glittering generality

_____ **1.** Campaigning for the 2012 Republican nomination, multimillion-aire Mitt Romney said, "It's for the great middle class—the 80 to 90 percent of us in this country."

_____ **2.** "Join our effort to defeat breast cancer by drinking Joe's Coffee. For every cup of coffee you buy, Joe's Coffee will donate a dime to the Susan G. Komen for the Cure Organization."

_____ **3.** My opponent is a weak-minded liberal.

_____ **4.** Mariah Carey advertises how she lost weight using the Jenny Craig program.

_____ **5.** Everyone smokes marijuana, so it should be legalized.

_____ **6.** An advertisement for State Farm Insurance says, "Like a good neighbor, State Farm is there."

_____ **7.** The Internet is one of the greatest tools of democracy and should be cherished and protected as a basic American right to access information. Stop censorship of the Internet in public libraries.

_____ **8.** Identify the propaganda technique used in this advertisement.
 a. plain folks
 b. bandwagon
 c. testimonial
 d. transfer
 e. name-calling
 f. glittering generality

B. Read the following fictitious advertisements. Identify the detail from each list that was **omitted** from each advertisement for the purpose of card stacking.

_____ **9.** For sale: A 2012 white Malibu with low mileage. Maintenance work has been done on a regular basis. All new tires. AM/FM radio with CD player and Aux input. Power steering. Only $13,999.
 a. The car has had only one owner, an elderly woman who didn't often drive.
 b. The car was recently in a wreck and has had major repairs.
 c. The car seats five people comfortably and has an adequate amount of trunk space.

_____ **10.** Be the gorgeous redhead you have always wanted to be. ColorLife Russet will turn your hair a luscious shade of auburn while leaving it soft and manageable. Turn heads your way with ColorLife Russet.
 a. ColorLife Russet is a temporary color that must be reapplied every two to three weeks.
 b. ColorLife Russet meets the Food and Drug Administration's recommended levels of lead acetate.
 c. ColorLife Hair Color comes in 26 other shades as well.

Name _____ Section _____

Date _____ **Score** _____ × 10 = _____

Visit MyReadingLab to take this test online and receive feedback and guidance on your answers.

A. Write the letter of the fallacy next to its definition.

a. begging the question   d. false cause
b. personal attack   e. false comparison
c. straw man   f. either-or

_____ **1.** In this fallacy, the original argument is replaced with a weaker version that is easier to challenge than the original argument.

_____ **2.** This fallacy assumes that two things are similar when they are not.

_____ **3.** This fallacy assumes that because events occurred around or near the same time, they have a cause-and-effect relationship.

_____ **4.** This fallacy assumes that only two sides of an issue exist.

_____ **5.** This fallacy restates the point of an argument as the support and conclusion.

_____ **6.** This fallacy uses abusive remarks in place of evidence for a point or argument.

B. Write the letter of the fallacy used in each of the following items.

_____ **7.** The truly patriotic citizen supports all elected officials.
a. straw man   c. false comparison
b. begging the question   d. either-or

_____ **8.** My opponent says he opposes prayer in public schools. What does he have against religion?
a. straw man   c. begging the question
b. false comparison   d. false cause

_____ **9.** I knew I was going to see you today because my horoscope said that I was going to meet with someone special today.
a. either-or   c. begging the question
b. false cause   d. straw man

_____ **10.** I love going to the movies because watching movies is my favorite
leisure time activity.

a. straw man

b. false cause

c. either-or

d. begging the question

13 Summary of Key Concepts about Advanced Argument: Persuasive Techniques

LO1 Assess your comprehension of advanced arguments and persuasive techniques.

- A fallacy is an _____.

- Irrelevant details draw attention away from logical thought by _____ _____.

- Inadequate details _____ the issue and do not _____ _____.

- Propaganda is an act of persuasion that systematically spreads _____ _____ that is designed to _____ a person, product, cause, or organization.

- _____ is the arousal of emotions to give meaning or power to an idea.

- Supply the definitions for the following terms:

  - Personal attack _____ _____.

  - Straw man _____ _____.

  - Begging the question _____ _____.

  - Name-calling _____.

  - Testimonials _____ _____.

  - Bandwagon _____

  - Plain folks _____ _____.

▪ Either-or _____

_____

_____

▪ False comparison _____

_____.

▪ False cause, also known as post hoc, _____

_____.

▪ Card stacking _____

_____.

▪ Transfer _____

_____.

▪ Glittering generalities _____

_____.

Test Your Comprehension of Advanced Argument: Persuasive Techniques

Respond to the following question. Answers may vary.

LO2 LO3 LO4 LO5 LO6 LO7 In your own words, explain the relationships among the following terms: *fallacy, irrelevant details, emotional appeal, inadequate details,* and *propaganda.* How will recognizing persuasive techniques help you improve your reading

comprehension? _____

_____

_____

_____

_____

2

Additional Readings

Textbook
Skills

Textbook
Skills

LO1   Evaluate the Connection Between Reading and Writing

The link between reading and writing is vital and natural. Written language allows an exchange of ideas between a writer and a reader. Thus, writing and reading are two equal parts of the communication process. In fact, reading is a form of listening or receiving information. And writing is like speaking—the sending of information. So an effective reader makes every effort to understand and respond to the ideas of the writer. Likewise, an effective writer makes every effort to make ideas clear so the reader can understand and respond to those ideas. Most writers find that reading improves their writing. Reading builds prior knowledge and fuels ideas for writing.

Because of this close relationship between reading and writing, both share similar thinking steps in their processes. In Chapter 1, you learned that the reading process has three phases: Before Reading, During Reading, and After Reading. The writing process also has three phases that occur before, during, and after writing: Prewriting, Drafting, and Proofing. By coordinating these two sets of process, you can improve both your reading and your writing. For example, the following statements sum up one way to connect reading and writing:

Reading is a prewriting activity. Drafting is an after reading activity.

Once you think of reading as a prewriting activity, you become a responsive or active reader during the reading process. In fact, you can begin using your writing skills as you read by annotating the text.

Annotating a Text

The word *annotate* suggests that you "take notes" in your book. If it's your own book, writing notes in the margin of a page as you read keeps you focused and improves your comprehension. You can quickly note questions where they occur, move on in your reading, and later return to clarify answers. In addition, after reading, your annotations help you review and respond to the material. The following suggestions offer one way to annotate a text:

How to Annotate a Text

- Circle important terms.
- Underline definitions and meanings.
- Note key ideas with a star or a check.
- Place question marks above words that are unknown or confusing.
- Number the steps in a process or items in a list.
- Write summaries at the ends of long sections.

- Write recall questions in the margins near their answers.

- Write key words and meanings in the margins.

⊙ **EXAMPLE** The following passage from a college health textbook is marked up as an example of an annotated text. Read the passage. Study the annotations. Then work with a peer or in a small group and create a summary of the text based on the annotations. See page 660 to review how to write a summary.

Textbook Skills

 Adapting to Stress

HEALTH SKILLS

Although there will always be some stress in your life, that does not mean you cannot do anything about it. In fact, the best medicine for stress appears to be learning how to adapt to or cope with stress.

Stress can be controlled!

(Coping) is adaptation to stress. In primitive times, coping with stress meant little more than exercising the basic (fight-or-flight reaction) to threatening situations. For example, if a tiger threatened a primitive man, he would either stand and fight (and do so with added strength and cunning brought about by the stress reactions described by the general adaptation syndrome) or run from the threat (also with the added strength and cunning brought about by the stress reaction).

What is "coping"? Describe "fight-or-flight." (F/F)

Today, we are not threatened by tigers. Threats come instead from difficult working situations, unexpected bills, and disappointing news. Although survival is still at issue, it is not as much the survival of an individual or the species as maintaining self-esteem in stressful situations. The fight-or-flight response still works well in some cases, as do (defense mechanisms) such as avoidance and denial. These responses, however, are usually effective only for the short term. In our complex society, more adaptive methods of coping are necessary for a long-term adaptation to stress. Fleeing or denying a stress situation might be very useful in diminishing the acute pain of an unhappy event, but it does not help you deal with the source of the stress over the long run.

What are two examples of defense mechanisms? (DM)

Summary: F/F and DM are 2 short-term ways to cope with stress.

Coping with Stress

There are several ways you can effectively minimize the negative effects of everyday stress, whether it is in school, on the job, or at home. One preventive action is to make sure that you take good care of your physical health. You do this by eating nutritiously, exercising, not smoking or using drugs, and getting an adequate amount of sleep. You will find tips on how to develop good health habits in the related chapters in this textbook. Being in good physical health can help your body fight the negative health effects that can accompany stress.

Healthy, long-term coping technique

Be Good to MYSELF!

—Reprinted from Pruitt, B. E., and Jane J. Stein. *Healthstyles: Decisions for Living Well,* 2nd ed., © 1999. Reprinted and Electronically reproduced by permission of Pearson Education, Inc., Upper Saddle River, New Jersey.

Writing a Summary

Writing a summary is an effective step in the reading and studying process.

A **summary** is a brief, clear restatement of a longer passage.

A summary includes only the passage's most important points. Often a summary is made up of the main idea and major supporting details. The length of a summary should reflect your study needs and the kind of passage you are trying to understand. For example, a paragraph might be summarized in a sentence or two, an article might be summarized in a paragraph, and a textbook chapter might be summarized in a page or two.

You can discover how well you understand a passage by writing a summary of it as an after reading activity. Use the annotations you make during reading to create your summary.

For example, read the following summary of the "Adapting to Stress" section of a college health textbook. Underline the words and phrases that were annotated in the earlier section:

> [1]By learning how to adapt to or cope with stress, stress can be controlled. [2]Two short-term ways to cope with stress are the fight-or-flight response and defense mechanisms. [3]During the primitive fight-or-flight response, a threat or stress creates a short-term burst of energy that allows a person to either stand and fight or turn and run with additional strength and skill. [4]Defense mechanisms include avoidance and denial. [5]However, healthy, long-term coping techniques for stress involve maintaining physical health. [6]To effectively cope with stress, eat a healthful diet, exercise, avoid use of tobacco and drugs, and get enough sleep.

This summary includes the author's main idea and the major supporting details. However, this summary also brings in a few minor supporting details. For example, sentence 3 explains the fight-or-flight reaction to stress. Including these details makes the summary longer than may be necessary. The following version includes only the main idea and the major supporting details.

> [1]Two short-term methods of adapting to stress include the fight-or-flight response and defense mechanisms such as avoidance and denial. [2]Healthy, long-term ways to cope with stress involve maintaining physical

health by eating healthfully, exercising, avoiding use of tobacco and drugs, and getting enough sleep.

Remember, the length of the summary depends upon your study needs as well as the length of the passage you are summarizing.

A Reading-Writing Plan of Action

Can you see how annotating a text lays the foundation upon which you can build a written response? The steps you take during reading feed into the process of writing a response after reading.

Remember, reading and writing is a conversation between the writer and the reader. One writes; the other reads. But the conversation often doesn't end there. A reader's response to a piece of writing keeps the dialogue going. When you write a summary, your response is to restate the author's ideas. It's like saying to the author, "If I understood you correctly, you said…" When you offer your own views about the author's ideas, you are answering the author's implied question, "What do you think?" In your reading and writing classes, your teacher often steps into the conversation. He or she stands in for the author and becomes the reader of your written response. In this case, your teacher evaluates both your reading and writing abilities. Your teacher checks your response for accuracy in comprehension of the author's message and development of your ability to write. The following chart illustrates this exchange of ideas.

The Conversation among Writers and Readers

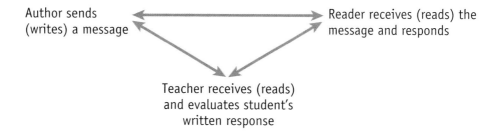

Author sends (writes) a message → Reader receives (reads) the message and responds → Teacher receives (reads) and evaluates student's written response

In each skill chapter of this textbook, the question "What Do You Think?" is posed after Review Tests 3 and 4. This question also appears after each reading selection in this section. The "What Do You Think?" writing assignments prompt you to respond to what you have read. This activity creates a writing situation and gives you a purpose for your written response. Just like a vocabulary word makes more sense in context than in a list, a writing assignment in context is more meaningful than an isolated topic or set of disconnected questions. The goal of "What Do You Think?" is to strengthen your connection between reading and writing. Because reading and writing are two distinct processes, it is helpful to have a guide that shows how to efficiently coordinate them. The following chart lays out a reading-writing plan of action. Note that the chart breaks the reading-writing process into a series of 6 steps. Keep in mind that any step can be repeated as needed. Also, you can move back and forth between steps as needed.

Study the 6-Step Reading-Writing Action Plan. Then work with a peer or small group of classmates and discuss the relationship between reading and writing, and how you will put this plan to use.

A 6-Step Reading-Writing Action Plan

Read		Write
1. Survey and Question **BEFORE**		**4. Prewrite**
Call on Prior Knowledge		Build Prior Knowledge*
Identify Topic		Gather Information*
Identify Key or New Words		Read and Annotate*
Identify Patterns of Organization		Brainstorm Ideas
Note Visual Aids		Choose Your Topic
Skim Introductions and		Generate Your Details
Conclusions		Create a Concept Map
		Outline Ideas
2. Read **DURING**		**5. Draft**
Monitor Comprehension		Write Introduction, Body,
Fix Confusion		and Conclusion
Annotate Text		
3. Review and Recite **AFTER**		**6. Revise and Proofread**
Recall Key Words and Ideas		Revise to Organize
Create Concept Maps		Revise for Exact Wording
Create Outlines		Correct Errors
Write a Summary		Fragments and Run-ons
Write a Response		Spelling
		Punctuation

*Prewriting steps accomplished during reading

1

Some are Semi-sweet and Some are Semi-not

Bob Schwartz

Bob Schwartz is an author and freelance humor writer whose popular writings have appeared in over 150 magazines and numerous newspapers. The following essay appears in his book *Would Somebody Please Send ME to MY Room! A Hilarious Look at Family Life.* As you read this passage, consider the following questions: Are you just like your family? Do you and your parents agree on most things? Have you ever been surprised by the ways in which you differ from your family or friends?

Vocabulary Preview

stupefied (paragraph 3): bewildered, confused, amazed
aversion (paragraph 4): strong dislike, distaste
blasphemous (paragraph 4): expressing disrespect for God or sacred
   things, improper
monumental (paragraph 5): large, significant
rendezvous (paragraph 5): meeting
hallucinogenic (paragraph 5): mind altered, delusional
revulsion (paragraph 8): disgust, loathing
renegade (paragraph 8): rebel, traitor

1   With two small words from our two-year-old, my wife and I began to question the entire validity of genetics. Having been introduced to chocolate for the first time, our daughter exclaimed the most inconceivable reaction by any child born into our Willie Wonka Biosphere.

2   She truly shook the very fabric of our bon-bon world. Upon tasting a chocolate brownie, she provided a very **animated** facial expression, which seemed to indicate that she was chewing lukewarm and hot pepper flavored sawdust. She then quite matter-of-factly said, "No like."

3   My wife and I stared at each other **stupefied**. Her older brothers reacted with jaw dropping disbelief as their Ho-Ho's fell from their hands and landed in their Cocoa Puffs.

4   Now we certainly do monitor the nutritional intake of our children's food consumption, but the fact was that our daughter had been born into a family of chocoholics. It seemed beyond comprehension that given her present **aversion** we'd have to work on

her taste buds for a little choco-conversion. Otherwise, we ultimately might be required to integrate our dessert table with the **blasphemous** flavors of vanilla and dare I even say it, butterscotch.

5   A little background regarding my Hershey's history might be in order. My **confectionery** confession is that I really didn't give much thought to chocolate until I met my wife. Up to that point, I think my lack of full commitment stemmed from a **monumental** event I'd had as a nine-year-old. It was then that my stomach had a mind-altering **rendezvous** with a breakfast plate of chocolate chip pancakes, laden with chocolate syrup and doused with chocolate whipped cream. My grandfather had treated me to this **ambrosial** delicacy at 7:00 a.m. at the International House of Sugar Overload. I was pretty much in a hyperactive **hallucinogenic** state the remainder of that year. To this day, I have only an extremely vague recollection of fourth grade.

6   My wife, on the other hand, grew up on Rocky Road in Loompaland. I didn't initially realize her chocolate dependence, since I had no idea of the truffles she'd seen. I slowly learned that her idea of a balanced diet was equal amounts of dark and white chocolate. She followed the twelve-step chocoholic program, which required that a person be no more than twelve steps from chocolate at any given time.

7   She slowly introduced me to cocoa butter and the **decadent** underworld of dark-chocolate mousse. And now, one of our children was rebuking everything we believed in—the very framework of our bumpy cake home! The next thing we knew our daughter might actually do the unthinkable. That's right, request green Jell-O for dessert.

8   We looked on the bright side and figured this was simply a toddler stage that she'd grow out of. We had preferred she'd instead exhibit the more familiar two-year-old acts of temper tantrums or extreme defiance. We could handle that. But a chocolate **revulsion**? The little radical. Perhaps this was the beginning of **renegade** behavior. Were we destined for demands for nose rings by age three, and a pink Mohawk haircut by age four from our little double fudge dessert **dissenter**?

9   Maybe we could sneak some crushed Oreos into her applesauce or mix some pieces of 3 Musketeer candy bars into her Cheerios to have her satisfy our Recommended Daily Allowance of chocolate.

10   Then again, we knew the right thing was just to let her go in her own sugar direction. She obviously marched to the sound of her own candy wrapper.

11   Perhaps she'd ultimately convert us a little. But I'm not sure I could ever look those jovial M & M fellas in the eye if I defected over to strawberry licorice.

—Schwartz, Bob. From "Some Are Semi Sweet and Some Are Not" in *Would Somebody Please Send Me to My Room! A Hilarious Look at Family Life* by Bob Schwartz. Reprinted by permission of Glenbridge Publishing Ltd.

Fill in the blank in each sentence with a word from the Vocabulary Preview.

Vocabulary Preview

1. Chocoholics Anonymous is a support group for people who are

    <u>stupefied</u> by their addiction to chocolate.

Vocabulary Preview

2. One group of Chocoholics Anonymous publically expressed their ___aversion___ to Tim Burton's film *Charlie and the Chocolate Factory* and demanded that the movie begin with a warning about the dangers of chocolate addiction.

Vocabulary Preview

3. Some claim that chocolate addiction is a **monumental** problem worse than addition to heroin or cocaine.

Vocabulary Preview

4. The real danger for a chocoholic is the ready availability of chocolate—no secret ___rendezvous___ is needed to get a fix—just a trip to the local grocery store.

Vocabulary Preview

5. Chocolate contains the chemical phenylethylamine; this compound has ___hallu___ properties similar to amphetamines.

For items 6 through 10, choose the best meaning of each word in *italics*. Use context clues to make your choice.

Vocabulary in Context ___b___ **6.** "Upon tasting a chocolate brownie, she provided a very *animated* facial expression, which seemed to indicate that she was chewing lukewarm and hot pepper flavored sawdust." (paragraph 2)
a. lifeless
b. lively
c. distasteful
d. eager

Vocabulary in Context ___d___ **7.** "My *confectionery* confession is that I really didn't give much thought to chocolate until I met my wife." (paragraph 5)
a. baking
b. pastry
c. candy making
d. food candies

Vocabulary in Context ___b___ **8.** "My grandfather had treated me to this *ambrosial* delicacy at 7:00 a.m. at the International House of Sugar Overload." (paragraph 5)
a. fruity
b. delightful
c. bland
d. offensive

Vocabulary in Context ___a___ **9.** "She slowly introduced me to cocoa butter and the *decadent* underworld of dark-chocolate mousse." (paragraph 7)
a. self-indulgent
b. wild
c. corrupt
d. innocent

Vocabulary in Context ___c___ **10.** "Were we destined for demands for nose rings by age three, and a pink Mohawk haircut by age four from our little double fudge dessert *dissenter*?" (paragraph 8)
a. follower
b. criminal
c. rebel
d. delinquent

Central Idea   c   **11.** Which of the following sentences states the central idea of the passage?
a. "With two small words from our two-year-old, my wife and I began to question the entire validity of genetics." (paragraph 1)
b. "She truly shook the very fabric of our bon-bon world." (paragraph 2)
c. "Upon tasting a chocolate brownie, she provided a very animated facial expression, which seemed to indicate that she was chewing lukewarm and hot pepper flavored sawdust." (paragraph 2)
d. "Perhaps this was the beginning of renegade behavior." (paragraph 8)

Supporting Details   d   **12.** The author's two-year-old said "No like" upon tasting
a. Ho-Ho's.   c. Cocoa Puffs.
b. 3 Musketeer candy bars.   d. a chocolate brownie.

Supporting Details   c   **13.** According to the author, his wife's idea of a balanced diet is
a. truffles.
b. chocolate mousse.
c. equal amounts of dark and white chocolate.
d. Cocoa Puffs and Cheerios.

Transitions   a   **14.** "Her older brothers reacted with jaw dropping disbelief as their Ho-Ho's fell from their hands and landed in their Cocoa Puffs." (paragraph 3)

The relationship of ideas **within** this sentence is
a. cause and effect.   c. comparison and contrast.
b. time order.   d. generalization and example.

Transitions   c   **15.** "To this day, I have only an extremely vague recollection of fourth grade. My wife, on the other hand, grew up on Rocky Road in Loompaland." (paragraphs 5 and 6)

The relationship of ideas **between** these sentences is
a. cause and effect.   c. comparison and contrast.
b. time order.   d. generalization and example.

Thought Patterns   a   **16.** The main thought pattern of the passage is
a. time order.   c. comparison and contrast.
b. classification.   d. definition and example.

Fact and Opinion   a   **17.** "My grandfather had treated me to this ambrosial delicacy at 7:00 a.m. at the International House of Sugar Overload." (paragraph 5)

This sentence is a statement of
a. fact.   c. fact and opinion.
b. opinion.

Tone and
Patterns
___b___ **18.** The overall tone and purpose of the author is
  a. to inform the reader about his struggles as a parent.
  b. to entertain the reader with an amusing personal story about parenting.
  c. to persuade the reader of the value of chocolate.

Inferences
___b___ **19.** Based on the details in paragraph 3, we can infer that
  a. the author's two-year-old is an only child.
  b. the author's two-year-old is the youngest child.
  c. the author has only three children.
  d. the author's two-year-old is the only daughter in the family.

Argument
___a___ **20.** The humor in paragraph 8 is based on the use of the persuasive technique
  a. false analogy.   c. transfer.
  b. bandwagon.   d. glittering generalities.

Mapping DON'T DO IT!
Complete the following story web with information from the passage.

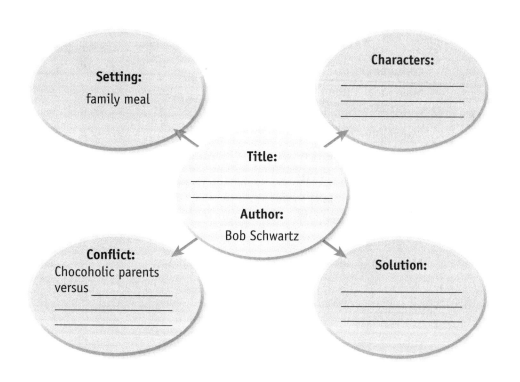

Setting:
family meal

Characters:
_____
_____
_____

Title:
_____
_____
Author:
Bob Schwartz

Conflict:
Chocoholic parents
versus _____
_____
_____

Solution:
_____
_____
_____

WHAT DO YOU THINK?

The humor of this essay comes from the author's use of irony—both verbal and situational. In what ways does the author use verbal irony? Give examples. In what ways is the situation described by the author ironic? Are you surprisingly different from your family? Or do you know someone who is ironically different from his or her family? Assume you are volunteering with troubled youth through a local branch of an organization such as the YMCA, Big Brothers, or Big Sisters. You have been asked to write an article of encouragement to post on the group's blog. Write an essay that relays a funny story about being different or about accepting someone else who is different.

EFFECTIVE READER SCORECARD

"Some are Semi-sweet and Some are Semi-not"

Skill	Number Correct	Points		Total
Vocabulary				
Vocabulary Preview (5 items)	_____	$\times$ 10	=	_____
Vocabulary in Context (5 items)	_____	$\times$ 10	=	_____
		Vocabulary Score		_____
Comprehension				
Main Idea (1 item)	_____	$\times$ 8	=	_____
Supporting Details (2 items)	_____	$\times$ 8	=	_____
Transitions (2 items)	_____	$\times$ 8	=	_____
Thought Patterns (1 item)	_____	$\times$ 8	=	_____
Fact and Opinion (1 item)	_____	$\times$ 8	=	_____
Tone and Purpose (1 item)	_____	$\times$ 8	=	_____
Inferences (1 item)	_____	$\times$ 8	=	_____
Argument (1 item)	_____	$\times$ 8	=	_____
Mapping (4 items)	_____	$\times$ 5	=	_____
		Comprehension Score		_____

2 Fifth Chinese Daughter

Jade Snow Wong

> Jade Snow Wong, the daughter of Chinese immigrants who settled in San Francisco, became a renowned author and ceramic artist. In her two volumes of autobiography, *Fifth Chinese Daughter* and *No Chinese Stranger*, she chronicled her life growing up in California in the 1930s and 1940s. Wong describes her traditional Chinatown family and her struggle to succeed both as an American woman and as the daughter of an immigrant family. The following passage is an excerpt from *Fifth Chinese Daughter*. Have your parents ever forbid you to do something you thought important? How did you respond? Did you honor your parents' wishes or did you rebel and do as you wanted?

Vocabulary Preview

conventional (paragraph 2): traditional, typical
subsist (paragraph 2): live, survive
mediocrity (paragraph 2): ordinariness, weakness
incurred (paragraph 4): acquired, suffered, experienced
derived (paragraph 6): resulting
perpetual (paragraph 6): unending, ongoing
nepotism (paragraph 7): bias in favor of family or friends, particularly in granting power and position
revered (paragraph 12): respected, honored
innuendos (paragraph 14): an indirect remark or gesture that usually suggests something improper
devastated (paragraph 15): overwhelmed, distressed
perplexed (paragraph 16): puzzled, confused, baffled

1   By the time I was graduating from high school, my parents had done their best to produce an intelligent, obedient daughter, who would know more than the average Chinatown girl and should do better than average at a conventional job, her earnings brought home in repayment for their years of child support. Then, they hoped, she would marry a nice Chinese boy and make him a good wife, as well as an above-average mother for his children. Chinese custom used to decree

that families should "introduce" chosen partners to each other's children. The groom's family should pay handsomely to the bride's family for rearing a well-bred daughter. They should also pay all bills for a glorious wedding banquet for several hundred guests. Their daughter belonged to the groom's family and must henceforth seek permission from all persons in his home before returning to her parents for a visit.

2   But having been set upon a new path, I did not **oblige** my parents with the expected **conventional** ending. At fifteen, I had moved away from home to work for room and board and a salary of twenty dollars per month. Having found that I could **subsist** independently, I thought it regrettable to terminate my education. Upon graduating from high school at the age of sixteen, I asked my parents to assist me in college expenses. I pleaded with my father, for his years of encouraging me to be above **mediocrity** in both Chinese and American studies had made me wish for some undefined but brighter future.

3   My father was briefly **adamant**. He must conserve his resources for my oldest brother's medical training. Though I desired to continue on an above-average course, his material means were insufficient to support that ambition. He added that if I had the talent, I could provide for my own college education. When he had spoken, no discussion was expected. After this **edict**, no daughter questioned.

4   But this matter involved my whole future—it was not simply asking for permission to go to a night church meeting (forbidden also). Though for years I had

accepted the authority of the one I honored most, his decision that night embittered me as nothing ever had. My oldest brother had so many privileges, had **incurred** unusual expenses for luxuries which were taken for granted as his birthright, yet these were part of a system I had accepted. Now I suddenly wondered at my father's interpretation of the Christian code: was it intended to discriminate against a girl after all, or was it simply convenient for my father's economics and cultural prejudice? Did a daughter have any right to expect more than a fate of obedience, according to the old Chinese standard? As long as I could remember, I had been told that a female followed three men during her lifetime: as a girl, her father; as a wife, her husband; as an old woman, her son.

5   My indignation mounted against that tradition and I decided then that my past could not determine my future. I knew that more education would prepare me for a different expectation than my other female schoolmates, few of whom were to complete a college degree. I, too, had my father's unshakable faith in the justice of God, and I shared his unconcern with popular opinion.

6   So I decided to enter junior college, now San Francisco's City College, because the fees were lowest. I lived at home and supported myself with an after-school job which required long hours of housework and cooking but paid me twenty dollars per month, of which I saved as much as possible. The thrills **derived** from reading and learning, in ways ranging from chemistry experiments to English compositions, from considering new ideas of sociology to the logic of Latin, convinced me that I had

made a correct choice. I was kept in a state of **perpetual** mental excitement by new Western subjects and concepts and did not mind long hours of work and study. I also made new friends, which led to another painful incident with my parents, who had heretofore discouraged even girlhood friendships.

7   The college subject which had the most jolted me was sociology. The instructor fired my mind with his interpretation of family relationships. As he explained to our class, it used to be an economic asset for American farming families to be large, since children were useful to perform agricultural chores. But this situation no longer applied and children should be regarded as individuals with their own rights. Unquestioning obedience should be replaced with parental understanding. So at sixteen, discontented as I was with my parents' apparent indifference to me, those words of my sociology professor gave voice to my sentiments. How old-fashioned was the dead-end attitude of my parents! How ignorant they were of modern thought and progress! The family unit had been China's strength for centuries, but it had also been her weakness, for corruption, **nepotism**, and greed were all justified in the name of the family's welfare. My new ideas festered; I longed to release them.

8   One afternoon on a Saturday, which was normally occupied with my housework job, I was unexpectedly released by my employer, who was departing for a country weekend. It was a rare joy to have free time and I wanted to enjoy myself for a change. There had been a Chinese-American boy who shared some classes with me. Sometimes we had found each other walking to the same 8:00 A.M. class. He was not a special boyfriend, but I had enjoyed talking to him and had confided in him some of my problems. Impulsively, I telephoned him. I knew I must be breaking rules, and I felt shy and scared. At the same time, I was excited at this newly found forwardness, with nothing more purposeful than to suggest another walk together.

He understood my awkwardness and 9 shared my anticipation. He asked me to "dress up" for my first movie date. My clothes were limited but I changed to look more graceful in silk stockings and found a bright ribbon for my long black hair. Daddy watched, catching my mood, observing the dashing preparations. He asked me where I was going without his permission and with whom.

I refused to answer him. I thought 10 of my rights! I thought he surely would not try to understand. Thereupon Daddy thundered his displeasure and forbade my departure.

I found a new courage and I heard my 11 voice announce calmly that I was no longer a child, and if I could work my way through college, I would choose my own friends. It was my right as a person.

My mother had heard the com- 12 motion and joined my father to face me; both appeared shocked and **incredulous**. Daddy at once demanded the source of this **unfilial**, non-Chinese theory. And when I quoted my college professor, reminding him that he had always felt teachers should be **revered**, my father denounced that professor as a foreigner who was disregarding the superiority of our Chinese culture, with its sound family strength. My father did not spare me; I was condemned as an ingrate for echoing dishonorable opinions which should only be temporary whims, yet nonetheless inexcusable.

13   The scene was not yet over. I completed my proclamation to my father, who had never allowed me to learn how to dance, by adding that I was attending a movie, unchaperoned, with a boy I met at college.

14   My startled father was sure that my reputation would be subject to whispered **innuendos**. I must be bent on disgracing the family name; I was ruining my future, for surely I would yield to temptation. My mother underscored him by saying that I hadn't any notion of the problems endured by parents of a young girl.

I would not give in. I reminded them 15 that they and I were not in China, that I wasn't going out with just anybody but someone I trusted! Daddy gave a roar that no man could be trusted, but I **devastated** them in declaring that I wished the freedom to find my own answers.

Both parents were thoroughly angered, 16 scolded me for being shameless, and predicted that I would someday tell them I was wrong. But I dimly perceived that they were conceding defeat and were **perplexed** at this breakdown of their training. I was too old to beat and too bold to intimidate.

—Wong, Jade Snow. From *Fifth Chinese Daughter* by Jade Snow Wong. Copyright 1945 by Jade Snow Wong. Reprinted by permission of Curtis Brown, Ltd.

Fill in the blank in each sentence with a word from the Vocabulary Preview.

Vocabulary Preview   **1.** San Francisco's Chinese community is _____ as the oldest, largest, and most visually recognizable urban Chinese American district in the world.

Vocabulary Preview   **2.** Many early Chinese immigrants were able to _____, as workers on farms, railroad construction crews, and in low-paying industrial jobs.

Vocabulary Preview   **3.** The Chinese brought with them _____ Chinese beliefs, values, and practices that defined their daily lives.

Vocabulary Preview   **4.** Early on, Chinese immigrants _____ the wrath of labor unions because the Chinese were willing to work hard and skillfully for low wages.

Vocabulary Preview   **5.** Despite hostility and discrimination, a _____ flow of Chinese immigrants poured into California to gain whatever opportunities awaited them in America.

For items 6 through 10, choose the best meaning of each word in *italics*. Use context clues to make your choice.

Vocabulary in Context   _____ **6.** "But having been set upon a new path, I did not *oblige* my parents with the expected conventional ending." (paragraph 2)
    a. accommodate   c. assist
    b. hinder   d. comfort

Vocabulary in Context _____ **7.** "My father was briefly *adamant*." (paragraph 3)
a. agreeable   c. inflexible
b. stingy   d. concerned

Vocabulary in Context _____ **8.** "After this *edict*, no daughter questioned." (paragraph 3)
a. disappointment   c. suggestion
b. command   d. reversal

Vocabulary in Context _____ **9.** "My mother had heard the commotion and joined my father to face me; both appeared shocked and *incredulous*." (paragraph 12)
a. calm   c. convinced
b. unquestioning   d. disbelieving

Vocabulary in Context _____ **10.** "Daddy at once demanded the source of this *unfilial*, non-Chinese theory." (paragraph 12)
a. surprising   c. civil
b. disrespectful   d. independent

Main Idea _____ **11.** Which of the following sentences states the central idea of the passage?
a. "But having been set upon a new path, I did not oblige my parents with the expected conventional ending." (paragraph 2)
b. "My indignation mounted against that tradition and I decided then that my past could not determine my future." (paragraph 5)
c. "How old-fashioned was the dead-end attitude of my parents!" (paragraph 7)
d. "I was too old to beat and too bold to intimidate." (paragraph 16)

Supporting Details _____ **12.** Which college course had the greatest influence on the author's thinking and actions as described in the passage?
a. chemistry   c. sociology
b. Latin   d. English composition

Supporting Details _____ **13.** According to the author's father, the superiority of Chinese culture was
a. the strength of the family.   c. its loyalty to male children.
b. its emphasis on education.   d. its devotion to religion.

Transitions _____ **14.** "Though I desired to continue on an above-average course, his material means were insufficient to support that ambition." (paragraph 3)

The relationship of ideas **within** this sentence is
a. time order.   c. comparison and contrast.
b. cause and effect.   d. generalization and example.

Transitions _____ 15. "Both parents were thoroughly angered, scolded me for being shameless, and predicted that I would someday tell them I was wrong. But I dimly perceived that they were conceding defeat and were perplexed at this breakdown of their training." (paragraph 16)

The relationship of ideas **between** these sentences is

a. cause and effect.   c. comparison and contrast.

b. time order.   d. generalization and example.

Thought Patterns _____ 16. The main thought pattern of the passage is

a. time order.   c. comparison and contrast.

b. classification.   d. definition and example.

Fact and Opinion _____ 17. "So I decided to enter junior college, now San Francisco's City College, because the fees were lowest." (paragraph 6)

This sentence is a statement of

a. fact.   c. fact and opinion.

b. opinion.

Tone and Purpose _____ 18. The overall tone and purpose of the author is

a. to inform the reader about her life growing up as a Chinese American female.

b. to entertain the reader with an amusing personal story about growing up as a Chinese American female.

c. to persuade the reader to challenge authority and become independent.

Inferences _____ 19. Based on the details in the passage, we can infer that

a. the author's parents loved her brother more than they loved her.

b. the author's father thought his son more intelligent than his daughter.

c. educating a daughter was unwise since she is expected to leave the family once she marries.

d. the author disliked her parents.

Argument _____ 20. "How old-fashioned was the dead-end attitude of my parents! How ignorant they were of modern thought and progress!" (paragraph 7)

Identify the logical fallacy used in these claims.

a. plain folks   c. transfer

b. straw man   d. personal attack

Mapping

Complete the following story web with information from the passage.

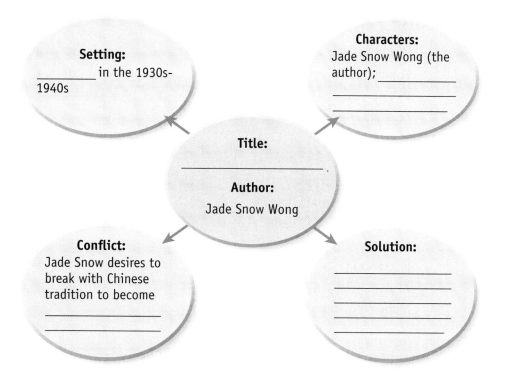

Setting:
_____ in the 1930s-1940s

Characters:
Jade Snow Wong (the author); _____
_____
_____

Title:
_____

Author:
Jade Snow Wong

Conflict:
Jade Snow desires to break with Chinese tradition to become
_____
_____

Solution:
_____
_____
_____
_____

WHAT DO YOU THINK?

In this "coming of age" passage, Wong describes two powerful influences in her life: her family and education. How did what she learned in class affect her relationship with her parents? How did family and education help her come of age or initiate her into adulthood? Have you learned something in an academic class that changed your values or view of the world? Have you experienced a moment in your life when you felt you had to stand up for yourself as a responsible adult? Assume you are taking a sociology course, and you are studying how young people transition into adulthood. Write an essay on one of the following topics: "An important lesson I've learned from a class or an elder" or "The moment I knew I was an adult." If you prefer, you should feel free to write about someone else that you have observed.

EFFECTIVE READER SCORECARD

"Fifth Chinese Daughter"

Skill	Number Correct		Points		Total
Vocabulary					
Vocabulary Preview (5 items)	_____	×	10	=	_____
Vocabulary in Context (5 items)	_____	×	10	=	_____
			Vocabulary Score		_____
Comprehension					
Main Idea (1 item)	_____	×	8	=	_____
Supporting Details (2 items)	_____	×	8	=	_____
Transitions (2 items)	_____	×	8	=	_____
Thought Patterns (1 item)	_____	×	8	=	_____
Fact and Opinion (1 item)	_____	×	8	=	_____
Tone and Purpose (1 item)	_____	×	8	=	_____
Inferences (1 item)	_____	×	8	=	_____
Argument (1 item)	_____	×	8	=	_____
Mapping (5 items)	_____	×	4	=	_____
			Comprehension Score		_____

3 Social Networking Sites: Online Friendships Can Mean Offline Peril

The Federal Bureau of Investigation

> On its official website, the Federal Bureau of Investigation (FBI) describes itself as "an Intel-driven national security and law enforcement agency, providing leadership and making a difference for more than a century." The agency posted the following article as part of its mission to "help protect you, your children, your communities, and your businesses from the most dangerous threats facing our nation—from international and domestic terrorists to spies on U.S. soil . . . from cyber villains to corrupt government officials . . . from mobsters to violent street gangs . . . from child predators to serial killers."

Vocabulary Preview

predators (paragraph 3): hunters, killers
extort (paragraph 4): force, obtain under threat
gender (paragraph 6): sex, sexual characteristic and role
demeaning (paragraph 7): humiliating, degrading
functionality (paragraph 24): the range of operations that can be run on a computer or other electronic system, being suited to serve a purpose

1   One thing is for sure: teens love the new **myriad** of online social networking sites. In fact, there are tens of millions of registered users. But, as with just about any kind of cyberspace communication, there are risks involved. And you should know what they are.

2   **What are social networking sites exactly?** They are websites that encourage people to post profiles of themselves—complete with pictures, interests, and even journals—so they can meet like-minded friends. Most also offer chat rooms. Most sites are free; some restrict membership by age.

3   **So what's the problem?** These sites can be appealing to child sexual **predators**, too: all that easy and immediate access to information on potential victims. Even worse, kids want to look cool, so they sometimes post suggestive photos of themselves on the sites.

677

4   **How pervasive is the problem?** Even with all the media attention on the dangers of social networking, we still receive hundreds of complaints per year about children who have been victims of criminal incidents on social networks. These incidents include but are not limited to:

- Adults posing as children who are about the same age as the victim who later travel to abuse the child; and

- Adults posing as children who convince the child to expose himself herself and/or perform sexual acts over webcam and later **extort** the child to perform additional acts.

5   According to an Internet safety pamphlet recently published by the National Center for Missing and Exploited Children (NCMEC), a survey of 12 to 17 year olds revealed that 38 percent had posted self-created content such as photos, videos, artwork, or stories. Another survey of 10 to 17 year olds revealed 46 percent admit to having given out their personal information to someone they did not know. The likelihood that kids will give out personal information over the Internet increases with age, with 56 percent of 16 to 17 year olds most likely sharing personal information.

6   Social networking websites often ask users to post a profile with their age, **gender**, hobbies, and interests. While these profiles help kids connect and share common interests, individuals who want to victimize kids can use those online profiles to search for potential victims. Kids sometimes compete to see who has the greatest number of contacts and will add new peo-

ple to their lists even if they do not know them in real life.

7   Children often don't realize that they cannot "take back" the online text and images they post. They also may not know that individuals with access to this information can save and forward these postings to an unlimited number of users. Kids may not realize the potential **ramifications** of their online activities. They can face consequences for posting harmful, explicit, dangerous, or **demeaning** information online, including being humiliated in front of their families and peers, suspended from school, charged criminally, and denied employment or entry into schools.

What can you do to keep your children safe, especially if they are visiting networking sites?

Most importantly, be aware and involved.

- Monitor your children's use of the Internet; keep your Internet computer in an open, common room of the house.   8

- Tell your kids why it's so important not to disclose personal information online.   9

- Check your kids' profiles and what they post online.   10

- Read and follow the safety tips provided on the sites.   11

- Report inappropriate activity to the website or law enforcement immediately.   12

- Explain to your kids that once images are posted online they lose control of them and can never get them back.   13

14 ▪ Only allow your kids to post photos or any type of personally identifying information on websites with your knowledge and consent.

15 ▪ Instruct your kids to use privacy settings to restrict access to profiles so only the individuals on their contact lists are able to view their profiles.

16 ▪ Remind kids to only add people they know in real life to their contact lists.

17 ▪ Encourage kids to choose appropriate screen names or nicknames.

18 ▪ Talk to your kids about creating strong passwords.

19 ▪ Visit social networking websites with your kids, and exchange ideas about acceptable versus potentially risky websites.

20 ▪ Ask your kids about the people they are communicating with online.

21 ▪ Make it a rule with your kids that they can never give out personal information or meet anyone in person without your prior knowledge and consent. If you agree to a meeting between your child and someone they met online, talk to the parents/guardians of the other individual first and accompany your kids to the meeting in a public place.

22 ▪ Encourage your kids to consider whether a message is harmful, dangerous, hurtful, or rude before posting or sending it online, and teach your kids not to respond to any rude or harassing remarks or messages that make them feel scared, uncomfortable, or confused and to show you the messages instead.

23 ▪ Educate yourself on the websites, software, and apps that your child uses.

▪ Don't forget cell phones! They often have almost all the **functionality** of a computer.

—FBI. "Social Networking Sites: Online Friendships
Can Mean Offline Peril."

Choose the best meaning of each word in *italics*. Use context clues to make your choice.

Vocabulary
in Context   _____   **1.** "One thing is for sure: teens love the *myriad* of online social networking sites." (paragraph 1)

    a. excitement   c. danger
    b. lack   d. large number

Vocabulary
in Context   _____   **2.** "Kids may not realize the potential *ramifications* of their online activities." (paragraph 7)

    a. results   c. causes
    b. difficulties   d. actions

Implied
Central Idea   _____   **3.** Which sentence best states the author's implied central idea?

    a. Social networking sites pose risks to children.

    b. The public should know the risks of cyberspace communication and how to keep children safe who access networking sites.

    c. Parents can take steps to protect their children.

    d. Predators use social networking sites to victimize children.

Supporting
Details   _____   **4.** According to the article, children post suggestive photos of themselves on social networking sites because they

    a. like to take risks.   c. want to look cool.

    b. are predators.   d. want to meet new friends.

Supporting
Details   _____   **5.** According to the article, which age group has the highest percentage of individuals most likely to share personal information on a social networking site?

    a. 10 to 12 year olds   c. 12 to 17 year olds

    b. 10 to 17 year olds   d. 16 to 17 year olds

Supporting
Details   _____   **6.** According to the article, how many complaints does the FBI receive about children victimized on social networks?

    a. thousands daily

    b. tens of millions in recent years

    c. hundreds per year

    d. too many to count.

Transitions   _____   **7.** "While these profiles help kids connect and share common interests, individuals who want to victimize kids can use those online profiles to search for potential victims." (paragraph 6)

The primary relationship of ideas **within** this sentence is

    a. time order.   c. contrast.

    b. cause and effect.   d. generalization and example.

Transitions   _____   **8.** "These incidents include but are not limited to:

Adults posing as children who are about the same age as the victim who later travel to abuse the child . . ." (paragraph 4)

The primary relationship of **between** these ideas is

    a. cause and effect.   c. comparison and contrast.

    b. listing.   d. classification.

Transitions   _____   **9.** "In fact, there are tens of millions of registered users. But, as with just about any kind of cyberspace communication, there are risks involved." (paragraph 1)

The relationship of ideas **between** these sentences is
a. cause and effect.
c. contrast.
b. time order.
d. generalization and example.

Thought Patterns _____ **10.** The main thought pattern used in paragraph 2 is
a. definition.
c. space order.
b. cause and effect.
d. comparison and contrast.

Thought Patterns _____ **11.** The main thought pattern of paragraphs 8–24 is
a. comparison.
c. listing.
b. cause and effect.
d. generalization and example.

Fact and Opinion _____ **12.** "One thing is for sure: teens love the myriad of online social networking sites." (paragraph 1)

This sentence is a statement of
a. fact.
c. fact and opinion.
b. opinion.

Fact and Opinion _____ **13.** "And you should know what they are." (paragraph 1)

This sentence is a statement of
a. fact.
c. fact and opinion.
b. opinion.

Fact and Opinion _____ **14.** Paragraph 5 mainly presents
a. facts.
c. facts and opinions.
b. opinions.

Tone and Purpose _____ **15.** "The tone of paragraph 5 is
a. objective.
c. worried.
b. shocked.
d. hopeful.

Tone and Purpose _____ **16.** The overall tone of the entire passage is
a. informal.
c. argumentative.
b. formal.
d. alarmed.

Tone and Purpose _____ **17.** The overall purpose of the author is
a. to entertain the reader with information about social networking sites.
b. to inform the reader about the dangers of social networking sties and ways to protect children.
c. to persuade the reader to keep children off of social networking sites.

Inferences _____ **18.** Based on the details in the passage, we can infer that
   a. most parents closely monitor their children's activities on social networking sites.
   b. most parents are aware of the dangers of social networking sites.
   c. parents also face dangers on social networking sites.
   d. some parents are not aware of the pervasive dangers of social networking sites.

Inferences _____ **19.** Based on the details in passage, we can infer that
   a. children can access social networks on their cell phones.
   b. children do not have access to social networks without their parental permission.
   c. most children use privacy settings on their social networks.
   d. children are more aware than their parents of the dangers of social networking sites.

Argument _____ **20.** The following statements from paragraph 7 list a claim and supports for that claim. Which sentence states the claim?
   a. "Children often don't realize that they cannot 'take back' the online text and images they post."
   b. "They also may not know that individuals with access to this information can save and forward these postings to an unlimited number of users."
   c. "Kids may not realize the potential ramifications of their online activities."
   d. "They can face consequences for posting harmful, explicit, dangerous, or demeaning information online, including being humiliated in front of their families and peers, suspended from school, charged criminally, and denied employment or entry into schools."

Outlining
Complete the following outline with information from the passage.

Social Networking Sites

   I. _____

   II. _____

   III. _____

   IV. _____

Assume you are the parent of teenagers who visit social networking sites. You also write a blog that is followed by your teenagers, their friends, and their parents. You want to educate them all about information provided in this article by the FBI. Write two paragraphs that explain some of the dangers of social networking sites and list specific ways teenagers can protect themselves.

EFFECTIVE READER SCORECARD

"Social Networking Sites : Online Friendship Can Mean Online Peril"

Skill	Number Correct		Points		Total
Vocabulary					
Vocabulary in Context (2 items)	_____	×	4	=	_____
Comprehension					
Implied Central Idea (1 item)	_____	×	4	=	_____
Supporting Details (3 items)	_____	×	4	=	_____
Transitions (3 items)	_____	×	4	=	_____
Thought Patterns (2 items)	_____	×	4	=	_____
Fact and Opinion (3 items)	_____	×	4	=	_____
Tone and Purpose (3 items)	_____	×	4	=	_____
Inferences (2 items)	_____	×	4	=	_____
Argument (1 items)	_____	×	4	=	_____
Outlining (4 items)	_____	×	5	=	_____
			Comprehension Score		_____

4 Toys R Us

Bucky McMahon

A nationally known adventure travel writer, Bucky McMahon has written for magazines such as *Outside*, *Esquire*, and *GQ*. He is also the author of *Night Diver*, a collection of personal essays. In this essay, he explores the emotions and meanings of childhood toys. Did you or someone you know have a favorite toy or childhood possession? What made that toy or possession so special?

Vocabulary Preview

fetlocks (paragraph 1): a horse's leg joint with a tuft of hair
sphagnum (paragraph 1): a type of moss
tundra (paragraph 1): a plain in the Arctic zone
conking (paragraph 4): hitting on the head
aura (paragraph 4): atmosphere
steeplechase (paragraph 5): a horse race involving jumping
titans (paragraph 6): giants, powerful people
cannon-fodder (paragraph 6): soldiers who are treated as expendable in battle
blather (paragraph 7): foolish and lengthy talking
eco-conscious (paragraph 8): to be aware of ecology and the sustainability of the
   natural planet
avatar (paragraph 8): an image who represents a person in virtual reality
nurturance (paragraph 10): the giving of loving care and attention
diminuendo (paragraph 10): to shrink or diminish in power
babicules (paragraph 10): tiny babies
churls (paragraph 11): rude people
half-life (paragraph 12): the time required for material to lose half of its effectiveness or radioactivity; a brief period of power before dying out
huckleberries (paragraph 13): a blueberry-like fruit that grows on a bush in
   clusters
cosmos (paragraph 13): the universe, immeasurable in time and space

1   When I was small I had a tiny tin moose. It was brown. Animal brown. Wild brown. Except where someone in Taiwan had hastily dipped it into black enamel up to the **fetlocks** in front and to the rump in the rear. The limbs were not posable, but I unwisely posed them a few times, as if to make my moose paw at the loose **sphagnum** of the **tundra**, in anticipation of the trumpeting rut, perhaps, or after whirling, as I'd read it must, to face the pack of timber wolves that had singled it out for age or infirmity, or because of their own desperation, and one limb broke off in my grubby little fingers.

2   The tiny tin moose never stood on its own again, unless it leaned against its companion, a little plastic dog that could be made to puff little paper cigarettes (this was in the days when dogs stilled smoked). I kept the tiny tin moose with me in a matchbox, bedded down on cotton. My sweet sister offered an aspirin, which rattled hollowly in the box in my pocket with the tiny three-legged tin moose. I became known as Moose ("the kid with the moose. Moose") among the three boys who **constituted** my society, until we moved, and I lost those boys, and that name, and that miniature moose as well.

3   Love of the miniature, so natural to the child, nourishing our tender personal devotion to the huge, to the cosmic, the infinite that miniaturizes all of us—I went in quest to Toys R Us for the little, the littler, the littlest of all.

4   Take for instance the horse, the real-life horse, stomping, farting, making large caca, the heavy horse of coarse mane, strong square teeth, **conking** hooves of horn, exuding its **aura** of hay and heat; and trace its descent in the child's imagination from the stick-horse (a stick-moose here, too)—a forward looking horse, all head and wish and child's pounding sneakers—to the $100 rocking horse, the $80 rocking horse, down to the fuzzy $40 rocking horse with child-seat; down to the scale model of the breeds; down to My Little Pony; down, down to The Adorable Li'l Pretty Perfume Pony, a mere thumbnail nub of a horse.

5   I like to think of the gulf between the real and its most pathetic imaging, and how the child's mind, surging with gigantic, oceanic forces, bridges that gulf in a bold leap worthy of a **steeplechase**.

6   Take the warrior, too, the boys' tool and **fool**. Of the men in bags: large green molded army men, **titans** among tykes, three to a bag, with faces like a favorite uncle; and the faceless **cannon-fodder** in bags of two dozen; and the traditional antagonists, the red and yellow cowboys and Indians, bow-legged, with mounts. Action figures, fist-sized, with posable limbs, have especially proliferated, and been given the power of speech—a risk, and a mistake.

7   Listen to the Warriors of M. P.A.C.T.: "Destroy it!"; "Hit the switch!"; and, eerily, "Lock 'em up!" G.I. Joe, the fashion-plate fighter, says, "Let's party!" and "Eat lead!" and makes battle sounds: "Blast!" "Boom!" "Zeeeooom!" But what will become of the boys' art of battle **blather** ("I'm hit!") and sound effects, the long-practiced and finally perfected near-miss ricochet: "Beeerunngh!"

8   It seems anything can be drafted into battle these days: the Turtles, of course, and the co-mutant, **eco-conscious** Toxic Warriors, and Bucky O'Hare of the Toad Wars, the Noid, Kevin Costner, Hulk Hogan, Jack

Nicholson, Beetlejuice and even Julia Roberts. Police Academy, Swamp Thing, the X-Men, He-Men, the Rocketeers and the Food Fighters—Fat Frenchy the bag of fries, Meenie Weiner, Lieutenant Legg the egg, Bad Bacon, and his earlier **avatar** Hamfat Lardo, the bazooka-wielding pig of Barnyard Commandos, victim/assailants of the universal draft.

9   The Dino Warriors have strapped what looks like a convenience store onto a brontosaurus, an inevitable wedding of prehistory and Pentagon spending. Weirdest are the Squirt Heads: Hulk Hogan, again; and Kevin Costner, again; the Squirt Head Killer Tomatoes.

10   One aisle over in Little Girl World and it's all pink **nurturance** in **diminuendo**: from the uncanny realism of baby-sized La Baby, down to Cherry Merry, Muffin, Tummy Luv, Li'l Softskin, the infestation of The Quints, Cutie Fruity Cupcakes; down, down to the sinister Tiny Teens, Toodles, Snookees, Baby Beans, and ending with the wee wee Kidgettes, perfumed **babicules**. All of this, I'm afraid, prepares girls all too well for the intentions of the Squirt Heads.

For an alternative to motherhood, 11 girls still get Barbie and the other high-maintenance Material **Churls** (available with Ferrari-Testarossa): single, age twenty-nine, on perpetual tiptoes to look over your head at a party for someone with more power.

I went looking for the small at Toys R 12 Us, for the miniature, the pocket-sized, for everything that has been taken from me by time, that big bully. I was looking for my tiny tin moose, too, lost somewhere between Atlanta and Miami, between age six and the **half-life** of tin, and time's nosedive into eternity. Irretrievably lost, as everything will be until dreamed again.

Elemental moose! I see you bursting 13 from the big red toy box of oblivion and raging in miniature up from the molten center of the earth, blasting out of that trap at the end of the world, flung into space in moose particles still pursued by the gray wolves of **form**, turning at last to face them in triumph, pawing suns, whole constellations hanging from your antlers like **huckleberries**, you bellowing your challenge to the **cosmos**. Well done, tiny tin moose! Oh, well done indeed!

—McMahon, Bucky. "Toys R Us" from *Night Diver* by Bucky McMahon.
Copyright © 2008. Reprinted by permission of Anhinga Press.

Choose the best meaning of each word in *italics*. Use context clues to make your choice.

Vocabulary in Context _____ **1.** "I like to think of the *gulf* between the real and its most pathetic imaging, and how the child's mind, surging with gigantic, oceanic forces, bridges that gulf in a bold leap worthy of a steeplechase." (paragraph 5)

a. swallowing
b. a wide distance
c. any body of water
d. scariness

Vocabulary in Context _____ **2.** "One aisle over in Little Girl World and it's all pink nurturance in diminuendo: from the uncanny realism of baby-sized La Baby, down to Cherry Merry, Muffin, Tummy Luv, Li'l Softskin, the *infestation* of The Quints, Cutie Fruity Cupcakes; down, down to the sinister Tiny Teens, Toodles, Snookees, Baby Beans, and ending with the wee wee Kidgettes, perfumed babicules." (paragraph 10)

a. troubling invasion by small things
b. to behave like an infant
c. to become a member of a group
d. to act like an insect or bug

Central Idea _____   **3.** Which of the following sentences best states the central idea of the passage?

a. "Love of the miniature, so natural to the child, nourishing our tender personal devotion to the huge, to the cosmic, the infinite that miniaturizes all of us—I went in quest to Toys R Us for the little, the littler, the littlest of all." (paragraph 3)
b. "Action figures, fist-sized, with posable limbs, have especially proliferated, and been given the power of speech—a risk, and a mistake." (paragraph 6)
c. "All of this, I'm afraid, prepares girls all too well for the intentions of the Squirt Heads." (paragraph 10)
d. "I was looking for my tiny tin moose, too, lost somewhere between Atlanta and Miami, between age six and the half-life of tin, and time's nosedive into eternity." (paragraph 12)

Central Idea _____   **4.** Which of the following sentences states the central idea of paragraphs 6–9?

a. "Take the warrior, too, the boys' tool and fool." (paragraph 6)
b. "Action figures, fist-sized, with posable limbs, have especially proliferated, and been given the power of speech—a risk, and a mistake." (paragraph 6)
c. "But what will become of the boys' art of battle blather ('I'm hit!') and sound effects, the long-practiced and finally perfected near-miss ricochet: 'Beeerunngh!'" (paragraph 7)
d. "The Dino Warriors have strapped what looks like a convenience store onto a brontosaurus, an inevitable wedding of prehistory and Pentagon spending." (paragraph 9)

Supporting _____   **5.** According to the author, which action battle figure toy name subconsciously appeals to the as-yet undeveloped male sexuality of boys?
Details

a. The Toxic Warriors   c. The Food Fighters
b. The Turtles, of course   d. The Squirt Heads

_____   **6.** According to the author, what social role do most girl toys prepare young
females for?
    a. dating   c. independence
    b. business careers   d. motherhood

_____   **7.** "Love of the miniature, so natural to the child, nourishing our tender
personal devotion to the huge, to the cosmic, the infinite that miniaturizes all of us—I went in quest to Toys R Us for the little, the littler,
the littlest of all." (paragraph 3)

The relationship of ideas **within** this sentence is
    a. time order.   c. description.
    b. cause and effect.   d. definition and example.

_____   **8.** "All of this, I'm afraid, prepares girls all too well for the intentions of the
Squirt Heads. For an alternative to motherhood, girls still get Barbie and
the other high-maintenance Material Churls (available with Ferrari-
Testarossa): single, age twenty-nine, on perpetual tiptoes to look over your
head at a party for someone with more power." (paragraphs 10 and 11)

The relationship of ideas **between** these sentences is
    a. cause and effect.   c. comparison and contrast.
    b. time order.   d. definition.

_____   **9.** The thought pattern of paragraph 4 is
    a. time order.   c. generalization and example.
    b. cause and effect.   d. comparison and contrast.

_____   **10.** The overall thought pattern of the passage is
    a. time order.   c. comparison and contrast.
    b. cause and effect.   d. generalization and example.

_____   **11.** "Action figures, fist-sized, with posable limbs, have especially proliferated, and been given the power of speech." (paragraph 6)

This sentence is a statement of
    a. fact.   c. fact and opinion.
    b. opinion.

_____   **12.** "Action figures, fist-sized, with posable limbs, have especially proliferated, and been given the power of speech—a risk, and a mistake."
(paragraph 6)

This sentence is a statement of
    a. fact.   c. fact and opinion.
    b. opinion.

Tone and Purpose _____ **13.** "For an alternative to motherhood, girls still get Barbie and the other high-maintenance Material Churls (available with Ferrari-Testarossa): single, age twenty-nine, on perpetual tiptoes to look over your head at a party for someone with more power." (paragraph 11)

The tone of this sentence is
a. objective.
b. sarcastic
c. scientific.
d. persuasive.

Tone and Purpose _____ **14.** The overall tone of the passage is
a. objective.
b. persuasive.
c. argumentative.
d. reflective.

Tone and Purpose _____ **15.** The overall purpose of the author is
a. to describe the toys at the store.
b. to entertain the reader with little-known facts.
c. to persuade the reader that toys are silly.
d. to help the reader see the meaning of playing.

Inferences _____ **16.** Based on the details in paragraphs 6, 7, and 8, we can infer that
a. boy toys help boys become more social and talkative.
b. boy toys sell best when they are modeled on celebrities.
c. boy toys appeal to male interests in war.
d. boy toys teach boys to show off to their friends.

Inferences _____ **17.** Based on the details in paragraphs 1 and 2, we can infer that
a. the author will find his toy moose at Toys R Us.
b. the author is too old to think about toys.
c. the boy's love for his toy is foolish.
d. playing with the toy moose encouraged the author to use his imagination.

Inferences _____ **18.** Based on the details in the passage, we can infer that the author's memories of his toy moose
a. encouraged him to admire the Space Shuttle program.
b. represent for him how the childish imagination can conquer time and space.
c. made him bored at Toys R Us when he didn't find his toy.
d. made him hopeful that gender differences are vanishing.

Argument _____ **19.** The following sentence from paragraph 9 contains a claim and a detail of support for that claim: "The Dino Warriors have strapped what looks like a convenience store onto a brontosaurus, an inevitable wedding of prehistory and Pentagon spending."

Which part of the sentence states the claim?
a. "The Dino Warriors have strapped what looks like a convenience store onto a brontosaurus"
b. "an inevitable wedding of prehistory and Pentagon spending"

Argument   _____   **20.** Paragraph 12 states a claim and supports for that claim. Which is the claim?
a. I went looking for the small at Toys R Us, for the miniature, the pocket-sized, for everything that has been taken from me by time, that big bully.
b. I was looking for my tiny tin moose, too, lost somewhere between Atlanta and Miami, between age six and the half-life of tin, and time's nosedive into eternity.
c. Irretrievably lost, as everything will be until dreamed again.

Outlining

Complete the following outline with information from the passage:

I. Introduction: The author introduces _____

_____

II. Thesis: _____

_____

    A. Toy horses

       1. Large real horses

       2. Pretend horses

       3. Small scale models of horses

       4. _____

    B. Boy action figures

    C. _____

III. Conclusion: The author states his love for his _____.

WHAT DO YOU THINK?

What do you remember and feel about your own childhood play? Did you have a favorite toy or possession? Or are you like many adults who outgrow their interest in children's toys, but still collect grownup toys to play with such as DVDs, video games, cars, bikes, or even clothes? Share with a reader a favorite toy you had as a child or a favorite possession you have now. Write about how that object reflects your interests, your personality, and the meaning that possession has for you.

EFFECTIVE READER SCORECARD

"Toys R Us"

Skill	Number Correct	Points	Total
Vocabulary			
Vocabulary in Context (2 items)	_____	× 4 =	_____
Comprehension			
Central Idea (2 items)	_____	× 4 =	_____
Supporting Details (2 items)	_____	× 4 =	_____
Transitions (2 items)	_____	× 4 =	_____
Thought Patterns (2 items)	_____	× 4 =	_____
Fact and Opinion (2 items)	_____	× 4 =	_____
Tone and Purpose (3 items)	_____	× 4 =	_____
Inferences (3 items)	_____	× 4 =	_____
Argument (2 items)	_____	× 4 =	_____
Outlining (5 items)	_____	× 4 =	_____
		Comprehension Score	_____

5 Curbing College Drinking Starts with a Change in Attitude

by Sara Fritz

College drinking is often seen as a harmless rite of passage into adulthood for American youth. Yet statistics reveal the seriousness of this behavior in the number of deaths, injuries, and assaults that occur each year in connection with college drinking. Sara Fritz, Washington Bureau Chief for the *St. Petersburg Times*, explores the problems of this long-standing dilemma and possible solutions for it.

Vocabulary Preview

trustee (paragraph 4): board member
intractable (paragraph 8): stubborn

1   Drinking by college students has long been seen as a relatively harmless rite of passage for young people. But we now have solid statistics that demonstrate the seriousness of the problem.

2   Each year, about 1,400 college students between ages 18 and 24 die of alcohol-related injuries, including auto accidents, alcohol poisoning and suicide. Another 500,000 sustain injuries under the influence of alcohol. More than 600,000 students are assaulted by a student who has been drinking, and about 70,000 of those are sexual assaults.

3   Of course, these statistics do not begin to portray the incredible loss that is felt on a campus or within families when young people with promising lives are killed while partying. These students are dying or killing themselves at the very moment when their lives are beginning to flourish. These are people who might otherwise find cures for disease, become our next political leaders or, at minimum, get married and raise children of their own.

4   As a college **trustee**, I have spent many long hours in discussions with students about this problem. Even though they frequently see fellow students being carried out of the dorm by paramedics after long bouts of excessive drinking, many of them still think the problem is being exaggerated.

5   "Our parents drank, did drugs and partied in college," they say, "so why are they trying to prevent us from doing the same thing?"

6   There are a couple of answers to this very good question. First, many of their parents have come to regret the excesses of their youth. Some have struggled with drug and

alcohol problems ever since. Second, because we now talk more openly about date rape and sexual assault, the real consequences of college drinking binges are better understood than they were two or three decades ago.

7   Nearly every college and university tries to do something to curb the problem, especially after a student dies. They appoint a counselor for students who get in trouble while abusing alcohol or they post signs or distribute brochures outlining the dangers of alcohol. Some campuses even establish chapters of Alcoholics Anonymous.

8   When these measures fail to curb reckless drinking, college administrators conclude it is an **insoluble** problem. "With each failed effort," says a new NIH report, "the image of college drinking as an **intractable** problem is reinforced, administrators are **demoralized**, and the likelihood that schools will devote resources to prevent programs decreases."

9   Now we have a group of social scientists who think their discipline can help solve the problem of college drinking. The group issued a report last week outlining a number of approaches that promise to change the drinking culture on college campuses.

10   What a concept! You'd think the nation's academics might have thought of

using the tools of their trade on a problem in their own back yard long before now.

11   "We need not accept high-risk drinking on our campuses as inevitable," says Mark Goldman, a researcher at the University of South Florida and co-chairman of the NIH task force working on this problem. "If colleges and communities work together, they can change these harmful drinking patterns."

12   The key to solving the problem, according to Goldman's task force, is to attack the problem from three different angles. The approach must try to change the entire student population, the environment in which they exist and the specific at-risk drinkers. This means there is probably no college or university in the country that is doing enough. Goldman and the task force deserve thanks for their work, even though their findings seem somewhat self-evident. But my guess is their report will be lost in the blizzard of paper that arrives on college campuses from the government.

13   Before any such program can succeed, students must be convinced that binge drinking is not normal behavior. Parents and college administrators have to be convinced that it is possible for them to influence students' behavior.

—Fritz, Sarah. "Curbing College Drinking Starts with a Change in Attitude" b Sarah Fritz, *St. Petersburg Times*, April 15, 2002.

Choose the best meaning of each word in *italics*. Use context clues to make your choice.

Vocabulary in Context _____ 1. "When these measures fail to curb reckless drinking, college administrators conclude it is an *insoluble* problem." (paragraph 8)
   a. college
   b. family
   c. impossible to solve
   d. easily solved

The best definition of **proactively** is

_____.

   a. after the fact
   b. in advance

▶ SADD works *proactively* to
stop college binge drinking.

Vocabulary
in Context   _____   **2.** " 'With each failed effort,' says a new NIH report, 'the image of college
drinking as an intractable problem is reinforced, administrators are
demoralized, and the likelihood that schools will devote resources to
prevent programs decreases.'" (paragraph 8)
   a. right   c. inspired
   b. uninvolved   d. discouraged

Central Idea   _____   **3.** Which sentence is the best statement of the implied central idea of the
and Main Idea   passage?
   a. Drinking by college students is a serious problem.
   b. A recent study suggests a program to address the serious and
       stubborn problems posed by college drinking.
   c. College drinking is an insoluble problem.
   d. Nearly every educational institution of higher learning is
       attempting to solve the problem of college drinking.

Central Idea   _____   **4.** Which sentence is the best statement of the main idea of
and Main Idea   paragraph 12?
   a. "The key to solving the problem, according to Goldman's task
       force, is to attack the problem from three different angles."
   b. "The approach must try to change the entire student population,
       the environment in which they exist and the specific at-risk
       drinkers."
   c. "This means there is probably no college or university in the
       country that is doing enough."
   d. "Goldman and the task force deserve thanks for their work,
       even though their findings seem somewhat self-evident."

Supporting Details _____ **5.** The estimated number of students between the ages of 18 and 24 who die each year due to alcohol-related injuries is
- a. 70,000.
- c. 500.
- b. 600,000.
- d. 1,400.

Supporting Details _____ **6.** The author, as a college trustee,
- a. participated in Goldman's NIH study about college drinking.
- b. drank, did drugs, and partied in college.
- c. spent many long hours in discussion with students about college drinking.
- d. feels that she is doing her part to solve the problem of college drinking.

Thought Patterns _____ **7.** The main thought pattern for the overall passage is
- a. comparing and contrasting drinking college students to non-drinking college students.
- b. discussing the causes of college drinking.
- c. listing and discussing the problems associated with college drinking and possible solutions.
- d. a narrative account of college drinking.

Thought Patterns _____ **8.** The thought pattern for paragraph 6 is
- a. comparison and contrast.
- c. time order.
- b. listing.

Transitions _____ **9.** "Each year, about 1,400 college students between ages 18 and 24 die of alcohol-related injuries, including auto accidents, alcohol poisoning and suicide. Another 500,000 sustain injuries under the influence of alcohol." (paragraph 2)

The relationship of ideas between these two sentences is
- a. addition.
- c. effect.
- b. contrast.

Transitions _____ **10.** "Before any such program can succeed, students must be convinced that binge drinking is not normal behavior." (paragraph 13)

The relationship of ideas within this sentence is
- a. time order.
- c. cause and effect.
- b. example.

Fact and Opinion _____ **11.** Overall, the ideas in this passage
- a. are based on research and statistics.
- b. are based on the personal experiences of the author.
- c. are based on a mix of statistics, research, and the personal experiences of the author.

Fact and
Opinion
_____ **12.** "These are people who might otherwise find cures for disease, become our next political leaders or, at minimum, get married and raise children of their own."

This sentence from paragraph 3 is a statement of
a. fact.   c. fact and opinion.
b. opinion.

Tone and
Purpose
_____ **13.** The overall tone of the passage is
a. pessimistic.   c. angry.
b. enthusiastic.   d. aloof.

Tone and
Purpose
_____ **14.** The tone of paragraph 10 is
a. admiring.   c. ungrateful.
b. sarcastic.   d. pleased.

Tone and
Purpose
_____ **15.** The tone of paragraph 13 is
a. forceful.   c. bitter.
b. unsure.   d. pleading.

Tone and
Purpose
_____ **16.** The author's main purpose in this article is
a. to persuade students, parents, and educators to change the culture that leads to college binge drinking.
b. to entertain readers with a personal reflection about a current issue.
c. to inform the readers about the serious problem of college binge drinking.

Inferences
_____ **17.** From paragraphs 5 and 6, we can conclude that
a. some students who drink in college think that their parents' objections to college drinking are hypocritical.
b. most parents don't mind if their college-aged students drink alcohol.
c. all parents "drank, did drugs and partied in college."
d. college students are spoiled and selfish.

Inferences
_____ **18.** From the details in paragraph 2, we can conclude that
a. college drinking is on the rise.
b. college drinking is an isolated problem.
c. over a million students suffer serious problems as a result of college drinking each year.
d. the problem of college drinking cannot be solved.

Inferences _____ **19.** The article implies that
   a. students are the only ones who can solve the problem of college drinking.
   b. solving the problem of college drinking will require the efforts of students, parents, and educators.
   c. the problem of college drinking cannot be solved.
   d. the problem of college drinking is exaggerated.

Argument _____ **20. Claim:** Parents should share with their children their hard-won wisdom about college drinking.

Which statement does not support this claim?
   a. Many parents have come to regret the excesses of their youth.
   b. The real consequences of college drinking binges are better understood now than they were two or three decades ago.
   c. No college or university in the country is doing enough to solve the problem of college binge drinking on their campuses.
   d. Students who are at risk will not listen to their parents about college binge drinking.

Outlining

Complete the following study outline with information from the passage.

   I. The problem is very serious.

   II. _____ a question.

   III. Colleges and universities respond to the problem.

   IV. Social scientists study the problem.

      A. _____

      B. Attack problem from three angles

         1. Change the _____

         2. _____

         3. _____

   V. Students, parents, and college administrators must change attitudes and work together to solve the problem.

WHAT DO YOU THINK?

Is binge drinking a problem at the college you attend? How does the college respond to student drinking? Does binge drinking occur in places not related to college? How should one respond to a person or group involved in binge drinking? Assume you are a member of your college's Student Government Association. The administration is developing a policy about binge drinking and substance abuse. You have been asked to participate as a student representative on a college-wide committee. Write a report for the committee about the status of substance abuse by the student population. Recommend a plan of action.

EFFECTIVE READER SCORECARD

"Curbing College Drinking Starts with a Change in Attitude"

Skill	Number Correct	Points		Total
Vocabulary				
Vocabulary in Context (2 items)	_____	× 4	=	_____
Comprehension				
Central Idea and Main Idea (2 items)	_____	× 4	=	_____
Supporting Details (2 items)	_____	× 4	=	_____
Thought Patterns (2 items)	_____	× 4	=	_____
Transitions (2 items)	_____	× 4	=	_____
Fact and Opinion (2 items)	_____	× 4	=	_____
Tone and Purpose (4 items)	_____	× 4	=	_____
Inferences (3 items)	_____	× 4	=	_____
Argument (1 item)	_____	× 4	=	_____
Outlining (5 items)	_____	× 4	=	_____
		Comprehension Score		_____

6

To the Power of a Persevering Teacher

D. J. Henry

> Low self-esteem, the struggle to fit in, turmoil at home, and poor academic performance are a few of the barriers to success the author had to face. The following essay gives tribute to two teachers who inspired, motivated, and taught her to believe in herself.

Vocabulary Preview

persevering (title): determined, tireless
transmuted (paragraph 1): changed
careened (paragraph 2): swayed, swerved
curriculum (paragraph 5): set of courses, program of study
cajoled (paragraph 6): coaxed, gently persuaded
soldering (paragraph 7): a process to join metals, uniting, melting together

1   I was such a Dork. No really, that was my nickname—gleefully given by a pack of peers who **transmuted** "Dorothy" to "Dork." Certainly understandable. Why, I wore glasses before I could walk. As an adolescent, I loomed tall above all. My hair took the shape of my mother's favorite style: the "pixie." Braces corralled my buckteeth, and due to an out-of-my-mind decision, a bold pair of glasses with glittery wingtips hid my eyes. Mostly quiet, yet if startled into laughter, I could be heard blocks away. No lie, what a Dork! Goofy and awkward and different.

2   My early academic career **careened** along a treacherous edge and inevitably involved a few learning wrecks. I shall never forget the elementary teacher who ripped up my spelling test in front of the whole class because she thought I had cheated to have improved so much. I shall never forget one teacher unceasingly mocking my **dialect** before the whole class: Once I dared to ask our location in the textbook with what I thought was a reasonable question: "Where are we at?" His response? "Where are we *at, Dor-ra-thee, where are we at* . . . I don't know where we are *at,* for I don't know where *at* is. Educated people do not end their sentences with a preposition!" No, I shall never forget the large, red letters of another teacher's note scrawled on one of my essays for all to see as the paper passed down the row to me, "This is unacceptable work!!!" Oh, how I feared I really was a Dork; everyone agreed! A poem best expresses such fears:

A View From Within

> Stupid me
> Full of stops, and nos, and don'ts and cant's
> Stalked by failure
> Running from rejection
> Tripping over needs
> Stubbing against most everything.
> Sometimes the striving goes hard:
> I hope against hope (maybe it's my
>   mama's hope)
> here today in your class
> beneath your scrutiny
> that the glint in your teacher eye
> comes from a good light,
> while that bear fierce fear breathes hot
>   down my neck
> and my brain freezes to stupor.
> I don't think my slowness to rise
> comes from any dullness in my head.
> After all, I can be sly survivor
> but then again stupid me
> got this far knowing nothing, so most
>   think.
> So, show me, I dare you, Go on!
> Show me
> My worth!

3   Though those moments remain most painful memories, caring teachers orchestrated my most profound experiences—two of those teachers deserve honor here. My twelfth grade English teacher, Mrs. Bauer, traveled with me during one of the most difficult journeys of my life. I have never since walked such a dark path: the year my father committed suicide and left himself for me to find. Much about that year is lost in a murky mist, but one of her assignments remains vibrant in memory.

4   Every day for six weeks we were to write in a personal journal. Never successful at such disciplined behaviors, I would start with good intentions, then falter into **inertia**, ultimately producing nothing. However, that journal I completed, perhaps out of the deep need to vent or to connect with myself, the events, another human, the reader. Though long lost, my journal, surely recorded a deeply painful personal confession—some might say an inappropriate self-disclosure. However, Mrs. Baur's note, "God bless, you!" gave me a satisfying sense of affirmation. Her dignified, heart-felt response roused up hope. Emily Dickinson wrote:

> Hope is the thing with feathers
> That perches in the soul,
> And sings the tune without the words,
> And never stops at all.

5   The great Greek dramatist Aeschylus said, "The meaning I picked, the one that changed my life: Overcome fear, behold wonder." Often, we students struggle to find wonder in two places: the **curriculum** and the self. A dedicated teacher can guide us into the wonder of knowing. Joseph Campbell said, "The job of an educator is to teach students to see the vitality in themselves." A beloved college teacher did just that for me. In truth, he was an answer to my mother's prayers.

6   Dr. Charles R. Hannum and I began our time at Judson College, Marion, Alabama, the same year: he as sole professor in the brand new theatre department, I as his student. He taught the 30-plus assortment of freshman through senior

girls how to design and build sets, plan and hang lighting, set up and work sound systems, and perform classics such as Moliere, Shakespeare, and Tennessee Williams. He kept us working late yet expected us to not only show up for 8 o'clock classes but also to do well. Still undisciplined and disconnected and reeling from trauma, I often skipped classes, never read textbooks until the night before exams, and often turned in works of first drafts hastily done last minute. He tried everything to make me mend my ways. He **cajoled**, threatened, reasoned with me, and gambled on me. He taught me to orally interpret the great classics. This ancient tradition of oral literacy through story telling lit my path to literacy. Hannum knew this and took every opportunity to spotlight my strengths. His program gave me a place to thrive.

7   I think I taught him patience. For instance, one day he directed me to drill a hole in a broomstick for the witch in *Hansel and Gretel*. Well, I had never, ever worked with tools, and really, I was too embarrassed and afraid to ask him for help, so after he left the room, I grabbed a tool that I thought would do and set about drilling the hole. After a few minutes, he returned and asked me, "Just what the heck are you doing with that **soldering** iron?" I was such a Dork!

8   Carl Jung once stated, "One looks back with appreciation to the brilliant teachers, but with gratitude to those who touched our human feelings. The cur-

riculum is so much necessary raw material, but warmth is the vital element for the growing plant and for the soul of the child."

Hannum, A God-gifted Teacher

I have always known
You—a Gift
From God no less,
Because always
In the first and from all our moments
That flow between us
Electric shock around, arching above
    and beyond
You make me know
You see something in me
Some value worth
The work to express itself,
And your sight
Gave me eyes
And now a voice
Urges on a body of work.
I have always known
You—Your great gift,
And only yesterday I prayed,
God give me a poem, a poem I could
    give to you.
Then hope fluttered within and softly
    breathed—
"You are my poem to him"

9   Oh how I still reap benefits from all he taught us. Oh, how I thank God for this man, and for all the caring, persevering teachers who strive by our sides to open our eyes. Oh, how I endeavor to be such a teacher for my own students.

Choose the best meaning of each word in *italics*. Use context clues to make your choice.

Vocabulary in Context _____

1. "I shall never forget one teacher unceasingly mocking my *dialect* before the whole class: " (paragraph 2)
   a. question
   b. intellect
   c. behavior
   d. speech pattern

Vocabulary in Context _____

2. "Never successful at such disciplined behaviors, I would start with good intentions, then falter into *inertia*, ultimately producing nothing." (paragraph 4)
   a. inaction
   b. difficulty
   c. activity
   d. unrest

Central Idea _____

3. Which sentence best states the author's central idea?
   a. "I was such a Dork." (paragraph 1)
   b. "My early academic career careened along a treacherous edge and inevitably involved a few learning wrecks." (paragraph 2)
   c. "Though those moments remain most painful memories, caring teachers orchestrated my most profound experiences—two of those teachers deserve honor here." (paragraph 3)
   d. "Oh, how I endeavor to be such a teacher for my own students." (paragraph 9)

Main Idea _____

4. Which of the following sentences states the main idea of paragraph 2?
   a. "My early academic career careened along a treacherous edge and inevitably involved a few learning wrecks."
   b. "I shall never forget the elementary teacher who ripped up my spelling test in front of the whole class because she thought I had cheated to have improved so much."
   c. "I shall never forget one teacher unceasingly mocking my dialect before the whole class."
   d. "No, I shall never forget the large, red letters of another teacher's note scrawled on one of my essays for all to see as the paper passed down the row to me."

Main Idea _____

5. Which of the following sentences states the main idea of paragraph 6?
   a. "Dr. Charles R. Hannum and I began our time at Judson College, Marion, Alabama, the same year: he as sole professor of the brand new theatre department, I as his student."
   b. "This ancient tradition of oral literacy through story telling lit my path to literacy."

   c. "Hannum knew this and took every opportunity to spotlight my strengths."

   d. "His program gave me a place to thrive."

Supporting Details _____ **6.** According to the passage, the author's father
   a. supported the family.   c. committed suicide.
   b. committed criminal acts.   d. deserted the family.

Transitions _____ **7.** "Every day for six weeks, we were to write in a personal journal." (paragraph 4)

The primary relationship of ideas **within** this sentence is
   a. time order.   c. space order.
   b. cause and effect.   d. generalization and example.

Transitions _____ **8.** "Though long lost, my journal, surely, recorded a deeply painful personal confession—some might say an inappropriate self-disclosure. However, Mrs. Baur's note, "God bless, you!" gave me a satisfying sense of affirmation." (paragraph 4)

The primary relationship of ideas **within** this sentence is
   a. cause and effect.   c. contrast.
   b. time order.   d. generalization and example.

Transitions _____ **9.** "I think I taught him patience. For instance, one day he directed me to drill a hole in a broomstick for the witch in _Hansel and Gretel_." (paragraph 7)

The relationship of ideas **between** these sentences is
   a. cause and effect.   c. comparison and contrast.
   b. time order.   d. generalization and example.

Thought Patterns _____ **10.** The main thought pattern used in paragraph 1 is
   a. space order.   c. definition and example.
   b. cause and effect.   d. comparison and contrast.

Thought Patterns _____ **11.** The overall thought pattern of passage is
   a. time order.   c. comparison and contrast.
   b. cause and effect.   d. definition and example.

Fact and Opinion _____ **12.** "I was such a Dork." (paragraph 1)

This sentence is a statement of
   a. fact.   c. fact and opinion.
   b. opinion.

Fact and Opinion _____ **13.** "My twelfth grade English teacher, Mrs. Bauer traveled with me during one the most difficult journeys of my life" (paragraph 3)

This sentence is a statement of
a. fact.   c. fact and opinion.
b. opinion.

Fact and Opinion _____ **14.** "Dr. Charles R. Hannum and I began our time at Judson College, Marion, Alabama, the same year: he as sole professor of the brand new theatre department, I as his student." (paragraph 6)
a. fact.   c. fact and opinion.
b. opinion.

Tone and Purpose _____ **15.** "The overall tone of paragraph 1 is
a. objective.   c. boastful.
b. self-critical.   d. cruel.

Tone and Purpose _____ **16.** The main tone of the entire passage is
a. unbiased.   c. argumentative.
b. bitter.   d. inspiring.

Tone and Purpose _____ **17.** The overall purpose of the author is
a. to entertain the reader with a personal story from her past.
b. to inform the reader about the powerful impact caring teachers had on her life.
c. to persuade the reader to honor teachers.

Inferences _____ **18.** Based on the details in paragraph 2, we can infer that
a. the author has forgiven the teachers who embarrassed her.
b. the teachers embarrassed her as a way to help her learn.
c. the teachers who embarrassed her damaged her self-esteem.
d. the author didn't want to learn.

Argument _____ **19.** Read the following claim. Then identify the detail that does not support the claim.

Claim: "The job of an educator is to teach students to see the vitality in themselves.'" (paragraph 4)
a. "I shall never forget one teacher unceasingly mocking my dialect before the whole class." (paragraph 2)
b. "However, Mrs. Bauer's note 'God bless, you!' gave me a satisfying sense of affirmation." (paragraph 4)

c. "Hannum knew this and took every opportunity to spotlight my strengths." (paragraph 6)

d. "His program gave me a place to thrive." (paragraph 6)

Argument _____ **20.** Which logical fallacy is used in the following sentence?

"No really, that was my nickname—gleefully given by a pack of peers who transmuted my name from 'Dorothy' to 'Dork.'" (paragraph 1)

a. either-or   c. false comparison

b. personal attack   d. false cause

Outlining

Complete the following outline with information from the passage.

To the Power of a Persevering Teacher

   I. I was such a _____

  II. _____

 III. Poem: "A View from Within"

 IV. Mrs. Bauer and the _____

  V. Literary references

    A. Poem by _____

    B. Quote of Greek dramatist Aeschylus

    C. Quote of Joseph Campbell

 VI. _____

VII. Quote of Carl Jung

VIII. Poem: "Hannum, a God-gifted Teacher"

WHAT DO YOU THINK?

Have you ever had a teacher who impacted your education? Have you ever had to overcome personal difficulties in order to achieve success? Write an essay that analyzes your academic experience. In your essay, describe your past experiences with teachers. They may be good, bad, or both. Explain why these relationships stand out, or how they affected you. Then identify some of your own behaviors that help or hinder your education. Explain why these behaviors are beneficial or harmful to your success.

EFFECTIVE READER SCORECARD

"To the Power of a Persevering Teacher"

Skill	Number Correct	Points		Total
Vocabulary				
Vocabulary in Context (2 items)	_____	× 4	=	_____
Comprehension				
Central/Main Idea (3 items)	_____	× 4	=	_____
Supporting Details (1 item)	_____	× 4	=	_____
Transitions (3 items)	_____	× 4	=	_____
Thought Patterns (2 items)	_____	× 4	=	_____
Fact and Opinion (3 items)	_____	× 4	=	_____
Tone and Purpose (3 items)	_____	× 4	=	_____
Inferences (1 item)	_____	× 4	=	_____
Argument (2 items)	_____	× 4	=	_____
Outlining (5 items)	_____	× 4	=	_____
		Comprehension Score		_____

7 The Quest for Peace and Justice
Nobel Lecture, December 11, 1964
Dr. Martin Luther King, Jr.

Dr. Martin Luther King, Jr. was awarded the Nobel Prize for Peace in 1964. At age 35, Dr. King was the youngest person to have received the Nobel Peace Prize. In the presentation of the award, Gunnar Jahn, Chairman of the Nobel Committee, offered the following praise of Dr. King. "Today we pay tribute to Martin Luther King, the man who has never abandoned his faith in the unarmed struggle he is waging, who has suffered for his faith, who has been imprisoned on many occasions, whose home has been subject to bomb attacks, whose life and the lives of his family have been threatened, and who nevertheless has never faltered." The following passage presents the introduction and the third major point of King's Nobel Lecture. To read his entire speech go to Nobelprize.org.

Vocabulary Preview

unfathomable (paragraph 1): impossible to measure, profound, unknowable
subjugates (paragraph 3): overpowers, overcomes, subdues
constitutes (paragraph 4): makes up, forms, composes
infantilism (paragraph 4): childishness, immaturity
inextricably (paragraph 4): inseparably, totally
annihilation (paragraph 5): total destruction, extinction
proneness (paragraph 6): tendency to do or be affected by something
inexorably (paragraph 6): unstoppable, unavoidably
inferno (paragraph 6): blaze, fire, hellhole
Dante (paragraph 6): a noted Italian poet of the Middle Ages
genocidal (paragraph 7): murderous
impotence (paragraph 8): powerlessness, inability, weakness
expulsion (paragraph 10): dismissed from a place of membership
cosmic (paragraph 11): vast, global, heavenly
elegy (paragraph 11): funeral song, mournful poem
ecumenical (paragraph 13): universal

Nietzsches (paragraph 14): followers of Fredrick Nietzsche, a German philosopher, poet, and critic, noted for his concept of the superman and his rejection of traditional Christian values

1   This evening I would like to use this lofty and historic platform to discuss what appears to me to be the most pressing problem confronting mankind today. Modern man has brought this whole world to an awe-inspiring threshold of the future. He has reached new and astonishing peaks of scientific success. He has produced machines that think and instruments that peer into the **unfathomable** ranges of interstellar space. He has built gigantic bridges to span the seas and **gargantuan** buildings to kiss the skies. His airplanes and spaceships have dwarfed distance, placed time in chains, and carved highways through the stratosphere. This is a dazzling picture of modern man's scientific and technological progress.

2   Yet, in spite of these spectacular strides in science and technology, and still unlimited ones to come, something basic is missing. There is a sort of poverty of the spirit which stands in glaring contrast to our scientific and technological abundance. The richer we have become materially, the poorer we have become morally and spiritually. We have learned to fly the air like birds and swim the sea like fish, but we have not learned the simple art of living together as brothers.

3   Every man lives in two realms, the internal and the external. The internal is that realm of spiritual ends expressed in art, literature, morals, and religion. The external is that complex of devices, techniques, mechanisms, and instrumentalities by means of which we live. Our problem today is that we have allowed the internal to become lost in the external. We have allowed the means by which we live to outdistance the ends for which we live. So much of modern life can be summarized in that arresting **dictum** of the poet Thoreau: "Improved means to an unimproved end." This is the serious **predicament**, the deep and haunting problem confronting modern man. If we are to survive today, our moral and spiritual "lag" must be eliminated. Enlarged material powers spell enlarged peril if there is not proportionate growth of the soul. When the "without" of man's nature **subjugates** the "within," dark storm clouds begin to form in the world.

4   This problem of spiritual and moral lag, which **constitutes** modern man's chief dilemma, expresses itself in three larger problems which grow out of man's ethical **infantilism**. Each of these problems, while appearing to be separate and isolated, is **inextricably** bound to the other. I refer to racial injustice, poverty, and war.

***

5   A third great evil confronting our world is that of war. Recent events have vividly reminded us that nations are not reducing but rather increasing their arsenals of weapons of mass destruction. The best brains in the highly developed nations of the world are devoted to military technology. The proliferation of nuclear weapons has not been halted, in spite of the Limited Test Ban Treaty. On the contrary, the detonation

of an atomic device by the first nonwhite, non-Western, and so-called underdeveloped power, namely the Chinese People's Republic, opens new vistas of exposure of vast multitudes, the whole of humanity, to **insidious** terrorization by the ever-present threat of **annihilation**. The fact that most of the time human beings put the truth about the nature and risks of the nuclear war out of their minds because it is too painful and therefore not "acceptable," does not alter the nature and risks of such war. The device of "rejection" may temporarily cover up anxiety, but it does not bestow peace of mind and emotional security.

6 So man's **proneness** to engage in war is still a fact. But wisdom born of experience should tell us that war is obsolete. There may have been a time when war served as a negative good by preventing the spread and growth of an evil force, but the destructive power of modern weapons eliminated even the possibility that war may serve as a negative good. If we assume that life is worth living and that man has a right to survive, then we must find an alternative to war. In a day when vehicles hurtle through outer space and guided ballistic missiles carve highways of death through the stratosphere, no nation can claim victory in war. A so-called limited war will leave little more than a calamitous legacy of human suffering, political turmoil, and spiritual disillusionment. A world war—God forbid!—will leave only smoldering ashes as a mute testimony of a human race whose folly led **inexorably** to ultimate death. So if modern man continues to flirt unhesitatingly with war, he will transform his earthly habitat into an **inferno** such as even the mind of **Dante** could not imagine.

7 Therefore, I venture to suggest to all of you and all who hear and may eventually read these words, that the philosophy and strategy of nonviolence become immediately a subject for study and for serious experimentation in every field of human conflict, by no means excluding the relations between nations. It is, after all, nation-states which make war, which have produced the weapons which threaten the survival of mankind, and which are both **genocidal** and suicidal in character.

8 Here also we have ancient habits to deal with, vast structures of power, indescribably complicated problems to solve. But unless we **abdicate** our humanity altogether and succumb to fear and **impotence** in the presence of the weapons we have ourselves created, it is as imperative and urgent to put an end to war and violence between nations as it is to put an end to racial injustice. Equality with whites will hardly solve the problems of either whites or Negroes if it means equality in a society under the spell of terror and a world doomed to extinction.

9 I do not wish to minimize the complexity of the problems that need to be faced in achieving disarmament and peace. But I think it is a fact that we shall not have the will, the courage, and the insight to deal with such matters unless in this field we are prepared to undergo a mental and spiritual reevaluation—a change of focus which will enable us to see that the things which seem most real and powerful are indeed now unreal and have come under the sentence of death. We need to make a supreme effort to generate the readiness, indeed the eagerness, to enter into the

new world which is now possible, "the city which hath foundations, whose builder and maker is God."

10   We will not build a peaceful world by following a negative path. It is not enough to say "We must not wage war." It is necessary to love peace and sacrifice for it. We must concentrate not merely on the negative **expulsion** of war, but on the positive affirmation of peace. There is a fascinating little story that is preserved for us in Greek literature about Ulysses and the Sirens. The Sirens had the ability to sing so sweetly that sailors could not resist steering toward their island. Many ships were lured upon the rocks, and men forgot home, duty, and honor as they flung themselves into the sea to be embraced by arms that drew them down to death. Ulysses, determined not to be lured by the Sirens, first decided to tie himself tightly to the mast of his boat, and his crew stuffed their ears with wax. But finally he and his crew learned a better way to save themselves: they took on board the beautiful singer Orpheus whose melodies were sweeter than the music of the Sirens. When Orpheus sang, who bothered to listen to the Sirens?

11   So we must fix our vision not merely on the negative expulsion of war, but upon the positive affirmation of peace. We must see that peace represents a sweeter music, a **cosmic** melody that is far superior to the discords of war. Somehow we must transform the dynamics of the world power struggle from the negative nuclear arms race which no one can win to a positive contest to harness man's creative genius for the purpose of making peace and prosperity a reality for all of the nations of the world. In short, we must shift the arms race into a "peace race." If we have the will and determination to mount such a peace offensive, we will unlock hitherto tightly sealed doors of hope and transform our imminent cosmic **elegy** into a psalm of creative fulfillment.

12   All that I have said boils down to the point of affirming that mankind's survival is dependent upon man's ability to solve the problems of racial injustice, poverty, and war; the solution of these problems is in turn dependent upon man squaring his moral progress with his scientific progress, and learning the practical art of living in harmony. Some years ago a famous novelist died. Among his papers was found a list of suggested story plots for future stories, the most prominently underscored being this one: "A widely separated family inherits a house in which they have to live together." This is the great new problem of mankind. We have inherited a big house, a great "world house" in which we have to live together— black and white, Easterners and Westerners, Gentiles and Jews, Catholics and Protestants, Moslem and Hindu, a family unduly separated in ideas, culture, and interests who, because we can never again live without each other, must learn, somehow, in this one big world, to live with each other.

13   This means that more and more our loyalties must become **ecumenical** rather than sectional. We must now give an overriding loyalty to mankind as a whole in order to preserve the best in our individual societies.

14   This call for a worldwide fellowship that lifts neighborly concern beyond one's tribe, race, class, and nation is in reality a call for an all-embracing and unconditional love for all men. This oft misunderstood and misinterpreted concept so readily dismissed

by the **Nietzsches** of the world as a weak and cowardly force has now become an absolute necessity for the survival of man. When I speak of love I am not speaking of some sentimental and weak response which is little more than emotional bosh. I am speaking of that force which all of the great religions have seen as the supreme unifying principle of life. Love is somehow the key that unlocks the door which leads to ultimate reality. This Hindu-Moslem-Christian-Jewish-Buddhist belief about ultimate reality is beautifully summed up in the First Epistle of Saint John:

15
> Let us love one another: for love is of God; and everyone
> that loveth is born of God, and knoweth God.
> He that loveth not knoweth not God; for God is love.
> If we love one another, God dwelleth in us, and His
> love is perfected in us.

16   Let us hope that this spirit will become the order of the day. As Arnold Toynbee says: "Love is the ultimate force that makes for the saving choice of life and good against the damning choice of death and evil. Therefore the first hope in our inventory must be the hope that love is going to have the last word." We can no longer afford to worship the God of hate or bow before the altar of retaliation. The oceans of history are made turbulent by the ever-rising tides of hate. History is cluttered with the wreckage of nations and individuals that pursued this self-defeating path of hate. Love is the key to the solution of the problems of the world.

Let me close by saying that I have the   17 personal faith that mankind will somehow rise up to the occasion and give new directions to an age drifting rapidly to its doom. In spite of the tensions and uncertainties of this period something profoundly meaningful is taking place. Old systems of exploitation and oppression are passing away, and out of the womb of a frail world new systems of justice and equality are being born. Doors of opportunity are gradually being opened to those at the bottom of society. The shirtless and barefoot people of the land are developing a new sense of "some-bodiness" and carving a tunnel of hope through the dark mountain of despair. "The people who sat in darkness have seen a great light." Here and there an individual or group dares to love, and rises to the majestic heights of moral maturity. So in a real sense this is a great time to be alive. Therefore, I am not yet discouraged about the future. Granted that the easygoing optimism of yesterday is impossible. Granted that those who pioneer in the struggle for peace and freedom will still face uncomfortable jail terms, painful threats of death; they will still be battered by the storms of persecution, leading them to the nagging feeling that they can no longer bear such a heavy burden, and the temptation of wanting to retreat to a more quiet and serene life. Granted that we face a world crisis which leaves us standing so often amid the surging murmur of life's restless sea. But every crisis has both its dangers and its opportunities. It can spell either salvation or doom. In a dark confused world the kingdom of God may yet reign in the hearts of men.

—King, Jr., Martin Luther. " The Quest for Peace and Justice", Nobel Lecture, December 11, 1964. © The Nobel Foundation 1964. Reprinted by permission of Nobel Media AB.

Fill in the blank in each sentence with a word from the Vocabulary Preview.

Vocabulary
Preview

1. Henry David Thoreau, Mahatma Gandhi, and Dr. Martin Luther King, Jr. believed in the _____ power of nonviolent resistance to oppression.

Vocabulary
Preview

2. A tyrant _____ the values, way of life, and beliefs of the powerless.

Vocabulary
Preview

3. Nonviolent resistance leads to the _____ of tyranny.

Vocabulary
Preview

4. Non-cooperation, such as refusal to pay taxes, _____ one part of nonviolent resistance.

Vocabulary
Preview

5. Gandhi also fought for the equality of women, an end to poverty, and the _____ of India's unfair social order based on classes or the caste system.

For items 6 through 10, choose the best meaning of each word in *italics*. Use context clues to make your choice.

Vocabulary
in Context

6. _____ "He has built gigantic bridges to span the seas and *gargantuan* buildings to kiss the sky." (paragraph 1)
   a. huge
   b. gorgeous
   c. ugly
   d. many

Vocabulary
in Context

7. _____ "So much of modern life can be summarized in that arresting *dictum* of the poet Thoreau: 'Improved means to an unimproved end.'" (paragraph 3)
   a. fact
   b. saying
   c. plan
   d. formula

Vocabulary
in Context

8. _____ "This is the serious *predicament*, the deep and haunting problem confronting modern man." (paragraph 3)
   a. event
   b. part
   c. dilemma
   d. solution

Vocabulary
in Context

9. _____ "On the contrary, the detonation of an atomic device by the first non-white, non-Western, and so-called underdeveloped power, namely the Chinese People's Republic, opens new vistas of exposure of vast multitudes, the whole of humanity, to *insidious* terrorization by the ever-present threat of annihilation." (paragraph 5)
   a. sinister
   b. obvious
   c. sincere
   d. harmless

Vocabulary
in Context   _____   **10.** "But unless we *abdicate* our humanity altogether and succumb to fear and impotence in the presence of the weapons we have ourselves created, it is as imperative and urgent to put an end to war…" (paragraph 8)
a. accept   c. secure
b. understand   d. abandon

Main Idea   _____   **11.** Which of the following sentences states the central idea of paragraphs 1 through 4?
a. "This evening I would like to use this lofty and historic platform to discuss what appears to me to be the most pressing problem confronting mankind today." (paragraph 1)
b. "Every man lives in two realms, the internal and the external." (paragraph 3)
c. "If we are to survive today, our moral and spiritual 'lag' must be eliminated." (paragraph 3)
d. "This problem of spiritual and moral lag, which constitutes modern man's chief dilemma, expresses itself in three larger problems which grow out of man's ethical infantilism." (paragraph 4)

Supporting
Details   _____   **12.** According to Dr. King, what is the third great evil confronting our world?
a. racial injustice   c. spiritual and moral lag
b. war   d. poverty

Supporting
Details   _____   **13.** According to Dr. King, man's internal realm includes
a. morals.   c. devices.
b. poverty.   d. progress.

Transitions   _____   **14.** "We must concentrate not merely on the negative expulsion of war, but on the positive affirmation of peace." (paragraph 10)

The relationship of ideas **within** this sentence is
a. cause and effect.   c. comparison and contrast.
b. time order.   d. generalization and example.

Transitions   _____   **15.** "This is a dazzling picture of modern man's scientific and technological progress. Yet, in spite of these spectacular strides in science and technology, and still unlimited ones yet to come, something basic is missing." (paragraphs 1 and 2)

The relationship of ideas **between** these sentences is
a. cause and effect.   c. comparison and contrast.
b. time order.   d. generalization and example.

Thought Patterns   _____ 16. The main thought pattern of paragraph 10 is
  a. time order.
  c. comparison and contrast.
  b. classification.
  d. definition and example.

Fact and Opinion   _____ 17. "If we assume that life is worth living and that man has a right to survive, then we must find an alternative to war." (paragraph 6)

This sentence is a statement of
  a. fact.
  c. fact and opinion.
  b. opinion.

Tone and Purpose   _____ 18. The overall tone and purpose of the author based on this passage is
  a. to inform the world community about the evils of war.
  b. to entertain the world community with lofty thoughts about war and peace.
  c. to persuade the world community to study and apply the strategies of nonviolence.

Inferences   _____ 19. Based on the passage, we can infer that Dr. King
  a. accepts war as a means to ensure peace.
  b. opposes war as an option under any circumstance.
  c. holds little hope for the future of mankind.
  d. has great faith in the science and technology progress of mankind.

Argument   _____ 20. The persuasive technique used in paragraph 1 is
  a. glittering generalities.
  c. a testimonial
  b. transfer.
  d. false cause.

Summary

Complete the following summary of the excerpts from the 1964 Nobel Lecture of Dr. Martin Luther King, Jr.

In his 1964 Nobel Lecture "The Quest for Peace and Justice," Dr. Martin Luther King, Jr. asserts that mankind's chief moral dilemma is the _____

_____ that leads to racial injustice, poverty, and war. Dr. King further asserts that mankind's survival is dependent upon its ability to solve these problems.

Dr. King believes that man must align his _____ progress with his

_____ progress and learn to live in harmony. To avoid the annihilation made possible by nuclear arms, Dr. King suggests the study and application of _____ in conflicts between peoples and nations. Finally, Dr. King calls for a worldwide fellowship based on the unifying principle of life: _____.

WHAT DO YOU THINK?

In the introduction of his speech, Dr. King states, "The richer we have become materially, the poorer we have become morally and spiritually." Do you agree with this statement? Why or why not? Assume you are interested in public service, and you have decided to support a cause that will improve life in your local community. You also want to inspire others to join the cause as well. Identify a local cause such as homelessness, pollution, recycling, drug abuse, or graffiti removal. To gain public support for your cause, write an entry for the community blog sponsored by your local newspaper. In your posting, define the cause and call for specific action from your readers.

EFFECTIVE READER SCORECARD

"The Quest for Peace and Justice"

Skill	Number Correct		Points		Total
Vocabulary					
Vocabulary Preview (5 items)	_____	×	10	=	_____
Vocabulary in Context (5 items)	_____	×	10	=	_____
			Vocabulary Score		_____
Comprehension					
Main Idea (1 item)	_____	×	8	=	_____
Supporting Details (2 items)	_____	×	8	=	_____
Transitions (2 items)	_____	×	8	=	_____
Thought Patterns (1 item)	_____	×	8	=	_____
Fact and Opinion (1 item)	_____	×	8	=	_____
Tone and Purpose (1 item)	_____	×	8	=	_____
Inferences (1 item)	_____	×	8	=	_____
Argument (1 item)	_____	×	8	=	_____
Summary (5 items)	_____	×	4	=	_____
			Comprehension Score		_____

I am Adam Lanza's Mother

Liza Long

On December 14, 2012, twenty-year-old Adam Lanza fatally shot twenty children and six adults and wounded two at Sandy Hook Elementary School in Newtown, Connecticut. Before driving to the school, Lanza had killed his mother Nancy at their home. As first responders arrived at the school, Lanza committed suicide. The tragedy ignited a national discussion on violence and gun control in America. Liza Long, a writer based in Boise and single mother of four, one of whom is a special needs child, posted the following article in her blog *The Anarchist Soccer Mom*. The article was also published at *The Blue Review*, a web-based journal from the Boise State University College of Social Sciences and Public Affairs. Immediately, Long's article, with its focus on mental illness, went viral on the web and received over one million Facebook likes.

Vocabulary Preview

Zyprexa (paragraph 8): an antipsychotic drug used to treat certain severe mental illnesses

autism (paragraph 9): a mental condition that impairs social relationships and communication

antipsychotic (paragraph 9): refers to a type of medication used to treat severe mental illness

pharmaceuticals (paragraph 9): drugs, medicines

mythology (paragraph 10): folklore, ancient story, legend

Einsteinian (paragraph 10): refers to the work of scientist Albert Einstein

Newtonian (paragraph 10): refers to the work of scientist Isaac Newton

chaotic (paragraph 29): disordered, confused

pathology (paragraph 29): disease, condition that is not normal

incarcerated (paragraph 29): in prison

stigma (paragraph 31): shame, humiliation

1   Three days before 20 year-old Adam Lanza killed his mother, then opened fire on a classroom full of Connecticut kindergartners, my 13-year old son Michael (name changed) missed his bus because he was wearing the wrong color pants.

2   "I can wear these pants," he said, his tone increasingly **belligerent**, the black-hole pupils of his eyes swallowing the blue irises.

3   "They are navy blue," I told him. "Your school's dress code says black or khaki pants only."

4   "They told me I could wear these," he insisted. "You're a stupid bitch. I can wear whatever pants I want to. This is America. I have rights!"

5   "You can't wear whatever pants you want to," I said, my tone **affable**, reasonable. "And you definitely cannot call me a stupid bitch. You're grounded from electronics for the rest of the day. Now get in the car, and I will take you to school."

6   I live with a son who is mentally ill. I love my son. But he terrifies me.

7   A few weeks ago, Michael pulled a knife and threatened to kill me and then himself after I asked him to return his overdue library books. His 7 and 9 year old siblings knew the safety plan—they ran to the car and locked the doors before I even asked them to. I managed to get the knife from Michael, then **methodically** collected all the sharp objects in the house into a single Tupperware container that now travels with me. Through it all, he continued to scream insults at me and threaten to kill or hurt me.

8   That conflict ended with three burly police officers and a paramedic wrestling my son onto a gurney for an expensive ambulance ride to the local emergency room. The mental hospital didn't have any beds that day, and Michael calmed down nicely in the ER, so they sent us home with a prescription for **Zyprexa** and a follow-up visit with a local pediatric psychiatrist.

9   We still don't know what's wrong with Michael. **Autism** spectrum, ADHD, Oppositional Defiant or Intermittent Explosive Disorder have all been tossed around at various meetings with probation officers and social workers and counselors and teachers and school administrators. He's been on a slew of **antipsychotic** and mood altering **pharmaceuticals**, a Russian novel of behavioral plans. Nothing seems to work.

10   At the start of seventh grade, Michael was accepted to an accelerated program for highly gifted math and science students. His IQ is off the charts. When he's in a good mood, he will gladly bend your ear on subjects ranging from Greek **mythology** to the differences between **Einsteinian** and **Newtonian** physics to *Doctor Who*. He's in a good mood most of the time. But when he's not, watch out. And it's impossible to predict what will set him off.

11   Several weeks into his new junior high school, Michael began exhibiting increasingly odd and threatening behaviors at school. We decided to transfer him to the district's most restrictive behavioral program, a contained school environment where children who can't function in normal classrooms can access their right to free public babysitting from 7:30–1:50 Monday through Friday until they turn 18.

12   The morning of the pants incident, Michael continued to argue with me on the drive. He would occasionally apologize and seem remorseful. Right before we turned into his school parking lot, he said, "Look, Mom, I'm really sorry. Can I have video games back today?"

13   "No way," I told him. "You cannot act the way you acted this morning and think you can get your electronic privileges back that quickly."

14   His face turned cold, and his eyes were full of **calculated** rage. "Then I'm going to kill myself," he said. "I'm going to jump out of this car right now and kill myself."

15   That was it. After the knife incident, I told him that if he ever said those words again, I would take him straight to the mental hospital, no ifs, ands, or buts. I did not respond, except to pull the car into the opposite lane, turning left instead of right.

16   "Where are you taking me?" he said, suddenly worried. "Where are we going?"

17   "You know where we are going," I replied.

18   "No! You can't do that to me! You're sending me to hell! You're sending me straight to hell!"

19   I pulled up in front of the hospital, frantically waiving for one of the clinicians who happened to be standing outside. "Call the police," I said. "Hurry."

20   Michael was in a full-blown fit by then, screaming and hitting. I hugged him close so he couldn't escape from the car. He bit me several times and repeatedly jabbed his elbows into my rib cage. I'm still stronger than he is, but I won't be for much longer.

21   The police came quickly and carried my son screaming and kicking into the bowels of the hospital. I started to shake, and tears filled my eyes as I filled out the paperwork—"Were there any difficulties with . . . at what age did your child . . . were there any problems with . . . has your child ever experienced . . . does your child have . . ."

22   At least we have health insurance now. I recently accepted a position with a local college, giving up my freelance career because when you have a kid like this, you need benefits. You'll do anything for benefits. No individual insurance plan will cover this kind of thing.

23   For days, my son insisted that I was lying—that I made the whole thing up so that I could get rid of him. The first day, when I called to check up on him, he said, "I hate you. And I'm going to get my revenge as soon as I get out of here."

24   By day three, he was my calm, sweet boy again, all apologies and promises to get better. I've heard those promises for years. I don't believe them anymore.

25   On the intake form, under the question, "What are your expectations for treatment?" I wrote, "I need help."

26   And I do. This problem is too big for me to handle on my own. Sometimes there are no good options. So you just pray for grace and trust that in hindsight, it will all make sense. I am sharing this story because I am Adam Lanza's mother. I am Dylan Klebold's and Eric Harris's mother. I am James Holmes's mother. I am Jared Loughner's mother. I am Seung-Hui Cho's mother. And these boys—and their mothers—need help. In the wake of another horrific national tragedy, it's easy to talk about guns. But it's time to talk about mental illness.

27   According to *Mother Jones*, since 1982, 61 mass murders involving firearms have occurred throughout the country. Of these, 43 of the killers were white males, and only one was a woman. *Mother Jones* focused on whether the killers obtained their guns legally (most did). But this highly visible sign of mental illness should lead us to consider how many people in the U.S. live in fear, like I do.

28   When I asked my son's social worker about my options, he said that the only

thing I could do was to get Michael charged with a crime. "If he's back in the system, they'll create a paper trail," he said. "That's the only way you're ever going to get anything done. No one will pay attention to you unless you've got charges."

29   I don't believe my son belongs in jail. The **chaotic** environment **exacerbates** Michael's sensitivity to sensory stimuli and doesn't deal with the underlying **pathology**. But it seems like the United States is using prison as the solution of choice for mentally ill people. According to Human Rights Watch, the number of mentally ill inmates in U.S. prisons quadrupled from 2000 to 2006, and it continues to rise—in fact, the rate of inmate mental illness is five times greater (56 percent) than in the non-**incarcerated** population.

30   With state-run treatment centers and hospitals shuttered, prison is now the last resort for the mentally ill—Rikers Island, the LA County Jail and Cook County Jail in Illinois housed the nation's largest treatment centers in 2011.

31   No one wants to send a 13-year old genius who loves Harry Potter and his snuggle animal collection to jail. But our society, with its **stigma** on mental illness and its broken healthcare system, does not provide us with other options. Then another tortured soul shoots up a fast food restaurant. A mall. A kindergarten classroom. And we wring our hands and say, "Something must be done."

32   I agree that something must be done. It's time for a meaningful, nation-wide conversation about mental health. That's the only way our nation can ever truly heal.

33   God help me. God help Michael. God help us all.

—Long, Liza. "I am Adam Lanza's Mother."
The Blue Review. 15 Dec. 2012.

Fill in the blank in each sentence with a word from the Vocabulary Preview.

Vocabulary Preview **1.** Childhood _____ is more widespread than previously believed.

Vocabulary Preview **2.** The use of _____ drugs to treat children with mental illness concerns many due to their serious side effects.

Vocabulary Preview **3.** Leigh established a set of rules to bring order to the _____ household.

Vocabulary Preview **4.** Samuel was _____ for years for selling illegal drugs.

Vocabulary Preview **5.** The _____ of mental illness keeps many from seeking help.

For items 6 through 10, choose the best meaning of each word in *italics*. Use context clues to make your choice.

Vocabulary
in Context _____   **6.** "'I can wear these pants,' he said, his tone increasingly *belligerent*, the black-hole pupils of his eyes swallowing the blue irises." (paragraph 2)

   a. humble   c. hostile
   b. engaged   d. friendly

Vocabulary
in Context _____   **7.** "'You can't wear whatever pants you want to,' I said, my tone *affable*, reasonable." (paragraph 5)

   a. coldly   c. angrily
   b. friendly   d. fearfully

Vocabulary
in Context _____   **8.** "I managed to get the knife from Michael, then *methodically* collected all the sharp objects in the house into a single Tupperware container that now travels with me." (paragraph 7)

   a. logically   c. secretly
   b. spitefully   d. carelessly

Vocabulary
in Context _____   **9.** "His face turned cold, and his eyes were full of *calculated* rage." (paragraph 14)

   a. natural   c. counted
   b. uncontrollable   d. planned or intended

Vocabulary
in Context _____   **10.** "The chaotic environment *exacerbates* Michael's sensitivity to sensory stimuli and doesn't deal with the underlying pathology." (paragraph 29)

   a. insults   c. worsens
   b. improves   d. soothes

Central Idea _____   **11.** Which of the following sentences states the central idea of the passage?

   a. "Three days before 20 year-old Adam Lanza killed his mother, then opened fire on a classroom full of Connecticut kindergarteners, my 13-year old son Michael (name changed) missed his school bus because he was wearing the wrong color pants." (paragraph 1)
   b. "I live with a son who is mentally ill." (paragraph 6)
   c. "We still don't know what is wrong with Michael." (paragraph 9)
   d. "It's time for a meaningful, nation-wide conversation about mental health." (paragraph 32)

Supporting Detail _____ **12.** According to the passage, Michael pulled a knife and threatened to kill his mother and himself because
  a. he had on the wrong color pants.
  b. his mother asked him to return library books.
  c. his mother grounded him from using electronics for the day.
  d. his mother threatened to take him to a mental hospital.

Supporting Detail _____ **13.** According to the passage, how old is Michael, the author's son?
  a. 43   b. 13   c. 20   d. 18

Transitions _____ **14.** "By day three, he was my calm, sweet boy again, all apologies and promises to get better." (paragraph 24)

The relationship of ideas **within** this sentence is
  a. cause and effect.   c. comparison and contrast.
  b. time order.   d. generalization and example.

Transitions _____ **15.** "I love my son. But he terrifies me." (paragraph 6)

The relationship of ideas **between** these sentences is
  a. cause and effect.   c. comparison and contrast.
  b. time order.   d. generalization and example.

Thought Patterns _____ **16.** The main thought pattern of the passage is
  a. time order.   c. comparison and contrast.
  b. classification.   d. definition and example.

Fact and Opinion _____ **17.** "With state-run treatment centers and hospitals shuttered, prison is now the last resort for the mentally ill—Rikers Island, the LA County Jail and Cook County Jail in Illinois housed the nation's largest treatment centers in 2011." (paragraph 30)

This sentence is a statement of
  a. fact.   b. opinion.   c. fact and opinion.

Tone and Purpose _____ **18.** The overall tone and purpose of the author is
  a. to inform the public about her mentally ill son Michael.
  b. to entertain the public with interesting details about her experiences with her son Michael.
  c. to persuade the public to address the need for improved mental health care in this country.

Inferences _____ **19.** Based on the details in paragraphs 29–30, we can infer that
   a. there exists a strong link between mental health and crime.
   b. all prison inmates are mentally ill.
   c. prison is the best place to receive mental health care.
   d. mentally ill people always commit crimes.

Argument _____ **20.** The following items from paragraph 27 contain a claim and a list of supports for that claim. Which sentence states the claim?
   a. "According to *Mother Jones*, since 1982, 61 mass murders involving firearms have occurred throughout the country."
   b. "Of these, 43 of the killers were white males, and only one was a woman."
   c. "*Mother Jones* focused on whether the killers obtained their guns legally (most did)."
   d. "But this highly visible sign of mental illness should lead us to consider how many people in the U.S. live in fear, like I do."

Mapping

Complete the following story web with information from the passage.

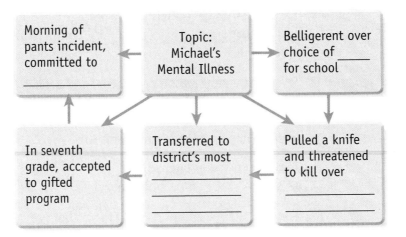

WHAT DO YOU THINK?

While many praised Liza Long as brave for focusing much needed attention on mental illness, others accused her of exploiting a tragedy for personal fame. Her critics claim she shared too much personal and damaging information about her son. One critic, Sarah Kendzior, pointed out that Long did little to protect her son's identity and damaged his reputation by promoting him as a future mass murderer. Do you think Liza Long was brave to publish her struggles and worries as the mother of a mentally ill child? Or do you agree with critics who accuse her of damaging her son's reputation? Assume you read Long's article online and chose to respond in the discussion forum that appeared at the end of the article. Write several paragraphs in which you support or oppose Liza Long's decision to write about her son's mental illness in her blog.

EFFECTIVE READER SCORECARD

"I am Adam Lanza's Mother"

Skill	Number Correct		Points		Total
Vocabulary					
Vocabulary Preview (5 items)	_____	×	10	=	_____
Vocabulary in Context (5 items)	_____	×	10	=	_____
			Vocabulary Score		_____
Comprehension					
Main Idea (1 item)	_____	×	8	=	_____
Supporting Details (2 items)	_____	×	8	=	_____
Transitions (2 items)	_____	×	8	=	_____
Thought Patterns (1 item)	_____	×	8	=	_____
Fact and Opinion (1 item)	_____	×	8	=	_____
Tone and Purpose (1 item)	_____	×	8	=	_____
Inferences (1 item)	_____	×	8	=	_____
Argument (1 item)	_____	×	8	=	_____
Mapping (4 items)	_____	×	5	=	_____
			Comprehension Score		_____

9 Psychological Disorders

Richard J. Gerrig and Philip G. Zimbardo

> The following selection is an excerpt from the college textbook *Psychology and Life*, 19th ed., by Richard J. Gerrig with Philip G. Zimbardo. In the preface to the textbook the authors state, "more often than not, students come into our course filled with misconceptions about psychology" based on "the infusion of 'pop psychology' into our society." Before you read, explore your own views. What do you believe and think about mental illness? Are you aware of the different types of mental illness? How many people suffer from mental illness? How does the public view someone with a mental illness? What causes mental illness? As you read, look for answers to these same questions. Also, identify and correct any misconceptions or mistaken views you may have had before reading.

Vocabulary Preview

psychopathological functioning (paragraph 2): disruptions in emotional, behavioral, or thought processes that lead to personal distress or block one's ability to achieve important goals

abnormal psychology (paragraph 2): the area of psychological investigation concerned with understanding the nature of individual pathologies of mind, mood, and behavior

pathologies (paragraph 2): diseases, studies of diseases

stigma (paragraph 2): the negative reaction of people to an individual or group because of some assumed inferiority or source of difference that is degraded

personality disorder (paragraph 4): a chronic, inflexible, maladaptive pattern of seeing, thinking, and behaving that seriously impairs one's ability to function

maladaptive (paragraph 4): poorly adapted or adjusted, unsuitable or unfit

borderline personality disorder (paragraph 5): a disorder defined by instability and intensity in personal relationships as well as confused emotions and impulsive behaviors

antisocial personality disorder (paragraph 5): a disorder characterized by stable patterns of irresponsible or unlawful behavior that violates social norms

impulsivity (paragraph 6): tendency to act on sudden urges

prevalence (paragraph 6): occurrence, rate, amount

concordance (paragraph 8): similarity or agreement

etiology (paragraph 9): study of causes, cause of disease

comorbid (paragraph 11): the presence of one or more disorders in addition to a main disorder or disease

attention-deficit hyperactivity disorder (ADHD) (paragraph 15): a disorder of childhood characterized by inattention and hyperactivity-impulsivity

autistic disorder (paragraph 15): a developmental disorder characterized by severe disruption of children's ability to form social bonds and use language

neurotransmitter (paragraph 19): chemical that carries signals between nerves

1   Have you ever worried excessively? Felt depressed or anxious without really knowing why? Been fearful of something you rationally knew could not harm you? Had thoughts about suicide? Used alcohol or drugs to escape a problem? Almost everyone will answer yes to at least one of these questions. Almost everyone has experienced the symptoms of a psychological disorder. This chapter looks at the range of psychological functioning that is considered unhealthy or abnormal, often referred to as psychopathology or psychological disorder.

2   **Psychopathological functioning** involves disruptions in emotional, behavioral, or thought processes. These disruptions lead to personal distress or block one's ability to achieve important goals. The field of **abnormal psychology** is the area of psychological investigation concerned with understanding the nature of individual **pathologies** of mind, mood, and behavior.

3   Our discussion focuses on the nature and causes of psychological disorders. We will discuss what they are, why they develop, and how we can explain their causes. The following sections discuss personality disorders, the psychological disorders of childhood, and the **stigma** of mental illness.

Personality Disorders

4   A **personality disorder** is a long-standing (chronic), inflexible, **maladaptive** pattern of perceiving, thinking, or behaving. These patterns can seriously impair an individual's ability to function in social or work settings. These patterns can cause great distress. They are usually seen by the time a person reaches adolescence or early adulthood. Personality disorders are coded on *Axis II of the Diagnostic and Statistical Manual of Mental Disorders, Fourth Edition, Text Revision* (DSM-IV-TR). DSM-IV-TR organizes 10 types of personality disorders into three clusters.

5   Diagnoses of personality disorders have sometimes been debatable. The debate occurs because of the overlap among the disorders. Some of the same behaviors lead to diagnoses of different disorders. In addition, researchers have tried to understand the relationship between normal and abnormal personalities. They ask, at what point does an extreme on a particular dimension of personality indicate a disorder (Livesley & Lang, 2005)? For example, most people are somewhat dependent on other people. When does dependence become extreme enough to signal dependent personality disorder? Clinicians must understand when and

how personality traits become maladaptive. They must understand when and how those traits cause either the person or society to suffer. To illustrate this point, we will focus on **borderline personality disorder** and **antisocial personality disorder**.

Borderline Personality Disorder

6   Individuals with *borderline personality disorder* experience great instability and intensity in personal relationships. These difficulties arise in part from difficulties controlling anger. The disorder leads people to have frequent fights and temper tantrums. In addition, people with this disorder display great **impulsivity** in their behaviors. They are mostly impulsive with respect to behaviors that can relate to self-harm, such as substance abuse or suicide attempts. Among adults in the United States, the **prevalence** of borderline personality disorder is about 1.6 percent (Lenzenweger et al., 2007).

7   One important aspect of borderline personality disorder is an intense fear of abandonment (Lieb et al., 2004). People with this disorder engage in frantic behaviors to prevent abandonment. For example, they make frequent phone calls. And they are physically clinging. However, they struggle with emotional control. Thus, they are likely to engage in behaviors that isolate them. Angry outbursts and bouts of self-harm make it quite difficult to maintain relationships with them. One study followed people with borderline personality disorder over the course of two years. The study found impaired social functioning across the whole period (Skodol et al., 2005). This research suggests that borderline personality disorder remains stable over time.

Causes of Borderline Personality Disorder

As with other disorders, researchers 8 have focused on both the nature and nurture of borderline personality disorder. Twin studies provide strong evidence in favor of a genetic contribution (Distel et al., 2008). For example, one study compared the rate of **concordance** for monozygotic (one cell) versus dizygotic (two cell) twins (Torgersen et al., 2000). When one MZ twin had borderline personality disorder, 35.3 percent of their siblings also had the disorder. For DZ twins, only 6.7 percent of their siblings also had the disorder.

Still, research suggests that environ- 9 mental factors make a strong contribution in the **etiology** of borderline personality disorder (Cohen et al., 2008; Lieb et al., 2004). One study compared the incidence of early traumatic events for 66 patients with the disorder to 109 healthy controls (Bandelow et al., 2005). The patients had greatly different lives. For example, 73.9 percent of the patients with borderline personality disorder reported childhood sexual abuse. Only 5.5 percent of the controls did so. The patients reported, on average, that the abuse started at age 6 and lasted for 3-1/2 years. That early trauma likely contributed to the incidence of the disorder. However, not all people who endure childhood sexual abuse develop borderline personality disorder. For example, the 5.5 percent of control participants in this study survived childhood sexual abuse. They did not develop the disorder. It is likely that a combination of genetic risk and traumatic events explains the etiology of the disorder.

Antisocial Personality Disorder

10   *Antisocial personality disorder* is marked by a long-standing pattern of irresponsible or unlawful behavior that violates social norms. Lying, stealing, and fighting are common behaviors. People with antisocial personality disorder often do not experience shame or remorse for their hurtful actions. Violations of social norms begin early in their lives. Behaviors include disrupting class, getting into fights, and running away from home. Their actions are marked by indifference to the rights of others. Among adults in the United States, the frequency of antisocial personality disorder is about 1.0 percent (Lenzenweger et al., 2007).

11   Antisocial personality disorder is often **comorbid** with other pathologies. For example, in one study of adults with histories of alcohol or drug abuse the prevalence of antisocial personality disorder was 18.3 percent for men and 14.1 percent for women. These findings are considerably higher than the 1.0 percent prevalence for the general population (Goldstein et al., 2007). In addition, antisocial personality disorder also puts people at risk for suicide. This risk exists even without major depressive disorder (Hills et al., 2005). This suicide risk is likely to be a product of the impulsivity and disregard for safety that marks the disorder.

Causes of Antisocial Personality Disorder

12 Researchers have used twin studies to examine genetic parts of specific behaviors linked with antisocial personality disorder. For example, one study examined the similarities in behaviors for 3,687 pairs of twins (Viding et al., 2005). Teachers responded to statements about each twin. The state-ments described callous-unemotional traits (such as "Does not show feelings or emotions") and antisocial behavior (such as "Often fights with other children or bullies them"). The comparisons of MZ and DZ twins suggested that the tendency to display callous-unemotional traits had a strong genetic component. In addition, for twins who displayed high levels of those callous-emotional traits, genetics also made a strong contribution to antisocial behavior.

Research has also focused on the envi- 13 ronmental circumstances that give rise to personality disorders (Paris, 2003). Consider this study of the relationship between parenting practices and antisocial personality traits.

A team of researchers assessed 742 men and women for personality traits that met DSM-IV criteria for antisocial personality disorder (Reti et al., 2002). The participants reported on their parents' behaviors toward them during childhood by completing the Parental Bonding Instrument (PBI). The PBI posed a range of questions. Participants responded on a 4-point scale. Some of the questions measured the extent to which parents showed caring for the child (for example, "Could make me feel better when I was upset"). Other questions measured the extent to which parents restricted the child's behavior (for example, "Let me dress in any way I pleased"). A third type of question measured the extent to which parents allowed the child psychological freedom (for example, "Tried to control everything I did"). The researchers looked for relationships between the participants' responses on the PBI and the extent to which they showed antisocial personality traits. The researchers found that the people who reported low levels of parental care had high levels of antisocial personality traits. Also, those individuals who believed that their mothers had been particularly overprotective also had high levels of antisocial personality traits.

The researchers were quick to assert that this link does not indicate a cause. It's possible that parenting behaviors brought about antisocial personality traits. It's also possible that children with antisocial traits negatively affected the way their parents behaved toward them. Still, the results suggest that researchers could observe family patterns to determine what children might be at risk to develop adult forms of antisocial personality disorder.

Psychological Disorders of Childhood

14   Our discussion so far has largely focused on adults who suffer from **psychopathology**. However, many begin to experience symptoms of mental illness in childhood and adolescence. Researchers have recently intensified their study of the time course with which psychopathology emerges in young lives (Zahn-Waxler et al., 2008). Researchers often try to identify behavior patterns that allow for early diagnosis and treatment. For example, problems with social functioning may provide clues that children and adolescents are at risk for schizophrenia (Tarbox & Pogue-Geile, 2008).

DSM-IV-TR also identifies a range of 15 disorders that are "usually first diagnosed in infancy, childhood, or adolescence." Here, we focus on **attention-deficit hyperactivity disorder** and **autistic disorder**.

Attention-Deficit Hyperactivity Disorder

The definition of *attention-deficit* 16 *hyperactivity disorder (ADHD)* refers to two clusters of symptoms (DSM-IV-TR, 2000). First, children must show a degree of inattention that is not consistent with their level of development. They might, for example, have difficulty paying attention in school. Or they often lose items such as toys or school assignments. Second, children must show signs of hyperactivity-impulsivity that, once again, is not consistent with their developmental level. Hyperactive behaviors include squirming, fidgeting, and excessive talking. Impulsive behaviors include blurting out answers and interrupting. A diagnosis of ADHD requires that children have shown these patterns of behavior for at least six months before age 7.

Researchers estimate the prevalence 17 of ADHD to be 3–7 percent of school-age children in the United States (Root & Resnick, 2003). Many studies suggest that more boys than girls experience ADHD. However, research also suggests that cultural biases (for example, expectations of gender differences) lead to fewer diagnoses of ADHD among girls than are justified. This bias makes it difficult to provide an exact estimate of the gender difference. However, in one large-scale study of adults, 3.2 percent of women and 5.4 percent of men met diagnostic criteria for

ADHD (Kessler et al., 2006a). These figures may accurately reflect gender differences across the life span. When they are diagnosed with ADHD, boys and girls show much the same patterns of problem behavior (Biederman et al., 2005). Some children overcome ADHD as they grow older. In one sample of 133 children diagnosed as hyperactive at ages 4 to 12, 42 percent did not meet criteria for ADHD at age 21 (Fischer et al., 2005). The 58 percent of young adults who still had ADHD performed less well than controls on a variety of mental tasks.

18   The diagnosis of ADHD is complicated by the fact that many children are prone to episodes of inattention, hyperactivity, or impulsiveness. For that reason, the diagnosis has sometimes been controversial. People have worried that children's normal disorderliness was being labeled as abnormal. However, there is now agreement among clinicians that some children's behavior reaches a level at which it is maladaptive. These children are unable to control their behavior or complete tasks. There has often been a popular perception that ADHD is overdiagnosed. However, research evidence contradicts that perception (Sciutto & Eisenberg, 2007). In fact, as we noted earlier, ADHD might actually be underdiagnosed for girls.

19   As with the other disorders we've described, researchers have considered both the nature and nurture of ADHD. Twin and adoption studies have provided strong evidence for the heritability of the disorder (Biederman & Faraone, 2005). Researchers have started to document relationships between specific genes that affect the brain's **neurotransmitter** function and the symptoms of ADHD (Smoller et al., 2006). There

are also important environmental variables associated with ADHD. For example, children who come from families with economic disadvantages or families with high levels of conflict are more likely to experience the disorder (Biederman et al., 2002). Some environmental variables have greater impact on children in different birth positions. For example, the eldest children in families that lack unity are more at risk for ADHD than are younger siblings in such families (Pressman et al., 2006). In these families, members are not committed to providing support to each other. Results of this sort suggest that parenting experience has an impact on the incidence of ADHD.

Autistic Disorder

20   Children with *autistic disorder* present severe disruption in their ability to form social bonds. They are likely to have greatly delayed and very limited development of spoken language. They also have very narrow interests in the world. Consider a report on a child who was diagnosed with this disorder:

> [Audrey] seemed frightened by nearly any changes in her customary routine, including the presence of strange people. She either shrank from contact with other children or avoided them altogether. She was seemingly content to engage in nonfunctional play by herself for hours at a time. When she was with other children, she seldom engaged in joint play or even copied any of their motor movements. (Meyer, 2003, p. 244)

Many children with autistic disorder also engage in repetitive and ritualistic behaviors: They might, for example, place objects in lines or balanced patterns (Greaves et al., 2006).

21   Research suggests that the prevalence of autistic disorder (and related disorders) is about one out of 150 children (Centers for Disease Control and Prevention, 2007). Many of the symptoms of autistic disorder relate to language and social interaction. Thus, it has often been difficult to diagnose the disorder. Parents must first notice that their children are failing to use language or interact. However, recent research has begun to document behaviors in the first year of life. These behaviors predict later diagnoses of autistic disorder. For example, children at risk are less likely to smile and respond to their names than are other children.

22 **Causes of Autistic Disorder** As with ADHD, autistic disorder has a large genetic component. In fact, researchers have begun to identify the variations in the human genome that may predispose individuals to experience the disorder (Bartlett et al., 2005; Liu et al., 2008). Researchers have also discovered brain markers of the disorder. For example, individuals with autistic disorder experience more rapid brain growth than do their peers (Amaral et al., 2008). The ongoing question is how such brain abnormalities bring about the symptoms of the disorder.

23   Researchers have suggested that individuals who suffer from autistic disorder have an inability to develop an understanding of other people's mental states (Baron-Cohen, 2008). Under ordinary circumstances, children develop what has been called a *theory of mind*. At first, they interpret the world only from their own perspective. However, with rapid progress

between ages 3 and 4, children develop an understanding that other people have different knowledge, beliefs, and intentions than they do. Research suggests that individuals with autistic disorder lack the ability to develop this understanding. Without a theory of mind, it is quite difficult for people to establish social relationships. Individuals with autistic disorder find it virtually impossible to understand and predict other people's behavior. This inability makes everyday life seem mysterious and hostile.

The Stigma of Mental Illness

One of our most important goals for this 24 chapter has been to demystify mental illness—to help you understand how, in some ways, abnormal behavior is really ordinary. People with psychological disorders are often labeled as deviant. However, the deviant label is not true to prevailing realities:

When 46.4 percent of adults in the 25 United States report having experienced some psychiatric disorder in their lifetime (Kessler et al., 2005a), psychopathology is, at least statistically, relatively normal.

Even given the frequency with which 26 psychopathology touches "normal lives," people who are psychologically disordered are often stigmatized in ways that most physically ill people are not. A **stigma** is a mark or brand of disgrace. In the psychological context, it is a set of negative attitudes about a person that places him or her apart as unacceptable (Hinshaw & Stier, 2008). One patient had this to say: "The patient and public, in my [opinion] needs to be educated about mental illness because people ridicule and mistreat, even misunderstand us at crucial times." Another recovered patient wrote, "For me, the stigma of mental illness was as devastating as the experience of hospitalization itself. Repeated rejections, the awkwardness of others around me, and my own discomfort and self-consciousness propelled me into solitary confinement" (Houghton, 1980, pp. 7–8). Negative attitudes toward the psychologically disturbed come from many sources. The mass media portray psychiatric patients as prone to violent crime. Jokes about the mentally ill are acceptable. Families deny the mental distress of one of their members. Legal terminology stresses mental incompetence. People also stigmatize themselves by hiding current psychological distress or a history of mental health care.

27   Researchers have documented a number of ways in which the stigma of mental illness has a negative impact on people's lives (Hinshaw & Stier, 2008). In one sample of 84 men who had been hospitalized for mental illness, 6 percent reported having lost a job because of their hospitalization. 10 percent reported having been denied an apartment or room. 37 percent reported being avoided by others. And 45 percent reported that others had used their history of mental illness to hurt their feelings. Only 6 percent of the men reported no incidents of rejection (Link et al., 1997). This group of men went through a yearlong course of treatment that resulted in considerable improvement in their mental health. Even so, at the end of that year, there were no changes in their perception of stigma. Despite their improvements in functioning, the patients did not expect to be treated any more kindly by the world. This type of research shows the great duality of many people's experience with mental disorders. Seeking help—allowing one's problems to be labeled—generally brings both relief and stigma. Treatment improves quality of life. At the same time, that stigma degrades it (Rosenfield, 1997).

28   An added difficulty is that people with mental illness often adopt expectations of rejections that may, in turn, bring about negative interactions (Pachankis, 2007). Consider this classic experiment.

> Twenty-nine men who had formerly been hospitalized for mental illness volunteered to participate in this study. They believed that the research concerned the difficulties ex-psychiatric patients have with finding jobs. The participants were informed that they would interact with a personnel trainee recruited from a business establishment. Half of the participants were told that the trainee knew of their status as ex-psychiatric patients. The other half were told that the trainee believed they had been medical or surgical patients at the hospital. In fact, the "trainee" was a partner of the experimenter who did not have any prior information about the participants' beliefs about his knowledge. That is, he did not know which participants thought that he knew that they were ex-patients. Therefore, any differences in the interactions during the time the participants and "trainee" spent together can be attributed to the participants' expectations. In fact, the participants who believed themselves to have been labeled as ex-psychiatric patients talked less during the session and performed worse on a cooperative

task. Furthermore, the "trainee" rated members of this group as more "tense and anxious." Again, the "trainee" did not know which group each participant was in (Farina et al., 1971).

The important conclusion here is that people who believe that others have attached the "mental illness" label to them may change their interactions in a way that brings about genuine discomfort. The expectation of rejection can create rejection. Mental illness can be another of life's unfortunate self-fulfilling prophecies.

29   A final note on stigma. Research suggests that people who have had prior contact with individuals with mental illnesses hold attitudes that are less affected by stigma (Couture & Penn, 2003). For example, students who read a short essay about a man named Jim who had recovered from schizophrenia were more optimistic about Jim's future prospects when the students had had prior contact with someone who suffered from a mental illness (Penn et al., 1994). Similarly, students' ratings of the dangerousness of patients with schizophrenia were lower when they had had prior contact (Penn et al., 1999). We hope that one effect of reading this chapter and the next will be to help modify your beliefs about what it means to be mentally ill and what it means to be "cured." We hope to increase your tolerance and compassion for mentally ill individuals.

—Adapted from Gerrig, Richard J.; Zimbardo, Philip G., *Psychology and Life*, 16th ed. pp. 442, 459–462, 471–472. © 2002. Printed and Electronically reproduced by permission of Pearson Education, Inc., Upper Saddle River, New Jersey.

Choose the best meaning of each word in *italics*. Use context clues to make your choice.

Vocabulary in Context _____   **1.** "In addition, people with this disorder display great *impulsivity* in their behaviors." (paragraph 6)
      a. abruptness   c. variety
      b. rashness   d. thoughtfulness

Vocabulary in Context _____   **2.** "Among adults in the United States, the *prevalence* of borderline personality disorder is about 1.6 percent." (paragraph 6)
      a. decline   c. rate
      b. increase   d. depth

Central Idea _____   **3.** Which of the following sentences best states the central idea of paragraphs 4–15?
      a. "A *personality disorder* is a long-standing (chronic), inflexible, maladaptive pattern of perceiving, thinking, or behaving." (paragraph 4)
      b. "Clinicians must understand when and how personality traits become maladaptive." (paragraph 5)

c. "Individuals with *borderline personality disorder* experience great instability and intensity in personal relationships." (paragraph 6)

d. "*Antisocial personality disorder* is marked by a long-standing pattern of irresponsible or unlawful behavior that violates social norms." (paragraph 10)

Main Idea _____ **4.** Which of the following sentences states the main idea of paragraph 16?

a. "The definition of *attention-deficit hyperactivity disorder (ADHD)* refers to two clusters of symptoms (DSM-IV-TR, 2000)."

b. "First, children must show a degree of inattention that is not consistent with their level of development."

c. "They might, for example, have difficulty paying attention in school."

d. "Second, children must show signs of hyperactivity-impulsivity that, once again, is not consistent with their level of development."

Supporting Details _____ **5.** According to the authors, children who engage in repetitive or ritualistic behaviors suffer from

a. attention-deficit disorder.   c. antisocial personality disorder.

b. autistic disorder.   d. borderline personality disorder.

Supporting Details _____ **6.** According to the authors, what percentage of adults in the United States report having experienced some psychiatric disorder in their lifetime?

a. 73.9 percent   c. 46.4 percent

b. 1.6 percent   d. 6 percent

Transitions _____ **7.** "The debate occurs because of the overlap among the disorders." (paragraph 5)

The relationship of ideas **within** this sentence is

a. time order.   c. comparison and contrast.

b. cause and effect.   d. definition and example.

Transitions _____ **8.** "Researchers have also discovered the brain markers of the disorder. For example, individuals with autistic disorder experience more rapid brain growth than do their peers." (paragraph 22)

The relationship of ideas **between** these sentences is

a. cause and effect.   c. comparison and contrast.

b. time order.   d. generalization and example.

Thought
Patterns   _____   **9.** The overall thought pattern of paragraphs 6–7 is
　　　　　　　　　　　a. time order.　　　　　　　c. definition and example.
　　　　　　　　　　　b. cause and effect.　　　　d. comparison and contrast.

Thought
Patterns   _____   **10.** The overall thought pattern of paragraphs 8–9 is
　　　　　　　　　　　a. time order.　　　　　　　c. comparison and contrast.
　　　　　　　　　　　b. cause and effect.　　　　d. definition and example.

Fact and
Opinion   _____   **11.** "Almost everyone has experienced the symptoms of a psychological
　　　　　　　　　　　disorder." (paragraph 1)

　　　　　　　　　　　This sentence is a statement of
　　　　　　　　　　　a. fact.　　　　　　　　　　c. fact and opinion.
　　　　　　　　　　　b. opinion.

Fact and
Opinion   _____   **12.** "Among adults in the United States, the prevalence of borderline
　　　　　　　　　　　personality disorder is about 1.6 percent." (paragraph 6)

　　　　　　　　　　　This sentence is a statement of
　　　　　　　　　　　a. fact.　　　　　　　　　　c. fact and opinion.
　　　　　　　　　　　b. opinion.

Tone and
Purpose   _____   **13.** "We hope to increase your tolerance and compassion for mentally ill
　　　　　　　　　　　individuals." (paragraph 29)

　　　　　　　　　　　The tone of this sentence is
　　　　　　　　　　　a. objective.　　　　　　　　c. disbelieving.
　　　　　　　　　　　b. sarcastic　　　　　　　　d. positive.

Tone and
Purpose   _____   **14.** The overall tone of the passage is
　　　　　　　　　　　a. academic.　　　　　　　　c. argumentative.
　　　　　　　　　　　b. appreciative.　　　　　　d. sentimental.

Tone and
Purpose   _____   **15.** The overall purpose of the author is
　　　　　　　　　　　a. to inform the reader about the types and causes of certain
　　　　　　　　　　　　　psychological disorders.
　　　　　　　　　　　b. to entertain the reader with new information about the types
　　　　　　　　　　　　　and causes of certain psychological disorders.
　　　　　　　　　　　c. to persuade the reader to recognize and get help for certain
　　　　　　　　　　　　　psychological disorders.

Inferences   _____   **16.** Based on the details in paragraph 28, we can infer that
　　　　　　　　　　　a. people with mental illness expect to be rejected.
　　　　　　　　　　　b. people with mental illness have negative interactions.
　　　　　　　　　　　c. people with mental illness perform worse on cooperative tasks.
　　　　　　　　　　　d. people with mental illness expect certain outcomes, and may
　　　　　　　　　　　　　create interactions to fulfill those outcomes.

Inferences _____ 17. Based on the details in the passage, we can infer that many psychological disorders are the result of
a. genetics or inherited traits (nature).
b. the environment or life experiences of the individual (nurture).
c. abuse or trauma (nurture).
d. genetics and the environment (nature and nurture).

Inferences _____ 18. Based on the details in paragraphs 10 and 11, we can infer that
a. all criminals suffer from antisocial personality disorders.
b. people who suffer from antisocial personality disorders are always violent.
c. people who suffer from antisocial disorders may be dangerous to themselves and others.
d. most alcoholics and drug abusers suffer from antisocial personality disorders.

Inferences _____ 19. Based on the details in the passage, which of the following behaviors would not generally support a diagnosis of attention-deficit hyperactivity disorder?
a. The child blurts out answers during class activities.
b. The child loses his toys and school assignments.
c. The child squirms and fidgets in the classroom.
d. The child cries when other children tease him.

Argument _____ 20. The following items from paragraph 26 contain a claim and list of supports for that claim. Which sentence states the claim?
a. "Negative attitudes toward the psychologically disturbed come from many sources."
b. "The mass media portray psychiatric patients as prone to violent crime."
c. "Jokes about the mentally ill are acceptable."
d. "Families deny the mental distress of one of their members."

Outlining

Complete the following outline with information from the passage.

Personality Disorders

I. _____

    A. _____

    B. Antisocial Personality Disorder

II. _____

    A. Attention-Deficit Hyperactivity Disorder

    B. _____

III. _____

WHAT DO YOU THINK?

Assume your professor has assigned the following activity: Ask several people (who are not psychology professionals) to define the following terms: *mental illness, personality disorder, attention-deficit hyperactivity disorder (ADHD), autism.* Ask them to describe behaviors that characterize each term. How do their definitions compare with the ones in your text? What can you conclude about the attitudes and understanding of mental illness shown by the people you interviewed? Write an article for the college newspaper that raises awareness about mental illness based on what you have learned by reading this passage and interviewing others.

EFFECTIVE READER SCORECARD

"Psychological Disorders"

Skill	Number Correct	Points	Total
Vocabulary			
Vocabulary in Context (2 items)	_____	× 4 =	_____
Comprehension			
Central Idea and Main Idea (2 items)	_____	× 4 =	_____
Supporting Details (2 items)	_____	× 4 =	_____
Transitions (2 items)	_____	× 4 =	_____
Thought Patterns (2 items)	_____	× 4 =	_____
Fact and Opinion (2 items)	_____	× 4 =	_____
Tone and Purpose (3 items)	_____	× 4 =	_____
Inferences (4 items)	_____	× 4 =	_____
Argument (1 item)	_____	× 4 =	_____
Outlining (5 items)	_____	× 4 =	_____
		Comprehension Score	_____

Diversity in U.S. Families

Excerpt from *Sociology: A Down-to-Earth Approach*, 9th Edition

James M. Henslin

Do you like to watch people and try to figure out why they do what they do? Have you thought about how our society and the groups to which we belong affect us? If so, you think like a sociologist. Sociology is fundamentally the study of life in groups. In the preface to the book from which this passage is taken, James M. Henslin states the study of life in groups "pries open the doors of society so you can see what goes on behind them." Henslin believes that as we study life in groups, "we gain new insights into who we are and how we got that way." The following passage is a section of the chapter "Marriage and the Family."

Vocabulary Preview

machismo (paragraph 7): emphasis on traits usually regarded as male: physical strength, courage, aggressiveness, and lack of emotional response

acculturated (paragraph 8): adjusted into the culture of another group, learning and adapting the practices and customs of another culture

emigrated (paragraph 9): left to live in another country

Confucian (paragraph 10): related to the teachings of Confucius, emphasis on personal, social, and political order

humanism (paragraph 10): belief in human-based moral codes, concern for people

collectivity (paragraph 10): state of being together, people or things work together to form a whole

permissive (paragraph 13): allowing freedom of behavior, lenient, tolerant

deferred (paragraph 14): postponed, delayed, overdue

conceptual (paragraph 24): theoretical, abstract, unapplied

1   It is important to note that there is no such thing as the American family. Rather, family life varies widely throughout the United States. The significance of social class, noted earlier, will continue to be evident as we examine diversity in U.S. families.

African American Families

2   Note that the heading reads African American families, not the African American family. There is no such thing as the African American family any more than there is the white family or the Latino family. The primary distinction is not between African Americans and other groups, but between social classes (Willie and Reddick 2003). Because African Americans who are members of the upper class follow the class interests reviewed in Chapter 10—preservation of privilege and family fortune—they are especially concerned about the family background of those whom their children marry (Gatewood 1990). To them, marriage is viewed as the merger of family lines. Children of this class marry later than children of other classes.

3   Middle-class African American families focus on achievement and respectability. Both husband and wife are likely to work outside the home. A central concern is that their children go to college, get good jobs, and marry well—that is, marry people like themselves, respectable and hardworking, who want to get ahead in school and pursue a successful career.

4   African American families in poverty face all the problems that cluster around poverty (Wilson 1987, 1996; Anderson 1990/2006; Venkatesh 2006). Because the men are likely to have few skills and to be unemployed, it is difficult for them to fulfill the cultural roles of husband and father. Consequently, these families are likely to be headed by a woman and to have a high rate of births to single women. Divorce and desertion are also more common than among other classes. Sharing scarce resources and "stretching kinship" are primary survival mechanisms. People who have helped out in hard times are considered brothers, sisters, or cousins to whom one owes obligations as though they were blood relatives; and men who are not the biological fathers of their children are given fatherhood status (Stack 1974; Fischer et al. 2005). Sociologists use the term **fictive** kin to refer to this stretching of kinship.

5   From Figure 1 you can see that, compared with other groups, African American families are the least likely to be headed by married couples and the most likely to be headed by women. Because African American women tend to go farther in school than African American men, they are more likely than women in other racial-ethnic groups to marry men who are less educated than themselves (South 1991; Eshleman 2000).

Latino Families

6   As Figure 1 shows, the proportion of Latino families headed by married couples and women falls in between that of whites and African Americans. The effects of social class on families, which I just sketched, also apply to Latinos. In addition, families differ by country of origin. Families from Mexico, for example, are more likely to be headed by a married couple than are families from Puerto Rico (Statistical Abstract 2007: Table 44). The longer that Latinos have lived in the United States, the more their families resemble those of middle-class Americans (Saenz 2004).

7   With such a wide variety, experts disagree on what is distinctive about Latino

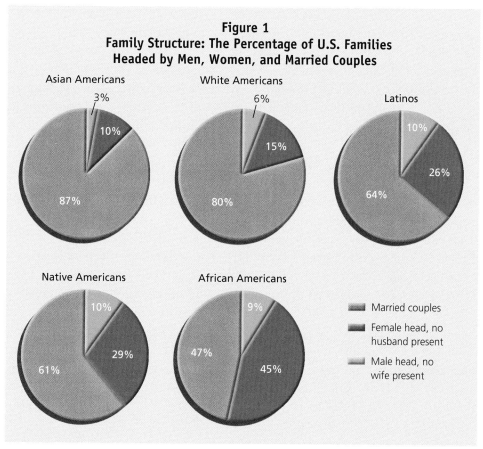

Figure 1
Family Structure: The Percentage of U.S. Families Headed by Men, Women, and Married Couples

Source: By the author. For Native Americans, "American Community . . ." 2004. For other groups, *Statistical Abstract* 2007:Tables 41, 44, 62. Data for Asian Americans are for families with children under 18, while the other groups don't have this limitation. Totals may not equal 100 percent due to rounding.

families. Some point to the Spanish language, the Roman Catholic religion, and a strong family orientation coupled with a disapproval of divorce. Others add that Latinos emphasize loyalty to the extended family, with an obligation to support the extended family in times of need (Cauce and Domenech-Rodriguez 2002). Descriptions of Latino families used to include **machismo**—an emphasis on male strength, sexual vigor, and dominance—but current studies show that machismo now charac-terizes only a small proportion of Latino husband-fathers (Torres et al. 2002). Machismo apparently decreases with each generation in the United States (Hurtado et al. 1992; Wood 2001). Some researchers have found that the husband-father plays a stronger role than in either white or African American families (Vega 1990; Torres et al. 2002). Apparently, the wife-mother is usually more family-centered than her husband, displaying more warmth and affection for her children.

8   It is difficult to draw generalizations because, as with other racial-ethnic groups, individual Latino families vary considerably (Contreras et al. 2002). Some Latino families, for example, have **acculturated** to such an extent that they are Protestants who do not speak Spanish.

Asian American Families

9   As you can see from Figure 1 on the previous page, Asian American children are more likely than children in any other racial-ethnic group to grow up with both parents. As with the other groups, family life also reflects social class. In addition, because Asian Americans **emigrated** from many different countries, their family life reflects those many cultures (Xie and Goyette 2004). As with Latino families, the more recent their immigration, the more closely their family life reflects the patterns in their country of origin (Kibria 1993; Glenn 1994).

10   Despite such differences, sociologist Bob Suzuki (1985), who studied Chinese American and Japanese American families, identified several distinctive characteristics of Asian American families. Although Asian Americans have adopted the **nuclear** family structure, they have retained **Confucian** values that provide a framework for family life: **humanism**, **collectivity**, self-discipline, **hierarchy**, respect for the elderly, moderation, and obligation. Obligation means that each member of a family owes respect to other family members and is responsible never to bring shame on the family. Conversely, a child's success brings honor to the family (Zamiska 2004). To control their children, Asian American parents are more likely to use shame and guilt rather than physical punishment.

11   The ideal does not always translate into the real, however, and so it is here. The children born to Asian immigrants confront a bewildering world of incompatible expectations—those of the new culture and those of their parents. As a result, they experience more family conflict and mental problems than do children of Asian Americans who are not immigrants (Meyers 2006).

Native American Families

12   Perhaps the single most significant issue that Native American families face is whether to follow traditional values or to **assimilate** into the dominant culture (Garrett 1999). This primary distinction creates vast differences among families. The traditionals speak native languages and emphasize distinctive Native American values and beliefs. Those who have assimilated into the broader culture do not. . . .

13   In general, Native American parents are **permissive** with their children and avoid physical punishment. Elders play a much more active role in their children's families than they do in most U.S. families: Elders, especially grandparents, not only provide child care but also teach and discipline children. Like others, Native American families differ by social class.

14   From this brief review, you can see that race-ethnicity signifies little for understanding family life. Rather, social class and culture hold the keys. The more resources a family has, the more it assumes the characteristics of a middle-class nuclear family. Compared with the poor, middle-class families have fewer children and fewer

unmarried mothers. They also place greater emphasis on educational achievement and **deferred gratification**.

One-Parent Families

15   Another indication of how extensively U.S. families are changing is the increase in one-parent families. From Figure 2, you can see that the percentage of U.S. children who live with two parents (not necessarily their biological parents) has dropped sharply. The concerns that are often expressed about one-parent families may have more to do with their poverty than with children being reared by one parent. Because women head most one-parent families, these families tend to be poor. Most divorced women earn less than their former husbands, yet about 85 percent of children of divorce live with their mothers ("Child Support" 1995; Aulette 2002).

16   To understand the typical one-parent family, then, we need to view it through the lens of poverty, for that is its primary source of strain. The results are serious, not just for these parents and their children but also for society as a whole. Children from one parent families are more likely to drop out of school, to get arrested, to have emotional problems, and to get divorced (McLanahan and Sandefur 1994; Menaghan et al. 1997; McLanahan and Schwartz 2002; Amato and Cheadle 2005). If female, they are more likely to become sexually active at a younger age and to bear children while still unmarried teenagers.

Families Without Children

17   While most married women give birth, about one of five (19 percent) do not (DeOilos and Kapinus 2003). The number of childless couples has doubled from what it was 20 years ago. As you can see from Figure 3, this percentage varies by racial-ethnic group, with whites and Latinas representing the extremes. Some couples are infertile, but most childless couples have made a choice to not have children. Why do they make this choice? Some women believe they would be stuck at home—bored, lonely, with dwindling career opportunities. Some couples perceive their marriage as too fragile to withstand the strains that a child would bring (Gerson 1985). A common reason is to attain a sense of freedom—to pursue a career, to be able to change jobs, to travel, and to have less stress (Lunneborg 1999; Letherby 2002).

Figure 2
The Decline of Two-Parent Families

The percentage of children under 18 who live with both parents

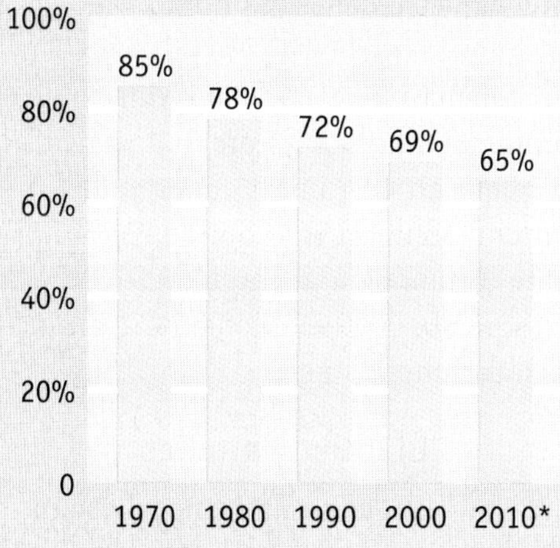

*Author's estimate

Source: By the author: Based on *Statistical Abstract* 1995: Table 79; 2007: Table 62.

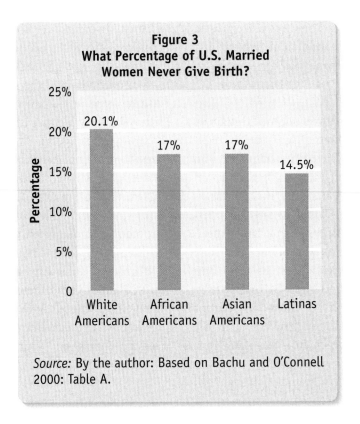

Figure 3
What Percentage of U.S. Married Women Never Give Birth?

Source: By the author: Based on Bachu and O'Connell 2000: Table A.

18   With trends firmly in place—more education and careers for women, advances in contraception, legal abortion, the high cost of rearing children, and an emphasis on possessing more material things—the proportion of women who never bear children is likely to increase. Consider this statement in a newsletter:

19   We are DINKS (Dual Incomes, No Kids). We are happily married. I am 43; my wife is 42. We have been married for almost twenty years… Our investment strategy has a lot to do with our personal philosophy: "You can have kids—or you can have everything else!"

Many childless couples, in contrast, are 20 not childless by choice. Desperately wanting to have children, they keep trying to do so. Coming to the soul-searching conclusion that they can never bear children, the most common solution is adoption. As featured in the Sociology and the New Technology box, some turn to solutions not available to previous generations.

Blended Families

The blended family, one whose mem- 21 bers were once part of other families, is an increasingly significant type of family in the United States. Two divorced people who marry and each bring their children into a new family unit become a blended family. With divorce common, millions of children spend some of their childhood in blended families. One result is more complicated family relationships. Consider this description written by one of my students:

22   I live with my dad. I should say that I live with my dad, my brother (whose mother and father are also my mother and father), my half sister (whose father is my dad, but whose mother is my father's last wife), and two stepbrothers and stepsisters (children of my father's current wife). My father's wife (my current stepmother, not to be confused with his second wife who, I guess, is no longer my stepmother) is pregnant, and soon we all will have a new brother or sister. Or will it be a half brother or half sister?

23   If you can't figure this out, I don't blame you. I have trouble myself. It gets very complicated around Christmas. Should we all stay together? Split up and go to several other homes? Who do we buy gifts for, anyway?

Gay and Lesbian Families

24   In 1989, Denmark became the first country to legalize marriage between people of the same sex. Since then, several European countries have passed such laws. In 2004, Massachusetts became the first of the U.S. states to legalize same-sex marriages. Walking a fine **conceptual** tightrope, other states have passed laws that give legal rights to "registered domestic partnerships." This is an attempt to give legal status to same-sex unions and yet sidestep controversy by not calling them marriages.

25   At this point, most gay and lesbian couples lack both legal marriage and the legal protection of registered "partnerships." Although these couples live throughout the United States, about half are concentrated in just twenty cities. The greatest concentrations are in San Francisco, Los Angeles, Atlanta, New York City, and Washington, D.C. About one fifth of gay and lesbian couples were previously married to heterosexuals. Twenty-two percent of female couples and 5 percent of male couples have children from their earlier heterosexual marriages (Bianchi and Casper 2000).

26   What are same-sex relationships like? Like everything else in life, these couples cannot be painted with a single brush stroke. As with opposite-sex couples, social class is significant, and orientations to life differ according to education, occupation, and income. Sociologists Philip Blumstein and Pepper Schwartz (1985) interviewed same-sex couples and found their main struggles to be housework, money, careers, problems with relatives, and sexual adjustment—the same problems that face **heterosexual** couples. Some also confront discrimination at work, which can add stress to their relationship (Todosijevic et al. 2005). Same-sex couples are more likely to break up, and one argument for legalizing gay marriages is that the marriage contract will make these relationships more stable. If they were surrounded by laws, same-sex marriages would be like opposite-sex marriages—to break them would require negotiating around legal obstacles.

Sociology and the New Technology

The Brave New World of High-Tech Reproduction: Where Technology Outpaces Law and Sometimes Common-Sense

Jaycee has five parents—or none, depending on how you look at it. The story goes like this. Luanne and John Buzzanca were infertile. Although they spent more than $100,000 on treatments, nothing worked. Then a fertility clinic mixed a man's sperm with a woman's egg. Both the man and the woman remained anonymous. Pamela Snell agreed to be a surrogate mother, and a surgeon implanted the fertilized egg in Pamela, who gave birth to Jaycee (Davis 1998a; Foote 1998).

At Jaycee's birth, Pamela handed Jaycee over to Luanne, who was waiting at her bedside. Luanne's husband, John, decided not to be there. He had filed for divorce just a month before.

Luanne asked John for child support. John refused, and Luanne sued. The judge ruled that John didn't have to pay. He said that because Jaycee had been conceived in a petri dish with an egg and sperm from anonymous donors, John wasn't the baby's father. The judge added that Luanne wasn't the baby's mother either.

Five parents—or none? Welcome to the brave—and very real—new world of high-tech reproduction. Reproductive technologies have laid a trap for the unsuspecting, calling into question even what a mother is. Although Pamela Snell gave birth to Jaycee, she is not a mother. How about the donor of the egg? Biologically, yes, but legally, no. Is Luanne a mother? Fortunately, for Jaycee's sake, a higher court ruled that she is.

—Henslin, James M. *Sociology: Down-to-Earth Approach*, 9th ed., pp. 479–480 © 2008. Reprinted and Electronically reproduced by permission of Pearson Education, Inc., Upper Saddle River, New Jersey.

Fill in the blank in each sentence with a word from the Vocabulary Preview.

Vocabulary Preview

1. The distinctly dressed Mormons are not _____ to current American society.

Vocabulary Preview

2. United Nations Ambassadors Angelina Jolie and Natalie Portman promote _____ in business; they call for commerce that raises the world's poorest people out of poverty.

Vocabulary Preview

3. Some view the 1960s in the United States as a time of rapid moral change that led to a more _____ society.

Vocabulary Preview

4. The cyborg as played by Arnold Schwarzenegger in *The Terminator* is _____ gone high-tech.

Vocabulary Preview

5. "We Are the World" is a song and charity single that celebrates the

_____ of the human experience. Fans enjoy hearing racially and musically diverse recording artists singing together on one track to raise money for those in dire need across the globe.

For items 6 through 10, choose the best meaning of each word in *italics*. Use context clues to make your choice.

Vocabulary in Context _____ **6.** "Sociologists use the term *fictive* kin to refer to this stretching of kinship." (paragraph 4)

    a. real   c. invented

    b. desired   d. true

Vocabulary in Context _____ **7.** "Although Asian Americans have adopted the *nuclear* family structure, they have retained Confucian values…" (paragraph 10)

    a. energized   c. secondary

    b. explosive   d. central

Vocabulary in Context _____ **8.** "… they have retained Confucian values that provide a framework for family life: humanism, collectivity, self-discipline, *hierarchy*, respect for the elderly, moderation, and obligation." (paragraph 10)

    a. authority   c. independence

    b. individuality   d. humiliation

Vocabulary in Context _____ **9.** "Perhaps the single most significant issue that Native American families face is whether to follow traditional values or to *assimilate* into the dominant culture." (paragraph 12)

    a. segregate   c. parrot

    b. integrate   d. impress

Vocabulary in Context _____ **10.** "They also place greater emphasis on educational achievement and deferred *gratification*." (paragraph 14)

    a. satisfaction   c. disappointment

    b. repayment   d. demands

Central Idea _____ **11.** Which of the following sentences states the central idea of the passage?

    a. "Rather, family life varies widely throughout the United States." (paragraph 1)

    b. "The primary distinction is not between African Americans and other groups, but between social classes." (paragraph 2)

    c. "From this brief review, you can see that race-ethnicity signifies little for understanding family life." (paragraph 14)

    d. "Another indication of how extensively U.S. families are changing is the increase in one-parent families." (paragraph 15)

Supporting Details _____ **12.** According to Figure 1, "Family Structure," which family group has the largest percentage headed by married couples?

    a. White Americans   d. Asian Americans

    b. Native Americans   e. African Americans

    c. Latinos

Supporting Details _____ **13.** According to Figure 3, "What Percentage of U.S. Married Women Never Give Birth?" which group has the lowest percentage of women who never give birth?

    a. White Americans   c. Asian Americans

    b. African Americans   d. Latinas

Transitions _____ **14.** "Compared with the poor, middle-class families have fewer children and fewer unmarried mothers." (paragraph 14)

The relationship of ideas within this sentence is

    a. cause and effect.   c. comparison and contrast.

    b. classification.   d. generalization and example.

Transitions _____ **15.** "It is difficult to draw generalizations because, as with other racial-ethnic groups, individual Latino families vary considerably (Contreras et al. 2002). Some Latino families, for example, have acculturated to such an extent that they are Protestants who do not speak Spanish." (paragraph 8)

The relationship of ideas between these sentences is

    a. cause and effect.   c. comparison and contrast.

    b. classification.   d. generalization and example.

Thought Patterns _____ **16.** The overall thought pattern for the passage is

    a. cause and effect.   c. comparison and contrast.

    b. classification.   d. definition and example.

Fact and Opinion _____ **17.** "While most married women give birth, about one in five (19 percent) do not (DeOilos and Kapinus 2003)." (paragraph 17)

This sentence is a statement of

    a. fact.   c. fact and opinion.

    b. opinion.

Tone and
Purpose
_____ **18.** The overall tone and purpose of the author is
a. to inform by offering a balanced overview of family groups based on expert opinions and factual detail.
b. to please each family group with positive descriptions.
c. to argue in favor of diversity in families.

Inferences
_____ **19.** Based on the details in "The Brave New World of High-Tech Reproduction" in the *Sociology and the New Technology* box, we can infer that
a. reproductive technology is harmful to families.
b. reproductive technology has complicated the definition of *family*.
c. reproductive technology should be banned.
d. reproductive technology is a widespread method of conceiving children.

Argument
_____ **20.** Read the claim and supports taken from "The Brave New World of High-Tech Reproduction" in the *Sociology and the New Technology* box. Then identify the detail that does not support the claim.

Claim: "Reproductive technologies have laid a trap for the unsuspecting, calling into question even what a mother is."
a. The judge added that Luanne wasn't the baby's mother.
b. Although Pamela Snell gave birth to Jaycee, she is not the mother.
c. How about the donor of the egg? Biologically yes, but legally no.
d. Is Luanne the mother? Fortunately, for Jaycee's sake, a higher court ruled that she is.

Outlining

Complete the following outline with information from the passage "Diversity in U.S. Families."

Central Idea:

I. African American Families

II. _____

III. _____

IV. _____

V. One-Parent Families

VI. _____

VII. Blended Families

VIII. _____

WHAT DO YOU THINK?

How did you respond to this passage? Do you agree with this classification of families? Why or why not? With artificial insemination becoming more common, many children are aware of the method of their conception and want to meet other children from the same sperm donor. To help locate their (half) brothers and sisters, they can consult a website, the Donor Sibling Registry. If your biological father were a sperm donor, would you want to meet him? How about your biological siblings? Why or why not? Assume your state is considering a law that requires open records for children of sperm donors. The law would require sperm donors to register and give a complete medical history. Write a letter to the editor of your local newspaper or to a state representative. In your letter, take a stand for or against a law for open records of sperm donors.

EFFECTIVE READER SCORECARD

"Diversity in U.S. Families"

Skill	Number Correct	Points		Total
Vocabulary				
Vocabulary Preview (5 items)	_____	× 10	=	_____
Vocabulary in Context (5 items)	_____	× 10	=	_____
		Vocabulary Score		_____
Comprehension				
Central Idea (1 item)	_____	× 8	=	_____
Supporting Details (2 items)	_____	× 8	=	_____
Transitions (2 items)	_____	× 8	=	_____
Thought Patterns (1 item)	_____	× 8	=	_____
Fact and Opinion (1 item)	_____	× 8	=	_____
Tone and Purpose (1 item)	_____	× 8	=	_____
Inferences (1 item)	_____	× 8	=	_____
Argument (1 item)	_____	× 8	=	_____
Outlining (5 items)	_____	× 4	=	_____
		Comprehension Score		_____

3

Combined-Skills Tests

Part Three contains 5 tests. The purpose of these tests is twofold: to track your growth as a reader and to prepare you for the formal tests you will face as you take college courses. Each test presents a reading passage and questions that cover some or all of the following skills: vocabulary in context, central ideas, supporting details, thought patterns, fact and opinion, tone and purpose, inferences, and argument. These tests—and 5 additional combined skills tests—can be found in MyReadingLab. By taking the tests in MyReadingLab, you will not only get additional practice and preparation, you will also receive feedback to right and wrong answers. This feedback will help reinforce why an answer is correct, and it will help you understand why an answer is incorrect.

TEST 1

Read the following passage, and then answer the questions.

Against All Odds, Hope, Determination, and Generosity Win

by Sandra Offiah-Hawkins

[1]Life has its ways of attempting to deter one's hopes, dreams, and **aspirations**; however, my life illustrates the power of hope and determination. [2]My lesson begins in Picayune, a little southern town in Mississippi.

[3]You see, at the very young, easy-to-influence age of fifteen, I became pregnant while attending a church conference in Biloxi, Mississippi. [4]As an eleventh grade African American high school student in my hometown, my educational process would normally have been discontinued until after the birth of the child. [5]Therefore, I opted to keep my **predicament** a secret that I shared only with a close friend, Carolyn—to whom I offered many excuses about why I could not tell my parents; however, the most important one, I thought, was that they would kill me—I was determined to stay in school. [6]Although Carolyn did not disclose my secret, for she had been sworn to secrecy, each day she tried to convince me that honesty in this case was indeed the best policy and that sooner or later the truth would inevitably be revealed.

[7]During this time, I contemplated suicide. [8]My logic: I didn't want to "disappoint" my family. [9]If I had told the school counselor, who was a close family friend, he would have told my parents and suggested I remain out of school until the birth of the baby the following year.

[10]Finally, after a great deal of thought—and the fact that I was literally running out of time—I decided to tell my mother. [11]She was deeply saddened. [12]I shall never forget what she said to me on that day, "Baby, everyone makes mistakes; just don't make it a habit." [13]My mother told my father, who was crushed by the news; I had always been the closest to him of his five daughters. [14]Carolyn and I were both relieved when the pressure of secrecy ended. [15]My daughter, Daphne, was born, and my education had not been interrupted.

[16]I had never been an "A" student, but I was always an outgoing, witty, and determined "B" student. [17]During my senior year of high school, I longed to try out for the part of Mama in *A Raisin in the Sun* by Lorraine Hansberry. [18]For a while I gave excuses why I could not take the part: the

baby needed me, I had no time to study lines, and yes, I was pregnant with baby number two.

[19]Many people facing this new crisis would say to hell with the play, but I decided to take the lead role in *A Raisin in the Sun*. [20]Although I was six months pregnant and only days away from high school graduation, I played the part of Mama in what others told me was a "breathtaking performance," and I felt as though everyone in my African American community was there. [21]Today, people in Picayune still talk about my performance that evening, and during my graduation ceremony, I received a trophy for best actor.

[22]I had thought I might get a college scholarship. [23]Since seventh grade, I had been playing the trombone in Carver High School's marching and concert bands. [24]By the time I became a senior, my band director, Mr. Simmons, was convinced I would receive a full band scholarship to Jackson State University and become a member of the Sonic Boom of the South. [25]Because of my latest pregnancy, I knew that I would be unable to attend summer camp in preparation for the fall semester, so I had to inform the band director that I was unable to take advantage of the opportunity my talent and hard work had earned me.

[26]There didn't appear to be any hope of receiving a college education with one child and another on the way, especially given my family's financial situation. [27]Yet, I did hope. [28]I was determined to get an education.

[29]A few days after graduating from high school, I moved to Jackson, Mississippi, to live with my sister and her family in a cramped one-bedroom apartment. [30]A couple of months later, my parents generously offered to take care of my daughter, for it was almost time for the new baby.

[31]Two weeks after the birth of my son, I started college at Utica Junior College in Utica, Mississippi. [32]For the next two years, I commuted to college 45 miles on a 6:00 A.M. bus.

[33]My sister, who taught at the school, informed the band director of my musical abilities. [34]He offered to pay for my tuition and books if I would join the band. [35]Although I had planned to stop playing the instrument after the birth of my second child, I agreed to become captain of the trombone section in the marching and concert bands.

[36]Later, faced with the problem of finding a place for my son and me to live, I met an elderly woman, Ms. Woods, who ran a day care center and rented rooms to 18 college girls. [37]Ms. Woods agreed to share her room with us until a bed became available. [38]We stayed in that room with her for more than a year. [39]For the first four years of his life, Ms. Woods's home was the only home my son ever knew.

⁴⁰Upon completion of my A.A. Degree, I transferred to Jackson State, which was located only two blocks from where we lived. ⁴¹The girls in the house would care for my son, Nick, while I worked and went to class. ⁴²By working two jobs to put myself through my last two years of college, I received a B.A. in English Literature. ⁴³I could not wait to finally have both my children living under the same roof, so I moved back home.

⁴⁴After returning home and teaching at East Side Elementary School for one year, I decided to uproot my small family and return to Jackson State to obtain certification in Reading and English. ⁴⁵A year and a half later, I received my M.A.T. in English and Reading.

⁴⁶I have taught English and Reading at two different colleges now for more than 23 years and am currently a professor and the Assistant Chair of the English Department. ⁴⁷I give thanks to God Almighty for all the many generous blessings He continues to bestow upon me—including hope and determination.

—Offiah-Hawkins, Sandra. "Against All Odds, Hope, Determination and Generosity Win" by Sandra Offiah-Hawkins. Reprinted by permission of the author.

Vocabulary   _____   **1.** The best meaning of the word **aspirations** as used in sentence 1 is
         a. barriers.   c. thoughts.
         b. ambitions.   d. differences.

Vocabulary   _____   **2.** The best meaning of the word **predicament** as used in sentence 5 is
         a. position.   c. opportunity.
         b. dilemma.   d. contradiction.

Central Idea   _____   **3.** Choose the sentence that best states the author's central idea.
         a. sentence 1   c. sentence 3
         b. sentence 2   d. sentence 47

Main Idea,   _____   **4.** Sentence 9 is
Details
         a. a main idea.   c. a minor supporting detail.
         b. a major supporting detail.

Thought   _____   **5.** Which thought pattern is suggested by the relationship between
Patterns   sentences 4 and 5?
         a. cause and effect   c. contrast
         b. classification   d. example

Transitions   _____   **6.** What is the relationship of ideas within sentence 40?
         a. contrast   c. space order
         b. classification   d. example

Purpose _____ **7.** The author's purpose is
  a. to entertain readers with lively details from her life.
  b. to inspire readers by sharing personal experiences of overcoming life's challenges.
  c. to inform readers about the difficulties of life.

Argument _____ **8.** We can conclude that the author's driving goal was
  a. to become a mother.
  b. to receive a college education.
  c. to become a musical performer.
  d. to get off of welfare.

Tone _____ **9.** The tone of sentence 8 is
  a. matter-of-fact.   c. ironic.
  b. bitter.   d. reflective.

Fact and Opinion _____ **10.** Sentence 16 states
  a. fact.   c. fact and opinion.
  b. opinion.

TEST 2

Read the following passage about teenage use of technology. Then answer the questions that follow.

Teens and Technology

[1]Several reports in recent years by the Pew Internet & American Life Project have documented some dramatic changes in teenagers' use of the Internet. [2]No longer are youths tied to a desktop in a building. [3]Now most carry mobile devices that enable "always-on" connections anywhere they go.

[4]According to the most recent report *Teens and Technology 2013*, a survey of hundreds of parents and their teenagers (12-years-old to 17-years-old) indicate that 78% of teens own cell phones, and half of those own smartphones. [5]This means that 37% of all teens own a smartphone, up from 23% in 2011.

[6]Most teenagers still own and use other types of devices. [7]According to *Teens 2012*, 80% teens have a desktop or laptop computer. [8]Nearly one-quarter (23%) of teens have a tablet computer. [9]Among the 20% of teens who do not have their own computer, two-thirds (67%) have access to one at home that they share with family. [10]Thus the report concludes, 93% of teens have a computer or access to one.

[11]However, despite access to such a variety of devices, the cell phone is rapidly gaining popularity as the main way teenagers access the Internet. [12]One in four teens identify themselves as "cell mostly" Internet users (*Teens and Technology 2013*).

[13]Additionally, social media drives teen use of the Internet: 81% use some kind of social media; 77% access Facebook. [14]And 24% use Twitter, a figure that is up from 16% in 2011, which was up from 8% in 2010 (*Pew Internet: Teens 2012*).[15]Obviously, Twitter is a growing **niche** for teen users.

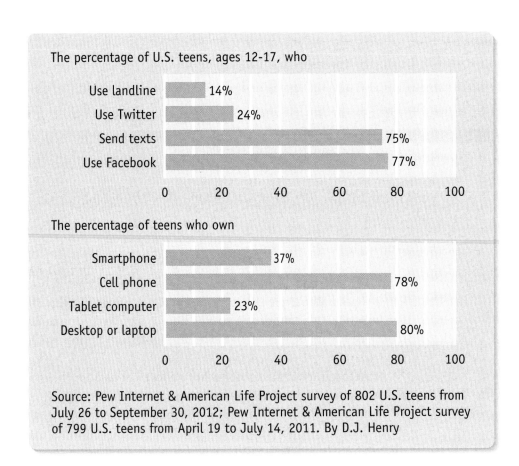

The percentage of U.S. teens, ages 12-17, who

Use landline	14%
Use Twitter	24%
Send texts	75%
Use Facebook	77%

0   20   40   60   80   100

The percentage of teens who own

Smartphone	37%
Cell phone	78%
Tablet computer	23%
Desktop or laptop	80%

0   20   40   60   80   100

Source: Pew Internet & American Life Project survey of 802 U.S. teens from July 26 to September 30, 2012; Pew Internet & American Life Project survey of 799 U.S. teens from April 19 to July 14, 2011. By D.J. Henry

¹⁶The report *Teens, Smartphones & Texting 2012* indicates that 75% of all teens text, and 63% send text messages everyday. ¹⁷The number of texts they send has also risen from 50 texts a day in 2009 to 60 texts for the average teenage user. ¹⁸In contrast, the use of landlines has **plummeted** to half of what it was in 2009. ¹⁹Only 14% of all teens admit to daily use of a landline to talk with friends, in contrast to the 30% who claimed to do so in 2009. ²⁰Nearly a third (31%) of teens say they never use or do not have access to a landline. ²¹Surprisingly, only 26% of all teens claim to talk daily with friends on their cell phone, down from 38% of teens in 2009.

²²One teen recently interviewed about her take on this trend said, "Everybody has a smartphone—it's the only way to go!"

Vocabulary _____ **1.** The best meaning of the word *niche* in sentence 15 is
a. role.   c. recess.
b. problem.   d. device.

Vocabulary _____ **2.** The best meaning of the word *plummeted* in sentence 18 is
a. climbed.   c. dropped.
b. thrust.   d. held.

Central Idea _____ **3.** The sentence that best states the central idea of the passage is
a. sentence 1.   c. sentence 3.
b. sentence 2.   d. sentence 4.

Supporting Details _____ **4.** According to the chart, which device is a teen least likely to use?
a. smartphone   c. tablet computer
b. cellphone   d. desktop

Supporting Details _____ **5.** According to the chart, teenagers most use technology to
a. use Twitter.   c. call others on a landline.
b. send text messages. d. use Facebook.

Transitions _____ **6.** The relationship of ideas between sentence 10 and sentence 11 is
a. time order.   c. cause and effect.
b. addition.   d. contrast.

Thought Patterns _____ **7.** The main thought pattern of the passage is
a. time order.   c. generalization and example.
b. cause and effect.   d. contrast.

Tone   _____   **8.** The overall tone of the passage is
                        a. biased.   b. objective.

Purpose   _____   **9.** The overall purpose of the passage is
                        a. to inform the reader about recent research findings about teen use of technology.
                        b. to amuse the reader with information about teen use of technology.
                        c. to persuade the reader to change his or her use of technology based on recent research.

Fact and   _____   **10.** Sentence 21 states
Opinion
                        a. a fact.   c. fact and opinion.
                        b. an opinion.

Argument   _____   **11.** The statement, "Everybody has a smartphone—it's the only way to go!" (sentence 22) is an example of the fallacy
                        a. name-calling
                        b. false cause.
                        c. transfer.
                        d. bandwagon.

TEST 3

Read the following passage, and then answer the questions.

Anorexia Nervosa

¹People who deliberately starve themselves or severely restrict their food intake suffer from an eating disorder called **anorexia nervosa**. ²The disorder usually begins around the time of puberty and leads to extreme weight loss—at least 15 percent below normal body weight. ³Those who struggle with this problem also have an intense fear of becoming fat, even though they are underweight. ⁴Many people with the disorder look **emaciated**, yet they are convinced that

they are overweight. ⁵Sometimes they must be hospitalized to prevent death by starvation. ⁶Still, they often continue to deny that they have a problem or face any health risk. ⁷Food and weight become obsessions. ⁸For some, the compulsiveness shows up in strange eating rituals or the refusal to eat in front of others. ⁹It is not uncommon for people with anorexia to collect recipes and prepare lavish gourmet feasts for family and friends but not partake in the meals themselves. ¹⁰They may adhere to strict exercise routines to keep off weight. ¹¹Ninety percent of all anorexics are women.

¹²The most important thing that family and friends can do to help individuals with anorexia is to love them unconditionally. ¹³Talk to physicians or counselors for help in determining the best way to approach and deal with the situation. ¹⁴People with anorexia will beg and lie to avoid eating and gaining weight; achieving a cure means giving up the illness and hence giving up the control. ¹⁵Family and friends should not give in to the pleadings of an anorexic patient but should not nag the person **incessantly** either. ¹⁶Anorexia is an illness that cannot be controlled by simple willpower; professional guidance is needed. ¹⁷Most important is to support the individual without supporting the person's actions.

—Adapted from National Women's Health Information
Center, "Anorexia Nervosa."

Vocabulary _____ **1.** The best meaning of the word *emaciated* as used in sentence 4 is
    a. wasted.   c. embarrassed.
    b. heavy.   d. willful.

Vocabulary _____ **2.** The best meaning of the word *incessantly* as used in sentence 15 is
    a. endlessly, all the time.   c. with violence.
    b. in silence.   d. with good intentions.

Main Idea _____ **3.** Which sentence best states the main idea of the second paragraph?
    a. sentence 12   c. sentence 14
    b. sentence 13   d. sentence 15

Implied
Central Idea _____ **4.** What is the implied central idea of the passage?
    a. Many people suffer from the condition known as anorexia nervosa.
    b. Anorexia nervosa is an eating disorder that has horrible consequences.
    c. The person suffering from anorexia nervosa faces mental and physical problems and requires the support of others.

d. Those who suffer from anorexia nervosa often deny that they have a life-threatening disorder.

Transitions _____ **5.** The relationship between sentences 5 and 6 is one of
    a. time order.   c. contrast.
    b. example.   d. cause.

Inferences _____ **6.** Choose the inference that is most soundly based on the information in the passage.
    a. Anorexia nervosa is not a serious problem.
    b. Anorexia nervosa is the result of childhood trauma.
    c. People who suffer from anorexia nervosa are seeking some sort of control over their lives.
    d. People who suffer from anorexia nervosa are selfish.

7–10. Complete the idea map based on the information in the passage.

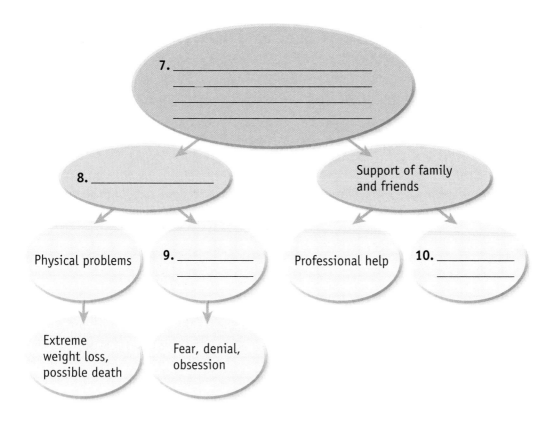

TEST 4

Read the following passage, and then answer the questions.

The Health of Routines and Rituals

[1]Routines and rituals are alive and well in the United States—and keeping people well in the process. [2]That's the claim of a review of 50 years of research that appears in the December 2002 issue of the *Journal of Family Psychology*. [3]Many Americans take part in routines and rituals, and these practices help to improve their mental and physical health and sense of belonging, according to the researchers who did the analysis of 32 studies. [4]Routine events, such as evening dinners eaten together as a family, provide comfort simply by being predictable events people can count on, says study author Barbara Fiese, a psychologist at Syracuse University in New York.

[5]Routines are acts done regularly that need to be done, such as eating or preparing for bed, and take time but are seldom thought about afterward, she says. [6]"Having some predictability in life around routines is positive," Fiese says. [7]Children flourish when they can predict things in their life, such as family dinners or regular bedtimes, the study found. [8]Regular family dinners, even if only for 20 minutes a day, are the most common routine. [9]"If you look at dinner time, for example, it's not happening seven days a week but usually four or five times," Fiese says. [10]"Even that short period of time has a positive effect. [11]It's related to physical health in infants and children and academic performance in elementary children."

[12]Rituals, on the other hand, are symbolic practices people do or celebrate that help define who they are—and about which they often **reminisce**, she notes. [13]Every ritual stands for something, such as marriage, which is an entrance into a family. [14]The meaningful, symbolic parts of rituals seem to help emotional development and satisfaction with family relationships. [15]When rituals are continued during times of stress, such as a divorce, they lessen the negative impact. [16]"They have the potential to protect kids from risks associated with one-parent families," Fiese says. [17]"It seems that at points of transition, such as school or marriage, rituals can increase one's sense of security."

—Adapted from Deutsch, Nancy. "A Slave to Routine?" by Nancy Deutsch, *HealthDay News*. Copyright © 2013 HealthDay. All Rights Reserved. Reprinted by permission.

Vocabulary _____ **1.** The best meaning of the word *reminisce* as used in sentence 12 is
  a. guess.   c. remember.
  b. harp.   d. stare.

Central Idea _____ **2.** The sentence that best states the central idea of the passage is
  a. sentence 1.   c. sentence 5.
  b. sentence 2.   d. sentence 12.

Transitions _____ **3.** The relationship between sentences 11 and 12 is one of
  a. definition and example.
  b. cause and effect.
  c. time order.
  d. comparison and contrast.

Transitions _____ **4.** The relationship of the ideas within sentence 5 is
  a. definition and example.   c. time order.
  b. cause and effect.   d. comparison and contrast.

Thought _____ **5.** Which thought pattern does the passage use in addition to definition?
Patterns
  a. comparison   c. time order
  b. effect

Supporting _____ **6.** Sentence 16 is a
Details
  a. central idea.   c. minor supporting detail.
  b. major supporting detail.

Purpose _____ **7.** The author's main purpose in the passage is to
  a. inform.   c. persuade.
  b. entertain.

Tone _____ **8.** The tone of the passage is
  a. excited.   c. objective.
  b. bossy.   d. pessimistic.

9–10. Complete the study outline with information from the passage.

Central idea: _____

_____

   I. Routines

      A. Definition: acts done regularly that need to be done and take time but
         are seldom thought about afterward

B. Examples

   1. _____

   2. Preparing for bed

C. Effects

   1. Improve physical health in infants and children

   2. Improve academic performance in elementary children

II. Rituals

A. Definition: symbolic practices people do or celebrate that help define who they are—and about which they often reminisce

B. Example: Marriage

C. Effects

   1. Protect children from risks linked to one-parent families

   2. Increase sense of security

TEST 5

Read the following passage, and then answer the questions.

"Boyhood Days"

Taken from *Up from Slavery* by Booker T. Washington

[1]From the time that I can remember having any thoughts about anything, I recall that I had an intense longing to learn to read. [2]I determined, when quite a small child, that, if I accomplished nothing else in life, I would in some way get enough education to enable me to read common books and newspapers. [3]Soon after we got settled in some manner in our new cabin in West Virginia, I **induced** my mother to get hold of a book for me. [4]How or where she got it I do not know, but in some way she procured an old copy of Webster's "blue-back" spelling-book, which contained the alphabet, followed by such meaningless words as "ab," "ba," "ca," "da." [5]I began at once to devour this book, and I think

that it was the first one I ever had in my hands. [6]I had learned from somebody that the way to begin to read was to learn the alphabet, so I tried in all the ways I could think of to learn it,—all of course without a teacher, for I could find no one to teach me. [7]At that time there was not a single member of my race anywhere near us who could read, and I was too timid to approach any of the white people. [8]In some way, within a few weeks, I mastered the greater portion of the alphabet. [9]In all my efforts to learn to read my mother shared full my ambition, and sympathized with me and aided me in every way that she could. [10]Though she was totally ignorant, so far as mere book knowledge was concerned, she had high ambitions for her children, and a large fund of good hard, common sense which seemed to enable her to meet and master every situation. [11]If I have done anything in life worth attention, I feel sure that I inherited the **disposition** from my mother.

[12]In the midst of my struggles and longing for an education, a young coloured boy who had learned to read in the state of Ohio came to Malden. [13]As soon as the coloured people found out that he could read, a newspaper was secured, and at the close of nearly every day's work this young man would be surrounded by a group of men and women who were anxious to hear him read the news contained in the papers. [14]How I used to envy this man! [15]He seemed to me to be the one young man in all the world who ought to be satisfied with his attainments.

[16]About this time the question of having some kind of a school opened for the coloured children in the village began to be discussed by members of the race. [17]As it would be the first school for Negro children that had ever been opened in that part of Virginia, it was, of course, to be a great event, and the discussion excited the widest interest.

* * *

[18]This experience of a whole race beginning to go to school for the first time presents one of the most interesting studies that has ever occurred in connection with the development of any race. [19]Few people who were not right in the midst of the scenes can form any exact idea of the intense desire which the people of my race showed for an education. [20]As I have stated, it was a whole race trying to go to school. [21]Few were too young, and none too old, to make the attempt to learn. [22]As fast as any kind of teachers could be secured, not only were day-schools filled, but night-schools as well. [23]The great ambition of the older people was to try to learn to read the Bible before they died. [24]With this end in view, men and women who were fifty or seventy-five years old would often be found in the night-school. [25]Sunday-schools were formed soon after freedom, but the principal book studied in the Sunday-school was

the spelling-book. [26]Day-school, night-school, Sunday-school, were always crowded, and often many had to be turned away for want of room.

Booker T. Washington, *Up from Slavery: An Autobiography.* New York: Doubleday, Page, 1901; Bartleby.com, 2000. www.bartleby.com/1004/. 30 July 2007.

Vocabulary _____ **1.** The best meaning of the word *induced* in sentence 3 is
    a. offered.   c. persuaded.
    b. stopped.   d. allowed.

Vocabulary _____ **2.** The best meaning of the word *disposition* in sentence 11 is
    a. situation.   c. problem.
    b. character.   d. need.

Central Idea _____ **3.** Which sentence best states the central idea of this passage?
    a. sentence 1   c. sentence 9
    b. sentence 2   d. sentence 15

Transitions _____ **4.** The relationship between sentences 12 and 13 is one of
    a. time order.   c. contrast.
    b. effect.   d. example.

Main Ideas, _____ **5.** Sentence 14 is a
Details
    a. main idea.   c. minor supporting detail.
    b. major supporting detail.

Fact and _____ **6.** Sentence 15 is a statement of
Opinion
    a. fact.   c. fact and opinion.
    b. opinion.

Inferences _____ **7.** Based on the information in the passage, we can infer that Booker T. Washington
    a. was a hardworking student.
    b. neglected work and chores to learn to read.
    c. was ashamed because he couldn't read.
    d. was one of many of his race who could read.

8–10. Complete the following time line with information from the passage.

    I. Washington determines to learn to read

   II. The influence of his **(8)** _____

  III. His envy of a man who can **(9)** _____

  IV. The opening of a **(10)** _____

    V. The whole race learns to read

Text Credits

Agee, Warren K., et al., *Introduction to Mass Communications.* © 1997. Reprinted and Electronically reproduced by permission of Pearson Education, Inc., Upper Saddle River, New Jersey.

Altshuler, Michael L., From "The Management Quotes: Recognizing the Importance of Time Management," Time-Management-Central.net. Reprinted by permission of the author.

Anderson, Lydia E. and Bolt, Sandra B., *Professionalism: Skills for Workplace Success,* 2nd ed., © 2011. Printed and Electronically reproduced by permission of Pearson Education, Inc., Upper Saddle River, New Jersey.

Aronson, Elliot, *Social Psychology,* 8th ed. © 2013. Printed and Electronically reproduced by permission of Pearson Education, Inc., Upper Saddle River, New Jersey.

Audesirk, Teresa, Audesirk, Gerald, and Byers, Bruce E., *Biology: Life on Earth,* 5th ed. © 2009. Reprinted and Electronically reproduced by permission of Pearson Education, Inc., Upper Saddle River, New Jersey.

Audesirk, Teresa, Audesirk, Gerald, and Byers, Bruce E., *Biology: Life on Earth with Physiology,* 9th ed. © 2011. Printed and Electronically reproduced by permission of Pearson Education, Inc., Upper Saddle River, New Jersey.

Benokraitis, Nijoke, *Marriage and Families: Changes, Choices and Constraints.* © 2002. Printed and Electronically reproduced by permission of Pearson Education, Inc., Upper Saddle River, New Jersey.

Bergman, Edward and Renwick, William H., *Introduction to Geography: People, Places and Environment,* 4th ed. © 2008. Printed and Electronically reproduced by permission of Pearson Education, Inc., Upper Saddle River, New Jersey.

Berman, Audrey J., Snyder, Shirlee, Kozier, Barbara J., and Erb, Glenora, *Kozier & Erb's Fundamentals of Nursing,* 8th ed. © 2008. Printed and Electronically reproduced by permission of Pearson Education, Inc., Upper Saddle River, New Jersey.

Bittinger, Marvin L. and Beecher, Judith A., *Introductory and Intermediate Algebra: A Combined Approach,* 2nd ed. © 2003. Printed and Electronically reproduced by permission of Pearson Education, Inc., Upper Saddle River, New Jersey.

Blake, Joan, *Nutrition and You,* 2nd ed. © 2012. Reprinted and Electronically reproduced by permission of Pearson Education, Inc., Upper Saddle River, New Jersey.

Brownell, Judi, *Listening: Attitudes, Principles, and Skills,* 2nd ed. © 2002. Reprinted and Electronically reproduced by permission of Pearson Education, Inc., Upper Saddle River, New Jersey.

Carl, John D., *Think Sociology*, 11th ed. © 2011. Reprinted and Electronically reproduced by permission of Pearson Education, Inc., Upper Saddle River, New Jersey.

Carlson, Neil, and William Buskist, *Psychology: Science of Behavior,* 5th ed. © 1997. Reprinted and Electronically reproduced by permission of Pearson Education, Inc., Upper Saddle River, New Jersey.

Ciccarelli, Saundra K. and White, J. Noland, *Psychology: An Exploration,* © 2010. Printed and Electronically reproduced by permission of Pearson Education, Inc., Upper Saddle River, New Jersey.

DeVito, Joseph A., *The Essential Elements of Public Speaking,* 4th ed. © 2012. Printed and Electronically reproduced by permission of Pearson Education, Inc., Upper Saddle River, New Jersey.

DeVito, Joseph A., *Essentials of Human Communication,* 5th ed. © 2002. Reprinted and Electronically reproduced by permission of Pearson Education, Inc., Upper Saddle River, New Jersey.

DeVito, Joseph A., *Essentials of Human Communication,* 7th ed. © 2002. Printed and Electronically reproduced by permission of Pearson Education, Inc., Upper Saddle River, New Jersey.

DeVito, Joseph A., *Human Communication: The Basic Course,* 12th ed. © 2102. Reprinted and Electronically reproduced by permission of Pearson Education, Inc., Upper Saddle River, New Jersey.

DeVito, Joseph A. *Interpersonal Communication Book.* © 2009. Reprinted and Electronically reproduced by permission of Pearson Education, Inc., Upper Saddle River, New Jersey.

DeVito, Joseph A., *The Interpersonal Communication Book*, 10th ed. © 2004. Printed and Electronically reproduced by permission of Pearson Education, Inc., Upper Saddle River, New Jersey.

DeVito, Joseph A., *Messages: Building Interpersonal Communication Skills.* © 2004. Reprinted and Electronically reproduced by permission of Pearson Education, Inc., Upper Saddle River, New Jersey.

Divine, Robert A., Breen, T. H. H., Frederickson, George M., and Williams, R. Hal. *The American Story,* 16th ed. © 2002. Printed and Electronically reproduced by permission of Pearson Education, Inc., Upper Saddle River, New Jersey.

DiYanni, Robert, and Pat C. Hoy II, *The Scribner Handbook for Writers,* 3rd ed. Copyright © 2001, 1998, 1995 by Allyn and Bacon. Reprinted and Electronically reproduced by permission of Pearson Education, Inc., Upper Saddle River, New Jersey.

Donatelle, Rebecca J., *Access to Health,* 12th ed. © 2012. Reprinted and Electronically reproduced by permission of Pearson Education, Inc., Upper Saddle River, New Jersey.

Donatelle, Rebecca J., *Health: The Basics,* 5th ed. © 2003. Printed and electronically reproduced by permission of Pearson Education, Inc., Upper Saddle River, New Jersey.

Donatelle, Rebecca J., *Health: The Basics, Green Edition.* Reprinted and Electronically reproduced by permission of Pearson Education, Inc., Upper Saddle River, New Jersey.

Donatelle, Rebecca J. and Davis, Lorraine G., *Access to Health,* 7th ed. © 2002. Reprinted and Electronically reproduced by permission of Pearson Education, Inc., Upper Saddle River, New Jersey.

Eshleman, J. Ross and Richard A. Bulcroft., *The Family,* 12th ed. © 2010. Printed and Electronically reproduced by permission of Pearson Education, Inc., Upper Saddle River, New Jersey.

Garraty, John A. and Mark C. Carnes, *American Nation Single Volume Edition.* © 2000. Reprinted and Electronically reproduced by permission of Pearson Education, Inc., Upper Saddle River, New Jersey.

Gerrig, Richard J. and Zimbardo, Philip G., *Psychology and Life,* 16th ed. © 2002. Printed and Electronically reproduced by permission of Pearson Education, Inc., Upper Saddle River, New Jersey.

Giannetti, Louis, *Understanding Movies*, 12th ed. © 2011. Printed and Electronically reproduced by permission of Pearson Education, Inc., Upper Saddle River, New Jersey.

Griffin, Ricky W. and Ebert, Ronald J., *Business*, 8th ed. © 2006. Printed and Electronically reproduced by permission of Pearson Education, Inc., Upper Saddle River, New Jersey.

Hames, Joanne and Yvonne Ekern. *Introduction to Law*, 4th ed. Upper Saddle River: Pearson Education, 2010, p. 24.

Henslin, James M., *Sociology: A Down-to-Earth Approach*, 9th ed. © 2008. Reprinted and Electronically reproduced by permission of Pearson Education, Inc., Upper Saddle River, New Jersey.

Hewitt, Paul G., *Conceptual Physical Science*, 2nd ed. © 2010. Printed and Electronically reproduced by permission of Pearson Education, Inc., Upper Saddle River, New Jersey.

Hopson, Janet L. *Get Fit, Stay Well!* © 2009. Printed and Electronically reproduced by permission of Pearson Education, Inc., Upper Saddle River, New Jersey.

Janaro, Richard and Altschuler, Thelma, *The Art of Being Human: The Humanities as a Technique for Living*, 10th ed. © 2012. Printed and Electronically reproduced by permission of Pearson Education, Inc., Upper Saddle River, New Jersey.

Kelly, Marilyn, *Communication @ Work*. Boston: Allyn & Bacon, 2006, p. 70.

Kennedy, X. J. and Gioia, Dana, *Literature: An Introduction to Fiction, Poetry, and Drama*, 8th ed., Interactive Edition. Copyright © 2002 by X. J. Kennedy and Dana Gioia. Reprinted and Electronically reproduced by permission of Pearson Education, Inc., Upper Saddle River, New Jersey.

Kosslyn, Stephen M. and Rosenberg, Robin S. *Psychology: The Brain, The Person, The World*. © 2001. Reprinted and Electronically reproduced by permission of Pearson Education, Inc., Upper Saddle River, New Jersey.

Lilienfield, Scott O., Lynn, Steven J., Namy, Laura L., and Woolf, Nancy J., *Psychology: A Framework for Everyday Thinking*, © 2010. Printed and Electronically reproduced by permission of Pearson Education, Inc., Upper Saddle River, New Jersey.

Lutgens, Frederick K., Tarbuck, Edward J., and Tasa, Dennis G., *Foundations of Earth Science*, 5th ed. © 2008. Printed and Electronically reproduced by permission of Pearson Education, Inc., Upper Saddle River, New Jersey.

Madura, Jeff, *Personal Finance Update*, 2nd ed. © 2006. Reprinted and Electronically reproduced by permission of Pearson Education, Inc., Upper Saddle River, New Jersey.

Maier, Richard, *Comparative Animal Behavior: An Evolutionary and Ecological Approach*. Boston: Allyn & Bacon, 1998.

Marieb, Elaine N., *Essentials of Human Anatomy and Physiology*, 9th. ed. © 2009. Printed and Electronically reproduced by permission of Pearson Education, Inc., Upper Saddle River, New Jersey.

Martin, James Kirby, Roberts, Randy J., Mintz, Steven, McMurry, Linda O. and Jones, James H., *America and Its People: Volume II: A Mosaic in the Making*, 3rd ed. © 1999. Printed and Electronically reproduced by permission of Pearson Education, Inc., Upper Saddle River, New Jersey.

Maslow, Abraham H., Frager, Robert D., and Fadiman, James, *Motivation and Personality*, 3rd ed. © 1987. Printed and Electronically reproduced by permission of Pearson Education, Inc., Upper Saddle River, New Jersey.

McGuigan, F. J., *Encyclopedia of Stress*. © 1999. Printed and Electronically reproduced by permission of Pearson Education, Inc., Upper Saddle River, New Jersey.

O'Connor, Karen and Larry J. Sabato, *American Government: Continuity and Change*. © 2000. Printed and Electronically reproduced by permission of Pearson Education, Inc., Upper Saddle River, New Jersey.

Parkay, Forrest, W. and Stanford, Beverly, *Becoming a Teacher*. © 1995. Reprinted and Electronically reproduced by permission of Pearson Education, Inc., Upper Saddle River, New Jersey.

Potter, Patricia, et al., *Fundamentals of Nursing*, 8th ed., p. 940. © 2008. Reprinted and Electronically reproduced by permission of Pearson Education, Inc., Upper Saddle River, New Jersey.

Powers, Scott K. and Stephen L. Dodd, *Total Fitness and Wellness*. © 2003. Printed and Electronically reproduced by permission of Pearson Education, Inc., Upper Saddle River, New Jersey.

Pruitt, B. E. and Jane J. Stein, *Healthstyles: Decisions for Living Well*, 2nd. ed. © 1999. Printed and electronically reproduced by permission of Pearson Education, Inc., Upper Saddle River, New Jersey.

Sayre, Henry M., *Discovering the Humanities*. © 2010. Reprinted and Electronically reproduced by permission of Pearson Education, Inc., Upper Saddle River, New Jersey.

Schmalleger, Frank J., *Criminal Justice: A Brief Introduction*, 9th ed. © 2012. Printed and Electronically reproduced by permission of Pearson Education, Inc., Upper Saddle River, New Jersey.

Schmalleger, Frank J., *Criminal Justice Today: An Introductory Text for the 21st Century*, 10th ed. © 2009. Printed and Electronically reproduced by permission of Pearson Education, Inc., Upper Saddle River, New Jersey.

Schwartz, Mary Ann A. and Scott, Barbara Marliene, *Marriage and Families: Diversity and Change*, 6th ed. © 2010. Printed and Electronically reproduced by permission of Pearson Education, Inc., Upper Saddle River, New Jersey.

Solomon, Michael R., Poatsy, Mary Anne, and Martin, Kendall, *Better Business*, 2nd ed. © 2012. Printed and Electronically reproduced by permission of Pearson Education, Inc., Upper Saddle River, New Jersey.

Tarbuck, Frederick K., Lutgens, Edward J., and Tasa, Dennis G., *Essentials of Geology*, 11th ed. © 2012. Reprinted and Electronically reproduced by permission of Pearson Education, Inc., Upper Saddle River, New Jersey.

Van Syckle, Barbara and Tietje, Brian, *Anybody's Business*. © 2010. Reprinted and Electronically reproduced by permission of Pearson Education, Inc., Upper Saddle River, New Jersey.

Walker, John R., *Introduction to Hospitality Management*, 3rd ed. © 2010. Printed and Electronically reproduced by permission of Pearson Education, Inc., Upper Saddle River, New Jersey.

Walker, John R. and Walker, Josielyn T., *Tourism: Concepts and Practices, 1st Edition*, © 2011. Reprinted by permission of Pearson Education, Inc., Upper Saddle River, NJ.

Withgott, Jay H. and Scott R. Brennan, *Essential Environment: The Science Behind the Stories*, 3rd ed. © 2009. Printed and Electronically reproduced by permission of Pearson Education, Inc., Upper Saddle River, New Jersey.

Wood, Samuel E., Wood, Ellen Green, and Boyd, Denise, *Mastering the World of Psychology*, 3rd ed. © 2008. Reprinted and Electronically reproduced by permission of Pearson Education, Inc., Upper Saddle River, New Jersey.

Zimbardo, Philip G., Johnson, Robert L., and Hamilton, Vivian McCann, *Psychology: Core Concepts*, 7th ed. © 2012. Printed and Electronically reproduced by permission of Pearson Education, Inc., Upper Saddle River, New Jersey.

Photo Credits

p. 19, Michael Drager/Shutterstock; pp. v, 28, Creativ Studio Heinemann/Alloy/Corbis; p. 31, Lori Adamski Peek/Stone/Getty Images; p. 48, Ian Hooton/Science Photo Library/Corbis; p. 49, MedicalRF.com/Corbis; p. 57, pryzmat/ Shutterstock; pp. vi, 89, Frank Burek/Corbis; p. 106, Ocean/Corbis; p. 110, Designua/Shutterstock; p. 115, Juan Medina/Reuters/Corbis; p. 140, Barry Mason/Alamy; pp. vii, 150, Punchstock/ Getty Images; p. 159, Frenzeny and Tavernier/Historical/Corbis; p. 167, Anna Maloverjan/Shutterstock; p. 208, Dennis MacDonald/Superstock; p. 226, U.S. Fire Administration/FEMA; pp. viii, 232, Jim Ruymen/Reuters/Corbis; p. 244, Romilly Lockyer/ The Image Bank /Getty Images; p. 244, iStock/Thinkstock; p. 251, Vincent Laforet/ Pool/ Reuters/Corbis; p. 273, O Driscoll Imaging/Shutterstock; p. 286, corepics/Shutterstock; p. 293, ArteSub/Alamy; pp. ix, 305, Bill Ross/ Cusp/Corbis; p. 310, MedicalRF.com/Corbis; p. 316, Alessandro Saffo/ Latitude/Corbis; p. 330, StevenRussellSmithPhotos/Shutterstock; p. 333, Dann Tardif/Bridge/Corbis; p. 373, Walter Geiersperger/ Encyclopedia/Corbis; p. 410, Paul Souders/ Documentary Value/Corbis; p. 412, Jimmy Margulies/Cagle Cartoons, Inc.; p. 418, Brian Snyder/Reuters/Corbis; p. 421 left, Library of Congress Prints and Photographs Division[LC-USZ62-72266]; p. 421 right, INTERFOTO / Personalities/INTERFOTO/Alamy; p. 425, right and left, Cumberland County Historical Society; p. 428 top, iStockphoto/Thinkstock; p. 428 bottom, AstroBoi/Fotolia; p. 442, moodboard/Superstock;

p. 458, Katie Orlinsky/Corbis News/Corbis; p. 464, moodboard/Corbis; p. 480, John Cole/Cagle Cartoons, Inc.; p. 484, Robert Mankoff / The New Yorker Collection/www.cartoonbank.com; p. 492, Ralf-Finn Hestoft/Corbis News/Corbis; p. 502, Martin Harvey/ Documentary Value/Corbis; pp. xi, 505, JEON HEON-KYUN/Newscom; p. 507, Jeff Parker/Cagle Cartoons, Inc.; p. 510, Trinette Reed/ Blend/Corbis; p. 511, Rafiqur Rahman/Reuters/Corbis; p. 513, WaterFrame/Alamy; p. 519, Dilbert @ 1997 Reprinted by permission of United Features Syndicate, Inc.; p. 526, Donald Reilly/The New Yorker Collection/ Cartoonbank; p. 532, Dariush M.,2010/ Used under license from Shutterstock.com; p. 542, Christophe Boisvieux/ Documentary Value/Corbis; p. 542, Jeff Metzger/iStock/Thinkstock; p. 553, Larry Wright/Cagle Cartoons, Inc.; p. 558, National Fluid Milk Processor Promotion Board; p. 561, Ildi/Fotolia; p. 572, JJAVA/Fotolia; p. 576, Lauri Patterson/E+/Getty Images; p. 582, Exactostock/Superstock; p. 594, REUTERS/Daniel Munoz; p. 600, Medioimages/Photodisc/ Getty Images; p. 602, Bob Daemmrich/Corbis; pp. xii, 617, CARLOS BARRIA/ Reuters/Corbis; p. 621, National Archives and Records Administration; p. 625, AP Photo/Globe Gazette, Deb Nicklay; p. 631 left, LBJ Photo by the Democratic National Committee; p. 631 right, AP Photo/U.S. Air Force; p. 650, National Library of Medicine; p. 652, akg-images/Newscom; p. 694, AP Photo/Brett Coomer; p. 773, Brand X Pictures (RF)/Jupiterimages.

Photo Credits

p. 19, Michael Drager/Shutterstock; pp. v, 28, Creativ Studio Heinemann/Alloy/Corbis; p. 31, Lori Adamski Peek/Stone/Getty Images; p. 48, Ian Hooton/Science Photo Library/Corbis; p. 49, MedicalRF.com/Corbis; p. 57, pryzmat/ Shutterstock; pp. vi, 89, Frank Burek/Corbis; p. 106, Ocean/Corbis; p. 110, Designua/Shutterstock; p. 115, Juan Medina/Reuters/Corbis;p.140,Barry Mason/Alamy;pp.vii, 150,Punchstock/Getty Images;p.159,Frenzeny and Tavernier/Historical/Corbis; p. 167, Anna Maloverjan/Shutterstock; p. 208, Dennis MacDonald/Superstock; p. 226, U.S. Fire Administration/FEMA; pp. viii, 232, Jim Ruymen/Reuters/Corbis; p. 244, Romilly Lockyer/ The Image Bank/Getty Images; p. 244, iStock/Thinkstock; p. 251, Vincent Laforet/Pool/ Reuters/Corbis; p. 273, O Driscoll Imaging/Shutterstock; p. 286, corepics/Shutterstock; p. 293, ArteSub/Alamy; pp. ix, 305, Bill Ross/Cusp/Corbis; p. 310, MedicalRF.com/Corbis; p. 316, Alessandro Saffo/ Latitude/Corbis; p. 330, StevenRussellSmithPhotos/Shutterstock; p. 333, Dann Tardif/Bridge/Corbis; p. 373, Walter Geiersperger/ Encyclopedia/Corbis; p. 410, Paul Souders/ Documentary Value/Corbis; p. 412, Jimmy Margulies/Cagle Cartoons, Inc.; p. 418, Brian Snyder/Reuters/Corbis; p. 421 left, Library of Congress Prints and Photographs Division[LC-USZ62-72266]; p. 421 right, INTERFOTO / Personalities/INTERFOTO/Alamy; p. 425, right and left, Cumberland County Historical Society;p.428 top, iStockphoto/Thinkstock;p.428 bottom, AstroBoi/Fotolia; p. 442, moodboard/Superstock; p. 458, Katie Orlinsky/Corbis News/Corbis; p. 464, moodboard/Corbis; p. 480, John Cole/Cagle Cartoons, Inc.; p. 484, Robert Mankoff / The New Yorker Collection/www.cartoonbank.com; p. 492, Ralf-Finn Hestoft/Corbis News/Corbis; p. 502, Martin Harvey/ Documentary Value/Corbis; pp. xi, 505, JEON HEON-KYUN/Newscom; p. 507, Jeff Parker/Cagle Cartoons, Inc.; p. 510, Trinette Reed/ Blend/Corbis; p. 511, Rafiqur Rahman/Reuters/Corbis; p. 513, WaterFrame/Alamy; p. 519, Dilbert @ 1997 Reprinted by permission of United Features Syndicate, Inc.; p. 526, Donald Reilly/The New Yorker Collection/ Cartoonbank; p. 532, Dariush M.,2010/ Used under license from Shutterstock.com; p. 542, Christophe Boisvieux/ Documentary Value/Corbis; p. 542, Jeff Metzger/iStock/Thinkstock; p. 553, Larry Wright/Cagle Cartoons, Inc.; p. 558, National Fluid Milk Processor Promotion Board; p. 561, Ildi/Fotolia; p. 572, JJAVA/Fotolia; p. 576, Lauri Patterson/E+/Getty Images; p. 582, Exactostock/Superstock; p. 594, REUTERS/Daniel Munoz; p. 600, Medioimages/Photodisc/ Getty Images; p. 602, Bob Daemmrich/Corbis; pp. xii, 617, CARLOS BARRIA/ Reuters/Corbis; p. 621, National Archives and Records Administration; p. 625, AP Photo/Globe Gazette, Deb Nicklay; p. 631 left, LBJ Photo by the Democratic National Committee; p. 631 right, AP Photo/U.S. Air Force; p. 650, National Library of Medicine; p. 652, akg-images/Newscom; p. 694, AP Photo/Brett Coomer; p. 773, Brand X Pictures (RF)/Jupiterimages.